D1433231

art

The World of Art, from Aboriginal to American Pop,
Renaissance Masters to Postmodernism.

Publisher and Creative Director: Nick Wells
Chief Editor: Karen Fitzpatrick
Designer: Lucy Bradbury
Editors: Michelle Clare, Vicky Garrard, Christine Kidney, Sonya Newland, Tom Worsley
Editorial Consultant: Andrea Belloli
Picture Researcher: Frances Bodiam

Special thanks to: Amanda Leigh, James Mackay, Ursula Payne, Belinda Wanis

Flame Tree Publishing
Crabtree Hall, Crabtree Lane
Fulham, London, SW6 6TY
United Kingdom

www.foundry.co.uk/flametree

First Published 2002

02 04 05 03

1 3 5 7 9 10 8 6 4 2

Flame Tree is part of the Foundry Creative Media Company Limited
Crabtree Hall, Crabtree Lane, Fulham, London. SW6 6TY

© 2002 the Foundry Creative Media Company Ltd

All rights reserved. No part of this publication may be reproduced or transmitted, in
any form or by any means, without the prior permission in writing of the publisher.

The CIP record for this book is available from the British Library.

ISBN 1 903 817 994

Every effort has been made to contact copyright holders.
We apologize in advance for any omissions and would be pleased to
insert the appropriate acknowledgment in subsequent editions of this publication.

While every endeavour has been made to ensure the accuracy of
the reproduction of the images in this book, we would be grateful to
receive any comments or suggestions for inclusion in future reprints.

art

The World of Art, from Aboriginal to American Pop,
Renaissance Masters to Postmodernism.

General Editor: Dr Robert Belton
Foreword by Christopher Rothko

FLAME TREE
PUBLISHING

Contents

How to Use this Book

The reader is encouraged to use this book in a number of different ways, each of which caters for a range of interests, knowledge and uses:

- The main A–Z section is organised by artist so that a familiar name can be found quickly.
- The A–Z format allows the reader to discover unusual or unknown art, next to the more familiar Impressionists, Pre-Raphaelites or Renaissance artists.
- The side boxes provide the reader with a snapshot of an artist's lifetime and allow further exploration with influences and movements that can be discovered elsewhere in the book.
- The Introduction and accompanying essays cover modern and world art in some depth, while the methods and techniques section reveals insights into the effects achieved by the artists and the movements to which some adhered.
- The Art Resources section includes books and website which can provide further, detailed information on the artists, paintings and issues discussed within the book.

1. Name of the artist, by Surname then Christian name
2. Details of the artist's life and works
3. Title of painting. Occasionally the origins of a painting are uncertain. We have used a number of terms to describe the artist where the name is not definite: 'studio', 'school of' and 'circle of' reveal that the actual painter had direct contact, perhaps studied with or under, the name attributed. 'Follower of' is usually used to indicate that the painter worked in the years after the attributed name. 'After' means a copy of a known work by the named artist.
4. Date of painting (if known)
5. Name of the movement to which the painting/ artist belongs
6. Other works by the artist
7. Other artists who influenced the featured painter
8. Birth date, and place of birth (if known), of artist
9. Geographical region(s) where artist worked
10. Date of artist's death, and place of death (if known)
11. Name of artist by Christian name, then surname
12. Picture credit

Foreword

Foreword

The years of the nineteenth and twentieth centuries were increasingly dominated by technology: technology that propelled an entirely new scale of building and expansion; technology that made possible unprecedented carnage and destruction. The art of these centuries documents both of these trends quite thoroughly in ways both direct and indirect. As we examine nineteenth- and twentieth-century art more carefully, however, we find a more subtle but perhaps more profound impact of technology: revolutions in travel and publishing allowed artists to see, for the first time, the full extent of their own cultural heritages and the art of peoples, places and times which had, up to that point, been largely the subject of myth.

For us today, at times overwhelmed with data in the midst of the information age, it can be difficult to recognize the extent of the new vistas opened for these artists, as their worlds were profoundly changed and enlarged. The evidence of these new horizons permeates their work, however: Picasso's transfigured faces are an echo of the African masks; Dubuffet's childlike figures are distilled in part from the art of prehistoric times; a brighter palette of colour is brought to the prints of Hiroshige by imported western pigments. The work of each of these artists, among so many others, embodies and testifies to the richness of this cross-pollination.

The book that you hold in your hands is very much a product of the information age, and it is in many ways a product of the type of cultural confluence I have just described. Witnessing these important trends, the book brings together, in a single volume, art from around the globe and throughout history. It is perhaps the first book to undertake the full spectrum of art; across time, across place, across culture and style. It crosses boundaries in an attempt to render a complete picture of the history of the art of humankind. The mass, volume and indeed, the title of the book, are a reflection of the breadth and depth of this venture. Ambitious? Absolutely. Encyclopedic? Decidedly. Exhaustive? Impossible, but a very substantial approximation.

Fully and beautifully illustrated with examples of great art from around the world, *The Art Book* will look terrific on a coffee table, but it should not linger there. This is a serious reference tool, designed to place at the fingertips essential information about hundreds of influential artists, the movements they created, the cultures and other artists they learned from and inspired. With its numerous entries on different epochs, traditions and trends, *The Art Book* makes it equally easy to place the artists in their cultural context, or to find the prime movers in important artistic schools.

Organized alphabetically, *The Art Book* places Dadaists next to Ming Dynasty masters, Fra Angelico next to Francisco Amighetti. The surprising juxtapositions that often result are part of the aim of the volume. To the degree possible, *The Art Book* breaks down classifications and cultural boundaries between artists and nations or national styles. The result is something more democratic and nonhierarchical than is the norm, where no particular art form or culture is placed before another.

The alphabetical arrangement also allows for artists to rub shoulders, as it were, breaking free from groupings which often confine them and placing them in a wider context of world art, whose influences on them may be many, disparate and indeed unconscious. This is particularly important for artists of this century who have grown up with not only unprecedented access to masterworks of their own tradition but who have encountered, absorbed and often espoused techniques, ideas and even styles from remote traditions and historical periods. It also allows the reader to encounter the artists free from some of the accumulated baggage of 'isms' and artistic fellow travellers, which can often obscure as much as enlighten his or her view of a particular artist.

Ultimately, however, *The Art Book* is a book for people who love to explore. It's shear breadth allows even the most knowledgeable reader to make unexpected discoveries, while each page will hold new acquaintances for people making a first venture into the world of art. The alphabetical listings provide fertile ground for serendipitous encounters, much as one makes discoveries thumbing through dusty volumes on a library shelf. In this way, *The Art Book* is a generalist's guide that even specialists will find extreme useful; one which can broaden anyone's horizons.

For all its emphasis on breaking the moulds of artistic ghettoization and moving across art historical categories, one should not assume that the book's mission, or indeed method, is more anarchic than scholarly. While the book presents information in new and stimulating ways, the editorial decisions have been guided, and the texts have been prepared, by leading scholars in the history of art.

In the end, *The Art Book* is a reference to *use* and *enjoy*. It may be all too tempting with such a work to focus on what is not here and who has been left out. Inevitably there will be omissions. It is the spirit of inclusiveness which has fuelled the production of this work, however, and used in that spirit all will find great wealth and many hidden treasures.

CHRISTOPHER ROTHKO

Introduction

For most people the process of viewing something aesthetically pleasing can be a momentarily life-enriching experience. The same people might also feel that there is a big difference between looking at a painting for its own sake, and accepting the concept of art as a medium conveying a set of intellectual theories and arguments, and many would ask why should we bother with art? The enjoyment provided by the visual is an acceptable motivation in itself. However, it does not tell us very much about anything – after all, sweets can provide enjoyment too.

Leonardo da Vinci, Mona Lisa

Unlike sweets, though, art has the potential to enrich life in a manner that goes well beyond mere enjoyment, agreeable décor or a more superficial gratification through popular imagery. Moreover, because the art of our own time often simply reaffirms our own values and expectations, being familiar with the art of other times and places is a useful portal into others' aesthetics, ideologies, morals, philosophies, politics and social customs. This familiarity, in turn, may well invite us to question our own ideologies and social customs; in fact, much art was never meant to be *enjoyed* at all, in the common sense of the word. Art's most fundamental importance is therefore not as décor but as an avenue of intellectual communication. This makes insight into art an invaluable part of an advanced comprehensive education.

For a long time there was little doubt that one of the higher expressions of a culture was its advanced visual art. For the layperson, the word 'Renaissance' remains to this day more likely to conjure up the works of Leonardo da Vinci and Michelangelo than those of, for example, the composers Heinrich Isaac and Josquin des Préz. However, it is difficult to say the same of the visual art of our own time, unless we are speaking specifically of the mass media. With a few notable exceptions, such as Picasso, modern and contemporary art is much less likely than that of the Renaissance to spring to average people's minds as an example of their own culture's higher accomplishments. For the purposes of this book, when we talk about art we are really referring to paintings, since for most 'lay' people paintings act as their first serious introduction into art interpretation, and for many it is the medium that they find most accessible.

Why is Art Difficult?

Why is it that much recent art – even that deemed very important by the critical community of visual arts professionals – simply does not engage the imagination of the average person in the same way as traditional art? One conventional explanation is that over the past 150 years art has increasingly moved away from the familiarity and comfort of resemblance, in part because artists felt photography and film freed them from having to stick to straightforward representation. Another is that instead of clarity in the discourse around new and unfamiliar work, explanations are increasingly, and deliberately, obscure. This implies that what went into the making of the art object is more important than what it says to, or the effect it has on, an observer.

The development of the mass media means that a larger proportion of the population is exposed to visual art on a daily basis, and consequently exposed to the accompanying argument. In other words, art that was once intellectually challenging is now part of mainstream culture, and in order for those artists pursuing art as a pure 'academic' exercise, to push the boundaries of learning, the questions they ask have to become more cryptic. Yet another reason that more recent art fails to engage the populace is a general mistrust for the people who create the art, and a perception of them and their work as elitist, only inviting in a narrow section of the population to engage in the discourse.

The average person's apparent alienation from the advanced art of the late twentieth and early twenty-first centuries puzzles the professionals, for it seems to be based on several faulty assumptions. The most basic of these is that what makes art 'art' is how accurately it resembles something. This misapprehension ignores the fact that part of what makes even traditional art 'art' is its symbolism, codes and composition, regardless of the accuracy of its representation. A well-crafted object with nothing to say is impoverished as art, whereas something that shows intelligence, imagination and creativity can sometimes be good art even if its technique is ostensibly poor.

Attributing too high a value to the *making* of art is clearly what lies behind frequently heard objections like 'my five-year-old daughter could do that', but these are not complaints that have been levelled solely at difficult contemporary art. The nineteenth-century sculptor Harriet Hosmer was criticized for her figures of heroines from history and literature because she did not make the final stone versions of her sculptures with her own hands. She defended herself by explaining that art is not the technique but the 'design' – the intellectual component of the work. The average person's resistance to art is based on the presumption that art is not the design but the technique – that what makes art 'art' is its 'craft', glorifying the means over the end.

A related faulty assumption is that because the art of the last century is almost invariably accompanied and explained by words, the meaning of the piece resides in the words rather than the object itself. This position fails to recognize that traditional art was often accompanied by words and that the words themselves are merely a part of the context in which the piece exists. More will be said about this context presently. As for class-based mistrust, yes, there are those who traffic in very expensive art less as expressions of an artist's motives than as trophies of their own status, but this is also true of other signs of material wealth and it has no bearing on the meaning or intrinsic value of the art itself. In other words, this too is merely an expression of a contextual matrix surrounding the art.

What is Art and What is Art For?

We must begin by asking several questions about context, the most basic of which are 'What is art?' and 'What is art for?' The average person might say, 'Art is decoration' or, more awkwardly, 'Art is the technically skilful representation of something absent in such a way as to create an illusion of its presence.' However, these answers ignore a host of important pieces that are not particularly attractive, realistic or well made. The history of art is filled with brilliant examples of disturbing and violent imagery, stylized or inaccurate likenesses, and objects that require constant care in order to prevent deterioration.

In addition to adornment and beautification, art's purposes have included:
- aggrandizing oneself or others
- arranging disordered or dissimilar things
- associating one thing with another thing
- communicating
- complementing education and training
- contrasting familiarity and surprise for aesthetic excitement
- creating codes
- creating illusions
- documenting things and events
- educating the illiterate
- employing the thoroughly known characteristics of one thing as metaphors of the less well known characteristics of another to shed light on the latter by comparison
- enlivening a dull existence with change and variety
- entertaining
- executing a premeditated purpose
- exhibiting technical skill
- flattering patrons
- giving form to therapy
- heightening experience
- illustrating ideas and narratives
- indulging in fantasy
- indulging in sensuousness
- reconciling differing ideologies
- passing on folklore or family histories
- passing the time
- providing a means of personal expression
- providing an opportunity for self-examination
- persuading
- propagandizing
- providing testimony
- redefining reality
- redefining art itself

This is a list of ends or purposes, and while it is possible that they might all be achieved using only one means – for example, realistic painting – in practice artists have used many techniques, styles and approaches. The result is that a definition of art based primarily on means is particularly unsatisfactory. All the definitions of art offered over the centuries include some notion of human agency, whether through manual skills (the art of sailing, painting or photography), intellectual manipulation (the art of politics) or public or personal expression (the art of conversation). As such, the word is related to 'artificial' – that is, produced by human beings rather than by nature. But it doesn't stop there: this definition of art is correct in a limited way but it is also essentially flawed because it does not allow one to distinguish the defined term from something else that correctly exemplifies the definition. 'A vacuum cleaner is a household appliance' is insufficient as a definition of a vacuum cleaner because 'vacuum cleaner' can be correctly replaced with 'refrigerator', and a vacuum cleaner is not a refrigerator. Saying 'Art equals artificial

Mary Cassatt, The Young Mother

Art

equals human-made things' fails to distinguish art from other things produced by human beings. It gives us a start, however, for it makes it clear that infinitely realistic painting would simply replicate the world. In so doing, realistic painting says nothing much about human agency and thereby ceases to be art in all but the most bankrupt way. It would be similarly unsatisfactory to try to understand art while limiting oneself to only one or two of the ends above. 'Art is decoration' fails to distinguish advanced art from simple ornament, and 'Art is the exhibition of technical skill' fails to distinguish art from sports and woodworking.

Thomas Mukarobgwa, Landscape

To fail to remain open to the wide range of art's purposes is to be indifferent to its contextual variations, even before we get to the seemingly infinite variety of means and ends. This cripples one's understanding of and openness to art. For example, those who say that art's goal is accurate representation ignore many cultures (such as African, indigenous Australian and Islamic, not just the modern West) in which realism is subordinate to emotional exuberance, imaginative visions anchored in faith or the expression of an idea. Some would declare that art, by definition, has to be beautiful, arbitrarily excluding innumerable depictions of social injustice, violence and tragedy. Still others might maintain that art's only real identity lies in redefining what constitutes art, but that is surely not what was on the mind of an artist whose work is effectively an anguished outburst.

Interpreting Art

So, the answers to the questions 'What is art?' and 'What is art for?' are that art is a particular way of saying something or producing an effect in an observer, and art is 'for' whatever it says or produces as an effect in an observer. The judges of what art is for must be the observers themselves, who are in some ways interpreters of this art. It does not follow, however, that one interpretation is just as good as the next one. Historians and older academics tend to encourage interpreters to 'perform the art' (the word 'interpret' means 'to perform' in some languages) subject to the constraints provided by the work itself. They do so because they believe that this produces more of a statement about the work itself than about the observer. However, observers have the right to interpret as they feel

– like a musician improvising around a theme, i.e., they can pretty much refuse to 'perform the art' subject to its constraints, allowing themselves to be inspired in a way that produces more of a statement about themselves than about the work. Both attitudes, and every position between them, can be seen in current writing about art. This might all seem very complicated, but bear in mind that there are in fact only three categories of statements one can make about a work of art: Context, Form and Content. However, there are numerous possibilities for interaction between the elements within each category (for example, Form to Form), exponentially more possibilities for interaction between the categories themselves (for example, between Form and Content) and virtually infinite possibilities brought to one layer in one of the categories (Context), so we shall consider each of these in turn.

Context

'Context' refers to the circumstances surrounding the production and reception of a work of art rather than anything physically present in the work itself. Whether an artist was a man or a woman, religious or secular, academically trained or self-taught, is not something *in* the work, but it provides additional information that can certainly affect our understanding *of* the work. Whether the work was produced for public consumption in a religious establishment or for the cabinet of a private collector also affects our interpretation and understanding of the piece. We would have to interpret a work made during the time of the Spanish Inquisition differently from a hypothetically identical one made, say, during the expansion of the railways in the New World because we would need to keep in mind the very different cultural expectations behind them.

Recognizing a contextual code can help an observer understand a lot more about a piece of art. In the absence of this knowledge, a conventionally representational painting might still give us something to look at, even though we do not really understand it at all. In a work that departs from the conventional – for example, art that uses scratchy, unpolished-looking graffiti marks and codes – we do not even have the comfortable familiarity of the contemporary *Zeitgeist* on art. If we do not know that a certain mark means 'the people who live here are friendly to the homeless', for example, then we do not understand the piece and we may have no meaningful experience of it. Without contextual information our interpretation is likely to be insufficient at best and faulty at worst.

Information about the artist is one of the major factors in the Context category. Although some might argue that details about the artist's social world are more significant, society in general did not produce the actual work, however much it may have influenced or affected its creation. Since there would be no work without its maker, primary Context is that which describes the circumstances of the work's production at the level of the individual artist. Contextual information is not a description of the production of the piece of art itself; it is the artist's attitudes and beliefs, education and training, gender and sexual preference, likes and dislikes, lifestyle and philosophy, politics and religion, social standing and personal wealth. As with all Context, none of these things has to appear in the work, but they all affect our understanding of it. For example, Artemisia Gentileschi (1593–1653) did not paint her experience of rape by her tutor Agostino Tassi in 1612, but knowing this detail of her life gives us license to interpret her depictions of male decapitations in a certain way.

We can consider secondary Context to be the broader cultural expectations, such as the philosophy, politics and religion of the observers or patrons of the work, which of course the artist might have shared. Again, none of these things appear in the work, but they can change our interpretation of it. For example, it can help us to understand that a swastika – a Greek cross with its arms bent in the same rotary direction – can be interpreted in one way in twentieth-century Europe where it is associated with Nazism, and in a completely different way in ancient China, India and Tibet where it is inextricably linked to Buddhism, Jainism and Hinduism.

The information we gain about a piece of art's context must be accurate and relevant (the sexual assault mentioned above is relevant, for example, whereas knowing that that artist was fond of a particular type of cheese would not be). One of the fascinating things about art history, however, is the way that later generations of observers sometimes retrieve and reuse an aspect of Context that an earlier generation found irrelevant. Every observer brings to a work his or her own secondary Context, and in this way the art is a reflection of ourselves. Secondary Context is theoretically infinite, unless we arbitrarily restrict our interpretations to a given range – for example, the lifetime of the artist or the patron. Because we have difficulty deciding where the boundary falls between acceptable and unacceptable circumstantial evidence, the proliferation of secondary Context makes the meanings of art seem inexhaustible.

Form

The second of the three basic categories, Form, differs fundamentally from Context. While the latter, by definition, does not appear in the work, Form *is* the work and its constituent elements, independent of any meaning they might have. For example, a work's colour, light, medium, shape, size, technique, and texture are all aspects of Form. The basic formal elements are primary when they are treated in isolation. For example, to speak of the character of a single shape in a painting as organic, geometric, static or dynamic is to refer to an aspect of primary Form. When we say something about how that shape relates to another shape, we shift to a secondary level of Form, in which elements relate to each other, as in balance, composition, contrast, distance, perspective, space, and so on. When we recognize shapes as particular things with particular identities – for example, identifying an arrangement of coloured stripes as a flag – we assign them a meaning and move from Form to Content. The mechanism that makes the change in the flag example is Context, because we know that certain stripes (Form) indicate a flag (Content) within the horizon of expectations of a particular culture. Moving from Form to Content is so natural to us that we find it difficult to distinguish between the categories. It is, however, a useful exercise, for Form, however interesting on its own, plays an important role in actually *creating* Content.

Content

'Content' refers to what a work says and the effects it produces in an observer. Some of these may actually be 'meanings' (in the sense that the artist meant or intended to convey them), and some may be better described as 'significances' (pseudo-meanings not intended or controlled by the artist but peculiar to an individual observer). Like the other categories, Content has primary and secondary levels. Primary Content corresponds approximately to the literal level of language – attributes, events, facts, objects, people, places and things, all representing what they appear to represent, as opposed to symbolizing something else. As soon as we point out that one thing symbolizes or stands for something else, we shift to a secondary level of Content. Every competent performer of a language instinctively understands that figurative expressions are not to be taken as literal. 'She was on cloud nine' does not refer to someone

Vincent Van Gogh, Portrait de l'Artiste sans Barbe

A good many of these tropes, as they are known, are conventional and widely understood by the culture or society in which the work has been produced. 'She was on cloud nine' would not be figuratively meaningful in a culture that had not standardized the expression. Other tropes are invented by the artist rather than simply borrowed from culture in general. Observers may recognize these spontaneously, or they may have to work at understanding them by filling in the gaps in their knowledge of the artist. That an observer's knowledge of the artist is never complete is another of the many ways in which the meanings of art seem to be inexhaustible.

Relationships between Context, Form and Content

That Form consists of elements independent of meaning does not mean that it does not affect the meaning of a piece of art. Just as Context influences Content, pushing it from primary to secondary, Form also affects Content, although it uses a less familiar method of category-shifting that we might call 'paralinguistic'. Though the term strictly applies to the spoken language, the same principles can be applied to the visual image. The term refers to the way changes in individual delivery (or performance) of a statement lead to changes in our understanding of what is meant. If one changes the Form of a literal image (that is, the way in which it is delivered or performed), one can produce a corresponding change of the literal meaning of the image to a metaphorical one. Like tropes, some of these shifts can be conventional, evoking an immediate response that is mediated by secondary Context. For example, in Western culture everyone spontaneously recognizes the difference between the look, sound, and meaning of 'fire' spoken normally and 'FIRE!' screamed loudly, even though the core meaning is the same. Moreover, everyone can tell the difference between 'fire!' yelled in a crowded theatre and 'fire!' shouted next to a line of aiming soldiers. Someone who fails to understand the difference has overlooked something important about the culture in which the expressions have achieved currency.

However, artists do not limit themselves to illustrating those paralinguistic shifts that are already part of the popular culture. They routinely invent them for expressive and aesthetic purposes. This is most immediately apparent in works of an expressionist sort – for example, Van Gogh's *Starry Night*. Because of the painting's departure from conventional depictions of the night sky (and from Van Gogh's own usual style), it seems to evoke a deeply emotional response, and the scene almost cries out in mystical ecstasy. Trying to unravel the

floating in the sky; it pushes beyond the primary to a secondary layer of Content, 'happiness'. This is the core flaw in the theory that the value of art lies in its ability to render something accurately: to praise a work solely for its realism is to ignore the codes that may be utterly obvious to an observer who shares its artist's horizon of expectations. In other words, what you see may not be what you (are supposed to) get.

There are several mechanisms by which primary Content becomes secondary Content. Probably the most common of these is symbolism – the comparison of a literal element in the picture to another element, whether present or implied, until a different level of meaning emerges. Devices such as the metaphor work in exactly this way. A child blowing a bubble is just that if we take the scene literally, but if we are prepared to see it as a comparison of the child and the bubble, a metaphor is produced. The understood characteristics of the bubble – its beauty and fragility – imply something less immediately apparent but no less true about the child.

meaning-effects of contextual codes and formal nuances without falling prey to the assumption that good art is realistic, is key to understanding art as art, rather than art as craft.

No matter how complicated, then, all works of art involve the interplay of these three categories. This realization provides a way to create a workable definition of visual art that brings us at least a little closer to sufficiency. That is, visual art is the manipulation and interrelation of visible Form, invisible Context and primary Content to create secondary Content – that is, to say something or to produce an effect in the observer that goes beyond the literal – for the purpose of accomplishing one or more of the various ends listed above.

What is Good Art?

Notice that the new definition of art carefully avoids the question 'What is good art?'. This is because definitions of 'good' are always mediated by the values of secondary Context, the circumstances in which the piece is seen rather than in which it is created. One set of secondary cultural expectations sees goodness as 'quality', for example. But in one culture quality is defined as formal orderliness whether or not it is really appropriate for the Content, and in another culture quality is interpreted as whether or not artists have achieved what they set out to achieve. Where some cultures have not seemed to care whether an artist's use of symbolism is purely conventional or original, another culture highly prizes 'innovation' – the deliberate striving of the artist to invent a new and unconventional way of expressing something. Today, innovation is in the ascendant and it is manifest in only about three ways. First, artists can innovate by portraying primary Content with Form that is unexpected and, ideally, previously unused in this connection in such a way that new secondary Content is produced. As raw subject matter, Picasso's famous weeping women are nothing new, but his inventive Form shifts them until they say something new and produce a new effect in the observer. Second, artists innovate by making unusual combinations of secondary Context. Judy Chicago's famous *Dinner Party* of 1979 (in which place-settings are decorated with flower motifs that pun on female genitalia) retrieves old associations – for example, women's art as flower painting – and reinvents them within the set of cultural assumptions that constitutes feminism. Third, artists innovate by developing and depicting idiosyncratic aspects of primary Context. Because this involves personal motivations that are often difficult to pinpoint, this third way to innovate is another contribution to the impression that art's meanings are inexhaustible.

The Purpose and Structure of this Book

You may be wondering what the relevance is to this book, of this reflection on art's definition, purpose, characteristics, and potential for interpretation. The answer lies in the fact that an artwork's Form and its primary Content actually appear in the work, while its Context has to be brought to the work to give the observer a full and sufficient experience. This does not mean that experience of a work without knowing its Context is invalid any more than the statement 'A Hoover is a household appliance' is invalid. It is simply insufficient. So the purpose of this book is to introduce the general reader to a wide sample of artists and artworks from around the world, along with some basic tools for their interpretations in the form of brief notes on art's Context, Form and Content.

We begin with a stellar example. Christopher Rothko writes of his illustrious father Mark Rothko, whose art is certainly among the more celebrated in Western culture in spite of its absence of conventional representational cues. Rothko's later paintings are popular because they are near-perfect examples of how to make meaningful art without succumbing to the misconception that realistic depictions are the only good art – that is, they say something by producing an effect in the observer for the purpose of accomplishing one or more of the various ends of art. For example, Rothko's paintings certainly adorn and beautify, but they also provide opportunities for aesthetic excitement, association, communication, entertainment, a heightening of experience, personal expression, sensuous indulgence, and so on. Moreover, they provide an atmospheric space that seems to invite viewers to enter an introspective, meditative state – all steps towards art's goal of providing viewers with an opportunity for self-examination.

We follow with Perspectives on Modern Art by Dr. Julia Kelly. Though it may seem unusual to start with such a specific area of art, it is perhaps the type of art that is currently given most coverage by the media, and often the most baffling for the art novice, despite its supposed links with contemporary life. The twentieth century ushered in a period of rapid transition, with more scientific, technological and political change than at any other time. Dr Kelly outlines the dramatic effect these changes had on the development of art, describing the sociological environment and historical factors that gave rise to the

Mark Rothko, Untitled

modern art movements, and discussing whether modern art is a reaction against, or a reflection of modern society.

The art of the modern world tends to dwell on the internal world of the artist, more than that of any other era, so that instead of the art movements that reflected the consensus of a group of artists, modern art conveys many intensely personal messages, which can be baffling to the observer. Dr Kelly elucidates the logic behind the modern art movements, such as conceptual art, using individual works as examples and explaining the reasoning behind them, especially in cases where a movement or style might be considered by many to be particularly incomprehensible or enigmatic.

The next section explores the physical constituents of art and their interrelations (or Form), through an investigation of methods and techniques. Here we present sketches of many of the more important

George Seurat, Model in Profile

techniques that have inspired artists and facilitated their expressions over the centuries. We provide brief technical explanations and descriptions of artists' processes, so that general readers can at least know how a print is created, and become wise to retailers promoting 'limited-edition prints' that are not true prints at all. Readers will also want to know how various techniques, in and of themselves, have 'voices' that inflect a work's Content.

We then move on to the task of providing Context in a variety of ways. First, we address the need to keep our minds open to others' aesthetics and social customs by learning about the art of other times and places. Ihor Holubizky contributes 'Perspectives on World Art', in which he considers what the expression 'World Art' implies in the light of differences in the viewpoints of the dominant European-American Context and what that Context deems somehow Other – that is, 'World' cultures. He briefly introduces a selection of artists from countries not often listed in general books of this sort in order to trace the wide variety of Contexts surrounding artists working in countries outside the western Hemisphere. He also touches on the interesting distinction between

world artists who work essentially within their indigenous traditions and those who consciously accept and manipulate international influences.

Curiously, the lay person seems to have less difficulty dealing with objects made by the indigenous branch of world artists than with works by those who accommodate and/or reinvent European-American approaches. One explanation is that average viewers might be thinking of the objects less as art per se than as ethnographic objects or charming curiosities. They might be tempted to justify this by alluding to the absence of a word equivalent to 'art' in some cultures, but some cultures probably also do not have a word for 'cystic fibrosis', the worldwide prevalence of which would not necessarily mean that the ailment cannot occur within their societies. So it is with art, which appears to be everywhere whether we know it by that name or not.

Perhaps the average person is more comfortable with indigenous objects than avant-garde objects because they do not expect the former to be art, so they do not run afoul of the perceptual fallacy that has been previously highlighted and therefore do not expect indigenous art to be a realistic portrayal of a subject or object. The same reasoning may lead some viewers to reject unconventional artworks from the European-American tradition, on the grounds that they don't accept such pieces as examples of a craft, preferring to think of them as some sort of fraudulent commodity at best, or tomfoolery at worst. In order for them to accept a craft there has to be a quality in the technique applied to the creation of the piece. They would hold that art is craft, and would reject some pieces of advanced art on these grounds.

If these hypothetical average viewers think of unconventional artworks in the Western tradition neither as craft nor as ethnographic objects, then it is possible to speculate that thinking of non-Western artworks as anthropological trophies is nothing more than a strategy to avoid engagement with them as works of art. This strategy of containment is exactly the opposite of our goal to keep our minds open to others' aesthetics and social customs. In fact, we should be so open to this that we pass beyond grounding our identity in self and other altogether, because there are those who think this process, however well-meaning, is parochial and in dire need of redefinition.

It is all the more important, then, to explore works in which world artists accommodate and transform Western models, because in them we see postcolonial approaches to contemporary art that might provide instructive models for future interpretations. In Africa, Australasia, Central America and South America indigenous artists were influenced by the trends of the European settlers, who worked in the prevailing European styles. It was only the course of the twentieth century that indigenous art, some of it with traditions going back many centuries, received a wider audience. This resulted in distinctive national or regional movements that either paint traditional themes using Western techniques or blend ethnic motifs with Western styles; but it is only within relatively recent times that the arts of Africa, Asia, Australasia or Polynesia have inspired artists working in Europe and America, as part of the ongoing quest for distinctive styles arising out of a riotous mixture of eclecticism.

We round off these sections with some convenient timelines – not a prescriptive index but a general guide against which to measure the works we meet here and encounter elsewhere.

Our next section provides explanations of the main art movements. Here Dr James Mackay surveys 30 of the more important historical categories, which are illustrated with artworks from each movement. Many of these are readily identified by sets of stylistic traits, as in the ubiquitous paint-dots of Pointillism, which is to say that some movements are best characterized by aspects of Form. Other movements can be characterized as well by aspects of Content, as in Symbolism's preoccupation with 'clothing the Idea in sensual, perceptible form', to paraphrase Jean Moréas (French Poet 1856–1910). In other words, an idea or emotion became the starting point for the piece, and was expressed through the selective use of color (for artists) and words (for poets) so that the idea attained a physical form. Still other movements can be characterized by Context, as in Surrealism's preoccupation with Freudian thought and Postmodernism's reliance on abstruse literary, political and other theories. Ultimately, all movements are in fact contextual entities because they are historically specific. If we describe the work of an artist of the 1990s in terms of Cubism, which flourished 80 years earlier, we are probably addressing only its Form. Such a work is likely outdated and of little significance, although it is possible that the artist is trying to accomplish some other end that would have to be unearthed through contextual analysis.

How to Read this Book

We invite readers to make use of this book in any way they see fit. We do, however, ask them to keep in mind that its final purpose is to see art as a way to exercise our hearts, imaginations and minds, not only to expand our knowledge of others' ideologies and social customs but also to question our own. These poles of respect and critique provide the parameters within which this book will achieve its purpose.

You may find that you end up reading this book, or at least sections of it, more than once. Dipping into the A–Z entries selectively will allow you to be drawn into the subject of art through the artists, or pieces, that most appeal to you. Reading through the introductory sections at a slightly later stage will then allow you to learn more about the lie of the land in general. Each of the essays in this introductory section has its own distinct style, but all are united by a common theme; that they ask demanding questions of art, and of the biases that exist within the subjects of art history and interpretation. You may even find that in some instances more questions are asked than answered. Some of those questions could not be feasibly answered within this book, forming the basis for an entire field of study, whilst others are merely designed to engage you in the interpretive discourse.

The concepts introduced in these sections will equip you to teach yourself more about the pieces on display as you work your way around a gallery as well as enable you to gain a deeper understanding of the works included in the A–Z section, by seeing how their components work in sympathy with one another. Lastly, we discourage you from thinking of the book's selection of works as the final word on the subject – art history's canonical 'greatest hits', as it were. Think of them instead as exercises to prepare you for the great adventure of art – to explore a world that could never be encapsulated within the covers of one book.

Dr Robert Belton

Christopher Rothko
on his Father

The artwork of my father, Mark Rothko (1903–70), has evoked dramatically polarized responses ever since his work first garnered significant attention in the early 1950s. On the one hand, one encounters an almost cultish worship, an ardor from his devotees that exceeds a typical enthusiasm for art. On the other, one finds a derisive dismissal, a deep resentment of a painter who would presume to present work so simple a child could produce it.

An art-lover by inheritance and a psychologist by training, I have long been intrigued by the strength of reaction to my father's work. My father's primary preoccupation throughout his career was to communicate with his audience. I believe that by examining some of the methods he adopted to do so we may discover causes for this polarity, and also learn something more generally about the interface between art and viewer.

Rothko began, and indeed ended, his career with the desire to express the 'human condition' through his work. This might not be immediately apparent in his best-known paintings, which present great expanses of saturated color, often beautifully juxtaposed. He maintained, however, that it was the 'human drama' which occupied him, that he was not interested in making decorative work, in the relationships of colour and space or in beauty *per se*. Instead he adhered firmly to the rather Romantic notion – despite his modernist techniques – that art has the power to dramatically affect those who engage with it. He believed that art must communicate something to those who see it, and that great art is that which is constantly striving to do so.

In the early years of his painting (*c.* 1925–37), Rothko pursued this goal by depicting urban scenes; figures often struggling within the social, cultural and economic confines of the American city. As 1940 approached, however, my father looked for a new, explicitly more universal language and turned, like many of his American colleagues, to Surrealism. He embraced this style because he believed it linked him to more primal elements basic to all people – the world of dreams and 'primitive' art to which all have at least unconscious access. Through the use of mythical subjects, my father also hoped to use a common vocabulary familiar to all.

Ultimately Rothko chose to abandon figuration altogether, moving to pure abstraction in the course of the year 1945. By 1949 his signature style, comprising of two or three rectangles of colour floated on a coloured background, was fully established. By stripping away all recognizable images, my father looked to communicate on a more elemental level, to appeal directly to the emotions with sensation as the only mediator. Here, he believed, was a truly universal language; a way

Mark Rothko, Untitled

to speak to that which is most essentially human without the interference of cultural referents and social conventions.

It was in many ways a risky leap and, I think, the primary reason why his work is so revered and so misunderstood. For those willing – and indeed capable – of interacting with a painting on this type of raw, visceral level, the experience can be deeply rewarding, even overwhelming (hence witness the many people who cry before Rothko paintings). For those primed to see paintings through established cultural norms, those desiring something more explicitly narrative in the work they view, those too emotionally guarded to take the suggested 'journey', or those simply on a different affective page from a given work on a given day, my father's attempt at communication will fail. The works will seem merely 'pretty', or empty, or even silly in their admixture of grandiosity and simplicity.

Rothko's work ultimately makes explicit what all art assumes: that what the artist presents is only a portion of the artistic experience; the rest must be supplied by the viewer, drawn from his or her own thoughts, experience, cultural grounding, emotional disposition. My father's gamble was to place a much heavier burden on the viewer to complete the interaction. The pay-off is that by reducing the obstructions of cultural specificity, by eliminating the need for translation, he could reach a broader spectrum of people.

Rothko's complicated relationship with his viewer and the demands it makes upon him or her bear many similarities to the difficulties in cross-cultural encounters between art and public. Because most people approach artwork with a group of culturally derived expectations, engagement with art from different worlds or periods often provokes confusion. This 'foreign' artwork, be it from the Pacific Rim or from 'Western' sources but 1,200 years removed, plays by different rules. It expresses (or defies) its own cultural norms, speaks from its own social lexicon, builds upon, or at least gestures towards, its own artistic traditions. Ultimately these works draw on and address a different set of human experiences and, like my father's painting, begin with different assumptions of what art is, what cultural role it plays and how it interacts with the viewer.

For example, medieval iconography may paint stylized expressions across the faces of martyred saints or the Virgin in mourning, expressions which may seem to us incongruous and unconvincing but which in those times served as a gloss for a whole catalogue of standard interpretations and established truths. They are masks, much like those of West Africa or the No theatre – frozen and seemingly limited in expression, but embodying cultural referents that go well beyond the physical piece. They are full of meaning to those schooled in their vocabulary and deeply rewarding to those who make the effort to learn.

My father sought to circumvent this chain of representations and symbols in order to broaden understanding of what he hoped to communicate. Yet the process is not so easy, for we all rely on these cultural cues to interpret what we see. How does one make sense of emotion not expressed through people? How does one understand the purpose of the art in the absence of narrative? Thus Rothko may have found a universal language, but it is one that some will remain unaware that they know how to speak. Much like that initial interaction when one exits the aeroplane thousands of miles from home, it requires a certain openness, a certain boldness to utter those first words in a foreign landscape.

Be it art of one's own time and country, or art greatly removed by time and place, my father believed emphatically in the importance of taking that step, of putting oneself forward into active communication with art. He would have been very happy to see a volume such as *The Art Book*, which not only invites, but in truth demands, a venture into the unfamiliar. There are great riches to discover in what may initially seem closed. I am sure he would have wished you a Bon Voyage.

Christopher Rothko

Modern Art

The twentieth century saw many radical changes in people's lives: an increased pace of technological and industrial change; the rapid spread of large urban centers; the development of new means of transportation and communication; innovative scientific discoveries such as the X-ray and the theory of relativity; the growth of consumerism on a large scale; and the chilling reality of mass warfare. Against this background of social, political and technological developments, Western art also underwent a series of radical shifts. For the preceding four centuries, painting in Europe had been based on illusionism – a desire to represent external reality through a series of pictorial conventions, such as single-point perspective and the modelling of depth through light and dark tones. In the twentieth century, however, these conventions were abandoned and a whole new range of possibilities opened up with regard to the effects and meanings that could be created in paint on a two-dimensional surface. Painting no longer had to take on the task of recording historical events – one of its central nineteenth-century roles – as this function was now fulfilled by the newer media of photography and especially film. Changes in the structure of the art market, too, away from the grand public 'Salons' which promoted large-scale works, to a system of private galleries and collectors, meant that paintings could be smaller, more personal and more experimental. Artists could respond to the changing reality around them in a variety of ways: embracing modern experience, reacting against it, or seeking to make an impact upon it through their art. They could also aim to be 'modern': to produce paintings that were innovative and exciting, different from anything that had been seen before, full of radical new effects and new meanings. Art in the twentieth century, like the social environment in which it was produced, would undergo a process of constant and rapid change.

From Symbolism to the Fauves and the Expressionists

In 1890, the French painter Maurice Denis (1870–1943) famously claimed: 'a picture before being a battle horse, a nude woman or some anecdote, is essentially a flat surface covered in colours arranged in a certain order.' Denis' definition has been seen as ultimately pointing towards abstract painting, but at the time he made this comment he was more concerned with downplaying the need for realism in art in favour of effects of line and colour. His paintings were of recognizable subjects

Paul Gauguin, Nave Nave Moe

– religious scenes, women in forest settings, bathers – but depicted in heightened, unreal colours bounded by flowing, decorative contours. His compatriot Paul Gauguin (1848–1903) used strong, contrasting colours and dark outlines around the different elements of his compositions, drawing attention away from the subject depicted and towards the artist's use of paint. Symbolism was a broad artistic movement that encompassed painting, literature, music and theatre in the late nineteenth and early twentieth centuries, and manifested itself in a diverse range of styles. Painting associated with the movement, such as that by Denis and Gauguin, was often based on literary themes, myths and legends, but also on personal fantasy and dream. A striking tendency within Symbolist works was a move away from narrative, away from the depiction of scenes that could 'tell a story' in an accessible way, in favour of the evocation of a mood or feeling. A common motif in Symbolist painting is a group of figures who do not interact in any straightforward way, whose eyes do not meet and whose gestures and gazes suggest that each one is lost in their own private reverie. The arrangement of a Symbolist composition can thus seem more artificial than truthful, more about art than about reality. In the works of Gauguin and Denis, this sense of artificiality is heightened by an emphasis on colour and line and on the ways in which different parts of the painting relate to one another within an overall 'pattern'.

The Symbolist interest in colour in painting as an evocative element in its own right was crucial to the development of the young painter Henri Matisse (1869–1954). Matisse trained in the studio of Gustave Moreau (1826–1898), a Symbolist artist who created extraordinary jewel-like effects in his paintings, building up layers of coloured paint, sometimes squeezing it directly on to the canvas, to evoke luxuriant details of dress and architectural décor within biblical and mythological scenes. In 1905, Matisse exhibited a painting that caused a great stir in the Salon des Indépendants, an artist-run and unjuried exhibition forum in Paris; this painting, *Luxe, calme et volupté* (painted in 1904) is now seen as one of the key Fauvist works. (Fauvism was characterized by a primitive style in which intense colours were used, often to create deliberate clashes. This technique completely freed colour from its depictive role, so that it could be truly expressive.) The piece took its title from a refrain in a poem by Charles Baudelaire (1821–67), who was himself a Symbolist. Matisse did not attempt to 'illustrate' this poem – a suggestive homage to the sensual pleasures of travel; rather he created his own vision of a beach scene with a moored boat and a group of languid female nudes. The whole composition was made up of small patches of colour, a technique known as 'Pointillism' which had been developed in the nineteenth century by Georges Seurat (1859–91). At a distance, these colour patches would fuse to suggest effects of light and volume, but seen close to, the painting would begin to break up into a series of juxtaposed markings. Matisse exaggerated this effect, making some marks bigger than others, as well as distorting the forms of his nudes using thick curving contours. The subject matter of *Luxe, calme et volupté* was ostensibly serene and restful – a lunch party on the beach – but Matisse's handling of the paint and treatment of the human figure were expressive and almost violent.

In the autumn of 1905, an exhibition of works by artists including Matisse, André Derain (1880–1954) and Maurice de Vlaminck (1876–1958) earned them the name 'Fauves' or 'wild beasts'. This term, coined by the art critic Louis Vauxcelles (b. 1870), was intended as derogatory, a response to what he saw as a spontaneous and reckless handling of paint and use of colour. Derain produced landscapes full of striking contrasting colours, reds and greens, which appeared to have been painted very freely and quickly, while Vlaminck aimed to express himself instinctively, after the model of the painter he most admired, Vincent van Gogh (1853–90), later describing himself as a 'tender-hearted savage, filled with violence'. The Fauves generally chose traditional subject matter in their paintings – landscapes, nudes and portraits – which they made modern through their radical treatment. A powerful example of this is Matisse's 1906 portrait of his wife, whose composition is brought to life by a bold green stripe extending down from her forehead and along her nose.

In Germany in 1905, a group of painters based in Dresden who called themselves 'Die Brücke' ('the bridge') felt a similar desire to inject youthful vigour and energy into the practice of painting as the Fauves did. Die Brücke also admired Van Gogh, as well as the Norwegian Edvard Munch (1863–1944) and the art of non-Western cultures, particularly Africa, all of whom to them achieved a kind of untrammelled expressiveness. Artists such as Ernst Ludwig Kirchner

(1880–1938) and Karl Schmidt-Rottluff (1884–1976) painted portraits and landscapes in bright colours with large, simplified forms, and were drawn to depictions of nudes in outdoor settings, suggesting a return to nature and to basic origins. Emil Nolde (1867–1956), who was associated with the group for a few months, used distorted forms and angry combinations of colour to explore his own religious beliefs. The term 'Expressionism' was first used in 1911, primarily in relation to art in France, and then to refer to the painters of Die Brücke, who by 1913 had drifted apart. It would continue to be applied to the work of artists like the Austrian Oskar Kokoschka (1886–1980) and the German painter Max Beckmann (1884–1950). Beckmann translated his traumatic experience during the first World War into distorted self-portraits and figure scenes, such as his disturbing vision of torture and murder *The Night* (1918–19). His later paintings depicted circus performers, with himself as clown or king, reflecting the anxiety caused by the social events that surrounded him.

The use of painting as a means of communicating personal experience and emotion – a central aim of the Expressionists – was manifested in a more subtle and controlled way in the work of the painters of the Munich-based group Der Blaue Reiter ('the blue rider'). In an almanac published in 1912, the Blauer Reiter artists, including Franz Marc (1880–1916), Wassily Kandinsky (1866–1944) and Paul Klee (1879–1940), put forward their vision of new ways of self-expression, including art, design, poetry and music. Kandinsky's painting, inspired by Fauvism, began to focus less on subject matter than on the lyrical force of colour and the strokes of his brush, seeking to communicate with the viewer in a direct and spontaneous way in the manner of a piece of music. Kandinsky's works of 1910 to 1914, such as *Improvisation No. 23*, are considered to be the first abstract paintings of the twentieth century. Klee's awareness of the evocative use of colour was encouraged by a trip to Tunisia in 1914, and he went on to create small-scale paintings of exotic landscapes, still-lifes and figure scenes, all depicted in a schematic and magical child-like way, a style that he described as 'taking a line for a walk'.

Franz Marc, *Springendes Pferd*

Cubism

Cubism was one of the most influential twentieth-century art movements, and one whose works can seem the most 'difficult' and inaccessible to the observer. Cubist works would provide a radical challenge to the painterly conventions for producing an illusion of depth, and they would attack the tradition of 'high' art by including within two-dimensional paintings and collages a range of extraneous, materials not traditionally associated with high art, such as newspaper clippings, scraps of sheet music and stencilled lettering. Cubism flourished in Paris between 1907 and the outbreak of the First World War in 1914, and its impact was felt in artistic developments throughout Europe during this period.

George Braque, Verre et as de Trefle,

The French painter Georges Braque (1882–1963) had worked initially in a Fauvist style, but after seeing a major retrospective exhibition of the work of Paul Cézanne (1839–1906) in Paris in 1907, he pursued a new artistic vision. Cézanne's work was an inspiration, particularly in its use of 'passages', the unification of parts of the picture surface through colour and tone, which meant that the difference between foreground and background was no longer sharply maintained. Braque made trips to the village of L'Estaque in southern France to paint the same sites depicted by Cézanne, and his resulting series of landscapes were exhibited in Paris in 1908, showing houses, trees and roads as simplified geometric forms squeezed into a shallow picture space. The box-like appearance of houses in these landscapes led the critic Vauxcelles – who had been quick to label the Fauves – to describe them mockingly as 'cubes', inspiring the term 'Cubism'.

In 1907 Braque had also made the acquaintance of the Spaniard Pablo Picasso (1881–1973), who that same year had produced his extraordinary large-scale painting *Les Demoiselles d'Avignon*. This work managed to bring together several radical and shocking elements. It showed five prostitutes with sharply distorted naked bodies within a room whose space seemed shattered into fragmentary shards, while the women's faces derived from Egyptian, Iberian and African art, the latter still viewed as something crude and savage in this period. Picasso's friends and collectors were unable to accept this painting, which they felt was 'mad' and 'monstrous', and it remained rolled up in his studio for almost 10 years. To the dizzying handling of space inspired by Cézanne's landscapes, Picasso added a disregard for the European canonical treatment of the human body influenced by his interest in African art, preferring startling deformations and exaggerations to idealized proportions.

By the end of 1909, Picasso and Braque were close friends, and often painted together, producing works very similar in appearance. The period of 'Analytical Cubism', which lasted until 1912, saw the creation of paintings that took traditional motifs, such as still-life elements, landscapes and nudes, and broke these up into a series of facets, often incorporating fragmentary glimpses of an object or figure from different points of view. These motifs could sometimes become barely recognizable within an overall fluctuating mass of planes, painted in a limited colour palette of greys and browns, suggesting an emphasis on the conceptual process of coming to terms with the subject depicted. The practice and problems of painting became the content and meaning of these Cubist works, where the central question was no longer what to represent, but how to represent it. The need to create an illusion of depth ceased to concern Picasso and Braque as painters; in fact they deliberately drew attention to the point that their explorations of objects in space were in themselves as paintings completely flat. In *Pitcher and Violin* (1909–10), Braque included a trompe-l'oeil nail at the top of the canvas, as if to suggest that the painting itself was simply tacked to the wall, and in 1911 he began to include stencilled lettering in his oil paintings. Picasso created the first Cubist collage in May 1912 when he included a piece of imitation chair-caning in a still-life of a table top. This fragment of oil cloth, painted to give the illusion of a chair seat, seemed to imply that all oil painting was a game, a means of fooling the spectator into believing what he or she sees. Cubist works after 1912 began to include pasted papers, textures such as sand and a greater range of colours – a phase known as 'Synthetic Cubism'. If 'analysis' consisted in breaking objects down from their starting point in the real world, 'synthesis' meant that they were built up again from the basis of the simple geometrical forms of a piece of collaged paper or a block of colour. The Spanish-born Juan Gris (1887–1927), who came to Paris in 1906 and was strongly influenced by Picasso, produced synthetic Cubist works using a variety of colours and collage elements such as wallpaper and newspaper which were carefully cut and positioned, creating the impression of meticulous control over the objects depicted.

Picasso and Braque produced no manifesto, and in their later careers gave little explanation of their Cubist works. Many of their paintings and collages were small-scale, experimental works, which were not necessarily intended for public view. They did not exhibit during the Cubist period, relying instead on the support of the dealer Daniel-Henry Kahnweiler (1884–1979), who agreed to buy the whole of their output at fixed prices, giving them financial security and encouraging experimentation. But this private orientation did not mean that the Cubism of Picasso and Braque declined to engage with the outside world. In fact, their Cubist works are full of references to popular culture, to music hall, café life and advertisements. From 1912 to 1913, Picasso produced a series of pasted papers using newspaper clippings that referred to the Balkan Wars then raging in central Europe.

Cubism did, however, have a public face in the form of the so-called 'Salon Cubists', a group of artists who exhibited together and whose leading figures, Jean Metzinger (1883–1956) and Albert Gleizes (1881–1953), produced a theoretical tract, *On Cubism*, in 1912. The group included the young Marcel Duchamp (1887–1968) along with his two older brothers, as well as Robert Delaunay (1885–1941) and Fernand Léger (1881–1955). Léger had learned from Cézanne's distortions of pictorial space, and broke the forms in his paintings up into cylindrical geometrical shapes, which were dubbed 'tubist'. In 1913 he began to produce a series of works entitled *Contrasting Forms* – lively compositions based on abstracted discs highlighted with primary colours; red, blue and yellow. These paintings were inspired by Léger's interest in the shiny metallic forms of machines, and in the simplified designs on advertising billboards, both of which for him epitomized the dynamic potential of new, modern experience. Delaunay and his wife Sonia Delaunay-Terk (1885–1979) also began to create paintings using circles and arcs of contrasting colour which aimed to capture effects of light and movement. Their work was based initially on scenes of modern city life, particularly the motif of the Eiffel Tower, but paintings such as Robert Delaunay's 1912 *Circular Forms* relied less on recognizable subject matter, reflecting Sonia's abstract designs for fabrics and book-bindings. Delaunay's use of colour, as well as the Cubist handling of space, were both important inspiration for the Russian painter Marc Chagall (1887–1985), who lived in Paris between 1910 and 1914. Chagall combined these effects and modern motifs like the Eiffel Tower with subject matter drawn from his own upbringing to produce dream-like poetic paintings.

The poet Guillaume Apollinaire (1880–1918), a crucial supporter of modern art before the First World War, called the Delaunays' work 'Orphic', a variant of Cubism which would rely on colour and form rather than subject matter for its meaning; the name was drawn from the ancient myth of Orpheus, who created a kind of 'pure' music. In his seminal collection of writings *The Cubist Painters* (1913), Apollinaire claimed: 'We are moving towards an entirely new art which will stand, with respect to painting as envisaged up to now, as music stands to literature. It will be pure painting, just as music is pure literature.' The painters of Orphism, who also included Francis Picabia (1879–1953), did not, however, produce purely abstract works: 'pure painting' should rather be understood as a desire to create works which had their own internal coherence independent of the motif represented, and which could convey some of the dynamism of modern experience that to these painters was much more important than the depiction of external reality.

Futurism and Vorticism

'Dynamism' was one of the names considered by the Italian writer Filippo Tommaso Marinetti (1876–1944) for a new movement which he planned to establish; he eventually opted for 'Futurism', which also suggested his fascination with the technology and speed of the modern world. Futurism was the first major twentieth-century art movement to be launched explicitly through a series of written manifestos, sets of ideas which preceded the development of new ways of painting. Marinetti lived and worked in Milan, but he published his 'Founding Manifesto of Futurism' in French on the front page of *Le Figaro* in February 1909, as he wished to make an impact upon Paris, still the most important centre for art in Europe. This manifesto was a passionate and provocative attack on culture and tradition, calling for the destruction of museums and libraries and for the glorification of rioting crowds, violent revolutions and war. Beauty in this period, for Marinetti, was to be found in the products of modern technology and industry, and above all in speed, and he claimed that a car was superior in this respect to one of the Louvre's most prized and famous antique statues: 'a screaming automobile that seems to run on grape shot, is more beautiful than the *Winged Victory of Samothrace*'.

The exaggerated rhetoric of the Futurist manifestos was an important part of their aim to raise the maximum publicity for themselves, and to communicate their ideas to as wide an audience as possible. The Futurist group included the artists Umberto Boccioni (1882–1916), Giacomo Balla (1871–1958) and Carlo Carrà (1881–1966), who were involved in a series of widespread publicizing

Giacomo Balla, Grand Fiore Futurista

events. Futurist evenings were staged, which could include the showing of paintings, the reading of manifestos, theatrical sketches or the painter Luigi Russolo (1885–1947) playing his cacophonous 'Noise Machines'. These evenings would often begin with the Futurists hurling insults at their audience, and sometimes ended in brawls and street fights, reported – to their delight – in the press the following day. Between 1912 and 1914 an 'Exhibition of Futurist Painters' toured extensively, from Paris via Berlin and London to Chicago and Moscow, accompanied by a series of lectures and publications.

Futurist painting was just one part of an overall assault on the art world, and was intended above all to illustrate ideas laid out in? Futurist manifestos. Boccioni's 'Technical Manifesto of Futurist Painting' of 1910 sought to overthrow the art of the past, and described the swift succession and perceptual overloading of images of the modern world

that this new art should strive to capture: galloping horses which appeared to have 20 legs; hurtling trams that seemed to merge with the houses around them; the human body becoming part of the furniture on which it is sitting. Balla's *Dynamism of a Dog on a Leash* (1912) drew upon time-lapse photography to evoke the successive movements of a woman walking a small dog. Boccioni's *The Street Invades the House* (1911) showed a woman

leaning from a balcony, her form merging with the tumultuous activity in the street below. Futurist painters used vibrant colours, thrusting diagonals and energetic, swirling compositions in order to convey speed and movement. They drew upon painterly techniques that had already been established in the late nineteenth century, such as the principle of colour divisionism, a variant of Pointillism, as well as taking inspiration from Cubism. The faceted appearance of Futurist works, where the subject represented began to disappear beneath an overall pattern of shifting planes, and the use of lettering in the work of Carrà and the Paris-based Gino Severini (1883–1965), both derived from Cubist painting. To some extent Futurist painting could not live up to the strident requirements of its manifestos, and it relied more on other artistic developments than may have been intended.

The impact of Cubism and Futurism was felt in many European countries, and in Britain just before the First World War the dynamic treatment of the forms of the modern world found expression in the works of the Vorticist movement. The Futurist Boccioni had stated that

all art should find its source in what he called an 'emotional vortex', and this terminology was taken up by the poet Ezra Pound (1885–1972) to describe a kind of imagery which would not be flat 'surface art', but 'a VORTEX, from which, and through which, and into which ideas are constantly rushing'. The paintings of Wyndham Lewis (1882–1957), the central figure of Vorticism, are a good illustration of Pound's definition. Lewis used simplified angular forms suggestive of cityscapes in his compositions, arranged in such a way as to create the impression of plunging recessions and vertiginous depths. Edward Wadsworth (1889–1949) painted abstracted intersecting shapes of buildings, while David Bomberg (1890–1957), an associate of the group, fragmented his motifs, initially based on groups of moving figures, into a brightly coloured overall grid-like pattern. Bomberg's paintings were the most radical in appearance: *In the Hold* (1913–14) was made up of a myriad of jostling flat triangles of colour, its original subject matter indicated only by its title. Vorticism crystallized around the publication of the periodical *BLAST*, which appeared in two issues in 1914 and 1915, and which proclaimed the aim of these artists was to overthrow the legacy of Victorian Britain in an aggressive and violent way. The brutal energy that was one of Vorticism's central principles, along with its interest in machine technology, strikingly prefigured the mass warfare that brought the movement to an abrupt end.

Suprematism and Constructivism

Cubism had initiated the idea of reducing a motif from the external world to its most basic elements, and of presenting a motif in a painting in such a way as to make apparent the canvas's inevitable flatness. The Cubist style became familiar to Russian artists via the numerous exhibitions of Western contemporary art in Moscow, from 1912 onwards. Both Matisse and Picasso were patronised by wealthy Russian merchants, who exibited their works to the public. The Suprematism of the Russian artist Kasimir Malevich (1878–1935) took the essential aspects of Cubist painting to their extremes. Malevich believed that art could be free from the representation of recognizable figures and objects. By no longer having to worry about how to depict external reality, art could develop its own language of forms and create new realities 'no less significant than the realities of nature itself'. The key elements of Suprematist art for Malevich were the straight line and the square, which reflected his emphasis on the man-made rather than the forms found in nature. In Leningrad in 1915 the artist exhibited a series of works that he claimed he had worked on since 1913, including a notorious painting of a black square on a white background. The square was a form not to be found in nature; it was a deliberate negation of artistic illusionism as well as a provocative comment on the art of the past. Painted canvasses themselves are on the whole flat, square and rectangular forms; Malevich's squares, however, were also intended to carry their own meanings for the artist himself, mainly of a spiritual nature. The elementary act of painting a line or square was, for Malevich, a gesture of humility, and he talked about the empty backgrounds of his compositions in terms of infinite spaces. After a series of coloured compositions with groups of diagonally placed rectangular shapes, Malevich produced a series of 'White on white' paintings in 1918. These works, which suggested a kind of ultimate freedom from the material world, took painted representation to its limits, and proved a crucial inspiration for later generations of artists.

While Malevich felt strongly that art should have no connection with society, and that the artist should be able to pursue spiritual ideas in complete independence, other painters in Russia in this period, known broadly as the 'Constructivists', had a more pragmatic and rigorous approach to non-representational painting. In around 1911, Mikhail Larionov (1881–1964) had developed a style he called 'Rayonnism', a means of breaking up objects through rays of light, colours and textures, which was also explored in the work of his partner Natalia Goncharova (1881–1962). Alexander Rodchencko (1891–1956) worked on paintings based on abstract principles, which he would later call 'non-objective', such as a series of works created in 1914 with the help of a ruler and compass. Lyubov Popova (1889–1924) produced linear architectonic compositions. All of these painters were involved in the applied arts, creating theatre designs, book-bindings, textiles and posters, so that their artistic experiments had a public, practical application.

After the Russian Revolution of 1917, the concerns of 'non-objective' art as something divorced from reality were justified as 'laboratory research' – a means of trying out ideas which ultimately would contribute to the progress of the new socialist state. Some of the most important works of Constructivism would be posters and photomontages destined for a mass audience, but more significant even than these were the sculptural and architectural projects, which could directly benefit the public. Designs for constructions and buildings had their roots, however, in radical developments in painting, as explorations in three dimensions of the spatial possibilities of the painted surface. El Lissitzky (1890–1941) had trained as an architect and in the 1920s produced a series of paintings based around his concept of 'Proun', taken from the Russian word meaning 'new art forms'. Proun was a means of working in which the fundamentals of form such as space, proportion, flatness and rhythm were allied to function in the creation of utilitarian objects. Lissitzky's paintings, such as *Proun 99* (*c.* 1924), resembled architectural plans, depicted through rectilinear shapes and in muted tones. Lissitzky also travelled widely in the 1920s and was an important disseminator of Russian Constructivist theories to artists throughout Europe.

Purism

In France after the First World War, concern with the functionality of objects and links to architectural principles were central to the development of Purism. The movement was conceived in relation to Cubism, seen as a logical successor to it in the book *After Cubism* (1918), written by the painters Amédée Ozenfant (1886–1966) and Charles Edouard Jeanneret (1887–1965), now better known as the architect Le Corbusier. The Purists took up the still-life motifs from the Cubism of Picasso and Braque – bottles, glasses and guitars – which they saw as 'type objects' uniting the positive qualities of precision and simplicity. Ozenfant and Jeanneret were critical of the development of Cubism towards decoration, and they called for a return to the values of order and objectivity which they felt it had originally pursued. These values were also to be found in the material world of man-made and machine-made things, which for the Purists were a much more fascinating subject for art than the human figure; this, they believed, suggested too many associations and feelings and was thus distracting. Both Ozenfant and Jeanneret painted still-lifes in mainly interior settings, consisting of groups of bottles, cups, vases, pipes and musical instruments (all traditional still-life motifs, from the seventeenth century onwards), depicted in muted pastel colours. Their works appear quite similar, as both used a smooth painted finish in order to maintain an impersonal, objective effect. In works such as Jeanneret's *Still Life* of 1920, the round openings at the top of these objects were shown as a series of full circles placed around the canvas, ignoring traditional perspective as the Cubists had done, and creating a sense of rhythmic regularity and order. The Purist periodical *L'Esprit nouveau* ('The New Spirit') appeared between 1921 and 1925,

Liubov Popova, Pictorial Architectonic

and acted as a vehicle for the celebration of architecture, engineering and industrial design as key elements of a new functionalism and efficiency. Jeanneret began to pursue architectural projects in the early 1920s under the name Le Corbusier, famously declaring in 1923 that 'a house is a machine for living in'. Purism also had a noticeable influence on the design principles of the German Bauhaus school of architecture and design, which had been founded in 1919 by Gropius.

De Stijl and Neoplasticism

Several artists in the first decades of the twentieth century, such as the Delaunays, Kandinsky and Malevich, had experimented with non-representational paintings. In France, Matisse had progressed from his Fauvist works to paintings like *The Piano Lesson* (1916), which asserted the flatness of the picture plane, eliminating depth and volume in favour

Piet Mondrian, Composition with Red, Blue and Yellow

of the abstract play of lines and colours. These developments, however, were to find their most extensive and coherent exploration in the work of the Dutch artist Piet Mondrian (1872–1944), and of the group to which he belonged, De Stijl ('the style'), active between 1917 and 1932.

Mondrian's early work was inspired by Fauvist painting, showing brightly coloured and expressively painted landscape motifs, and between 1911 and 1914 he lived and worked in Paris, absorbing the new developments in Cubist art. A group of works based on single trees from this period show the artist's paring down of his motif, reducing the leaves and branches to a series of schematic markings or signs on a flat surface, and creating an overall pattern which appears to be held in place by fragments of rectangular and squared-off lines. The abstract paintings that Mondrian produced in these years had their origins in landscapes or still-life, which were now totally integrated into a rhythmic grid of squares and rectangles composed in muted shades of grey, pale blue and ochre. In the most extreme works of 1914–17, the shapes of the sea and pier at Scheveningen, near The Hague, were indicated only through a succession of monochrome 'plus' and 'minus' shapes. In his writings, Mondrian felt that this point of departure in nature was hindering his art, as nature aroused feelings and emotions that got in the way of what he called 'universal harmony'. He wanted to reduce the markings of his paintings even further, and create a new harmonious reality using elements of form and design.

Around 1917, Mondrian met the painter Theo van Doesburg (1883–1931), who was the leading figure behind the founding of the De Stijl group and the editor of a journal of that name through which ideas could be propagated. For van Doesburg and for the designer Gerrit Rietveld (1888–1964), another member of the group famous for his *Red-blue Armchair* (1917–18), colour was crucial. Under their influence, Mondrian began to use colour as a fundamental part of his compositions in its most basic form: the three primary colours of red, yellow and blue; and the three non-colours black, white and grey. According to his own theory of what he termed 'Neoplasticism', published in *De Stijl* in 1919, Mondrian's ultimate aim in painting was to reduce representation to its most elementary function: 'In painting you must first try to see *composition, colour and line* and not the representation *as representation*. Then you will finally come to feel the subject matter a hindrance.' Mondrian's best-known works pursue this aim, consisting of a series of rectangles in primary colours separated by a grid of black vertical and horizontal lines. These separating lines were necessary so that a painted rectangle would not suggest any illusion of depth. Paintings such as *Composition with Red, Yellow, Blue and Black* (1921) were intended to be completely impersonal, controlled and harmonious, creating a sense of balance that for Mondrian had a strong spiritual meaning. Mondrian would maintain his austere artistic vision rigorously throughout the rest of his career, developing variations on the essential principles of his compositions, such as lozenge-shaped canvasses as the basis for his groupings of lines and colours. Towards the end of his life, in 1940, he moved to New York, where the excitement of the metropolis was captured in the vibrant patterns of paintings such as *Broadway Boogie-Woogie* (1942–43), based on much smaller units to create a greater sense of movement and jazz-like rhythm.

Van Doesburg's work had made a crucial contribution to the development of De Stijl in his use of a strong asymmetricality, shown, for example, in his painting *The Cow* (1917), with its carefully placed flat blocks of colour – in this case pink, blue, yellow and black – on a plain white background. Van Doesburg also created a series of compositions based on diagonal forms, whose pattern of horizontal and vertical lines and rectangles were shifted through 90 degrees, to dynamic effect. Mondrian's belief in contrasting pictorial elements was extended by Van Doesburg to a vision of all of the arts: painting, sculpture, music and architecture. Architecture and applied design, particularly interior décor, furniture and typography, were an important part of De Stijl's overall programme. A style with clean, straight lines and no decoration was in part a reaction against the flowing qualities of Art Nouveau, and an assertion of the dominance of the man-made over the forms of nature. Van Doesburg's interest in design and in the creation of functional objects also led him, in a manifesto of 1923 entitled 'The End of Art', to praise everyday items like bicycles, cars, irons and bathrooms, and to pronounce any attempt to renew art as it had previously existed as bankrupt: 'Let us rather create a new life-form which is adequate to the functioning of modern life.'

Dada

The urgent need to liberate art from its past was nowhere more strongly felt in the early twentieth century than among the artists and writers internationally who were associated with the Dada movement. For the Dadaists, the 'end of art' was already taken for granted: art had been discredited by its connection with the world of consumerism, and was the preserve of the 'bourgeoisie' – a past generation whose values were seen to be stifling and defunct. The Dadaists reacted strongly against the generation of their parents and its associated morality, and responded to what they saw as the absurdity and mindless horror of the First World War. Dada came into being in Zurich in 1916, when a group of expatriate young artists in refuge from the war, including the Romanian writer Tristan Tzara (1896–1963) and the Alsatian Hans Arp (1887–1966), founded an arts center called the 'Cabaret Voltaire'. The name 'Dada' was taken either from a dictionary definition of a child's term for a rocking horse, or from the Romanian for 'yes'; either way it was intended to be deliberately child-like and nonsensical. The Cabaret Voltaire was a forum for artistic events: readings of nonsense poetry, recitals of folk songs and performances of raucous music, frenetic dancing and the display of new pictures. There was no stylistic principle to these manifestations: Dada was not a style but an attitude. Its tone caught on in other European centres, as well as in the United States during the war, where Duchamp and Picabia had got to know the artist Man Ray (1890–1977).

Arp was a poet as well as an artist and he later talked about the need to find an elementary means of creation which would save mankind from the madness of the times, by responding in an appropriate manner, summed up in his paradoxical claim 'Dada wanted to replace the logical nonsense of the men of today with the illogically senseless'. Arp used words and sentences chosen at random from newspapers in his poetry, and began to produce compositions based on torn-up pieces of paper dropped in chance formations. He also made woodcuts, reliefs, and later paintings and sculptures based on simple,

organic forms, often with absurd titles, like the relief *Navel, Shirt and Head* (1926). The principle of random combinations was also central to the work of Kurt Schwitters (1887–1948), a Dada artist working in Hanover. Schwitters used the term 'merz', a fragment from the word 'Kommerzbank' ('corporate bank'), to describe his collage works, which consisted of scraps of coloured paper and discarded bits of rubbish arranged in two and three dimensions.

Marcel Duchamp, Nude Descending a Staircase 2

An emphasis on the absurd and on chance was one of the means by which Dada artists responded to events in the wider world; a very particular attitude towards modern technology was another. Back in 1912, Duchamp had submitted a strange canvas entitled *Nude Descending a Staircase* to a Cubist exhibition called the 'Golden Section'. The painting had been rejected, and in a series of subsequent paintings had shown combinations of human and machine parts with titles that evoked love and desire. In contrast to the celebration of the machine that underpinned Futurism, Duchamp, along with Picabia, Man Ray and the German artist Max Ernst (1891–1976), produced works which ironized the new mechanized society. Picabia's diagrammatic drawings of mechanical parts, complete with labels, depicted nonsense machines which would never work in reality. The title of his painting *Amorous Parade* (1917) suggests that the dysfunctional collection of isolated parts he represents – levers, a piston and a large screw – are ironically symbolic of modern sexual relationships. Paintings like these had the appearance of scientific diagrams, precise and neutral, deliberately lacking any sense of the artist's unique powers of expression, as a commentary upon the nature of art itself. Ernst, working in Cologne, used a wide range of source materials in his paintings, drawings and collages, including illustrations from encyclopedias and engravings from technical manuals and sales catalogues, which he would juxtapose with other elements to create new and bizarre combinations. In his painting *The Elephant Celebes* (1921), a large metal corn bin is transformed into a grotesque imaginary creature.

Central to the Dadaist attitude was the nonsense gesture, intended to turn the very idea of art on its head. Duchamp presented for exhibition in New York in 1917 under a pseudonym an upturned urinal that he entitled *Fountain*: this man-made object was rejected from the show, an outcome that was undoubtedly intended. Duchamp

Art

Otto Dix, Kupplerin, A Woman Smoking

turned his back on painting in 1912, preferring to concentrate on 'ready-mades' like *Fountain*, and on interventions into famous paintings, like his addition of a moustache and an obscene caption to Leonardo da Vinci's *Mona Lisa*. The sanctity of great works of art was rudely undercut by Dada: Duchamp also once suggested that a Rembrandt could be used as an ironing board. Picabia's painting *L'Oeil cacodylate* (1921) was an intentional mockery of the financial value attached to the artist's signature: a piece of untreated canvas covered in the scrawled signatures, dedications and cut-out photographs of his friends and Dada associates.

In post-World War I Berlin, Dada took the form of a virulent political protest against society, and against the moral values of the Weimar Republic. The writer Richard Hülsenbeck (1892–1974) had been a founder member of Zurich Dada, and in 1917 he returned to his native Germany. In his 'First German Dada Manifesto' he claimed that: 'The highest art will be that which in its unconscious content presents the thousandfold problems of the day'. The 1920 Berlin Dada fair – an art exhibition which showed paintings and collages accompanied by slogans painted on the gallery walls – included a stuffed effigy of a Prussian officer with a pig's head suspended from the ceiling. George Grosz (1893–1959) produced drawings and paintings which brutally satirized figures of authority – the police, the army and the clergy – showing them as morally corrupt, greedy and sexually depraved, in line with his Communist convictions. In the hands of Hannah Höch (1889–1978) and John Heartfield (1891–1968), photomontage became a powerful tool for social commentary, for absurd and grotesque juxtapositions of words and images. Heartfield continued to use photomontage in the 1930s, to mock and undermine Hitler's regime.

Germany's moral decay was also evoked in the work of Otto Dix (1891–1969), whose paintings depicted subjects such as war cripples and prostitutes, figures on the margins of society who represented the fallout from a materialistic state. Dix often worked in tempera on wooden boards – an Old Master technique – and used a realistic style heightened by minutely observed details. This close attention to immediate surroundings, treated in an uncompromising and even 'ugly' way, was a feature of a painting style which developed in Germany in the 1920s, known as 'Neue Sachlichkeit' ('new objectivity'), and represented by artists like Grosz, Dix and Christian Schad (1894–1982), whose portrait paintings have smoothly worked surfaces and an almost photographic realism.

Surrealism

The term 'surrealism' was first used by the poet Apollinaire in 1917 to suggest a heightened sense of realism, but in Paris in the mid-1920s it came to designate a new art movement, whose influence was widespread and lasting. Dada activities in Paris, centering around Francis Picabia, had fizzled out by 1922, and a group of young artists and writers led by the poet André Breton (1896–1966) had begun to search for a more positive means of expression – one that would say 'yes' where Dada had said 'no'. The former Dadaist Max Ernst settled in Paris in 1922, and his work was praised by Breton for its strange juxtapositions, but above all for the new poetic vision of reality that these suggested. In order to try to stimulate new visions and ways of seeing, Breton, Ernst and a group of writers including the poets Paul Eluard (1895–1952) and Louis Aragon (1897–1982) experimented with mind-altering drugs and hypnotic trances. In 1924 Breton produced the 'First Surrealist Manifesto', in which he set out a definition of Surrealist activity as 'pure psychic automatism', a way of thinking that would be completely free of 'any control exercised by reason', as well as 'exempt from any aesthetic or moral concern'. As a kind of philosophical belief, Surrealism also set store by 'the superior reality of certain forms of previously neglected associations' and by 'the omnipotence of dream'.

Surrealism was primarily a literary movement, dominated by writers and poets, and the definitions of its manifestos were intended to apply to writing more than to painting. The Surrealists set out to produce 'automatic writing' – a free-flowing chain of thoughts and associations coming from the subconscious mind, inspired in part by treatments for psychiatric patients. Some members of the group questioned whether painting could ever be free of conscious control, as it was dependent on the artist's technical and compositional intentions. However, some artists did produce work which was seen to be – to some degree – 'automatic'. Surrealist journals such as *The Surrealist Revolution*, a crucial means by which the movement could express its ideas, were full of reproductions of drawings by the artist André Masson (1896–1987). Masson's paintings and drawings such as *Birth of the Birds* (1925), used flowing calligraphic lines to evoke figures, fruit, birds, fish and radiant suns caught up in a kind of swirling flux.

Surrealist artists found ways of creating works which suggested the absence of a controlling rationality. Masson also experimented with sand and paint poured on to the canvas, taking inspiration from the random forms which resulted. Ernst used the technique of 'frottage' ('rubbing'), in which he took the patterns of wood graining, stones or leaves as a starting point to create pencil or wax crayon rubbings which could then become the basis of mysterious compositions such as *The Great Forest* (1927). The Catalan artist Joan Miró (1893–1983) created paintings using simplified marks and signs – schematic stick figures, body parts, animals and insects, suns and stars – combined with drawn lines and sometimes written inscriptions. These paintings, for example *The Hunter* (1923–24), had a child-like and spontaneous appearance, as if they were a more basic means of expression, freed from the limitations of a 'civilized', Western mentality.

Surrealism and the Subconscious Mind

The Surrealists looked to the creativity of children and the mentally disturbed as models of an untrammelled vision – the eye in a 'savage' state, as Breton once wrote. But they also looked within themselves, to the subconscious world opened up by the writings of the Viennese psychoanalyst Sigmund Freud (1856–1939), and to the manifestation of this world in dreams and desires. The Surrealists were fascinated by the work of the Italian artist Giorgio de Chirico (1888–1978): they interpreted his paintings of deserted sunlit Italian piazzas with isolated statues, looming dark arcades and tall chimneys, such as *The Enigma of a Day* (1914), as full of hidden sexual symbolism. The dream-like atmosphere of de Chirico's works also had a great influence on Surrealism, realistically painted and subtly disorienting the spectator through shifting points of perspective. The Spaniard Salvador Dalí (1904–89) produced works which suggested dream scenarios, and which explored his own sexual fantasies and fears. He used his own personal symbols to evoke taboo themes such as masturbation and castration anxiety: a hand swarming with ants; the sticky insides of an egg; a floppy extended limb supported by a crutch; and a snarling lion's head to represent his feared father. Dalí's oil paintings were meticulous in their use of illusionistic detail, a technique that was crucial to his development of what he called 'paranoiac-critical' activity, the cultivation of painted double images. In *The Metamorphosis of Narcissus* (1937), a large hand holding an egg is echoed by the forms of a crouching figure and its reflection in a lake, suggesting the power of the mind to play tricks and reveal hidden subconscious thoughts.

The paintings of the Belgian artist René Magritte (1898–1967) also took up the idea of art as an illusion. Magritte used striking distortions of scale, paintings within paintings and strange juxtapositions (a bottle becoming a carrot), to force his viewers to question what they saw. He also explored contradictory combinations of images and words. *The Key of Dreams* (1930) depicted a series of objects including a hat, a shoe and a candle alongside handwritten labels which did not designate them at all.

The Surrealist 'revolution' in ways of seeing went beyond painting, moving into the fields of photography, film and object-making, and its combination of the cultivation of new artistic techniques along with new attitudes to social morality based on an acceptance of unconscious desires, was an inspiration to artists internationally. The exploration of personal, autobiographical events and feelings through disturbing imager, was a key feature of the work of artists such as the American painter Dorothea Tanning (b. 1910) and the Mexican Frida Kahlo (1907–58). Kahlo's paintings evoked her own anxieties and physical distress using strange details, such as the scattered locks of her own hair in her *Self-Portrait with Cropped Hair* (1940). The Chilean artist Roberto Matta (b. 1911) expressed his own subconscious feelings in paintings of free-floating forms suggesting scenes of violence and bodily deformation, which he called 'psychological morphologies'. Matta worked first in Paris, then from 1939 in the United States, and his work was an important influence on a new generation of American artists after the Second World War.

Roberto Matta, *Abstracto*

Surrealism was also a significant context for the development of the work of Picasso in this period. The surrealist leader André Breton had praised Picasso's Cubist works as seminal precursors in their creation of a 'window' on to a new world. In his large painting *The Three Dancers* (1925), Picasso combined flattened areas of colour and an interior setting deriving from Cubism with an evocation of magic ritual, violence and sexuality. Human figures in his paintings, particularly women based on his wife, Olga, and his lover, Marie-Thérèse Walter, began to be grotesquely deformed, with swollen limbs, bulging faces and screaming mouths. These expressive distortions were used to powerful effect in Picasso's 1937 painting *Guernica*. In response to the bombing of a Basque town by General Franco's forces during the Spanish Civil War, Picasso produced a horrific vision of an assault upon humanity. Twisted bodies and terrified women and children are depicted in a fragmented way suggesting the shattering impact of an air attack, in a black-and-white palette recalling newspaper photographs. The new painting styles of the twentieth century made possible visually striking and disturbing reactions to social and political events.

Paris Post War and Tachisme

Picasso remained in Paris during the German Occupation, producing still-lifes and figure studies which reflected the physical constraints and deprivations of wartime. Painting in Paris in the post-war period was marked by a sombre mood: subject matter that suggested the isolation of the individual, often executed in a limited palette. The existentialist philosophy of Jean-Paul Sartre (1905–80) began to reach a wide audience in 1945, and emphasized the absurdity of human existence and the importance of personal responsibility. Sartre also wrote on art, providing prefaces for exhibitions of the work of Swiss artist Alberto

Alberto Giacometti, Annette Assise

Giacometti (1901–66). Giacometti had created Surrealist sculptures in the 1930s, and had spent the war in neutral Switzerland. On his return to Paris, he began to produce a series of tall, elongated figure sculptures with roughly modelled surfaces, and in the 1950s he worked on painted portraits of his mother, wife and writer friends. These paintings show single figures almost disappearing beneath a mass of crosshatched lines, situated against yawning backgrounds which seem about to swallow them up. Giacometti used muted shades of brown and grey, and fine white lines to pick out the volumes of his figures. His mother in the painting *The Artist's Mother* (1951) takes on a skeletal, ghostly appearance.

Existentialism seemed to account, above all, for the experience of urban living: the alienating feeling of struggling alongside a mass of other individuals. The theme of urban existence was explored in the paintings of the French artist Jean Dubuffet (1901–85), who depicted single figures against graffiti-scrawled walls, or bustling group scenes full of men in suits and hats failing to interact with one another, such as *The Busy Life* (1953). Dubuffet developed a radical and characteristic painting technique, using thick, encrusted layers of paint which looked like smeared mud, sometimes enhanced with added glue, plaster or asphalt, and which were described by critics as 'living matter' and 'filth'. Dubuffet's technique sprang from his rejection of art-school training and of conventional notions of artistic beauty: he had abandoned art for almost 20 years to run the family wine business. He cultivated a

deliberately naïve style, depicting the human body in a child-like way, as a simple outline with caricatural, often grimacing features. Dubuffet had a strong interest in the art of children as a source of authentic expression, and in the art of the insane, assembling an important collection of what he termed *art brut* ('raw art').

A thick surface impasto or textured pigment was also a feature of the paintings of Jean Fautrier (1898–1964), where it took on harrowing connotations. Fautrier had heard the cries of tortured prisoners from his studio just outside Paris during the war, and the series of works that he produced with the title *Hostages* reflected this experience. In these paintings, light-coloured oil paint was built up to create rugged fragmentary heads and torsos, whose flesh looked mottled and bruised, while areas of red paint suggested bleeding wounds. The artistic treatment of the human body as a formless mass of matter, and the expressive improvised lines in Fautrier's compositions were characteristics of a style known as 'art informel' ('art without form'). The tendency towards abstracted markings suggesting emotive states of mind in French painting of this period was also known more specifically as 'Tachisme', from the French word *tache* ('blot' or 'mark'). The watercolours of Henri Michaux (1899–1984), evoking primordial mental states and sometimes produced under the influence of hallucinatory drugs, and the explosive scratched and scribbled paintings of the German-born Wols (1913–51), were representative of this style.

Abstract Expressionism

The expressive qualities of paint's colours and textures were an essential feature of the movement that developed in the United States during the 1940s that became known as Abstract Expressionism. The Abstract Expressionists were a loose grouping of painters in New York, working in varying styles, but sharing a desire for a freedom from traditional artistic values. Art in the United States had begun to evolve in the 1930s and 40s, rising to prominence over that emerging from the old centre of Paris, as European imperial dominance began to wane, and with it cultural dominance over the old art of the West. In addition a new community of artists and intellectuals had begun to arrive from Europe, fleeing political upheaval and persecution, and including some of the major exponents of the Purist-Abstract and Surrealist art movements. American artists were receptive to both styles, so that the previously mutually distinct movements were assimilated into a third, new style.

One of the dominant tendencies in 1930s American painting had been a realistic and often documentary style, depicting rural and small-town life, epitomized by the work of the Iowa-based Grant Wood (1892–1942). The Abstract Expressionists reacted against what they saw as the conservatism and dryness of this kind of painting, preferring spontaneous and personal expression. Cubism and Surrealism were important sources for the development of this new movement. The Armenian painter Arshile Gorky (1905–48) was a close friend of Roberto Matta, and developed in his own work strong personal imagery using brightly coloured biomorphic forms. In paintings such as *One Year the Milkweed* (1944), Gorky created a bursting mass of daubed shapes overlaid with blurring, dripping colours full of emotional and irrational intensity. Gorky wrote about his paintings as transcriptions of childhood recollections, as well as explorations of joy, anxiety and pain. Gorky was a significant link between the European art movements and the new generation of American painters. The artist Hans Hofmann (1880–1966) also had a considerable influence. Hofmann, born in Germany, had worked in Paris and Munich before moving to New York in 1932, where he taught some of the artists that would rise to prominence in the following decade. Hofmann's paintings of still-lifes and landscapes bore the marks of Cubism, but he also began to experiment with bold brushwork, strong colours and most importantly, with techniques of dripping and dribbling paint on to the canvas.

Jackson Pollock (1912–56) developed an abstract style based initially on mythic imagery inspired by the work of Picasso, Masson and Miró, and evoking sexual and violent themes expressed in a spontaneous way similar to Surrealist 'automatism'. Pollock had undergone psychoanalysis based on the teachings of the Swiss psychologist Carl Gustav Jung (1875–1961), which revolved around a series of collective, subconscious archetypes, such as the opposition of male and female qualities. Powerful, universal forces were suggested in the large-scale paintings that Pollock began to produce from 1946. He placed his canvasses horizontally on the floor and poured paint on to them in splashes and dribbles from all directions. Works like *Full Fathom Five* (1947) present a rhythmic mass of dripped paint, supplemented with small found objects such as cigarettes, nails and buttons, without any recognizable subject matter. Great arcs and curving forms reflect Pollock's vigorous gestures in creating the work, moving freely around the canvas using dried-out brushes, sticks and trowels to apply his paint from a distance. This process was known as 'action painting'. Pollock's work had great significance within the development of modern painting through its insistent treatment of the canvas as a flat – in this case horizontal – surface, and through its emphasis on the painter's own processes of creation.

Gestural energy and an emotive 'unfinished' appearance were important features of the painting of other artists associated with Abstract Expressionism, such as Lee Krasner (1911–84), Pollock's wife, and the Dutch-born Willem de Kooning (1904–97). De Kooning's work maintained a tension between abstraction and figuration, using the female nude in particular as the basis for compositions in violent reds and pinks. De Kooning was less interested in the processes of 'automatic' creation than in the relationship between the flat picture surface and the illusion of volume of the human figure, between the drawn line and the fleshy presence of colour. These concepts he had derived from Cubism, and from the work of Picasso in particular, whose grotesque deformations of women's bodies were a forceful inspiration upon De Kooning's *Woman* series of the early 1950s. The exuberance of this strain of Abstract Expressionism had a formative influence on the work of the 'Cobra' group of young painters in Europe, which included the Dutchman Karel Appel (b. 1921), with his stridently coloured, child-like animal and figure scenes, and the Dane Asger Jorn (1914–73), whose paintings are full of furious brushstrokes and disorderly forms in primary colours. The American Cy Twombly (b. 1928) was also inspired by the spontancity of Abstract Expressionism as well as by the child-like vision of Paul Klee, creating complex scribbled works midway between painting and drawing.

The Colour-Field Technique

A very different tone and tendency was explored in New York in the work of Clyfford Still (1904–80), Barnett Newman (1905–70) and Mark Rothko (1903–70). All three passed through a stage of experimenting with mythic themes – chaotic, archetypal landscapes and primordial forms – to eventually develop personal abstract works known collectively as 'colour-field' paintings. In colour-field paintings the artists applied pure pigments to the canvas to create subtle variations in colour that were evocative of mood. From 1945, Still began to produce paintings using large planes of colour which dominated most of the canvas, at its edges making room for jagged fragments of other layers of paint. Still used a palette knife to apply paint evenly, creating a sense of emptiness, particularly in the centre of the canvas where we would expect the focus of a composition to be. He was adamant in his rejection of a painterly

Willem De Kooning, Woman

tradition, which he characterized as 'dust and filing cabinets', and he was scathing of the spectator's attempts to be comforted or uplifted by art. Still's works are deliberately inaccessible and difficult to read, an assertion of his own perception of his 'solitary' and 'outside' status.

Barnett Newman was more receptive to the spiritual potential of his abstract paintings. In *Onement I* (1948) Newman laid a strip of masking tape painted orange-red vertically down the centre of his rectangular, deep-red canvas, originally intending to remove it later, but liking the result so much that it remained. A series of works ensued, known as the 'zip paintings' because of their single vertical stripes. These stripes echoed the edges of the canvas, making the process of framing the composition an integral part of the painting. The use of the whole canvas is a crucial characteristic of colour-field painting, and Newman once described how he reached a stage with his work 'where I got to the edge and didn't fall off'. Newman frequently gave his works suggestive titles, often on biblical themes, imparting to his paintings the sense of a search for simple, elemental forms.

Mark Rothko, who was of Russian origin, also talked in terms of 'ritual' and 'a transcendent realm' with regard to his paintings after 1947. His works were conceived to be seen up close in an atmosphere of silence, in order to encourage an intimate response. Their large scale was a corollary of this, allowing the spectator to enter into the experience of viewing them, as Rothko suggested: 'A large picture is an immediate transaction: it takes you into it.' The artist used veil-like layers of colour of varying warmths and coolnesses, creating an effect of soft depth which seems to engulf the onlooker. Patches of luminous colour are characteristically arranged as a stacked series of horizontally aligned rectangles in Rothko's works of the 1950s, such as *Number 10* (1950), creating an impression of calm meditation and otherworldly mystery. Warm reds and maroons gave way to more sombre colours in Rothko's later work as he succumbed to depression. The artist thought of his paintings not as totally abstract, but he was interested in how they could convey basic human emotions.

Pop Art

Pop Art first emerged in the mid-1950s in both America and Britain. In part it was a reaction against the emotional seriousness and introspection of Abstract Expressionism, which had been affected by the experience of the Second World War. In the United States, John F. Kennedy's presidency, which began in 1960, marked a new era of optimism and a celebration of middle-class consumer values. The term

'Pop Art' was coined by the British-born critic and curator Lawrence Alloway (1926–90) in 1954 to describe the 'popular art' and imagery produced by a mass culture which 'high' art had begun to pick up and use: flags, jukeboxes, badges, advertising logos, comic strips and magazines. This interest in 'low' art forms as a means of rejuvenating artistic tradition had its precursors in American modern art in the work of earlier painters like Charles Demuth (1883–1935) and Stuart Davis (1894–1964). Demuth's painting *I Saw the Figure Five in Gold* (1928), for example, had recalled the industrial look of mechanically produced billboard lettering. After the intensity of Abstract Expressionism, Pop Art favoured irony and impersonal techniques in the creation of art works, as well as a return to figurative painting.

Bridging the Gap: Abstract Expressionism to Pop Art

The work of Robert Rauschenberg (b. 1925) and Jasper Johns (b. 1930) was influenced by the use of everyday, 'found' materials in Cubist collage and in the 'ready-mades' of Marcel Duchamp. From 1954, Rauschenberg began to produce works that incorporated collage elements and everyday objects, existing part way between two and three dimensions. For the artist, the activity of making these works was somewhere between art and life. In *Bed* (1955), Rauschenberg suspended a bed vertically on a wall and splashed it with coloured paint, a parody of the Abstract Expressionists' 'drip paintings', suggesting that their ideas had been brought into the realm of the banal and the everyday. The 'all-over' effect created by Rauschenberg's combines, where no single element appeared compositionally more important than the others – whether painted, reproduced or found – was also similar to the 'all-over' paintwork of Abstract Expressionism.

A painterly style deriving from Abstract Expressionism was employed by other artists of the so-called 'Beat generation' of the 1950s, such as the jazz musician-turned-painter Larry Rivers (b. 1923) and the performance artist Jim Dine (b. 1935). Jasper Johns, too, in his paintings referred ironically to the mode that he had pursued in his early work, by using expressive, gestural brushstrokes. His individualistic technique, however, was characteristically applied to subject matter common to everyone: familiar mass imagery such as flags and targets. In the painting *Three Flags* (1958), Johns depicted three American flags of decreasing size, one on top of the other, creating an image that was at once recognizable, but also formed a kind of abstract pattern. In works like this, attention was drawn away from the subject represented, with its well-known forms and colours, towards the handling of the paint itself. The representation and incorporation of real objects in Johns' paintings, and his sculptures of beer cans and flashlights in real-life scale and detail, raised the issue of art as a process of thought, making Johns an important forerunner of Conceptual Art. His use of bold, iconic imagery, however, was a crucial inspiration for the Pop artists.

The world of advertising and graphic design was a major source for Pop Art. James Rosenquist (b. 1933) worked as a billboard painter before incorporating the large-scale, clear-cut forms and slick realism of advertising into his works. The painting *F-111* (1965) put together a jumble of images from the mass media, including a jet bomber and a child's smiling face, to suggest the jarring juxtapositions of modern urban life. Ed Ruscha (b. 1937) painted isolated words and signs as striking graphic elements in their own right. Most famously, Andy Warhol (1928–87) first worked as an illustrator producing advertisements and fashion designs, creating in the early 1960s a series of stencilled paintings using industrial paint which depicted cans of Campbell's tomato soup, dollar bills and Coca-Cola bottles. Warhol, like Johns, deliberately chose motifs that were part of a common American culture, and he developed a technique of screen-printing his images so that they could be mass reproduced.

A stylistic neutrality and lack of emotion were important aspects of Warhol's paintings, so that they maintained a deliberate distance from the realm of 'fine' or 'high' art. His studio, known as 'The Factory' and comprising many acolytes and hangers-on, produced a large amount of work in an intentionally machine-like way. Warhol also used repetition to emphasize this idea of industrial-style production and, in his works depicting famous personalities like Marilyn Monroe and Elvis Presley, to suggest the superficiality of celebrity and media culture. His painting *Marilyn Diptych* (1962), created just after the film star's death, evoked a melancholy sense of the inadequacy of the iconic image through the blurring and fading of Marilyn's repeated face.

The importance of the visual image as a form of mass communication which had superseded the written word, in the form of film, television and comics, was a key feature of the work of Roy Lichtenstein (1923–98). Lichtenstein's paintings were composed of a series of tiny, meticulously painted 'Ben Day' dots – the basic components of printed imagery – and they depicted isolated comic-strip frames, often complete with words and captions. The painting *Girl with Hair Ribbon* (1965) showed a glamorous blue-eyed blonde with an anxious expression, suggesting the small-scale mundane dramas of American suburban life.

Roy Lichtenstein, Kiss II

Pop Art in Britain as it developed in the early to mid-1950s expressed a desire for an American lifestyle of consumer plenty, in contrast to the atmosphere of post-war rationing and privation. In a collage entitled *"Just what is it that makes today's homes so different, so appealing?"* (1956), the artist Richard Hamilton (b. 1922) put together magazine images including an advertisement for a vacuum cleaner, a tin of preserved ham, a Ford motor-car insignia and a muscle-bound bodybuilder as an ironic, but also celebratory, homage to aspirational consumerism. The Scottish-born Eduardo Paolozzi (b. 1924) also drew upon popular American magazines, using a spicy women's magazine called 'Intimate Confessions' in his early piece *I Was a Rich Man's Plaything* (1947). Peter Blake (b. 1932) took inspiration above all from popular music, using collaged photographs, but also the traditional technique of oil paint on canvas or board, to represent magazine covers featuring Elvis or Bo Diddley. His own role as a fan and collector of pop ephemera and souvenirs is evoked in the painting *Self-Portrait with Badges* (1961), which suggests a certain nostalgia rather than an enthusiastic embrace of modern technology. Blake's association with pop music was cemented by his creation of the album cover for the Beatles' *Sergeant Pepper's Lonely Hearts Club Band* in 1967.

The early work of David Hockney (b. 1937), born in the north of England, drew upon popular culture, most notably in the form of graffiti, but after he visited and eventually settled in California from the mid-1960s his painting style became flatter, reflecting a shift from oil paint to smooth acrylics. Hockney used simplified shapes – the horizontal forms of houses, lawns, hedges, pools and the blue Californian sky – in a series of works depicting the different movements of water. His painting *A Bigger Splash* (1967), showing a white spray of water from an immaculate swimming pool, evoked a wealthy and laid-back lifestyle, while in *Sunbather* (1966), a homoerotic male nude lies beside a calm pool, its shimmering surface suggested by graphic undulating lines. Hockney was an important mediator between British and American Pop Art.

Nouveau Réalisme

The use of found objects and remnants of everyday life, as well as an ironic attitude towards the new consumer society, were features that Pop Art shared with the work of a group of artists in France in the 1960s, known as the Nouveaux Réalistes ('new realists'). These artists, who included Yves Klein (1928–62), Arman (b. 1928) and Jean Tinguely (1925–91), wanted to involve contemporary society directly in their work through references to consumerism and the mass media, in an attempt to engage with 'the passionate adventure of the real'. To this end, they experimented with performances and events, and with three-dimensional 'assemblages' based on the principle of collage. The artist Niki de Saint-Phalle (b. 1930) created a series of 'shooting paintings': large collections of assembled objects at which she and fellow artists would fire small cloth bags filled with paint, to produce a spattered, violent effect. Born into a society family, Saint-Phalle rebelled

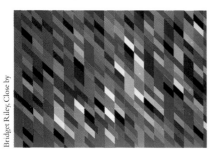

against the traditional female roles that were expected of her, depicting grotesque 'crucified' women in a combination of paint and other media.

Bridget Riley, Close by

Yves Klein, who had no formal art training, made paintings which had a direct link to performance. He produced a series of charred works on paper, made with the aid of a blowtorch. His *Anthropometries*, whose title suggested the scientific measuring of human proportions, were based on the bodily imprints of nude models on paper or canvas, and were often created during notorious public 'happenings'. These paintings were both literally figurative – a kind of portraiture of each individual body – and also abstract, an effect reinforced by Klein's predominant use of the colour blue. His favourite shade was patented as 'International Klein Blue': the cultivation of his provocative personality was an important part of his artistic activity. The Italian artist Piero Manzoni (1933–63) met Klein in 1957, and under his influence moved away from figurative painting to the creation of plain canvasses enhanced with simple details such as a covering of white objects, which he called 'Achromes' ('without colour'). *Achrome* (1960) was a canvas covered in a fine clay material and bunched up into horizontal folds in the centre of the composition, and Manzoni also slashed and stitched his canvasses to draw attention to them as objects in themselves. The notion of art as performance, central to Nouveau Réalisme, was taken up by Manzoni in his famous gestures of signing balloons filled with his own breath, and tins containing his own faeces.

Op Art

While Pop Art relied on recognizable images to get across its celebration or parody of contemporary culture, the 1960s tendency known as 'Op Art' was uncompromisingly abstract. Op Art had its sources in Russian Constructivism and in the Suprematism of Malevich, in developing a painting style that was all about the spectator's perception of abstract forms and about the sensations and illusions that these could provoke. The term 'Op' is a shortening of 'optical', and Op Art aimed to explore the effects of different kinds of retinal stimulation, using closely spaced black-and-white or coloured patterns. In line with other modern developments, Op Art sought not to provide the illusion of representation – one of painting's traditional roles – but to make the viewer question his or her processes of seeing. But Op Art was not only confined to the realm of 'high' art: when the term was first coined in the American media in 1964, it also quickly came to refer to a characteristic design scheme used for fabrics, wallpaper and other household objects.

The Hungarian-born painter Victor Vasarély (1908–97), who worked for most of his life in France, trained as a graphic designer, creating works in black and white, before devoting his career from the late 1940s onwards to abstract painting using optical effects to suggest movement and depth. He believed that the standardized forms in his works could lead to a new, urban art replacing easel painting. Vasarély's coloured works with their pulsating squares and circles came to be seen as the epitome of Op Art. In Britain, Bridget Riley (b. 1931) also had a background in commercial design and advertising, going on to produce works like *Burn* (1964) – a composition in emulsion on hardboard, using repeated black-and-white triangles, which appear to fluctuate and move, disorienting the viewer. Riley's paintings combine a neutral and meticulous technique with a spectacular and psychologically affecting visual result.

Minimalism

Minimalism or Minimal Art of the late 1950s and early 1960s sought to eliminate all self-expression from the work of art. Like Op Art, it looked to earlier twentieth-century movements like Suprematism and the Neoplasticism of Mondrian as precedents in the creation of works that were meaningful in their own right without representing anything, and that were conceived in the artist's mind rather than found in nature. The painter Agnes Martin (b. 1912), born in Canada but working in New York in the 1960s, entitled a work of 1965 *Harvest*, which consisted of a fine grid of criss-crossing pencil lines on a plain cream canvas. Martin created these thousands of lines with a ruler, to produce a geometric work which was emotionless and impersonal, bearing an oblique relation to the natural motif of its title.

Minimal Art had in part evolved out of Abstract Expressionism, from the increasingly pared-down paintings of Barnett Newman. Ad Reinhardt (1913–67) had been a close associate of the Abstract Expressionists, but partly through the inspiration of Oriental art had begun to produce paintings using a single colour and simple symmetrical rectilinear forms. In 1960, Reinhardt created a series of 'black paintings' which consisted of nine even squares of black paint on a canvas, only barely distinguishable from each other, to make the shape of a cross. In a statement of 1962 entitled 'Art as art', Reinhardt claimed that the only aim of abstraction could be to make art 'purer and emptier, more absolute and more exclusive'. The young artist Frank Stella (b. 1936) also produced 'black paintings'. In 1959 an exhibition at the Museum of Modern Art in New York included four large radical works by Stella, then aged 23. These paintings, such as *Die Fahne hoch!* ('The Flag High!') of 1959, were based on symmetrical patterns of regular pinstripes. Stella applied stripes of black enamel using a housepaint brush, leaving small gaps between them through to the canvas beneath. The evocative titles of these works, with their potential for private associations in the mind of the spectator, sat uneasily with their blank formal effects. The title *Die Fahne hoch!*, for example, derived from a German Nazi anthem, while the work's cruciform pattern recalled a 1923 painting by Malevich called *Black Cross*. These paintings also stood out from the walls against which they were displayed to an unusual extent, due to Stella's use of thick stretcher bars for his canvasses, making them more like three-dimensional objects. Many of the artists associated with Minimalism turned away from painting towards sculpture, including Donald Judd (1928–94) and Carl Andre (b. 1935), famous for his floor-based groups of commercial firebricks.

Conceptual Art

Both Pop artists and Minimalists had been concerned to some degree with art as a means of thinking – 'art as idea' – which could go beyond the boundaries of the traditional media of painting, drawing and sculpture to include gestures, performances and happenings. The common starting point of these different manifestations was the rejection of the conventional art object: something tangible and unique that could be exhibited and sold. The work of Marcel Duchamp in the 1910s was a crucial inspiration for this, through his designation of objects – a bicycle wheel, a bottle rack and a row of coat pegs – as well as transactions – a cheque for his dentist, a bond for a roulette game – as 'art'. Conceptual Art, an international movement bridging the 1960s and 1970s, often resulted in events and activities which were short-lived, existing for posterity only in the form of photographs, film or written documentation. However, painting was also used by Conceptual artists to raise questions in the mind of the observer, whose role now became more important than ever by participating in and 'completing' the work of art.

A shift of emphasis away from the art object itself and towards a set of ideas about the role and function of art led to the frequent use of language as an integral part of an art work. The Italian-born artist Ben Vautier (b. 1935), working in France, painted bold slogans in acrylic on canvas which were intended as a kind of anti-establishment propaganda. The painting *Art is Useless, Go Home* (1971) consisted of the sentence 'L'art est inutile rentrez chez vous' in large white capital letters on a bright red background, a playful and provocative piece which transforms painting into a paradoxical 'anti-art' activity. The American artists Joseph Kosuth (b. 1945) and Lawrence Weiner (b. 1940) used words printed on the gallery wall or as images to be reproduced in different contexts such as billboards or even advertisements in newspapers. Kosuth characteristically employed dictionary definitions, blown up in large scale and printed white on black, of words related to his art-making processes, such as 'idea'. The British group Art and Language, which included the artists Michael Baldwin (b. 1945) and Mel Ramsden (b. 1944), saw the production of communal texts as an integral part of their art practice, as well as producing ironic paintings based on Socialist Realist icons like Lenin and Stalin in the style of Pollock's Abstract Expressionism.

If ideas were the main subject of Conceptual Art, the process of creating a work became just as important as the 'finished' result. The Japanese artist On Kawara (b. 1933), based in New York, has worked since 1966 on a series of 'date paintings', each of which is a neutral white-on-black transcription of the date on which the work is made, in the language of the country he is working in. The Pole Roman Opalka (b. 1931) began in 1965 an extensive series of paintings called *1 to*

Ad Reinhardt, Untitled Gouache on Paper

Infinity, in which canvasses are filled with infinite sequences of numbers, each one recorded into a tape player at the same time as it is painted. Each of Opalka's paintings in this series is regarded as a 'detail' from the larger overall work. The work of these two artists shares an emphasis on painting which is almost anonymous, a vehicle rather than an end in itself. The French artist Daniel Buren (b. 1938) reduced his paintings to simple stripes as a protest against individual artistic style, and in 1966 decided that he would henceforth use only stripes of white and one colour and of a consistent width, in all his subsequent work. Buren uses his striped format on paintings, billboards or on panels of fabric to be shown in spaces both inside and outside the art gallery, in order to criticize the elitism of the art world.

Conceptual Art was often austere and unrelenting in its appearance and its attitude towards artistic tradition, seen as ideologically loaded and unacceptable. The movement began to fade in the mid-1970s, when artists began to take a renewed interest in painting's materials and subject matter. It had, however, brought to the fore the use of irony, humour and autobiographical content which would all be taken up by new generations of artists.

New Painting and Neo-Expressionism

The late 1970s saw a concerted return to painting as a central artistic concern, in reaction to the explosion of different kinds of art activity in previous decades, such as photography, video and installation art. The painting that was produced differed in style, often harking back to earlier twentieth-century modes. One common feature was a rejection of the conception of painting seen as a specifically flat medium, whose subject matter and treatment should reflect this inevitable flatness. The

Anselm Kiefer, Noch Ist Poten Nicht Verloren IV

so-called 'New Painting' of the late 1970s and 1980s turned away from this emphasis on flatness, which had been seen as key aspect of the development of pictorial abstraction, preferring to use painting to represent external reality in its traditional function as a 'window on to the world'. The resurgence of painting took place primarily in the then West Germany, Italy, the United States and Britain.

One of the features of the revival of painting was a reappraisal of the work of an older generation of artists whose work had always been figurative, despite changing artistic fashions. In London in 1976, the artist R. B. Kitaj (b. 1932), who had been born in America and who had played an important role in British Pop Art, organized an exhibition of figurative painting that included the work of Lucian Freud (b. 1922) and Francis Bacon (1909–92), painters known together as the 'School of London'. Kitaj's own work comprised landscapes and figure scenes, often quoting from 'high' art sources like Renaissance paintings, with a stress on painting's narrative content. Freud's paintings were nude studies and portraits, often seen close to or from unusual angles, with a powerful, painterly handling of flesh and an honest, sometimes frankly ugly, treatment of the naked human body. Freud's visceral and psycho-logically unnerving approach to the figure has continued in his painting up to the present day. Since the late 1940s, Francis Bacon had painted in an expressive mode, using distorted depictions of the human body to evoke sharpened emotions of pleasure and pain. Bacon had a strong interest in portraiture, particularly self-portraiture, and in narrative history painting. In his painting *Triptych – August 1972*, Bacon used a traditional religious format to depict three different views of his friend George Dyer in an austere empty room, both seated, and in the central panel, apparently writhing on the floor. The artist's use of paint to create flesh which is beautiful and repulsive simultaneously was part of his aim to 'bring the figurative thing up onto the nervous system more violently and more poignantly'. It was significant for these artists of the School of London that the human figure had never gone away as one of painting's central concerns.

In the United States, the painter Leon Golub (b. 1922) had also worked in a figurative style, in line with his deep left-wing political commitments. In 1976 he began a series of paintings called *Mercenaries*, whose raw realism was intended to reflect the violence of international conflicts – in Vietnam, Africa and Latin America. Golub used press and media photographs for details of weapons, uniforms and even bodily gestures, but believed that his large-scale paintings had a role as a kind of modern history painting, despite the extensive media coverage of wars and atrocities, which he saw as manipulated and tendentious. His works, with their bold coloured backgrounds and scraped-away painted flesh (an effect achieved by Golub's use of a small meat-cleaver as a painting tool) were intended to be shocking. Through their large size, the figures depicted – laid-back killers or interrogators – are, Golub insisted, 'inserted into our space and we're inserted into their space', forcing the spectator into confrontation.

History painting, which had been the dominant mode of nineteenth-century painting, was rejected in the first half of the twentieth century in favour of more intimate and experimental modes. In the work of the German Neo-Expressionists in the late 1970s and early 1980s, however, it was revived as a means of commenting upon Germany's past and of expressing distrust for political developments like the desire for the unification of East and West. These painters used exuberant brushstrokes and bright colours in their works, prompting identification with the early twentieth-century Expressionist movement, as well as with Fauvism through the designation 'Neue Wilden' ('the new wild ones').

Investigating Concepts of Art

The artist Jörg Immendorff (b. 1945) had been trained under the seminal Conceptual artist Joseph Beuys (1921–86), who drew heavily upon his German roots in the creation of a personal mythology. Beuys served in the Luftwaffe during the Second World War, and was shot down over the Crimea in 1943. His rescue by nomads was to shape his philosophy as an artist; the felt and fat in which they covered him, enduring as two of his favourite materials (expressing warmth and comfort), and their Shamanic beliefs influencing his view that the role of an artist was akin to that of a Shaman: channelling energy through objects to give them symbolic power.

Immendorff's large, complex compositions, such as his *Café Deutschland* series, brought together military and political characters like Lenin, Stalin and Hitler, as well as using symbols of German identity such as flags, eagles and tanks. Anselm Kiefer (b. 1945) included the name of Joseph Beuys alongside those of the Romantic painter Caspar David Friedrich and the composer Richard Wagner in his 1973 painting *Spiritual Heroes of Germany*. His large-scale works of the 1980s also explored the theme of Germany's past, often evoking myths in a

manner deliberately and pointedly reminiscent of the Nazis. Kiefer used highly textured, expressive surfaces, but combined with problematic and distancing subject matter, questioning painting's role as direct self-expression. The artist Georg Baselitz (b. 1938) distanced the viewer from his emotionally charged brushwork by turning his compositions upside down, counteracting conventional ways of looking at art. Unlike that of Immendorff and Kiefer, Baselitz's art is sensual and anti-intellectual, focused on the act of painting and breaking down the barriers between abstraction and figuration, in order to be, as the artist put it, 'delivered of all ballast, delivered from tradition'.

The Italian painter Francesco Clemente (b. 1952) produced highly eclectic works drawing on a range of different religious, cultural and mythological motifs, using the traditional fresco technique of painting into wet plaster that had been perfected in the Renaissance. Working in different international locations, principally Italy, India and New York, Clemente created paintings in the 1980s that took on references specific to the place in which he found himself. Clemente was seen as the foremost representative of a new *Transavanguardia* ('beyond the avant garde'). The principle of referring to different artistic subjects and styles within the same painting was characteristic of the so-called 'Bad Painting' that developed in the United States in the 1980s. The young artist Julian Schnabel (b. 1951) was one of the leaders of this trend, creating energetic large-scale paintings in which 'high' art themes such as motifs from the Classical tradition are mixed with 'low', popular art forms like broken crockery. His work *Blue Nude with Sword* (1979–80) used a dramatic fragmented surface of smashed plates upon which were painted Classical columns and a vigorous squatting male nude brandishing a sword. Schnabel also attached unconventional materials such as lino, velvet and fake fur to his canvases which, along with his fragmentary quotations from Old Master paintings, created a confusing and even infantile effect.

The work of Keith Haring (1958–90) and Jean-Michel Basquiat (1960–88) also employed a child-like style, derived from the popular cultural forms of graffiti and street art. Haring was trained as an artist, but began his career decorating empty advertising hoardings in the New York subway before his brightly coloured scenes of dancing cartoon-like figures were accepted by art galleries and museums. A series of untitled works in acrylic on muslin from 1984 combined his trademark figures with motifs from the world of comic books and pop culture – aeroplanes, flying saucers and computers – rendered in simple thick black outlines. Basquiat, of Puerto-Rican and Haitian parentage and born in Brooklyn, brought to his paintings his favourite boyhood obsessions: cars, weapons, war, old movies, Richard Nixon and J. Edgar Hoover, as well as referring to Cajun, Hispanic and black American culture. Basquiat used a combination of acrylic, oil paint and wax crayons, enclosing his simplified figures and symbols with white lines, like chalk on a blackboard. His figures' grimacing, skeletal faces, in paintings like *Profit I* (1982), recall the caricatural style of the French artist Jean Dubuffet, while his graffiti-like scratches and scribbles suggest an ironic take on 'primitive' art.

In contrast to the profuse, energetic style of Schnabel, Haring and Basquiat, other American painters associated with the revival of figurative painting, preferred a more neutral, realistic mode. Eric Fischl (b. 1948) used a relaxed, casual style to depict subjects full of simmering repressed desires such as *Bad Boy* (1981). The directness of his scenes of young adolescent boys in sexual situations, combined with subtle lighting effects, makes the viewer a prurient voyeur of these explorations of suburban American anxieties. The artist Mark Tansey (b. 1949) created deadpan figure scenes which play tricks on the viewer in the manner of the paintings of René Magritte. *Action Painting II* (1984) was realistically painted in a monochrome range of blues, like a black-and-white photograph, and shows a group of easel painters depicting the launch of a space rocket in mid-air: the visual joke is that they could not possibly have captured their motif so quickly. The work refers both to American patriotism, through its inclusion of a flag and the space shuttle, and to the classic American art movement Abstract Expressionism in its title. Realistic painting was used with an ironic awareness of previous modern art movements.

Postmodernism and Contemporary Currents

One of the issues at stake in the revival of painting was the sense that in the wake of the profusion of artistic experimentation of the twentieth century, no really new and original style could be created. Rather, hybrid forms of painting and pastiches of former styles were the only way forward, a belief which fully acknowledged the impossibility of the artistic expression of real, 'authentic' feelings and emotions – so central a principle in the creation of 'modern' art. The term 'post modernism' signalled that this belief in originality and authenticity was now defunct, and that assumptions about what art could be were no longer valid in a new era of cynicism. In the mid-1980s, the cultural theorist Jean Baudrillard described the dominance of what he called 'hyperreality' in our experience of images. In the face of the ever-increasing growth and saturation of the mass media and the commercial world, the existence of something 'real' behind this surface proliferation of imagery was being called into doubt. The 'postmodern' artist would knowingly play with this 'hyperreal', exploring the impact of its simulated reality.

Postmodernism can be used to describe the work of a variety of artists from the mid-1970s up to the present. 'Neo-Expressionism' and American 'Bad Painting', in particular the work of Julian Schnabel, have features that can be seen as postmodern. The idea of making a painting by copying another visual source is a striking way of suggesting the end of art's uniqueness, a postmodern trait which had its roots in Dada and Pop Art. The German artist Gerhard Richter (b. 1932) used amateur snapshots from the 1960s onwards as the basis for blurry grey images made with paint dragged across the surface of the canvas, and talked about the liberating effect for his art of discovering 'that a stupid, ridiculous thing like copying a postcard could lead to a picture'. Richter's 'photographic' paintings, such as *Venice – Stairs with Isa (586-3)* (1985), are deliberately perverse: knowingly creating the appearance of photographs by the wrong means. Richter also creates abstract paintings with striking colours spread over the canvas using squeegees and spatulas, avoiding the unique touch of the artist's hand. Richter often worked closely with the Polish-born Sigmar Polke (b. 1941), another artist originally associated with German Pop. Polke's works of the 1980s used incongruous superimpositions of illustration-like motifs and decorative surfaces like wallpaper, blankets and screen-printed 'Polke' dots, his trademark feature. The painting *Alice in Wonderland* (1983) combined references to sport, opium smoking and the children's story, carefully mixing different visual registers – the poetic and the trivial, the manually produced and the industrially manufactured – to create an overwhelming blend of changing images. The German artist Rosemarie Trockel (b. 1952) ironized painting techniques in her computer-knitted paintings of the 1980s, reproducing familiar imagery like the Playboy bunny or the Soviet hammer and sickle in a way that raised the question of women's artistic production. The contemporary British artist Chris Offili (b. 1968) uses collage elements from pornographic and celebrity magazines, as well as beads and elephant dung, heavily varnished, to provocatively tackle the Western perception of the black body.

The work of the postmodern American 'Neo-Geo' artists blurred the boundaries between artistic and industrial manufacture. The abstract paintings of Peter Halley (b. 1953) use fluorescent paints and metallic paints alongside acrylic and Roll-a-Tex to create a mixture of smooth and rough surfaces reminiscent of institutional paintwork and décor effects. The term 'Neo-Geo' was used in the 1980s to suggest a revival of geometric abstraction stripped of its spiritual meanings. For Halley, Day-Glo paint represented 'low-budget mysticism', while the austere rectilinear forms in works like *CUSeeMe* (1995) were intended to evoke the confining architectural spaces of prisons, hospitals, schools and cheap motels. Halley's fellow New York artist and friend Ross Bleckner (b. 1949) drew upon Op Art to produce abstract works which were ironic, but also had a curious spiritual quality in their treatment of radiant lighting effects.

In Britain, the painter Gary Hume (b. 1962) originally produced life-size paintings of hospital doors in grim institutional colours. In the mid-1990s he began to create works in household paint on aluminium, based on celebrities, supermodels, angels or the shape of leaves and flowers, reduced to simplified areas of high-gloss colour. Hume feels his paintings – such as *Kate* (1996), based on the model Kate Moss – to be about beauty and without deep meaning, claiming 'all you ever get from me is surface'. Another Young British Artist, Fiona Rae (b. 1963), samples different abstract styles in her paintings: large, expressive brushstrokes, neat circular forms, splashes and dribbles, dragged and smeared paint. Her work combines an appearance of spontaneity with carefully calculated composition, giving a sense of vibrant energy without recognizable meaning.

While the label 'postmodern' might suggest a certain shallowness in art and the presentation of diversity without any commitment on the part of the artist, contemporary painters working in a whole range of styles do create work that communicates meanings and moods as well as taking account of the long painting tradition behind them. The British artist Howard Hodgkin (b. 1932), a member of an older generation of contemporary artists, creates abstract paintings on wood which are full of personal resonances, transforming motifs like landscapes and still-lifes into a luxuriantly-coloured array of forms. Hodgkin refers to artistic tradition by painting his frames as part of his compositions, in the manner of the late nineteenth-century painter Georges Seurat. His paintings are not ironic, however, but intimate and contemplative, painted slowly over a period of years. Marlene Dumas (b. 1953), born in South Africa but based in Amsterdam, works from photographic materials to capture the poses of her models, as well as taking subjects from art history. Of paramount concern in her works is their emotional effect, more than the familiarity of her figure subjects.

Her four-panel painting *The First People (I-IV) (The Four Seasons)* (1990) is based on photographs of her first child, shown in awkward poses on plain backgrounds, with putrid and deathly flesh tones which create a strong sense of anxiety. Dumas' works suggest a process of coming to terms with human vulnerability, without moral or social judgment. The Belgian Luc Tuymans (b. 1958) also bases his paintings on photographs as well as film. His disturbing images, often close-ups which impose themselves on the spectator such as *Der Diagnostische Blick IV* (1992), use badly applied cheap paint in washed-out empty colours, creating an air of desperation. The content of his work refers to Flemish, American and German history, and Tuymans regards his role as artist not as the documenter of events, but as a potential perpetrator. His paintings evoke a troubled detachment, drawing their effect from what Tuymans describes as a 'tremendous intensity of silence ... the silence before the storm'.

Howard Hodgkin, Dinner at the Grand Palais, 1975

The variety and diversity of painting at the end of the twentieth and beginning of the twenty-first centuries reflect the artists' own individual approaches. The pursuit of personal ideas and feelings in painting seems more important today than the artistic allegiances and rivalries of painters previously, throughout the twentieth century. Painting is seen as less 'cutting-edge' than other artistic forms, such as video and installation art, and painters now are less caught up in the trends and fashions of the art world. Painting has also come a long way since the start of the twentieth century, from its traditional format of oil on canvas, to embrace all sorts of other materials, often taken from outside the realm of 'fine' art. The range of experimentation with content and technique that continues today demonstrates that painting's scope has most certainly not been exhausted.

Painting Techniques

So often people look at a picture – the end-product of an artist's endeavour – for the form and content, and do not focus on the technicalities. What materials did he or she use and how were they applied? On what substance was the picture painted? A knowledge of the methods, techniques and materials and how they interact provides an invaluable insight into the art of different periods and styles as well as a better understanding of the individual artist. The materials available at different times and in different places have often had an important bearing on both the subject matter and the manner in which the work was painted.

To take one example (which, incidentally, spans the entire period of art in human history), for thousands of years Australian Aborigines

Clifford Possum Tjapaltjarri, Water Dreaming

have been employing the careful arrangement of soils and sands of different colours and textures to create pictures whose patterns and symbolism relate to the stories and myths of the ancestral Dreamtime and tribal history or customs. Today there are native Australian painters working with conventional Western materials such as oils or acrylics on canvas or board to produce stunning visual effects, in the very forefront of modern art, but which have adapted traditional, age-old imagery to contemporary techniques. This is, perhaps, an extreme case; but in the course of the past century alone it seems as if all the methods, techniques and materials from many different civilizations and periods have come together. In the never-ending search for something new, art has become more eclectic than ever.

By contrast, the art of the world up to the end of the nineteenth century followed fairly defined patterns and courses. There are many factors – aesthetic, social, economic and political – that have governed the various movements and styles in art through the ages, but many of them also evolved out of changes in technique and they, in turn, arose

because of the introduction or invention of new materials. Although this survey is primarily concerned with methods and techniques it is essential that we also examine the materials available to artists at different times and in different parts of the world. These are the basic ingredients of a painting and they play an important part not only in what is possible or impossible but also in how the painter approaches the subject, or even what type of subject is available. There are other factors which, at various times in different places, have affected methods and techniques. Regional variations in climate should be obvious, yet their effects on how people painted, and in what media, have often been overlooked or ignored.

Paleolithic Techniques

The oldest forms of two-dimensional art (as opposed to sculpture) found in Europe are the paintings that have been discovered in caves from north-western Spain to southern Russia. These pictures, executed over thousands of years during the Old Stone Age (Paleolithic period) vary considerably in size and style. Some are very small while others are life-size representations of animals. What is more important in this context, however, is the manner in which these pictures were produced and the materials used.

Many of these pictures on the walls and ceilings of caves were first engraved using a sharpened flint tool, rather like the burin used by etchers and engravers to this day. In the Trois Frères cave in southern France one such flint tool was discovered on a ledge below an engraving of a lion. One can imagine the artist putting it down while standing back to admire his handiwork, or perhaps he went off for the Stone Age equivalent of a lunch-break and forgot where he had left it. And there it would lie for perhaps 10,000 years until some pot-holer stumbled across it. Having created the outlines of the picture, the artist would then colour them in. The pigments used varied considerably from district to district, depending on what mineral oxides were available. Iron oxides produced a wide range of shades from bright red, through chestnut to darker brown, while manganese oxides provided the darker colours from blue to black. Iron carbonates yielded the yellows and vermilions. Carbon-dating has confirmed what early archaeologists could only surmise: that the greatest variety of different colours belong to the most recent period, around 10,000 BC. Burnt wood and bone produced primitive forms of charcoal pencil, which were also used to sketch the outline and sometimes to produce the effects of tones and shading. Although the black arising out of carbonized materials was less permanent than manganese oxides it has survived surprisingly well in those caves which were not exposed to the weather or climatic extremes. These oxides and carbonates were ground to a fine powder and then mixed with animal fat or oils. Tubes of paint fashioned from bones, and even palettes of slate or flat bones, have been discovered in these caves, showing how the paints were prepared and mixed. How they were applied is not known for certain, but they were probably laid on with the fingers and palms of the hands, although in some cases it appears that they were applied with sticks or pads made from pieces of fur or hide.

We tend to think of Stone Age painters merely adorning the walls of their living quarters, but many of these caves extend for considerable distances and it is astonishing that paintings have been discovered in extremely inaccessible places where the artist would have had to crawl through narrow spaces. Working in total darkness, illuminated only by some primitive stone lamp using animal oil and a moss wick, the Palaeolithic artists often created their masterpieces in extraordinary conditions. What drove them to do this is not known but we may speculate that their art had some mystical or quasi-religious significance.

What of the techniques employed by these cave dwellers? From the outset they strove to record their impressions of animals and hunting scenes. We can see the evolution of human figures, for example, from 'matchstick men' – not unlike the earliest attempts at drawings by little children to this day. In the most primitive works there was no correlation between the hunters and the hunted, but later some attempt was made to depict them in an appropriate scale, although these cave painters never seem to have progressed beyond the stage of creating images in direct proportions as if side by side. Movement is one illusion that they tried to recreate, although this never got beyond the simple convention of painting animal and human figures slanted upwards or downwards or, in the most sophisticated examples, by an attempt to convey such actions as running or jumping by the arrangement of the limbs.

Similar methods and techniques have been discovered in the cave paintings of primitive civilizations nearer the present time in many parts of the world, notably central Australia, where the Stone Age culture of the Aborigines has many affinities with that found in Paleolithic Europe. That there is a huge gap between the Old Stone Age and the art of the great civilizations of the Middle and Near East may be explained by the fact that paintings that were not preserved in remote and inaccessible caves would not have stood the test of time.

Fresco

Paintings dated to around 3,000 BC were used to decorate the walls of tombs and temples. Paint was probably also applied to the murals in palaces and villas as well, but none has survived. Like the earlier cave-paintings, tomb-paintings survived because they were not exposed to sunlight or weather. Similar paintings have been recorded in the Minoan civilization of Cyprus at a slightly later date and the same techniques continued through the Classical periods of Greece and Rome. The technique invented by the Egyptians and perfected by later civilizations is known as fresco (the Italian word for 'fresh'). It may be defined as painting on wet lime plaster using pigments mixed with water and lime. As the water evaporates, the setting of the lime binds the pigment to the plaster. The process is completed by chemical reaction: exposure to the air converts the lime to carbonate of lime and this has the effect of fixing the pigment, just as if the painting on a piece of pottery was glazed and fixed by firing in a kiln.

The pigments used by the earliest Egyptians were basically the same as those used by the prehistoric cave-dwellers, but gradually the range was extended to include ochre (reds and browns) and malachite (greens and blues). These minerals were ground to a very fine powder and mixed with water and lime, but the Greeks, and possibly also the Minoans of Knossos, gave body to their painting materials by adding egg yolk, size, gum arabic or beeswax. The earliest written account of the technique of fresco painting was given by Vitruvius, who stated that the Romans borrowed the practice from the Greeks. Immense care was taken in the preparation of Roman plaster, which was several inches thick. The basis was composed of the *arriccio*, a mixture of crumbled bricks, sand and lime, on top of which were several layers of lime and powdered marble, progressively finer and smoother and carefully applied with a trowel to create a highly polished surface. It has been argued that only the ground colouring was applied in a mixture of pigment and lime water, and that the final painting was executed in an emulsion, but it is impossible to say for certain. Roman painters also used a technique whereby colours with a wax base were applied by some kind of heat treatment, and there is some evidence to suggest that this refinement was used to create the astonishingly colourful frescoes at Pompeii.

This technique, however, seems to have been uncommon, and when fresco-painting was revived at Rome in the thirteenth century the usual method was either to apply the paint to the still-wet plaster or to dampen dry plaster immediately prior to painting. Whichever was the case, there was no way in which frescoes could be repainted and there was no margin for error on the part of the painter. This method of painting continued more or less unchanged until the fifteenth century and the great era of ecclesiastical decoration. By that time the Italian painters were distinguishing between *fresco secco*, the art of painting in watercolours on dry plaster, and *buon fresco*, the more traditional technique of mixing pigments with lime and water applied to fresh wet plaster. Because of the haste with which the painter had to work, he would plan the exact design in pencil on paper or parchment as a preliminary cartoon (from the Italian *cartone*, literally 'a little card') – long before this term took on the more specialized meaning of a satirical drawing. The cartoon was often overlaid with grid lines, corresponding, on a larger scale, to a pencil drawing on the plaster itself, known as the *sinopia* (from the Greek *synopsis*, meaning 'overview'). In the case of large murals a thin layer of wet plaster (*intonaco*) was applied to an area sufficient for each day's painting, working from the top left-hand corner to the bottom right-hand corner, in daily sections known as *giornate*. Whatever portion remained unpainted at the end of the day was carefully scraped away and the edges undercut, the process being repeated the following day. A careful examination of late medieval frescoes will often reveal the joins in the plasterwork. *Buon fresco* might be used for the principal subjects. Such features as the texture of clothing, hair and fur could be suggested with the point of a very fine hard brush.

Treatises on painting dating from the fifteenth century give various recipes for both lime and the mixture of pigments. The exact proportions of lime and sand (a ratio of 1:2) were just as important as the preparation of the lime itself, which could take years to mature correctly. White colouring was known as *bianco sangiovanni* ('St John's white') and was produced from little cakes of slaked lime exposed to air and sunlight for several months. To the basic pigments of the ancients, the Italians added raw or burnt sienna, *terra verte*, metallic oxides such as chrome yellow and the cobalt blues and greens. The Germans invented smalt (*Schmalte*), a deep blue pigment which revolutionized the appearance of stained glass and enamels, but which was also adapted to fresco painting. Previously the Italians had obtained this colour from ground azurite, which tended to turn green with exposure to the atmosphere and the carbonic acid in the lime. This chemical reaction was countered to some extent by mixing the powdered azurite with egg-yolk, but to achieve a true deep-blue effect only ultramarine (an expensive substance produced by grinding lapis lazuli) would suffice. Fresco painting has been revived in recent times; notable exponents include the Italian José Clemente Orozco (1883–1949) and the Mexican muralist Francesco Clemente (b. 1952).

Tempera

Broadly speaking tempera (Italian for 'temper') was a process that involved some sort of binding material (other than oil). Traditionally this was egg-yolk, a substance that was also extensively used in fresco painting, but any albuminous, gelatinous or colloidal material could be mixed with pigments to achieve similar results. The terms fresco and tempera are sometimes used as if they were synonymous, but the distinction lies not so much in the mixture but the material to which it was applied. Thus tempera is more commonly associated with the paintings on mummy cases and papyrus rolls in pharaonic Egypt, or medieval paintings on ivory or wood panels, although some wall paintings in ancient Egypt, Knossos, Mycenae and Classical Rome probably relied on this technique. Egg-yolk, sometimes diluted by a little vinegar, was the preferred medium, though a thin glue produced by boiling animal skins was also extremely effective, while Pliny mentions milk as a binding substance.

Although tempera is mainly associated with relatively small paintings executed on wood panels, the paint was not applied directly on to the wood. The surface had to be prepared and this entailed a process that was not unlike the plastering of walls, but on a much smaller scale. It was more refined than fresco and called for a greater degree of preparation. First of all, only certain types of close-grained timber were suitable for this purpose – lime, poplar and willow being preferred. Panels were carefully planed and any graining, knots or other blemishes filled with a mixture of size and sawdust and rubbed to a smooth surface. The panel was then covered with a piece of old linen affixed by glue. A material known as gesso (Italian for 'gypsum' or 'chalk', mixed with animal glue) was then added in up to eight layers. First came the *gesso grosso* ('heavy plaster'), evenly spread with a spatula or broad-bladed knife, and finally the *gesso sottile* ('subtle plaster'), diluted with water and mixed with size, was applied by means of a broad brush. When this surface was perfectly dry it could be painted with tempera paints.

Because the paints were readily absorbed by the gesso and dried rapidly, tempera was a technique that called for great skill and extreme rapidity on the part of the painter. In unskilled hands, tempera often appears as very flat, but the best practitioners were capable of amazing results. By the technique known as *chiaroscuro* (from the Italian words for 'light' and 'dark') tone and shade could be achieved, either by hatched strokes, as in fresco painting, or more usually by repeated coats of paint on the precise area until the desired depth and darkness was achieved. Tempera was a popular medium for icons and religious triptychs and looked particularly effective when the painted areas contrasted with gold surrounds. This called for a separate technique in which the areas to be gilded were given several coats of red bole to which the gold leaf was firmly affixed with egg white.

Egg tempera on wood was the preferred medium of such Renaissance artists as Cimabue, Duccio, Fra Lippo Lippi, Ghirlandajo and Botticelli, while others, such as Piero della Francesca, Titian and Tintoretto employed it in their underpainting, using oils for the final painting. Tempera was widely used before the advent of oil painting which spread from northern Europe, but though the Italian artists were the last to abandon it generally in favour of oils, paradoxically tempera continued for several generations among the primitive painters of Germany and the Low Countries.

Although largely superseded by oil painting, tempera survived fitfully over the years and enjoyed a new lease of life in the nineteenth century, as part of the general revival of interest in the arts and crafts of the late Middle Ages, and in more recent years the technique of tempera has been combined with oils. Dry colours with a tempera medium were also used extensively in commercial art from the early twentieth century, the pigments mixed with a compound of glycerine and gum arabic to produce colours of greater depth and intensity than was generally possible with watercolours. Like fresco, this modern version of tempera is a direct process which dries quickly and does not permit the artist second thoughts.

Oil Painting

Although the mixture of pigments with oil revolutionized the art of painting, the distinction between tempera and oil painting is not as clear-cut as is often stated, any more than it can positively be said that it was invented by any one man (although Jan Van Eyck generally gets the credit). There is ample evidence to suggest that oil-based paints were employed in the painting and preservation of timber in houses and boats long before the technique was applied to decorative painting. In paintings executed in tempera there are early examples in which portions of the panel were done in oils, either to enhance the central figure or, to paint the large surfaces of boats. In addition, it should be noted that some tempera paintings were subsequently given a thin coating of oil which not only enhanced the brilliance of the colours but made them more durable. Indeed, the principles of oil painting were first enunciated as early as 1100 by a German monk named Theophilus, a fact which implies

that the technique, in various forms, was in use long before the 1420s when the brothers Hubert and Jan Van Eyck first employed it. It may be no accident that oil painting developed in northern Europe, where the climate was unsuitable for frescoes. For the same reason, painting in oils on canvas developed more rapidly in places – such as Venice – that had a damp climate unsuited to either frescoes or large wood panels. The chief drawback about oil paint was the inordinate time it took to dry, a point made by Theophilus himself, and it is now considered that over the ensuing three centuries artists experimented with oils and various materials in order to accelerate the drying process.

What is important is that oil paints freed artists from the limitations imposed by fresco and tempera painting for the simple reason that oil paints adhered more readily to a wide variety of surfaces and therefore did not require the costly and time-consuming preparation of these media. The most popular bases for oil painting have been wood and canvas, although other materials, including paper, pasteboard, ivory and metal (notably copper plates) have also been employed at various times right up to the present day. Until the end of the Renaissance period, wood was by far the most common support for oil painting. Although many different timbers have been recorded, the Italian artists preferred the white poplar whereas the Van Eycks and other members of the Flemish School used oak; from the seventeenth century onwards, however, hardwoods such as mahogany and lignum vitae were considered more desirable because they did not split or crack as thin panels of oak were prone to do.

Jan Van Eyck, Portrait of Giovanni Arnolfini and Wife (Arnolfini Marr)

Wood panels were suitable for small pictures but when larger works were contemplated this material was impractical unless (as in the case of the *Magi* by Rubens) it was possible to construct a huge surface from a number of transverse sections. For most practical purposes, however, canvas was, and still is, the preferred basis for oil paintings. Here again, the type and quality of canvas is very important. While there are examples of oil paintings on everything from sailcloth to old burlap sacks, the choice of the right materials is all-important, especially for the durability of the painting. In earlier centuries it was found that canvas of pure hemp was ideal, but by the eighteenth century linen canvas of unbleached flax fibre was widely regarded as the finest medium. Canvas that contained cotton fibres, on the other hand, was found to be much less suitable because of the tendency of cotton to expand and contract according to changes in temperature and relative humidity, thereby causing stresses which led to the priming of the paint flaking off and, in extreme cases, cracking the painting.

The surface of a wood panel or a canvas generally required some preparation, known as priming. In wood, for example, this entailed the application of an undercoat which would readily adhere to the wood and facilitate the application of oil paints. Early devotees of oil painting borrowed a practice from frescoes and applied a coating of carbonate of lime, but later a mixture called white lead (which might actually range from grey to brownish-red in colour) was used, either on its own or as a second coat over the lime. Jan Van Eyck, for example, favoured a ground composed of animal glue and chalk, completely covering the wood and rubbed down to produce a very smooth base. From the late seventeenth

Peter Paul Rubens, Two Saints

century, however, a couple of coats of white lead were regarded as the normal practice. The first coat would be applied quite thickly in order to fill up and conceal the weave of the fabric, followed by a thin coat to impart greater smoothness; some painters, however, preferred several fairly thin coats, with a period for thorough drying between each, to achieve the desired flexibility.

The actual pigments were derived from various mineral or vegetable substances and after the development of oil painting the range was infinitely extended. From the nineteenth century onwards scientific research into the properties of coal tar resulted in the vivid aniline colours as well as the combination of various substances such as sodium sulphide and alumina silicates to produce the vivid ultramarine so vital to Renaissance artists but so very expensive at that period.

Strangely enough, white was one of the most difficult colours to procure satisfactorily. Flake white, as it was called, was a lead carbonate, which had a distressing tendency to go yellow and, in extreme cases, turned black as a result of sulphur in the atmosphere. Other colours that were affected by oxidation or sulphurization included pigments from zinc, chromium and cadmium, which were particularly prone to atmospheric chemical reaction, changing colour, turning black or opaque. At one time a form of mineral tar known as bitumen (or rather bituminous pigments which included various hydrocarbons) was widely used, notably by Rubens, Rembrandt and other members of

the Flemish and Dutch Schools, to produce those transparent shades of brown that characterize their paintings. But far too late in the day it was realized that bitumen never dries and thus is inherently unstable. When it came in contact with quick-drying varnishes the combination could be harmful.

The grinding of colours and mixing them with oil was a long and laborious task which was quite an art in itself. The degree of skill attained might make a considerable difference to the painting itself, and there have been numerous cases of beautiful paintings marred by inattention to this preparatory process. There was also considerable variation in the colours produced by mixing the pigments with different oils. Olive oil was extensively used in Italy chiefly because it was so cheap and readily available, but it fell into disfavour because it dried very slowly. Linseed oil, on the other hand, dried rapidly – perhaps too rapidly – and a happy medium was effected by the use of copal oil, although poppy oil, both light and almost colourless, has been preferred since the mid-nineteenth century. The practice of grinding and mixing colours by hand continued until the beginning of the twentieth century, when the supply of oil paints in tubes, ready-mixed, became prevalent.

Developments in Technique

Paint was generally applied by brushes. Until the nineteenth century these were rounded, but flat brushes were adopted at this time, being more suited to the technique of brushwork that was then coming into fashion, and enabling the artist to paint in separate touches with a full brush. Brushes composed of sable hairs were preferred for fine work while those made of hogs' bristles were more suitable for large expanses of the canvas requiring a broad and vigorous surface. Brushes of this type were first used in Venice because they were better adapted to the rather coarse canvasses popular there. Broad brushes with a rounded head were sometimes employed to blend paint when still wet and soften harsh outlines. Even at quite an early stage in the development of oil painting, artists frequently used their fingers and palms to achieve certain effects, especially in the underpainting. Finger painting was also used extensively in the nineteenth century. Many painters from El Greco onwards occasionally used a fine trowel or a knife with a very thin flexible blade to apply an even groundwork, although it seems to have been Gustave Courbet who took this a stage further and began laying on slabs of paint with a palette knife – a technique that has been applied by many modern painters to create an almost three-dimensional effect.

Conversely Edouard Manet frequently scraped or pared away the thick impasto areas of his paintings with a knife before reworking them. Other techniques devised in relatively recent times include the saturation of the canvas with paint rather than sizing and priming it first, and even creating unusual effects by dripping paint on to the canvas or throwing paint at it apparently at random.

Considerable variation can be imparted to the canvas according to the fundamental colours chosen for the groundwork, on which the overall appearance of the finished painting may depend. Among the great masters, for example, there were those who had a preference for a particular shade, such as the distinctive grey used by Poussin or the warm pink favoured by Boucher. Rubens, on the other hand, used a groundwork of grey, yellow, brown or some greenish tint as well as plain white, at various times and to suit different circumstances. By contrast many of the paintings on a red or deep brown ground, or the sombre hues approaching black, have not worn well because whatever colours are painted over them have either faded or have been overcome by the dominance of these strong underlying tones. Conversely, pictures with a predominantly white groundwork have generally retained the freshness of their colour harmonies much better. Although oil painting has one obvious advantage over fresco and tempera painting, in that it is possible to paint over one's mistakes and even make quite radical alterations to the composition of a picture, there is always the possibility that in the fullness of time the original detail is going to rise to the surface because the colours have become transparent with the passage of time. There are numerous examples of what the French call *repentirs*, in which the artists' original thoughts prove unfortunately to be much stronger than their changes.

The only solution to this age-old problem was to sketch out on the canvas a fairly detailed outline, in pencil or charcoal, and then paint over it. This was particularly advisable in the case of large canvases and murals. A good example of this is provided by the enormous paintings by Stanley Spencer, where the drawings can still be seen in the unfinished areas of the canvas. Artists either prepared a cartoon to guide them, just as the fresco painters did in the Renaissance period, or prepared sheets of paper on which each of the squares from the cartoon was suitably enlarged. Then the details from the sheets were 'pounced' (pricked out) on to the canvas and the lines joined up.

In his great Arnolfini masterpiece, Jan Van Eyck sketched a detailed outline in watercolour which was then coated with drying oil. This fixed the drawing and provided an impervious basis for the actual painting. Other artists have sketched out a rough outline of the composition in a light monochrome wash, greatly diluted so that the form is barely discernible against the bare canvas but will never obtrude in the finished painting. This technique is extremely useful in

Stanley Spencer, Angels of the Apocalypse

landscapes where the large masses of light and shade in the sky, cloud formations, hills and fields, lakes and rivers, can be lightly sketched in and the principal lines mapped out before final and detailed painting takes place. Here again, great care has to be taken to ensure that the light monochrome wash does not clash with any of the colours of the final painting. The pitfalls that beset the artist in achieving the right combination of groundwork and final painting are too numerous to elaborate here, and no amount of genius ever compensated for ignoring the basic rules. Moreover, painting over an area before it had sufficiently dried out caused cracking at a later date, and the same problem arose when the priming was too smooth.

A very important aspect of oil painting is the varnish applied to the finished canvas to protect the surface from atmospheric pollution and also to give the colours their sparkle and richness of tone. The varnish, in fact, compensates for the loss of oil in the original paintwork, either through natural evaporation as the picture proceeds or because some of the oil seeps through the layers of paint to the canvas. Ideally the varnish should be applied by the artist rather than be left to the art dealer (as was often the case). The varnish should be regarded as an integral part of the painting and deserves to be applied with as much care as the actual choice of colours or the brushwork. Unfortunately inadequate or far too lavish a coating of varnish, or perhaps application before the paint has sufficiently dried and hardened, has so often spoiled the final effect. Not all of the problems attributed to faulty varnish, however, are really due to this. Instead the fault may lie in the use of oil of the wrong consistency or the wrong proportion of oil to pigment. Delacroix and Prud'hon are always cited as examples of artists who paid insufficient attention to this matter, with the result that many of their paintings have suffered irremediable damage through cracks.

It was the Impressionists who began exploring new ways of working oils on canvas. Claude Monet was the arch exponent of this style, who succeeded in conveying the illusion of spontaneity, the image captured at a single moment in time. Obviously the actual execution of any painting, however rapidly it is carried out, takes more than a few moments. The secret lay in the preparation of the groundwork. Monet used a fine-weave canvas with a thin basic wash, on top of which he painted broad areas in two or three basic colours. Next he applied opaque paint in patches which allowed a glimpse of the underlying blocks and then used a wide variety of different brushwork, putting fresh paint on still-wet surfaces or dragging pure, almost dry paint, across the surface to create special effects and textures, often by using the wooden point of his brushes to let the pale ground show through. The resulting variety of colours and the scintillating play of light and reflection give his canvases their instantaneous character. The Impressionists in general made extensive use of wet-on-wet techniques to soften the edges of contrasting colours, or softened the lines by rubbing them or painting over them with a thin opaque coat of colour – a practice known as 'scumbling'.

Pierre-Auguste Renoir was the first painter of his generation to explore the potential of warm-cool colour contrasts which he used to great advantage in his nude studies. He also employed rubbing and staining to build up form, colour and depth. In the second half of the nineteenth century, scientists like James Clerk Maxwell studied the physical properties of light and colour and painters followed these developments closely. One of these was Georges Seurat who, in 1884, adopted a palette of 11 colours arranged in the sequence in which they

Pierre-Auguste Renoir, Les Baigneuses

appear across the spectrum, from raw sienna to yellow ochre, combined with white to enhance the effects of light. He strove for an opaque impression and deliberately left his paintings unvarnished to heighten the matt effect. Taking his interest in the composition of colour to its logical conclusion he began in 1885 to build up different hues using patterns of dots. Whereas traditionally artists had mixed yellow and blue pigments to produce shades of green, Seurat aimed at the same effect by placing dots of yellow and blue paint in close proximity, varying the intensity of the colour accordingly. The result, however, was seldom as he intended, for he failed to realize that the eye picked up the signal as a fusion of pigment rather than a blending of light. Camille Pissarro was the other ardent practitioner of Pointillism, but in his case it proved to be an extremely laborious way of achieving subtle shades. Paul Signac (1863–1935) modified this, using broader dabs of colour to achieve

similar results. In the twentieth century Paul Klee was also preoccupied with the scientific theories of colour and used a mosaic or cloisonné technique, involving tiny cells of different pigments, to build up colour harmonies, which attained fruition in his painting entitled *Ad Parnassum* (1932).

Watercolour

Although sometimes looked down on as a minor art compared with oil painting, watercolour painting is one of the oldest techniques known to humankind. It was the medium used by the artists of China and Japan from the third century AD, if not earlier, and appears to have developed in India and Persia about five centuries later when the rulers of Turkestan began commissioning Chinese artists, from whom the technique spread further west and south. Interestingly, some of the earliest watercolours of China have an affinity to the tempera of the Mediterranean civilizations, although subsequently the Chinese preferred clear watercolour to the opaque forms associated with tempera. Just as the brushes used by European painters were made of sable or hogs' hair, depending on the quality of work desired, so too the Chinese used these materials in their brushes, but with the salient difference that the latter were infinitely finer as befitted the extremely delicate nature of their brushwork. By these means, Chinese painters and calligraphers achieved an extraordinary range of styles, from the most refined, almost microscopic styles to coarse, vigorous forms.

Another important difference between Chinese and Occidental painting was that the Chinese were primarily concerned with design, while colour was always of secondary importance. The versatility of watercolours was suited to the materials on which they were executed. Whereas Western artists relied on wood panels and canvasses, the Chinese preferred paper and silk panels from the outset. The earliest papers were relatively coarse, and were fashioned from the bark of certain trees. Later came a type of paper made from silk fibres and later still a very tough, hard rice-paper. Then sheets of silk were glued to layers of paper and this seems to have proved to be the most satisfactory medium, for it remained more or less constant for many centuries. Black ink was mainly employed although deep shades of sepia were also used, but under the influence of Buddhism sumptuous colours were introduced as well as a lavish use of gold leaf. Poetic suggestion rather than representation was the watchword of Chinese watercolour compositions in the Song dynasty. An interest in landscape also developed and would become the dominant feature of later Chinese art. Colours were now more subdued and used sparingly. Many artists were also poets who decorated their exquisite paintings with fine calligraphy. Having reached the acme of perfection around AD 1000, Chinese watercolour painting remained relatively static for centuries, and the hand-scrolls and wall-hangings executed in this medium continued with little stylistic difference until the influence of Western art began to make itself felt at the end of the nineteenth century.

Diffusion of the Chinese Style

The technique of watercolour painting spread to Japan in the middle of the sixth century and, until about AD 850, slavishly followed Chinese patterns and techniques; but then there began to develop a distinctly Japanese style which was encouraged by the establishment of a number of schools. There was a revival of the Chinese style from the fifteenth to the late seventeenth centuries, when a new popular style emerged. This gradually gave way to a more naturalistic style, influenced to some extent by ideas brought by the Portuguese and later the Dutch from Europe but harnessed to the particular parameters of Japanese watercolour painting. The heyday of the Japanese watercolour was from the late seventeenth century onwards, following the establishment of the art school founded by Hishigawa Moronobu (1646–1713). Landscapes, portraits of the actors of the Kabuki theatre, geishas and court scenes which make up the *Ukiyo-e* ('pictures of the floating world') formed the bulk of watercolour painting and inspired the production of block prints which were hand-coloured. From about 1875, Western influences in watercolour painting can be detected in the greater use of *chiaroscuro* and linear perspective, as well as a greater concentration on the exact reproduction of form, a matter which had previously been of secondary importance.

The Persians learned the technique of watercolours via the Chinese artists who brought their craft to Turkestan, but very little appears to have survived from this early period. Even watercolour miniatures from the period of the Mongol invasions are very rare. At Herat, however, a great school of art was founded in the fourteenth century and from this developed the exquisitely jewelled manuscripts that reached their peak of perfection in the time of the Mughal emperors and accompanied them southwards to India. In the period from the sixteenth to eighteenth centuries Indian watercolour art

expanded to include small-scale murals executed on paper and employing the techniques of fresco and tempera as well as clear colours. Various methods of treating or glazing the surface of the paper evolved, mainly in order to enhance the appearance of portraits.

Watercolour painting developed in Europe during the Middle Ages and was widely practised in monasteries and other religious foundations. The vast majority of these miniature paintings were executed on parchment, seldom as individual works and generally forming the embellishment of manuscript books. An offshoot of this was the development of the portrait miniature, done on smooth card or small ivory plates, watercolours being the preferred medium. The miniature continued in fashion until the 1840s, when it was ousted by the daguerreotype, one of the earliest photographic techniques.

Painting on silk, board, card or paper often includes fresco and tempera as well as clear colour and although the finished painting was left as it was, it was occasionally coated with shellac or some form of wax to give it greater permanence. Between the early sixteenth century, when illuminated manuscripts went out of fashion with the dissolution of the monasteries, the art of watercolour painting (apart from miniature portraits) virtually disappeared in Britain, but it was revived at the beginning of the eighteenth century. At first it was confined mainly to monochrome pictures, known as pen-and-wash, but soon browns and other colours came into use and by the end of the century the palette was greatly extended. Pigments in powdered or cake form were mixed with water and applied to paper, the form often being strengthened by pen drawing. Later watercolours took on greater depth following the introduction of opaque, gouache or body colour, although these techniques were difficult to master and the results were often harsh and raw, with uncomfortable ridges of colour. Making a virtue of necessity, however, artists exploited these qualities, painting on coarse paper or papers with a grey or tinted tone and sometimes combining watercolours with crayons or chalks for varied effect.

Watercolour sketches and preliminary cartoons are known to have been produced by some of the greatest masters, from Rubens and Rembrandt to Dürer and Daumier, but the watercolour as an art form in its own right only really came to prominence in the second half of the eighteenth century. What started as an amateur pastime was given a much higher status in the hands of such artists as Paul Sandby (1725–1809), Samuel Scott (1710–72) and Thomas Malton (1748–1804), the last-named producing some remarkable pictures of architectural subjects. The heyday of the English watercolour ran from

1780 until 1850, and produced some landscapists of the first rank, such as John Robert Cozens (1752–97), Peter de Wint (1784–1849), John Sell Cotman (1782–1842), Thomas Girtin (1775–1802) and Cornelius Varley (1781–1873).

Artists who worked in oils and other media, notably John Constable and William Blake, also produced outstanding watercolours, but the most prominent artist who may be said to have made the watercolour his very own medium was J. M. W. Turner, and it would be true to say that his exploration of the techniques of this medium considerably enhanced his work in oils. The range of his watercolours is incredible and reveals Turner as a bold and imaginative innovator. In the second half of the nineteenth century and the twentieth century, watercolour was an important aspect of British art in the hands of such painters as Sir William Orpen, Samuel Palmer, Sir Alfred Munnings, Wilson Steer, Frank Brangwyn and many others. Nor should it be forgotten that watercolour was extensively used by the Pre-Raphaelites and their successors, notably Sir Edward Burne-Jones, whose paintings in this medium have an exquisite jewelled quality.

Perhaps under English influence, watercolour painting also became extremely popular in the United States. Examples are known from pre-revolutionary times and consist mainly of rather naïve landscapes and still-lifes, but the movement received tremendous impetus during the Civil War, rivalling the new-fangled camera as a method of recording the scenes of battle and military life. An immediate outcome was the formation in 1866 of the American Water Color Society, based in New York, with separate groups arising in Boston and Philadelphia a few years later. Although this medium was regarded as more within the realm of the amateur and the dilettante, it should be noted that major artists such as Winslow Homer produced some excellent work in this medium. Early American watercolours tended to be rather dry and not particularly rich in colour, slavishly emulating their English counterparts, but in the last four decades of the nineteenth century a much freer, more colourful style developed.

Among the outstanding watercolourists of this period were John F. Kensett (1818–73), S. R. Gifford (1823–80) and Thomas Hicks (1823–90). They were followed by artists who appreciated that this medium could be used to convey rapid and dramatic work, full of pace and movement. First and foremost was John Singer Sargent (1856–1925) who was actually born in Italy and spent much of his life in England, but who exerted enormous influence in the United States, especially in raising the standard of watercolours. Other artists who excelled in this medium include John Ward Dunsmore (1856–1945) who concentrated on historical subjects, Henry B. Snell (1858–1943) who developed the so-called scrub method which gave his pictures a certain luminosity, Arthur B. Davies (1862–1928) whose paintings veered towards the mystical and fantastic, Dodge McKnight (1860–1950), the leading figure among the Boston watercolourists, and Rockwell Kent (1882–1971), one of America's latter-day Renaissance men who excelled as an engraver, lithographer, book designer, illustrator, explorer, sailor and writer as well as a watercolourist of note who advocated greater use of painting outdoors from life. Horatio Walker (1858–1938) was the prime exponent of watercolour painting in Canada, exhibiting an uncanny grasp of atmosphere in his quaint and romantic studies of the Canadian countryside.

Some artists started their careers in watercolours before moving on to oils. In this group may be named Norman Rockwell (1894–1978), who developed a realistic technique of idealizing small-town America, especially in his covers and illustrations for such periodicals as *The Saturday Evening Post* (1916–63). John Marin (1875–1953) branched out and created watercolours in a highly distinctive style before adapting the medium to Cubist concepts. Other European and American artists of more recent times who made extensive use of watercolours include Edward Burra, Mark Tobey, and Otto Dix. Gouache, a type of opaque watercolour thickened with gum, was employed by Joan Miró and Egon Schiele.

If watercolour lacks the lustrous depths and sumptuous colours of which oils are capable, it is a medium that is ideally suited to the lightning sketch and for that reason, if for no other, it would deserve notice for truly capturing the fleeting moment, a principle grasped by the Chinese and the Japanese so many centuries ago.

Miniatures

The word miniature has passed into the English language as a synonym for something tiny, or a representation of something on a much-reduced scale. In fact the word is derived from the Latin *minium*, which had nothing to do with size at all, but was the word used to describe cinnabar or red lead, used in the decoration of the borders of medieval manuscripts and the initial letters around which were woven tiny pictorial elements. Later the word miniature came to apply to these decorations rather than the red lines and, in turn, to signify any painting executed on a very small scale. In the sixteenth and seventeenth centuries such works were often described as 'paintings in little' or 'limnings' and the artists who practised this craft were known as limners, a corruption of the French *enluminer* and Latin *illuminare* (the verbs 'to paint'). The art of miniature painting has a long, if at times sketchy, history that stretches all the way back to the fragments of the Egyptian *Book of the Dead* and some scraps from Roman Imperial times – tantalizing glimpses of an accomplished art which perished because the materials used have themselves barely survived. Miniature paintings worked in tempera and watercolours but it was their skilful use of gold leaf (and more rarely silver foil) to embellish their illustrations that gave them their distinctly sumptuous qualities. The illuminated manuscripts of medieval Europe represent an astonishing range of styles and techniques. The manuscripts of the Irish monks, for example, exhibit a highly idiosyncratic blend of Celtic and Norse art, totally different from the Anglo-Saxon art practised in the monasteries of England. Out of the craft of the limners working in the Byzantine, Gothic and Romanesque traditions developed the art of painting which has already been noted. Persia, the Mughal Empire of India and Turkey were centres of miniature paintings, which could be wrapped up and transported easily by the substantial nomadic populations. The paintings were often produced as collections illustrating the lives and exploits of great rulers and bound in book form.

Content and the Miniature

Miniature painting for its own sake and not primarily as illustration to the written word developed in Europe in the sixteenth century at a time when the illuminated manuscript was nearing the end of its life. Most of the earliest practitioners of portrait miniatures probably learned their craft as limners, and merely adapted the techniques of tempera, watercolours and oils to the confines of these tiny portraits, executed on thin flakes of ivory and, later, highly glazed card. The earliest centres of European miniature paintings in this period were Ghent and Bruges in Flanders, Paris and Tours in France and Ferrara and Florence in Italy, but from these places the art spread rapidly to other parts of the continent. Although the traditional illumination of manuscripts lingered on for about a century after the introduction of the printed book, its exponents soon diversified from the sacred to the secular and created tiny portraits for patrons drawn from the rising middle classes as well as the royal court.

Portraits of living persons may be found in illuminated manuscripts from the fourteenth century, gradually at first and later much more frequently, in copies of books commissioned by wealthy patrons. One of the greatest of the earliest miniaturists was Hans Holbein, who had already established his reputation for easel-paintings on wood panels. Between 1532, when he settled in England, and his death 11 years later he produced a number of these tiny masterpieces, although only a dozen or so of the 50 miniatures attributed to him are undoubtedly his work. Although his name is pre-eminent in this medium, he was by no means the only sixteenth-century artist who produced dainty little portraits of this type, and some of them – like Benninck and Teerlinc – also migrated from Flanders to England. Holbein worked in tempera, mixing his colours with both the white and yolk of eggs and giving them greater body with albumen mixed with a little vinegar.

Among Holbein's successors in England, Nicholas Hilliard (*c.* 1547–1619) provides an interesting insight into an art in transition, for his portraits, using opaque colours mixed with gum arabic or honey and a great deal of gold leaf, have a flatness and absence of shadows which place them firmly in the tradition of the illuminated manuscripts. The very fine work of this and later miniaturists was executed with a brush using squirrel hair. Isaac and Peter Oliver (father and son) carried on the tradition but during their working life it took on a new maturity. Isaac (*c.* 1567–1617) learned his craft from Hilliard himself, while Peter (1594–1647) was his father's pupil. They evolved the technique of imparting a roundness of form to the likenesses of their subjects and greatly enlivened the medium. Whereas Holbein and Hilliard painted very small miniatures, suitable for mounting in jewellery, the Olivers literally expanded the miniature, often producing paintings that were the size of a book page. The miniatures of these early artists were truly two-dimensional but what they lacked in naturalism they made up in the astonishing attention to the minute details of jewellery, lacework or embroidery in the costume of their sitters – truly a triumph of technique over art.

Hans Holbein, Henry VIII

John Hoskins (d. 1664) and his nephew Samuel Cooper (1609–1702) were the outstanding miniaturists of the next generation. The last of the original school of illuminators died out in the middle of the seventeenth century and this freed the portrait miniature from the stereotypes of that discipline. Hoskins pioneered the use of rich masses of colour, a greater and more intelligent approach to light and shade, and was probably the first miniaturist to capture the true flesh tints. Cooper trained under his uncle, but also spent some time in Holland and France perfecting his technique. His miniatures were true works of art, as accomplished as any full-scale painting but rendered exquisitely in a small format. He was also more adventurous than his predecessors in his use of colour.

The preferred medium for portrait miniatures until the middle of the eighteenth century was a glazed card – the plain backs of playing cards were often used for this purpose – but occasionally a very fine parchment made from the skin of chickens was employed. Cooper tried to find a more satisfactory but cheap substitute and experimented with painting on the flat bones of sheep, but early in the eighteenth century plaques of ivory came into fashion. This material was relatively expensive at first and it was a long time before it completely ousted the use of card or vellum. In the same period there was a certain vogue in Italy and the Netherlands for miniatures painted in oils on copper or silver plates, but these works were seldom, if ever, signed and very little is known about the artists who produced them. It should be noted that some miniaturists also painted in enamels on copper or porcelain, then fired or fused in a kiln and used in the manufacture of snuff-boxes and other objects of *vertu*, but these paintings belong more in the realm of the decorative arts than fine art. In the early 1760s there was a fashion for very small miniatures mounted as jewellery. The best of these microscopic miniatures – arguably fine art in its smallest form – were painted by Gervase Spencer (d. 1763).

Samuel Cooper, Miniature of James II as the Duke of York

The greater popularity of ivory more or less coincided with the development of transparent colours perfected in France. These materials eventually spread to England and triggered off a new and more sumptuous phase in miniature painting, given enormous impetus by the foundation of the Royal Academy in 1768. In the late eighteenth century the leading exponent of the art in Britain was Richard Cosway (1742–1821), whose miniatures were distinguished by the jewel-like brilliance of their colours. Andrew Plimer (1763–1857) produced many very engaging portraits, despite uneven draughtsmanship and attempts at *chiaroscuro* which did not always achieve the desired results. Probably the most successful, and certainly the most prolific, of the English

miniaturists was George Engleheart (1750–1819), whose account books indicate that he painted almost 4,000 portraits. It should also be noted that Sir Thomas Lawrence and Sir Henry Raeburn both produced excellent miniatures in the early stages of their illustrious careers.

The heyday of this rather restricted medium was the eighteenth century, and by the 1770s every town in the British Isles of any importance had at least one studio catering to the needs of the rising middle classes, who might not be able to afford a full-scale oil painting, but for whom the miniature was an admirable substitute. This movement received tremendous impetus during the French Revolutionary and Napoleonic Wars, when it was customary for young officers to have their portrait painted before going off on campaign. The great garrison towns of England, Scotland and Ireland were the centres of the miniature industry. Often only the actual features of the sitter would be painted by the master, the uniform and other details being filled in by one of his numerous assistants. This technique carried on even after the Battle of Waterloo. Although this mass-production technique was detrimental to the miniature as a work of art, there were still artists of this period – incuding Ozias Humphrey, Nathaniel and Horace Hone, Peter Paillou and William Wood – who produced excellent individual pieces. The advent of photography in the middle of the nineteenth century rapidly led to the demise of the portrait miniature.

The Growth of the Miniature

The artist Andrew Robinson realized that if the public regarded a studio photograph as a perfectly adequate substitute for a tiny miniature, the solution might be to give them something larger, if not a full-sized portrait. He pioneered miniatures which were similar to small oil paintings but were executed on stout cartridge paper using the new range of watercolours which were capable of a much darker, deeper and altogether more brilliant appearance than their predecessors, enhanced by setting the portrait against a very dark ground to give it greater dignity and force. The process of flattening out curved slices of ivory under hydraulic pressure enabled the new wave of miniature painters to combine the special qualities of ivory with the much larger format. Sir William Ross and Edward Chalon, among others, produced miniatures which ranged between octavo and quarto in size. While Chalon worked in broad masses of colour, Ross preferred a very laborious technique of microscopic detail which required special brushes and a high-powered magnifying glass.

Miniature painting also had immense appeal in North America.

The pioneer of the portrait miniature in the American colonies was John Watson who, in about 1715, began producing some exquisite little works drawn in pencil and Indian ink. The leading exponent of the art was Charles Willson Peale (1741–1827), who seems to have been equally versatile in miniatures and life-size portraits. Many of his 17 children, all of whom were named after famous artists and, not surprisingly, followed their father's profession, also painted miniatures – the best of these being by the appropriately named Rembrandt Peale. Archibald and Alexander Robertson (both Scots) and Walter Robertson (an Irishman) settled in the United States and produced excellent miniatures as well as giving encouragement to artists of the next generation, including E. G. Malbone of Rhode Island, Benjamin Trott of Boston and Charles Fraser of Charleston. At the end of the eighteenth and beginning of the nineteenth centuries the foremost miniaturists included Alban Clark of Massachusetts and R. M. Staigg of Newport. Although the art of the miniature declined with the advent of photography, there were still artists producing excellent work in a dwindling market. As in Britain, there were artists who gained their reputations in full-scale painting but who also dabbled in miniatures.

If portrait miniatures found the greatest favour in the English-speaking world, they were by no means confined to it. The Flemish painter Jean Clouet (c.1485–1541), who settled in France, produced a number of miniatures painted on card or vellum. His son François (c.1516–72), who succeeded him as court painter, also excelled in this medium. Although both Clouets and Jean Fouquet made their reputations as painters of large-scale portraits they also helped to popularize the art of the miniature. In the time of Louis XV and XVI, with the exception of a few miniatures by Nicolas Lancret (1690–1743), François Boucher (1703–70) and Jean-Baptiste Greuze (1725–1805), French painters of the first rank showed little or no interest in this restrictive medium, and it is significant that many of the best French miniatures of that period were actually painted by Peter Adolf Hall (a Swede) and Heinrich Füger (an Austrian). To be sure, there was a handful of French artists who concentrated on miniatures and their works are very much sought-after nowadays. In this group must be named Jean-Baptiste-Jacques Augustin (1759–1832), François Dumont (1751–1831), Antoine Sergent (1751–1817) and especially Jean-Baptiste Isabey (1767–1855), who continued to produce first-class miniatures almost to the end of his long life. Elsewhere in Europe there was little interest in miniatures, far less the development of any national styles, though it should be noted that Rosalba Carriera (1675–1757),

the celebrated Venetian pastellist was also a notable miniaturist, while the ever-versatile Francisco Goya of Spain included portrait miniatures in his vast repertory.

Pastel

Drawing in crayons or coloured chalks is the simplest method of putting colour on a surface, usually paper or cardboard. It has the advantage over other methods in that the artist can see immediately how the picture is progressing and how it will look when completed, whereas in those methods where pigments are mixed with oil or water, the end result is never obvious until the paint has dried. The chief drawback about pastel, however, is that the colour, essentially fine chalk dust, does not penetrate the medium but lies on the surface and is therefore easily disturbed. Lay one sheet on top of another and you will get an offsetting of the colours on the back of the top sheet. Pastels are prone to rubbing or surface disturbance unless carefully preserved under glass, and even then there is always a tendency for the colours to migrate. The fugitive nature of the chalk can be used to create subtle tones by gently rubbing with the fingers to blend one colour with another. In recent years, moreover, there have developed various types of soluble pencil which combine the control of a top-quality chalk with the natural fluidity of watercolour, releasing an infinite range of tonal variations. It is possible to create a picture with 'dry' pencils then go over it lightly with a wet brush to produce a watercolour effect which, because it penetrates the paper, becomes truly permanent. Or one can work with crayons dipped in water to produce a watercolour effect from the outset, or use a mixture of both techniques.

Although their composition is different, coloured wax crayons are used in the same manner as chalks to create pictures. The wax substances have a more adhesive quality than chalk but are less permanent than oil paints or watercolours, but the application of heat melts the wax so that it penetrates the paper and is thus fixed permanently, and the same heat treatment is used to merge the colours and soften the edges.

Just as the invention of oil painting is often credited to Jan Van Eyck, so also the invention of pastel or crayon has been attributed to various people, notably Johann Alexander Thiele (1685–1752), a landscape painter and etcher of

Jean Fouquet, The Nativity

note, or two ladies from Danzig (now Gdansk) named Vernerin and Heid who were exact contemporaries of Thiele. French art historians, on the other hand, credit the portraitist Robert Nanteuil with the invention. Dietrich Moyer of Switzerland (1572–1658) was a great innovator who experimented with various techniques, and these certainly included drawings in coloured chalks, though he is better remembered as the alleged inventor of soft-ground etching. It may well be the fact that one or other of these persons devised a method of producing coloured chalks in the form of sticks, but chalk drawing had certainly existed long before their time, for Hans Holbein (1497–1543) and Guido Reni (1575–1642) both created some portraits in this medium.

Whatever the precise origins of pastel, it triggered a distinctive movement in portraiture in France which, in the years leading up to the

Rosalba Carriera, Portrait of Prince Charles Edward Stuart

Revolution, enjoyed immense popularity and attracted the serious attention of many oil painters, notably Watteau, Boucher, Chardin and Greuze, although the leading artists in this medium were those who concentrated on it. The pastellists were led by Louis Tocque (1696–1772), the son-in-law of Nattier (1685–1766) who was one of the first artists to exhibit pastels at the Salon (in 1747). Another leading exponent was Hubert Drouais (1699–1767), who exhibited five pastel portraits at the Salon of 1746. However, the greatest French master of this medium was Maurice Quentin de la Tour (1704–88), who employed pastels very effectively in portraiture. He was, in fact, was a portraitist, first and foremost, for whom pastel was the ideal medium for capturing the fleeting expression of his sitters, and the results vividly bring to life the sparkle, wit and gaiety of French society of the Ancien Regime. In this regard the only artist who came close to him was Jean-Baptiste Perroneau (1715–83), who produced many pastels, remarkable for their use of colour. Pastel was virtually the closed preserve of the portraitist, although Simon Lantara (1729–78) pioneered the use of pastels in landscapes.

The Venetian artist Rosalba Carriera (1675–1757) was equally at home working in oils or pastels. During her time in Paris she was attracted to the freshness and lightness of the latter medium, and in her later career she produced a considerable number of quite remarkable portraits in pastels. During her extensive travels around Europe she did much to popularize the new medium. Indeed, her success encouraged other female artists to follow suit – the most notable being Vigée Le Brun, who executed many fine pastels in addition to her portraits in oils on canvas.

In Switzerland – where Moyer had led the way with his chalk drawings of the early seventeenth century – the principal exponent of pastels was Jean Étienne Liotard (1702–89), arguably one of the greatest pastellists of all time, whose portraits entitled *La Belle Chocolatière* (1745) and *La Belle Liseuse* (1746) established his reputation.

Painting with crayons was well established in England at an early date. John Riley (1646–91) produced numerous portraits in this medium, many of them formerly attributed to Sir Peter Lely. Francis Knapton (1698–1778) produced a prodigious quantity of pastel portraits, particularly of royalty and nobility. William Hoare of Bath (*c.* 1707–92) studied pastel in Paris and Rome and raised the English technique to new heights. Francis Cotes (*c.* 1725–70) studied under Rosalba Carriera and helped to develop a purely English style of pastel painting. This medium attained its peak in the hands of Cotes' pupil John Russell (1745–1806), who displayed an unsurpassed grace and elegance in his many fine portrait studies. Russell worked primarily in pastels and greatly extended the range of the medium, producing excellent groups as well as genre and historical subjects. There were many other artists working in pastels who demonstrated vividly that, in skilled hands, this medium was the equal of oils. Richard Cosway (1742–1821) and his wife Maria (1759–1838) – though perhaps better known as miniaturists – were also masters of this technique.

Decline and Resurgence

Interest in pastels declined at the beginning of the nineteenth century. It continued to be practised by amateurs, but the only professional British artist of note to make a major contribution to the medium was Henry Bright (1814–73), who concentrated on landscapes. Interest revived in the 1860s and led to the foundation of the Société des Pastellistes at Paris in 1870. The medium attracted the serious attention of artists whose reputation in other fields was already assured. Foremost in this group were James McNeill Whistler, Jean François Millet and Edgar Degas. Indeed, Degas made pastels very much his own medium. Although he painted in oils on canvas, he explored colour and texture and in the course of his experiments he turned to pastels, developing his own highly distinctive technique which involved the application of fine chalk lines, criss-crossing like a woven fabric, often superimposing one colour on another in such a manner that the earlier colours peeped through. Degas experimented with a very fine spray of water covering the chalk that he then worked up into a paste which he could manipulate with his fingers or a brush with stiff bristles. He also experimented with steam or heat to melt the pigments and achieve similar effects. Ironically, Degas turned more and more to pastels as his eyesight failed, but his innovations helped to stimulate renewed interest in the medium and reveal exciting possibilities which were taken up by other artists.

By the end of the nineteenth century pastel-painting was well established once more and attracted the serious attention of many artists of the first rank who further extended the medium. There were artists, such as Odilon Redon in France, who applied pastels to vellum or parchment. Aristide Maillol was primarily a sculptor, but he used coloured wax crayons to sketch his ideas for those splendid nude figures he modelled, and nowadays these crayons are regarded as great artworks in their own right. Émile Wauters in Belgium achieved a notable success with his numerous life-size portraits whose strength, vitality and sophistication had an immense impact at the turn of the century and in more recent years his fellow countryman Léon Spillaert has successfully combined pastels with watercolours. In Britain the leading pastellists of the modern movement include Henry Tonks, McLure Hamilton, Anning Bell, Walter Crane and William Rothenstein. The technique found an enthusiastic response in America, where excellent work in pastels was produced by Thomas Dewing, Robert Blum, Jerome Myers and James Alden Weir as well as Mary Cassatt, who is much better known for her oil paintings. Wifredo Lam combined chalks and oils on paper which was then pasted on to canvas.

Perspective

No account of methods and techniques would be complete without some reference to perspective – which is defined by the Oxford English Dictionary as, 'The art of representing three dimensional objects on a two dimensional surface, so as to convey the impression of height, width and relative distance.'. Perspective was blithely ignored by the earliest primitives; even if Greek paintings of the sixth century BC are no longer extant, we have the startling example of Athenian coins in which the goddess Athena, depicted in profile, has an eye that stares straight out of the coin at us. This is decidedly disconcerting, and must have seemed so at the time; yet it remained unchanged throughout the Archaic period. Interestingly, this position of the eye was a characteristic of many of Picasso's Cubist paintings of the early twentieth century as

he tried to show several different aspects of the subject simultaneously. In the art of the past two millennia artists were originally concerned with rhythm and harmony in composition, then changing from a static pose of figures (as shown on the friezes of Egypt and Greece) to an impression of movement when it was realized that the arrangement of figures within the confines of the picture could make a considerable difference to its overall appearance.

After the Romans, the problem of perspective was not confronted again until the Renaissance. Significantly the first painters to study this were those who had trained in a sculptural medium and were primarily concerned to convey in the two dimensions of flat painting the impression of three dimensions. They knew that a straight road with parallel sides ran in a straight line and that at the end the sides were as far apart as ever; yet when they gazed along it they had the impression that the lines drew closer together and eventually reached a point at which they vanished altogether. Paolo Uccello (1397–1475) is credited with being the first painter to have grasped the basic principles of perspective and apply them successfully to his pictures. In the early part of his career he had worked with the sculptor Lorenzo Ghiberti, whose great bronze bas-reliefs exhibit an early and probably subconscious understanding of the concept of converging lines.

Paolo Uccello, The Flood and the Subsidence of the Waters

It should be emphasized that Uccello was by no means the first artist to make a successful attempt to convey perspective – Chinese artists had been doing just that for hundreds of years – but he was the first to explain and interpret it. The Florentine architect Filippo Brunelleschi (1377–1446) exhibited a mastery of perspective in the design of the high-domed cupola of Florence Cathedral and wrote treatises on the subject. Other painters, such as Alberti and da Vinci, quickly developed the theories of Uccello and Brunelleschi, and it was Piero della Francesca who brought the concept to a triumphant conclusion by discovering the principle of the vanishing point, the point at which receding parallel lines appear to meet when represented in linear perspective. Uccello himself showed his understanding of this principle in his great panoramic view of *The Hunt in the Forest*, painted in the early 1460s.

Other notions, such as the apparent diminution in size of objects farther distant and foreshortening (the deliberate compacting of a detail to create the illusion of depth), were refined within a few years.

Understandably the perspective of curves and circles took longer to grasp. Globes and balls, for example, may appear as ovals or even irregular shapes, depending on the angle from which they are perceived. Subconsciously artists realized this, but without some knowledge of advanced geometry they did not understand why it should be so, and therefore the creation of the correct illusion was not always achieved. However, One artist, Masaccio (1401–28), showed an early and precocious understanding of the perspective of curves, triumphantly exhibited in his *Trinity* (1425), which inspired one of the most perceptive passages in the writings of Giorgio Vasari, describing the barrel vault 'drawn in perspective, and divided into squares with rosettes which diminish and are foreshortened so well that there seems to be a hole in the wall'.

Nevertheless, Uccello's discoveries were quite revolutionary. Suddenly artists realized that they could not just show the outline of a subject but depict it in the round. Hitherto this could only be hinted at by the adroit use of highlights and shadows, but until the geometry of perspective was understood paintings could not take on the illusion of three dimensions. From the time of Uccello and his colleagues onwards, however, people could not just look *at* a picture, they could now look *into* it as well.

Georges de la Tour, The New Born Child

Later generations of painters would refine the principles of perspective by using light and shadow to give greater depths to their pictures, a notable exponent of light and darkness being Georges de la Tour (1593–1652). In general the scenes depicted were at the eye-level of the spectator, but Rembrandt, in his great canvas *The Blinding of Samson* (1636), employed a very unusual angle, as if looking directly down on the scene, in order to heighten its dramatic effect.

Avant-garde Developments

The techniques and methods of painting evolved over hundreds of years; whatever the styles of painting at different periods, the techniques involved in their production followed clearly defined lines. All that had gone before would become liable to sudden and dramatic change, if not outright rejection, and over the past century successive generations of artists have sought ways of breaking away from the rules and regulations that governed their predecessors. We find a hint of this in the paintings of Edouard Manet, who has been described as 'the father of modern art'. At first glance his great masterpiece, *The Picnic* (1863), seems technically conventional, even if his choice of subject-matter raised eyebrows at the time; but closer examination reveals that he had flouted the rules of perspective, with the female figure in the background of undiminished size.

Once the notion of the Post-Impressionists was accepted – that what we see depends on how we see it – the floodgates opened and artists exercised their prerogative to interpret everything in their own way. This paved the way for the multiplicity of psychological approaches of Surrealism, Futurisim, Dadaism and all the other 'isms' right up to the present day. In this free-for-all, methods and techniques have changed radically. There are probably more painters at work today than throughout all the ages from the Renaissance to the Impressionists put together, and we are confronted with a bewildering array of styles as artists of each decade strive to find something that has never been tried before. It is a veritable maelstrom and yet most artists are still governed by certain principles in laying paint on canvas, regardless of what they do with it or how they lay it out.

Nevertheless, there have been radical departures in the past 50 years. One of these relates to the use of photography to create fine art. Visual aids, such as the camera obscura, had been used by some painters for centuries, and from the 1840s many artists resorted to photography rather than the sketch-pad in generating the preliminary work for their paintings. The Scottish landscapist, David Octavius Hill was a prime exponent of this technique; today his paintings are all but forgotten but his place as one of the great pioneer photographers is assured. In more recent times Andy Warhol made extensive use of photographs or photographic treatments to replicate endlessly images of the famous, of which his 1962 masterpiece portraying Marilyn Monroe is a good example. *Girlie Door* by Peter Blake (1959) is a collage of pin-up photographs and other objects mounted on a board painted to resemble a bright red door. Marlene Dumas is one of a number of contemporary artists who has used polaroid photographs in her compositions. Conversely, what appears to be a photograph in the work of Chuck Close is actually a meticulously painted image of photographic intensity.

The materials may change but the basic principles are still adhered to. Many painters work in acrylics and there are others who have achieved spectacular results with metallic paints, commercial paints normally employed in painting houses or bridges, enamels and Day-Glo or wax substances. Peter Halley (b. 1953) favours a combination of metallic and Day-Glo acrylics with a type of artificial stucco known as Roll-a-Tex applied to canvas, to give his paintings an unusual architectural texture. Lacquer, paper and acrylic on canvas has been the preferred combination of Sigmar Polke (b. 1941) in such works as *Opium Smoker* (1983). Niki de Saint-Phalle (1930–85) created very striking artworks in painted polyester. The paintbrush may give way to the paint-spray and the aerosol can, while traditional canvas may be supplanted by masonite or celotex panels and plywood boards. Arman (b. 1928) created a work entitled *Crusaders* (1968) which consisted entirely of silver glue brushes mounted on polyester and Plexiglass, while Richard Hamilton (b. 1922) has made extremely effective use of plastic film combined with black ink, watercolour and graphite on paper. Roy Lichtenstein's paintings in oils and magna on canvas appear as blow-ups of strip cartoons, in which the original shading, composed of Ben Day dots, are meticulously reproduced.

Materials and the Fusion of Forms

Sometimes the boundaries between artistic media are blurred. Are the creations of Stanley William Hayter (1901–88) prints or paintings? They combine elements of both, in that they are basically combinations of engraving, soft-ground etching and scorper, often overlaid by paint. Increasingly also the lines between painting and sculpture are becoming blurred, as in the works of Eva Hesse (1936–70), which combined cheesecloth, fibreglass and latex to evoke metaphors for femininity. Yves Klein (1928–62) used broad swathes of oil paint on partially burned and charred paper to create his *Anthropometry* series. Piero Manzoni (1933–63) drenched pleated canvas in kaolin mud to produce his work entitled *Achrome* (literally 'uncoloured').

The Dadaists set the precedent for the technique of some modern artists in the accumulation of ordinary, everyday objects and even discarded refuse from which to create a montage or collage. *Sacking and Red* by Alberto Burri (1915–55) consists of scraps of old sacks glued to the canvas and surrounded by bright red slabs of vinyl paint, while Anselm Kiefer (b. 1945) has combined oil and charcoal worked on burlap which is then mounted on canvas. Serge Poliakoff (1906–69) was another painter who found the coarse texture of burlap well-suited to his brand of abstract painting. Jean Dubuffet's *Dimpled Cheeks* (1955) combined various media with a montage of butterfly wings. The ultimate materials in mixed media compositions designed primarily to shock the spectator are those in which the olfactory as well as the visual senses are involved. Pig's guts (Helen Chadwick), blood (Marc Quinn) and faeces, both animal and human, must surely represent the ultimate materials in the creation of works of art.

As its name suggests, collage (from the French verb *coller*, 'to stick') is a form of mixed media in which painting is combined with various objects that have been glued to the canvas or board. The German artist Kurt Schwitters (1887–1948) was a pioneer of this technique, producing severely geometric collages in the 1920s. One of the best-known examples of more recent years is *Flag,* which the American artist Jasper Johns (b. 1930) painted between 1954 and 1956 – the latter date is obvious since some of the pieces of newspaper which appear under the Stars and Stripes bear the date 15 February 1956, although Johns himself dated the painting to 1955. In his masterpiece *Smiling Landscape* of 1967, Jiri Kolá (b. 1914) took the *Mona Lisa* and a Dutch landscape, cut them into vertical strips, and then glued them together alternately so that both pictures are distorted yet retain their separate identity. The end result is not unlike those modern electrically powered billboards where the image is constantly changing. Other artists who have made very effective

Jean Dubuffet, *Cortege*

Art

use of collage in their paintings include Jean Metzinger (1883–1956). The ultimate application of this technique seems to be the paintings of Robert Rauschenberg (b. 1925), who has made extensive use of pieces of magazines and all manner of objects apparently stuck at random on board. The American artists Tim and Kos Rollins used pages torn from a Czech novel as the basis for their *Amerika* series of paintings in the 1980s, adding a mixture of watercolours and acrylics with charcoal and pencil drawing. Frank Stella (b. 1936) has worked in mixed media on etched magnesium whereas the Australian Imants Tillers (b. 1950) prefers a mixture of oilstick, gouache and synthetic polymer paint on a number of small boards which combine to form a large work.

Most of the artists working in mixed media are highly individu-alistic and no two painters adopt the same technique. It is only when one examines the art being produced in the countries of the so-called

Jessie Oonark, Angagok Conjuring Birds

Third World that one finds entire schools pursuing their own distinctive methods. Many of the Australian Aboriginal artists of the past 50 or 60 years have successfully combined not only the themes but the actual materials of their age-old traditions. Thus traditional sand painting, arguably the most ephemeral art form ever devised, has been transformed and made permanent by combining sand patterns with oils, acrylics and other substances laid on board or canvas. Interestingly, this technique was borrowed by Antoni Tàpies (b. 1923) in some of his paintings, which combine oils on canvas with sand and asphalt. Jessie Oonark is only the

best-known of the Baker Lake Inuit artists of northern Canada, who create remarkable artworks using traditional skills in caribou hide decoration. Visually the most exciting of all these schools is the sequin painting of Haiti. Arguably the poorest and least-privileged country in the world, it has nevertheless produced a number of artists who, in recent years, have created dazzling pieces in which thousands of tiny sequins are built up, like mosaics, to create masterpieces of Voodoo art.

In many modern paintings, paint itself often assumes a secondary role. Jackson Pollock pioneered the vast canvas on which enormous swathes of paint were sloshed haphazardly, with buttons, nails and even cigarette butts embedded at random. Known as 'Jack the Dripper' from his custom of laying the canvas on the studio floor and then dripping the paint on to it, he has inspired many painters of a later generation to

follow suit. Gillian Ayres (b. 1930), for example, has adapted Pollock's technique in her own huge abstracts, but going a step further by using her hands and knees to mould and knead the paint on unstretched canvas. Jean-Paul Riopelle's *Abstractions* are a positive riot of vibrant primary colours squirted straight from the tube on to the canvas in clusters and clumps which therefore take on a sculptural effect.

Mixed media open up seemingly limitless possibilities. Ashley Blickerton's *Le Art (Composition with Logos)* of 1987, a clever assemblage of modern brand logos sending up industrial design, was actually hand-crafted in silkscreen and acrylic with lacquer on plywood and aluminium. In *Wiring the Unfinished Bathroom* (1962) Jim Dine combines tiny metal lamps, toothbrushes and patches of paint on the canvas to make a very witty statement about DIY and the 'when I get round to it' syndrome. John Lennon's widow Yoko Ono (b. 1933) combined sumi ink, string, cloth, seeds and a bamboo screen to create her *Painting for the Wind* (1961) . She has joined forces with other avant-garde artists such as Claes Oldenburg and Jim Dine in recent years in performance art, involving the burning of canvasses and jumping around on canvasses dripping with wet paint.

The Conceptual Art movement of the 1960s, whose fundamental premise was that the idea behind a work was of greater importance than the work itself, resulted in such very unusual combinations. Zvi Goldstein, for example, combined silkscreen with a painted aluminium relief in creating such works as *Future* (1985) depicting functionless objects. On Kawara, a Japanese Conceptualist, has used a substance called Liquitex on canvas to produce his 'date paintings' recording the passage of time. It has even reached the point at which art, such as Andy Goldsworthy's pictures created from flowers and leaves, has become a thing of the fleeting moment, but thanks to photography it can be recorded for posterity.

World Art

There has been image and mark making by humankind for a very long time. It predates history as well as the current notion of what constitutes art. Many cultures still do not have a specific word for art or artist. What we think of as art tends to be that art produced by urban civilizations, and more specifically Western, urban civilizations. Art within this setting and its function within Western society and culture can be dated (by some) to the beginning of the social revolutions – the separation of Church and State, for example. The French Revolution established a new form of rule by the people, distinct from that of Ancient Greece, and modelled on the American Revolution. The American art historian Linda Nochlin described the creation of the first art museum – the Louvre – as a radical upheaval, 'conceived in the optimistic days of the Enlightenment and borne to the shore by the waves of the French Revolution. In a sense it was also a token of art's impotence, its final severance from the social structure, setting it apart, like religion, for weekend worship.'[1] Nochlin also explored the role of the museum as a mechanism to spread knowledge and thus aid in the emancipation of the public. A new world of art emerged that would establish a Western hegemony on the idea of art, and export it to the world. The 200 years since can rightfully be called the age of art museums, even though artists of the modern age would consistently rage against them – calling them irrelevant and anachronistic. They were established in the far reaches of Empire – a sign of civilization, a model of good breeding and a compound social service – and finally becoming a business like any other commodity: witness the branch plants of the Tate and Guggenheim museums in the 1990s. Many will argue that this plays into the now-questioned European model of what art is, and continues the Empire of Western Art, which has traced its aesthetic roots to the Golden Age of Greece, thereby linking empires in an apparent form of continuous legacy.

The European bias has also been reinforced in general readership books which, until recently, have excluded the contemporary art histories of other cultures. These books have become accepted as the guide, and form the curriculum reading in schools. A more curious shaping appears in the 1979 Phaidon Press reference book *Key Dates in Art History, from 600 BC to the Present*. The chronology follows a column format of categories – painting, architecture, sculpture and key events (that is, history itself) – broken into European regions and North America. North America excludes Canada, and no mention is made of Latin America, let alone Asia. Yet the book is 'designed to help anyone in search of a chronological skeleton, either in order to arrive at a fuller understanding of the art of the past or as a means of using that art to create new works'.[2] This is not to point an accusatory finger at one book, but it is symptomatic of how art history is formulated. Key dates and events defy a simple truth, not only the diversity of cultural expression: artists travel, gain new experiences and change the face of art. History, as is often said, is written by the winners, and chronology is not the only governing factor. Being the first is only a beginning and shaping is always done from a place, a perspective and often after the original event has taken place.

Michelangelo, Creation of Adam

Closely aligned to the emergence of the museum was the role of city as art centre. There was a precursor battle between Rome and Florence for claims to the Renaissance, but the urban epoch begins with the emergence of Paris as a world art centre from the mid-nineteenth century through to the mid-twentieth. Why one city should claim the title over another is a difficult question to answer, but large cities are centres of power, generating wealth, surplus capital and many other conditions for a cultural milieu, a hot-house effect. There are minor centres in this mix over the past 150 years – Zurich, Moscow, Berlin, Milan – from which ideas have issued forth that have galvanized the cultural imagination. Urban size, however, is not the only factor. A by-consensus critical mass has not appeared out of Cairo, São Paulo, Beijing or Calcutta. Tokyo emerged as a world art centre in the 1980s due to the impact of the Japanese industrial boom. Wealthy corporate collectors purchased Western modern masters in highly publicized auctions for extraordinary prices, and then the Western gallery world turned its attention to the new Japanese art. If London has emerged as a centre in the late 1990s, some of that is the result of museum expansion – the opening of the Tate Modern. New York grabbed the centre title from Paris in the 1950s. The United States was the new economic power and the 'mother of invention' in the latter half of the twentieth century, but also the site of vigorous museum building: the Museum of Modern Art in 1929; the Whitney Museum of American Art in 1931

Norman Lewis, *Evening Rendezvous*

(when the donation of the Whitney private collection was turned down by the Metropolitan Museum of Art); the Guggenheim Museum in 1959, marrying the spectacle of modern art and Frank Lloyd Wright's architecture. This last was equalled only for notoriety by Frank Gehry's design for the Bilbao Guggenheim, opened in 1997. Finally, almost inevitably, there had to be a New Museum, which was established in 1977 to 'reflect the global nature of art today, and span a vast array of cultural activities and media … guided by the conviction that contemporary art is a vital social force that extends beyond the art world into the broader culture' (from the New Museum's mission statement). The New Museum teamed up with the Museum of Contemporary Hispanic Art and the Studio Museum in Harlem (also New York) in the production and presentation of The Decade Show in 1990. A Hispanic or Harlem Museum would have been unthinkable prior to 1980. They are a sign of a changing cultural perspective.

Forever and Forever

The world is a big place, and its art has increasingly taken on proportions unimaginable to the first art historians, leaving a daunting task to those who wish to revise that history, or add to it. One can liken art in the world to the presence of water, its properties and actions, as water covers much of our world. The earliest cartographers were obsessed with the outline, and circumnavigation was the best way to determine the shape of a land mass. So, too, for the obsession of art historians. But because art has been mapped through individuals, forming schools and movements of type and style, the modern art geology tree as a visual aid was first proposed in 1936 by Alfred Barr, the founding director of the Museum of Modern Art, New York. Another mapping approach has been by chronology, stratified by regions of

activity. As events and information accumulate faster than our ability to provide historical perspective, the same is true for world art. The modern age, beginning in the mid-nineteenth century, has much unfinished business and unexplored terrain, let alone coming to a field theory of what it all means. Much of the modern period is written from the *tsunami* perspective. It is 'the shock of the new' as Ian Dunlop wrote of key modernist exhibitions in 1972.

To extend the water world analogy, there are many streams, pools and eddies – some flow into the big rivers, and finally into the world's oceans. The dilution – or 'derivation', in art terms – is not the art or idea, but our ability to discern one wave from another. As in nature, the cycle of a critical mass alters our perception of the waves and tides of art making. A high tide is not necessarily better than a low tide, but is thought to be so in art history, hence the lament for high times of production, the 'golden ages' and the appearance of the remarkable. Low tides also have their value and meaning. Artists do not stop working because the art world periodically loses interest, or proclaims the death of a movement (waiting for the next one), or has a limited attention span. That span can be compared to building a bridge. It must span calm as well as troubled waters. Moreover, the high and low tides are simply different points in a cycle, and river sources come as trickles from remote areas. So too for art. The streams are practitioners who may themselves not be prominent but, over time, actions accumulate and wear down the shorelines. The cartographer/art historian cannot walk away but must return periodically to see what has happened to the original line.

This is not the only metaphor: the American George Kubler described art history as a vast mining operation. Modernism – the first and only art movement to take the world's stage – may have dug a hole for itself, but it also opened the floodgates. Kubler brings forth another problem, 'if the fullness of history is forever indigestible, the beauty of art is ordinarily incommunicable. The rhapsodist can suggest a few clues to the experience of a work of art [but] can communicate nothing to persons not ready to travel the same path.' The role of the historian, Kubler continues, has been to uncover the shape of time – cultural activity that is only known to us by the things we make, or the things that survive.

A Canadian artist, who recently travelled on an official trade and diplomatic mission, and visited art and history museums in Russia, commented in a letter to the author, 'with all the dislocation and horror of humanity it is staggering to see and understand what has been protected – more sacred than life itself'.

Artists and the Life of the City

Twentieth-century revisionist historians have argued that entire sections of artists and art production have been ignored: those considered to be regionalists, not of the city; women; and non-Europeans. A considerable amount of scholarly effort has taken place over the past 20 to 30 years to revisit this art and provide a social argument for the inclusion of this work. But the role of the artist as exemplary model cannot be underestimated. Picasso's life and work, for example, is so enmeshed with the creation myth of modern art that to speak of his Spanish-Catalan origins is almost beside the point. Picasso is the model of modern art, much in the same way The Beatles are the standard of measurement for popular music/youth culture in the early 1960s. Picasso borrowed liberally from African and ancient Mediterranean cultures – not surprising, as Spain is part of that culture – and from his precursors, the old masters. So too for The Beatles: their repertory until 1965 (considering their impact, a surprisingly short recording career, 1962–71) borrowed so heavily on Black America's rhythm and blues, that had they been an American group, they might have been dismissed as a cover band with odd-looking hair and a few charming original songs about youthful love. The Beatles were distinct enough: their accents and behaviour (irrepressible, as is the art world's vanguard) were a model for success. American bands imitated The Beatles, as did aspiring musicians elsewhere in the world. The appeal crossed national and cultural barriers. Once this happens, there is no way to stop it, nor can one predict when the next wave will take place. There is always a new wave, a term used for the new American jazz in the early 1960s (and French cinema of the 1960s), and the new British/American music of the early 1980s. Was it really new or just a different wave, the same waters, the same gravitational pull? So too for the waves and movements of art in the twentieth century.

What made Picasso remarkable, among other things, was being a foreigner at the centre of the art world. It was Picasso, and not his French counterpart, Georges Braque, who made the lasting impression. Yet Braque and Picasso shared so many similarities in the formative Cubist period that their work c. 1911–12 is interchangeable, like a brilliant comedy team trading straight lines and punch lines. The interchangeability is comparable for The Beatles. Their hair styles, a 'French cut,' became The Beatles Cut and a global sign of youth rebellion; their Spanish-heeled boots became Beatles boots. The Beatles were also responsible for popularizing a hitherto 'minor' instrument, the electric guitar. The Beatles were a distorted cultural mirror:

everyone could reflect in it and enjoy themselves without wondering who is really fat or thin. One can also say this of the monumental impact of Claude Monet's paintings. His version of Impressionism became the paradigm, above all others, even that of the formative modern painter Paul Cézanne. Artists from around the world flocked to Monet's home at Giverny, and an artist's colony was established there between 1887 and 1914, when it was suspended because of the First World War.

The circulation of cultural ideas, the lure of the unknown and the exotic, may be the beginning of World Art as we now experience it. In the Americas, Asia-Pacific and the African continent, itinerant European artists – often members of exploration and expeditionary forces – were depicting 'new' worlds for the 'old' world. Dutch artist Albert Eckhout (c. 1612–c. 1665) painted portraits of Mameluke, Tupi, African and Tarairiu natives of Brazil in 1641. All are women, two are shown with children. The shock (of the new) is the Tarairiu, a cannibal, gracefully holding a severed hand as if a fan, and a foot sticking out of her head basket. These are not journal illustrations but on the scale of royal portraiture, each painting over 2.5 metres high, life-size, thereby brought to life. The New World stories are evident in the Casta paintings of Colonial Latin America, Mexico, Peru, Bolivia, and spanning the eighteenth century, and done by 'named' and anonymous artists. The paintings portray the process of *mestizaje*, or race-mixing and intermarriage between Indian, Spanish and Black peoples. However one wishes to analyze them – art or social anthropology – they depict the emergence of a different world, and a portent of the new political order in the nineteenth century.

Paul Cézanne, Still Life With Apples

In 1960, Australian professor Bernard Smith published *European Vision and the South Pacific*, a subject predated by his published writings from 1945. In the preface to the second edition in 1985, Smith responded to the issue of vision – images of the exotic, or what is commonly referred to as the 'noble savage'. Smith writes, 'the use of the term "European vision" declared a belief in a cognitive theory of perception: that seeing is conditioned by knowing. But the [original] book nowhere suggested that Europeans (or for that matter the members of any other ethnic or cultural groupings) are incapable as individuals of seeing what is actually before them, or that they are incapable of knowing that they are in the presence of the (for them) new, though they may well find and usually do find, difficulty in assembling appropriate words, images, symbols, and ideas to describe accurately their experience.'[3] Smith was not hiding the historical fact of a fatal encounter, that Europeans did disrupt and destroy Aboriginal societies. The same can be said of any encounter of humankind, where a dominant power establishes territorial control. Human nature is such, but why blame the artist for bad behaviour, insensitivity, or accuse them of being a pawn in the game of world domination?

Rude Awakenings

Concurrent with the age of museums was the appearance and invention of the here-and-now exhibition. If wrought independently – the museum at the outset was essentially a storehouse of treasures – they would soon combine as the museum recognized the value of audiences drawn to the spectacle. Ian Dunlop noted that 'In the nineteenth century people [Europeans and Americans] were passionately interested in the art of their contemporaries. New paintings and sculpture could arouse strong feelings.'[4] Those strong feelings also meant commissions and a livelihood for the celebrated artists – an ultimate prize. Dunlop examined landmark exhibitions that are commonly accepted as having had seismic impact in establishing the world of modern art: The Salon de Refusés (1863); The First Impressionist Exhibition (1874); The Salon

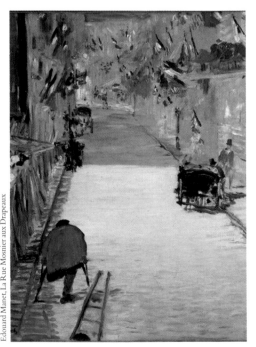

Édouard Manet, La Rue Mosnier aux Drapeaux

d'Automne (1905); The Post-Impressionists (1910); The International Exhibition of Modern Art, commonly referred to as The Armory Show (1913); The International Surrealist Exhibition (1938); Entartete Kunst (1937).

The first three were staged in the centre of the art world at the time – Paris – but the Post-Impressionism exhibition took place in London. It is not only notable for its change of scene, but also for the appearance of the independent curator, the art historian, curator and artist Roger Fry. Whereas 'Impressionism' was

the term that became attached to the new art of 1863 (although not sanctified until 1874), it originated from a critic of the new art. Fry coined the term 'Post-Impressionism' and thereby set the course for more naming by curators. Artists would continue to name themselves, but often these terms have fallen into disuse. The Armory Show of 1913 was another quantum locality leap, taking place in New York, an outpost of the art world and, moreover, the home of artists who wanted to distance themselves from the Old World. The Surrealist exhibition of 1938 returns Paris to the forefront, titled 'International' (as was the Armory Show), although referring more to the aspirations of those associated with Surrealism rather than a view of practitioners in the world. The last, Entartete Kunst, was a landmark by default. Instigated by Adolf Hitler, it was to be the proof that modern art was degenerate. It resulted in the loss and destruction of many works of art, the persecution of many of the artists, and has become a cause célèbre for artistic freedom against the mechanisms of totalitarian power.

The Salon des Refusés has developed its own creation mythology, perhaps a misreading of the term 'refusés'. It came about as a union of convenience: the rejection of Edouard Manet and the 'new' painters from the official Salon, but also the refusal of work by regular exhibitors who felt it their right to be entered. Napoleon III was petitioned for, and granted, an edict, in essence an official sanction. It is unlikely that Napoleon III felt any sympathy towards this art or any other, but saw it as a popular and liberal decision – to endear himself to Paris. It provided the public a first opportunity to decide for themselves, and proved to have the opposite effect of the sanctioned intentions, allowing the 'refused' to damn themselves in public. It was a runaway success. The rest is history. If the first shot, it was not the overthrow of the Ancien Régime. Squabbling is a hallmark of the avant garde – keeping it forever young and angry.

Manifestos

The early part of the twentieth century may also be seen as an age of manifestos, interwoven with the emergence of the museum as cultural broker and the landmark exhibition. They are declarations of independence and a call to arms. While most have lost their then-contemporary sense of urgency, perhaps even been accepted in the general consensus, they serve as important historical documents, to track the temperament of the times. There is no particular commonality, but a defence of the new in relationship to the past, often looking to the future world, and the belief in some form of essential truth.

The Italian poet and *agent-provocateur* Filippo Tommaso Marinetti, published the *Futurist Manifesto* in Paris in 1909. He was not promoting a different form of art, but a new, anti-aesthetic vision: 'We affirm that the world's magnificence has been enriched by a new beauty; the beauty of speed. A racing car whose hood is adorned by great pipes, like serpents of explosive breath – a roaring car that seems to run on shrapnel – is more beautiful than the *Victory of Samothrace* [also know as *Winged Victory*, a Greek artifact in the Louvre collection]. We sing of great crowds excited by work, by pleasure, and by riot; we will sing of the multicoloured, polyphonic tides of revolution in the modern capitals.' And so on.

Umberto Boccioni (1882–1916) was one of the artists who took up Marinetti's challenge. He published his *Technical Manifesto of Futurist Sculpture* in 1912; in it he wrote about the difference between real form and ideal form, the new form (of Impressionism) and the traditional concept. Unlike Marinetti, he offered some prescriptive advice for the would-be sculptor of the future: 'The straight line is the only means that can lead us to the primitive virginity of a new architectonic construction of sculptural masses and zones.' As naïvely ludicrous as this may seem, it would be taken up by a generation of American artists in the 1960s, under another 'ism' – Minimalism. Another Futurist-associated artist, Gino Severini (1883–1966), would publish his own Futurist manifesto in 1913.

Albert Gleizes (1881–1953) and Jean Metzinger (1883–1956) co-wrote a Cubist manifesto in 1912. Ironically they are minor artists in the modern reckoning, but neither of the prime players – Picasso and Braque – entered the heated debate. Gleizes and Metzinger recounted the recent past, ranking artists and movements in degrees of importance relative to Cubism, starting with Gustave Courbet as the end to 'secular realism'. They criticized Impressionism for its 'feeble' drawing and declared 'imitation is the only error possible in art; it attacks the law of time, which is Law'. Cubism, they write, is 'painting itself'.

Kasimir Malevich (1878–1935), the founder of Suprematism in 1913, published his treatise *The Non-Objective World* in 1927: 'To the Suprematist the visual phenomena of the objective world are, in themselves, meaningless; the significant thing is feeling, as such, quite apart from the environment in which it is called forth.' Malevich went on to deride 'academic naturalism', the Impressionists and the Cubists.

Architect Le Corbusier (born Charles Edouard Jeanneret, 1887–1965) and painter Amédée Ozenfant (1886–1966) articulated their doctrines of Purism, first published in conjunction with the Purist

Amédée Ozenfant, Nature Morte aux Verres, Bouteilles et Pot Blanc

exhibition held at Galerie Thomas, Paris, in 1917. They wrote, 'the goal of art is not simple pleasure, rather it partakes of the nature of happiness [and] the means of executing a work of art in a transmittable and universal language.'[5]

It is important to note that these ideas, and the many others there were, came to the surface in little more than a decade, and that the authors are of the same generation, born between 1881 and 1887. In each manifesto there is an assertion that art can appear and be meaningful anywhere in the world – an idealism perhaps, but these ideas did take root quickly in many places, inflected by locality and regionality. Manifestos are the winds upon which the seeds of the modern idea are borne.

There are other manifestos – minor because they appear at the outposts of the modern empire, and Europe, yet important because of the battle for freedom from the local 'tyranny'. In 1928 the São Paulo writer and poet Oswald de Andrade issued the *Manifesto Anthropófago*, with a provocative opening salvo 'Only anthropophagy [cannibalism] unites us [Brazilians]'. The text is ripe with poetic satire, puns and linguistic twists: a rage against the vestiges of European colonialism and Catholicism while inviting the mysteries of that 'which does not belong to me', to quote another line.[6] The carnal allusions to cannibalism and anthropophagy drive Andrade's textual engine. Cannibalism is the act of eating human flesh and the finale in a war of supremacy and a cultural destruction of the other (the word itself does not appear in the manifesto). Anthropophagy also involves the consumption of human flesh but is differentiated as a form of cultural communion, to assimilate what is deemed as worthy or a noble attribute, the eating of souls. As a form of appropriation it leads to hybridization. In the modern world cannibalism suggests a metaphor of international capitalism (as the inheritor of imperialism and colonialism), and anthropophagy as the voracious appetite of cultural discourse. In vernacular terms, this can be likened to raiding the cultural icebox.

The manifesto 'Refus Global' was delivered in 1948 to Canada, a settler country with twin founding colonizing nations – France and England. The architect of the manifesto was Montreal painter Paul-Emile Borduas. His declaration began with the descendants of those who arrived 'by resistance to the conqueror' and maintained 'an irrational attachment to the past, self-indulgence and sentimental pride and other compulsions.' Borduas wrote: 'Forbidden readings circulate, spreading solace and hope.' Citing the French, Russian and Spanish revolutions, he shouted on the page, 'Make way for Magic! Make way for objective mysteries! Make way for life! Make way for necessities!... We foresee a future in which man is freed for useless chains....' Nowhere does he describe or promote a style or style of art. It is a humanist, liberating exclamation.[7]

In Australia, the opening salvo came later. Time, as noted, is relative in the world – and consciousness can come to different places at different times. A group of young artists in Melbourne, including Arthur Boyd, John Brack, Charles Blackman and the 'theorist' of the group, the aforementioned Bernard Smith, issued the 'Antipodean Manifesto' for an exhibition in 1959. 'Modern art has liberated the artist from his bondage to the world of natural appearances; it has not imposed upon him the need to withdraw from life. The widespread desire, as it claimed, to 'purify' painting has led many artists to claim that they have invented a new language. We see no evidence at all of the emergence of such a new language nor any likelihood of its appearance. Painting for us is more than paint.'[8] The manifesto appeared on contested ground – not pitting figurative painting against abstraction or non-objective painting, but suggesting that the last should be the predominant form, and counters the claim that the past – that image-making – was no longer useful. Smith later claimed that he

was not proposing a regressive (anti-abstract) modern national school for Australia, but the manifesto has been thought of as such by observers, and perhaps encoded into that historical view and the emergence of an independent Australian art.

Arthur Boyd, Expulsion

Manifestos are one thing, but they must also find an agent – a visual statement – or they may remain empty words. Italian artists such as Giacomo Balla would take up Marinetti's Futurist calling, but the challenge would spread to the Americas and Japan (and undoubtedly other places, too). The explanation is both simple and complex – we were all living in that Future World, even if at different degrees of intensity.

Brazilian Modernism first emerged in a week-long festival staged in São Paulo in 1922, and the first Modernist house was built there in 1927 by Russian émigré architect Gregori Warchavchik. But it is Tarsila do Amaral (1886–1973) who is credited with giving Andrade's manifesto a pictorial equivalence. While studying in Paris in the early 1920s she received a letter from his brother Mario, imploring her to 'abandon' Juan Gris and André Lhote – two of her European influences – and return to 'the virgin forest' (*matavirgismo*), spiritually and physically. Do Amaral was already conscious of her Brazilianness and on returning to São Paulo in the late 1920s 'presented' Andrade with tropical morphology, a fleshy indigenous-referenced figuration in her 1928 painting titled *Abaporu* and mythicized (non-European and non-Cubist) landscapes.

Other calling cards are not as easy to identify. Paul-Emile Borduas' stark white-and-black, non-objective paintings have important sign value in Canadian art, even if people never bother to read the 'Refus Global', and even if Borduas' Automatiste abstraction – 'derived' from the French movement – was overshadowed by American artists of the time. Moreover, the battle for abstraction was still being waged in the 1950s. The same is true in Australia. It is difficult to extract a single image from the 'Antipodean Manifesto', but the face of the new age can be seen in the dark history revisited by Sidney Nolan in the late 1940s, his Ned Kelly series (the mythologized nineteenth-century outlaw) and in Russell Drysdale's painting of white settlers in the outback. It is not the civilizing element, but one of stark survival, and in the background – invisible – is Aboriginal life and culture.

Back and Forth

Lest this commentary revert to the description of landmarks only, other factors must be taken into account. While Paris, and other European centres, attracted artists from the outposts, they participated and returned as agents of modernity. The example of Tarsila do Amaral has already been cited, but the two-way traffic began much earlier. Juan Manuel Blanes (1830–1901) was born in Montevideo, Uruguay, two years after that country's independence from Spain. Blanes began to paint at an early age – self-taught but with talent – and in 1854 he established a studio, devoting much of his time to portraiture (a profession in the outpost). In 1860 he received a grant to study in Europe and spent five years in Florence and Rome, arriving at a time of great artistic, political and social turmoil in the form of the rebellions of the Risorgimento that eventually resulted in the unification of Italy. On his return, Blanes had a new technical facility, social awareness and a vision to paint the images of nationhood, rather than mythical allegorical paintings in the European academic tradition. The subject matter included disease, death and revolution, but like any good historian, Blanes picked his moments: there are heroic battle scenes, as well as pieces like *The Death of General Venancio Flores* (1868). The moment is the giving of absolution by a priest over the general's body; the street is empty except for the two men; the painting makes a stark contrast between the white buildings and road and the black garb of priest and general – a balance between form and content. In *The Paraguayan Woman* ('La Paraguaya', *c.* 1879), a woman in native garb stands alone on the battlefield with bodies strewn around her. It is not a hysterical portrait, nor even a historical moment, but the conflation of matriarchy and nationhood. It occupies a space between the past and future – a modern painting. To know the painting one must first know history, and through that painting know more about history.

David Burliuk (1882–1967) was born a native Ukrainian (there was actually no nation of Ukraine at the time, but there had existed 1,000 years of language and culture distinct from that of Russia). His studies took him to Munich and Paris before 1904, and then to Moscow. He became a founding member of Der Blaue Reiter group, along with Kandinsky, in Munich in 1911, and the following year he co-authored the Russian Futurist Manifesto, entitled 'A Slap in the Face of Public Taste'. The civil war that followed the 1917 Bolshevik Revolution spilled into a battle for the territorial control of Ukraine (Kyiv was captured and recaptured by five different groups in an eight-month period between in 1919 and 1920). Burliuk escaped through Siberia in 1918 and then travelled to Japan, where he stayed long enough to be influential in the establishment of Japanese Futurism. He arrived in the United States by way of Canada in 1922. Burliuk remained active in the avant-garde tradition and authored the 'Manifesto Radio-Style' in 1926, which ends with a very non-Futurist thought: 'We need to train our mind to see things slowly, yet see much. The Chinese see things on a different – a slower – scale than our highly "civilized" artists. We have acquired with our civilization a [sic] algebraic vision. The Chinese painters see distinctly each feather on the wing of a flying bird.'

Ian Fairweather (1891–1973) was born in Scotland. He studied art in Switzerland, Holland and Munich. In 1926 he set off to Canada, working as a farm hand, and finally raised enough money for a passage to Shanghai in 1929. From there he travelled though Southeast Asia and arrived in Melbourne in 1934. By no real intent, Australia was to become his home, but he returned to Asia (and England) before resettling on the east coast of Australia, on Bribie Island, north of Brisbane, in 1953. What happened on his return is not clearly understood except by that unknown thing – hated by art historians – an epiphany. He began to merge styles; he professed interest in Cézanne's Modernism but also incorporated his first-hand Asian experience into his work. In 1962, at the age of 71, Fairweather was proclaimed Australia's greatest living artist by an art critic (echoing Jackson Pollock's sainthood by the American press). The issue is not of greatness – Fairweather was all but unknown to the rest of the world – but of the resonance that such an artist would have, a professed hermit, idiosyncratic, independent and living simply, but with purpose. It was, again, evidence that a Western artist could draw from other wells of culture. He was not the only Australian to do so, if indeed, Fairweather can be called 'Australian'. In 1941, the painter Margaret Preston declared that 'the art of the aborigine has for too long been neglected. The attention of Australian people must be drawn to the fact that it is great art and the foundation of a national culture for this country'.[9] The nation was 40 years old at the time: she was speaking of a culture that had been on the land for at least 40,000 years.

Ian Fairweather, Roi Soleil or Sun King

Our understanding of time, then, is shaped by our consciousness – when we are ready to receive the signal, and what we perceive that signal to be. Likewise, wandering is nothing new for artists. Often such artists are written out of the history books because they are not associated with any particular place, but driven by their own, portable intellectual property.

Art

The New Outposts

In the post Second World War era, national survey exhibitions proliferated on the international stage, signalled elsewhere by the arrival of the United Nations as a global body, quite different from the club nomenclature of its failed predecessor, the League of Nations. Art became a political-national calling card, and artists continued to move to the centre – at that time, New York – but even the centre itself was shifting and changing. Betty Parsons championed artists such as Barnett Newman (1905–70), Jackson Pollock (1912–56), Ad Reinhardt (1913–67) and Mark Rothko (1903–70), but when she opened her New York gallery in September 1946 it was with an exhibition of Northwest Coast Indian Art. She represented a young Japanese artist Kenzo Okada (1902–82), who had arrived in New York in the late 1940s. New York was something of a Mecca for

Mark Rothko, Untitled

Japanese artists after the war, but the traffic began earlier. The best-known is Yasuo Kuniyoshi (1889–1953), who arrived in the United States in 1906. The American-born Isamu Noguchi (1904–88) was not afraid to express his cultural roots, and paved a path for two-way cultural traffic. One of the early survey exhibitions, The New Japanese Painting and Sculpture, was organized by the Museum of Modern Art in New York, and circulated the United States from 1965 to 1967. It must also be noted that non-Western countries were also paying attention to their modern movements. The first museum of modern art in Japan was built in Kamakura in 1951. An Asian art exhibition was mounted in Fukuoka in 1979, with work by 230 artists from India, China and Japan. It was followed up the next year by a more comprehensive look at contemporary Asian art: 471 artists were represented from Bangladesh, China, India, Indonesia, Korea, Malaysia, Nepal, Pakistan, the Philippines, Singapore, Sri Lanka, Thailand and Japan. This has evolved into the Fukuoka Asian Art Triennial, mounted in 1999 and 2002.

International artist residency programs and facilities sprang up to facilitate global traffic – not surprisingly in Paris with the founding of the Cité des Arts in 1965, and through the Deutscher Akademischer Austauschdienst (DAAD) in Berlin, a private, publicly funded, self-governing organization of higher education institutions in Germany,

promoting international academic relations and co-operation. Such institutions also appeared in the mountains – the Banff Centre, Canada (founded in 1933, with the arts programming beginning in 1953)– and the desert – Mishkenot Sha'ananim in Jerusalem, which started in the late 1960s. International artists' residencies have become part of the mix for many cultural funding agencies. International biennials and triennials have multiplied. The Venice Biennale was founded in 1893, but the post-1950 outings saw the construction of permanent national pavilions by non-European nations, building new worlds, so to speak, in the garden of the old world. The São Paulo *Biennale* was founded in 1951 and the Sydney *Biennale* in 1973. There were more than 20 international biennials mounted around the world in 1997 and 1998. Moreover, there were exhibitions exploring all manner of the Diaspora and regionality. More than a rush to mimic cultural tourism, this is also an indication that, everywhere, there is a desire to know more about 'the Other', even if it is only to look over the cultural fence.

Arguably the first world exhibition was The Family of Man, organized by Edward Steichen (1879–1973) for the Museum of Modern Art in New York. Steichen, who had already established himself as a photographer of reputation with the Photo Secession group in New York in the early twentieth century, began planning the exhibition in 1951. It was, as some have suggested, his antidote to the Cold War and used what Steichen felt was a universal language – photography. There was an open invitation for photographs, and Steichen received more than two million pictures from around the world. They were edited to 503 photographs by 273 photographers from 68 countries, based on his themes of love and faith, birth, work, family, education, children, war and peace. First mounted at the Museum of Modern Art in 1955, it circulated internationally until 1964, drawing more than nine million visitors. The exhibition was reassembled in the 1990s.

Bernard Rudofsky's (1905–88) exhibition Architecture Without Architects was shown at the Museum of Modern Art in 1964. Rudofsky wrote: 'Architectural history, as written and taught in the Western world, has never been concerned with more than a few select cultures. [This exhibition] attempts to break down our narrow [Western] concepts of the art of building by introducing the unfamiliar world of non-pedigreed architecture.'[10] Rudofsky then delivered the stunning revelation that since so little was known about it, there could be no name and no category. He proposed vernacular, anonymous, spontaneous, indigenous, rural, on a case-by-case basis. Rudofsky was careful to avoid the 'primitive' label, the charming, picturesque principle, which has been admired for centuries, and used the term 'exotic' in its original sense of 'alien'. Rather than an admiration exercise, he delivered an important lesson – instead of trying to conquer nature, indigenous builders adapted to the terrain, responded to the climate, solved problems with the materials at hand with engineering skills that were no less accomplished than those of the steel-and-glass age. There is an aesthetic beauty in the sense that the proportions and design embellishments have a harmony and give pleasure in the looking. Rudofsky is his own example of itinerancy. Born in Vienna, he studied and worked in architecture in Austria, Germany and Italy, and the United States before moving to Brazil in 1941. He settled permanently in the United States in 1942, but was a guest professor in Japan in 1961 and Denmark in the late 1970s.

Curator Jean-Hubert Martin mounted Magiciens de la Terre at the Centre Georges Pompidou, Paris, in 1989. It was the first global art perspective (a distinction to the photo documentary aspect of Steichen's exhibition), done with a seven-person curatorial team selecting work by 100 artists from Africa, Oceania and non-Western regions. North American, white and indigenous, and European artists were also included. More than 10 years later, the exhibition is still the subject of much discussion and debate. The German curator René Block, himself no stranger to the world of international art, suggested that 'unorthodox exhibitions ... remain etched in our memories for a long time as one tries to rationalize and identify why they failed to fulfil their promise. The greatest of these exhibitions [was] Magiciens de la Terre. However, why did this exhibition – the most important I have ever witnessed – fail in its endeavour to confront the works of artists from Africa, Oceania and the world's other "peripheral" cultural zones with those of their counterparts in the key artistic centres of Western Europe or the USA on an equal basis? Today we can furnish a simple explanation: because the cultural setting of these works was simply too diverse in order to conduct a meaningful dialogue.'[11]

Land Spirit Power was the first major international exhibition of contemporary art by artists of native ancestry to be held at the National Gallery of Canada, in 1992. One of the contributors, artist Robert Houle (b. 1947) – a member of the Saulteaux Nation based in the southern Manitoba (Canada) area – explored the issues of mythic time and its relevance to contemporary culture, but he also spoke as an artist educated in Western culture: 'The lack of a linear chronology in myth, storytelling, and dreams, the interchangeable grammar and the

Lin Onus, Jimmy's Billabong

interchangeability of perception is what makes wonderful, rhythmical patterns of thought in the oral traditions of the ancient ones. These constituted patterns of thought have been etched into the psyche of their descendants through the human voice, thus leaving a legacy with which to affirm one's being and one's place in the scheme of things.'

He continued: 'To detach them [contemporary indigenous artists] from this ethnic specificity, its subjectivity, by subsuming it in the master narrative of Christian patriarchal hegemony [and] western European ethnocentricity, is to disinherit them, to deny their inherent right to the land their ancestors have always enjoyed and respected. Because there has always gaped so terrifying a chasm between the basic needs of humankind and our knowledge of the world as we first became conscious beings, we have always reached towards ways of understanding and controlling our environment. Theological explanations have been superseded in the modern age by scientific and technological proof – the new poetry of belief.' He concluded, by no means a conclusion: 'There is certainly a language the artists [in the exhibition] understand, for any attempt to move away from the Renaissance imagery of figures and objects contributes to their struggle to open and reopen the discussion over the nature of beauty.'[12]

Houle was speaking of more than the battleground of beauty as seen in art, that which the West has claimed from the Greek Classical ideal; he was speaking of how to alter the model and allow other models of culture to co-exist. It is difficult because many of those histories are open wounds. Australian curator Djon Mundine examined this problem in an exhibition with an explicit title, Tyerabarrbowaryaou, I Shall Never Become a White Man. Organized for the Museum of Contemporary Art, Sydney, in 1992, it circulated in Australia and was remounted for the 5th Havana Biennal in 1994. Mundine deliberately intended that the show would be more confrontational than people would expect; he wanted to shock his white observers. He strongly felt

David Alfaro Siqueiros, El Botero

through the world, and wherever they are now [they] have always been in exile in relation to the place they were in before. The younger generations don't actually lose that. There is a kind of melancholia, a nostalgia for something which, finally, is the world.'[14]

Cartographies, a survey of contemporary Latin American art, was mounted by the Winnipeg Art Gallery, Canada, and circulated in the Americas from 1993 to 1995. The Brazilian curator Ivo Mesquita echoes the George Kubler statement cited at the outset: 'The exhibition ... requires of the visitor the traveller's disposition: a being with history and identity, guided by the senses through the territories he traverses and discovers. It proposes that each visitor transform himself into a cartographer and invent his own territory. For, by extension, it also intends to make explicit an attitude towards life: to be a traveller means to seek an almost permanent existence in the present, in constant displacement and in the condition of the eternal foreigner, with roots not in nationality but in those territories under the rule of desire, sensibility and knowledge. After all, it is of life we speak when we think about art.'[15] Paulo Herkenhoff provided an 'Incomplete Glossary' for the neophyte reader of Latin American history and culture. If liberties were taken with the conventions of taxonomy, Herkenhoff showed that Latin America is a site of world intersections, both painful and positive. His B section started with entries for Banana, Bandits, Baroque, Blindness, Body, Books and Brancusi. Herkenhoff includes regional-deprecating wit. For the entry on Soccer, he admitted, 'Latin America produces no good art connected to soccer in spite of winning the world championship seven times'.

Herkenhoff was the Chief Curator for the 1998 Bienal of São Paulo. Its theme was based on the 1928 Manifesto of Oswald de Andrade. The exhibition peeled back colonial history (500 years in the year 2001), to reveal the deep connective tissue to Modernism and 'inviting' Europe while maintaining a relative distance from Eurocentricity. The theme of curatorial cannibalism was interwoven throughout the Bienal building: representing 264 living and dead artists; 33 curators; and four distinct exhibition components. The historical section was subdivided into 27 sections and 68 countries were represented in the nations section. Cannibal pictorialism flowed through the European work of Théodore Géricault, Gustave Moreau, Francis Bacon, René Magritte to post Second World War. American artists Louise Bourgeois, Eva Hesse, Robert Smithson, Dennis Oppenheim, Bruce Nauman and others. David Siqueiros and Roberto Matta were two of the Latin American artists given prominence in the

the injustice of the 'dispossession' of the Aboriginals by the Europeans and understood their spiritual affinity with their land. The connection of land and spirit is the power that keeps culture alive, not merely as an artifact, but in a vital living way.

Coincidentally, and concurrent with the Museum of Contemporary Art and National Gallery of Canada exhibitions – proof that similar ideas and thinking were in the air – was Routes of Wandering, mounted at the Israel Museum, Jerusalem, in 1991. In the foreword, Chief Curator Yigal Zalmona explained that the exhibition was not about the local versus the universal – the *ad nauseam* cringe of international aspirations for 'local art', but the distinction between 'a yearning for a crystallization of a distinctive collective identity and a condition of floating identity'.[13] The distinguished Egyptian-born writer Edmond Jabès (1912–91) was interviewed for the catalogue. He recounted his interpretation of the Jewish existential condition of wandering and exile. 'Even in Israel the Jew is a nomad ... his wanderings are part of his thought ... even when they were dispersed selection. Contemporary Brazilian work was integrated – as if the outsider, jeering. Tunga's 'club-shaped' two-metre-high steel and magnet assemblage *TaCePe* (1986–87) was propped up near Eckhout's seventeenth-century painting *Dança Tapuia* and in view of Bruce Nauman's neon *Eat/Death* (1972). Cildo Meireles's four-metre-long wooden folding ruler object (appearing normal except for non-sequential numbering), sat inside a wall vitrine at knee level to the right of a Van Gogh landscape. Vik Muniz's cibachrome print 'chocolate' portrait of Sigmund Freud hovered over a section of European Surrealism. Arthur Barrio's *Bloody Bundles* object (1969) was set in a wall vitrine insert at floor level in the Francis Bacon section. Herkenhoff contended that Barrio's work 'selected' Bacon, resonating with the carnal phenomenology. If an off-hand comment, the truth of the reversed cultural order was plausible and visible. In another section, Alberto Giacometti's work was counter-posed by the sculpture of Brazilian Maria Martins (1900–73). The work of Hélio Oiticica (1937–80) and Lygia Clark (1920–88) brought the Brazilian cultural context forward. By the 1960s both had abandoned studio practice conventions for installations, interventions and participation, to integrate art and everyday experience. The Roteiros section (translated as 'routes' and repeated seven times, as in Andrade's manifesto) was the global dialogue – that which unifies and points to difference. Seven curators examined regions of Oceania, Latin America, Asia, Africa, the Middle East, Europe and Canada/United States.

All the World's a Museum

The multi-voiced curatorial model is becoming one of the new museum and exhibition models, as in the Asia Pacific Triennial, mounted by the Queensland Art Gallery in Brisbane, starting in 1993. The 1999 Triennial listed 48 contributing curators and 80 writers, outnumbering the 77 artists. A precursor Gallery exhibition – Japanese Ways, Western Means – was mounted in 1989 in collaboration with the Museum of Modern Art in Saitama, Japan. Masayoshi Homma, Director of the Saitama Museum of Modern Art, wrote of the shaping of Japanese art and culture from the outside, China and Korea, though its history, and interdependent histories. He described the 'rural heart' of Japan, 'surrounded by natural beauty and ... blessed with an abundant supply of pure water. Nature is like a mother to the Japanese people, who have had a close affinity with it for centuries.'[16] This, of course, is the case for every culture, remarkable when we also think of the modern world as the built and congested environment, preoccupied

with denying or controlling nature, to build higher, control waters and repurify the elements that we have polluted.

As much as Eurocentricity is held up as a problem in coming to terms with the unruly business of art, there is a lack of a model by which to organize and categorize effectively the diversity of cultural histories – their particular quality and interchange. We are in the midst of a scientific, secular age with no possibility of a return to an idyllic state. Moreover, the nature and design of the modern state is inherently unstable. New alliances, fraternities, agendas and ambitions continuously arise and shift. Traditional ways of life become destabilized and torn apart by modernists who see them as archaic and an impediment to progress. In turn, modern nationalism feeds internationalism – be it democratic or totalitarian and all the political shades of right, centre and left (one and the same for the disadvantaged) – and an international standard as irony feeds the art of this century in the form of internationalism.

With or without irony or its confrontational temperament, contemporary art is often the orphan sitting on the margins of analysis and descriptions of nation and culture. The Paris-based writer/curator Simon Njami has stated that debate on African contemporary art has only just begun, and in turn has questioned whose history are we referring to when the History of Art is spoken of – the history of the African continent can be measured in millennia. Even the term 'post-colonial' is fraught with problems if considered in historic time. That period began in the early nineteenth century in Latin America; in the 1960s in Africa; but only in the early 1990s for the former Soviet republics. These are new nations with old cultures, and have survived the twentieth-century exile from a homeland as a hyphenated culture in the Americas: a melting pot in the United States and a cultural mosaic in Canada. The difference may not be that great. The question of place brings its shadow and nemesis, displacement. To ask about one is to uncover the other. Everyone has a Diaspora.

In attempting to journey to the beginning of any cultural history, the concept of place is often framed in terms of continuous habitation. The migration of populations is not new and has accelerated since the emergence of the

Chéri Samba, Mobali Ya Monyato

Art

modern state. Cultures can thrive in displacement; others are marginalized, shrivel or wither, to disappear or merge with a dominant culture – to 'feed' that culture which itself may be a transformed and a 'displaced' hybrid. The best answer for the prosperous scenario is that the source culture provides a richness of signs, symbols and signifiers, enough to plant the banner afar and proclaim 'now we are here'. This is certainly the case with former Imperial European cultures and nations – literature (which can survive translation), music, design and cuisine – adapting, adjusting and being vulgarized in the fertile ground of new urban environments without losing sight of essential, defining qualities.

Ways of knowing the world and looking at the world may be different things, and yet converge, as in the water metaphor proposed at the outset. For the 1970 Information exhibition at Museum of Modern Art, New York, the Brazilian artists Cildo Meireles and Hélio Oiticica

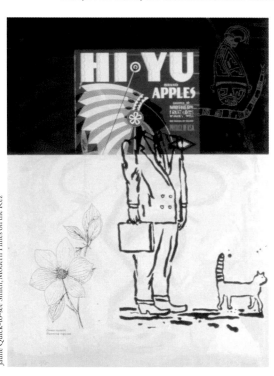

declared that they were not representing nationality. They were not denying their nationality – evident in the texture and meaning of their work – but not promoting a political-national agenda. A work by Israeli artist Zvi Goldstein (b. 1947), *Sirocco-day 4*, was shown at the 1998 São Paul Bienal, a black painted and anodized aluminium construction as if vernacular 'minimal', but including a framed statement, the brittle counterpart to a globalizing view of art: 'Postmodern plurality remains an opulent theory, protected by the economical security of late capitalism and the status quo of Western Democracy. At the same time, the Third World is figured as a Postmodern society without modernism.'[17] The Canadian artist Greg Curnoe (1936–92) – a staunch regionalist – lettered on to to one of his text works of the late 1960s 'THIS IS TRULY GREAT ART BECAUSE IT WAS NOT MADE BY AN AMERICAN'. The Haitian-born artist Roland Jean (b. 1955), wrote on a 1993 photographic self portrait work, 'I am not proud of my roots and I'm not proud of anybody's roots'.

Radical Forms and Culture

Do radical forms come from the dispossessed or disenfranchised? Jazz is a way of looking at this perplexing question. Music, like Steichen's assertion for photography, is near to a universal language. The relationship of jazz to modern art has been written about since jazz first appeared. It was important to avant-garde white artists in America and can be rightfully claimed as a major cultural contribution to world culture. Jazz entered into the stream rapidly – a fuel for the modern age, the speed that the Futurists spoke of – but the question of a 'pure' and 'true' form is impossible to determine. There are innovators, as in any art form, but the followers are not necessarily minor derivations. There is no pure jazz; it emerged 'adulterated' – the spirituals of black slaves in America, being Christianized (i.e. 'civilized'). The South African-born pianist-composer Abdullah Ibrahim (b. 1936) recalled his formative years in Cape Town: 'We played a lot of boogie-woogie back then. It had a structure very similar to our native songs. We never regarded this music as foreign; it was just the music of our brothers and sisters in another part of the world. And in our corner there were great piano players; they didn't play jazz however; they played tradition ... pure African tradition.'[18] Does it matter that the piano is not a native African instrument? It is a tool, like canvas and paint, given meaning by the artist.

In 1969, Charlie Haden, a White American bass player, formed the Liberation Music Orchestra, conceived by synchronicity, upon hearing the songs of the Spanish Civil War of 1936–37 and then witnessing the struggle at the 1968 Democratic Party Convention over the issue of Vietnam. In his liner notes – a form of manifesto – he wrote, 'this music ... is dedicated to creating a better world; a world without war and killing, without poverty and exploitation; a world where men of all governments realize the vital importance of life and strive to protect rather than destroy it. We hope to see a new society of enlightenment and wisdom where creative thought becomes the most dominant force in all people's lives.'[19]

These might be noble words, but they can be lost in the hubris of commerce and continuing tribal conflict. In that sense, Marshall McLuhan's 'global village' has its dark and tragic side. The world of art is contested, in some places more vigorously than others. There is the battle for national symbols, and the reconciliation with indigenous cultures, which can be turned into symbols of the nation for export. Even the rehabilitation of Australian Aboriginal art is contested – is it art or ethnography? Artist Gordon Bennett (b. 1955) operates between worlds – his Australian suburban upbringing and his Aboriginal

Jaune Quick-to-see Smith, Modern Times on the Rez

genealogy. The works have visual references to artists of the West – Jackson Pollock and Kasimir Malevich (the East-West) – but also to the outsider on the inside, the black American artist Jean-Michel Basqiat (1960–88). Raiding the icebox, as Bennett does, has been an axiom throughout time. The world changed at first contact: people from one village visiting another, learning something, adapting an idea or thing, and finding a way to communicate. Orientalism may have taken foothold in Europe in the late nineteenth century, the age of Euro-exploitations, but it began on Marco Polo's return from the East in 1295, another example of raiding the icebox. The personification of art and culture will continue because it is much easier to identify with a person than a national sensibility, hence the lionization of Picasso. Griel Marcus wrote that Elvis Presley was the first singer to change the world, not just the face of music. Elvis spawned imitators, and rabid devotees, but the claim can also be made for tenor Enrico Caruso at the beginning of the twentieth century. It was his voice that gave credibility to the nascent recording industry (a minor invention, even its inventor Thomas Edison barely understood its value and future use), to a dominant thing in our lives. Whether the millions of records that sold during Caruso's lifetime (and the phonographs) ever made it to the mountains and deserts is not the point. Eventually, recording technology did appear, and was used to record the cultures of place.

One of the many stumbling blocks in coming to a deeper understanding and appreciation of art in the world, or even the world of art, is that we have been conditioned to receiving our views and constructing perspectives in large digestible chunks. Often the flavour of the particular is masked. What does it mean to stare into the face of a Bronzino portrait, and then into the 'face' of a Kasimir Malevich Suprematist abstraction? Then stare into an Andrew Wyeth face, a Frida Kahlo self-portrait and the face made by an anonymous carver/craftsman of Egypt, Asia or Oceania. What do we think when we stare into the face of an artist's vision unknown to us? Can we instantly know the world, or do we have to take the history of the world one artist, one object at a time? In trying to unravel the mystery of the museum and audience, British curator Bryan Robertson wrote that 'it is not easy for museums, eager to please a large public, to avoid betrayal of the works of art and the values entrusted to them', but he also cited the impossibility of a contemplative communication in a society that promotes the voracious appetite: 'A great painting or sculpture denotes forces in our imagination which transform life.'[20] It cannot happen in an instant, and the promotion of the few is done at the expense of the many.

In the Cartographies glossary Paulo Herkenhoff devotes 42 entries in exploring the 'theme' of time, with respect to Latin American art. Reading them takes time and, to state the obvious, understanding them, appreciating them can take a lifetime. Can we separate the experience of time from the experience of the world? Like rivers, they flow into greater bodies, and return as rain, again and again.

Footnotes

1. Linda Nochlin, 'Museums and radicals: A history of emergencies' in Brian O'Doherty (ed.) *Museums in Crisis* (New York: George Braziller, 1972), 8.
2. Peter Murray et. al., Phaidon Press (Oxford, 1979), 7. There is, in addition, a puzzling disclaimer in the preface: 'works of art appear under the region where they were executed, rather than according to the nationality of the artist. Works executed outside the geographical areas are not included (Gaughin's Tahiti paintings, for instance).'
3. Bernard Smith, *European Vision and the South Pacific* (Melbourne: Oxford University Press, 1989), vii.
4. Ian Dunlop, *The Shock of the New* (London: American Heritage Press, 1972).
5. All quotes from Robert L. Herbert (ed.), *Modern Artists On Art* (New Jersey: Prentice-Hall, Inc., 1964). Marinetti quote from Robert Hughes, *The Shock of the New* (London: British Broadcasting Corporation, 1980, 1981 reprint), 43.
6. See XXIV Bienal de São Paulo, 1998, Núcleo Historico volume.
7. François-Marc Gagnon, Paul-Emile Borduas, *Writings, 1942-1958* (Halifax: the Press of the Nova Scotia College of Art and Design, 1978), 45–54.
8. Robert Hughes, *The Art of Australia* (Australia, Penguin Books, 1966, reprinted 1981), 246–247.
9. Frances Lindsay, 'Antipodean Antecedent: An Accent of the Present' in *1988 Australian Biennale*, 14.
10. Bernard Rudofsky, *Architecture Without Architects* (New York: Doubleday & Company Inc., 1964), 2.
11. Rene Block opened a gallery in Berlin in 1964, and then in New York in the 1970s. He directed the Berlin Artists Residence Program of the DAAD. from 1982–92, and since has been the director of biennials in Istanbul, Sydney and Gwangju, Korea. Quote from www.gwangju-biennale.org/last-biennale/2000/english/mainex-concept-eu.html.
12. Robert Houle, 'The Spiritual Legacy of the Ancient Ones' in *Land, Spirit Power, First Nations at the National Gallery of Canada* (Ottawa: National Gallery of Canada, 1992), 44–45.
13. *Routes of Wandering, Nomadism, Journeys and Transitions in Contemporary Israeli Art* (Jerusalem: The Israel Museum, 1991), 258.
14. Ibid., 252.
15. Ivo Mesquita, *Cartographies*, op. cit., 17.
16. *Japanese Ways, Western Means* (Brisbane: Queensland Art Gallery, 1989), 11.
17. XXIV Bienal de São Paulo, 1998, Representações Nacionais volume, 282.
18. See *Circling the Mountain 1*, www.junior.apk.net/~hoon/6dAl_Bio.html.
19. Impulse! records AS-9183. Re-released on CD as IMPD-188, 1996.
20. Bryan Robertson, 'The museum and the democratic fallacy' in *Museums in Crisis* (op. cit.), 85–86.

Timelines

Artists lives rarely exist in a vacuum. They are often a reflection or a product of their time, sometimes caught up in the events of history in the making, like William Blake and his responses to the French and American Revolutions at the turn of the 18th Century. Western art in the 1200s was almost exclusively defined by its association with the Christian church, depicting events from the bible and other acts of worship. As the world changed through wars, empires and the diversification of civilisations, by the 19th Century artists were expressing themselves through an astonishing range of subjects, forms and media, affected by historical events of their time and influencing each other. This series of timelines sketches some of the political, scientific and cultural events which occurred during the lives of many of the artists in the main A–Z of this book, providing a useful background to the overall development of art.

Cimabue *b* 1240

Giotto di Bondone *b* 1267

Duccio di Buoninsegna *b* 1278

c.1200– Islamic architecture spreads to India
- Incas develop sophisticated weaving and dying techniques
- Ife, in Nigeria, produces its famous terracotta heads, and bronze and brass castings
- The Japanese sculptor, Unkei, flourishes
1203– The building of *Mont-Saint-Michel* begins
1205– Layamon, an English priest the Norman French *Roman de Brut* into English
1208– The *Gesta Danorum* was completed by Saxo Grammaticus

1211– The construction of the cathedral at Reims begins

1220– *Aucassin et Nicolette*, a romance, written by an anonymous French poet
- work begins on Salisbury cathedral
- work begins on the Gothic cathedral at Burgos in Spain
1225– The *Out Minar* tower constructed near present day Delhi
- *Sumer is icumen* is the earliest known English round song

1235– The first part of the *Roman de la Rose* is written by Guillaume de Lorris

1248– Construction of the *Alhambra Palace* near Granada, Spain begins

1252– The Buddhist bronze image of *Amida*, nearly 50 feet high is erected at Kamakura
1257– The Persian poet Sa'adi publishes his classic *Bustan*

1260– Emir Khusro introduces Persian and Arabic elements into Indian music

1270– The Naumburg Master completes the ten figures representing the founders of the Naumburg Cathedral

1283– James of St George begins work on Caernarvon and Harlech castles
1285– French composer Adam de la Halle writes comic opera *Le Jeu de Robin et de Marion*

1200– Emergence of Hausa city states
- Aztecs occupy the valley of Mexico
1204– Fourth Crusade
1206– Genghis Khan and the mongols begin conquest of Asia

1212– Battle of Las Navas de Tolosa
1215– Magna Carta signed
1216– Foundation of Dominican order

1220– Emergence of first Thai kingdom
1225– The Inquisition in Europe
1226– Death of St Francis of Assisi
1228– Hafsid dynasty established at Tunis

1234– Mongols destroy Chin empire
1237– Mongols invade and conquer Russia

1241– Mongols invade Poland, Hungary and Bohemia
1242– Alexander Nevsky defeats Teutonic Order

1250– Collapse of imperial power in Germany and Italy
- Mayapan becomes dominant Maya city of Yucatán
1258– Mongols sack Baghdad; end of Abbasid caliphate

1260– Expulsion of Jews from England
- Kublai Khan makes Peking his capital
1261– Greek empire restored in Constantinople
1264– Kublai Khan founds Yüan
1265– Japanese swordmakers create Tachi (slashing swords) that can behead with one stroke.

1272– Death of St Thomas Aquinas
1274– Mongol attack on Japan defeated
1275– Marco Polo arrives in China
1276– Papermaking begins in Italy
1279– Mongols conquer southern China

1288– Guns invented in China
1289– Mongol attacks on Pagan defeated

1291 Glassmakers learn to produce clear glass
1299– Ottoman Turks expansion in Anatolia

d 1302

d 1318

d 1337

Andrei Rublev *b* 1360

Fra Angelico *b* 1395
Paolo Uccello *b* 1397

c.1300– Miracle and Mystery plays begin to come under control of local trade guilds
1306– Giotto completes series of Frescoes in Padua
1307– Work begins on the Forbidden City in Peking
1309– Work begins on the Doges' Palace in Venice

1314– The golden age of *Ge'ez literature* begins in Ethiopia
1320– Walter of Evesham describes the medieval knowledge of music in *De Speculatione Musices*

1321– Dante finishes *The Divine Comedy*
– The first French guild of minstrels is formed
1325– Aztecs of Mexico build their capital city, Tenochtitlan

1339– Building of the Kremlin

1341– Italian poet Petrarch is crowned as poet laureate in Rome
1348– Italian poet Giovanni Boccaccio begins writing the *Decameron*

1350– The Leaning Tower of Pisa is finished
– Japanese cultural revival
– Lo Kuan-Chung completes *The Story of the Three Kingdoms*, the first major Chinese historical novel
1353– Peter Parler appointed architect of Prague Cathedral

1368– Work begins on a porcelain factory at Ching-t'ou-chiang in China

1370– William Langland writes *Piers the Plowman*
1374– Francesco Petrach, Italian poet and author of *Rime* dies
1375– First appearance of Robin Hood in English legends
1375-9– Jehan of Bruges designs the *Tapestry of the Apocalypse*
1377– Guillaume de Machaut, French poet, musician and composer dies

1384– Motokiyo Se'ami turns the *No* drama of Japan into standard entertainment of the samurai.
1387– Chaucer starts *The Canterbury Tales*

1390– The first *emaki*, or narrative scrolls are produced in Japan
1392– Death of Hafiz, Persian lyric poet
1397– Francesco Landino, composer of *ars nova* dies

1300– Mechanical clocks invented in Europe
– The Italian renaissance begins
1305– Papacy moves from Rome to Avignon

1314– Battle of Bannockburn: Scotland defeats England
1315-17– Great famine in northern Europe

1325– Ivan I begins recovery of Moscow

1333– End of Minamoto shogunate: civil war in Japan
1335– Sultan Muhammad ibn Tughluq rules most of India
1337– Start of Hundred Years' War between England and France

1342– 'Black Death' starts in Asia
1346-49– The Black Death sweeps through Europe
1349– First Chinese settlement at Singapore; beginning of Chinese expansion in southeast Asia

1350– Golden age of Majapahit empire in Java
1354– Ottomans Turks capture Gallipoli
1358– Peasant rising in France known as *Jacquerie*

1360– Stringed keyboard instruments developed– the Clavichord and Harpsichord
1368– Ming dynasty founded in China

1370– Hindu state of Vijayanagar dominant in south India
1375– Chimú conquest of central Andes begins
1378-1417– Great Schism in West

1380– Tamerlane begins conquests
1386– Union of Poland and Lithuania
1389– Battle of Kosovo: Ottomans gain control of Balkans

1392– Korea reduced to vassal status
1394– Thais invade Cambodia
– Expulsion of Jews from France
1397– Union of Kalmar (Scandinavia)

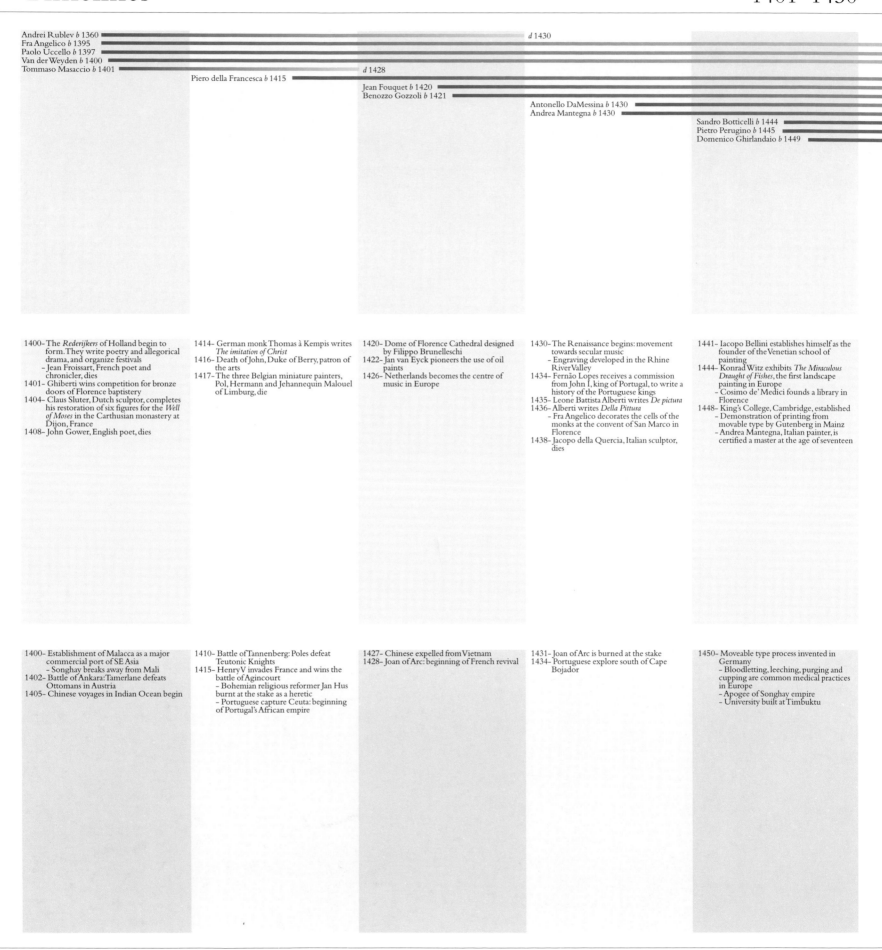

Andrei Rublev *b* 1360   *d* 1430
Fra Angelico *b* 1395
Paolo Uccello *b* 1397
Van der Weyden *b* 1400
Tommaso Masaccio *b* 1401   *d* 1428

Piero della Francesca *b* 1415

Jean Fouquet *b* 1420
Benozzo Gozzoli *b* 1421

Antonello DaMessina *b* 1430
Andrea Mantegna *b* 1430

Sandro Botticelli *b* 1444
Pietro Perugino *b* 1445
Domenico Ghirlandaio *b* 1449

1400– The *Rederijkers* of Holland begin to form. They write poetry and allegorical drama, and organize festivals
   – Jean Froissart, French poet and chronicler, dies
1401– Ghiberti wins competition for bronze doors of Florence baptistery
1404– Claus Sluter, Dutch sculptor, completes his restoration of six figures for the *Well of Moses* in the Carthusian monastery at Dijon, France
1408– John Gower, English poet, dies

1414– German monk Thomas à Kempis writes *The imitation of Christ*
1416– Death of John, Duke of Berry, patron of the arts
1417– The three Belgian miniature painters, Pol, Hermann and Jehannequin Malouel of Limburg, die

1420– Dome of Florence Cathedral designed by Filippo Brunelleschi
1422– Jan van Eyck pioneers the use of oil paints
1426– Netherlands becomes the centre of music in Europe

1430– The Renaissance begins: movement towards secular music
   – Engraving developed in the Rhine River Valley
1434– Fernão Lopes receives a commission from John I, king of Portugal, to write a history of the Portuguese kings
1435– Leone Battista Alberti writes *De pictura*
1436– Alberti writes *Della Pittura*
   – Fra Angelico decorates the cells of the monks at the convent of San Marco in Florence
1438– Jacopo della Quercia, Italian sculptor, dies

1441– Iacopo Bellini establishes himself as the founder of the Venetian school of painting
1444– Konrad Witz exhibits *The Miraculous Draught of Fishes*, the first landscape painting in Europe
   – Cosimo de' Medici founds a library in Florence
1448– King's College, Cambridge, established
   – Demonstration of printing from movable type by Gutenberg in Mainz
   – Andrea Mantegna, Italian painter, is certified a master at the age of seventeen

1400– Establishment of Malacca as a major commercial port of SE Asia
   – Songhay breaks away from Mali
1402– Battle of Ankara: Tamerlane defeats Ottomans in Austria
1405– Chinese voyages in Indian Ocean begin

1410– Battle of Tannenberg: Poles defeat Teutonic Knights
1415– Henry V invades France and wins the battle of Agincourt
   – Bohemian religious reformer Jan Hus burnt at the stake as a heretic
   – Portuguese capture Ceuta: beginning of Portugal's African empire

1427– Chinese expelled from Vietnam
1428– Joan of Arc: beginning of French revival

1431– Joan of Arc is burned at the stake
1434– Portuguese explore south of Cape Bojador

1450– Moveable type process invented in Germany
   – Bloodletting, leeching, purging and cupping are common medical practices in Europe
   – Apogee of Songhay empire
   – University built at Timbuktu

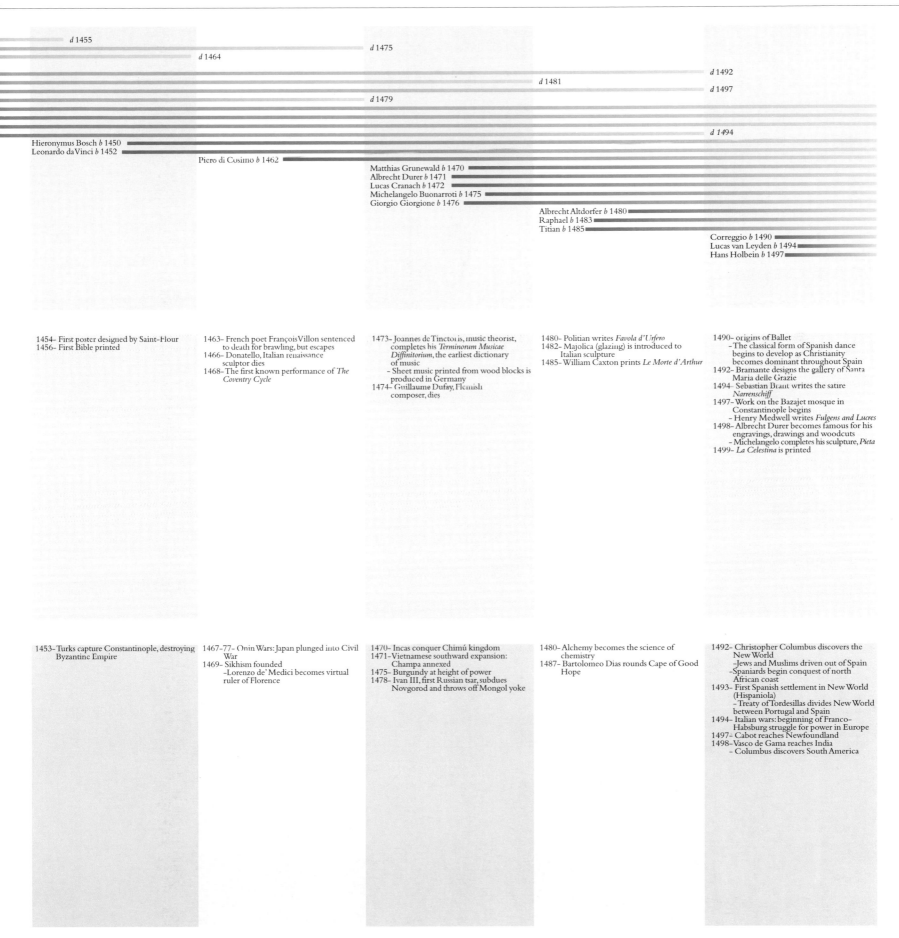

d 1455

d 1464

d 1475

d 1492

d 1481

d 1497

d 1479

d 1494

Hieronymus Bosch *b* 1450
Leonardo da Vinci *b* 1452

Piero di Cosimo *b* 1462

Matthias Grunewald *b* 1470
Albrecht Durer *b* 1471
Lucas Cranach *b* 1472
Michelangelo Buonarroti *b* 1475
Giorgio Giorgione *b* 1476

Albrecht Altdorfer *b* 1480
Raphael *b* 1483
Titian *b* 1485

Correggio *b* 1490
Lucas van Leyden *b* 1494
Hans Holbein *b* 1497

1454- First poster designed by Saint-Flour
1456- First Bible printed

1463- French poet François Villon sentenced
    to death for brawling, but escapes
1466- Donatello, Italian renaissance
    sculptor dies
1468- The first known performance of *The
    Coventry Cycle*

1473- Joannes de Tinctoris, music theorist,
    completes his *Terminorum Musicae
    Diffinitorium*, the earliest dictionary
    of music
    - Sheet music printed from wood blocks is
    produced in Germany
1474- Guillaume Dufay, Flemish
    composer, dies

1480- Politian writes *Favola d'Urfeo*
1482- Majolica (glazing) is introduced to
    Italian sculpture
1485- William Caxton prints *Le Morte d'Arthur*

1490- origins of Ballet
    - The classical form of Spanish dance
    begins to develop as Christianity
    becomes dominant throughout Spain
1492- Bramante designs the gallery of Santa
    Maria delle Grazie
1494- Sebastian Brant writes the satire
    Narrenschiff
1497- Work on the Bazajet mosque in
    Constantinople begins
    - Henry Medwell writes *Fulgens and Lucres*
1498- Albrecht Durer becomes famous for his
    engravings, drawings and woodcuts
    - Michelangelo completes his sculpture, *Pieta*
1499- *La Celestina* is printed

1453- Turks capture Constantinople, destroying
    Byzantine Empire

1467-77- Onin Wars: Japan plunged into Civil
    War
1469- Sikhism founded
    -Lorenzo de' Medici becomes virtual
    ruler of Florence

1470- Incas conquer Chimú kingdom
1471- Vietnamese southward expansion:
    Champa annexed
1475- Burgundy at height of power
1478- Ivan III, first Russian tsar, subdues
    Novgorod and throws off Mongol yoke

1480- Alchemy becomes the science of
    chemistry
1487- Bartolomeo Dias rounds Cape of Good
    Hope

1492- Christopher Columbus discovers the
    New World
    -Jews and Muslims driven out of Spain
    -Spaniards begin conquest of north
    African coast
1493- First Spanish settlement in New World
    (Hispaniola)
    - Treaty of Tordesillas divides New World
    between Portugal and Spain
1494- Italian wars: beginning of Franco-
    Habsburg struggle for power in Europe
1497- Cabot reaches Newfoundland
1498- Vasco de Gama reaches India
    - Columbus discovers South America

Andrea Mantegna *d* 1506

Sandro Botticelli *d* 1510

Pietro Perugino *d* 1523

Hieronymus Bosch *d* 1516
Leonardo da Vinci *d* 1519

Piero di Cosimo *d* 1521
Matthias Grunewald *d* 1528
Albrecht Durer *d* 1528

Lucas Cranach *d* 1553

Giorgio Giorgione *d* 1510

Albrecht Altdorfer *d* 1538

Raphael *d* 1520

Correggio *d* 1534
Lucas van Leyden *d* 1533

Hans Holbein *d* 1543
d 1540

Francesco Parmigianino *b* 1503
Agnolo Bronzino *b* 1503

Jacopo Tintoretto *b* 1518

Peter Bruegel *b* 1525
Paolo Veronese *b* 1528
Giusseppe Arcimboldi *b* 1528

Sofonisba Anguissola *b* 1532

El Greco *b* 1541

---

c.1500– Tudor style of architecture emerges
– White glass, instead of oiled paper, is first used by the French in their windows
1503– Leonardo da Vinci paints the *Mona Lisa*
1504– *L'Arcadia* composed by Jacopa Sannazzaro
1506– Bramante begins rebuilding of St Peters's, Rome
1508–12– Michelangelo paints the ceiling of the Sistine Chapel

1515– Giovanni Giorgio Trissino publishes *Sophonisba*
1517– Heinrich Isaak, Flemish composer, dies

1521– Josquin Deprès, Flemish composer, dies
1526– The *Kogan Pyo* by Shin Rat-hta-tha-ra, a Burmese poet, appears
1528– Castiglione: *The Book of the Courtier*

1532– *Pantagruel* is published by François Rabelais
1533– The *First Book of Madrigals* is printed in Rome

1543– Benvenuto Cellini makes golden salt cellars for the King of France
1545– Mikolaj Rej publishes *Zywot Józefa*
– First book fair held in Liepzig, Germany
1546– Francis I begins rebuilding Louvre, Paris
1548– Building of the Pitti Palace, Florence
1549– Joachim du Bellay publishes *Défense et Illustration de la Langue Française*

1500– Ambroise Paré devises artificial limbs for injured soldiers
– The Reformation
– Shah Ismail founds Safavid dynasty in Persia
1503– Julius II becomes Pope
1505– Portuguese establish trading posts in east Africa
1507– America appears on a map for the first time
1509– Watch invented by Peter Henle

1510– First African slaves arrive in America
1511– Portuguese take Malacca
1516– Ottomans overrun Syria, Egypt and Arabia
1519– Charles V becomes Holy Roman Empire
– Cortés begins conquest of Aztec empire

1520– Martin Luther excommunicated
– Magellan crosses Pacific
1522– The Spanish discover the Inca Empire
– First circumnavigation of the globe completed by Sebastian de Cano
1523– Collapse of Union of Kalmar; Sweden independent
1526– Mughal Empire founded in India
– Turks defeat Lajos II at the Battle of Mohács and take control of Hungary for the next 150 years
1527– Sack of Rome
1529– First Ottoman siege of Vienna

1531 Pizarro begins conquest of Inca empire for Spain
1533– Ivan the Terrible becomes Grand Duke of Moscow
1534– Henry VIII breaks with Rome

1541– John Calvin founds reformed church at Geneva
1543– Copernicus lays the foundations of modern astronomy
– Portuguese traders arrive in Japan
1545– Council of Trent begins
– Discovery of silver mines at Potosí (Peru) and Zacatecas (Mexico)
1546– Mali empire destroyed by Songhay

Annibale Carracci *b* 1560
Artemisia Gentileschi *b* 1563

Michelangelo Caravaggio *b* 1571
Guido Reni *b* 1575
Peter Rubens *b* 1577

Frans Hals *b* 1582
Hendrick Terbrugghen *b* 1588

Jose Ribera *b* 1591
Il Guercino *b* 1591
Gerrit Honthorst *b* 1592
Jacob Jordaens *b* 1593
Nicolas Poussin *b* 1594
Jan van Goyen *b* 1596
Pieter Claesz *b* 1597
Francisco Zurbaran *b* 1598
Sir Anthony van Dyck *b* 1599
Diego Velaxquez *b* 1599

Michelangelo Buonarroti *d* 1564

Titian *d* 1576

Agnolo Bronzino *d* 1572

Jacopo Tintoretto *d* 1594

Peter Bruegel *d* 1569

Paolo Veronese *d* 1588

Giusseppe Arcimboldi *d* 1593

1550- Vasari's *Lives of the Artists* published
 - The K'un-ch'ü school is founded in Kiangsu
1557- *Songs and Sonnets* printed by Richard Tottel

1561- Louis Bourgeois, French musician, dies
1562- Pope Pius IV restores church music to its pure vocal form by eliminating all instruments except the organ
 - Giovanni Da Palestrina writes *Pope Marcellus Mass*
1563- Accademia del Disegno founded in Florence
1564-1616- Shakespeare writes 37 plays, including *Hamlet, Romeo and Juliet* and *The Merchant of Venice*
1565- Castration emerges as a way of preserving choir-boy's voices
 - Lope de Rueda, Spanish dramatist, dies
1567- Palladio's Villa Rotunda begun

1571- Benvenuto Cellini, Italian sculptor, dies
1572- Luis de Camöens of Portugal writes his epic poem *Os Lusíado*
1577- The Gelosi Troupe arrive at Blois to perform for Henry III, king of France

1580- Andrea Palladio, Italian architect, dies
1587- Christopher Marlowe writes *Tamburlaine the Great*
1588- The English Madrigal School is established producing some of the most delightful secular music ever heard

1590- Robert Greene becomes well known
1591- Vincenzo Galilei, Italian composer, dies
1596- Ju Tzayyuh publishes the *Book of Songs*
1598- Jacopo Peri writes *Dafne*, the first Italian Opera
1599- The Globe theatre opens in London

1550- Mongol, Altan-Khan, invades northern China; Japanese 'pirate' raids in China
1555- Charles V abdicates and divides inheritance
1556- Earthquake kills hundreds of thousands in China
 - Ivan IV of Russia conquers Volga basin
1557- Portuguese enclave established at Macao (China)
1559- Tobacco first introduced into Europe

1560- Portuguese begin sugar cultivation in Brazil
1561- Philip II makes Madrid the capital of Spain
1562-1598- Wars of religion in France
1563- Nordic Seven Year's War
1565- Pencil invented
 - Akbar extends Mughal power to Deccan
 - Introduction of potato from south America to Europe
1568- Mercator produces his projection for the drawing of maps
1569- Union of Lublin unites Poland and Lithuania

1570- Potatoes introduced to Europe
1571- Battle of Lepanto: end of Turkish sea power in central Mediterranean
 - Portuguese colony established in Angola
 - Spanish conquer Philippines
1572- Dutch revolt against Spain
1578- Battle of Al-Kasr al-Kebir: Moroccans destroy Portuguese power in northwest Africa

1580- Sir Francis Drake completes circumnavigation of the world
1581- Yermak begins Russian conquest of Siberia
1584- William the Silent, Chief architect of Dutch independence, assassinated in Delft
1588- Spanish Armada defeated by Francis Drake

1590- Microscope invented
 - Galileo publishes his treatise on motion
1591- Battle of Tondibi: Moroccans destroy Songhay kingdom
1596- Invention of the water closet
1598- Edict of Nantes defines rights of Protestants at end of Wars of Religion in France

Annibale Carracci *d* 1609

Artemisia Gentileschi *d* 1639

Michelangelo Caravaggio *d* 1610

Guido Reni *d* 1642
Peter Rubens *d* 1640

Hendrick Terbrugghen *d* 1629

Sir Anthony van Dyck *d* 1641

Salomon Ruysdael *b* 1600
Rembrandt *b* 1606
Judith Leyster *b* 1609
Samuel Cooper *b* 1609

Ferdinand Bol *b* 1616
Bartolome Murillo *b* 1617
Peter Lely *b* 1618
Gong Xian *b* 1619
Willem Kalf *b* 1619

Albert Cuyp *b* 1620
Fabritius Carel *b* 1622
Jan Vermeer *b* 1628
Pieter DeHooch *b* 1629

Yun Shouping *b* 1633
Meindert Hobbema *b* 1638

Andrea Pozzo *b* 1642

Sofonisba Anguissola *d* 1625

El Greco *d* 1614

1600– Mahmud Baki, Turkish poet, dies
c.1600– Kabuki theatre becomes popular in Japan
– The Baroque period in music: strict forms and highly ornamental works
1605– *Don Quixote* published
1606– John Lyly, English writer, dies
1607– Monteverdi's *La Favola d'Orfeo* establishes opera as an art form

1611– Authorized version of the Bible
– Royal mosque at Isfahan, Persia is built
1616– Cervantes, Spanish novelist, dies
– William Shakespeare dies
1619-22– Inigo Jones builds Whitehall Banqueting House

1623– Death of William Byrd, English composer
1625– Francesca Caccini finishes the opera-ballet *La Liberazione di Ruggiero*
– Orlando Gibbons, English composer, dies
1629– Kabuki theatre banned because female performers were considered immoral

1630– Apogee of Netherlands art
1631– John Donne, English poet, dies
1633– John Milton writes *L'Allegro* and *Il Penserosa*
1637– Ben Jonson dies
– Corneille writes *Le Cid*
1639–The first comic opera, *Chi Soffre Speri* by Virgilio Mazzocchi and Marco Marazzoli, premieres in Rome

1640– Francesca Caccini, Italian composer, dies
1645– Gianlorenzo Bernini starts *Ecstasy of St Teresa*
1648– Académie Royale de Peinture et de Sculpture founded in Paris
– Alexis I Mikhailovich, czar of Russia, decreed a ban on all amusements

1603– Beginning of Tokugawa shogunate in Japan
– Union of Crowns between England and Scotland
1605– The Gunpowder Plot
1607– First permanent English settlement in America
1608– French colonists found Quebec
1609– Dutch Republic effectively wins freedom from Spain
– Telescope invented

1610– Galileo studies the stars and planets with his telescope
– Scientific revolution begins in Europe
1618-48– Thirty Years War
1619– Foundation of Batavia (Jakarta) by Dutch: start of Dutch colonial empire in East Indies

1620– The *Mayflower* sails to America
– First weekly newspapers in Europe
1625– Dutch settle in New Amsterdam

1630– Gustavus Adolphus of Sweden intervenes in Thirty Years' War
1636–Foundation of Harvard College in North America
1638– Russians reach Pacific

1641– Dutch capture Malacca from Portuguese
1642– English Civil War begins
1645– Tasman circumnavigates Australia and discovers New Zealand
1648– Peace of Westphalia ends Thirty Years' War
1649– First Anglo-Dutch War: beginning of Dutch decline
– Charles I executed. England becomes a republic under Cromwell

Frans Hals *d* 1666

Jose Ribera *d* 1652

Il Guercino *d* 1666

Gerrit Honthorst *d* 1656

Jacob Jordaens *d* 1678

Nicolas Poussin *d* 1665

Jan van Goyen *d* 1656

Pieter Claesz *d* 1660
Francisco Zurbaran *d* 1664

Diego Velaxquez *d* 1660

Salomon Ruysdael *d* 1670

Rembrandt *d* 1669
Judith Leyster *d* 1660

Samuel Cooper *d* 1672

Ferdinand Bol *d* 1680
Bartolome Murillo *d* 1682
Peter Lely *d* 1680
Gong Xian *d* 1689

Willem Kalf *d* 1693
Albert Cuyp *d* 1691

Fabritius Carel *d* 1654

Jan Vermeer *d* 1691

Pieter DeHooch *d* 1684

Yun Shouping *d* 1690

Ogata Korin *b* 1658

Rachel Ruysch *b* 1664

Rosalba Carriera *b* 1675

Hua Yan *b* 1682
Antoine Watteau *b* 1684

Giovanni Tieopolo *b* 1696
William Hogarth *b* 1697
Giovanni Canaletto *b* 1697
Jean-Baptise-Siméon Chardin *b* 1699

1652- Inigo Jones, English architect, dies
   - Gregorio Allegri, Italian musician, dies
   - Vienna opens its first opera house
1653- Taj Mahal completed

1660- Samuel Pepys begins his diaries
1661- Louis XIV begins enlarging chateau of Versailles
   - The Drury Lane Company uses women to play female roles for the first time
1662- Royal Society founded in London
1666- Académie Française founded in Paris
   - The first Stradivarius violins emerge from Antonio Stradivari's workshop in Cremona, Italy
1667 Johann Froberger, Viennese composer, dies
   - The colonnaded square of St Peter's, Rome is completed

1672- Bellori, *Lives of the Modern Painters*
   - John Bannister holds the first public concert for which admission was charged, at his home in London
1673- Molière, French playwright, dies
1674- John Milton, English writer, dies
1675- Wren rebuilds St Paul's Cathedral, London
   - Mathew Locke composes *Psyche*
1677- John Dryden is England's leading poet

1680- La Rochefoucault, French author, dies
1685- Bach and Handel are born
   - Pieter de Hooch, Dutch painter, dies
1689- Purcell's *Dido and Aeneas* opens in London

1690- Charles le Brun, French painter and architect, dies
1695- Henry Purcell, English composer, dies

1652- Foundation of Cape Colony by Dutch
1654- Ukraine passes from Polish to Russian rule
1657- Dutch astronomer Huygens designs the first accurate clock regulated by a pendulum

1660- Restoration of the English monarchy
1662- Royal Society founded in London
1664- New Amsterdam taken by English from Dutch (later renamed New York)
1666- Fire of London
   - Academy of Sciences founded in Paris
1667- Beginning of French expansion under Louis XIV

1674- Sivaji creates Hindu Maratha kingdom

1683- Turkish siege of Vienna
1684- La Salle explores Mississippi and claims Louisiana for France
1687- Isaac Newton's *Principia*
1688- 'The Glorious Revolution'; constitutional monarchy in England
1689- Treaty of Nerchinsk between Russia and China
   - 'Grand Alliance' against Louis XIV

1690- Foundation of Calcutta by English
1693- Gold discovered in Brazil
1697- Chinese occupy Outer Mongolia
1699- Treaty of Carlowitz: Habsburgs recover Hungary from Turks

François Boucher *b* 1703

Allan Ramsay *b* 1713

Joshua Reynolds *b* 1723
Jean-Baptiste Greuze *b* 1725
Thomas Gainsborough *b* 1727

Jean-Honoré Fragonard *b* 1732
Hubert Robert *b* 1733
Joseph Wright *b* 1734
George Romney *b* 1734
John Copley *b* 1738
Benjamin West *b* 1738

Angelica Kauffman *b* 1741
Henry Fuseli *b* 1741
Francisco Goya *b* 1746
Jacques-Louis David *b* 1748

Meindert Hobbema *d* 1709
Andrea Pozzo *d* 1709

Ogata Korin *d* 1716

Antoine Watteau *d* 1721

1703- Vivaldi becomes violin master at Venice's La Pietà orphanage
 – Charles Perrault, French writer, dies
 – Samuel Pepys, English writer, dies
1705- Reinhard Keiser uses French horns for the first time in opera in his production of *Octavia*

1710- Meissen porcelain factory founded
 – Building of St Paul's Cathedral, London
1712- Yusuf Nabi, Turkish poet, dies
1716- First theatre in colonial America constructed in Williamsburg, Virginia
1719- Daniel Defoe writes the first part of *Robinson Crusoe*

1720- Rococo style of decoration begins
1721- J.S. Bach composes the *Brandenburg Concertos*
1723- Christopher Wren, English architect, dies
1725- Vivaldi writes *The Four Seasons*
 – Chikamatsu Monzaemon, Japanese playright, dies
1726- Jonathan Swift publishes *Gulliver's Travels*
1729- William Congreve, English dramatist, dies
 – Bach composes his *St Matthew Passion*

1731- Daniel Defoe, English writer, dies
1732- Theatre Royal opens in London
1735- Imperial ballet school in St Petersburg opens
1737- England begins censorship of plays

1741- Antonio Vivaldi, Italian musician, dies
1742- Handel's *Messiah* premieres in Dublin
1747- Samuel Johnson begins work on his dictionary
1748- Royal Danish Ballet formed in Copenhagen
1749- Henry Fielding publishes *Tom Jones*

1700- Rise of Ashanti power
1700-21- Great Northern War
1702-13- War of Spanish succession
1703- Peter the Great founds St Petersburg
1707- Act of Union unites England and Scotland
 – Death of Aurangzeb: decline of Mughal power in India
1709- Battle of Poltova: Peter the Great of Russia defeats Swedes
 – Abraham Darby discovers coke-smelting technique for producing pig iron

1713- Treaty of Utrecht ends War of Spanish Succession
 – Fahrenheit begins the use of mercury in thermometers
1718- New Orleans founded by France

1722- Last Safavid Shah overthrown by Afghan rebels
1728- Bering begins Russian reconaissance of Alaska

1730- Revival of the ancient empire of Bornu (central Sudan)
1735- Wahabite movement to purify Islam begins in Arabia
 – Linnaeus, *System of Nature*
1739- Nadir Shah invades India and sacks Delhi

1740- Frederick II becomes ruler of Prussia
1740-48- War of the Austrian Succession
1747- Ahmad Khan Abdali founds kingdom of Afghanistan

François Boucher *d* 1770

Allan Ramsay *d* 1784

Joshua Reynolds *d* 1792

Thomas Gainsborough *d* 1788

Joseph Wright *d* 1797

Torii Kiyonaga *b* 1752
Kitagawa Utamaro *b* 1753
Vigee Lebrun *b* 1755
Henry Raeburn *b* 1756
William Blake *b* 1757

Katsushika Hokusai *b* 1760
Joshua Johnston *b* 1765
Anne-Louis Girodet de Roucy *b* 1767
John Crome *b* 1768
Marie Benoist *b* 1768
Sir Thomas Lawrence *b* 1769

Antoine Jean Gros *b* 1771
Caspar Friedrich *b* 1774
Thomas Girtin *b* 1775
JMW Turner *b* 1775
John Constable *b* 1776

Jean-Auguste-Dominique Ingres *b* 1780
Sir David Wilkie *b* 1785
John Martin *b* 1789

Rachel Ruysch *d* 1750
Rosalba Carriera *d* 1757
Hua Yan *d* 1756

Theodore Gericault *b* 1791
John Linnell *b* 1792
Jean-Baptiste-Camille Corot *b* 1796
Paul Delaroche *b* 1797
Ando Hiroshige *b* 1797
Eugène Delacroix *b* 1798

Giovanni Tieopolo *d* 1770

William Hogarth *d* 1764
Giovanni Canaletto *d* 1768

Jean-Baptiste-Siméon Chardin *d* 1779

1750– Bach dies and the Baroque period ends
1753– Thomas Chippendale begins producing furniture
1755– Montesquieu, French political philosopher, dies
1759– Voltaire's *Candide* published

1761– Haydn becomes vice-Kapellmeister to the Esterhazy family
1762– J.J. Rousseau's *Social Contract*
1763– Wu Ching-Tzu, Chinese author, dies
1768– Royal Academy of Arts founded in London

1773– Johann von Goethe writes the first version of *Faust*
1778– La Scala Opera House opens in Milan
    – Death of Voltaire

1780– Urdu literature reaches its height with the Poets Sauda, Mir Hasan and Mir
1781– Emmanuel Kant: *Critique of Pure Reason*
1783– John Broadwood patented his improved piano pedals
1784– Denis Diderot, French encyclopedist, dies
1786– Mozart's *The Marriage of Figaro* premieres in Vienna
    – Robert Burns publishes his first book of poems
1787– Mozart's *Don Giovanni* debuts in Prague

1793– Building of the Capitol in Washington D.C. begins
1794– Ramón de la Cruz, Spanish playwright, dies
1796– Robert Burns, Scottish playwright, dies
1797– Schubert is born in Vienna

1751– China overruns Tibet, Dzungaria and Tarim Basin
1754– Renewed war between Britain and France for control of North America
1755– Alaungpaya founds Rangoon and reunites Burma
1756– Seven Years' War begins
1757– Battle of Plassey: British defeat the French

1760– New France conquered by British
1761– Capture of Pondicherry: British destroy French power in India
1763– Treaty of Paris
1765– British granted the revenues of Bengal by Mughal emperor
1768– Cook begins exploration of Pacific
    – First steam engine built by Watt

1772– First partition of Poland
1774– Treaty of Kuchuck Kainarji: beginning of Ottoman decline
    – Priestly discovers the nature of oxygen
1775– American revolution begins
1776– American Declaration of Independence
1778– France enters American War of Independence

1783– Russia annexes Crimea
1788– British colony of Australia founded
1789– French Revolution begins
    – George Washington becomes first president of USA

1791– Russia gains Black Sea steppes from Turks
1792– French republic proclaimed; beginning of revolutionary wars
    – Cartwright invents steam-powered weaving loom
1793– Attempts to reform Ottoman empire by Selim III
    – Decimal system introduced
1796– British conquer Ceylon
    – Jenner discovers smallpox vaccine
1798– Lithography invented
    – Napoleon attacks Egypt
1799– Napoleon becomes First Consul

Thomas Cole *b* 1801
Richard Parkes Bonnington *b* 1802
Samuel Palmer *b* 1805
Jean-Baptiste Greuze *d* 1805
William Dyce *b* 1806
Jean-Honoré Fragonard *d* 1806
Hubert Robert *d* 1808
Honoré Daumier *b* 1808
George Romney *d* 1802

Angelica Kauffman *d* 1807

Kitagawa Utamaro *d* 1806

Thomas Girtin *d* 1802

Robert Macpherson *b* 1811

Théodore Rousseau *b* 1812

Jean-François Millet *b* 1814
John Copley *d* 1815

Cornelius Krieghoff *b* 1815

Torii Kiyonaga *d* 1815
Adolf von Menzel *b* 1815

Richard Parkes Bonnington *d* 1828

Robert Duncanson *b* 1821
Benjamin West *d* 1820

Henry Fuseli *d* 1825
Francisco Goya *d* 1828
Jacques-Louis David *d* 1825
William Holman Hunt *b* 1827

Henry Raeburn *d* 1823
William Blake *d* 1827

Anne-Louis Girodet de Roucy *d* 1824
John Crome *d* 1821
Marie Benoist *d* 1826

Dante Gabriel Rossetti *b* 1828

Theodore Gericault *d* 1824

Sir John Everett Millais *b* 1829

Thomas Cole *d* 1848

Camille Pissaro *b* 1830

Gustave Doré *b* 1832
Édouard Manet *b* 1832
Sir Edward Coley Burne-Jones *b* 1833

James Whistler *b* 1834
Edgar Degas *b* 1834

Joshua Johnston *d* 1830
Winslow Homer *b* 1836
Alma Tadema *b* 1836
Paul Cézanne *b* 1839
Sir Thomas Lawrence *d* 1830
Antojne Jean Gros *d* 1835

Vigee Lebrun *d* 1842

Katsushika Hokusai *d* 1849
Odilon Redon *b* 1840

Claude Monet *b* 1840
Berthe Morisot *b* 1841
Caspar Friedrich *d* 1840

Grafton Brown *b* 1841

Sir David Wilkie *d* 1841

Pierre-Auguste Renoir *b* 1841

Henri Rousseau *b* 1844
Paul Gaugin *b* 1848
John William Waterhouse *b* 1849

1801- Haydn composes *The Seasons*
1806-09- Arc de Triomphe built
1807- Beethoven completes his *Symphony No5*

1810- Schumann is born in Germany
1814- Walter Scott writes *Waverley*
1815- Schubert writes *Der Erlkönig*
1816- Rossini's *The Barber of Seville* debuts in Rome

c.1820- Romanticism in European literature- Byron, Chateaubriand, Heine
1821- Von Weber's *Der Freischutz* debuts in Berlin
1822- Royal Academy of Music is founded in London
1824- National Gallery founded – Death of Byron
1826- Mendelssohn writes the overture to *A Midsummer Night's Dream*

1832- Daumier imprisoned for political satire
1835- Hans Christian Andersen publishes his first fairy tales
1836- Charles Dickens and *The Pickwick Papers*
1839- The New York Philharmonic is established

1843- Wagner writes *The Flying Dutchman*
1848- Pre-Raphaelite Brotherhood formed
1849- Death of Chopin

1800- Volta discovers a source of constant current electricity
1803- Louisiana Purchase nearly doubles size of US
1805- Battle of Trafalgar

1812- Napoleon invades Russia – Cylinder printing press invented
1813- British defeat Marathas and become rulers of India
1815- Congress of Vienna redraws frontiers of Europe
1818- Shaka forms Zulu kingdom in SE Africa
1819- First Atlantic steamship crossing

1823- Monroe Doctrine
1825- First passenger steam railway
1826- Joseph Niepce takes first photograph, Paris

1830- Russia begins conquest of Kazakhstan
1833- Slavery abolished in British Empire, first regulation of industrial working conditions (Britain)
1836- Birth of Ramakrishna
1838- First electric telegraph

1840- Samuel Morse devises his code for sending messages
1839-42- First Opium War: Britain annexes Hong Kong
1842- First Afghan War
1845- Irish famine, Texas annexed by US
1848- *Communist Manifesto* issued by Marx – Gold Rush in California

Walter Sickert *b* 1860
Gustav Klimt *b* 1862

Samuel Palmer *d* 1881
Ludwig Kirchner *b* 1880

Robert Macpherson *d* 1872
Piet Mondrian *b* 1872
Aubrey Beardsley *b* 1872

Aubrey Beardsley *d* 1998

William Dyce *d* 1864
Théodore Rousseau *d* 1867
Vassily Kandinsky *b* 1866

Honoré Daumier *d* 1879
Jean-François Millet *d* 1875
Robert Duncanson *d* 1872

Fernand Leger *b* 1881
Pablo Picasso *b* 1881
Georges Braque *b* 1882

Camille Pissaro *d* 1903

Cornelius Krieghoff *d* 1872

Edward Hopper *b* 1882
Gustave Doré *d* 1883
Édouard Manet *d* 1883

Egon Schiele *b* 1890
Stanley Spencer *b* 1891
Sir Edward Coley Burne-Jones *d* 1898

Adolf von Menzel *d* 1905
Vincent van Gogh *d* 1890
James Whistler *d* 1903

Vincent van Gogh *b* 1853

John Sargent *b* 1856

Bill Traylor *b* 1856

Dante Gabriel Rossetti *d* 1882

Otto Dix *b* 1891

JMW Turner *d* 1851

Raoul Dufy *b* 1877

Georges Seurat *b* 1859
John Martin *d* 1854

Jean-Auguste-Dominique Ingres *d* 1867

Amedeo Modigliani *b* 1884

Gustav Klimt *b* 1862

Georges Seurat *d* 1891

John Linnell *d* 1882

Max Ernst *b* 1891
Grant Wood *b* 1892

Paul Delaroche *d* 1856
Ando Hiroshige *d* 1858

Jean-Baptiste Camille Corot *d* 1875

Edvard Munch *b* 1863
Henri de Toulouse-Lautrec *b* 1864
Eugène Delacroix *d* 1863

Paul Klee *b* 1879

Sir John Everett Millais *d* 1896

Paul Gaugin *d* 1903

Pierre Bonnard *b* 1867
Frances Hodgkins *b* 1869
Henri Matisse *b* 1869

Max Beckmann *b* 1884
Lawren Harris *b* 1885
Sonia Delaunay *b* 1885
Diego Rivera *b* 1886
Oskar Kokoschka *b* 1886
Kurt Schwitters *b* 1887
Laurence Stephen Lowry *b* 1887
Marc Chagall *b* 1887
Georgia O'Keeffe *b* 1887

George Grosz *b* 1893
Joan Míro *b* 1893
Ben Nicholson *b* 1894
William Hawkins *b* 1895
Rene Magritte *b* 1898
Aaron Douglas *b* 1899

1851- Great Exhibition, London
1853- Richard Wagner publishes the librettos to *Der Ring des Nibelungen*
1854- Liszt conducts the first performance of his symphonic poems

c.1860- The slave trade introduces West African rhythms, work songs, chants and spirituals to America, which strongly influence blues and jazz
1860- George Eliot writes *The Mill on the Floss*
1864- Brunel's *Bristol Suspension Bridge* is finished
1865- Lewis Carroll and *Alice in Wonderland*
1869- Leo Tolstoy finishes *War and Peace*

1870- Jules Verne publishes *20,000 Leagues Under the Sea*
 - Metropolitan Museum in New York is founded
1874- Verdi's *Requiem* premieres in Milan
 - First Impressionist exhibition in Paris
1877- Ruskin sues Whistler
 - Saint-Saëns debuts *Samson et Dalila*

1880- Dostoevsky publishes The Brothers *Karamazov*
 - Tchaikovsky writes the *1812 Overture*
1881- Ibsen, *Ghosts*
1882- The Berlin Philharmonic is established
1883- Brooklyn Bridge by John Roebling is finished
 - Nietzsche, *Also sprach Zarathustra*
 - Royal College of Music is founded in London
1884- Mark Twain writes *Huckleberry Finn*
1885- Zola writes *Germinal*
 - Gilbert and Sullivan finish *The Mikado*
1886- New English Art Club founded in London
1887- Eiffel Tower by Gustave Eiffel
 - Verdi's *Otello*
1888- Strauss writes *Don Juan*

1893- Dvorak composes *From the New World*
1895- First film performance, Paris
 - Cézanne has one-man show in Paris
1896- Ragtime is born
 - Alfred Nobel's will establishes annual prizes for peace, science, and literature
 - Puccini, *La Bohéme*
1897- Bram Stoker's *Dracula*
 - Tate Gallery opens

1850-64- Taiping Rebellion in China
1851- The Great Exhibition in London
1852- Fall of French republic
1853- Haussmann begins rebuilding Paris
1857- Indian Mutiny
1859- Darwin and *The Origin of Species*
 - First Oil well drilled, Pennsylvania

1860- Pony Express is established in the US
1861- Outbreak of American Civil War
 - Kingdom of Italy proclaimed
1863- Slavery abolished in US
1865- Abraham Lincoln is assassinated
1868- End of Tokugawa shogunate
1869- Suez Canal opens
 - First transcontinental railway completed

1870- Franco-Prussian War
1871- Otto von Bismarck becomes chancellor of new German Empire
1872 - Zulu war in South Africa
1876- Korea becomes an independent nation
 - Queen Victoria becomes Empress of India
 - Alexander Bell invents the telephone
1877- Thomas Edison patents the phonograph
1878- Microphone is invented by David Hughes
1879- Second Afghan War
 - Dual alliance between Germany and Austria-Hungary

1880- German physician Karl Eberth discovers the Typhoid Bacillus
1881- Austro-Serbian treaty of alliance
1885- The Statue of Liberty arrives in New York from France
1886- Germany and Britain partition east Africa
1887- Daimler and Benz complete the first motor cars
1888- Dunlop invents pneumatic tyre
 - Jack the Ripper terrorizes London

1890- dismissal of Bismarck
1893- New Zealand becomes the first country to allow women to vote
1895- Guglielmo Marconi invents radio telegraphy
 - German physicist Wilhelm Röntgen discovers X rays
1897- Crete proclaims union with Greece
 - Rudolph Diesel produces the heavy oil engine
1898- Spanish-American War

Gustav Klimt *d* 1918

Alex Colville *b* 1920
Wayne Thiebaud *b* 1920

Gerhard Richter *b* 1932
Possum Tjapaltjarri *b* 1932
Ludwig Kirchner *d* 1938

Walter Sickert *d* 1942

Hale Woodruff *b* 1900

Piet Mondrian *d* 1944

Vassily Kandinsky *d* 1944

Alberto Giacometti *b* 1901

Egon Schiele *d* 1918

Lucian Freud *b* 1922

Joseph Matar *b* 1935

Jean DeBuffet *b* 1901
William Holman Hunt *d* 1910
Wilfredo Lam *b* 1902
Mark Rothko *b* 1903
John Piper *b* 1903

Leonora Carrington *b* 1917

Fateh Moudarres *b* 1922

Paula Rego *b* 1935

Edgar Degas *d* 1917

Odilon Redon *d* 1916

Alma Tadema *d* 1912
Jacob Lawrence *b* 1917

Roy Lichenstein *b* 1923
John Sargent *d* 1925
Antonio Tapies *b* 1923
Jean-Paul Riopelle *b* 1923
Thomas Mukarobgwa *b* 1924
Robert Rauschenberg *b* 1925
Claude Monet *d* 1926
Avigdor Arikha *b* 1929

Shusaku Arakawa *b* 1936
Frank Stella *b* 1936
David Hockney *b* 1937
Louis Maqhubela *b* 1939
Chuck Close *b* 1940

Winslow Homer *d* 1910

Paul Cézanne *d* 1906

Jaune Quick-to-See Smith *b* 1940

Bill Traylor *d* 1949

Grafton Brown *d* 1918

Amedeo Modigliani *d* 1920

Jasper Johns *b* 1930
Bridget Riley *b* 1931

Salvador Dalí *b* 1904

Gustav Klimt *d* 1918
Pierre -Auguste Renoir *d* 1919

Fernando Botero *b* 1932
Howard Hodgkin *b* 1932

Grant Wood *d* 1942
Edvard Munch *d* 1944

Henri de Toulouse-Lautrec *d* 1901
Arshile Gorky *b* 1904
Barnett Newman *b* 1905
Henri Rousseau *d* 1910
Antonio Berni *b* 1905

Kumi Sugai *b* 1919

Jackson Pollock *b* 1912

Arshile Gorky *d* 1948

John William Waterhouse *d* 1917

RB Kitaj *b* 1932

Pierre Bonnard *d* 1947
Frances Hodgkins *d* 1947

Max Beckmann *d* 1950

Kurt Schwitters *d* 1948

Frida Kahlo *b* 1907
Francisco Amighetti *b* 1907
Norman Lewis *b* 1909
Francis Bacon *b* 1909
Dorothea Tanning *b* 1910

Roberto Matta *b* 1911

Andrew Wyeth *b* 1917
Russell Drysdale *b* 1912
Ad Reinhardt *b* 1913
Meret Oppenheim *b* 1913
Romare Bearden *b* 1914
Hafiz Drubi *b* 1914
Faik Hassan *b* 1914
Sidney Nolan *b* 1917

Andy Warhol *b* 1928

Lin Onus *b* 1948

1900- Sigmund Freud's *The Interpretation of Dreams* is published
1901- Mahler's *Fourth Symphony* debuts in Munich
 - Sagrada Familia built in Barcelona
1904-The London Symphony Orchestra is established
1905- Fauvism launced at Salon d'Automne
 - First regular cinema opens in Pittsburgh
1907- Braque and Picasso evolve Cubism
1908- Schoenberg's *Book of Hanging Gardens* marks a major change in the style of classical music
 - Stravinsky completes *The Firebird*
1909- Marinetti launches Futurism

1910- Birth of abstract art
1911- Camden Town Group formed
 - Strauss's *Der Rosenkavalier* debuts in Dresden
1913- Marcel Proust, *Swann's Way* Stravinsky, *Rite of Spring*
 - *Billboard* magazine publishes a list of the most popular vaudeville songs
1914- Birth of Vorticism
 - Charlie Chaplin creates his film character in *The Tramp*
1915- Dadaism founded
1918- Claude Debussy, French composer, dies
1919- Bauhaus opens in Weimar

1920- Group of Seven founded
1922- James Joyce publishes *Ulysses*
1923- Bessie Smith records her first song
1924- First Surrealist manifesto
 - Ravel's *Bolero* and Gershwin's *Rhapsody in Blue* debut
1925- Kafka, *The Trial*
1927- The first 'talkie' film: *The Jazz Singer* with Al Jolson
 - The Theremin, the first electronic instrument, is invented
1929- Museum of Modern Art, New York, founded

1930- Buñuel: *L'Age d'Or*
1931- Courtauld Institute of Art founded in London
 - Chrysler building completed
1932- Empire State Building completed
1933- Duke Ellington writes *It Don't Mean a Thing, If it Ain't Got That Swing*
1936- International Surrealist Exhibition, London
 - Electric guitars debut
1937- JRR Tolkein publishes *The Hobbit*
 - Nazi exhibition of 'Degenerate Art'
 - Bartok's Music for *Strings, Percussion and Celesta* premieres in Basel

1942-The film *Casablanca* is released
1947- Institute of Contemporary Arts, London, founded
1948- Columbia records introduce the 33 1/3rpm LP
1949- George Orwell publishes *Ninety Eighty Four*

1900- Boxer uprising in China
 - Commonwealth of Australia is established
1903- First successful flight of petrol-powered aircraft
1905- First Morroccan crisis
1908- Bulgaria becomes independent
1910- Japan annexes Korea

1911- Chinese revolution
1912- Stainless steel invented
1914- Outbreak of First World War
 - Henry Ford begins mass production by conveyor belt of Model T car
1917- Revolution in Russia
 - The pop-up toaster patented in America
1918-20- Civil War in Russia. About 15 million Russians die
1919-The first nonstop transatlantic flight

1920- Start of prohibition
1920-2- Gandhi leads Indian non-cooperation movement
1921- Discovery of insulin
1922- USSR formed
 - Howard Carter discovers the tomb of Tutankhamen
1925- Television invented by John Logie Baird
1928- Alexander Fleming developed Antibiotics
1929- The Wall Street Crash

1930- German autobahn system developed
1933- Adolf Hitler is appointed Chancellor of Germany
 - Electron microscope invented
1936-9- Spanish Civil War
1937- Jet engine invented
1938- Ballpoint pen invented
1939- World War II begins
 - First helicopters built

1941- Japan attacks US at Pearl Harbour
1941-45- Six million Jews murdered by German Nazis
1942- Construction of first atomic reactor
1944- First digital computer completed
1945- US drops atom bombs on Japan
 - Germany surrenders
1947- *The Dead Sea Scrolls* are discovered in Israel
 - Microwave oven invented
 - Partition of India and Pakistan

Hale Woodruff *d* 1980

Fernand Leger *d* 1955

Pablo Picasso *d* 1973

Georges Braque *d* 1963
Alberto Giacometti *d* 1966
Edward Hopper *d* 1967

Stanley Spencer *d* 1959

Jean DeBuffet *d* 1985

Wilfredo Lam *d* 1982

Mark Rothko *d* 1970

John Piper *d* 1992

Julian Schnabel *b* 1951
Cheri Samba *b* 1956

Gabriel Orozco *b* 1962
Seraphine Pick *b* 1964

Otto Dix *d* 1969

Raoul Dufy *d* 1953

Salvador Dalí *d* 1989

Max Ernst *d* 1976

Kumi Sugai *d* 1996

Barnett Newman *d* 1970

Jackson Pollock *d* 1956

Antonio Berni *d* 1981

Henri Matisse *d* 1954

Lawren Harris *d* 1970
Sonia Delaunay *d* 1979

Diego Rivera *d* 1957

Oskar Kokoschka *d* 1980

Laurence Stephen Lowry *d* 1976

Marc Chagall *d* 1985
Georgia O'Keeffe *d* 1986

George Grosz *d* 1959

Joan Miro *d* 1983
Ben Nicholson *d* 1982

William Hawkins *d* 1990

Rene Magritte *d* 1967

Aaron Douglas *d* 1979

Frida Kahlo *d* 1954

Norman Lewis *d* 1979

Francis Bacon *d* 1992

Andy Warhol *d* 1987
Russell Drysdale *d* 1981

Ad Reinhardt *d* 1967

Meret Oppenheim *d* 1985
Romare Bearden *d* 1988

Hafiz Drubi *d* 1991
Faik Hassan *d* 1992
Sidney Nolan *d* 1992
Lin Onus *d* 1996

Keith Haring *b* 1958

Keith Haring *d* 1990

1950- United Nations building in New York City is completed
1951- JD Salinger: *The Catcher in the Rye*
1952- Samuel Beckett: *Waiting for Godot*
1954- Elvis Presley becomes a worldwide star
1957- Leonard Bernstein completes *West Side Story*

1960- John Coltrane forms his own quartet
1961- Pop Art introduced
   - Joseph Heller writes *Catch 22*
1965- The Beatles top the charts all over the world
1966- Floods destroy Florentine art treasures
   - New Metropolitan Opera House opens in New York City
1969- The Woodstock Music and Art Fair marks the zenith of the 'Hippy' era

1971-77- Pompidou centre built in Paris
1976- Philip Glass completes *Einstein on the Beach*

1982- Michael Jackson's Thriller spends 37 weeks at the top of the US chart and sells 40 million copies worldwide
1984- Malcolm Morley is first winner of the Turner prize
1985- Saatchi collection opens in London
   - Live Aid rock concert raises $60 million for African famine relief
1986- Wole Soyinka is the first black African to win the Nobel Prize for Literature

1995- Damien Hirst wins the Turner Prize

1948- Long-play record invented
   - Establishment of State of Israel: first Arab-Israeli war
1950- China invades Tibet
1953- Structure of the DNA molecule described
   - Military coup in Iran
1955- Contraceptive pill developed
   - Warsaw Pact
1956- Video recorder invented
   - Suez crisis

1957- Soviet Sputnik: world's first satellite
1958- 'Great Leap Forward' in China
1959- Castro seizes power in Cuba
1960- Laser invented
1961- Berlin Wall built
1962- Cuban missile crisis
1963- President Kennedy assassinated
1964- Nelson Mandela imprisoned
1965-75- Vietnam War

1966-76- Cultural Revolution in China
1968- Assassination of Martin Luther King
   - USSR invades Czechoslovakia
   - World wide student protests
1969- Neil Armstrong walks on the moon
1976- First flight of Concorde
1978- Compact disc invented
1979- Fall of Shah of Iran
   - Civil war in Nicaragua and El Salvador
   - Soviet Army invades Afghanistan

1981- President Sadat of Egypt assassinated
   - First re-usable shuttle space flight
1982- AIDS becomes widespread
   - Israel invades Lebanon
1983- US occupies Grenada
1986- Chernobyl nuclear power station explodes
   - US bomb Libya
1987- World population reaches 5 billion
1989- Berlin Wall demolished

1990- Growth of the Internet
1991- Disintegration of the USSR
   - Gulf War
1991-96- Civil War fragments Yugoslavia
1993- Human embryos are cloned
1994- Nelson Mandela elected as president of South Africa
1999- European single currency (Euro) launched
2001- Terrorist attacks on New York: Planes fly into the World Trade Centre

Art Movements

Some movements, like the Pre-Raphaelite Brotherhood, were conscious attempts by a group of artists to make a particular statement; others, like the Renaissance were collected together retrospectively, characterised by the developments of the period. For those interested in painting or art in general such labels often seem arbitrary, meaningless and confusing, apparently interfering with the enjoyment and contemplation of the work, but it can be illuminating to understand the different responses of artists painting in the same tradition, at the same time. The following pages reveal a history of the main movements and explain some of the style, subject matter and techniques which distinguish them. The A–Z section takes a selection of the main and some of the newer movements, visually demonstrating the differences between, terms like the Impressionists, Expressionists and the Abstract Expressionists.

Main Art Movements

Art in one form or another has been in existence for thousands of years. There is ample evidence not only that cave painting and engraving were widespread in Palaeolithic times, but also that it spanned many centuries and reflected many different styles and purposes. It is fascinating to observe the development of technique over the centuries and the improvement in the materials used to create a wider range of colours and styles. It is clear that cave-dwellers executed these works of art partly for decoration, partly for self-expression and partly for some other motive, perhaps in connection with their religious beliefs. The Aboriginal art of Australia, which has developed along distinctive tribal and community lines for almost 40,000 years, offers the best example of art which, in form and content, has retained its essential character and is still very much a living force.

Ian Abdulla, Sowing Seeds at Nite

There is a huge gap between the cave paintings of the Old Stone Age and the art of the Middle Eastern civilizations. It should not be supposed that art did not exist in the interim, merely that the media in which it was executed have not survived. Certainly the applied and decorative arts from 10,000 BC onwards in Anatolia and Mesopotamia, in metalwork and pottery, for example, reveal a high degree of artistic attainment. The fine arts of painting and sculpture evolved gradually all over the world and eventually attained high levels of sophistication and aesthetic sensibility in those parts of the world where 'civilization' in the broadest sense reached its peak. Thus we may find a high degree of technical skill manifest in the temple and tomb murals of Pharaonic Egypt, the friezes of Babylon, the wall-hangings of China and the mosaics and frescoes of Crete and Mycenae. Out of the art of the Aegean, which flourished between 5,000 and 1,000 BC would develop the art of Greece and ultimately that of Rome. To the Greeks painting was a minor art, mostly confined to the decoration of vases but nevertheless revealing a very lively sense of composition and realism. The Etruscans derived their art from the Greeks but took it a stage further, reviving the art of painting on ceilings and walls – techniques later refined by the Romans. The murals of Pompeii and Herculaneum, engulfed by lava and volcanic ash in AD 79 and miraculously preserved as a result, are mute testament to the skills of Roman artists, notably in their clever use of line to create a three-dimensional effect.

Ancient Eastern Art

Isolated from the Mediterranean world by vast deserts, lofty and impenetrable mountain ranges, and the seas and oceans, China's artistic development was uninfluenced by that of any other civilization. Towns and cities emerged around 4,000 BC and by 2,750 BC pottery and silk-weaving were established. Metalwork, writing and the manufacture of writing materials developed in China quite independently of Europe and, indeed, Chinese technology in silks, ceramics, paper, gunpowder and many other fields would eventually enrich the Western world. Coinage arose more or less simultaneously in China and Asia Minor, though independently and subsequently developing along quite different lines. So, too, the art of painting. Whereas art in the Mediterranean civilizations ultimately strove to create – or re-create –a thing of beauty, with the human body as the acme of perfection, rendered in painting or sculpture as close to reality as the artist could achieve, Chinese art took a different approach; interpretation rather than representation was the keyword. Realizing the futility of the exact reproduction of, for example, a flower, a Chinese artist would seek to convey the impression that its fragrance made on him. The Chinese style influenced that of neighbouring Korea, which in turn influenced Japan over a period of several centuries through continued contact, which included the movement of people. The art of China, Japan and Korea, therefore, evolved along radically different lines from that of the Mediterranean. Through the centuries, much of the former has revelled in the wildness of nature, the rugged mountain scenery and the raging torrents of cascades and mountain streams. A twisted, stunted, gnarled old tree becomes a thing of beauty because it represents the finest ideals of Confucianism. The artists of the Mediterranean area had little interest in the beauties of nature, let alone scenery. Far from inspiring works of art, mountains were dangerous places which struck terror but did not inspire awe let alone any desire to create representations of them.

As in so many other aspects of life, the art of painting in China and Japan had reached such an apparent peak of perfection at an early stage that it would remain relatively static for many centuries thereafter. At a period when artists in Europe were still painting on walls or vases, the Chinese were already painting and drawing on silk, a material that enabled them to develop a very fine and delicate style. Although papyrus was used in Egypt and the Alexandrine Empire (332–323 BC) it was mainly confined to writing. By the second century BC the Chinese had developed a form of paper and later this was used as an alternative to silk for hand-scrolls. The invention of block printing provided a further impetus to the creation of pictures of exquisite draughtsmanship. The use of ideograms to convey words and meanings throughout a vast empire of many different languages led to the development of writing and, combined with painting, raised calligraphy to an art form in its own right. Creativity expressed itself in both the picture and the poetry that went along with it. Painting and poetry were regarded as the height of intellectual attainments; they gave expression to the philosophies of Buddhism, Taoism and Confucianism, and in turn, the development of Zen Buddhism had a dramatic impact on all forms of art, particularly painting and ceramics.

Although Japanese art arose from early contacts with China and the spread of Buddhism, strict isolation from other countries from 1192 onwards and the development of an extremely structured society with strict codes covering all aspects of life resulted in an artistic style radically different from the Chinese. At first, screens and wall-hangings were painted in bright colours embellished with gold and placing emphasis on figures rather than scenery. Out of this *Yamato-e* style developed the *Emakimono* ('story scrolls') from the eighth century onwards, which remained immensely popular until the eighteenth century. Under the military regime of the shogun warlords (1165-1867 AD), however, there developed a much more austere style, bound by the restrictions of monochrome ink. Paintings consisted mainly of hand-scrolls and wall-hangings executed on fine silks; these remained the preferred media right up until the second half of the nineteenth century, when China, Japan and Korea became more susceptible to Western influences.

Another great civilization began to emerge in India, at about the same time as those in Egypt and China, which reached its zenith around 800 BC. The Aryans (the root of the word 'Iran', the modern name for Persia) introduced the Sanskrit language and the fundamentals of Hinduism, both of which dominated Indian art for many centuries. The earliest paintings are the frescoes executed on plaster in the caves at Ajanta and other religious sites. Smaller works were later painted on palm leaves and this style continued on vellum and paper, reaching its greatest heights in the albums of miniatures commissioned by successive Mughal emperors and continued at the courts of the various noble families.

Although there were some notable exceptions, such as the Tang frescoes of Tunhuang, and the religious cave paintings of India,

Oriental, Middle Eastern and Indian art tended to be small in scale, eventually giving rise to such examples as the exquisite miniature paintings of Persia and the Mughal Empire. The art of Greece and Rome, on the other hand, was generally much larger in scale, consisting mainly of mosaics for floors, walls and ceilings as well as colossal murals and friezes to adorn the walls of palaces and temples.

Byzantine Art

As the Roman Empire pushed farther east it came in contact with the arts of the Orient and, after the collapse of the empire in the West in the fifth century, the Byzantine Empire increasingly looked to the East for both the form and content of its art. Silk-weaving, ivory-carving and glass mosaics all benefited from this Oriental influence. The sumptuously coloured illuminated manuscripts from the sixth century onwards, replete with gold leaf, reflect the influence of Persia, but it was not until the end of the ninth century that representational art, in the style of the Classical Greeks, was revived and then rose to new heights. Most of the surviving examples from the later Byzantine period are associated with imperial portraiture or the representation of saints, out of which developed the tradition for icon painting which continues in Orthodox countries to this day.

Although the western Roman Empire disintegrated under the incursions of the Goths, Vandals and other barbarian peoples and its civilization was destroyed, it did not vanish completely. Western Christianity, with its headquarters in Rome itself, was eventually embraced by the pagan tribes, and from this developed the petty kingdoms of the Dark Ages and the revival of empire under Charlemagne. Italy was reconquered (or liberated) by the Byzantines in the sixth century and in the ensuing period Ravenna and Venice became major centres of Byzantine art and architecture, noted for their religious mosaics. Although the Byzantine Empire briefly extended along the southern shores of the Mediterranean as far as Morocco, the rise of Islam in the seventh century gradually forced it back and Constantinople itself came under attack in the eighth century. Nevertheless, the Byzantine Empire endured until 1453, when its capital Constantinople fell to the Osmanli Turks. Its art had become somewhat stereotyped and what fresh impetus it had seems to have come from southern Russia (notably in the shape of icons), Turkey or Syria; but from the early 1300s there was a late flowering of Byzantine art, reflected in religious wall-painting, illuminated manuscripts and icons which, in turn, had a dramatic impact on Italian art in the fourteenth century.

Art

Gothic Art

As the political and cultural heir of the western Roman Empire, the Holy Roman Empire founded by Charlemagne consciously imitated the art and architecture of the period before the fall of Rome. In architecture particularly this imitation was often crude and barbaric, and was contemptuously dismissed by Renaissance writers as 'Gothic'. Although the term is grossly inaccurate and misleading, it has been retained as a convenient name for the art and architecture from the end of the first millennium to the start of the Renaissance.

The Gothic style arose primarily out of a desire by newly Christianized peoples to build churches, monasteries and cathedrals on a grand scale; consequently, Gothic is largely associated with extravagant vaulting, spires, flying buttresses and elaborate tracery. These edifices were distinguished by their huge, tall windows which encouraged the development of stained glass, but whose walls left relatively little scope for mural painting. Fine art in this period made advances through the medium of illuminated manuscripts, but this was a skill practised in every monastery. Working on parchment, the limners outlined their pictures in various coloured inks and used tempera (a mixture of various pigments with egg-yolk, oil and water) and gold leaf to create everything from an ornamental initial letter to a complete illustration in the manuscript copies of the Gospels, psalters and breviaries. Before the invention of printing from movable type, the only books were those laboriously copied by hand, a labour of love for the greater glory of God. Inevitably there was also a secular parallel development when kings, princes and great merchants commissioned prayer-books, known as 'books of hours', which differed from the monastic works in their greater use of scenes drawn from everyday life. These books were produced by artists who might have learned their craft in a monastery, but who operated in purely commercial workshops. It is significant that while we know little of the identity of the monastic limners and scribes, the earliest identifiable artists in western Europe were those like Jean Pucelle of Paris and the Limbourg Brothers of Flanders, the respective creators of the magnificent *Belleville Breviary* and the *Très Riches Heures du Duc de Berry*.

Fresco Painting

Long before the fall of Constantinople brought a flood of refugees to western Europe with the accumulated learning, skills and technology of the East, the Byzantine influence was making itself strongly felt. In the thirteenth century a change in Italian ecclesiastical architecture left more wall space, which demanded suitable decoration. We shall probably never know who was the genius who first stumbled upon the technique of painting on wet lime plaster, using colours ground and mixed with lime water. As the plaster dried the colours were fixed, just as if they had been applied to pottery then fired in a kiln. The problem with this technique was that the plaster set quickly, so fresco painting (as it was termed) had to be executed swiftly to a careful plan, because it was impossible to repaint once the plaster had dried. Although this style of painting was immensely popular all over Europe, by its very nature it was unsuited to the prevailing damp climate of northern Germany, the Low Countries or Britain, with the result that few medieval frescoes have survived intact. Even in Italy, many of the frescoes painted for churches have not stood the ravages of time and weather.

The greatest impetus to fresco painting came in the late thirteenth century, when the Franciscan order created the magnificent foundation at Assisi in honour of St Francis. The Franciscans recruited the best artists from all over Italy and thus Assisi briefly became an important centre where painters came together, argued and exchanged ideas. A large part of the decoration at Assisi was carried out by Benevieni di Pepo, nicknamed Cimabue ('ox-head'), in around 1280. Trained in the Byzantine tradition, Cimabue (*c.* 1240–*c.* 1302) transformed it and laid the foundations for a distinctive Italian style. Few frescoes by this Florentine painter have survived, but those that are still extant reveal his role in effecting the transition. The influence of Byzantine icon-painting is still very strong in his *Maestà* (1280), but the Madonna on her majestic throne has a much softer, more human expression than one would find in icons of the period. The artist's radical departure from the Byzantine tradition was continued by his pupil and successor Giotto di Bondone (1266–1337), who combined a more flexible approach to composition with portraiture, a style that conveyed both the feelings and character of the subject in a manner never previously attempted, far less achieved.

The Sienese School

Although there were at this time a number of artists at Rome who, like Cimabue and Giotto, had been schooled in the Byzantine tradition and who had turned from mosaics to painting, the work of Giunta Pisano (*c.* 1229–*c.* 1254), Coppo di Marcovaldo (*c.* 1225–*c.* 1274) and their colleagues did not immediately follow the new style. In Siena, however, there was Duccio di Buoninsegna (*c.* 1255–*c.* 1318), whose *Ruccellai Madonna* of 1285 was the equal of the masterpieces by Cimabue and

Giotto. Like his contemporaries, Duccio was raised in the Byzantine tradition, and he too breathed new life into it, independently of Cimabue and Giotto, with works that displayed an increased sense of spatial awareness and narrative. His studio in Siena became the well-spring for a school of art which developed along parallel lines with that of Florence. The Sienese artists of the next generation included Simone Martini (c. 1284–1344) and the Lorenzetti brothers Pietro (c. 1280–1348) and Ambrogio (d. 1348). The latter completed his art training in Florence which, by the middle of the fourteenth century, had emerged as the predominant force in Italian painting.

The Early Flemish School

Elsewhere in western Europe, the outstanding painter of his generation in Flanders was Jan Van Eyck (1390–1441). Not only did Van Eyck inject an unprecedented realism into his paintings, particularly in his delineation of the texture of robes and the surface of stone or brick, but he was also responsible for the introduction of painting in oils – a method that would revolutionize the medium. The appearance of his great altarpiece of the Mystic Lamb, with its 12 interior panels and matching exterior compartments was a *tour de force* that placed the Flemish School in the forefront of painting in northern Europe – a position it retained for more than a century – and even influenced developments in Italy itself. A prime example of this was the painting of himself and his wife, which was commissioned by Arnolfini at Bruges; this piece is still widely regarded as the exemplar of realism and precision that was the hallmark of Flemish painting. Rogier Van der Weyden (1400–64) and later Hugo Van der Goes (c. 1440–82) continued the tradition, adding their own special brand of pathos and expression.

Early Renaissance Art

Although France was at the nadir of its fortunes as a result of the Hundred Years' War with England (which occupied Paris itself), a few artists managed to maintain standards at Avignon, then a papal fief. Among them was Jean Fouquet (c. 1420–c. 1480), who raised portraiture to a new level (painting on canvas instead of the more usual wood support), in full-scale works as well as in miniatures, and demonstrated how, even in vicissitude, a country can still produce great art.

The wealth of the merchant princes who controlled the affairs of the great Italian cities created a patronage of the arts that has not been exceeded since. This period coincided with the rise of the papacy, and an unparalleled era of church building in the Italian style which yielded huge expanses of interior walls for decoration. This was the golden age of frescoes and elaborate altarpieces as artists vied with each other in painting the Holy Family and biblical scenes, into which was breathed the fresh air of the new Renaissance humanism. Religious works were given a contemporary slant and made free use of ordinary everyday scenes. A new realism pervaded these paintings, enhanced by much greater attention to detail. Pisanello (1380–1456) and Masaccio (1401–28) pioneered the study of the human form and made the nude figure a respectable subject for ecclesiastical decoration – a notion taken to its logical conclusion by Masolino da Panicale (1385–1447) in his great *Baptism of Christ*.

In the background architecture of Masaccio's paintings we can see the striving towards a mastery of perspective; had he not died so young, who knows what he might have achieved. As it was, it was his colleague Paolo Uccello (1397–1475) who solved the problem. Indeed, Uccello became obsessed with creating a three-dimensional illusion that might emulate the great bronze bas-reliefs of Lorenzo Ghiberti (1378–1455), in whose workshop he had originally been employed as a mosaicist. Andrea del Castagno (1423–57) also experimented with perspective and the use of space and lighting. Piero della Francesca (c. 1420–62), though not a Florentine, subsequently came under the influence of Uccello and Masaccio and likewise sought the solution to the problems of perspective, eventually writing a couple of treatises on the subject.

Piero della Francesca, Baptism of Christ

Painters were held in the highest esteem in the early Renaissance era, and the Dominican monk Fra Angelico (1387–1455) was even beatified by the Church in recognition of the profound effect his powerful but simple religious paintings had on those who saw them. By contrast, the Carmelite monk Fra Filippo Lippi (c. 1406–69) brought an earthy realism into his works and is best remembered for liberating the altarpiece, removing the artificial divisions of the centrepiece and side panels to create one large continuous surface.

High Renaissance Art

Painters who had begun their careers as stone carvers or sculptors included Sandro Botticelli (1444–1510), Antonio Pollaiuolo (c. 1429–98) and Andrea Verrocchio (1435–1488), and they too strove to achieve those attributes which would give their paintings a proper sense of

Art

distance. These artists came to the fore just at the time the Renaissance ideals of secularism and humanism were at their most pervasive, but were overshadowed by the next generation. Foremost, of course, was Leonardo da Vinci (1452–1519), whose life was synchronous with the High Renaissance and who was the most perfect example of the Renaissance man, excelling in an extraordinary diversity of disciplines, as an architect, sculptor, designer, military engineer and inventor as well as a painter. Not only did he produce one of the greatest masterpieces of all time, the *Mona Lisa*, but he was also one of the first Italian artists to employ landscape as an extension of the subject rather than merely to fill the background.

Michelangelo (1475–1564) had many of Leonardo's attributes, as well as being a poet of considerable ability. Though best known as a sculptor, in later life he produced paintings of such sublime power as to place him in the first rank; his decoration of the Sistine Chapel is rightly

regarded as one of the greatest masterpieces of all time. His near contemporary was Raphael (1483–1520), trained in the effete Umbrian School but later acquiring the positive qualities of the Florentine School, and having the good sense to graft on the best precepts from Leonardo and Michelangelo. The end result was a noble style that transcended the sum of its parts and was universally regarded as the quintessence of a pure and perfect harmony. The religious paintings of Raphael are so well known that it is difficult to realize how startlingly novel they struck his contemporaries. He breathed new life into the hackneyed subject of the Madonna and Child and other aspects of the Holy Family, which were an obligatory part of the repertory of every artist of the period. To Raphael more than any other artist of the High Renaissance is due the credit for establishing Rome as the artistic centre of the Western world – a position that remained unchallenged for more than 200 years.

Mannerism

It became the goal of every aspiring painter and sculptor to travel to Rome and study under the great masters. Returning to France,

Germany or the Low Countries, they would spread the teachings of Rome, a process that endured long after Rome's status as Europe's cultural capital had diminished. The rising powers of northern Europe compounded this by hiring Italian artists to decorate palaces which themselves were designed by Italians or slavishly followed the example of Italian architects. This Italian predominance led indirectly to the rise of Mannerism, a style that evolved in the sixteenth century as the successors of Michelangelo and Raphael tried to surpass them. The buzzword was *maniera* ('stylishness'), but in striving to achieve this its practitioners indulged in a rather self-conscious refinement which reached its peak in the 1570s. Exaggeration of form, colour and expression characterized the works of Andrea del Sarto (1486–1531) and his pupil Jacopo Pontormo (1494–1577) but culminated in the frescoes of Giorgio Vasari (1511–74), better known today as an art historian than an artist in his own right. Mannerism was relatively short-lived, and the reaction to it produced a return to more naturalistic styles.

The Later Flemish School

While the Italianate influence was accepted unquestioningly in France, it was not embraced quite so wholeheartedly in the Low Countries, where Quentin Metsys (1466–1530), founder of the Antwerp School, modified Italianism to produce a more humanist style imbued with natural expression and a distinctive grace. Hieronymus Bosch (c. 1450–1516) harnessed Italian techniques to his own highly idiosyncratic style, creating a brand of fantasy and visionary painting which in many respects anticipated the Surrealists by several centuries. Pieter Brueghel (c. 1520–69) accepted the basic tenets of the Italian style, but his approach to painting was wholly original. We may detect the influence of Bosch in his Gothic scenes, but his development of genre scenes, full of down-to-earth humour, was without precedent. His son, Pieter Brueghel the Younger, tried to go one better, with grotesque paintings of devils and hags which inspired terror in their beholders, but the wheel came full circle in the case of younger brother Jan, known as 'Velvet' Brueghel because of his anodyne paintings of flowers, still-lifes and religious themes that conformed to mainstream ideas.

The German School

Something of the anarchic attitudes of Bosch and Brueghel was also evident in the paintings of the German engineer, architect, engraver and artist Matthias Grünewald (c. 1470–1528), who rebelled against Roman Classicism. The parallel with da Vinci is very close: a man of

Raphael, School of Athens

many talents and prodigious intellect, whose visionary passion comes across vividly in his great masterpiece, the Isenheim altarpiece. His exact contemporary was Albrecht Dürer (1471–1528), whose Classical training never impeded his Germanic genius. If he lacked the versatility of Grünewald, he had da Vinci's enquiring mind and fascination for the minutiae of nature, evident in his numerous anatomical studies of animals and humans. Lucas Cranach (1472–1553) lived far longer, and for that reason his art was strongly influenced by the Reformation. Working as court painter at Wittenberg, he was an eye-witness to the dramatic events surrounding Martin Luther from 1517 onwards. Thus his earlier work, comprising mainly religious paintings and Classical allegories, gave way to portraits (including the reformers Luther and Melancthon) and more secular subjects, all imbued with a sense of realism and immediacy.

Portraiture had been comparatively neglected in the Italian convention, although there had been some outstanding exceptions – Leonardo's portraits of Ginevra di Benci (c. 1476) and the *Mona Lisa* (the wife of Zanoki del Gioconda) 30 years later were quite extraordinary examples of purely secular portraiture in an age when idealized pictures of the Holy Family and the saints were the norm. The example of Cranach was followed by Hans Holbein (1497–1543) who, though German by birth, trained in Italy then worked in Switzerland and finally in England. One of the first truly cosmopolitan artists, he combined Teutonic precision with Italian elegance to create some of the greatest documentary portraits of the early sixteenth century, notably his series devoted to Henry VIII and his wives. Holbein produced full-scale easel-paintings, but also helped to establish the tradition of the portrait miniature, which attained its zenith with Nicholas Hilliard (1547–1619) in the reign of Elizabeth I and continued unabated in Britain until the advent of photography in the middle of the nineteenth century.

The Venetian School

The Venetian School also developed in the fifteenth century. Its progenitor was Andrea Mantegna (c. 1431–1506), a native of Vicenza who learned his craft in Padua and worked mainly in Mantua and other towns and cities of northern Italy. Mantegna's influence spread to Venice via his connection with Giovanni Bellini, his brother-in-law. Bellini's early years as an artist were inspired by Mantegna's style; particularly his sculpturesque figure style and sense of composition. Although Mantegna was employed as a fresco painter – his finest works were the

series of tempera pictures *The Triumph of Caesar* and the ceiling of the Camera degli Sposi in Mantua – he exerted enormous influence on the next generation of northern Italian painters. Their vitality and exuberance brought renewed splendour to Italian painting at a time when the older-established schools were running out of momentum.

Actually the Venetian tradition can be traced back much further, to Gentile da Fabriano (c. 1370–c. 1427), who spent most of his life painting in Venice before studying in Rome, Florence and Siena in the 1420s. Gentile was the teacher of Jacopo Bellini (c. 1400–70), a Venetian artist whose few extant works reveal an intense fascination with landscape and architecture long before either subject was fashionable. Jacopo was the father of Gentile (c. 1429–1507) and Giovanni (c. 1430–1516), the Bellini brothers who helped to revolutionize and reinvigorate Italian painting in the late fifteenth century. Gentile Bellini was one of the first artists to appreciate the unique beauty of Venice and its canals, but he also excelled as a portraitist, and was invited to Constantinople in around 1480 to paint a portrait of Sultan Muhammed II. Giovanni Bellini was the first Italian artist successfully to wed figures to landscapes in a wholly naturalistic setting, and pioneered the naturalistic treatment of light.

Mantegna married Jacopo's daughter and was thus brother-in-law to Gentile and Giovanni, with whom he worked very closely. Also associated with them was Antonello da Messina (c. 1430–70), who migrated from southern Italy in the last decade of his life and was one of the first Italians to abandon tempera for oil paints and explore the potential of this Flemish innovation. Another early exponent of the Venetian School was Antonio Pisanello (c. 1395–c. 1455); working in a city in which the influence of the eastern Mediterranean was pervasive, Pisanello countered the prevailing Byzantine style with his own individual brand of International Gothic.

The leading figures in the next generation of Venetian painters included Vittore Carpaccio (c. 1460–c. 1525), who combined religious themes with contemporary Venetian urban landscape, and Giorgione (c. 1476–1510), a somewhat shadowy figure whose chief interest is that he bridges the gap between Giovanni Bellini and Titian, who assisted him on the frescoes of the Fondaco dei Tedeschi.

The Venetian School attained its finest flowering in the sixteenth century, in the hands of Tiziano Vecellio, known as Titian (c. 1490–1576). He succeeded Giovanni Bellini as Painter to the Most Serene Republic in 1516 and, like his predecessor, executed a number of large paintings and altarpieces for various churches in and around Venice. He also undertook commissions for wealthy patrons, in which he concentrated on Classical subjects which enabled him to develop the painting of the female nude. In Florence nudes were invariably shown as standing figures in static poses, but Titian liberated the nude; his Venuses were recumbent or reclining in languid poses, invested with a new sensuality. This was a definite turning point: and in works such as *Sacred and Profane Love* Titian freed painting from its religious didacticism and enabled his successors to explore the infinitely wider world of sentiment. In his later works the quality of his brushwork led to an exceptional combination of form and content; the manner in which he used paint poetically to attain sublimity of expression has rarely been equalled, far less surpassed.

Of all the Venetian painters, Jacopo Tintoretto (1518–94) came closest to scaling Titian's great heights, and he went even further in taming perspective. Tintoretto produced some of the largest painted works of all time, but despite their great size, the quality was undiminished and he excelled both as a portraitist and as an accomplished master of the human figure in every conceivable pose. The third of the great painters in this phase of the Venetian School was Paolo Veronese (*c.* 1528–88), noted for his great historical and biblical scenes conceived and executed on a heroic scale. Veronese pushed to the limits the secular treatment of religious subjects, an activity that led to charges by the Inquisition that he had treated sacred themes in a profane manner. His chief contribution to the development of painting was his exploration of colour and texture and the effects of light on different surfaces. The reflection of hard or polished surfaces such as metal and marble, the soft tones of human flesh, the sumptuous qualities of silks and brocades or the deep tones suggestive of velvet and fur or the glossy tints of human hair – these were attributes that the great Venetian masters raised to new levels, investing their paintings with qualities of pathos, nostalgia, melancholy, majesty or an inner radiance.

Italian Academicism

Throughout the course of the sixteenth century there was a great deal of cross-fertilization in the European art world. Venetians such as Titian worked in Rome on papal commissions. Others also found their way there: Sebastiano del Piombo (1485–1547), a pupil of Giovanni Bellini and Giorgione, assisted Michelangelo at Rome from 1510 onwards and was so strongly influenced by him that he was regarded as more Florentine than the Florentines. Conversely, there were also artists of great independence of spirit and originality of style flourishing in other parts of Italy. Antonio Correggio (*c.* 1499–1534) worked in Parma, a

skilled decorator on a vast scale but also an accomplished master of the smaller easel painting. Agostino (1557–1602) and Annibale Carracci (1562–1609) were artists who developed in Bologna, outside the mainstream of the large schools. Ironically, they founded an academy which attempted to train young artists to paint according to clearly defined principals and formulae, thereby giving rise to the rather stereotyped 'academicism' of the seventeenth and eighteenth centuries. The greatest of the independent artists, however, was Michelangelo da Caravaggio (1573–1610), a restless and untamed spirit in every sense, whose wild lifestyle forced him to move frequently and hurriedly. Perhaps this constant need to be one step ahead of his creditors or enemies dictated his passionate, rapid, almost frenzied style of painting. Caravaggio was the great master of genre scenes from everyday life, often so lowly that few would have considered them fit for depiction; but he also produced some sublime religious masterpieces in which the subjects were handled with great realism. Stripping Christ and the saints from the idealization of earlier generations, Caravaggio made them more acceptable at a time when reform and the questioning of traditional religious values were becoming more commonplace. His revolutionary style struck a responsive chord throughout Italy and beyond; Rembrandt was one of the northern painters to come under his spell.

Art in Spain

The chief reason for the preponderance of Italian art in the fifteenth and sixteenth centuries was that it was the part of western Europe that felt the greatest impact of the Renaissance. North of the Alps, a different set of forces were at work. The printing press revolutionized communications, enabling the rapid dissemination of new ideas in philosophy and religion, and the development of a humanism that challenged the teachings of the Church. In turn, this created the independent, free-thinking climate in which art developed along radically different lines. While Italian art continued to be dominated by religious paintings, in Germany and the Low Countries a more secular approach was reflected in the intimacy of small portraits, in the popularity of genre subjects and in the development of both landscapes and domestic interiors.

France went through a period of social and political upheaval before an uneasy peace between the Catholics and the Protestant Huguenots was agreed in the Edict of Nantes in 1598. Consequently, in the seventeenth century France gradually took over from Italy as the leading artistic centre. Spain, on the other hand, had only achieved political unity at the end of the fifteenth century. The expulsion of the

Moors and Jews took place in the very year that Columbus landed in the New World. Religious conformity – enforced in Spain more rigorously through the Inquisition than anywhere else in the Catholic world – was a major factor in the development of art in the sixteenth and seventeenth centuries, while the vast influx of precious metals from the mines of Mexico and South America produced a period of unparalleled wealth and prosperity, in which architecture, sculpture and painting flourished as never before.

If the disparate elements of Spain were brought together through the marriage of Ferdinand of Aragon and Isabella of Castile, the political unions of their offspring would lead rapidly to the ascendancy of the Habsburg dynasty and the emergence of Charles V as the ruler of a vast European empire. The resulting cross-fertilization in Spanish art far exceeded the eclecticism in Italy during the same period. It is significant that the leading Spanish painter of the early sixteenth century was Antonio Moro (c. 1517–77), who was actually born Anthony Mor van Dashorst at Utrecht in Holland and trained under Jan Scorel (1495–1562) at Antwerp. One of the first great, although somewhat underrated, cosmopolitans, Moro enjoyed a high reputation as a portraitist at the courts of Brussels and London before being summoned to Madrid. His style was eclectic, combining Flemish realism with Spanish romanticism and Italian classicism. The result betrays more than a hint of Mannerism, the style that developed initially in Italy in the second half of the sixteenth century. Originally this was clearly defined as a tendency to exaggerate or distort features or form for the sake of effect; in Moro's case this was reflected in the elegant aloofness and haughty expressions of his royal sitters, but in later generations mannerism (with a small 'm') became a general term denoting an affected adherence to a particular style.

It was another foreigner who brought the Spanish version of Mannerism to its fullest flowering. Domenikos Theotokopoulos (1541–1614) was a native of Crete, part of the Venetian dominions at that time, but ethnically and culturally Greek. Trained in the Byzantine tradition, El Greco ('the Greek') went to Venice where he became a pupil of Titian in the latter's declining years, came under the influence of Tintoretto and the Mannerist style of Andrea del Sarto, and studied the works of Michelangelo and Raphael in Rome before settling at Madrid in 1577. El Greco developed a highly individual style. Faces and bodies were elongated and features distorted and his style influenced Spanish portrait painters of the ensuing generations, notably Diego Velázquez (1599–1660) and Bartolome Murillo (1617–82).

The French School

Religious and political stability came to France in 1610 with the accession of Henri IV, but it was his grandson, Louis XIV (1638–1715), who left his mark on the seventeenth century and created the era that is still known as Louis Quatorze. This was the era that witnessed the great glories of Versailles and an extraordinary flowering of the applied and decorative arts, from Gobelins tapestries to Sèvres porcelain. The era of Louis XIV would become almost synonymous with the age of the Baroque.

In the fine arts, France had lagged behind both Italy and Spain. Since the time of Jean Fouquet in the fifteenth century there had been little of note in French painting, other than the Clouets, father and son. Jehan Clouet (c. 1483–1541) hailed from Flanders and was successively painter to the Duke of Burgundy and François I of France. His skills as a portraitist were exceeded by those of his son François

Nicolas Poussin, The Triumph of David

(c. 1516–72). Best remembered for his extraordinary portraits of Charles IX, Elizabeth of Austria and Mary, Queen of Scots, François also painted the remarkable *Lady in her Bath* (possibly the royal mistress, Diane de Poitiers), which betrays the influence of the Mannerists. There was no continuity such as existed in Italy at the same period, and the artists who emerged in the seventeenth century received their training elsewhere, or were influenced by the art of other countries. Simon Vouet (1580–1649) appears to have been self-taught, an infant prodigy whose skills by the age of 14 led to many international commissions which took him to England, Constantinople and Italy, where he worked in Venice, Florence and Genoa before being summoned by Louis XIII back to Paris in 1628. For the last 20 years of his life he ruled the French art establishment and although his own pictures are not highly appreciated nowadays, he had a tremendous influence on the development of French painting, not least on the work of Nicolas Poussin (1594–1665), who was only four years his junior. Poussin covered a wide range, from allegorical, classical and bacchanalian scenes in the first half of his career to great religious, heroic, historic and architectural subjects in his later years. Towards the end of his career (1648) he took up landscape painting. Poussin was precise and meticulous, every brushstroke clearly thought out, never indulging in whim and leaving nothing to chance. Not surprisingly, Poussin laid down the strict principles that would be slavishly followed by the Royal Academy of Painting and Sculpture (founded in 1648) until the closing years of the nineteenth century. By contrast, Claude Lorraine (1600–82) is classed as a French painter solely on grounds of birth, but early in his career he settled in Rome and spent most of his life there. Yet his landscapes were painted in a distinctive style that stands apart from the Roman manner. Regrettably, the demands of Louis XIV for colossal paintings designed to record the glories of France and depict the Sun King in the most heroic light did not inspire great or original painting.

The Flemish School

The marriage in 1495 of Joanna of Castile and Philip of Burgundy at Antwerp, and the birth of their son, the future Holy Roman Emperor Charles V, gave Spain control of the Netherlands. In 1579 the seven

predominantly Protestant provinces proclaimed their independence and became a republic, although they remained under the control of a hereditary Stadholder, the Prince of Orange. While the remaining provinces (later known as the Austrian Netherlands and now Belgium) declined in importance, the United Provinces became one of the leading maritime powers of the seventeenth century. Amsterdam and Rotterdam took over from Antwerp and Brussels as great trading centres, and the arts flourished accordingly.

Peter Paul Rubens (1577–1640) was born in Westphalia but was educated in Antwerp and throughout his life remained loyal to the Habsburg connection. A man of many talents, he was a scholar, antiquarian and career diplomat as well as one of the greatest European painters of all time. He was a devout Catholic and supporter of the Habsburgs and his greatest diplomatic achievement was the peace treaty he negotiated between Spain and England. It was as a result of his diplomatic activity that he was able to paint so many portraits in both Madrid and London, not to mention the extraordinary series of 21 large canvasses showing the life and times of Marie di Medici, Queen of France. An artist of the widest range, he was equally at home in intimate portraits and colossal heroic scenes and in his Antwerp studio he made use of a large number of pupils and assistants, including Anthony Van Dyck (1599–1641), Jacob Jordaens (1593–1678) and Frans Snyders (1579–1657); his influence on the later Flemish School was profound and long-lasting. Nor should it be overlooked that his style had a tremendous impact on such French painters as Eugène Delacroix (1798–1863) and Jean-Antoine Watteau (1684–1721).

Van Dyck was born at Antwerp and closely emulated the style of his master. Like Rubens, Van Dyck excelled as a portraitist and is best known for his magnificent paintings of Charles I and other members of the British royal family, as well as English nobles and celebrities of the early seventeenth century. In turn, Van Dyck exerted an enormous influence on the English portraitists, notably Thomas Gainsborough (1727–88).

The Dutch School

Long before the Dutch School emerged in all its glory, there were precursors whose originality and independence of mind set them apart from the main Flemish School. In this group may be named such painters as Lucas Van Leyden (1494–1533), whose portraits were boldly innovative, and Gerard de St Jean (c. 1465–93), a self-taught artist whose naïve religious paintings anticipate the Primitives of a much later period. But what led to a pronounced dichotomy between the older Flemish School and the emerging Dutch School were the social, political and religious differences that came in the wake of the Reformation.

The Reformers were iconoclasts who abhorred religious imagery of any kind. For this reason art was diverted from the religious subjects that dominated even secular painting in Catholic countries, and resulted in pictures that extolled the Christian virtues in a more subtle, natural manner. Dutch painters were free to indulge their passion for realism, constrained solely by what appealed to the increasingly wealthy middle classes. The rising bankers, merchants, manufacturers and ship-owners of Holland did not live in large palaces surrounded by opulence, but in relatively modest houses, which explains why Dutch paintings of the seventeenth century were generally small in scale. Despite this, there was still a vogue for large canvasses, commissioned by the wealthy guilds and corporations as well as the numerous paramilitary volunteer groups which stemmed from the protracted wars of independence. The personal element in Dutch painting ensured that portraiture assumed paramount importance. It is a singular fact that all the great Dutch masters were portraitists, first and foremost. Frans Hals (c. 1580–1666), a native of Antwerp who spent most of his life in Haarlem, is unusual in that he rarely painted anything else, although his work ranged from small individual portraits to those large militia groups that were a purely Dutch phenomenon.

The early Dutch masters reacted against the Mannerists and the religious painters by concentrating on genre scenes and landscapes. The artists in Haarlem who learned their trade from Frans Hals included

Anthony Van Dyck, Self Portrait with a Sunflower

Adriaen Brouwer (c. 1606–38), who specialized in genre subjects of a decidedly earthy, off-colour and sometimes downright vulgar character, which may be regarded as a healthy reaction against the extreme Calvinism of the period. Adriaen Van Ostade (1610–85) worked primarily as an etcher and watercolour artist, although he also executed a number of fine oil paintings. Like Brouwer, he had a penchant for Rabelaisian comedy, tinged in his case with satire, though his more serious work extolled the virtues of the peasantry. His pupil Jan Steen (1626–79) produced his own special brand of genre paintings, comic scenes of dysfunctional families in their disorderly homes – immensely popular with the Dutch who, in their own lives, were models of cleanliness and order.

Towering over all the others, however, is Rembrandt Van Rijn (1606–69), a native of Leyden who settled in Amsterdam at a time when that port was emerging as the most prosperous city in the Netherlands and the nation's commercial capital. Rembrandt was schooled by his master, Peter Lastman (1583–1633), in the traditions of the High Renaissance, but soon established his own distinctive style. Rembrandt was unusual in the Holland of his day in that he continued to paint large religious scenes long after they had fallen out of favour. Although he never went to Rome, he studied prints of the best classical works and in this manner imbibed the techniques of light and shade pioneered by Caravaggio. To his religious, mythological and historical subjects he brought a new realism, and these works are now regarded as his greatest masterpieces. In his own lifetime, however, what earned his daily bread were the portraits of individuals and groups. Even as the commissions dried up, Rembrandt continued to paint self-portraits and portraits of his family, including imaginary portraits derived from history or mythology. Like Dürer, he was also a prolific draughtsman who left a rich legacy of etchings and prints.

The generation of Dutch masters that followed Rembrandt was also noted for portraiture, but by the middle of the seventeenth century the prevailing fashion was for landscapes and domestic interiors – the sort of pictures that the Dutch bourgeoisie preferred to hang on their walls. The transition from the bonhomie of the militia groups and genre paintings of tavern scenes was almost imperceptible at first, Gerard Terborch (1617–81) having switched effortlessly from one to the other. Carel Fabritius (1622–54) was a pupil of Rembrandt who produced some unusual pictures which, in effect, combined still-life with landscape. The sort of pictorial geometry that delighted Fabritius also exercised painters like Samuel Van Hoogstraten (1627–78) and Pieter de Hooch (1629–84), the latter using this to good advantage in his domestic interiors, handling perspective with considerable skill. Jan Vermeer (1632–75) likewise specialized in domestic interiors of such precision that it has been speculated that he employed some form of camera obscura. The resulting paintings are highly objective, but lack feeling or passion, and their realism is counterbalanced by the lack of variety in texture and tone.

The Dutch painters, however, invented a style of art that had no motive beyond the precise reproduction of inanimate objects which had never excited any interest previously. These studies of still-life were generally small; they became very popular from the 1630s onwards and gave rise to a sub-school of Dutch painters who produced little else. In time the still-life was subdivided into distinct categories, so that there were artists who specialized in vases of flowers, dead fish or game, breakfast or banqueting compositions. Still others consisted of the careful juxtaposition of objects thath had some symbolic connotation. A popular theme, for example, was mortality, hence those pictures of human skulls and hour-glasses as a constant reminder that time was running out. Arrangements of crowns and jewels might symbolize the vanity inherent in the lust for wealth or power. Books and musical instruments were also popular subjects for pictures with a moral undertone. There were many exponents of still-life painting, but the most interesting works were produced by Davidsz de Heem (1606–83), whose use of a limited range of sombre colours emphasized the austerity of his subjects and emulated the work of Pieter Claesz (c. 1596–1661). Jan van Huysum (1682–1749) was a later exponent of the virtually monochrome still-life which at times veered towards the abstract. De Heem, however, later moved to Antwerp, where he was swept up in the Baroque fashion and switched to lavish still-life paintings, rich in colour and profuse in subject matter.

The Dutch painters were noted for their landscapes, and so diverse were the styles and their exponents that there was a tendency to specialize. Thus Aelbert Cuyp (1620–91) at Dordrecht and Jacob Van Ruysdael (c. 1628–82) from Haarlem produced vast landscapes that relied heavily on clouds and unusual lighting effects. Van Ruysdael's works often depicted rugged mountains in the background which, considering where he spent all his life, must have been largely a figment of his imagination. Cuyp's trademark was to depict cattle, sometimes individual cows but often herds, in the foreground. Other artists, such as Pieter Molijn (1595–1661) and Jan van Goyen (1596–1656), concentrated on seascapes and riverbanks, or placid views along the numerous canals of Holland. Jan Porcellis (*c.* 1584–1632) went a step further by creating dramatic stormy scenes in which ships featured prominently. Marine pictures became immensely popular later in the seventeenth century, reflecting national pride in the Dutch East India Company, which brought the wealth of the Indies and the Far East to Holland. Specialists in this medium included Willem Van de Velde the Younger (1633–1707), who painted particular ships and had a high reputation for pictures showing naval engagements.

Baroque Painting

The Baroque movement which swept across the rest of Europe in the seventeenth century was a marked contrast to the homely styles evolved by the Dutch School. It arose initially as a reaction against Mannerism in painting and sculpture and was triggered by the Caravaggisti, the followers of Caravaggio who were inspired by his dramatic naturalism. At its best, the Baroque style of painting resulted in a riot of colour which appealed to the emotions rather than the intellect. The Baroque style was extensively used in architecture and every aspect of the applied and decorative arts, and as such had an enormous impact which survives to this day. Significantly, many of the finest paintings in this manner were architectural in concept. Elaborate architectural forms can be seen in the great frescoes of Pietro da Cortona (1596–1669) and, most of all, in the illusionistic ceilings and murals of Andrea Pozzo (1642–1709). The finest exponent of the Baroque at its most extravagant was Gianlorenzo Bernini (1598–1680), the most accomplished master of all the artifice and illusionistic tricks. He was first and foremost an architect and sculptor, but he succeeded admirably in translating the three-dimensional to the two dimensions of painting and, by the clever use of lighting and perspective, creating masterpieces that seem to leap off the surface. Painting was also combined with stucco work to heighten the three-dimensional effect.

Elsewhere, there were many practitioners of the Baroque, but because of the sheer flamboyance of the style and the criticism heaped upon it in later periods, they have often been overlooked. In France, Baroque ideas fitted very neatly with the grandiose views held by Louis XIV, interpreted competently by such prolific painters as Hyacinthe Rigaud (1659–1743) and Nicolas de Largillière (1656–1746). Spanish painting of the comparable period, however, was so totally dominated by Velázquez, de Zurbarán and Murillo, that the Baroque style received short shrift. It made little impact on painting, though a noteworthy exception is the *Transparente* in Toledo Cathedral by Narciso Tomé

(*c.* 1690–1742), which echoes Bernini in its combination of stucco and painting. Baroque, in fact, was a style most closely associated with architectural painting and lent itself particularly to the huge ceilings of palaces. Good examples are to be found as far afield as the Banqueting Hall in Whitehall, London (painted by Rubens), and Drottningholm Palace, Stockholm (painted by David Klöcker Ehrenstrahl) appropriately entitled *Great Deeds of the Swedish Kings*.

Rococo Style

The term Rococo was derived from the French word *rocaille*, signifying the rockery and shell work which became immensely popular in sunken gardens, dells and grottoes in the late seventeenth and early eighteenth centuries. Indeed, a spin-off from the same movement was the Grotesque (literally pertaining to caves and grottoes). Just as the craze for all things Baroque swept across Europe like a plague, so also the fashion for Rococo assumed epidemic proportions. It manifested itself primarily in architecture and furniture, but soon extended to silver, glass, ceramics and all the minor decorative arts. Asymmetry was the key, with profuse application of scrollwork and curvilinear ornament. It fitted the mood of frivolity and gaiety that affected many countries during this period. On mainland Europe it mirrored the economic recovery after the long-term debilitating effects of the Thirty Years' War (1618–48), and in Britain it was a fitting climax to a liberalization in the arts that had begun with the Restoration of the monarchy in 1660 and attained its greatest heights in the reign of Queen Anne (1702–14).

More specifically Rococo developed in France in the closing years of the seventeenth century, when many of the noble families began to drift back to Paris from Versailles as the Sun King lost his brightness. The process was accelerated after the death of Louis XIV when the royal court no longer seemed to be the centre of the world. The aristocracy who built their villas and town houses in Paris laid out gardens to match, and it was in the artificial creation of 'natural' features such as dells and grottoes that the fashion for the Rococo developed.

The first painter to catch the spirit of the Rococo in a big way was Watteau, who neatly encapsulated all the wit, grace and elegance of the early eighteenth century – a time when France was the unchallenged arbiter of taste throughout the Continent. His paintings were neatly attuned to the boudoirs and salons of the aristocracy, in marked contrast to the great Baroque extravaganzas required for the grand palaces of Louis XIV. Watteau's paintings are frothy confections of light and colour, although towards the end of his very short life there is often an underlying air of melancholy, perhaps a premonition of the death from tuberculosis that lay ahead. He was an innovator whose *Fêtes galantes* ('pastoral scenes') reflected the obsession with rusticity when even the French royal family played at shepherds and shepherdesses. The delicacy of his brushwork was well-suited to subjects which were play-acting and pure fantasy, but underlying this was a keen observation of the ordinary and an uncanny feeling for human nature. He had a number of pupils and imitators, such as Nicolas Lancret (1690–1743) and Bonaventure de Bar, who did not take his style further but who enjoyed a certain vogue due to their lyrical quality, even if they seldom found their way beneath the surface as Watteau had done.

François Boucher (1703–70) was the leading French Rococo artist of the next generation. Compared with Boucher, Watteau seems a master of restraint, for the younger man created paintings which were a riot of colour, whose exuberance matched the extravagance of the subject. If there was an innocence about Watteau's *Fêtes galantes*, there was a much more sensual character to Boucher's bacchanals, derived from Classical mythology and therefore invariably executed in the best possible taste. Pink nudes suffused with golden light, cavorting all over the canvas, were perfectly acceptable so long as it was clear that they were classical gods and goddesses and not meant to represent real human beings. Under the patronage of Madame de Pompadour (the mistress of Louis XV) Boucher produced his greatest masterpieces dealing allegorically with the rising and setting of the sun, but there is no denying the eroticism of such paintings as *Odalisque*.

Significantly, interest in the Rococo style evaporated in France following the death of Madame de Pompadour in 1764, although it enjoyed a brief resurgence in the paintings of Jean-Honoré Fragonard (1732–1806). Early in his career he had copied the paintings of Boucher and the best of his later work was very much in the same style, even if the eroticism was generally more subtle as befitted the less licentious atmosphere in the reign of the worthy but dull Louis XVI who, along with his wife Marie Antoinette, were chief among Fragonard's patrons. In the 1770s and 1780s, the Rococo element in Fragonard's paintings was gradually replaced by something more sentimental.

Elsewhere, the great centre of Rococo art was Italy, where the style was nicely attuned to the lighter aspects of the Grand Tour. Italy in the eighteenth century had ceased to be a major player on the world commercial scene. Many of the great palaces and public buildings that had been erected in the heyday of the merchant princes and powerful prelates were now in decay, if not total ruin. Giovanni Battista Piranesi (1720–78) made a good living from his picturesque scenes of Roman ruins, although there was also a dark side to his art – the very antithesis of the Rococo – in his nightmarish visions, which were probably drug-induced. For Italianate Rococo at its frothiest we must turn instead to the ceilings and frescoes of Giovanni Battista Tiepolo (1696–1770). Elegance, lightness and grace are personified in the glorious decorations which he executed for the churches and palaces of his native Venice, as well as further afield all over northern Italy, southern Germany and latterly in Spain. However, Tiepolo was a deeply religious man who never strayed over the boundaries of decorum. His cherubim and putti may frolic all over the place but they are innocent and sexless. He also painted a number of large historical works derived from events of the Middle Ages but invariably (and rather incongruously) executed in the Rococo style. His brother-in-law, Francesco Guardi (1712–93), shows some affinity with the Rococo in his paintings, but this is more evident in the form than the content, for his forte was the urban landscape of Venice, a medium in which he was second only to Antonio Canaletto (1697–1768). While Canaletto travelled to England and produced some of the finest eighteenth-century paintings in London, his nephew Bernardo Bellotto (1720–80) went to

François Boucher, *La Cible D'Amour (Love Target)*

Poland where he introduced a late flowering of the Rococo to Warsaw in the dying years of the Polish kingdom. Many of his architectural paintings served as the basis for the meticulous post-war restoration of the Polish capital after its wholesale destruction in 1944.

French Academicism

There was a more serious side to the art of the eighteenth century, exemplified by Jean-Baptiste Chardin (1699–1779). Although in some respects one of the pedestrians of the French academic tradition, who spent much of his career as a sign-writer but who also worked on the restoration of the royal paintings at Fontainebleau, Chardin had his moments of glory. In 1728 he made his debut at the Academy with two large still-lifes which combined richness of colour and subtlety of draughtsmanship with a feeling of intimacy but, above all else, a lyric quality, a sense of rejoicing in the humble things of everyday life. These canvasses were a hint of things to come; Chardin would go on to paint

Art

pictures of peasant and domestic scenes imbued with charm and integrity. His pictures were wholesome but unpretentious and foreshadowedg the paintings of Jean-Baptiste Camille Corot (1796–1875) more than a century later. In the next generation this example would be taken up by Jean-Baptiste Greuze (1725–1805). In the first half of his career Greuze concentrated on historical subjects, but after visiting Rome in 1755 he switched to genre subjects, mainly featuring young women and often with an underlying edge of satire which redeemed his more sentimental works teetering on the edge of mawkishness.

The English School

Greuze is sometimes compared unfavourably with William Hogarth (1697–1764), an English engraver who turned to portrait painting but achieved renown with his great moral and satirical works, crammed

with detail and subtexts. Hogarth visited Paris in 1743 and thereafter concentrated on genre subjects drawn from low life. Hogarth, in fact, was the first great English indigenous painter. Britain, on the edge of Europe, produced very few painters of any eminence in earlier periods. Instead, the court and nobility relied on European artists to fill the gap. To Holbein, Mora, Rubens and Van Dyck may be added Pieter van der Faes (1618–80) and Gottfried Kniller (1646–1723), who anglicized their names as Peter Lely and Godfrey Kneller respectively.

Sir Anthony Van Dyck, ennobled by Charles I, may be regarded as the father of the English School. As Van Dyck was first and foremost a portraitist, it was in the realm of portraiture that the British artists excelled. The Reformation deprived them of the rich field of religious subjects, but Classical mythology was little known or understood in Britain and thus did not fill the gap. Like the Dutch, the British painters concentrated on portraits, followed by landscapes and genre subjects. Whereas the Dutch also perfected the intimate street scene and the small domestic interior, the British did not diversify from portraiture until relatively late in the eighteenth century. Nevertheless, artists of the calibre of Allan Ramsay (1713–84), Sir Joshua Reynolds (1723–92), George Romney (1734–1802), Sir Henry Raeburn (1756–1823) and Sir Thomas Lawrence (1769–1830), as well as Gainsborough, raised the art of portraiture to new levels. Gainsborough alone in this group was equally versatile as a landscape painter, and established the pattern later followed

William Hogarth, Beggars Opera

by John Constable (1776–1837) and J. M. W. Turner (1775–1851). Although lacking the formal guidance provided on the Continent by the guilds of St Luke and the various academies, the foundation of the Royal Academy in 1768 placed the English School on a proper footing at last. It should be noted that attempts to establish an Academy of St Luke in Edinburgh were short-lived and Scottish artists such as Ramsay and Raeburn gained their training, and to a large extent earned their living, in England.

Neoclassicism

In 1755 archeologists unearthed the ruins of Herculaneum and Pompeii, which had been engulfed by lava from Mount Etna in AD 79, and electrified the world by the beauty and naturalism of the mosaics and frescoes thus brought to light. Archeology was then in its infancy, but the notion of lost civilizations that lay just below the surface of the modern world fired the popular and artistic imagination. Johann Winckelmann (1717–68) studied theology then medicine before turning to art history, and it was while working as a librarian in Rome that he was inspired by the discoveries at Pompeii to embark on his great *History of the Art of Antiquity* (1764), which had a tremendous impact on the art world throughout the later years of the eighteenth century and right through the nineteenth century.

The first artist to exploit this resurgent interest in Classical subjects was J. M. Vien (1716–1809), whose paintings *Marchandes d'Amour* and *Belisaires* excited favourable comment. He and his pupils, Vincent and Regnault, took to heart Winckelmann's famous dictum that beauty depended on calmness, simplicity and correct proportion, exemplified in Greek sculpture. These qualities were the direct opposite of Rococo and the reaction against its excesses resulted in the great movement known as Neoclassicism.

Its finest exponent was another pupil of Vien, Jacques-Louis David (1748–1825). Ironically, he gained little from studying under Vien but was inspired by the writings of Quatremère de Quincy, who seized on Winckelmann's doctrine and expanded it for the benefit of his French audience. Greek painting of the Classical period had long since vanished but de Quincy urged French painters to study Greek statuary, and for this reason the earliest works by David and his contemporaries have a rather static appearance. Thus David's great painting *The Oath of the Horatii* (1785) bears an uncanny resemblance to a Classical bas-relief in which form triumphs over colour. It was an immediate sensation, whose vigour and austerity were hailed as shining examples of all that was best in 'republican virtues'. What was meant, of course, was the ideals of the Roman Republic, but the term would soon have an unfortunate resonance for France as the country was plunged into revolution. When the French Revolution erupted David shot to the top of the new artistic establishment, abolished the Academy and even designed a revolutionary uniform based on Classical lines. When Charlotte Corday stabbed Jean Paul Marat in his bath-tub, creating the first great martyr of the Revolution, David hastened to the gory scene to capture it in oils. His *Death of Marat* evoked patriotism in the highest Roman republican ideal, painted with noble simplicity in the best Classical tradition.

Ironically, the man who dictated the doctrinaire precepts of the new republican art ultimately found himself in prison, as the Revolution took an uglier twist, but he survived the ordeal and was restored to favour under Napoleon Bonaparte. In this period he concentrated on portraiture, his great masterpiece being *The Coronation of Napoleon I* (1804). Driven into exile after the decisive Battle of Waterloo, he spent the last years of his life in Belgium, where he helped found the Belgian School, which reached maturity just as Belgium won its independence from Holland in 1831. In France, David strongly influenced Pierre Narcisse Guérin (1774–1833), a Neoclassicist who outdid even David in his sense of the melodramatic. Both Guérin and Antoine Jean Gros (1771–1835) became pillars of the French art establishment and received peerages in recognition of their achievement. Guérin passed on his Neoclassicist principles to Théodore Géricault (1791–1824) and Delacroix, but they, like their master, later turned to Romanticism, unlike poor Baron Gros, whose attempts to keep Classicism alive led to his work being ignored – an unhappy situation that drove him to suicide. Infinitely more successful in fighting the rearguard action on behalf of Classicism was Jean-Auguste-Dominique Ingres (1780–1867), who studied under David and regarded himself as the custodian of the Davidian tradition. He succeeded because he strove towards a greater purity and in so doing created a style of expression that was all his own. But he was sometimes accused of being 'Gothic' or even 'Chinese', and he waged an artistic duel with Delacroix that lasted for many years. Ironically, Ingres did what Gros failed to do, and eventually moved with the times, producing portraits – thoroughly modern in their realism – of the self-satisfied upper middle classes of the Second Empire when he was in his eighties.

The chief exponent of Neoclassicism in Germany itself was Anton Raffael Mengs (1728–79), who painted religious and historical subjects conveying the restrained emotions and heroic style of the neo-classical period (working as a painter to the royal courts of Saxony, Poland, Naples and Spain). Mengs lacked the passion and patriotic fervour of David, but in the last years of his life he worked in Madrid, where he created the great *Apotheosis of the Emperor Trajan* for the dome of the grand salon in the Escorial. Perhaps his greatest contribution to the development of European art was the fact that he taught Francisco Goya (1764–1828). It should be noted that Goya, the spiritual heir of Velázquez, was very much his own man, who derived inspiration and technique from many sources and refashioned them in his own inimitable style, and it is significant that whatever Neoclassicism he had imbibed from Mengs was quickly subsumed in the extremely versatile range of Goya's output. The last of the great eighteenth-century painters, he was also the father of nineteenth-century art and the precursor of modern art.

The Age of Reason

A second Renaissance occurred in the middle of the eighteenth century, dominated by the pursuit of truth and knowledge. An entirely new, scientific approach was applied to every discipline. Archeology replaced the vague antiquarian pursuits of previous generations and led to a reappraisal of history. Mathematics, physics, chemistry, astronomy, biology, philosophy, logic, politics and economics were put under the spotlight of rational thought. This intellectual revolution went hand in hand with a technological revolution, as steam mechanized industry and soon transformed communications. The Age of Reason was therefore also the Age of Steam, of the industrial and agrarian revolutions and ultimately the overturning of long-accepted systems of government.

It was inevitable that these intellectual and technological upheavals should have a profound effect on the fine arts. Perhaps because Britain was at the cutting edge of the Industrial Revolution, it tended to be British artists who led the way. The prime example of an artist who revelled in the wonders of the Industrial Revolution was Joseph Wright of Derby (1734–97). Although an accomplished portraitist and painter of genre scenes, his reputation was secured by his exploration of – indeed revelling in – the great mechanical wonders of the age that were rapidly transforming the way that people lived and worked. Wright was also brilliant in his handling of artificial light, which considerably enhanced his treatment of the industrial subjects he drew from his environment. Other painters applied scientific procedures in furthering their art. George Stubbs (1724–1806) was not the first artist by any means to study anatomy as a prelude to painting human or animal subjects, but few artists went to the extremes of endlessly dissecting carcasses as he did, in order to impart greater realism to his work.

Even if he had acquired the most perfect knowledge of equine anatomy, Stubbs could not have produced such wonderful paintings had he not also possessed a powerful imagination. It was this attribute that marked out a number of other artists active in the second half of the eighteenth century and, letting their imagination, reveries and dreams run riot, they created some of the most extraordinary paintings of that or any other period. Many of the great symphonies of light and colour painted by Turner were in the latter part of his career, when he was becoming increasingly reclusive. In these paintings Turner used paint to recreate the effects of light, which was in turn used to convey the moods associated with his increasingly pessimistic vision of the world, as in *The Slave Ship* (1840).

Paradoxically, therefore, the Age of Reason also produced great paintings that seemed devoid of reason. Long before the time of Freudian psychoanalytical technique, painters were attempting to interpret their dreams and nightmares and record them on canvas. Henry Fuseli (1741–1825) was born in Switzerland, worked in England as a translator (1763–70) then studied painting in Italy (1770–78) before returning to London. Although best remembered for the two series of paintings illustrating the works of Milton and Shakespeare, he painted *The Nightmare* (1781), a truly disturbing work with its overtones of sexuality, sadism and death. It was the precursor of many other works that explored the deepest and darkest recesses of the mind. It was rumoured that Fuseli ate or drank certain substances to make his consciousness more receptive to these horrific images. He may therefore have been the first – but certainly not the last – artist to resort to drugs to conjure up the lurid or the psychedelic as the basis of their paintings.

There were also mystics and visionaries who rejected the theories of rational thought altogether and strongly objected to the scientists and mathematicians who would reduce everything to geometric principles. Foremost among the rebels against Reason was William Blake (1757–1827). Blake was essentially a poet, but he was also a competent engraver and illustrator. As a poet, he fought long and hard against the tyranny of rationalism and materialism and championed the freedom of the imagination, which eventually found expression in the 537 coloured illustrations that he produced for Edward Young's *Night Thoughts* (1797), as well as a number of individual works, such as *The Marriage of Heaven and Hell* (1791).

Blake inspired a veritable army of followers and imitators whose work carried on well into the nineteenth century and, in turn, influenced some of the artistic developments that come, broadly speaking, under the heading of the Romantic movement. John Martin (1789–1854) produced some highly disturbing images, charged with passion, in his illustrations for Milton's *Paradise Lost*. At one end of the spectrum was Samuel Palmer (1805–81), whose visionary paintings were ultimately more accessible (and therefore more successful) than Blake's because he managed to effect a compromise between an inner mystical vision and the external reality of nature. Furthermore, in an age when conformity was the watchword, eccentricity and idiosyncrasy in art might so easily be regarded as evidence of a deranged mind. In the nineteenth century there would be all too many examples of artists – from Richard Dadd to Louis Wain, from Vincent Van Gogh to Edvard Munch – who were mentally disturbed to a greater or lesser degree. In spite of, or perhaps because of, their affliction some of them at least would produce great art.

Romanticism

The year 1815 was one of the great watersheds of history. The defeat of Napoleon at Waterloo brought to an end his dreams of a European order, but the Congress of Vienna did not entirely turn back the clock. The archaic Holy Roman Empire disappeared, and in its place emerged new nation states. However, Belgium and Holland were forced into an uneasy union which would eventually be dissolved, while the struggle between Austria and Prussia for supremacy in the German-speaking world would be a source of instability in Central Europe. The unification of petty states to form Germany and Italy was a violent process spread over many years. Europe was engulfed by revolutions in 1848–49, but the only major continental conflict to involve Britain between 1815 and 1914 was the Crimean War (1853–56), a relatively localized campaign, while the wars with Denmark (1864), Austria (1866) and France (1870–71) which charted the rise of Prussia and the formation of the German Empire, were short-lived.

The period was one of relative peace and enormous material progress. Britain had a head start, being at the forefront of the Industrial Revolution. Britain took the raw materials from a third of the world and converted them into manufactured goods which were then exported to every country. The population and material wealth of the United Kingdom expanded out of all recognition throughout the nineteenth century. The fine arts flourished in Britain as never before, and for a time a country that had hitherto been on the fringes of artistic development now took on a more prominent role. Yet France, despite the demoralizing effects of defeat in 1815 and 1871, and punctuated by revolution and political instability in the intervening period, continued to be the centre of Western art in the widest sense, and Paris the Mecca that drew aspiring artists from every part of Europe and, increasingly, from the New World.

Thus it was in France that most of the great nineteenth-century art movements had their origins and their greatest exponents although, significantly, most of the others began in England. Neoclassicism was already on the wane when Napoleon commissioned large paintings – heroic in scale and content – to chronicle his imperial exploits. Confronted by the harsh reality of modern warfare, even a convinced Neoclassicist like Gros could not help depicting *The Plague House at Jaffa* (1804) as it really was; full of emaciated, dying men. But the artist who led the revolt against the Neoclassicism of David was Pierre Paul Prud'hon (1758–1823). Having trained at Dijon, he worked in Rome and thus was absent from France during the revolutionary period. He only returned to the latter part of the Empire when his skill as a portraitist brought him the patronage of Napoleon's empresses. He shared David's fascination for Classical sculpture without demonstrating David's dogmatism, and in his great allegorical works – noted for their rich colours, fluid composition and exquisite charm – he led the return to a style akin to that which was popular under the Ancien Régime, yet invested with a freshness that foreshadowed the Romantics.

François Gérard (1770–1837) was a pupil of David who started out as a staunch upholder of art in the service of the Revolution but who ended his career as a baron under Louis XVIII. His *Cupid and Psyche* (1798) is in the Neoclassicist mould, but relieved by an elegance that was quite distinctive. In contrast, his epic canvas of the *Battle of Austerlitz* (1808) was only one of several large works that marked a return to a more realistic approach. Paul Delaroche (1797–1856) was a pupil of Gros, from whom he learned the technique of executing vast historical canvasses. Apart from his murals for the École des Beaux-Arts, where he was a professor, he is chiefly noted for dramatic scenes from English history, such as *The Death of Queen Elizabeth* (1828) and *The Execution of Lady Jane Grey* (1834).

Géricault is another interesting artist who marks the transition from the rigidity of Neoclassicism to the flights of fancy characteristic of the Romantics. Though trained in the style of David, he was also influenced by the Flemish School and showed considerable originality, not to say unorthodoxy, in a number of paintings, notably the *Raft of the 'Medusa'* (1819). In this painting Géricault portrays the true and horrific story of the shipwreck of La Méduse. Nowadays this is regarded as one of those great seminal works that mark a turning point; here are realism and Romanticism wonderfully fused, a splendid example of inspiration at its loftiest. But it was greeted with outrage and vehement criticism which drove the artist into exile in England. Gérard and Géricault were the role models for Delacroix, one of the most intellectual artists of his generation, whose *Journal* provides a rare insight into his attitudes towards art in general as well as a careful analysis of his own and other painters' efforts.

Delacroix made his debut at the Salon of 1824 (the Salon was the name given to the official exhibition of members of the French Royal Academy of Painting and Sculpture) with *The Massacre at Chios*, an action-packed canvas alluding to an incident in the Greek struggle for independence, then at its height. Between this work and his great masterpiece, *The Taking of Constantinople by the Crusaders in 1204*, exhibited in 1840, Delacroix established himself as the undisputed champion of Romanticism. Unlike most other French painters of his generation, he drew on the great writers of English literature for inspiration, from Shakespeare to Byron and Scott. It may be said that while Delacroix never repudiated his Classicist origins, there was much of the Romantic in Ingres. In fact, their differences lay rather in their approach and individual character: the one instinctive where the other was intellectual, the former more concerned with form and the latter more interested in dramatic expression.

Théodore Géricault, Homme Nu a Mi-Corps Man

The Barbizon School

One aspect of the Romantics that hardly ever arose in earlier art movements in France was an interest in landscape for its own sake. This arose in the closing period of the Revolution, although it did not attain maturity for several decades after this, in the hands of a group of painters who were only born in the last years of the First Empire. The eldest of this group was Alexandre Gabriel Decamps (1803–60), a leading Romantic and a great colourist who specialized in Oriental scenery and biblical subjects and who broke new ground with his evocative landscape entitled *The Watering Place*. Jules Dupré (1811–89) studied in England under John Constable and went on to become one of the leaders of the Barbizon School. Théodore Rousseau (1812–67) had a conventional academic training but by 1833 was sketching from nature in the forest of Fontainebleau. Although he had a measure of success with his *Forest of Compiegne* (1834) he endured more than a decade of disappointment. In the 1840s he settled in the village of Barbizon, where he helped to found a colony of like-minded artists.

Unlike most of his colleagues, Jean-François Millet (1814–75) actually came from a peasant background and grew up with an appreciation of nature, while living and working with his father in a small farm at Gruchy, and he received his art education not in Paris or one of the other major centres but at Cherbourg. He continued his studies in Paris before settling in Barbizon and producing such works as *Peasants Grafting* (1855) and *The Gleaners* (1857). Masterpieces of social realism, they were regarded at the time as politically subversive for daring to treat peasants as noble subjects.

Charles François Daubigny (1817–78) specialized in moonlight scenes and river landscapes, of which his *Banks of the Oise* (1872) is a typical example. Constant Troyon (1810–65) injected interest into his landscapes by including animals. What the Barbizon painters had in

common, apart from their fascination with landscape, was a desire to represent nature in every aspect, from the awesome to the mundane and ordinary.

Although he also worked at Barbizon for many years, Camille Corot (1796–1875) differed quite radically from the other artists associated with this district. Corot by virtue of his training was more of a Classicist, interested in landscape only in so far as it served his purpose in achieving a harmony between sky and trees, the play of light and the composition of figures in the foreground. Corot, in fact, stood apart from the Romantics and anticipated the Impressionists.

Jean-François Millet, La Cardeuse

Naturalism and Realism

Millet's paintings of peasant subjects broke new ground and triggered a movement in France that combined naturalism with realism in order to make a statement with political undertones. France in the period of the Second Empire was still coming to grips with industrialization and the drift of the peasantry from the land to the burgeoning industrial towns. It was a period of great deprivation and social injustice. What Emile Zola and Victor Hugo achieved through their polemical novels, artists such as Gustave Courbet (1819–77) and Honoré Daumier (1810–79) sought to create through their paintings. Courbet believed that the common people

were the only true custodians of real values and simple truths, a viewpoint perhaps that comes across very vividly in the vigour and passion of his pictures. Not surprisingly, Courbet was severely criticized and reviled for coarseness and vulgarity when his paintings were exhibited at the Salon. Undaunted, Courbet persevered, and his later canvasses became even more dedicated to putting across his notions of primitive socialism. True to his principles, he took an active part in the ill-starred Paris Commune of 1870–71. Daumier went much further, neatly avoiding the cloying sentimentality that occasionally reduced the paintings of Corot and Millet to mawkishness. His chief forte was the lithograph, a medium that he used extremely effectively to put across his satirical and often savage comment on the ills of society. After the Revolution of 1848 he took up painting, and became increasingly strident in his attacks on the corruption and hypocrisy of the bourgeoisie after Louis Napoleon seized power. He was too satirical to be regarded as a Naturalist, but his use of Realism as social comment has never been surpassed.

Offshoots of Romanticism

Although France dominated the Romantic movement, as it had done Neoclassicism, it had its counterparts in other parts of Europe. The German artist Caspar David Friedrich (1774–1840) is usually regarded as belonging to this movement, although there was a fundamental difference between the French Romantics, who tended to regard nature as a substitute for God, and Friedrich, who saw painting as a medium for worshipping God. His preference was for grandeur of lofty and rugged mountains and wild places, invariably painted by moonlight or at dawn or sunset in order to make the most of the special effects of the sun's rays. He was something of a loner, supremely confident in his own talents without the need to seek out like-minded artists from whom he might learn, or to whom he could impart his ideas. To be sure, there was a group of German painters who sought a spiritual aspect to their work, but they were expatriates, working in Rome, where they formed a quasi-monastic order known as the Brotherhood of St Luke. This group was founded by Friedrich Overbeck (1789–1869) and Franz Pforr (1788–1812) as a reaction against the doctrinaire academicism of Vienna. After Pforr's death the group was reformed as the Nazarenes, whose later members included Peter Cornelius (1783–1867) and Julius Schnorr von Carolsfeld (1794–1872). Their paintings of biblical subjects and historic scenes were distinguished by their bright colours and deliberately medieval appearance.

The counterpart of the Nazarenes in Britain was the Pre-Raphaelite Brotherhood, founded in 1848 by Dante Gabriel Rossetti (1828–82), William Holman Hunt (1827–1910) and John Everett Millais (1829–96) as a reaction against the prevailing Neoclassicism of the Royal Academy. They consciously strove to return to the early Italian Renaissance, before the advent of Raphael (hence their name). Like the Nazarenes, they had a penchant for sharply incised outlines and brilliant colours. Although the Pre-Raphaelites soon went their individual ways, they exercised a profound influence on the next generation of English painters, notably Edward Burne-Jones (1833–98) and Lawrence Alma-Tadema (1836–1912), while their principles were also endorsed by William Morris (1834–96).

Impressionism

Although this term did not come into use until 1874 when Claude Monet exhibited a painting entitled *Impression, Sunrise, Le Havre* – provoking the comment by Louis Leroy that pictures of this kind were an 'impression' of nature, nothing more – the movement had been evolving for more than a decade. Camille Pissarro (1839–1903) had been a pupil of Corot, whose open-air landscapes pointed the way towards Impressionism. Edouard Manet (1832–83) had been influenced by Goya, whereas Edgar Degas (1834–1917) had studied under Ingres. Alfred Sisley (1839–99), Claude Monet (1840–1926) and Pierre-Auguste Renoir (1841–1919) were among the other leading figures. While they were primarily preoccupied with landscape, Renoir became one of the leading exponents of the female nude, while Manet excelled in animated groups and Degas was renowned for his paintings of ballet dancers. On the fringe of Impressionism was Paul Cézanne (1839–1906), who felt uneasy at the lack of discipline in this style and wished to return to a greater reliance on form and content without sacrificing the feeling for light and brilliant colours. Out of this evolved Post-Impressionism, a term that originally meant merely 'after Impressionism', but which became the springboard to all the varied 'isms' that come under the heading of modern painting and which, accordingly, belong more fittingly to a different section of this book.

Apart from Cézanne, the leading Post-Impressionists included Georges Seurat (1859–91). Neither of them was particularly concerned with the emotional content of their paintings, but this was the principal feature of the lithographs and paintings of Henri de Toulouse-Lautrec (1864–1901) and the works of Van Gogh and Gauguin.

World Art

From the seventeenth century onwards, European subjects occasionally appeared in Japanese paintings. Conversely, Europe had a passion for *chinoiserie* (the use of Chinese motifs and techniques in Western art) from the same century onwards, although this manifested itself mainly in the applied arts, such as porcelain and lacquer. The cross-fertilization of European and Oriental art took off in the mid-nineteenth century, when Japanese block prints first invaded the Parisian market. The ancient arts of Egypt were brought before the European public as a result of Napoleon's expedition of 1798 and it had a passing effect on Neoclassical painting.

On the other side of the world the Europeans who settled in the western hemisphere took with them their distinctive styles. While the American colonies (and later the United States) followed the trends of English painting, Canada was (and still is) more exposed to the prevailing fashions in France, and the countries of Latin America naturally looked to Spain for artistic guidance. Although excellent indigenous painters soon emerged in every part of the American continent they tended to follow the styles of their motherland, often receiving their training there and even, like John Singleton Copley (1738–1815), Benjamin West (1738–1820), John Singer Sargent (1856–1925) and James McNeill Whistler (1834–1903) settling there. Not surprisingly, portraiture and genre painting were little distinguishable from those of the mother countries, but the nineteenth-century development of interest in landscape and the way of life of the native Americans led to the emergence of distinctive styles, such as the Hudson River School. The outstanding painters of the second half of the nineteenth century included John Frederick Kensett (1816–72), Winslow Homer (1836–1910) and Thomas Eakins (1844–1916).

In Africa and Australasia the pattern was much the same. Indigenous art – despite its traditions, which stretched back many centuries – was largely ignored by the Western art establishment until the twentieth century, when it came to the attention of a more extensive audience. The result was a fusion of styles, in which traditional themes were depicted using western techniques. Nevertheless, it is only in the recent past that artists working in Europe and America have taken their inspiration from the art of Africa, Asia, Australasia and Polynesia, using ethnic motifs and themes to create eclectic and distinctive styles.

UNTIL 1939 the centre of the avant-garde art world was Paris, but with the outbreak of World War II this shifted to New York, whence many European painters fled from Nazi-occupied Europe. This influx of new ideas coincided with the project under Roosevelt's New Deal program of commissioning otherwise unemployed artists in the Depression period to paint large murals. Out of these factors emerged Abstract Expressionism, which may be defined as a style of painting in which the artist strove to express feelings and attitudes through non-representational means. Whether as refugees from persecution or as a result of hardship or social injustice, there was also a strong social message. The movement was divided between the Gesture Painters, such as Jackson Pollock, Robert Motherwell and Franz Kline, and the Colour Field Painters led by Clyfford Still and Mark Rothko. In the immediate post-war years Abstract Expressionism crossed the Atlantic, Antoni Tàpies and Jean Dubuffet taking the lead in giving it a more distinctively European slant born of the anxieties and uncertainties so prevalent in that period.

OTHER REFERENCES
Robert Motherwell, Jackson Pollock, Mark Rothko

INFLUENCES
Cubism, Constructivism

Franz Kline (1910–62)
Scudera, 1961

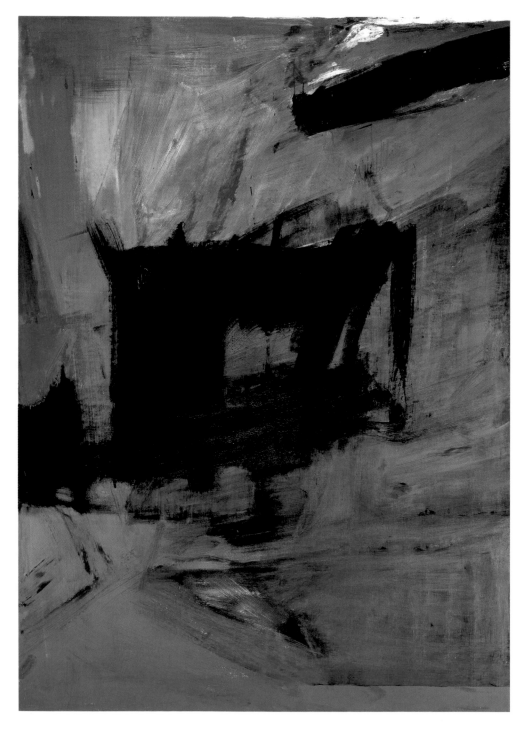

Courtesy of Private Collection/Christie's Images/© ARS, NY and DACS, London 2002

FRENCH FOR 'new art', this term was used in the English-speaking world to describe a style that came to prominence in about 1895 and continued until World War I, being derived from the Paris shop of that name opened by the Hamburg entrepreneur Samuel Bing. Paradoxically, in France it was generally known as *le style anglais* and in Italy more specifically as *lo stile Liberty*, after the London department store which did so much to promote it. In the German-speaking countries it was *Jugendstil* ('Youth Style'). All of these names embraced a style distinguished by its sinuous curves, swirling lines and ethereal quality. Figures were elongated and in some cases distorted and its practitioners relied heavily on plant forms; tulips, lily pads and thistle heads being particularly favoured. It manifested itself in every medium of the applied and decorative arts, from the architecture of Gaudi and Horta to the furniture of Mackintosh and the Wisteria glass of Tiffany. In the fine arts it was manifest in the drawings of Louis Anquetin and Aubrey Beardsley, and the paintings of Edward Burne-Jones, Alphonse Mucha and Jan Toorop.

OTHER REFERENCES
Sir Edward Burne-Jones
INFLUENCES
Symbolism, Pre-Raphaelites, Arts and Crafts Movement, Aesthetic Movement

Charles Rennie Mackintosh (1868–1928)
The Wassail, 1900

← 7½" →

Courtesy of Private Collection/Christie's Images

THE FRENCH word for 'irregular', derived from the Portuguese *barroco*, describing a misshapen pearl, Baroque was applied to a style in art and architecture very fashionable in the seventeenth century, and distinguished by extravagant forms and ornamentation which became so elaborate as to verge on the grotesque. Indeed, in its more extreme form, it described a style of decorative art allegedly derived from caves or grottoes and characterized by fantastic human or animal forms merged with natural motifs. The Baroque style manifested itself most noticeably in the florid decoration of buildings and furniture, but it spread to sculpture and painting through its most enthusiastic exponent, Gianlorenzo Bernini. However, Annibale Carracci and Michaelangelo Caravaggio reacted against the Mannerist style of the late sixteenth century by infusing their works with a new naturalism which, in turn, would lead to greater realism and the vogue for landscapes in the eighteenth century. Artemisia Gentileschi raised Baroque painting to a new level with her realism combined with a flair for dramatic composition.

OTHER REFERENCES
Andrea Pozzo, Annibale Carracci, Caravaggio
INFLUENCES
Architecture and sculpture of Gianlorenzo Bernini and Francesco Borromini

Pietro da Cortona (Berretini) (1596–1669)
Allegory of the Arts (Ceiling Painting)

Courtesy of Palazzo Barberini, Rome, Italy/Bridgeman Art Library

LARGELY A reaction against the florid, fussy styles in the applied arts of the late nineteenth century, the Bauhaus style developed in the early twentieth century under the inspiration and guidance of Walter Gropius, a German architect and designer who was influenced by the writings of John Ruskin and William Morris. Unlike these mentors, he did not reject mechanization but sought ways of harmonizing industrial methods to design. He was appointed Director of the Grand Ducal schools of art in Weimar in 1919, collectively known by the name Bauhaus (literally 'architecture house'). Gropius and his colleagues strove to marry form and function in the applied arts, architecture and industrial design. When the Nazis came to power Gropius and his disciples went to France, Britain and the USA, spreading the gospel and laying the foundations for the clean lines of modern industrial design. In the decorative arts their ideas influenced the development of Art Deco and Art Moderne in the 1920s and 1930s. Paul Klee and Wassily Kandinsky were among the artists who taught at the Bauhaus and were, in turn, imbued with its concepts, leading to the development of Abstract art.

OTHER REFERENCES
Paul Klee

INFLUENCES
Arts and Crafts Movement, John Ruskin

Wassily Kandinsky (see page 304)
Ship and Red Sun, 1925

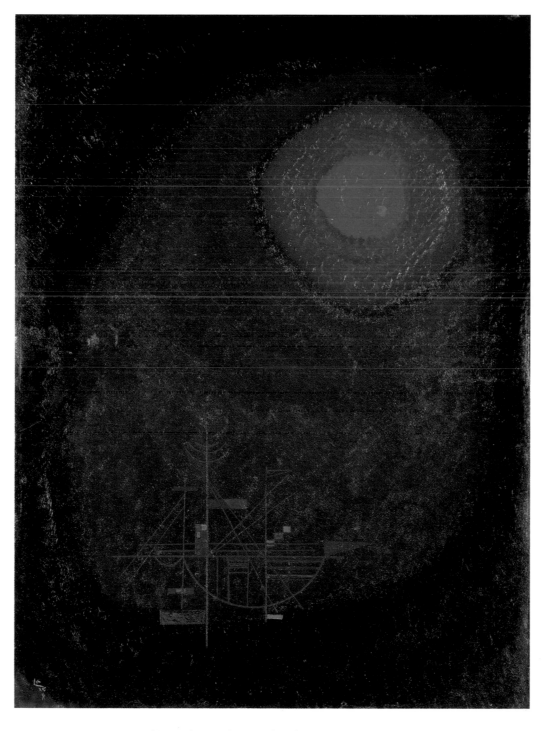

Courtesy of Private Collection/Bridgeman Art Library/© ADAGP, Paris and DACS, London 2002

Art Movement

THIS NON-FIGURATIVE movement originated shortly before World War I, at a time when avant-garde artists in Russia were experimenting with Cubism and Futurism. The shape of things to come was evident in Kazimir Malevich's sets for the futurist opera *Victory Over the Sun* (1913) and developed in his paintings from 1915 onwards, but the true founder of Constructivism was Vladimir Tatlin whose wire and metal 'corner reliefs' appeared in the same year. In 1919–20 he devised a monument to the Third International which was to be the Bolshevik equivalent of the Eiffel Tower.

The concept was rejected by Trotsky as wildly impractical and it is known only from photographs of the model. It did have a profound effect on the artists of the post-Revolutionary era, notably sculptors like Naum Gabo and painters like Alexander Rodchenko, who believed that art should have a practical application to everyday life. El Lissitzky, who had studied under Malevich, produced numerous graphic works and designs for book jackets in the Constructivist idiom, and was its outstanding exponent in painting.

OTHER REFERENCES
Kazimir Malevich, László Moholy-Nagy

INFLUENCES
Cubism and Futurism

El Lissitsky (1890–1941)
Neuer Plate 10 from Die Plastiche Gestaltung Der Elektro

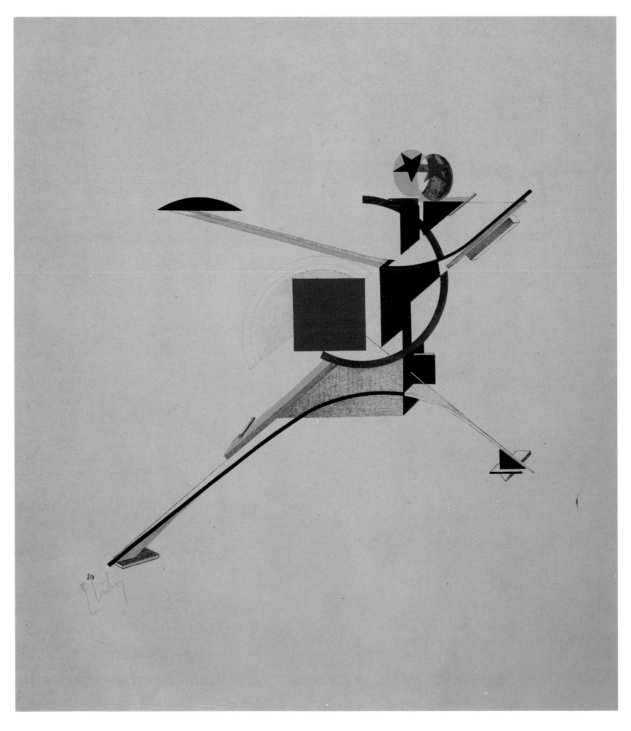

Courtesy of Private Collection/Christie's Images/© DACS 2002

Art Movement

IN 1907 Pablo Picasso and Georges Braque wrestled with the problem of representing three-dimensional figures and objects in the two-dimensional medium of painting. Their solution was to create an abstract form that could display two or more sides of an object simultaneously. The artists collaborated closely and worked at a frenetic pace without any predetermined concepts in their attempts to create recognizable images liberated from all the previous artistic conventions. Picasso's *Demoiselles d'Avignon* (1907) is regarded as the first Cubist painting, although his ideas were not fully developed until 1911 when both he and Braque exhibited at the Salon des Indépendants in Paris. Their example was rapidly followed by artists such as Léger and Delaunay and their ideas propagated in the writings of Apollinaire. Although many of the Cubist painters later moved on to more completely abstract work, the movement had an enormous impact on the development of twentieth century art and its echoes are to be found in architecture, graphic art and textile design up to the present time.

OTHER REFERENCES
Georges Braque, Robert Delaunay, Juan Gris Fernand Léger,

INFLUENCES
Paul Cézanne

Pablo Picasso (see page 386)
Violon, Bouteille et Verre, 1913

Courtesy of Private Collection/Christie's Images/© Succession Picasso/DACS 2002

THIS MOVEMENT began in neutral Switzerland in 1915, when most of the surrounding countries were embroiled in a conflict that threatened to destroy civilization. It arose as a form of protest by violently and shockingly rejecting all previously accepted artistic values. The term itself, one of the first sounds made by babies, symbolized its deliberate irrationality. At first it consisted of recitals of obscene or nonsensical verse, or performances that involved the destruction of sculpture or paintings. These activities were purely transient, but the thinking behind them found

expression in various periodicals and manifestos, deliberately crudely printed on coarse paper. Out of this developed the artistic medium, as avant-garde painters saw the possibilities of its anarchic nihilism. Jean Arp was the first to translate Dada into art, using pieces of paper torn up and haphazardly dropped on the floor. Marcel Duchamp took Dada across the Atlantic, exhibiting a urinal in New York and asserting that it was a work of art because he said so. Dada was short-lived, but it paved the way for Surrealism in 1924.

OTHER REFERENCES

Jean Arp, Max Ernst, Kurt Schwitters

INFLUENCES

Tristan Tzara

Jean Arp (1887–1966)
The Great Dancer, 1926

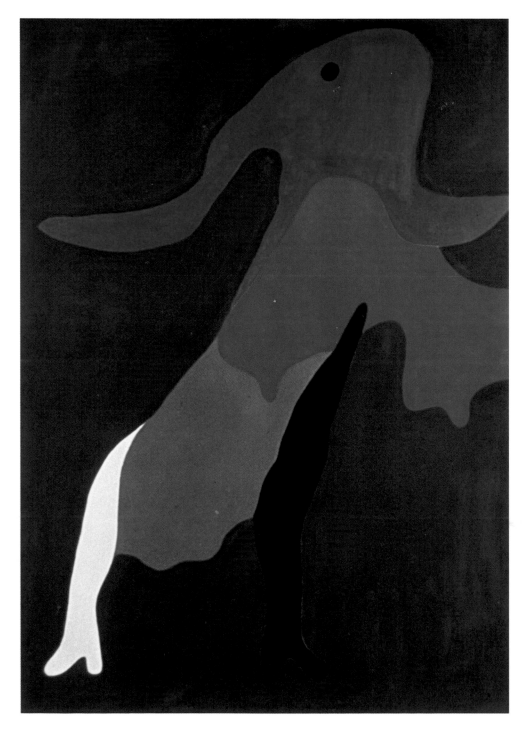

Courtesy of Musee National d'Art Moderne, Paris/Bridgeman Art Library/© DACS 2002

THE DUTCH words for 'the Style' denoted a group of artists and designers which was formed in the Netherlands in 1917 and took its name from a magazine edited by Theo van Doesburg. The other founder members included the painters Piet Mondrian and Bart van der Leck, the architect J. J. P. Oud and the furniture designer Gerrit Rietveld. It was a reaction against Art Nouveau (which had run its course by that time) and the excessively florid styles of the late nineteenth century, and sought to create a pure aesthetic based on straight lines and primary colours plus black and white. It was a conscious reminder of the austere qualities of seventeenth century Dutch Protestantism and the flat, regimented character of the Dutch landscape. Van Doesburg was the driving force of the movement, creating paintings that were strongly influenced by Constructivism and, in turn, making a major contribution to the development of modern typography. Rietveld gave De Stijl its public face through his startlingly modern furniture designs and architecture. In the fine arts, however, De Stijl found its purest manifestation in the paintings of Mondrian and their emphasis on straight lines and squares.

OTHER REFERENCES
Theo van Doesburg, Bart van der Leck

INFLUENCES
Kazimir Malevich, El Lissitzky

Theo Van Doesburg (1883–1931)
Vetrata Kompositie V in Lood, 1918

Courtesy of Private Collection/Christie's Images

THIS MODE of artistic expression attempts to depict the artist's subjective emotions and responses to objects and events. It developed in the early years of the twentieth century when some of the German avant-garde artists formed the group known as Die Brücke ('The Bridge'), which hoped to bridge the gap between academic and modern art. They were strongly influenced by the harshly disconcerting and tortured paintings and engravings of Edvard Munch. The group's prime mover was Ernst Ludwig Kirchner, whose paintings epitomize the ideals of the group by giving expression to the anxieties and sense of isolation felt by so many struggling young artists of his generation, trying to come to terms with the stresses of industrialized society and the modern world. Kirchner and his colleagues used colour and form to illustrate their feelings. Although the group was dissolved before World War I, it laid the foundations for the psychological paintings of the 1920s and 1930s. Many Expressionists were traumatized by their horrific experiences in the war and used their paintings as a means of expiating their obsessions.

OTHER REFERENCES
Die Blaue Reiter, Emil Nolde, Max Beckmann, Georg Grosz

INFLUENCES
Franz Marc, Max Pechstein

Edvard Munch (see page 368)
Madonna-Liebendes Weib, 1895

Courtesy of Private Collection/Christie's Images/© Munch Museum/Munch - Ellingsen Group, BONO, Oslo, DACS, London 2002

FEW ARTISTIC movements can be so precisely pinpointed as Futurism, which was launched in February 1909 when the young Italian poet Tommaso Marinetti published his Futurist Manifesto in Paris. Although Marinetti's primary concern was to give poetic expression to the dynamism and movement of machines in the age of speed, his concepts applied just as forcibly to painting and were immediately seized upon. To Marinetti a modern racing car was as much a thing of beauty as the *Winged Victory of Samothrace* in the Louvre and his message was taken up enthusiastically by his

compatriots, notably Gino Severini and Umberto Boccioni. *A Technical Manifesto of Futurist Painting* was drawn up in 1910 by Giacomo Balla, Luigi Russolo and Carlo Carra. Futurism was often linked to Mussolini's brand of Fascism in the 1920s, although most of the original exponents of the style, horrified by their experiences in World War I, later reverted to more conventional painting which lacked their original passion and raw energy. Futurism nevertheless dominated art in the totalitarian countries and exerted a powerful appeal everywhere else in the interwar years.

OTHER REFERENCES
Carlo Carra

INFLUENCES
Bauhaus

Giacomo Balla (see page 150)
Amorous Figures, 1923

Courtesy of Private Collection, Milan, Italy/Peter Willi/Bridgeman Art Library/© DACS 2002

THIS CANADIAN group of conceptual artists was formed in 1968 by A. A. Bronson (Michael Tims) of Vancouver, Felix Partz (Ron Gabe) of Winnipeg and Jorge Zontal (Jorge Saia) from Parma, Italy. Under these pseudonyms they worked in diverse media, including sculpture, photography, video and street theatre, with the aim of critically examining and, if possible, undermining the established social structure. The notion of working as a team, closely collaborating on each project, destroyed the stereotype of the artist as a loner, operating in isolation. One of their earliest targets was the beauty parade, lampooned in the *Miss General Idea Pageant* of 1970, and the success of this venture encouraged them to develop this concept, notably the public burning of the 1984 Pavilion at Kingston, Ontario (1977), the charred fragments being exhibited as art. This gave rise to similar manifestations in the 1980s before General Idea concentrated on the campaign to combat AIDS, which has occupied their creative energies in more recent years.

OTHER REFERENCES
Jean Arp, Max Ernst
INFLUENCES
Dadaism

Michael Tims (1946–), Ron Gabe (1945–) and Jorge Saia (1944–94)
One Year of AZT, 1991

© National Gallery of Canada, Ottawa, Purchased 1995/A. A Bronson

THIS TERM was coined pejoratively by the journalist Louis Leroy in 1874 and used in an article in the satirical magazine *Charivari* to attack the paintings of Claude Monet, which were exhibited that spring. The term derived, in fact, from one of Monet's canvasses simply entitled *Impression: Sunrise* leading the critic to dismiss it as 'an impression of nature, nothing more'. The Impressionists took ordinary subjects and used colour to illustrate the play of light and shadow on surfaces to suggest rather than delineate faithfully what they saw. In its heyday, between the late 1860s and about 1879, Impressionism was a remarkable revolution against Classicism, seeking to achieve immediacy and spontaneity, playing on the emotions as much as the imagination to achieve results. It lingered on fitfully till the end of the century, spawning such offshoots as the Neo-Impressionism of Pissarro and the Pointillism of Seurat, but most of its practitioners moved on to Post-Impressionism, with a greater concern for structure and content, while holding on to everyday subjects rendered in strong, bright colours.

OTHER REFERENCES
Paul Cézanne, Edouard Manet, Edgar Degas, Alfred Sisley, Camille Pissarro, Georges Seurat, Pierre-Auguste Renoir
INFLUENCES
Camille Corot, Eugène Boudin, Johann Barthold, Jongkind

Claude Monet (see page 361)
Le Palais Ducal vu de Saint George Majeur, 1908

Courtesy of Private Collection/Christie's Images

IT WAS the art historian and pupil of Michelangelo, Giorgio Vasari, who coined the term 'Gothic' to describe the art and architecture of the Middle Ages, assuming that this style had originated with the Goths, the Teutonic barbarians who attacked the Roman Empire. Gothic thus came to represent the opposite of Classic (the art which derived from Greece and Rome). Strange as it may seem, Vasari's theories were not dismissed until the nineteenth century, and the label Gothic has remained to describe the fantastic spires and grotesque ornament of cathedrals, as well as the style in stained glass,

tapestry and the applied arts. It found expression in the fine arts of the fourteenth and fifteenth centuries, mainly through the medium of the richly illuminated books of hours and other devotional works. The finest exponents of this art were the three brothers – Pol, Hermann and Janneken Malouel from Limbourg in Flanders (now Belgium) – who flourished around the end of the fourteenth century and executed many fine miniature paintings for Philip the Bold and his brother John, Duke of Berri. Pol studied in Italy and his style reflects the influence of contemporary artists there.

OTHER REFERENCES
Hubert and Jan van Eyck, Piero della Francesca

INFLUENCES
Gentile da Fabriano, Giotto di Bondone

Limbourg Brothers
Breviary of John the Fearless, c. 1415

Courtesy of British Library, UK/Bridgeman Art Library

THIS MODE of abstract art, consisting of simple geometric forms executed in an impersonal style, arose in the mid-1960s out of a wish to confront the viewer as directly as possible. Such paintings and sculpture could be understood at a glance, but taken out of the context of a group or entire exhibition of such works, individual pieces were often beyond the comprehension of the spectator. This was particularly true in the case of those paintings by Ad Reinhardt consisting of a solid black square or white on a white ground. This severely reductive style owes much to the Abstract Expressionists, such as Newman, Still and Rothko, particularly in those works that consist essentially of a single colour with perhaps only a solitary line in a contrasting colour down the centre. In the late 1950s Frank Stella produced simple patterns of uniform stripes. Robert Ryman's paintings are essentially white, enlivened by his exploration of different types of paint and other materials. In more recent years Minimalism sometimes incorporates other objects, such as Donald Judd's untitled work of 1994, comprising three sets of shelves in aluminium and plexiglass screwed to a plain wall.

OTHER REFERENCES
Ad Reinhardt, Robert Ryman, Donald Judd

INFLUENCES
Clyfford Still, Mark Rothko, Barnet Newman

Frank Stella (see page 448)
Untitled 1962

Courtesy of Private Collection/Christie's Images/© ARS, NY and DACS, London 2002

THE DISCOVERY of the ruins of Pompeii in 1748 triggered off an interest in and enthusiasm for the antiquities of Greece and Rome, given direction by the German archaeologist and art historian Johann Joachim Winckelmann, who argued that beauty depended on calmness, simplicity and correct proportion, the complete antithesis of the Rococo, which was then at the height of fashion. Neoclassicism was almost an inevitable reaction to the frivolity of Rococo and it was given a political dimension when it became the preferred style in France in the aftermath of the Revolution. Although Neoclassicism spread throughout Europe, it was therefore in France that it found its warmest reception. Ironically, the trend gained the royal seal of approval in 1785 when Louis XVI purchased *The Oath of the Horatii* by Jacques-Louis David, the outstanding exponent of the Neoclassical style. David would go on to record the assassination of Marat (1793) in this idiom and was at the height of his powers when he became Napoleon's favourite painter. Neoclassicism found expression in the sculptures of Canova, Thorwaldsen, Houdon and Flaxman, and in the vogue for architecture imitating Greek temples.

OTHER REFERENCES
Anton Raffael Mengs, Francisco de Goya

INFLUENCES
Greek classical architecture, Roman sculpture

Jacques–Louis David (see page 207)
The Oath of the Horatii, 1784

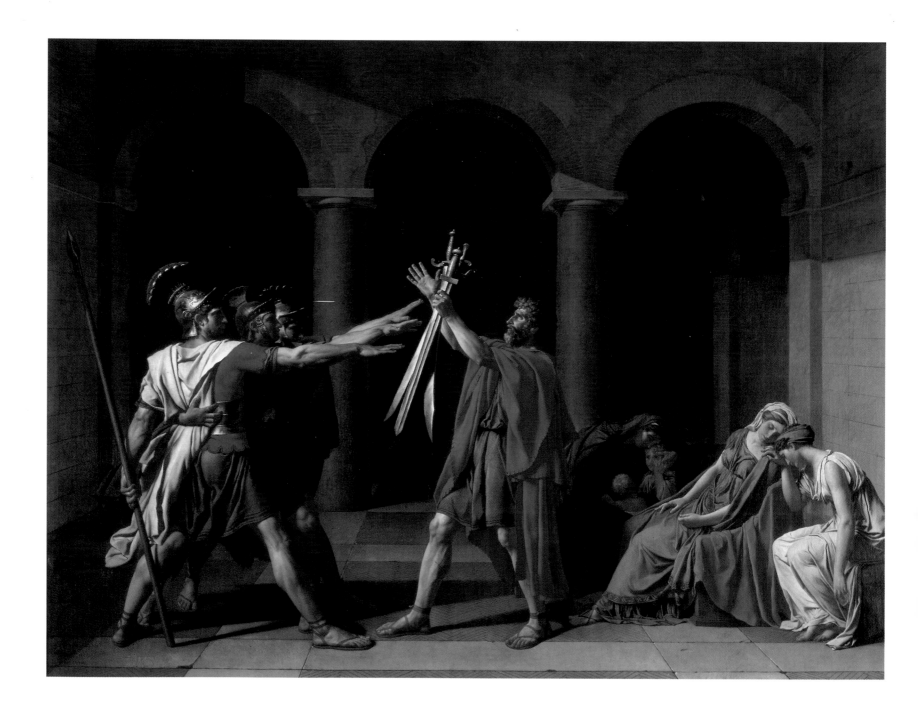

Courtesy of Louvre, Paris/Bridgeman Art Library

AN AVANT-GARDE art movement founded in Germany after World War I. Under the name of Neue Sachlichkeit, it remained to a large extent specific to Germany. Characterized by the harsh, uncompromising and often grotesquely distorted imagery, sometimes verging on the abstract but never ceasing to be figurative, it had a great impact on the viewer. It was born out of the mental and physical pain suffered by artists who had endured the horrors of trench warfare and who had either been hospitalized as a result or who bore the scars of their experiences into the postwar era.

Confronted by the free-wheeling materialism of the Weimar Republic and the increasing menace of Nazism, the practitioners of Neue Sachlichkeit lampooned and satirized the corruption and ever-present specter of militarism of Germany in the 1920s in their canvasses. The harsh, distorted imagery spilled over into portraits in which fingers and features were unnaturally elongated and bodies contorted. New Objectivism was inevitably condemned by the Nazis as degenerate art and its devotees fled abroad after 1933. A subsequent moderation of style proved influential in the development of Abstract Expressionism.

OTHER REFERENCES
Max Beckman, George Grosz, Christian Schad, Tamara de Lempicka
INFLUENCES
James Ensor, Max Beckmann

Otto Dix (see page 217)
Der Salon I, 1921

Courtesy of Christie's Images/© DACS 2002

PARALLEL WITH Pop Art, which rejected the abstract imagery of the 1940s and 1950s, was a style that utilized abstraction to experiment with the creation of optical effects, allowing the spectator to see things that are not there at all. Optical illusions are heightened by the use of bright, contrasting colours emphasized by hard edges, and the use of metallic pigments and substances such as dayglo to simulate the appearance of neon lights. This technique was pioneered in the United States by Morris Louis (1912–62) towards the end of his life, painting huge canvasses in which dazzling rivers appeared to be running down the edges and giving the impression of fluidity. He had a profound influence on such American painters as Kenneth Noland, Ellsworth Kelly and Al Held, originally under the label of Post-Painterly Abstraction. From this developed Op Art, which strives for a dazzling and optically disturbing effect. The foremost practitioners of Op Art include Victor Vasarely and François Morellet in France, Frank Stella in America and the British artist Bridget Riley. Riley's large paintings, with their kaleidoscopic patterns of strident colour, sear the eyeball and have, in extreme cases, allegedly brought on migraines.

OTHER REFERENCES
Frank Stella

INFLUENCES
Abstract Expressionism, Pop Art

Bridget Riley (see page 415)
Orient IV, 1970

Courtesy of Private Collection/Christie's Images/2002 © Bridget Riley, all rights reserved Courtesy Karsten Schubert, London

THIS TERM originally denoted an ancient Greek religion allegedly founded by Orpheus, but it was borrowed by Guillaume Apollinaire in 1913 to describe the paintings of Robert Delaunay, which he regarded as 'pure art'. This was a novel form of Abstract Art which was not rooted in reality but entirely independent in concept and execution. Delaunay had for some time previously been experimenting with blocks of pure colour to explore their emotional impact, a revolutionary concept at a time when the large majority of French artists remained firmly wedded to recognizable subjects. His paintings positively glowed with the prismatic effect of bright, contrasting colours. In turn Delaunay and his wife Sonia adopted Apollinaire's definition and expanded their concepts to create a movement under the name of Orphism. Although it had no immediate material effect on French painters, it strongly influenced the German avant-garde, notably the Blaue Reiter group in Munich, and manifested itself in the paintings of Franz Marc, Otto Freundlich and Wassily Kandinsky. There are echoes of Orphism in the Op Art of Frank Stella and Bridget Riley.

OTHER REFERENCES
Sonia Delaunay, Franz Marc, Otto Freundlich, Wassily Kandinsky, Bridget Riley, Frank Stella
INFLUENCES
Neo-impressionism, Fauvism

Robert Delaunay (see page 211)
Helice, 1923

Courtesy of Private Collection/Christie's Images/© L&M Services B.V. Amsterdam 20020512

Art Movement

PHOTOGRAPHY HAS been directly or indirectly connected with fine art almost since its inception in the 1830s and was originally used as a visual aid by landscapists such as David Octavius Hill, whose photographs are now more highly regarded than his paintings. In the 1920s photomontage was a technique favoured by such Dadaists as Raoul Hausmann and John Heartfield. While Cindy Sherman in the 1980s raised photography to the status of a fine art (but has since moved on to create horror and sex pictures incorporating foodstuffs and even vomit), Bruce Nauman and Bill Viola have experimented with video and mixed media. Conceptual artists like Duane Michals and Victor Burgin have used photographs with text superimposed or inscribed alongside. Photorealism in its purest form emerged in America in the paintings of Malcolm Morley, Robert Bechtle and especially Richard Estes, and the sculptures of John De Andrea and Duane Hanson. Other artists have used serial or overlapping images to convey movement. Although much admired for its clarity of imagery, the movement was relatively short-lived, most of its practitioners moving on to develop other styles.

OTHER REFERENCES

Chuck Close, Robert Mapplethorpe, Man Ray, Larry Clark

INFLUENCES

Marcel Duchamp, Raoul Hausmann, Nan Goldin, Pop Art

Richard Estes (1936–)

Williamsburg Bridge, 1987

Courtesy of Private Collection/Christie's Images/© Richard Estes, courtesy, Marlborough Gallery, New York

THIS TERM is derived from the French verb pointiller, to stipple, and neatly describes the technique of applying small strokes or dots of pure colour to a surface so that from a distance they appear to blend together. It unconsciously anticipated the screening process in such printing methods as offset lithography, half-tone and photogravure in which light and shade, colour and tone depend on the density of dots in one or more colour. An early practitioner of this technique was Georges Seurat, who called it Divisionism, but it attained its fullest flowering in the hands of Camille Pissarro. Encouraged by Corot, who advised him to study light and tonal values, he persevered with landscapes, painted out of doors from nature, in which he achieved extraordinary luminosity by his painstaking technique of applying colour in the form of dots and tiny dabs. Although he had some influence on Cézanne, Pissarro's technique was too laborious to attract many followers. He himself abandoned the technique for mainstream Impressionism in the last years of his life, when failing eyesight made pointillism impossible.

OTHER REFERENCES
Paul Cézanne

INFLUENCES
Georges Seurat, Camille Corot

Georges Seurat (see page 438)
Model in Profile, 1887

Courtesy of Musee d'Orsay, Paris, France/Bridgeman Art Library

POP ART is a term applied to a wide range of styles, techniques and artistic media. In effect, the painters and graphic artists who explored the possibilities inherent in everyday objects of the 1950s and 1960s were motivated by the growing affluence of the developed countries and the emergence of the throw-away society. Pop Art arose more or less at the same time in New York and London, and its essence was neatly summed up by the painter Richard Hamilton as popular (designed for a mass audience), transient (short-term solution), low cost, mass-produced, youth-oriented, 'witty, sexy, gimmicky, glamorous, Big Business'. The most high-profile exponents on both sides of the Atlantic were David Hockney and Andy Warhol; significantly both were originally inspired by packaging, by TyPhoo Tea and Campbell's Soup respectively. Roy Lichtenstein's paintings resemble giant comic strips. In addition to painting, photography and silk-screen printing were utilized in the creation of Pop Art; while other artists used pieces of discarded junk to build collages, but the ultimate aspect was Performance Art as practiced by Jim Dine and Robert Rauschenberg.

OTHER REFERENCES
David Hockney, Robert Rauschenberg, Andy Warhol
INFLUENCES
Abstract Expressionism, commercial art, graphic design of packaging

Jim Dine (see page 216)
The Heart called "Rancho Pastel", 1982

Courtesy of Private Collection/Christie's Images/© ARS, NY and DACS, London 2002

IN THIS movement of the 1980s and later decades, modern art has come full circle, its followers rejecting the constant search of the avant-garde for new forms and techniques, and taking a fresh look at styles and themes of earlier periods throughout the history of art. In the end Postmodernism is a synthesis of all kinds of styles and periods. The argument of the Postmodernists is that every conceivable avenue has been explored in the past century and there is hardly any scope for novelty or originality. Consequently they have embraced as many different styles and techniques as possible, often combining them in the same work. The leading exponents in the 1980s were Sigmar Polke in Germany, Jiri Dokoupil in the Czech Republic, Shinro Ohtake in Japan and David Salle in the United States. Ohtake's work in particular symbolizes the cross-culturalism of contemporary art. Although criticized for being derivative, these artists and their followers have, in fact, reinvented art in the most exciting and revolutionary style to emerge since Braque and Picasso formulated Cubism in the early 1900s.

OTHER REFERENCES
Keith Haring

INFLUENCES
Pop Art, Dada, Surrealism

David Salle (1952–)
Acralist, 1988

Courtesy of Private Collection/Christie's Images © David Salle / VAGA, New York/© DACS, London 2002

THIS TERM was coined by the art critic Clement Greenberg and used as the title of an exhibition which he organized in 1964 with the participation of Ellsworth Kelly, Helen Frankenthaler, Al Held, Morris Louis, Kenneth Noland, Jules Olitski and Frank Stella. What these artists had in common was an aversion to the painterly character of Abstract Expressionism; instead they painted flat coloured surfaces in their quest for the essential. The style was originated by Kelly who, since the 1940s, had been painting wooden reliefs in geometric shapes derived from elements of contemporary architecture. By the early 1960s these paintings had solid masses outlined in a contrasting colour. This was initially termed Hard-Edge Painting, which rather missed the point as Kelly was chiefly concerned with the relationship of shape to colour and the hard-edged lines were incidental. The style at that time was not very different from that of the Colour Field Painters, such as Still, Newman and Rothko. A notable feature of Post-Painterly Abstraction is the staining of canvasses with paint to eliminate brushstrokes.

OTHER REFERENCES
Frank Stella, Mark Rothko, Barnet Newman, Clyfford Still

INFLUENCES
Colour Field Painting

Ellsworth Kelly (1923–)
Orange Relief with Green, 1991

© Ellsworth Kelly/The Tate, London 2002

Art Movement

IN 1848, Dante Gabriel Rossetti, William Holman Hunt and John Everett Millais founded the Pre-Raphaelite Brotherhood, with the aim of restoring the principles and practices of the early Renaissance painters such as Botticelli and Filippo Lippi, before the time of Raphael, whose followers injected Mannerism into painting. The Pre-Raphaelites were imbued with literary romanticism, Rossetti in particular being inspired by his medieval namesake, while the poetry of Keats and Tennyson, especially *Idylls of the King* provided them with themes and subjects drawn from Arthurian legend. Scenes from the Bible and medieval legends were painted in sumptuous colours,

rich in detail and often with wry touches of humor, which sometimes shocked or outraged the viewer at the time. The movement was short-lived; Romanticism went out of fashion in the 1850s and the Brotherhood broke up, only Hunt remaining true to the Pre-Raphaelite precepts. Nevertheless, it had immense impact on later artists and craftsmen such as Morris and Burne-Jones. A somewhat parallel development was the Nazarenes, a group of German artists working in Rome, who originally formed the Brotherhood of St Luke and painted biblical subjects in a romantic medieval style reminiscent of Raphael.

OTHER REFERENCES
Dante Gabriel Rossetti, William Holman Hunt, John Everett Millais, Edward Burne-Jones
INFLUENCES
Sandro Botticelli, Filippo Lippi, the Nazarenes

Sir John Everett Millais (see page 354)
A Dream of the Past: Sir Isambras at the Ford

Courtesy of Private Collection/Christie's Images

Art Movement

REACTION AGAINST both the rather stereotyped Classicism and Romanticism gradually developed in France in the first half of the nineteenth century and resulted in a greater naturalism in subject matter and the manner in which it was presented. A turning point came in 1830, when Camille Corot painted Chartres Cathedral exactly as he saw it. At the same time Jean-François Millet began painting rural subjects in which the peasantry were imbued with the dignity which previously had been reserved for religious or heroic classical themes. This was taken a step further by Gustave Courbet, whose landscapes were inhabited by real people in everyday, often very humble, situations. His vigorous brushwork drips with passion and sincerity, laying the foundations of social realism. When his epic canvas of the *Burial at Ornans* was exhibited at the Salon in 1850 the art establishment was scandalized; but Realism had a significant impact on later developments such as Impressionism, while continuing to resonate through the early twentieth century as the principal medium for art as social criticism.

OTHER REFERENCES
Canille Corot, Jean-François Millet

INFLUENCES
Honoré Daumier, Pierre Proudhon

Gustave Courbet (see page 200)
Nuages sur la Lac Leman, c.1856

Courtesy of Private Collection/Christie's Images

Art Movement

THE FRENCH word meaning 'rebirth' alludes to the humanistic revival of the classical influence in Western Europe in the fourteenth to sixteenth centuries. Although the fall of Constantinople in 1453 and the consequent flight of intellectuals to the West is often cited as the starting point of the Renaissance, the 'rebirth of learning' had begun several generations earlier, as Arab arts and crafts filtered through Spain. It was marked by an unprecedented flowering of the arts and literature as well as the beginning of modern science. In the fields of the fine arts and architecture, the Renaissance had its greatest impact in Italy.

Significantly it was in the great mercantile centre of Florence, rather than in the religious centre of Rome that the movement developed initially and it was in the liberal world of the merchant princes that the new art flourished most vigorously. Wealthy patrons like the Medici, Sforza and Strozzi families encouraged the art of Leonardo and Michelangelo. The term 'Renaissance man', denoting a person of wide interests and expertise, was never truer than when applied to Leonardo da Vinci, who excelled as a sculptor, architect, inventor and military engineer, as well as a painter.

OTHER REFERENCES
Michelangelo, Donatello, Ghiberti, Brunelleschi, Masaccio, Gentile da Fabriano
INFLUENCES
Cimabue, Giotto, Duccio, the Lorenzetti

Leonardo da Vinci (see page 327)
Vitruvian Man, c. 1492

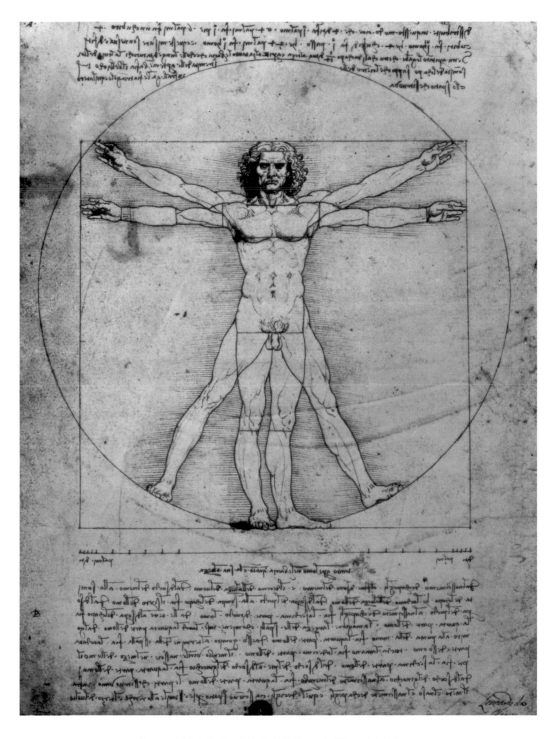

Courtesy of Galleria Dell'Accademia, Venice/Bridgeman Art Library/Christie's Images

THIS ITALIAN term is derived from the French *rocaille* ('rock work'), which describes the shell work decorating grottoes and rockery dells in French gardens in the late seventeenth and early eighteenth centuries, and which coincided with the drift of society back to Paris from Versailles. The new style, with its asymmetrical curves, lightness and frivolity, captivated the French and spread rapidly to Italy and other parts of Western Europe. It reflected the spirit of the age, when beliefs in religious dogma and the divine rights of kings were constantly being challenged. It influenced the style of architecture, furniture and a wide range of the applied and decorative arts. In painting it was reflected in the love of nature and the rise of the landscape, but it also impacted on the great allegorical compositions – especially ceilings and murals. Watteau, Boucher and Fragonard were its chief exponents in France, but it is also strongly evident in the frescoes of Tiepolo and the great architectural paintings of Canaletto and Guardi. It can be found as far afield as Frederick the Great's lavish palace of Sans Souci and David Ehrenstrahl's extravagant ceiling in Drottningholm Palace, Stockholm.

OTHER REFERENCES
Boucher, Watteau, Canaletto, Tiepolo, Guardi

INFLUENCES
Peter Paul Rubens, Gobelins tapestries, Sèvres porcelain

Jean-Honoré Fragonard (see page 239)
The Swing (Les Hazards heureux de L'Escarpolette), 1767

Courtesy of Wallace Collection, London, UK/Bridgeman Art Library

Art Movement

WHAT BEGAN as a literary and philosophical movement in the late eighteenth century soon involved the fine arts, as many painters and sculptors reacted against Neoclassicism and the sterile academic disciplines by emphasizing individual aspirations, feelings, emotion and atmosphere – especially the remote, rugged and exotic. The works of the great classical authors were out; the plays of Shakespeare, the poetry of Byron and the novels of Scott were in. Romanticism permeated the music of Beethoven and Mendelssohn and it inspired numerous painters. Its chief centre was Paris where the glories of Napoleon's victories found expression in the paintings of Delacroix, Géricault and Gros. Even a confirmed Classicist like Ingres was converted to Romanticism in old age. In Germany its chief exponent was Caspar David Friedrich, whose atmospheric landscapes were paralleled in England by Constable and reached their zenith in the magnificent oils and watercolours of Turner, with their recurring themes of man's puny struggle against the forces of nature. On the other side of the Atlantic the leading Romantics were Washington Allston, Frederick Church and Thomas Cole.

OTHER REFERENCES

William Blake, Albert Bierstadt, John Cozens, William Etty

INFLUENCES

Francisco de Goya, Pierre Guérin

J. M. W. Turner (see page 468)

Abergavenny Bridge

Courtesy of Private Collection/Christie's Images

THIS MOVEMENT in art has been defined as one that uses the incongruous images conjured by the unconscious to transcend reality as perceived by the conscious mind. While there had been elements of the surreal in the works of earlier painters – notably Bosch and Bruegel – Surrealism in its modern form arose out of Dada when some of its activists like Arp and Ernst settled in Paris in the 1920s. Like Dada, Surrealism rejected the necessity for rational thought and behavior but unlike Dada it had a relatively clear idea of its intentions, formulated by André Breton in his manifesto of 1924 'to resolve the previously contradictory conditions of dream and reality'. The ideas of Jung, Freud and Adler, from psychoanalysis to the interpretation of dreams, played a prominent part in Surrealist concepts and it was no accident that the dream sequence in the Hitchcock thriller *Spellbound* should have been created by Salvador Dalí, one of the outstanding masters of the genre. The illogicality and irrationality of Surrealist paintings was underscored by their almost photographic realism. Few pictures were wholly nightmarish, but in general the juxtaposition of images was unnerving.

OTHER REFERENCES
Jean Arp, Max Ernst, René Magritte, Joan Miró

INFLUENCES
Marcel Duchamp, Hieronymus Bosch, Pieter Bruegel

Salvador Dalí (see page 205)
Mirage, 1946

Courtesy of Private Collection/Christie's Images/© Salvador Dalí, Gala-Salvador Dalí Foundations DACS, London 2002

ORIGINALLY THE Symbolists were French writers and poets, notably Rimbaud, Verlaine, Baudelaire and Mallarmé, who used symbols to convey a subjective view of reality and particularly to give expression to abstract concepts. The literary movement found its voice in the Manifesto of Symbolism, proclaimed by the poet Moréas in 1886 as a reaction against materialism. But it was the novel *À Rebours*, published by Joris Huysmans in 1884, with its undertones of the exotic, sybaritic and perverse, that inspired painters to take notice. Husymans explored the world of artistic decadence and aspects of intellectual and spiritual life which had an immediate impact on such artists as Gustave Moreau and Odilon Redon and enabled them to give free reign to their imagination. In the next generation the leading exponents of Symbolism were Maurice Denis and Paul Gauguin in the early phase of his career. Although he started as an Impressionist he turned to Symbolism while working in Brittany and began to 'invoke beautiful thoughts with form and colour', painting his *Vision After the Sermon* in 1888. Later, of course, he would search for his ideals in the South Pacific, while other Symbolists joined the Nabis in the 1890s.

OTHER REFERENCES
Gustave Moreau, Maurice Denis, Odilon Redon

INFLUENCES
Joris Huysmans, Prosper Mallarmé, Arthur Rimbaud,

Paul Gauguin (see page 247)
Café at Arles, 1888

Courtesy of Pushkin Museum, Moscow, Russia/Bridgeman Giraudon

THE ONLY specifically English avant-garde movement to develop in the twentieth century, Vorticism was originated by Wyndham Lewis in 1914. The name was derived from a comment by the Italian art critic and Futurist painter Umberto Boccioni that 'all creative art emanates from an emotional vortex'. It was a synthesis of other movements, including elements of Cubism, Fauvism and Futurism, distinguished by uncompromising angularity and the juxtaposition of strident colours. Overlapping images from slightly different angles strove for a three-dimensional effect. At its best it pulsated with raw energy and passion; unfortunately it was prone to harsh excesses which became self-parodying and hastened its downfall. It flourished briefly, its mood being in tune with the terrible events of World War I but it was either rejected in the aftermath of war or overtaken by other movements. Traces of Vorticism, however, can be detected in much of the poster art produced in Britain in the 1920s. Some of Lewis's best work was done as an artist on the Western Front and there are muted echoes of this in the paintings of Paul Nash in the early phases of World War II.

OTHER REFERENCES
David Bomberg, Paul Nash

INFLUENCES
Pablo Picasso, Georges Braque

Percy Wyndham Lewis (see page 329)
The Room that Mary Lives In, 1949

Courtesy of Private Collection/Christie's Images

A-Z by Artist

Over 400 artists are presented here in alphabetical order, offering an enthralling selection of painted arts from 1250 AD to the present day, reflecting the broad cultural diversity of life through time and throughout the world. From America and Europe through to Africa, Asia and Australasia, there are artists from every continent, painting in every recognizable style, many of which are simply beautiful or striking in their own right. The book seeks to present the works of the artists as they are, without making value judgements about their origins or style, so that the reader can enjoy both familiar paintings and those new to them, created by artists painting in the widest possible range of traditional, indigenous or international styles. Some of the paintings chosen are not necessarily the best known because the book strives to combine the familiar with the new at every level. Some artists, like Monet or Michelangelo, are so prolific that no single painting can represent their work so the painting chosen conveys a flavour of their art with further examples provided for reference; in the case of Picasso his work is also represented in the Cubist entry of the Art Movements section. Museums, galleries, art collections, many private collections and the artists themselves have provided the works of art to further the aims of this exciting project.

The A-Z section can be used either to browse through, or to find a particular painter as a starting point; the book will then lead you to complementary artists or sections which illuminate the work, artist, method or a movement represented in each entry.

Abdulla, Ian

THIS ABORIGINAL ARTIST spent his boyhood in an idyllic riverside setting in South Australia, and consequently the river in all its aspects is a recurring theme in his paintings. He studied art in Adelaide and had his first one-man show in the Tandanya National Aboriginal Culture Institute in that city in 1990. He has since had one-man shows in many other parts of Australia and was declared South Australian Aboriginal Artist of the Year in 1991, winning the National Aboriginal Award for best painting five years later. His paintings are in all the major Australian galleries, including the

National Museum of Australia in Canberra. In more recent years he has achieved international fame with award-winning exhibits in Canada and Cuba. His paintings combine the traditional patterns and art forms of Aboriginal tribal culture stretching back thousands of years with Western techniques, creating both figurative and semi-abstract works in a highly distinctive style.

MOVEMENT
Modern Australian School
OTHER WORKS
Tyerabarrbowaryaou, I Shall Never Become a White Man
INFLUENCES
Aboriginal traditional art forms

Ian Abdulla   *Born* 1947 Swan Reach, South Australia
Painted in Australia

Courtesy of National Gallery of Australia, Canberra, purchased with funds from the Moet & Chandon Australian Art Foundation/© The Artist

Al Attar, Suad

SUAD AL ATTAR studied at the University of Baghdad, the California Polytechnic State University in San Luis Obispo, the Wimbledon School of Art and the Central School of Art and Design, London (where she took a degree in print-making). In 1965 she became the first female Iraqi artist to have a solo exhibition in Baghdad and has since received numerous awards at international exhibitions in Cairo, Brazil, London, Madrid and Poland. She paints in oils on canvas or card laid down on board and her work ranges from figures and still life to landscapes and decorative works which combine the classical Islamic art forms of the Middle East with modern Western influences. In the past decade she has painted a number of semi-abstract works inspired by images in the love poems of Mahmoud Darwish. She also creates tapestries with traditional Arab motifs.

MOVEMENT
Modern Iraqi School
OTHER WORKS
Abacus, Birds of Paradise, Blue Sunset Birds, Bustan Guardian
INFLUENCES
Classical Islamic art forms of the Middle East

Suad Al Attar   *Born* 1942 Baghdad, Iraq
Painted in Iraq

Courtesy of Sotheby's Picture Library

ALBERS TRAINED in the prevailing German academic tradition, at the art schools of Berlin, Essen and Munich. He combined their discipline in draughtsmanship with his own imaginative flair and innovative approach when he continued his studies at the Bauhaus in Weimar, subsequently working as an abstract painter and furniture designer. The advent of the Nazi regime forced him to leave Germany and settle in the United States, where he developed a style that gave free rein to the exploration of colours and their relationship to each

other. He held a series of important academic appointments, at the avant-garde Black Mountain College, North Carolina (1933–49) and at Yale University (1950–60). His work became increasingly non-figurative, and in the 1950s culminated in purely geometric canvasses, notably in his series entitled *Homage to the Square*. He was also one of the foremost colour theorists of the immediate post-war period, publishing a seminal work on the subject in 1963 which was influential in the subsequent rise of geometric abstract painting.

MOVEMENT
Abstract Expressionism
OTHER WORKS
Skyscrapers, Homage to the Square: Blue Climate, Apparition,
INFLUENCES
Walter Gropius, Kandinsky

Josef Albers *Born* 1888 Bottrup, Germany
Painted in Germany, USA
Died 1976 New Haven, Connecticut, USA

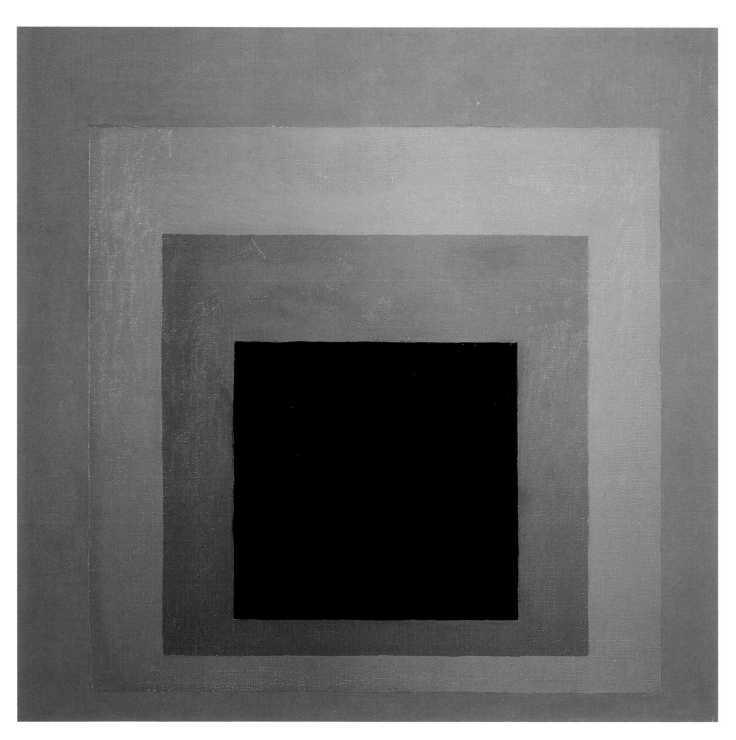

Courtesy of Private Collection/Christie's Images © DACS 2002

Alma-Tadema, Sir Lawrence

LAWRENCE ALMA-TADEMA trained at the Antwerp Academy of Art and later studied under Baron Hendryk Leys, an artist noted for his large historical paintings. In 1863 Alma-Tadema went to Italy, whose classical remains, notably at Pompeii, exerted a great influence on him. He moved to England in 1870, where he built up a reputation for narrative paintings in the Classical style. He was knighted in 1899. Three years later he visited Egypt and the impact of Pharaonic civilization had a major impact on the works of his last years. His large paintings brought everyday scenes of long-dead civilizations vividly to life through his extraordinary master of detail. He amassed a vast collection of ancient artefacts, photographs and sketches from his travels; the visual aids that enabled him to recreate the ancient world.

MOVEMENT
Neoclassical
OTHER WORKS
The Finding of Moses, The Conversion of Paula
INFLUENCES
Baron Hendryk Leys

Sir Lawrence Alma-Tadema *Born 1836*
Dronrijp, Holland *Painted in* Holland, England
Died 1912 Wiesbaden, Germany

Courtesy of Private Collection/Christie's Images

ALBRECHT ALTDORFER was born in Regensburg, Bavaria about 1480 and spent his whole life there. A Renaissance man in the true sense, he trained as an architect and was responsible for the design of many of the buildings in his native city, as well as rising to prominence in the city council. He also worked as an engraver, strongly influenced by Dürer, and was a pioneer of the technique of copperplate etching, but it is for his landscapes painted in oils on wood that he is best remembered. He specialized in biblical and historical subjects set in backgrounds, that gave free rein to his fertile imagination. After a prolonged tour of the Alps and Danube basin in 1511, however, he tended to concentrate on more realistic landscapes that were unusual for the time in that they were devoid of human figures and vividly conveyed a sense of atmosphere.

MOVEMENT
Danube School of German painting
OTHER WORKS
St George, Battle of Arbela, Landscape at Regensburg
INFLUENCES
Lucas Cranach, Albrecht Dürer

Albrecht Altdorfer   *Born c.* 1480
Painted in Regensburg, Bavaria
Died 1538 Regensburg

Courtesy of National Gallery, London/Bridgeman Art Library

BORN NEAR CAPIVARI, São Paulo State, Brazil in 1886, Tarsilo do Amaral was the daughter of a wealthy businessman and travelled to Europe several times in childhood. She began studying art in São Paulo in 1916 under Pedro Alexandrino and Fischer Elpons. She studied at the Académie Julien in Paris (1920–22) and on her return to Brazil became a prominent member of the short-lived art circle known as the Grupo dos Cinco. She then returned to Paris with Oswald de Andrade, where they were influnced by Picasso and Chirico. She later divided her time between Paris and Rio de Janeiro, bringing Brazilian art to Europe and taking Modernist ideas back to Brazil. Her paintings, in a style she dubbed 'Pau-Brazil', are an unusual blend of native Brazilian art forms, notably from the Tupi-Guarani tradition, with a geometric style influenced by Fernand Léger. Later she created a movement known as Antropofagia, which sought to replace the Portuguese colonial tradition with an indigenous style that was primitive and earthy.

MOVEMENT
Modern Brazilian School
OTHER WORKS
A Negra (The Black Woman)
INFLUENCES
Albert Gleizes, Picasso, Fernand Léger, Giorgio de Chirico

Tarsila do Amaral *Born* 1886 Sao Paulo, Brazil
Painted in São Paulo, Rio de Janeiro, Paris
Died 1973 São Paulo, Brazil

Courtesy of Museu de Arte Contemporaneo, São Paulo, Brazil/Index/Bridgeman Art Library

COSTA RICA was not a country with a rich artistic tradition, and something like a national school did not emerge till the end of the nineteenth century, when the development of the coffee trade gave rise to an affluent middle class, stimulated by contact with North America and Europe. At first painting tended to follow Neoclassicist lines, influenced by Spanish and German artists who taught in San José. The dead hand of the stereotyped Classicism was not removed until the 1920s when the so-called 'nationalist generation' of artists received their training at the Escuela de Bellas Artes. Amighetti, however, is largely self-taught but absorbed the stylistic development from Mexico, the United States and Europe (notably German Expressionism) as well as Japanese prints, evolving his own regional brand of painting to chronicle the everyday life of the Costa Rican peasantry in a luminous style which has been dubbed Creole Impressionism. Figures, animals and colourful adobe houses are painted in a style that mirrors his preoccupation with social problems.

MOVEMENT
Modern Latin American School
OTHER WORKS
Toro y Gente (Bull and People)
INFLUENCES
Japanese ukiyo-e prints

Francisco Amighetti   *Born* 1907 San José, Costa Rica
Painted in Costa Rica

Courtesy of Pinacoteca Digital- de Floria Barrionuevoy Maria Enriqueta Guardia

Andrea del Sarto

THE SON of a tailor (*sarto*), hence his nickname, Andrea was originally apprenticed to a goldsmith but his early aptitude for drawing led to him being sent to Piero di Cosimo for training in draughtsmanship and colouring. The measure of how well he learned his lessons is evident not only in his surviving works but also in the epithet applied to him in his lifetime as 'Andrea the Unerring'. Between 1509 and 1514 he was employed by the Brotherhood of the Servites to paint a series of frescos illustrating the life of the Servite saint Filippo Benizzi, and this established his reputation for his extraordinary mastery of colour and tone. Widely regarded as the finest fresco painter of his generation, Sarto was later commissioned by François I of France and spent some time in Paris before returning to Florence, where most of his later religious paintings were executed. As well as large wall paintings he excelled in smaller, more intimate portraits and he would undoubtedly have gone on to greater things had he not been struck down by the Plague at a relatively young age.

MOVEMENT
Florentine School
OTHER WORKS
Baptism of Christ, Dance of the Daughter of Herodias
INFLUENCES
Leonardo, Michelangelo, Franciabigio

Andrea del Sarto *Born* 1486 Florence, Italy
Painted in Florence and Paris
Died 1530 Florence

Courtesy of Predo, Madrid, Spain/Bridgeman Art Library

Angelico, Fra (Guido di Pietro)   The Annunciation (detail) *c.* 1420

FRA ANGELICO was one of a select band of Renaissance artists who combined the monastic life with a career as a professional painter. Little is known about his early years, apart from the fact that he was born at Vicchio, near Florence, and that his real name was Guido di Pietro. He became a Dominican friar *c.* 1418–21, entering the monastery of San Domenico in Fiesole. For the remainder of his life, he placed his art at the service of his faith, earning the nickname 'Angelic', by which he has become known to posterity.

Angelico's earliest surviving works are small-scale and betray an astonishing eye for detail, suggesting that he may have begun his career as a manuscript illuminator. They also display the influence of the International Gothic style, which was starting to fall out of fashion. The painter-monk learned quickly, however, absorbing Tommaso Masaccio's revolutionary ideas about the organization of space and perspective. He also tackled the most prestigious form of religious art: frescoe painting. In this field, Angelico's greatest achievement was a magnificent cycle of frescoes at the newly restored monastery of San Marco in Florence (c. 1438–45).

MOVEMENT
Renaissance
OTHER WORKS
The Annunciation, Linaiuoli Triptych, Coronation of the Virgin
INFLUENCES
Masaccio, Monaco

Fra Angelico   *Born c.* 1400
Painted in Italy
Died 1455

Courtesy of Prado, Madrid, Spain/Bridgeman Art Library/Christie's Images

SOFONISBA ANGUISSOLA was born into an aristocratic family. Her mother died when she was quite young, but her enlightened father ensured that Sofonisba and her four clever sisters received a sound classical education, including lessons in painting. Her extraordinary talent enabled her to overcome contemporary prejudices against female artists (reflected in the subterfuge of pretending that this self-portrait was the work of a male artist) and eventually her lifelike portraits secured her an appointment at the Spanish court. Her paintings range from formal studies of Spanish grandees to charming genre subjects, notably her earlier pieces, in which her sisters provided the models. It is these which are now most highly regarded, not only on account of the lively rendering of their subjects but also because of the attention to detail in dress and background. Anguissola remained active almost to the end of her very long life.

MOVEMENT
Spanish School of Portraiture

OTHER WORKS
Three Sisters Playing Chess, Portrait of a Young Nobleman

INFLUENCES
Titian, El Greco

Sofonisba Anguissola   *Born c.* 1527 Cremona Italy *Painted in* Cremona and Madrid *Died* 1625 Palermo, Italy

Courtesy of Muzeum Zamek, Lancut, Poland/Bridgeman Art Library

SHUSAKU ARAKAWA studied medicine and mathematics at Tokyo University but later switched to painting at the Musashino College of Art, and staged his first one-man show in the National Museum of Modern Art in 1958. Strongly influenced by the Dadaists of the early 1920s, he revived this movement in Japan and staged a number of 'happenings' from 1960 onwards to satirize the sickness and corruption in contemporary Japanese society. These activities caused a furore and Arakawa moved to the USA in 1961, settling in New York where he has lived ever since, working as a performance artist and film-maker as well as continuing to paint. Sending up those artists who produced works entitled *Untitled,* he produced a series under the name *Untitledness,* where blank spaces had pin marks where the object should be. A series entitled *Diagrams* consisted of spray-painted silhouettes of everyday objects. Later works explored the relationship between different forms of representation.

MOVEMENT
Dadaism
OTHER WORKS
Diagrams, Webster's Dictionary, The Mechanism of Meaning
INFLUENCES
Jean Arp, Kurt Schwitters, Man Ray

Shusaku Arakawa   *Born* 1936 Nagoya, Japan
Painted in Tokyo and New York

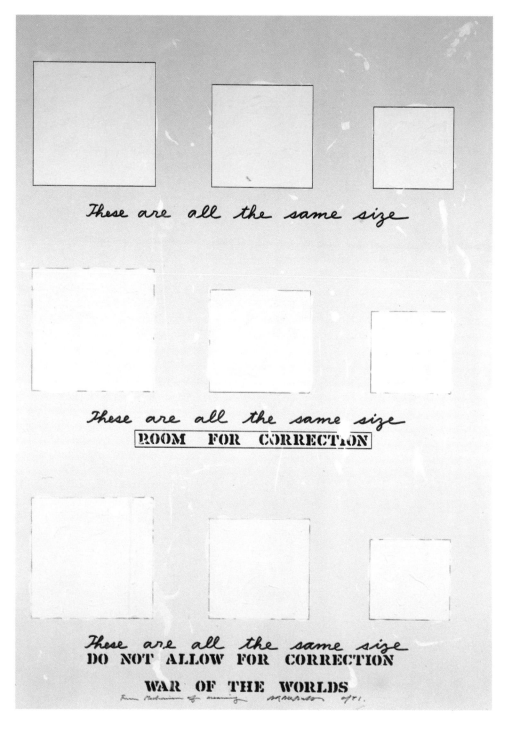

Courtesy of Private Collection/Christie's Images

GIUSEPPE ARCIMBOLDO began his artistic career by working on the stained-glass windows in the Duomo (Cathedral) in Milan. Later he moved to Prague which, under Charles V, became for a time the centre of the Holy Roman Empire, and here he was employed by the Habsburg rulers as an architect (of the civic waterworks among other public projects), impresario of state occasions, curator of the imperial art collection and interior designer. It was in Prague that he painted the works on which his reputation now rests. In his exploration of human portraits composed of non-human and inanimate objects he was far ahead of his time, anticipating the Surrealists by several centuries. His fantastic heads symbolizing the four seasons were made up of pieces of landscape, flowers, vegetables and animals, even pots and pans and other mundane articles from everyday life, all executed in brilliant colours with an extraordinary attention to detail.

MOVEMENT
Surrealism
OTHER WORKS
Summer
INFLUENCES
Medieval stained glass

Giuseppe Arcimboldo   *Born* 1527 Milan, Italy
Painted in Milan and Prague
Died 1593 Milan

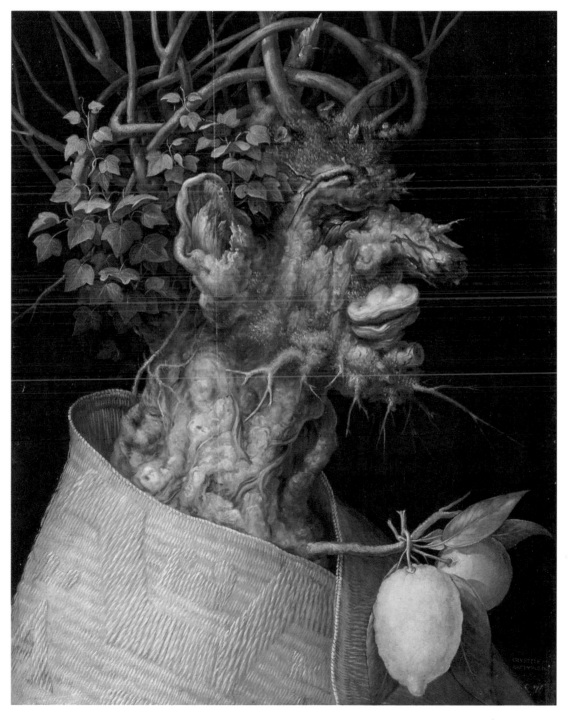

Courtesy of Kunsthistoriches Museum, Vienna/Bridgeman Art Library

Arikha, Avigdor   Alexander Frederick Douglas-Home, Lord Home of the Hirsel, 1988

AVIGDOR ARIKHA was born in 1929 in Bukovina (Romania), and survived the Holocaust thanks to the boyhood drawings he had created in deportation. He arrived in Palestine in 1944 where he received a Bauhaus art-education at Bezalel, Jerusalem, (1946-1949), and where he was also severely wounded in Israel's war of Independence (1948). He continued his art studies at the Ecole des Beaux-Arts in Paris (1949-1951) where he still mainly resides. His style, which was at first figurative, had evolved into abstraction in the late 1950s. He renounced abstraction in 1965 in favour of drawing and painting from observation, treating all subjects, whether they be still-lifes, landscapes, nudes or portraits (such as Lord Home and Queen Elizabeth the Queen Mother) in a single sitting. As an art historian, Arikha has curated exhibitions at the Louvre (Poussin, 1979) and the Frick Collection in New York (Ingres, 1986), among others. His writings include: *Peinture et Regard*, Paris, 1991 and *On Depiction*, London, 1995. Books about him include *Arikha* by Samuel Beckett, Robert Hughes et al., London, 1985 and *Avigdor Arikha* by Monica Ferrando and Arturo Schwarz, Bergamo, 2001.

MOVEMENT
International School
OTHER WORKS
Anne from the Back, 1973; The Square in June, 1983
INFLUENCES
Mondrian

Avigdor Arikha   *Born* 1929 Bukovina, Romania
Painted in Israel, France, England and USA

© The artist, courtesy of Scottish National Portrait Gallery, Edinburgh

BORN IN Dublin of English parents, Bacon left home at the age of 15, travelling to London, Berlin and Paris. In Paris he visited a Picasso exhibition, which inspired him to paint. In 1929, Bacon settled in London, where he designed Bauhaus-style furnishings and later, during wartime, joined the Civil Defence. His breakthrough as an artist came in 1945, when his *Three Studies for Figures at the Base of a Crucifixion* caused a sensation at the Lefevre Gallery. In this, as in many of his future works, elements of mutilation, pain and claustrophobia combined to create a highly disturbing effect.

From 1946 to 1950, Bacon resided in Monte Carlo, partly to satisfy his passion for gambling. His international reputation growing, he returned to London. His source material was very diverse, ranging from the work of other artists (Velázquez, Van Gogh) to films and photographs (Muybridge, Eisenstein) and autobiographical details. His studies of caged, screaming figures, for example, are often viewed as a reference to his asthma. Bacon's prevailing theme, however, is the vulnerability and solitude of the human condition.

MOVEMENT
School of London
OTHER WORKS
Sleeping Figure, Man with Dog
INFLUENCES
Picasso, Velázquez, Mathis Grünewald, Eadweard Muybridge

Francis Bacon *Born* 1909 Dublin
Painted in Britain, France and South Africa
Died 1992

Courtesy of Private Collection/Christie's Images/© Estate of Francis Bacon 2002. All rights reserved, DACS

Balla, Giacomo

AFTER A conventional art training in his native Turin, Giacomo Balla went to Paris in 1901, where he was strongly influenced by Impressionism and Divisionism. In 1910 he signed the Futurist Manifesto, publicizing his commitment to a form of art that would express the vibrant dynamism of the twentieth century. In his paintings Balla tried to convey the impression of speed through the use of overlapping images like time-lapse photographs. Futurism lost its freshness and idealism during World War I and in the 1920s it became increasingly stereotyped and associated with Fascism. As a result, Balla turned to more abstract forms and from 1930 onwards tended to return to the more mainstream styles of figural painting. Nevertheless, echoes of Balla's technique may be found in many works of the late twentieth century which use blurred or overlapping images to suggest rapid movement.

MOVEMENT
Futurism
OTHER WORKS
Girl Running on the Balcony, Dog on a Leash, Flight of Swallows
INFLUENCES
Umberto Boccioni, Carlo Carrà

Giacomo Balla   *Born* 1871 Turin, Italy
Painted in Italy
Died 1958 Rome, Italy

Courtesy of Private Collection/Christie's Images/Bridgeman Art Library/© DACS 2002

Bannister, Edward M.

THE SON of a West Indian and a woman from Canada's Maritime provinces, Edward Mitchell Bannister moved to Boston in 1848, working as a ship's cook and then as a barber. In the 1850s he joined the Crispus Attucks Choir and the Histrionics Club, a black drama group. His marriage to Christiana Carteaux, who owned a chain of high-class hair salons, gave him the financial freedom to pursue his artistic interests and he became the first black to attend art classes at the Lowell Institute. In 1870 the Bannisters moved to Providence,

Rhode Island, where Bannister took a prominent role in the circle of artists influenced by the Barbizon School. He regarded the rural landscape as an affirmation of harmony and spirituality, although he did not cavil at the advances of industrialization and painted such subjects with equal enthusiasm. In the last years of his life he produced a number of paintings of rural scenes and genre subjects.

MOVEMENT
American School
OTHER WORKS
Seaweed Gatherers, Dorchester, Massachusetts
INFLUENCES
Corot, Millet

Edward M. Bannister *Born* 1828 Canada
Painted in Boston, Providence and Rhode Island, USA
Died 1901 Providence

© Smithsonian American Art Museum, Washington, DC / Art Resource, NY

VERY LITTLE is known of this Hindu artist who flourished during the reign of Akbar the Great (1556–1605), but his name appears in the list of the top 17 painters in the Mughal Empire, compiled about 1590 by Abul Fazl, Akbar's chief minister, which presupposes that he was born around the middle of the century. Of the 17 artists, no fewer than 13 were Hindus and the others Muslims, revealing the grafting of Persian art on to the much older Indian stock. Akbar, raised a Muslim, took his role as Emperor of India very seriously and strove to unite his Hindu and Muslim subjects, art being one of the more obvious ways in which this was achieved. Basawan was the foremost of these painters, renowned for the utmost delicacy of his brushwork and the sumptuous quality of his colours. He contributed miniature paintings to virtually all of the collections commissioned by the Emperor, detailing the history and legends of both cultures in pictures full of action and crammed with detail.

MOVEMENT
Mughal or Indo-Persian School

OTHER WORKS
Razm Nama, Tuti Nama, Hamza Nama

INFLUENCES
Daswanth Kahar

Basawan   *Born c.* 1550 Delhi, India
Painted in Delhi
Died c. 1610 Delhi

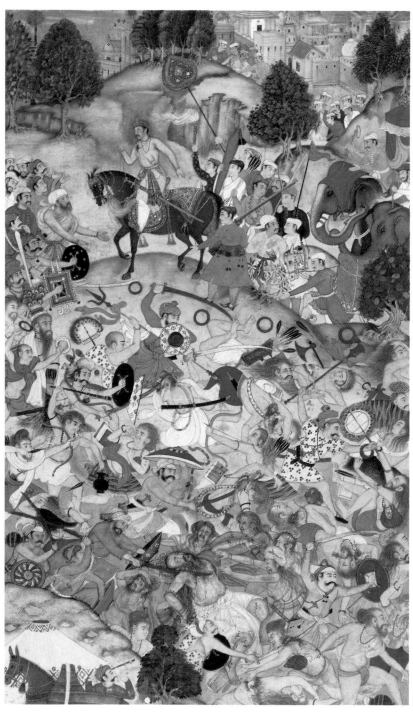

Courtesy of Victoria & Albert Museum, London/Bridgeman Art Library

Bearden, Romare H.

BORN IN Charlotte, North Carolina, in 1914, Romare Howard Bearden moved with his family to New York when he was three and eventually settled in Harlem. He began drawing cartoons at New York University, where he was also art editor of the student magazine *Medley*. Although originally intending a career in medicine, he switched to art and enrolled for evening classes at the Art Students' League where he studied under George Grosz. After military service in World War II the GI Bill enabled him to pursue his art studies at the Sorbonne, being particularly drawn to such masters as Duccio, De Hooch, Rembrandt and Manet. When he returned to the United States in 1952 he did not immediately take up creative painting, but from 1964 onwards he began producing collages. He is a versatile painter of landscapes and urban scenes, figures and abstracts, bringing to bear a highly intellectual approach in his work and drawing upon his southern roots for inspiration.

MOVEMENT
Modern American School
OTHER WORKS
Sunday After Sermon, Before the Dark, The Visitation
INFLUENCES
George Grosz

Romare Bearden   *Born* 1914 Charlotte, North Carolina, USA
Painted in New York and Paris

Courtesy of Art Resource, NY/© Romare Bearden Foundation / VAGA, New York/DACS, London 2002

Beardsley, Aubrey   The Peacock Skirt, Illustration for Oscar Wilde's play, 'Salome' 1894

ENGLISH GRAPHIC ARTIST, the epitome of *fin-de-siècle* decadence. Born in Brighton, Beardsley was a frail child and suffered his first attack of tuberculosis in 1879. He left for London at the age of 16, working initially in an insurance office, while attending art classes in the evening. In 1891 Edward Burne-Jones persuaded him to become a professional artist and, two years later, Beardsley received his first major commission, when J. M. Dent engaged him to illustrate Malory's *Morte d'Arthur*. The success of this venture gave him the opportunity to work on an even more prestigious project, the illustration of Wilde's *Salome*, while also producing images for a new journal, *The Yellow Book*.

Soon Beardsley developed a unique style, combining the bold compositional devices used in Japanese prints; the erotic, sometimes perverse imagery of the Symbolists; and an effortless mastery of sinuous, linear design, which prefigured Art Nouveau. A glittering career seemed to beckon, but in 1895 the scandal surrounding the Wilde trial led to his sacking from *The Yellow Book*. His tubercular condition flared up again and within three years he was dead.

MOVEMENT
Symbolism, Decadence, Art Nouveau
OTHER WORKS
The Toilet of Salome, How King Arthur saw the Questing Beast
INFLUENCES
Sir Edward Burne-Jones, Kitagawa Utamaro, Toulouse-Lautrec

Aubrey Beardsley   *Born* 1872, Brighton
Worked in England and France
Died 1898

Courtesy of Fogg Art Museum, Harvard University Art Museums, USA/Bridgeman Art Library

MAX BECKMANN is regarded as one of the greatest figurative artists of the twentieth century. He studied in Weimar and worked as a draughtsman and print-maker before moving to Berlin in 1904, where he embarked on large-scale paintings. During World War I he worked as a hospital orderly – a terrifying experience that shaped his subsequent art. There are Gothic overtones in his canvasses which starkly depict the hopeless struggle of the individual against evil. Not surprisingly, his work was dismissed by the Nazis as degenerate. In 1937 he fled to Holland and spent the last years of his life in the USA, a period in which his paintings expressed a new hope for the world. He was both prolific and versatile, his work ranging from still life and formal portraits to landscapes, abstracts and symbolic compositions, often bizarre and monstrous but always thought-provoking.

MOVEMENT
Expressionism
OTHER WORKS
Departure, Quappi with Parrot, The Night
INFLUENCES
George Grosz

Max Beckmann   *Born* 1884 Leipzig, Germany
Painted in Germany, Holland and USA
Died 1950 New York, USA

Courtesy of Private Collection/Christie's Images/© DACS 2002

FARUKH BEG is often referred to as Farukh the Qalmak (Kalmuck), which suggests that he hailed from that region of the Mughal Empire. Like other painters of the Indo-Persian School, little is known of his life, but he was one of the four Muslim artists named by Abul Fazl in the list of 17 court painters. Farukh contributed excellent miniature paintings to the Akbar Nama and was the author of a remarkable painting in three scenes, occupying a full page on the reverse of a folio in the Oriental collection at the British Library. He painted in the Persian manner, characterized by flatness and a fondness for surface patterns, extreme elegance in line and decorative detail. Farukh excelled in portraiture, reflecting the Emperor Akbar's total disregard of orthodox Muslim teaching, which forbade representation of living creatures, human or animal.

MOVEMENT
Mughal or Indo-Persian School
OTHER WORKS
Akbar Nama, Babur Nama, Sufi Pir at the Tavern Door
INFLUENCES
Mir Sayyid Ali, Abdus Samad

Farukh Beg *Born c.* 1550 Qalmakia, Persia
Painted in India
Died c. 1610 Delhi, India

Courtesy of Victoria and Albert Museum, London / Bridgeman Art Library

Benoist, Marie-Guillemine

MARIE-GUILLEMINE BENOIST was the daughter of a government official who recognized her talent and enrolled her as a pupil of Vigée-Lebrun in 1791; the latter's influence is very evident in Benoist's early works, mainly portraits done in pastels. Later she studied under Jacques-Louis David and as a result she began producing more ambitious works in oils. She made her debut at the Salon with two historical scenes and thereafter painted both portraits and historical subjects. She achieved a high reputation and received a gold medal and an annual government grant. Napoleon commissioned portraits of himself and his family from her. In the early 1800s she switched to painting genre subjects and sentimental domestic scenes which were immensely popular. Her best-known painting, a remarkable portrait of a young black woman painted in 1800, is believed to have been inspired by the decree of 1794 abolishing slavery.

MOVEMENT
French Romantic School

OTHER WORKS
Napoleon Bonaparte, The Imperial Family

INFLUENCES
Marie Vigée-Lebrun, David

Marie-Guillemine Benoist   *Born* 1768 Paris
Painted in Paris
Died 1826 Paris

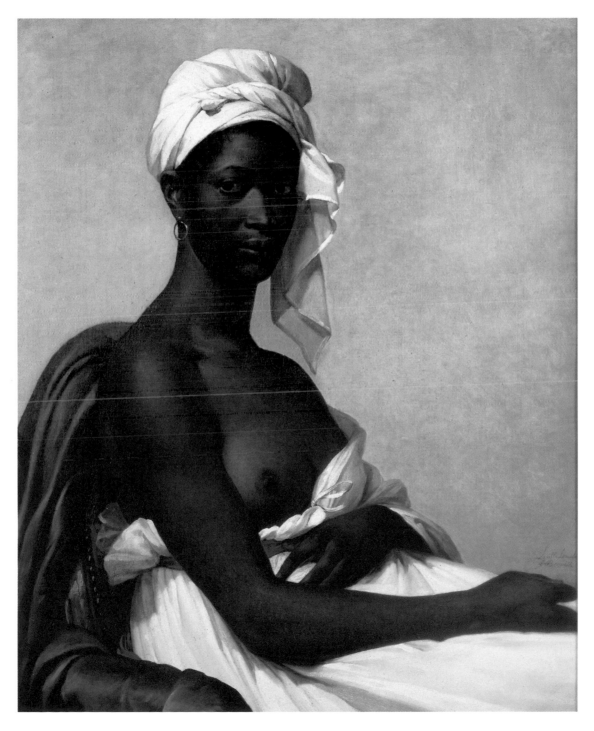

Courtesy of Louvre, Paris/Bridgeman Art Library

Berni, Antonio

AFTER A conventional art training in Buenos Aires, Antonio Berni travelled to Paris, where he continued his studies under Othon Friesz and André Lhote. With a number of other young Argentinian artists in the late 1920s formed the Grupo de Paris, through whom he also came under the influence of the Surrealists, De Chirico's Pittura Metafisica and the Italian muralists of the fifteenth century. More importantly, perhaps, he also imbibed the Marxist politics of the inter-war period and the course of the Spanish Civil War left a deep impression on him. On his return to Argentina he embarked on Surrealist works that concentrated on social themes ideally suited to the rugged material and technique. For these he used burlap (rough canvas) painted with distemper. The unusual perspective, foreshortened figures and a technique borrowed from film stills and religious icons combined to make his paintings truly distinctive.

MOVEMENT
Modern Latin American School
OTHER WORKS
Desocupados (Unemployed), Manifestación (Demonstration)
INFLUENCES
Giorgio de Chirico, Surrealism

Antonio Berni   *Born* 1907 Buenos Aires, Argentina
Painted in France and Argentina
Died 1981 Buenos Aires

Courtesy of Private Collection/Christie's Images

ONE OF the leading artists of the American West, George Caleb Bingham trained at the Pennsylvania Academy of Fine Arts in Philadelphia. His education was rounded off by a trip to Europe, followed by extensive travel round North America before he settled in Missouri, then on the western frontier. From here he explored the wilderness, recording landscape, sights and scenes of a rapidly vanishing way of life, although he is best remembered for his genre scenes of boatmen and trappers in Missouri. Regrettably he returned to Europe to improve his style, but the time spent in Düsseldorf had the opposite effect, stifling the homespun character of his painting with the rather stereotyped academicism of mid-nineteenth century Germany. As far back as 1848 he had been elected to the state legislature and by the time of the American Civil War he abandoned his palette altogether to concentrate on politics.

MOVEMENT
North American Frontier style

OTHER WORKS
Raftsmen Playing Cards, The Country Election

INFLUENCES
George Catlin, Seth Eastman

George Caleb Bingham   *Born* 1811 Augusta USA *Painted in* Missouri, USA *Died* 1879 Kansas City, USA

Courtesy of Metropolitan Museum of Art, New York/Bridgeman Art Library

VISIONARY POET and painter, one of the most individual talents to emerge from the Romantic movement. Blake lived in London for most of his life. He trained as a commercial engraver and briefly attended the Royal Academy Schools, although he soon felt stifled by the life classes; for him, the imagination was always far more important than the imitation of nature. Stylistically, Blake's art bore some of the hallmarks of Neoclassicism – particularly in its linear approach and its dramatic intent – but a classical sense of restraint was notably absent. His figures, meanwhile, owed much to the example of Michelangelo.

Blake's technique was highly inventive. He devised a system of 'illuminated printing', which enabled him to produce lavish editions of his books of poetry, and pioneered a form of tempera painting, in place of oils. His subject matter was largely drawn from the complex, personal mythology outlined in his verses. This baffled many of his contemporaries, who regarded him as an eccentric. Blake did have his admirers however, which included the group of young artists known as the Ancients.

MOVEMENT
Romanticism, Neoclassicism
OTHER WORKS
Glad Day, God Judging Adam, God Creating the Universe
INFLUENCES
Michelangelo, Henry Fuseli, John Flaxman

William Blake   *Born* 1757 London
Painted in England
Died 1827

Courtesy of Private Collection/Christie's Images

Bol, Ferdinand

FERDINAND BOL was the son of a master surgeon and was originally intended to follow in his footsteps. He learned the rudiments of painting from Jacob Cuyp (father of Albert Cuyp) in Utrecht and also studied for a time under Rembrandt in Amsterdam in the late 1630s. Bol established his own studio in Amsterdam by 1642 and soon built up a reputation for his portraits and large groups as well as allegorical, religious and classical works. He was Rembrandt's most talented pupil and painted in a style so close to that of his master that some of his paintings have been wrongly attributed to Rembrandt. As well as executing paintings for wealthy patrons he received a number of major civic commissions, including the decorations for the town hall, leper asylum and admiralty building. Bol was a prominent member of the Guild of St Luke, and became its governor in 1665. He appears to have painted nothing after 1669 when he married a wealthy widow and thereafter devoted himself to business and civic affairs.

MOVEMENT
Dutch School
OTHER WORKS
Vertumnus, Pyrrhus and Fabricius, Bacchus and Ariadne,
INFLUENCES
Jacob Cuyp, Rembrandt

Ferdinand Bol *Born* 1616 Dordrecht, Holland
Painted in Dordrecht, Utrecht and Amsterdam
Died 1680 Amsterdam

Courtesy of Private Collection/Christie's Images

Bonington, Richard Parkes

ENGLISH ROMANTIC ARTIST, mainly active in France. Born near Nottingham, Bonington migrated to France with his family in 1817. He learned watercolour techniques from Louis Francia before completing his training under Antoine-Jean Gros at the École des Beaux-Arts. While in Paris, he met Eugene Delacroix, with whom he later shared a studio. Both men were greatly impressed by John Constable's exhibits at the 1824 Salon, and they travelled together to England in the following year. By this stage, Bonington had already made his mark at the Salon, where he won a gold medal for his landscapes. These were acclaimed for their freshness, spontaneity and feeling for atmospheric effects – qualities which the artist had developed by making copious *pochades* (outdoor oil sketches). In addition to his landscapes, Bonington also produced a series of costume paintings, illustrating picturesque anecdotes from British history.

Bonington's promising career was cut short by ill health. He contracted tuberculosis and died in London, shortly before his twenty-sixth birthday.

MOVEMENTS
Romanticism
OTHER WORKS
Fish Market near Boulogne, Scene on the Coast of Picardy
INFLUENCES
Louis Francia, Eugene Delacroix, John Constable

Richard Parkes Bonington *Born* 1802
Painted in France, England, Italy and the Low Countries
Died 1828

Courtesy of Private Collection/Christie's Images

Bonnard, Pierre

PIERRE BONNARD settled in Paris in 1888, where he studied at the Académie Julien and the Ecole des Beaux-Arts. With Maurice Denis and Edouard Vuillard (with whom he shared a studio) he was influenced by Paul Gauguin's expressive use of colour and formed the group known as Les Nabis (from the Hebrew word for prophet) and later the Intimists. While other artists at the end of the nineteenth century were tending towards abstraction, Bonnard was influenced by Japanese prints and concentrated on landscapes and interiors which strove after subtle effects in light and colour at the expense of perspective. At the turn of the century he was moved by the intensity and passion in the paintings of Van Gogh and this led him to become a founder member of the Salon d'Automne in 1903. Thereafter he was influenced by Les Fauves (literally 'the wild beasts'), whose strident colours and distorted images he tamed and harnessed to his own style.

MOVEMENTS
Les Nabis, Intimism, Fauvism

OTHER WORKS
Mirror on the Washstand, The Open Window, The Table

INFLUENCES
Gauguin, Van Gogh

Pierre Bonnard *Born* 1867 Fontena-aux-Roses, France *Painted in* Paris, France *Died* 1947 Le Cannet, France

Courtesy of Private Collection/Christie's Images © ADAGP, Paris and DACS, London 2002

BORN JEROME VAN AKEN but known by the Latin version of his first name and a surname from the shortened form of his birthplace 's Hertogenbosch in North Brabant, where he spent his entire life, he painted great allegorical, mystical and fantastic works that combined the grotesque with the macabre. His oils are crammed with devils and demons, weird monsters, dwarves and hideous creatures, barely recognizable in human form. His quasi-religious and allegorical compositions must have struck terror in the hearts of those who first beheld them, but centuries later he would have a profound influence on the Surrealists. In more recent times there have been attempts to analyse his paintings in Jungian or Freudian terms, the theory being that he tried to put his more lurid nightmares on to his wood panels. This is his best-known work, executed on four folding panels, in which he develops the story of the Creation and the expulsion of Adam and Eve. At the core of the work is a vast sex orgy, symbolizing the sins of the flesh that caused man's downfall.

MOVEMENT
Surrealism
OTHER WORKS
The Temptation of St Anthony, Last Judgment
INFLUENCES
Gothic art

Hieronymus Bosch *Born c.* 1450, Holland
Hertogenbosch, Holland (now in Belgium)
Painted in Hertogenbosch, Holland
Died 1516 Hertogenbosch, Holland

Courtesy of Prado, Madrid, Spain/Bridgeman Art Library

THE OUTSTANDING Colombian artist of the twentieth century is Fernando Botero, who has attained a universal reputation in recent years. He studied the Great Masters of European art and the influence of such disparate artists as Uccello, Piero della Francesca, Mantegna, Velázquez and Rubens is discernible in his work, which exalts form while exploring new realities. His work is by no means rigidly classicist, but he has combined his studies of the Old Masters with a detailed examination of the popular indigenous art of Colombia. The extraordinary range of his work, encompassing figures, portraits, landscapes and genre subjects, is characterized by ironic humour and warm humanity, coupled with wry, shrewd observation of the scenes and people around him. Figures are often depicted in a curious pneumatic fashion with fixed expressions on their grossly inflated faces, deliberately producing a naive style. Botero has also produced a number of monumental sculptures, chiefly of female nudes.

MOVEMENT
Modern Latin American School

OTHER WORKS
Sunday Afternoon, Colombian Woman

INFLUENCES
Paolo Uccello, Piero della Francesca, Velázquez, Rubens, Goya

Fernando Botero   *Born* 1932 Medellin, Colombia
Painted in Colombia

Courtesy of Private Collection/Christie's Images

BORN ALESSANDRO Di Mariano dei Filipepi, he acquired his nickname ('little barrel') from his brother Giovanni, who raised him and who was himself thus named. From 1458 to 1467 he worked in the studio of Fra Lippo Lippi before branching out on his own. By 1480 he was working on the frescoes for the Sistine Chapel and his lesser works consist mainly of religious paintings, although it is for his treatment of allegorical and mythological subjects that he is best remembered. Outstanding in this group are his paintings *Primavera* (1477) and *The Birth of Venus* (1485), both now in the Uffizi. He also excelled as a portraitist, and provided the illustrations for Dante's *Divine Comedy*, which he executed in pen and ink and silverpoint (1402–5).

MOVEMENT
Florentine School

OTHER WORKS
Venus and Mars

INFLUENCES
Fra Lippo Lippi, Verrocchio

Sandro Botticelli *Born* 1445 Florence, Italy
Painted in Florence and Rome
Died 1510 Florence

Courtesy of Galleria Della Uffizi, Florence/Bridgeman Art Library/Christie's Images

Boucher, François

FRENCH PAINTER and designer, one of the greatest masters of the Rococo style. Born in Paris, Boucher was the son of a versatile, not particularly successful, artist and craftsman. As a result, he learned a wide variety of artistic techniques in his father's workshop before training more formally under François Lemoyne. Boucher's first significant job was to produce a set of engravings after Watteau's drawings, but he also found time to paint, winning the Prix de Rome in 1723. After making the traditional study-tour of Italy (1727–31), he began to gain official plaudits for his work. In 1735

he was granted his first royal commission and this secured his position as a court artist. This role governed the nature of Boucher's art. There were no grand, intellectual themes or moral dramas in his pictures. Instead, he painted light-hearted mythologies and pastoral idylls, which could serve equally well as paintings, tapestry designs or porcelain decoration. This is also evident in Boucher's work for his most distinguished patron, Madame de Pompadour. He immortalized her in a series of dazzling portraits, but also decorated her palace and designed sets for her private theatre.

MOVEMENT
Rococo

OTHER WORKS
The Triumph of Venus, Mademoiselle O'Murphy,

INFLUENCES
Watteau, Abraham Bloemaert, François Lemoyne

François Boucher   *Born* 1703, Paris
Painted in France and Italy
Died 1770

Courtesy of Private Collection/Christie's Images

ARTHUR MERRIC Bloomfield Boyd was born at Murrumbeena, Victoria, the younger son of the New Zealand-born painter Merric Boyd (1862-1940). He studied at the National Gallery of Victoria Art School, Melbourne, and at the Rosebud, Victoria. After war service he returned to Murrumbeena to work with his father and brother-in-law, John Perceval. From 1959 to 1972 he worked in London before becoming Fellow in Creative Arts at the University of Canberra. Although schooled in the Australian tradition, he came under European influence at an early age, both Van Gogh and Kokoschka being major sources of inspiration, which have given Boyd's paintings a more cosmopolitan character. Some of his more radical, avant-garde paintings were even confiscated by the Australian authorities during World War II. Later he concentrated on religious works, mixing the landscapes of Victoria with the imagery of Brueghel, Bosch and Stanley Spencer.

MOVEMENT
Australian Realism
OTHER WORKS
Shearers Playing for a Bride, The Mockers
INFLUENCES
Van Gogh, Oskar Kokoschka, Brueghel

Arthur Boyd   *Born* 1920 Victoria, Australia
Painted in Australia and England
Died 1999

Courtesy of Private Collection/Bridgeman Art Library

Braque, Georges

BORN IN Argenteuil, the son of a house-painter, Braque was initially trained to carry on the family business. In 1902 he switched to art, but retained a profound respect for craftsmanship and always ground his own pigments. Initially, he joined the Fauvist group, but his style altered radically after two key events in 1907. Firstly he was overwhelmed by an exhibition of Cézanne's work, then, later in the year, he saw *Les Demoiselles d'Avignon* in Picasso's studio and embarked on a unique collaboration with the Spaniard. Working, in Braque's words, 'like two mountaineers roped together', they created Cubism.

This artistic partnership was halted by the war, when Braque was called to the Front. He was decorated for bravery before being discharged with serious wounds in 1916. Unlike Picasso, who changed direction completely, Braque spent the remainder of his career refining his experiments with Cubism. These culminated in a magnificent cycle of paintings on *The Studio*, which he began in 1947. Braque also diversified into design work, producing ballet décors, stained-glass windows, book illustrations and, most notable of all, a ceiling for the Etruscan Gallery in the Louvre.

MOVEMENT
Cubism
OTHER WORKS
The Round Table, Guitar and Fruit Dish, Still Life with Violin
INFLUENCES
Picasso, Cézanne, Juan Gris

Georges Braque   *Born* 1882, France
Painted in France
Died 1963

Courtesy of Private Collection/Christie's Images © ADAGP, Paris and DACS, London 2002

Bronzino, Il

Madonna & Child with Infant Saint John the Baptist

BORN AGNOLO di Cosimo di Mariano, he became the leading court painter of the Florentine School in the mid-sixteenth century. He studied under Raffaellino del Garbo and Jacopo da Pontormo (working with the latter on religious frescoes) as well as being strongly influenced by Michelangelo. He spent his entire working life in Florence where he was court painter to Cosmo I, Duke of Tuscany. Second only to Andrea del Sarto among the Florentine portraitists, he also excelled as a painter of religious works. His talents extended to the written word, for he was also a notable poet and a member of the Florentine Academy. From Pontormo he developed a passion for light, resulting in the rich, brilliant colours that dominate his paintings. These are also striking on account of their fascination for the female nude, without precedent or parallel up to that time.

MOVEMENT
Mannerism
OTHER WORKS
Guidobaldo della Rovere, Eleanora Toledo and her Son
INFLUENCES
Raffaeline del Garbo, Jacope da Pontormo, Michelangelo

Il Bronzino *Born* 1503 Monticelli, Florence, Italy
Painted in Florence
Died 1572 Florence

Courtesy of Private Collection/Christie's Images

Brown, Grafton Tyler

(after) Gold Mining in California, 1861

GRAFTON TYLER BROWN was the first African American to work as a professional artist in California, where he settled in the 1850s. He worked as a draughtsman and later a lithographer for Kuchel & Dressel of San Francisco, but established his own company in 1867, producing lithographic views of buildings and landmarks, many of which appeared in stock certificates. In 1882 he took part in the Bowman geological survey of British Columbia, producing numerous sketches which he later reworked as watercolours. He lived in Portland, Oregon (1886–90) and from 1892 to 1897 was employed as a draughtsman by the United States Army Engineers in St Paul, Minnesota, where he died in 1918. His landscapes are very realistic and packed with detail, well deserving the comment by one early critic that he was 'the originator of intellectual and refined art'.

MOVEMENT
American Realism

OTHER WORKS
San Francisco

INFLUENCES
Northern Sung landscape artists of China

Grafton Tyler Brown *Born* 1841 Harrisburg, USA *Painted in* San Francisco and St Paul USA *Died* 1918 St Paul

Courtesy of Private Collection/Bridgeman Art Library

Brueghel, Pieter

ALSO KNOWN as Brueghel the Elder (to distinguish him from his son Pieter and younger son Jan), he was probably born about 1520 in the village of the same name, near Breda. He studied under Pieter Coecke van Aelst (1502–50) and was greatly influenced by Hieronymous Bosch, from whom he developed his own peculiar style of late-medieval Gothic fantasy. About 1550 he travelled in France and Italy before returning to Brussels, where his most important paintings were executed. He was nicknamed 'Peasant Brueghel' from his custom of disguising himself in order to mingle with the peasants and beggars who formed the subjects of his rural paintings. Although he was a master of genre subjects his reputation rests mainly on his large and complex works, involving fantastic scenery and elaborate architecture, imbued with atmosphere and a sensitivity seldom achieved earlier.

MOVEMENT
Flemish School
OTHER WORKS
Tower of Babel, Peasant Wedding
INFLUENCES
Pieter Coecke, Hieronymus Bosch

Pieter Brueghel *Born c.* 1520 Brögel, Holland
Painted in Breda and Brussels, Belgium
Died 1569 Brussels

Courtesy of Kunsthistoriches Museum, Vienna/Bridgeman Art Library/Christie's Images

Burne-Jones, Sir Edward

The Prince Enters the Briar Wood, 1869

EDWARD COLEY BURNE-JONES studied at Oxford where he met William Morris and Dante Gabriel Rossetti, who persuaded him to give up his original intention of entering holy orders and concentrate on painting instead. He was also heavily influenced by the art critic John Ruskin, who introduced him to the paintings of the Pre-Raphaelites and with whom he travelled to Italy in 1862. On his return to England he embarked on a series of canvasses that echoed the styles of Botticelli and Mantegna, adapted to his own brand of dreamy mysticism in subjects derived from Greek mythology, Arthurian legend and medieval romance. Burne-Jones, made a baronet in 1894, was closely associated with the Arts and Crafts movement, designing tapestries and stained glass for William Morris, as well as being a prolific book illustrator.

MOVEMENT
Romanticism and Mannerism

OTHER WORKS
King Cophetua and the Beggar Maid, The Beguiling of Merlin

INFLUENCES
Botticelli, Mantegna, Pre-Raphaelites

Sir Edward Burne-Jones   *Born* 1833
Birmingham, England *Painted in* England
Died 1898 London, England

Courtesy of Private Collection/Christie's Images

Burra, Edward

EDWARD BURRA was mainly educated at home on account of chronic ill health as a child, but in 1921 he enrolled at the Chelsea Polytechnic and later studied at the Royal College of Art. Later he travelled widely in Europe and America where he imbibed the ideas and techniques of the Surrealists and Dadaists, as well as German painters such as George Grosz. Bouts of ill health dogged him throughout his career and may explain the frenetic activity in his paintings and the exceptionally vivid colours, often placing his figures against exotic backgrounds. He had a keen eye for the absurd, the offbeat and the louche, and delighted in recreating scenes of low life in bars, brothels and nightclubs. By contrast, his pictures relating to the Spanish Civil War (1936–9) are stark and sombre, a prelude to his grim paintings of World War II. In the postwar period he turned to landscapes and still-life compositions. Burra also designed sets for ballet.

MOVEMENT
Surrealism
OTHER WORKS
The Snack Bar, Harlem, Soldiers
INFLUENCES
George Grosz, Dadaism, Surrealism

Edward Burra   *Born* 1905 London, England
Painted in London
Died 1976 Rye, Sussex, England

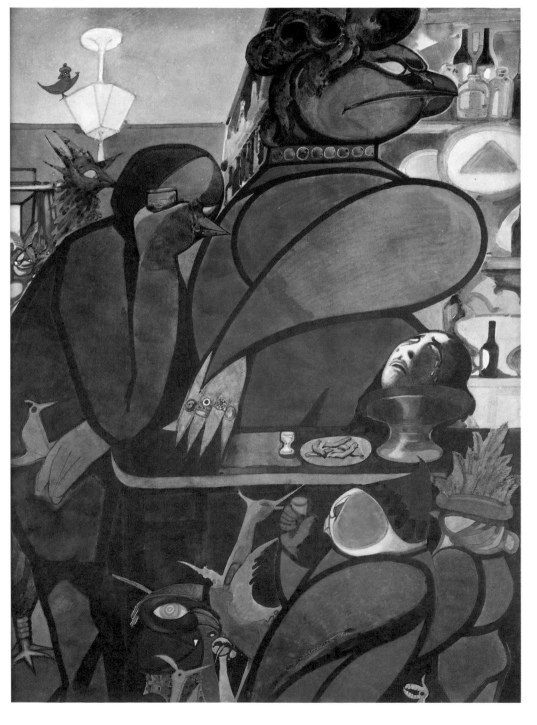

Courtesy of Private Collection/Christie's Images

Canaletto

ORIGINALLY NAMED Giovanni Antonio Canale, Canaletto was the son of a scene-painter in whose footsteps he at first followed. In 1719 he went to Rome to study architecture and on his return to Venice he began painting those great architectural masterpieces with which he has been associated ever since. Although most of his paintings illustrate the buildings and canals of his native city – executed as souvenirs for wealthy patrons from England making the Grand Tour – he lived mainly in London from 1746 to 1753. This is reflected in his paintings of the Thames and the City, and other views in the Home Counties. He then returned to Venice where he became a member of the Academy in 1763. He established a style of architectural painting that was widely imitated by the next generation of Italian artists, notably Francesco Guardi and his own nephew Bernardo Bellotto, who slavishly imitated him and even signed his works 'Canaletto'.

MOVEMENT
Venetian School

OTHER WORKS
Piazza San Marco, Regatta on the Grand Canal

INFLUENCES
Tiepolo

Canaletto *Born* 1697 Venice, Italy
Painted in Venice and London
Died 1768 Venice

Courtesy of Private Collection/Christie's Images

Caravaggio

BORN MICHELANGELO MERISI in the village of Caravaggio, Italy, he studied in Milan and Venice before going to Rome to work under the patronage of Cardinal del Monte on altarpieces and religious paintings. His patron was startled not only by Caravaggio's scandalous behaviour but also by his rejection of the Roman ideals and techniques in painting. Instead, Caravaggio headed the *Naturalisti* (imitators of nature in the raw), developing a mastery of light and shade and concentrating on realism, regardless of theological correctness. As a result, some of his major commissions were rejected and in 1606, after he had killed a man in an argument, he fled from Rome to Naples and thence to Malta. On his return to Italy in 1609 he contracted a fever and died at Pontercole, Sicily. The years of exile produced one of his greatest portraits, the full-length of the *Grand Master of the Knights*.

MOVEMENT
Baroque

OTHER WORKS
Christ at Emmaus, The Card Players

INFLUENCES
Annibale Carracci

Caravaggio   *Born c.* 1572 Caravaggio, Italy
Painted in Venice, Rome and Malta
Died 1610 Porto Ercole, Sicily

Courtesy of Galleria Degli Uffizi, Florence/Bridgeman Art Library/Christie's Images

Carr, Emily

EMILY CARR received her art education at the California School of Design in San Francisco (1891–94) and then went to England where she continued her studies at the Westminster School of Art (1899). She returned to Vancouver in 1904 to explore Indian sites in British Columbia, but a period in Paris (1910–11) had a profound effect on her art. She exhibited at the Salon d'Automne of 1911 and studied the works of the Impressionists, Post-Impressionists and Fauvists in particular. On her return to Vancouver she resumed her study of the art of the Indian communities of the north-west Pacific Coast and devoted much of her life to salvaging the remnants of their civilization, which permeated her later paintings. She painted nothing from 1912 until 1927 when she met the Group of Seven artists in Ottawa and was inspired by them to resume her artistic career. Her best work belonged to the ensuing decade. Following a heart attack in 1937 she spent the last years of her life mainly writing books.

MOVEMENT
Modern Canadian School

OTHER WORKS
Skidegate, British Columbian Indian Village

INFLUENCES
A.Y. Jackson, Lawren Harris

Emily Carr *Born* 1871 Victoria, British Columbia, Canada *Painted in* British Columbia *Died* 1945 Victoria, British Columbia

Courtesy of Art Gallery of Ontario, Toronto, Canada/Bridgeman Art Library

CARLO CARRÀ was largely self-taught, but at the beginning of the twentieth century he came under the influence of Giacomo Balla and signed the Futurist Manifesto of 1910. His paintings of this period show the futurist preoccupation with speed and movement. For a time, however, he also studied the works of Giotto. He served in the Italian army during World War I and while recuperating in a military hospital in 1917 he met Giorgio de Chirico, with whom he evolved a metaphysical style which in fact bordered on Surrealism.

From 1921 onwards, however, he switched to a more reflective mode into which he injected notions of heightened realism which he imbibed from his friend Giorgio Morandi. Back in the mainstream of Italian art, he taught at the Milan Academy and influenced the interwar generation of painters.

MOVEMENTS
Futurism, Metaphysical Painting
OTHER WORKS
Le Canal, Lot's Daughters
INFLUENCES
Giacoma Balla, Giorgio de Chirico, Giorgio Morandi

Carlo Carrà *Born* 1881 Quargnento, Italy
Painted in Milan, Italy
Died 1966 Milan

Courtesy of Private Collection, Switzerland/Bridgeman Art Library/© DACS 2002

Carracci, Annibale

THE GREATEST of a talented family (which included his brother Agostino and his cousin Ludovico), Annibale Carracci was self-taught to some extent, although he was influenced by Correggio and Raphael. The three Carraccis founded an academy of painting in Bologna in 1585 and exerted a tremendous influence on Baroque artists of the next generation. In 1595 Annibale went to Rome, where he was employed by Cardinal Farnese in the decoration of his palace with a series of great frescoes whose motifs were mainly derived from classical mythology – an achievement which is surpassed only by Michelangelo's work in the Sistine Chapel. Carracci also produced numerous paintings of religious subjects, often placing the Madonna and saints in somewhat idealized classical landscapes. He thus combined the traditions of classicism with the advances in naturalism in the late sixteenth century.

MOVEMENT
Neoclassical

OTHER WORKS
The Assumption of the Virgin, The Virgin Mourning Christ

INFLUENCES
Correggio, Raphael, Titian

Annibale Carracci   *Born* 1560 Bologna, Italy
Painted in Bologna and Rome
Died 1609 Rome

Courtesy of Private Collection/Christie's Images

Carriera, Rosalba

THE DAUGHTER of the painter Andrea Carriera, Rosalba was taught by her father and worked in pastels and oils. She painted mostly miniature portraits in oils on ivory both for framing and mounting in snuff-boxes, but by the beginning of the eighteenth century she had diversified into larger portraits mainly executed in pastels, and soon gained a high reputation in this medium. She was admitted to the Academy of St Luke at Rome in 1705. As well as formal portraits she painted genre subjects, mainly dealing with the everyday lives of women, latterly she also painted allegorical scenes and figures from classical mythology. Her style matured significantly from about 1711, and her portraits became much more expressive of the sitter's character. In 1720–22 she worked in Paris and was admitted to membership of the Académie Royale. From 1723 onwards she was much in demand at the courts of Europe to paint royal portraits.

MOVEMENT
Venetian School
OTHER WORKS
Antoine Watteau, Empress Amalia, Lady Cutting her Hair
INFLUENCES
Andrea Carriera, Federico Bencovich, Giovanni Pellegrini

Rosalba Carriera   *Born* 1675 Venice, Italy
Painted in Italy, France, Germany and Austria
Died 1757 Venice

Courtesy of Private Collection/Christie's Images

BORN IN Lancashire but brought up in London, Leonora Carrington came under the influence of the Surrealists in the 1930s and produced a number of paintings which combined scenes and images from her childhood with mystical and fairytale themes. In 1942 she crossed the Atlantic and settled in Mexico, where she shared a studio with Remedios Varo, a Spanish female painter of similar outlook, who shared her enthusiasm for the occult, alchemy and other magical subjects.

A feminist ahead of her time, Carrington attempted to explore and analyse the female psyche through the medium of painting. A recurring theme was woman as the life force at the heart of all creativity contrasted by malign forces in nature, which often gives her paintings a rather sinister undertone. There are echoes of the early Renaissance religious artists in her work, especially in the use of allegory and mythology, but these are often mingled with weird and bizarre elements that owe more to the Surrealists.

MOVEMENT
Surrealism
OTHER WORKS
Baby Giant, The Magic Works of the Mayas
INFLUENCES
Hieronymus Bosch, Dalì

Leonora Carrington   *Born* 1917 Clayton Green, Lancashire, England
Painted in England and Mexico

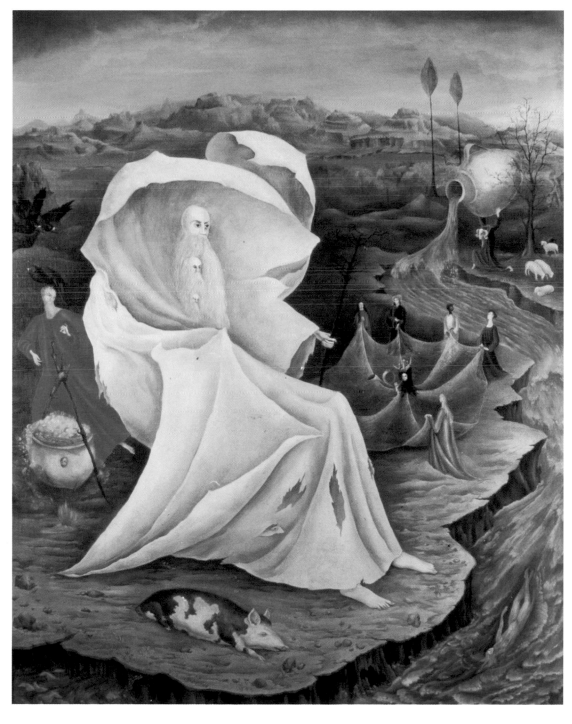

Courtesy of Private Collection, Christie's Images/© ARS, NY and DACS, London 2002

MARY CASSATT studied art at the Pennsylvania Academy of Art in Philadelphia from 1861 to 1865, but after the American Civil War she travelled to Europe, continuing her studies in Spain, Italy and the Netherlands before settling in Paris, where she became a pupil of Edgar Degas. Her main work consisted of lithographs, etchings and drypoint studies of genre and domestic subjects which often reflect her interest in Japanese prints; but her reputation now rests on her larger works, executed in pastels or oils, which explore the tender relationship between mother and child, although her mastery of technique (which owed much to her original teacher, Thomas Eakins) prevented her from descending into the banal or mawkish. After her death in Paris in 1926 her work was for some time neglected, but in more recent years it has been the subject of re-appraisal and her realistic but sensitive portraiture of women, girls and young children is now more fully appreciated.

MOVEMENT
Impressionism
OTHER WORKS
Mother and Child, Woman Sewing
INFLUENCES
Thomas Eakins, Degas

Mary Cassatt *Born* 1844 Pennsylvania, USA
Painted in USA and France
Died 1926 Paris, France

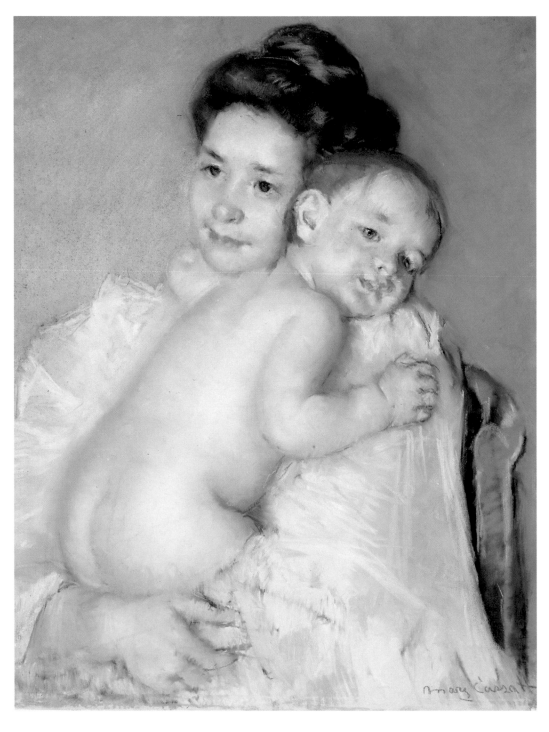

Courtesy of Private Collection/Christie's Images

Cézanne, Paul

FRENCH PAINTER, a leading member of the Post-Impressionists. Born in Aix-en-Provence, the son of a banker, Cézanne's prosperous background enabled him to endure the long struggle for recognition. He studied in Paris, where he met the future members of the Impressionist circle, although his own work at this time was full of violent, Romantic imagery. Cézanne did not mix easily with the group; he was withdrawn, suspicious and prey to sudden rages. Gradually, with Pissarro's encouragement, he tried *plein-air* painting and participated at two of the Impressionist

exhibitions. But, in art as in life, Cézanne was a solitary figure and he soon found the principles of the movement too restricting.

After his father's death in 1886, Cézanne returned to Aix, where he brought his style to maturity. His aim was to produce 'constructions after nature'. He followed the Impressionist practice of painting outdoors but, instead of the transient effects which they sought, he tried to capture the underlying geometry of the natural world. This was to make him a fertile source of inspiration for the Cubists.

MOVEMENT
Post-Impressionism
OTHER WORKS
Mont Sainte-Victoire, Apples and Oranges, The Card Players
INFLUENCES
Delacroix, Courbet, Pissarro

Paul Cézanne *Born* 1839 France
Painted in France
Died 1906

Courtesy of Private Collection/Bridgeman Art Gallery/Christie's Images

BORN INTO an Orthodox Jewish family in what was then known as Russian Poland, Marc Chagall studied in St Petersburg and Paris and returned to his native city on the eve of World War I. Initially he worked as a sign-writer but on his return to Russia he joined the Knave of Diamond group and participated in their 1917 exhibition, which was intended as an attack on the stuffy classicism of the Moscow School of Art. The Revolution broke out shortly afterwards and Chagall was appointed Director of the Vitebsk Art School before being summoned to Moscow to design sets for the Jewish Theatre. He left Russia in 1922 and settled near Paris. On the outbreak of World War II he moved to the USA where he designed sets and costumes for the ballet, as well as illustrating books and producing stained-glass windows, notably for the UN Building in New York and the Hadassah Hospital in Jerusalem. He also painted the murals for the Knesset (Israeli parliament). His paintings combine fantasy, folklore and biblical themes with an intensely surreal quality. Indeed, it is claimed that Guillaume Apollinaire originally coined the term 'Surrealist' to describe Chagall's paintings.

MOVEMENT
Surrealism
OTHER WORKS
Above the Town, I and the Village
INFLUENCES
Gauguin, The Fauves

Marc Chagall   *Born* 1887 Vitebsk, Russia
Painted in Russia, France and USA
Died 1985 Saint Paul-de-Vence, France

Courtesy of Private Collection/Christie's Images/© ADAGP, Paris and DACS, London 2002

Chardin, Jean-Baptiste-Siméon   A Ray - Fish, Basket of Onions, A Green Jug, A Copper pot, 1731

FRENCH PAINTER, specializing in still life and genre scenes. Chardin was born in Paris, where he spent most of his life. His father was a carpenter and, initially, he seemed destined to follow this trade, until his aptitude for painting became apparent. As a youth, Chardin trained under two very minor history painters, Pierre Cazes and Noel-Nicolas Coypel, but his real education came from copying Dutch and Flemish paintings in private art collections. These prompted him to concentrate on still-life pictures – a brave decision, since this type of painting had a low reputation and was very poorly paid.

Despite these drawbacks, Chardin's career flourished. In 1728, *The Skate* won such acclaim at a Paris exhibition that he was invited to become a full member of the Academy, an unprecedented honor for a still-life artist. Chardin was delighted and became a stalwart of the institution, holding the post of Treasurer for 20 years. Even so, he found it hard to make a living and, accordingly, extended his repertoire to include simple domestic scenes. These wonderful vignettes of everyday life displayed none of the affectation of the prevailing Rococo style, and proved enormously popular with the public.

MOVEMENT
Still life and genre
OTHER WORKS
Saying Grace, The Brioche
INFLUENCES
Nicolaes Maes, Jean-Baptiste Oudry

Jean-Baptiste-Siméon Chardin   *Born* 1699
Painted in France
Died 1779

Courtesy of Private Collection/Christie's Images

Cheng, Li

detail from 'A Buddhist Temple in the Mountains', 10th century

LI CHENG was one of the foremost scroll painters of the Northern Sung School and produced superb handscrolls, adapting the towering mountain subjects to the horizontal format in 'level-distance' pictures as well as the large vertical hanging scrolls which did full justice to the majestic scenery they depicted. He was particularly noted for his representation of gnarled, twisted trees (symbolic of the Confucian ideals of morality and uprightness) and distant views of rugged peaks and barren landscapes. His works were executed in saturated ink brushwork, ideally suited to the depiction of bare, spiky trees against awesome massifs, creating an intense atmosphere of grandeur. By contrast, he was very sparing in the use of colour for the background scenery, giving his paintings a three-dimensional quality. Li Cheng's style is unmistakable and was perpetuated by his most famous pupil, Guo Xi.

MOVEMENT
Northern Sung School, China
OTHER WORKS
A Solitary Temple Amid Clearing Peaks, Winter Forest
INFLUENCES
Wei Xian, Dong Yuan

Li Cheng   *Born c.* AD 919 Northern China
Painted in China
Died c. AD 967 Beijing, China

Courtesy of The Art Archive/Private Collection/The Art Archive

Chirico, Giorgio de

BORN IN north-western Greece of Venetian descent, Giorgio de Chirico studied in Athens and Munich, then worked in Paris and finally collaborated with Carrà in Italy, founding *Pittura Metaphisica*. About 1910 he began painting a series of pictures of deserted town squares, imbued with a dreamlike quality, characterized by incongruous figures and strange shadows which anticipated the style of the Surrealists, on whom he exerted tremendous influence. After suffering a breakdown during World War I he developed his metaphysical style of paintings, which conveyed an intensely claustrophobic impression. In the 1920s, however, his paintings often verged on the abstract before he returned to a more traditional style shortly before World War II – the complete antithesis of all he had done up to that time. He continued to embrace academic naturalism in the postwar period.

MOVEMENT
Metaphysical painting, Surrealism
OTHER WORKS
The Uncertainty of the Poet, The Archaeologists
INFLUENCES
Carlo Carrà

Giorgio de Chirico   *Born* 1888 Volo, Greece
Painted in France and Italy
Died 1978 Rome

Courtesy of Private Collection/Christie's Images/© DACS 2002

Cimabue, Giovanni

Angels from the Santa Trinita Altarpiece, 1280–90

CIMABUE WAS the nickname of Genni di Pepo or Peppi, who was born in Florence around 1240. He began his career by imitating the Byzantine styles then prevalent, but soon developed a style of his own which earned for him the title of 'Father of Italian Painting'. There were certainly distinctive Italian painters before his time, but he was the outstanding artist of his generation and a role model for his successors. His fame rested mainly on the enormous altarpiece in the chapel of the Rucellai in Santa Maria Novella, Florence,

although this was later proven to have been painted by Duccio. Works that are definitely attributed to him include the frescoes in the church of St Francis of Assisi and a number of paintings of the Madonna. He was the precursor of Giotto, whom he is supposed to have discovered as a 10-year-old shepherd boy and recognized his artistic potential.

MOVEMENT
Florentine School
OTHER WORKS
St John (Pisa Cathedral)
INFLUENCES
Byzantine, Romanesque

Cimabue *Born c.* 1240 Florence, Italy
Painted in Florence
Died c. 1302 Florence

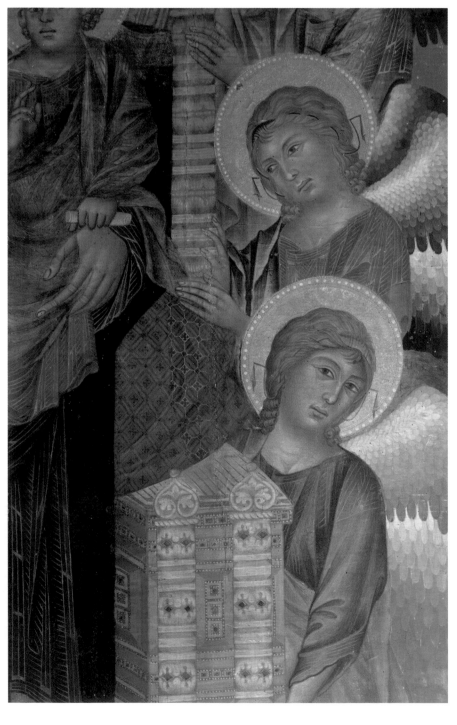

Courtesy of Galleria Degli Uffizi, Florence, Italy/Bridgeman Art Library

BORN AT Haarlem in the Netherlands in 1597 or 1598, Pieter Claesz grew up in a town which was the centre of the Dutch flower trade, so it was not surprising that he developed an early interest in floral painting. He grew up at a time when this style was being introduced to Holland by Flemish refugees, notably Ambrosius Bosschaert the Elder and Balthasar van der Alst. Claesz went on to develop the type of still life known as the breakfast or banquet picture – much less ebullient than the colourful flower paintings with more somber tones suited to the intimate atmosphere of domestic interiors. Claesz in fact took this further than his contemporaries, creating an almost monochrome effect and relying on the precise juxtaposition of each object which then took on a symbolic meaning. He pioneered a style that was emulated by many Dutch artists of the succeeding generation.

MOVEMENT
Dutch School

OTHER WORKS
Still Life with a Candle

INFLUENCES
Ambrosius Bosschaert, Balthasar van der Alst, Caravaggio

Pieter Claesz   *Born c.* 1597 Haarlem, Holland
Painted in Haarlem
Died 1660 Haarlem

Courtesy of Johnny van Haeften Gallery, London, UK/Bridgeman Art Library

Close, Chuck

CHUCK CLOSE studied art at Yale from 1962 to 1964 and settled in New York City in 1967. In that year, influenced by the photographic self-portraits produced by Claude Cahun in the 1920s, he began painting photographs of portraits, meticulously reproducing the tiniest detail. Every line and wrinkle, every pore and individual strands of hair are carefully delineated. In fact, appearances can be deceptive; closer examination often reveals slight distortion or blurring around the ears or shoulders in order to convey the impression that the face is looming towards the viewer. In this way the artist remedies the shortcomings of the camera lens. In more recent years he has taken this a stage further, combining this photo-realism with such techniques as finger-painting, a microscopic stippled effect and collages.

MOVEMENT
Hyper-realism
OTHER WORKS
John
INFLUENCES
Claude Cahun

Chuck Close   *Born* 1940 Monroe, Washington State, USA
Painted in New York

Courtesy of Private Collection/Christie's Images/© Chuck Close

Coldstream, Sir William

ENGLISH PAINTER, teacher and administrator, a leading member of the Euston Road School. Coldstream was born in Northumberland, the son of a doctor, and moved to London with his family in 1910. He trained at the Slade School and joined the London Group (a spin-off from the Camden Town Group), but remained uncertain about the direction of his art. For three years (1934–37), Coldstream turned to film-making until Kenneth Clark coaxed him back to full-time painting. At this stage, he joined the Euston Road School, which had recently been founded by Victor Pasmore and Claude Rogers. This group rejected the more radical elements of avant-garde art, preferring to teach and practice a figurative style of painting, which took account of social realities. This accorded well with Coldstream's own choice of subject matter: urban landscapes, portraits and nudes.

The school closed with the outbreak of war and, after a brief stint in the Royal Artillery, Coldstream became a war artist, based in Cairo and Italy. Subsequently, he distinguished himself in arts administration. The Coldstream Report (1960) reshaped the structure of art-school teaching in the UK.

MOVEMENT
Euston Road School
OTHER WORKS
St. Pancras Station, Mrs. Winifred Burger, Bolton
INFLUENCES
Walter Sickert, Graham Bell, Claude Rogers

Sir William Coldstream *Born* 1908, Northumberland *Painted in* England, Italy and Egypt *Died* 1987

Courtesy of Private Collection/Christie's Images

BORN IN Lancashire, England, Thomas Cole served his apprenticeship as an engraver of textile designs for calico printing. He emigrated with his family in 1818 and worked briefly as an engraver in Philadelphia before settling in Steubenville, Ohio, where he took lessons from an unknown travelling artist. In 1823 he returned to Philadelphia and enrolled at the Pennsylvania Academy of Fine Arts, then moved to New York in 1825. He began sketching along the Hudson River and through the Catskill Mountains, and his paintings of the American wilderness brought him fame and fortune. In 1829–32 he travelled all over Europe painting landscapes and classical ruins. On his return to New York he embarked on a colossal project – a series of large paintings that would chronicle the rise and fall of civilization. He took immense pride in his allegories and deprecated the landscapes which made his fortune and on which his reputation still rests.

MOVEMENT
Hudson River School
OTHER WORKS
Expulsion from the Garden of Eden, The Course of Empire
INFLUENCES
Washington Alliston

Thomas Cole   *Born* 1801, Lancashire, England
Painted in North America and Europe
Died 1848 Catskill, New York, USA

Courtesy of Private Collection/Christie's Images

Colville, Alex

ALTHOUGH BORN in Toronto, David Alexander Colville was raised in Amherst, Nova Scotia. At the age of nine he suffered a bout of pneumonia and during a long convalescence was encouraged to draw and paint. Later he studied under Stanley Royle, who persuaded him to abandon his plans for a career in law and politics and concentrate on art. In 1942 he was one of the first graduates in Fine Arts anywhere in Canada, and spent three years as an official war artist, an experience that shaped his later career. After the war he taught art at Mount Allison University until 1963, when he retired to paint full-time. A versatile artist, he has designed everything from Canadian coins and medals to album sleeves for folk singers. His realist style is executed in the manner of the French pointillists, using thousands of tiny brushstrokes to create an almost sculptural effect.

MOVEMENT
Modern Canadian School
OTHER WORKS
Horse and Train
INFLUENCES
Camille Pissarro, Seurat

Alex Colville   *Born* 1920, Toronto, Ontario, Canada
Painted in Amherst and Wolfville, Nova Scotia

Courtesy of Art Gallery of Ontario, Toronto/Bridgeman Art Library

A PIONEERING British artist who, together with Turner, raised the status of landscape painting in England. Constable enjoyed a happy childhood in his native Suffolk, and this region became the focus for most of his paintings. In Constable's day, however, landscape painting was a poorly paid profession and both his family and that of his lover, Maria Bicknell, were appalled by his choice of career. For many years, the couple were forced to meet in secret, until they eventually married in 1816. Constable's struggle for success was as difficult as his father had feared and, for a time, he was obliged to paint portraits for a living. In part, this was because he did not seek out romantic or picturesque views, but preferred to paint his local area, even though many regarded it as dull, agricultural land. He also paid unprecedented attention to atmospheric conditions, making copious sketches of individual clouds. These were so realistic that one critic joked that Constable's paintings always made him want to reach for his umbrella. Eventually, he found success with his 'six-footers' (i.e. six foot wide), gaining membership of the Royal Academy and winning a gold medal at the Paris Salon.

MOVEMENT
Romanticism
OTHER WORKS
The Hay Wain, Flatford Mill, Salisbury Cathedral
INFLUENCES
Thomas Gainsborough, Jacob van Ruisdael, Claude Lorrain

John Constable Born 1776, Suffolk, England
Painted in England
Died 1837

Courtesy of Private Collection/Christie's Images

Cooper, Samuel

SAMUEL COOPER is often regarded as the greatest painter of miniatures who ever lived; certainly he was instrumental in raising the status of miniature painting to new heights. He learned his skills from his uncle, John Hoskins. Pepys mentions Cooper frequently in his diaries and noted that he was a fine musician and a good linguist in addition to his artistic talents. He lived through turbulent times and had the distinction of holding official appointments both under the Commonwealth and later the Crown following the Restoration of 1660. He painted several portraits of both Oliver Cromwell and King Charles II, including the effigy of the King used for the coinage. As well as miniatures, painted on ivory or fine parchment, he was also a prolific draughtsman, his collection of chalk drawings being preserved in the Oxford University gallery.

MOVEMENT
English Miniaturists
OTHER WORKS
John Aubrey, Mrs Pepys, Self Portrait
INFLUENCES
John Hoskins

Samuel Cooper   *Born* 1609 London, England
Painted in London
Died 1672 London

Courtesy of Victoria & Albert Museum, London, UK/Bridgeman Art Library

Copley, John Singleton

BORN AT Boston, Massachusetts of Irish parents, John Singleton Copley was self-taught as an artist but by the late 1750s had established himself as a portraitist in his native city. A small painting of a boy with a squirrel was exhibited at the Royal Society of Arts in London 1760 and helped to spread his reputation across the Atlantic. In 1774 he visited Italy, and arrived in England just as the American War of Independence was erupting. Consequently he settled in London, became an associate of the Royal Academy in 1777 and an academician in 1783 following the exhibition of his best-known work, the dramatic *The Death of Chatham*. He is esteemed on both sides of the Atlantic, for his portraits of the British royal family and for his studies of the leading political and military figures in Boston society in the late-colonial period.

MOVEMENT
English School
OTHER WORKS
The Death of Major Pierson
INFLUENCES
Sir Joshua Reynolds

John Singleton Copley *Born* 1737 Boston USA *Painted in* Boston, USA and London, England *Died* 1815 London

Courtesy of Private Collection/Christie's Images

Corot, Jean-Baptiste-Camille

FRENCH PAINTER, specializing in landscapes in the classical tradition. Born in Paris, Corot was the son of a cloth merchant and initially followed his father's trade. For a time, he worked at The Caliph of Bagdad, a luxury fabric shop. Turning to art, he trained under Michallon and Bertin, both of whom were renowned for their classical landscapes. Indeed, Michallon was the first winner of the Historical Landscape category in the Prix de Rome, when it was introduced in 1817. This genre, which Corot was to make his own, consisted of idealized views, set in the ancient, classical world, and was inspired by the 17th-century paintings of Poussin and Claude Lorrain.

Corot's distinctive style stemmed from his unique blend of modern and traditional techniques. Each summer, he made lengthy sketching trips around Europe, working these studies up into paintings in the winter, in his Paris studio. He combined this traditional practice with a fascination for the latest developments in photography. The shimmering appearance of his foliage, for example, was inspired by the *halation* or blurring effects, which could be found in contemporary photos.

MOVEMENT
Romanticism, Barbizon School
OTHER WORKS
The Bridge at Narni, Gust of Wind, Recollection of Mortefontaine
INFLUENCES
Achille-Etna Michallon, Claude Lorrain, Constable

Jean-Baptiste-Camille Corot   *Born* 1796

Painted in France, Italy, Switzerland, England and Low Countries *Died* 1875

Courtesy of Private Collection/Christie's Images

ANTONIO ALLEGRI, known to posterity by his nickname of Correggio, was born in the town of that name in the duchy of Modena. Originally he began training as a physician and surgeon, and studied anatomy under Giovanni Battista Lombardi – believed to be the doctor portrayed in the painting entitled *Correggio's Physician*. In 1518 he embarked on his epic series of frescoes for the Convent of San Paolo in Parma, and followed this with the decoration of Parma Cathedral. He was the first Italian artist to

paint the interior of a cupola, producing *The Ascension* for the church of San Giovanni in Parma. He also executed numerous religious and biblical paintings, but also occasionally drew on classical mythology for inspiration. His wife Girolama (b 1504) is believed to have been his model for the *Madonna Reposing*, sometimes known as *Zingarella* ('Gipsy Girl').

MOVEMENT
Parma School
OTHER WORKS
Mystic Marriage of Saint Catherine, Ecce Homo
INFLUENCES
Leonardo da Vinci, Andrea Mantegna, Lorenzo Costa

Correggio *Born* 1494 Correggio, Italy
Painted in Correggio and Parma
Died 1534 Correggio

Courtesy of Prado, Madrid, Spain/Bridgeman Art Library

Cotman, John Sell

JOHN SELL COTMAN received his art training in London before returning to his native Norwich in 1806, where he became the foremost watercolourist among the group of East Anglian artists who came to be known as the Norwich School. In the early years of the nineteenth century he travelled extensively in England and Wales and his best work belongs to this period. Although chiefly remembered for his work in this medium he also executed a number of fine oil paintings during the time when he resided at Great Yarmouth (1811–23). Failing in business, however, he was forced to sell all his paintings and etchings and return to London, where he obtained a position as drawing master at King's College. There is an uncompromisingly austere character to his landscapes, very much ahead of his time and not at all in step with the fashions prevailing in Regency England, but his handling of light and shade was to have a profound influence on his followers.

MOVEMENT
English Landscape School
OTHER WORKS
Greta Bridge, Chirk Aqueduct, Duncombe Park
INFLUENCES
Thomas Girtin, Turner

John Sell Cotman *Born* 1782, Norfolk, England *Painted in* Norwich and London *Died* 1842 London

Courtesy of Christie's Images/Bridgeman Art Library

FRENCH PAINTER, the leader of the Realist movement. Courbet was born at Ornans in the Jura region, and remained fiercely loyal to this area throughout his life, featuring it prominently in his paintings. Although he later claimed to be self-taught, he actually studied under a succession of minor artists, but learned more from copying Old Masters in the Louvre. Initially, Courbet aimed for conventional success by exhibiting at the Salon, even winning a gold medal for his 1849 entry. After he showed *The Burial at Ornans*, however, official approval evaporated. Instead, this landmark realist picture was savagely criticized for being too large, too ugly and too meaningless. Worse still, in the light of the recent 1848 Revolution, the artist was suspected of having a political agenda.

Courbet revelled in the furore. In the following years, he gained greater recognition abroad, but remained antagonistic towards the French Establishment. He refused to exhibit at the 1855 World Fair, turned down the offer of a Legion of Honor, and served as a Councillor in the Paris Commune. The latter proved his undoing and he was forced to spend his final years exiled in Switzerland.

MOVEMENT
Realism
OTHER WORKS
The Painter's Studio, The Bathers
INFLUENCES
Le Nain brothers, Velázquez, Millet

Gustave Courbet   *Born* 1819 France
Painted in France, Switzerland and Germany
Died 1877

Courtesy of Musee Fabre, Montpelier, France/Bridgeman Art Library

Cozens, John Robert

AN ARTIST whose background was more colourful than his paintings (Cozens' artist father Alexander is believed to have been the illegitimate son of Peter the Great by an English girl while the Tsar was learning the shipbuilding trade at Deptford). John Robert Cozens studied under his father, the drawing master at Eton who wrote treatises on watercolours and is best remembered for his technique of incorporating accidental blots into his landscapes. In turn, his son evolved a style of watercolour painting that departed from his predecessors: impressionistic and decidedly atmospheric.

He was thus the forerunner of Girtin and Turner, the latter freely admitting his indebtedness to Cozens, while Constable's regard for his talent was effusive: 'the greatest genius that ever touched landscape.' In 1776 and 1782 Cozens travelled overland to Italy, sketching and painting prolifically en route, and providing the basis for his great landscapes and historical works. His colours were muted, often somber, and there is a dark, foreboding element in his paintings which reflect the severe depressive illness which led to his incarceration in a lunatic asylum in the last years of his relatively short life.

MOVEMENT
English Landscape School
OTHER WORKS
Landscape with Hannibal on his March over the Alps
INFLUENCES
Alexander Cozens

John Robert Cozens *Born* 1752, London,
Painted in England, Switzerland, Italy
Died 1797, London

Courtesy of Christie's Images, London, UK/Bridgeman Art Library

BORN AT Kronach in Germany, whence he derived his surname, Cranach learned draughtsmanship from his father. In 1504 his paintings came to the attention of the Elector of Saxony, who appointed him court painter at Wittenberg. Thereafter he designed altarpieces, etched copper, produced woodcuts and engraved the coinage and medal dies for the Saxon mint. In 1509 he visited the Netherlands and painted the portraits of the Emperor Maximilian and his son, the future Charles V. Although Cranach produced many religious paintings, it should be noted that he sided with the reformers and painted the earliest authentic likeness of Martin Luther, while also executing numerous paintings of an allegorical or mythological character. Nevertheless, it is as a painter of very life-like portraits that he is chiefly remembered, especially as a chronicler in oils of the leading personalities of the German Reformation. All three sons, including Lucas Cranach the Younger, were painters.

MOVEMENT
German School
OTHER WORKS
Jealousy, The Crucifixion
INFLUENCES
Albrecht Dürer

Lucas Cranach *Born* 1472 Kronach, Germany
Painted in Saxony
Died 1553 Weimar, Germany

Courtesy of Private Collection/Christie's Images

Crome, John

ENGLISH LANDSCAPE PAINTER, a leading member of the Norwich School. Crome was apprenticed to a coach-and-sign painter at the age of 15, before moving to London in 1790. There he learned his trade by copying pictures in the collection of his patron, Thomas Harvey. These included British artists Wilson and Gainsborough and the Dutch landscapists Ruisdael and Hobbema.

Crome travelled to Paris in 1814 to view the artworks looted by Napoleon, but the greater part of his career was spent in East Anglia. In 1803, he became one of the founder members of the

Norwich Society of Artists, serving as its President for many years. Despite his growing reputation, however, Crome still had to rely on teaching for much of his income. Stylistically, he was a transitional artist. Paintings such as his *Old Houses at Norwich* were still very much in the Picturesque tradition, though he also produced lyrical, moonlit scenes, which displayed a budding Romantic sensibility. He was often known to his contemporaries as Old Crome, to distinguish him from his son — another John — who was also an artist.

MOVEMENT
Romanticism, Norwich School
OTHER WORKS
Yarmouth Jetty, Mousehold Heath: Mill and Donkeys
INFLUENCES
Richard Wilson, Gainsborough, Hobbema

John Crome *Born* 1768
Painted in England
Died 1821

Courtesy of Private Collection/Christie's Images

Cuyp, Albert

ALBERT CUYP, or Cuijp, was the son of the painter Jacob Gerritsz Cuyp (1594–*c.* 1652), scion of a well-to-do family. Controversy continues to rage over the extent of his work, many paintings, particularly of still life, being merely signed with the initials AC. On the other hand, those paintings signed 'A Cuyp' are generally landscapes, whose startling lighting effects are very characteristic of his work. As the signed canvasses belong to his later period, it has been argued that the AC paintings are from his earliest years as a

painter. He never strayed beyond the Netherlands, and his landscapes are bounded by the Maas and the Rhine, but what the flatness of the scenery lacks in variety is more than compensated for by Cuyp's mastery of conveying the different seasons and even different times of day, at their best suffusing the figures of humans and animals with brilliant sunshine.

MOVEMENT
Dutch School
OTHER WORKS
Dordrecht Evening, Cattle with Horseman and Peasants
INFLUENCES
Van Goyen and Jan Both

Albert Cuyp   *Born* 1620 Dordrecht, Holland
Painted in Dordrecht
Died 1691 Dordrecht

Courtesy of Private Collection/Christie's Images

Dalí, Salvador

SPANISH PAINTER, graphic artist and film-maker – the most controversial member of the Surrealists. Dalí was born in Catalonia and studied at the Academy of Fine Arts in Madrid, until his outrageous behaviour caused his expulsion. Before this, he had already made contact with the poet Lorca and the film-director Buñuel. In the early 1920s, he dabbled in a variety of styles, including Futurism and Cubism, although it was the metaphysical paintings of De Chirico which made the deepest impact on him.

The key stage in Dalí's career came in 1929, when he made *Un Chien Andalou* with Buñuel, met his future wife Gala, and allied himself with the Surrealists. His relationship with the latter was rarely smooth and, after several clashes with Breton, he was forced out of the group in 1939. In the interim, he produced some of the most memorable and hallucinatory images associated with the movement, describing them as 'hand-painted dream photographs'. Dalí remained very much in the public eye in later years, gaining great celebrity and wealth in the US, but for many critics his showmanship overshadowed his art.

MOVEMENT
Surrealism
OTHER WORKS
The Metamorphosis of Narcissus, The Persistence of Memory
INFLUENCES
Pablo Picasso, Giorgio de Chirico, Yves Tanguy

Salvador Dalí   *Born* 1904 Catalonia, Spain
Painted in Spain, France, USA and Italy
Died 1989

Courtesy of Private Collection/Christie's Images/© Salvador Dalí, Gala-Salvador Dalí Foundation, DACS, London 2002

Daumier, Honoré

FRENCH GRAPHIC ARTIST, painter and sculptor, noted above all for his stinging caricatures. Daumier had a deprived childhood, which fuelled the campaigning nature of much of his art. His first job, in a bailiff's office, also left him with a permanent loathing for lawyers and bureaucrats. After learning lithography, however, he was soon in great demand as a political cartoonist, working principally for *Le Charivari* and *La Caricature*. A scurrilous drawing of Louis-Philippe in the guise of Gargantua made Daumier notorious, but also earned him a spell of imprisonment. Undaunted, he branched out into social satire, illustrating the foibles of contemporary society. During his lifetime, Daumier's paintings were virtually unknown and never provided him with a viable living. In their general outlook, as objective depictions of modern Parisian life, they can be linked with Courbet's Realist movement. Stylistically, however, Daumier was an isolated figure. His paintings were shaped by his graphic work, displaying a bold economy of form, subtle characterization and an overall lack of finish. In later years, his eyesight failed and he was only saved from absolute penury by the generosity of fellow painter, Corot.

MOVEMENT
Realism
OTHER WORKS
The Refugees, Chess Players, Ecce Homo
INFLUENCES
Charles Philipon, Gustave Courbet, Rembrandt

Honoré Daumier   *Born* 1808 France
Painted in France
Died 1879

Courtesy of Private Collection/Christie's Images

David, Jacques-Louis

FRENCH PAINTER, the leader of the Neoclassical revival. In both his art and his life, David displayed a tempestuous nature, possibly inherited from his father, who was killed in a duel in 1757. He trained under Vien, and his early paintings featured the same uncomfortable blend of Rococo sweetness and antique trappings as those of his master. After winning the Prix de Rome, however, David spent an extended study period in Italy (1775–80), where his art acquired a new dignity and grandeur. With their fiery patriotism and stern morality, David's paintings of the 1780s captured the rebellious mood

of the times. Indeed, his greatest picture, *The Oath of the Horatii*, has often been seen as a visual call to arms. During the Revolution, David was swept up in politics, joining the National Convention, where he became associated with Robespierre and Marat. After their fall, he was imprisoned and was only saved from the guillotine by his royalist wife. This experience did nothing to quell the artist's spirit, however, for he became equally involved with Napoleon. After the latter's defeat, David fled to Brussels, where he remained in exile for the rest of his days.

MOVEMENT
Neoclassicism
OTHER WORKS
Madame Récamier, Brutus and his Dead Sons
INFLUENCES
Gavin Hamilton, Joseph-Marie Vien, Anton Raffael Mengs

Jacques-Louis David   *Born* 1748 France
Painted in France, Italy and Belgium (then Holland)
Died 1825

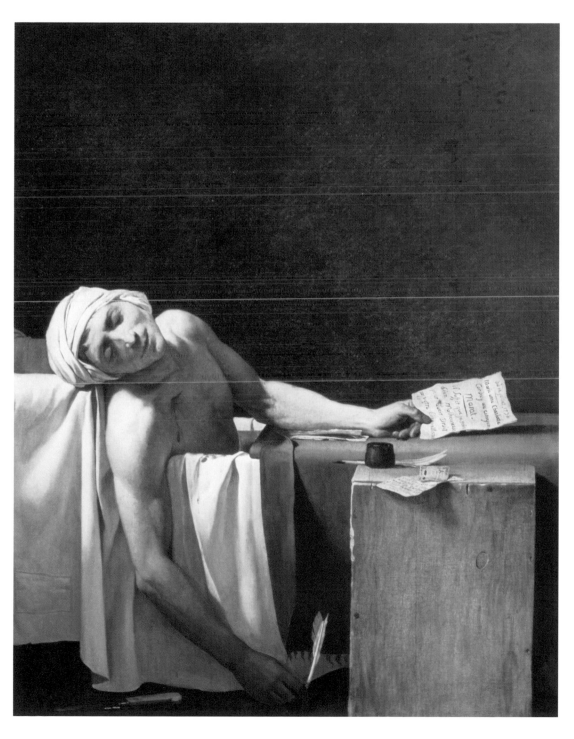

Courtesy of Musee des Beaux-Arts, Reims, France/Bridgeman Art Library/credit: Roger-Viollet, Paris

Degas, Edgar

FRENCH PAINTER and graphic artist, one of the leading members of the Impressionist circle. Originally destined for the law, Degas' early artistic inspiration came from the Neoclassical painter Ingres – who taught him the value of sound draughtsmanship – and from his study of the Old Masters. However, he changed direction dramatically after a chance meeting with Manet in 1861. Manet introduced him to the Impressionist circle and, in spite of his somewhat aloof manner, Degas was welcomed into the group, participating in most of their shows.

Degas was not a typical Impressionist, having little enthusiasm for either landscape or *plein-air* painting but he was, nevertheless, extremely interested in capturing the spontaneity of a momentary image. Where most artists sought to present a well-constructed composition, Degas wanted his pictures to look like an uncomposed snapshot; he often showed figures from behind or bisected by the picture frame. Similarly, when using models, he tried to avoid aesthetic, classical poses, preferring to show them yawning, stretching or carrying out mundane tasks. These techniques are seen to best effect in Degas' two favourite subjects: scenes from the ballet and horse-racing.

MOVEMENT
Impressionism
OTHER WORKS
The Dancing Class, Carriage at the Races, Absinthe
INFLUENCES
Jean-Auguste-Dominique Ingres, Edouard Manet

Edgar Degas   *Born* 1834 France
Painted in France, USA and Italy
Died 1917

Courtesy of Private Collection/Christie's Images

Delacroix, Eugène

A CHAMPION of the Romantic cause, legally Delacroix was the son of a politician but in reality he was probably the illegitimate child of Talleyrand, a celebrated diplomat. He trained under Guérin, a respected Neoclassical painter, but the dominant influence on his style came from Géricault, a fellow pupil. Delacroix watched the latter creating *The Raft of the Medusa*, one of the seminal works of the Romantic movement, and was overwhelmed by its raw, emotional power. He swiftly began to emulate this in his own canvasses, achieving his breakthrough with *The Massacre of Chios*.

Critics attacked Delacroix for his apparent fixation with violence and his lack of finish. They accused him of wallowing in scenes of brutality, rather than acts of heroism. In addition, they denounced his pictures as 'sketches', because he abandoned the smooth, linear finish of the Neoclassical style, preferring to build up his compositions with small dabs of colour.

Like most Romantics, Delacroix was fascinated with the exotic but, unusually, he actually visited the Arab world. As a result, his Orientalist paintings were more sober and realistic than most European fantasies.

MOVEMENT
Romanticism
OTHER WORKS
The Massacre at Chios, Women of Algiers, The Death of Sardanapalus
INFLUENCES
Rubens, Géricault, Constable

Eugène Delacroix *Born* 1798
Painted in France, England, Morocco, Spain, Algeria
Died 1863

Courtesy of Private Collection/Christie's Images

FRENCH PAINTER and sculptor, specializing in historical scenes. Delaroche trained initially as a landscapist, but turned to figure painting in 1817 after failing to win the Prix de Rome. He entered the studio of Gros and began exhibiting at the Salon in the early 1820s – at the very time when the rivalry between Romanticism and Classicism was at its fiercest. Delaroche steered a middle course between these two extremes. His historical subjects, which aimed at poignancy rather than grandeur, were typical of the Romantics, but were handled in a bland academic manner.

Neoclassical painters had taken their historical themes from ancient Greece and Rome, but for the Romantics British subjects were more appealing. This was largely due to the popularity of the novels of Sir Walter Scott. Certain themes also had a particular resonance for French spectators. Cromwell was often seen as a forerunner of Napoleon, while the beheading of Lady Jane Grey evoked memories of the French Revolution. After Delaroche's death, his melodramatic style fell completely out of favour although, in recent years, his reputation has undergone a minor revival.

MOVEMENT
Romanticism
OTHER WORKS
The Death of Queen Elizabeth, The Princes in the Tower
INFLUENCES
Antoine-Jean Gros, Richard Parkes Bonington

Paul Delaroche   *Born* 1797 France
Painted in France and Italy
Died 1856

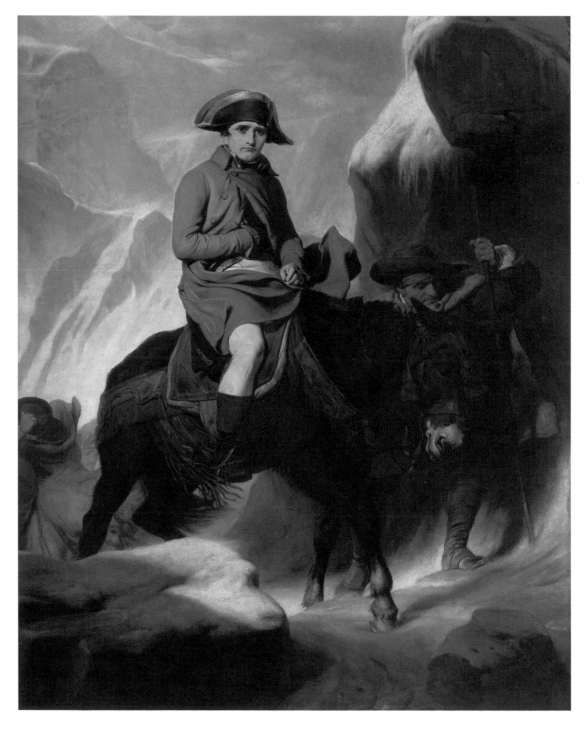

Courtesy of Private Collection/Christie's Images

Delaunay, Robert

AFTER A conventional art training in Paris, Robert Delaunay worked as a designer of sets for the theater and did not take up painting seriously until 1905–06, when he came under the influence of the Neo-Impressionists. Over the ensuing decade he was also closely associated in turn with the Fauves, the Cubists and especially Der Blaue Reiter in 1911–12. In the latter years, however, his experimentation with contrasting colour patterns resulted in the development of a distinctive style which his friend, the poet Guillaume Apollinaire, dubbed Orphism because of its lyrical, almost musical, harmony. In his initial period, Delaunay painted numerous landscapes in and around Paris – the Eiffel Tower being a favourite subject – but gradually he moved towards a more non-figurative style, and in his organization of contrasting colours he had a profound influence on the development of Abstract art in the 1920s. He collaborated with his wife Sonia, especially from 1918 onwards when he returned mainly to stage design.

MOVEMENT
Orphism

OTHER WORKS
Eiffel Tower, Sainte Severin, Political Drama

INFLUENCES
Picasso, Otto Freundlich, Franz Marc, Kandinsky

Robert Delaunay *Born* 1885 Paris, France
Painted in Paris
Died 1941 Montpellier, France

Courtesy of Private Collection/Christie's Images/DACS 2002 © L & M Services B.V. Amsterdam 20020512

BORN SONIA TERK STERN at Gradizhsk in the Ukraine, she was raised in St Petersburg and studied art in Karlsruhe, Germany and then, in 1905, attended the Académie de la Palette in Paris. In order to remain in France, in 1909 she contracted a marriage of convenience with the art critic Wilhelm Uhde but it was dissolved after a few months. In 1910 she married the French painter Robert Delaunay (1885–1941) with whom she founded the movement known as Orphism. Together they designed and painted sets and costumes for Diaghilev's Ballets Russes. Robert is chiefly remembered for his endless experiments in colour orchestration, which had a profound effect on abstract art, while Sonia concentrated on Art Deco textile designs. In the interwar period she also evolved a purity of expression using brightly contrasting colours in her paintings (mainly in watercolours) that influenced her textile designs and vice versa.

MOVEMENT
Orphism, Cubism
OTHER WORKS
Girls in Swimming Costumes
INFLUENCES
Robert Delaunay, Kandinsky

Sonia Delaunay *Born* 1885 Gradizhsk, Ukraine
Painted in France
Died 1979 Paris, France

Courtesy of Private Collection/Christie's Images/DACS 2002 © L & M Services B.V. Amsterdam 20020512

Delvaux, Paul

BORN NEAR Liège in Belgium Delvaux studied architecture then painting in Brussels, where he established his studio. In his early career he dabbled in Expressionism and Impressionism but later came under the influence of Giorgio de Chirico and especially his fellow-countryman René Magritte. He evolved his own distinctive style of Surrealism in which somnambulatory nudes and doe-eyed semi-nude figures are set alongside skeletons amid classical ruins while the artist, in conventional modern dress, looks on. This largest and most ambitious painting features the arrival of the artist, alighting from a ghostly train in silent cities in the dead of night, illumined only by the Moon, in which bodies sleep-walk or flit languorously. This combination of the classical and the contemporary gives these dreamlike paintings a timeless quality. Between 1950 and 1962 he was professor of painting at the École Nationale Supérieure d'Art et d'Architecture in Brussels. In 1982 the Paul Delvaux Museum was established at Sint-Idesbald.

MOVEMENT
Surrealism
OTHER WORKS
The Sleeping Town, The Call of the Night
INFLUENCES
Giorgio de Chirico, Magritte

Paul Delvaux   *Born* 1894 Antheit-lez-Huy, Belgium
Painted in Brussels, Belgium
Died 1994 Knokke-Heist, Belgium

Courtesy of Private Collection/Christie's Images/© Foundations P. Delvaux-St Idesbald, Belgium/DACS, London 2002

Derain, André

WHILE STUDYING art in Paris, André Derain teamed up with fellow student Maurice de Vlaminck with whom he shared a studio. Although very different in temperament they sparked radical ideas off each other regarding the use of colour and, encouraged by Matisse whom they met in 1899, they gradually evolved the style known as Fauvism, distinguished by its often violent and savage use of contrasting colours. In 1905 Ambroise Vollard, a prominent art dealer, encouraged Derain to travel to England and try to capture the strange lighting effects in the Pool of London. The results were startling but considered to be some of his greatest masterpieces. Later he toned down the adventurous use of colour and, under the influence of Cézanne, painted landscapes in a more Impressionist style. He also designed theatre sets, notably for Diaghilev, as well as working as a book illustrator.

MOVEMENT
Fauvism
OTHER WORKS
Houses of Parliament, Barges on the Thames, The Pool of London
INFLUENCES
Vlaminck, Matisse, Cézanne

André Derain *Born* 1880 Chatou, France
Painted in France and England
Died 1954

Courtesy of Private Collection/Christie's Images © ADAGP, Paris and DACS, London 2002

Diebenkorn, Richard

LIVING AND working on America's West Coast, well away from the mainstream of post-war artistic development, Richard Diebenkorn remained aloof and unaffected by the greatest fashions of the period, both Abstract Expressionism and Pop Art. In 1946 he enrolled at the California School of Fine Arts in San Francisco and subsequently taught there for some time. It would be more accurate to say that he was influenced by the Modernist trends coming from Europe in evolving his distinctive approach to landscape, reduced by broad swathes of thick colour to a semi-abstract form. Thus, although never losing sight of the landscape form, his paintings are imbued with his own passion and sensitivity. Latterly he came under the influence of the colour-field painters and produced canvasses that echoed the Symbolists in his mastery of sensation through the medium of colour and form.

MOVEMENT
Modern American School

OTHER WORKS
Ocean Park series, Berkeley series, City Scape

INFLUENCES
Matisse, Willem de Kooning, Piet Mondrian

Richard Diebenkorn *Born* 1922, Portland, Oregon, USA *Painted in* Oregon and California *Died* 1993, Portland

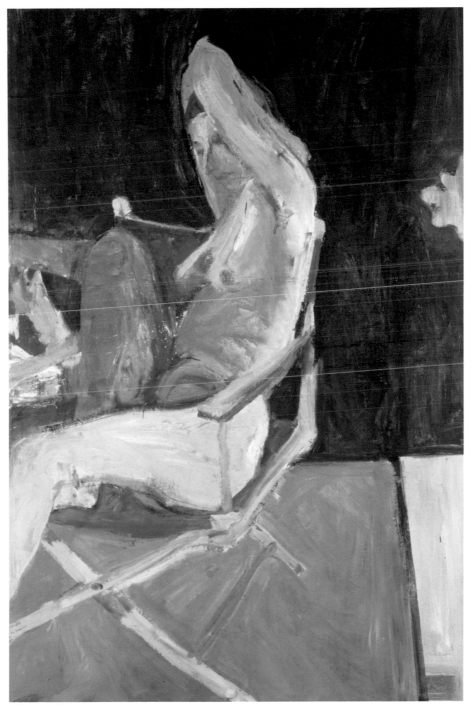

Courtesy of Private Collection/Christie's Images/Bridgeman Art Library

Dine, Jim

TRAINED AT the University of Cincinnati, the Boston Museum of Fine Arts School and the University of Ohio, Jim Dine was one of the foremost exponents of Pop Art. He held his first exhibition of objects as images in 1959, alongside Claes Oldenburg, with whom he subsequently collaborated on a number of projects. Like the Dadaists, he believed in the combination of many different media and the use of ready-made objects or fragments of them in creating his compositions. Taking this process to its logical conclusion in the late 1950s he began organizing a series of 'happenings', live performances which combined his art with his experience of life. These, in effect, were the forerunners of the Performance Art that came to fruition a few years later. In more recent years, however Dine has returned to a more representational and figurative style of painting. He has combined oils with collage, or etching and printing on hand-coloured paper.

MOVEMENT
Performance Art, Pop Art
OTHER WORKS
The Toaster, Wiring the Unfinished Bathroom
INFLUENCES
Dadaism, Surrealism, Abstract Expressionism,

Jim Dine *Born* 1935 Cincinnati, Ohio, USA
Painted in Cincinnati, Boston and New York

Courtesy of Private Collection/Christie's Images/© ARS, NY and DACS, London 2002

OTTO DIX studied art in Dresden, where he developed an intense interest in realism. Drafted into the infantry on the outbreak of World War I he experienced at first hand the horrors of trench warfare, and this was to have a profound effect on his work. After the war he continued his studies at Dresden and Düsseldorf, producing grimly shocking collages and etchings. In around 1925 he turned from these strident anti-war messages to social realism, producing paintings of beggars, the war-maimed and prostitutes, which earned him his place in the New Objectivity. Brilliant but devastating in his merciless criticism of the Weimar Republic's social and political shortcomings, he was intensely reviled by the Nazis, who dismissed him from his teaching post and condemned his works as degenerate. Persecuted by the Gestapo, he turned to romanticism and religious art and in his later years painted in an Expressionist style.

MOVEMENT
New Objectivity, Expressionism
OTHER WORKS
Die Grosstadt, Homage to Beauty, The War
INFLUENCES
George Grosz, Max Beckmann

Otto Dix   *Born* 1891 Gera-Unternhaus, Germany
Painted in Dresden, Germany
Died 1969 Konstanz, Germany

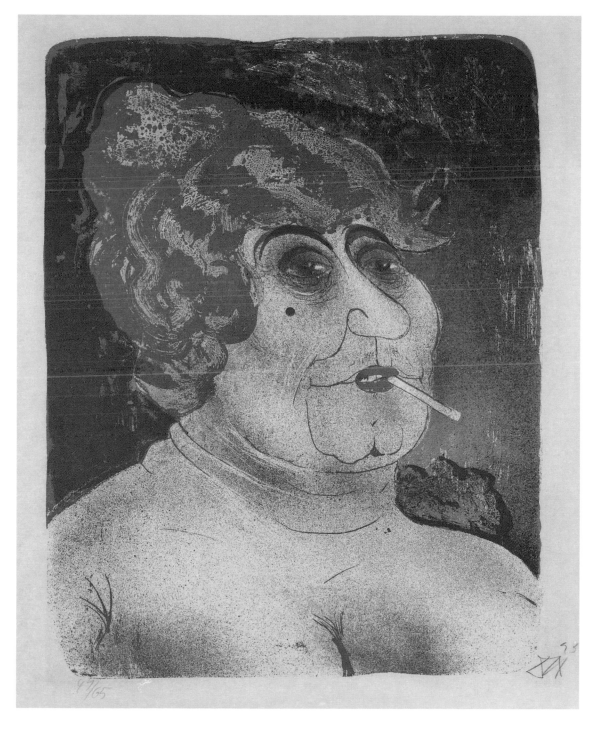

Courtesy of Private Collection/Christie's Images © DACS 2002

DORÉ WAS the most prolific and successful French illustrator of his age. Initially, he was drawn to caricature, spurred on by the encouragement of Philipon. As a teenager, Doré visited the Paris shop of this noted cartoonist and was briefly employed by him. He also began producing humorous drawings for *Le Journal pour Rire*. These precocious skills proved invaluable, when, following the death of his father in 1849 he became the family's main breadwinner.

Doré soon progressed to book illustrations. During the 1860s, his wood engravings for Dante's *Inferno* and Cervantes' *Don Quixote* made him famous. Stylistically, he owed much to the Romantics, excelling at depictions of the exotic and the macabre. This is particularly evident from his strange, glacial landscapes in the *Rime of the Ancient Mariner* and the grotesque beasts in the *Inferno*. Yet Doré could also be brutally realistic. His unflinching portrayal of the London slums attracted widespread praise and captured the imagination of the young Van Gogh. In later life, Doré produced some paintings and sculpture, but these are less highly regarded. His most successful venture in this field was the monument to his friend, the novelist Alexandre Dumas.

MOVEMENT
Romanticism
OTHER WORKS
London: A Pilgrimage
INFLUENCES
Charles Meryon, Grandville, Charles Philipon

Gustave Doré *Born* 1832, France
Worked in France and England
Died 1883

Courtesy of Private Collection/Christie's Images

Douglas, Aaron

THE LEADING exponent of the Harlem Renaissance, Aaron Douglas studied at the University of Kansas and from 1925 to 1927 studied art in New York under Winold Reiss, who encouraged him to accept and celebrate his black heritage. Throughout the 1920s he illustrated a number of books by emerging black authors, while drawings contributed to a number of magazines of the period show the influence of African art forms, putting Douglas in the forefront of the

Harlem Renaissance. In 1931 he went to Paris and studied at the Académie Scandinave under Despiau, and in 1938 he travelled all over the American South and Haiti. He later taught at Fisk University in Nashville, Tennessee. In the 1930s he executed a number of large murals for public buildings in Nashville and New York which drew on the black cultural tradition and history. He played a prominent role in the development of modern black consciousness.

MOVEMENT
Modern American School
OTHER WORKS
Aspects of Negro Life, From Slavery through Reconstruction
INFLUENCES
Winold Reiss, Charles Despiau

Aaron Douglas   *Born* 1899 Topeka, Kansas, USA
Painted in New York, Nashville and Paris
Died 1979 Nashville, Tennessee

© Schomberg Center, The New York Public Library / Art Resource, NY

BORN INTO a mercantile family in what was then a provincial backwater of the crumbling Ottoman Empire, Hafiz Drubi had a conventional art education but later came under the influence of the European avant-garde artists of the 1930s and 1940s. He gradually developed his own distinctive style, showing the influence of the Cubists. His paintings reflect his cultural roots in the exuberant display of colour and tone, although the composition is usually in the Western idiom. Little-known outside Iraq, he came to international prominence in the early 1960s, when his paintings were exhibited at Gallery One in Beirut. This gallery, founded by the poet Yusuf al Khal and his Lebanese-American wife Helen, gave many Middle Eastern artists their first real break and established Beirut as the art centre of the Arab world.

MOVEMENT
Modern Islamic Art
OTHER WORKS
Still Life (oil on canvas, 1979)
INFLUENCES
Picasso, Robert Delaunay, Max Beckmann

Hafiz Drubi   *Born* 1914 Baghdad, Iraq
Painted in Baghdad
Died 1991 Iraq

Courtesy of Sotheby's Picture Library

Drysdale, Sir George Russell

BORN AT Bognor, Sussex, where he received his early education, George Russell Drysdale emigrated with his parents to Australia in 1923 and settled in Melbourne, Victoria. He took up sketching while recovering from an eye operation as a boy and this led him to enrol at the George Bell Art School. He continued his studies at the Royal Academy School in London and then went to Paris, where he came under the influence of the Surrealists. On his return to Australia he began painting and drawing the desolate scenes of the Outback, drawing upon the styles and techniques of contemporary British artists in depicting the Australian wilderness with a rugged realism. His work was first exhibited in London in 1950 and immediately established him as one of the most promising Australian artists of his generation. Over the ensuing three decades he was the most influential figure in Australian art. He was knighted in 1969 and became a Companion of the Order of Australia in 1980.

MOVEMENT
Modern Australian School
OTHER WORKS
Back Verandah, The Walls of China
INFLUENCES
Surrealism

Sir George Russell Drysdale *Born* 1912
Sussex, England *Painted in* Australia
Died 1981 Sydney, Australia

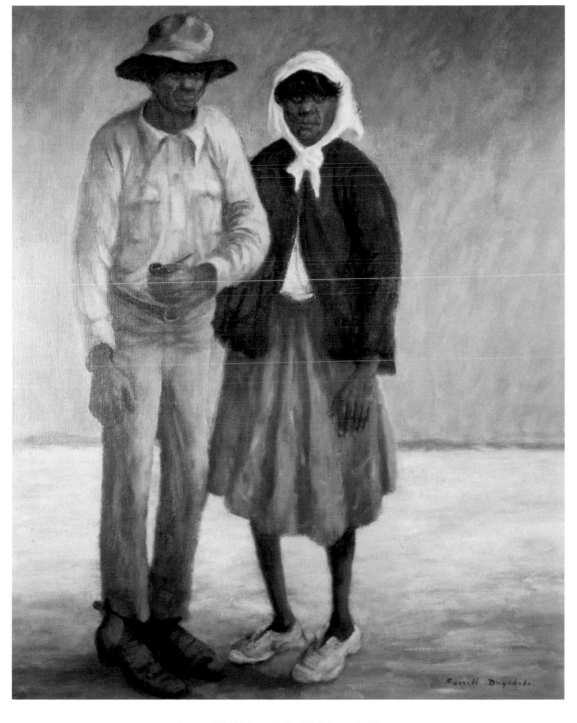

Courtesy of Christie's Images, London, UK/Bridgeman Art Library

JEAN DUBUFFET studied at the Académie Julien in Paris but, dissatisfied with the styles in 'new art' then being taught, branched out on his own and began exploring unusual materials and the deliberate use of coarse canvas and paint applied roughly. He believed that there was more truth in the art produced by the untrained, the childish or the psychotic and strove to recreate such effects. The synthesis of rough materials with discarded rubbish such as pieces of old newspapers and broken glass resulted in what he termed *Art Brut*

('raw art'), which was the antithesis of painterly perfection and aesthetic sensitivity. By this means Dubuffet confronted the spectator with the seamier side of life and nature in the raw. Though often derided, he exerted a tremendous influence on the next generation of artists and anticipated the Pop Art and neo-Dadaism of the 1960s.

MOVEMENT
Abstract Expressionism
OTHER WORKS
Man with a Hod, Villa sur la Route, Jazz Band
INFLUENCES
Antoni Tapiès, Alberto Giacometti

Jean Dubuffet   *Born* 1901 Le Havre, France
Painted in France
Died 1985 Paris, France

Courtesy of Private Collection/Christie's Images/© ADAGP, Paris and DACS, London 2002

Duccio di Buonisegna

WESTERN ART begins with Duccio di Buonisegna, who learned his craft from studying the illuminated manuscripts created by unknown Byzantine limners. His earliest recorded work, dating about 1278, was to decorate the cases in which the municipal records of Sienna were stored. In 1285 he was commissioned to paint a large Madonna for the church of Santa Maria Novella. This is now known as the Rucellai Madonna, for centuries attributed to Cimabue. Duccio painted the magnificent double altarpiece for the Cathedral of Siena, regarded as his masterpiece and one of the greatest paintings of all time. Many other works documented in the Sienese records have been lost, but sufficient remain to establish Duccio as the last and greatest of the artists working in the Byzantine tradition, as well as the founder of the Sienese School, and thus the progenitor of modern art. In his hands the degenerate painting of the Gothic style was transformed and the principles of expressive portraiture established.

MOVEMENT
Sienese School, Italy
OTHER WORKS
The Crucifixion, Majestas, Madonna with Three Franciscans
INFLUENCES
Byzantine illuminations

Duccio di Buonisegna   *Born c.* 1255 Siena, Italy
Painted in Siena and Florence
Died 1319 Siena

Courtesy of National Gallery, London, UK/Bridgeman Art Library

Duchamp, Marcel

ALTHOUGH HE produced relatively few artworks, Duchamp was a key figure in twentieth century art, playing a seminal role in the development of several different movements. Duchamp trained in Paris, and was briefly influenced by Cézanne and the Fauves. His first real masterpiece – *Nude Descending a Staircase* – was a potent blend of Cubism and Futurism, In 1913 he invented the *ready-made* – an everyday object, divorced from its normal context and presented as a work of art in its own right. Two years later, Duchamp moved to the US, where he became a leading light of the New York Dada movement. His work from this period displayed a mischievous sense of humour, whilst also challenging existing preconceptions about the nature of art. In *L.H.O.O.Q.,* for example, he added a moustache and a smutty inscription to the *Mona Lisa*. His most notorious *ready-made* was a urinal, which he exhibited under the title of *Fountain*. After receiving a legacy, Duchamp's output slowed dramatically but his later work has been seen as a foretaste of Kinetic art and Conceptual art.

MOVEMENT
Cubism, Dada, Conceptual Art
OTHER WORKS
Fountain, The Bride Stripped Bare by her Bachelors Even
INFLUENCES
Francis Picabia, Paul Cézanne, Man Ray

Marcel Duchamp   *Born* 1887, Normandy
Worked in France and the USA
Died 1968

Courtesy of Philadelphia Museum of Art, Pennsylvania, PA, USA/Bridgeman Art Library/© Succession Marcel Duchamp/ADAGP, Paris and DACS, London 2002

ALTHOUGH HE had a conventional training at the École des Beaux Arts in Paris, Raoul Dufy was attracted to the radical ideas of Matisse and Derain and for some time flirted with Impressionism, Cubism and Fauvism. In 1907 he turned away from painting to concentrate on textile patterns, graphic design and book illustrations, but in 1919 he took up painting again and settled on the French Riviera. There he was encouraged by his friend, the couturier Paul Poiret, to embark on a prolific series of paintings executed swiftly,

characterized by large areas of flat colour and sharply incised black lines after the manner of the Chinese calligraphic artists. He created a kind of *ukiyo-e*, pictures of transient scenes, on promenades and beaches, at regattas and race meetings. His greatest masterpiece was the vast mural for the Exposition Universelle in Paris, 1938, one of the largest works ever painted.

MOVEMENT
Modern French School
OTHER WORKS
The Paddock, The Pier and Promenade at Nice
INFLUENCES
Matisse, André Derain, Vlaminck

Raoul Dufy *Born* 1877 Le Havre, France
Painted in Paris and the French Riviera
Died 1953 Forcalquier, France

Courtesy of Galerie Daniel Malingue, Paris, France/Bridgeman Art Library/© ADAGP, Paris and DACS, London 2002

BORN IN upstate New York, the son of a Canadian Scot and a black mother, Robert Stuart Duncanson was taken to Canada as a boy and raised there by his father. It is believed that he received part of his education in Scotland before returning to America in 1841, when he went to live with his mother in Cincinnati. He was by that time an accomplished artist who showed three of his paintings in the art exhibition of 1842. He was a skilled and versatile artist, equally proficient in portraits as in the landscapes for which he is famous. He was the first black American to become a professional painter, producing a wide range of work, from still life to genre subjects. A grant from the Anti-Slavery League enabled him to travel to Italy, France and England in 1853 to further his studies. He was also an early exponent of photography, which he used as an aid to his landscapes.

MOVEMENT
American School
OTHER WORKS
Mount Healthy, Ohio, Belmont Murals
INFLUENCES
Thomas Cole

Robert Duncanson *Born c.* 1817 New York
USA *Painted in* Cincinnati
Died 1872 Cincinnati

Courtesy of The Detroit Institute of Arts, USA/Bridgeman Art Library

Dürer, Albrecht

ALBRECHT DÜRER was the son of a goldsmith who taught him the art of drawing in silverpoint. In 1484 he was apprenticed to the leading Nuremberg painter and book illustrator of his time, Michael Wolgemut (1434–1519), from whom he learned the techniques of woodcut engraving. He then travelled extensively in Italy, where the works of Leonardo, Bellini and Mantegna had a profound influence on his later career, both as a practicing artist and as an art theorist who wrote extensively on the subject. Dürer was thus responsible for introducing many of the ideas of the Italian Renaissance to northern Europe. Although now remembered chiefly for his engravings (including the *Triumphal Car*, at nine square metres the world's largest woodcut), he was an accomplished painter whose mastery of detail and acute observation have seldom been surpassed.

MOVEMENT
German School
OTHER WORKS
Wing of a Hooded Crow
INFLUENCES
Leonardo da Vinci, Bellini, Mantegna

Albrecht Dürer   *Born* 1471 Nuremberg, Germany
Painted in Nuremberg
Died 1528 Nuremberg

Courtesy of Private Collection/Christie's Images

Eakins, Thomas

THOMAS EAKINS studied at the Pennsylvania Academy of Fine Arts and took anatomy at Jefferson Medical College before going to Paris to study under J. L. Gérôme and Léon Bonnat at the École des Beaux-Arts. On his return to Philadelphia in 1870 he established his studio, later working as Professor of Anatomy at the Pennsylvania Academy of Fine Arts. In addition to figures, he painted numerous genre scenes, such as *Chess Players*, which was critically acclaimed when exhibited at the Centennial Exposition of 1876. His greatest masterpiece, illustrated here, shows his mastery of portraiture and anatomy as the eminent surgeon Professor Gross demonstrates an operation to a group of medical students. Eakins also excelled as a sculptor and many of his paintings have a sculptural quality. He painted athletes and sportsmen, black Americans and rural subjects.

MOVEMENT
American School
OTHER WORKS
The Swimming Hole, Max Schmitt in a Single Scull
INFLUENCES
Jean Léon Gérôme, Léon Bonnat

Thomas Eakins   *Born* 1844, Philadelphia, USA
Painted in Philadelphia and France
Died 1916

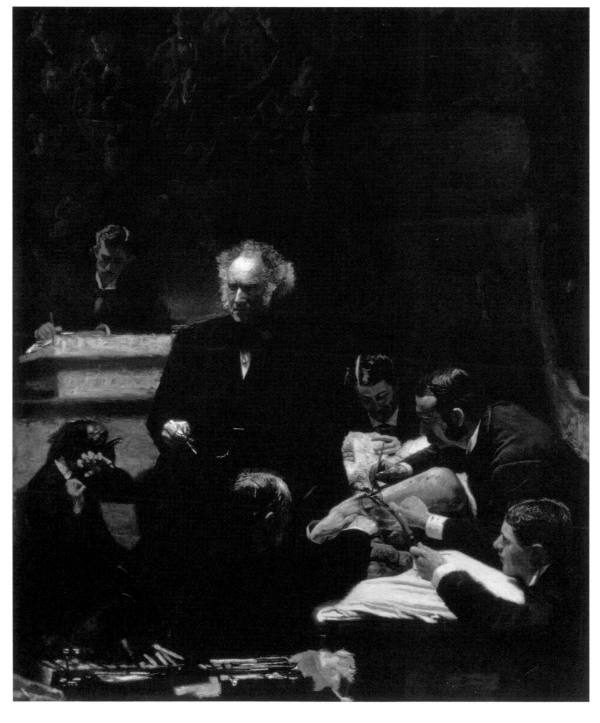

Courtesy of Jefferson College, Philadelphia, PA, USA/Bridgeman Art Library

El Greco

THIS NICKNAME, meaning 'the Greek' in Spanish, is the epithet by which Domenikos Theotokopoulos is better known. Born at Candia, Crete, which was then ruled by the Venetians, he worked as a painter of icons in the Byzantine tradition before moving to Italy, where he is believed to have become a pupil of Titian. He then settled at Toledo in Spain. His early portraits show the Venetian influence of his early training, but in Spain he evolved his own highly distinctive, mannered approach to portraiture, characterized by the elongation and distortion of the face and figure, combined with his penchant for sombre colours. These aspects are seen at their most dramatic and solemn in his large religious paintings, but they are also present to a lesser extent in his portraits of his contemporaries. Inevitably, his treatment of his sitters' portraits was considered controversial at the time. Many of his extant works are preserved in the Museo El Greco in Toledo where he spent the last 44 years of his life.

MOVEMENT
Spanish School
OTHER WORKS
Disrobing of Christ, Burial of Count Orgaz
INFLUENCES
Titian, Tintoretto

El Greco *Born* 1541 Candia, Crete
Painted in Toledo, Spain
Died 1614 Toledo

Courtesy of Private Collection/Christie's Images

Ensor, James

BORN IN Ostend, Belgium, of English parents, James Sydney Ensor is one of those painters whose art seems to have been wholly his own, with very little discernible influence from his contemporaries or predecessors, apart from some slight echoes of the Symbolists. In 1884 he founded the group known as Les Vingt ('The Twenty'), but he soon broke away from them. Essentially a loner, he reacted violently to the comments of art critics and the general public alike, who regarded his pictures as disturbed and macabre. Their obsession with corpses, grotesque masks and skeletons painted in garish colours, symbolized the corruption of society and the world around him. From about 1900, when he was no longer an 'angry young man', his paintings mellowed and became more conventional, and eventually he was back in the mainstream of Belgian art, recognized by his peerage in 1929 shortly after taking Belgian nationality. Nevertheless, it is for his satirical painting that he is remembered today, marking the transition from Symbolism to Expressionism and anticipating the Surrealism of Magritte.

MOVEMENT
Expressionism
OTHER WORKS
Death and the Masks, Entry of Christ into Brussels
INFLUENCES
Odilon Redon

James Ensor   *Born* 1860 Ostend, Belgium
Painted in Ostend and Brussels
Died 1949 Ostend

Courtesy of Private Collection/Christie's Images/© DACS 2002

Ernst, Max

GERMAN PAINTER and a leading Surrealist. Born near Cologne, Ernst studied psychology at Bonn University, taking a particular interest in the art of the insane. Before the war he befriended Arp and Macke, and mixed with the Blaue Reiter ('Blue Rider') group. Then, in 1919, he staged the first Dada exhibition in Cologne. Typically for this movement, visitors had to enter the show through a public urinal and were handed axes, in case they wished to destroy any of the exhibits. In 1922, Ernst moved to Paris and joined the Surrealist circle. His work in this style was incredibly varied. He made considerable use of the chance images, which were suggested by automatic techniques, such as *frottage* (rubbings of textured surfaces). At the same time, he exploited the 'poetic sparks', which were created by the juxtaposition of totally unrelated objects. These sometimes took the form of paintings, but were also produced as collages, drawn from popular magazines.

Ernst was interned during World War II and spent much of his later career in America.

MOVEMENT
Surrealism, Dada
OTHER WORKS
The Robing of the Bride, Europe after the Rain
INFLUENCES
August Macke, Hans Arp, Giorgio de Chirico

Max Ernst   *Born* 1891, Colgne, Germany
Painted in Germany, France and the USA
Died 1976

Courtesy of Private Collection/Christie's Images/© ADAGP, Paris and DACS, London 2002

Fabriano, Gentile Da   The Adoration of the Magi, detail of Virgin and Child with Three Kings, 1423

BORN IN the little north Italian town of Fabriano, Gentile worked as a painter mainly in Venice and later Brescia before settling in Rome in about 1419, although subsequently he also worked in Florence and Siena. There he executed a great number of religious paintings, although regrettably comparatively few of these works appear to have survived. His most important work was probably carried out at Florence where he enjoyed the patronage of Palla Strozzi, the richest magnate of the city in his day. About

1423 Strozzi commissioned him to paint the magnificent altarpiece depicting the Adoration of the Magi for the sacristy-chapel in the church of the Holy Trinity, intended by the patron as a memorial to his father Onofrio Strozzi. This is Gentile's undoubted masterpiece. The very epitome of the Italian Renaissance, it is now preserved in the Uffizi Gallery. It is an extraordinary work, crammed with figures – among whom we may discern the Strozzi family and their friends.

MOVEMENT
Florentine School
OTHER WORKS
Madonna and Child, Madonna with Angels
INFLUENCES
Filippo Brunneleschi

Gentile da Fabriano   *Born c.* 1370 Fabriano, Italy
Painted in Venice, Brescia, Rome, Florence and Siena
Died c. 1427 Venice

Courtesy of Galleria degli Uffizi, Florence, Italy/Bridgeman Art Library

Fabritius, Carel

CAREL FABRITIUS studied under Rembrandt in Amsterdam before settling in Delft in around 1650. His life was tragically cut short when he was killed in the great explosion which destroyed the arsenal and much of the town of Delft in 1654. The influence of his master is very evident in his paintings, although Fabritius developed the technique of lighting the subjects in order to convey an almost three-dimensional quality. His mature work was also characterized by sensitive brushwork and great care in composition. Though arguably the most talented of Rembrandt's pupils in portraiture, Fabritius also excelled in interiors and landscapes, noted for their careful proportions and perspectives.

MOVEMENT
Dutch School
OTHER WORKS
View of Delft with a Music Instrument Seller's Stall
INFLUENCES
Rembrandt

Carel Fabritius *Born* 1622 Amsterdam, Holland *Painted in* Amsterdam and Delft *Died* 1654 Delft

Courtesy of Private Collection/Bridgeman Art Library

REGARDED AS an Australian painter of Scottish birth, Ian Fairweather trained at the Slade School of Art in London. In 1924 he began wandering nomadically all over the world, living and working in Germany, Canada, India, China and Japan before settling in Australia. During World War II he served as a captain with the British Army in India, but returned to his adopted land in 1943 after being invalided out. An eccentric loner, in 1952 he hit the headlines when he sailed from Darwin to Indonesia on a home-made raft and a year later settled on Bribie Island in northern Australia. His paintings range from portraits to landscapes but he is particularly noted for genre subjects. Relatively few of his paintings have an Australian theme – the majority of his works being Chinese scenes decorated with calligraphy in the Oriental manner. After World War II he worked mainly in gouache before turning to synthetic polymers in 1958. His best work consists of the virtually monochrome abstracts of 1959–61.

MOVEMENT
Australian School
OTHER WORKS
Kite Flying, Monastery, Monsoon, Bathing Scene Bali
INFLUENCES
Chinese traditional art

Ian Fairweather   *Born* 1891 Scotland
Painted in Australia
Died 1974 Brisbane, Australia

Courtesy of The Art Archive/© Estate of Ian Fairweather 2002. All Rights Reserved, DACS

LYONEL CHARLES Adrian Feininger was born and died in New York City, but he is regarded more as a European than as an American artist. The son of German Jewish parents, he was educated in Germany and studied art in Munich, where he joined the Blaue Reiter group in 1913 and associated with Wassily Kandinsky, with whom he worked at the Bauhaus in Weimar and later Dessau. Following the advent of the Nazi regime he returned to the United States in 1935 and there helped establish the New Bauhaus in Chicago. His artistic career was very varied. Having started as a political cartoonist in the 1890s, he only turned to painting in 1907 when he moved to Paris. There he came under the influence of Cubism and was closely associated with Robert Delaunay, whose Orphism is reflected in Feininger's intense interest in the emotional qualities of colour.

MOVEMENT
Cubism, Orphism, Bauhaus
OTHER WORKS
Sailing Boats, Village Church, Gelmeroda
INFLUENCES
Picasso, Juan Gris, Robert Delaunay, Kandinsky, Giacomo Balla

Lyonel Feininger   *Born* 1871 New York, USA
Painted in Paris, Weimar, Dessau, Germany, Chicago and New York *Died* 1956 New York

Courtesy of Private Collection/Christie's Images/© DACS 2002

Fischl, Eric

EDUCATED AT the California Institute of the Arts (1969–72), Eric Fischl led the reaction against Op Art and Minimalism in the late 1970s and 1980s, calling for a return to a more purely figurative and representational style of painting which had strong echoes of the Social Realism of the New Deal era. What has marked out his work from his predecessors of the 1930s, however, is the psycho-sexual undertones of his compositions, in which the spectator becomes a voyeur, looking at scenes which may appear relatively simple and

straightforward on one level, but which reveal disturbing elements of anxieties, phobias, insecurities and a wide range of sexual hang-ups, invariably unexplained and thus open to individual interpretation. Although far less accomplished technically than the paintings of Tamara de Lempicka, for example, Fischl's sly exploration of repressed or ambivalent sexuality invites obvious comparison.

MOVEMENT
Neo-Figurative School
OTHER WORKS
Bad Boy, Sleepwalker, Pizza Eater
INFLUENCES
Tamara de Lempicka, Norman Rockwell, Walter Sickert

Eric Fischl   *Born* 1948 New York USA
Painted in New York

Courtesy of Private Collection/Christie's Images

Fontana, Lucio

BORN IN Argentina of Italian parents, Lucio Fontana was raised in Milan, where he studied art at the Brera Academy from 1927 to 1930. Five years later he was a signatory of the First Manifesto of Italian Abstract Artists. In the early part of his artistic career he concentrated on sculpture and did not turn to painting until after World War II, when he began producing canvasses in which he used a very restricted range of colours, verging on monochrome effects. In 1946 he produced his White Manifesto, launching a series of paintings in shades of white. He really came to prominence a year later when he developed a style which he called Spatialism, in which cuts and slashes in the canvas were combined with a plain painted surface, bringing a new dimension to bear on Minimal Art. The apparent simplicity of his paintings was deceptive and they had a profound influence on a later generation of conceptual artists.

MOVEMENT
Italian Abstract School
OTHER WORKS
Spatial Concept, New York 15, The End of God
INFLUENCES
Yves Klein, Mark Rothko

Lucio Fontana   *Born* 1899 Argentina
Painted in Italy
Died 1968 Varese, Italy

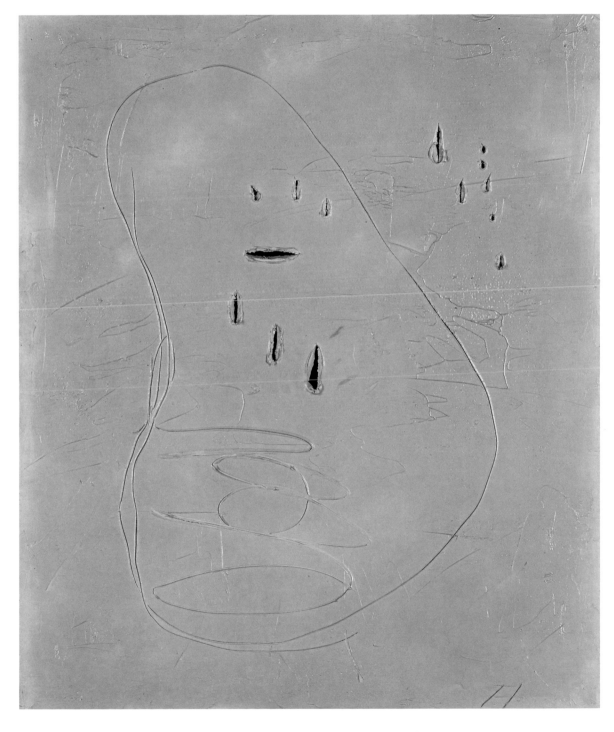

Courtesy of Hamburg Kunsthalle, Hamburg, Germany/Bridgeman Art Library

THE MOST representative French painter of the fifteenth century, Jean Fouquet originally came under the influence of Van Eyck, but a period in Italy – where he was commissioned to paint the portrait of Pope Eugenius IV – brought him in contact with the new styles emerging in Tuscany. On his return to France he combined the Flemish and Tuscan elements to create a wholly distinctive French style. Highly influential on the succeeding generation of French artists, Fouquet's supreme importance was not fully realized until

1904, when his surviving works were brought together for an exhibition in Paris. His painting combines the skills and precision acquired during his early career as a limner and miniaturist with a new-found expressiveness that places him in the forefront of the painters who could get behind the eyes of their subjects and reveal the underlying character.

MOVEMENT
French Primitives
OTHER WORKS
Virgin and Child, Saint Margaret and Olibrius, Jouvenal des Ursins
INFLUENCES
Van Eyck, Piero della Francesca

Jean Fouquet   *Born c.* 1420 Tours, France
Painted in France and Italy
Died c. 1481 Tours, France

Courtesy of British Library, London, UK/Bridgeman Art Library

Fragonard, Jean-Honoré   Portrait of Mademoiselle Guimard as Terpsichore, 1773-75

FRENCH PAINTER a leading exponent of the light-hearted Rococo style. Fragonard trained under Boucher (Madame de Pompadour's favourite artist) and won the Prix de Rome, both of which seemed to mark him out for a conventional career as a history painter. But he was too ill-disciplined to enjoy the business of copying Old Masters and his studies in Rome (1756–60) did not progress well. Instead, the Italian countryside awakened Fragonard's interest in landscape painting while, on his return to France, the success of *The Swing* led his art in a different direction.

The Swing demonstrated Fragonard's undoubted gift for playful eroticism, and it brought him a series of commissions for similar 'boudoir' pictures. Patrons were attracted by his dazzling, vivacious style and by his innate sense of taste, which strayed close to the margins of decency, but never crossed them. In this sense, Fragonard became the archetypal painter of the Ancien Régime and ultimately shared its fate. By the 1780s, Neoclassicism had all but supplanted the Rococo style and, although he received help from David after the Revolution (1789), Fragonard's later years were marred by poverty and neglect.

MOVEMENT
Rococo
OTHER WORKS
The Progress of Love, The Bolt, The Love Letter
INFLUENCES
François Boucher, Hubert Robert, Tiepolo

Jean-Honoré Fragonard   *Born* 1732 France
Painted in France and Italy
Died 1806

Courtesy of Private Collection/Christie's Images

Frankenthaler, Helen

AFTER A college education at Bennington in Vermont, Helen Frankenthaler studied art under the abstract print-maker Hans Hoffman and the Mexican painter Rufino Tamayo. While still at Bennington, however, she evolved her own highly distinctive technique of applying very thin, diluted paint to the unprimed canvas so that it soaked right through. These 'stain-soak' paintings were created with a series of applications in different colours and consistencies, the canvasses being laid flat on the studio floor. This technique created an unusual atmospheric effect and the subtle blending of forms (not unlike that of certain watercolours, a medium in which she also worked) which form the basis for her large abstracts are vaguely suggestive of landscapes or the natural world. From 1958 to 1971 she was married to Robert Motherwell, whose influence can be discerned in her own brand of Abstract Expressionism. In her more recent paintings, acrylics have been applied to give greater depth to the principal details.

MOVEMENT
Abstract Expressionism
OTHER WORKS
Black Frame, Door, The Other Side of the Moon
INFLUENCES
Rufino Tamayo, Jackson Pollock, Robert Motherwell

Helen Frankenthaler   *Born* 1928, New York
Painted in New York, USA

Courtesy of Private Collection/Christie's Images

NATURALIZED BRITISH painter; a leading member of the school of London. Freud was born in Berlin, the grandson of the famous psychoanalyst Sigmund Freud. As a Jewish family living in the shadow of Nazism, the Freuds left Germany in the 1930s, settling in London. Lucian joined the Merchant Navy, becoming an artist after he was invalided out of the service in 1942. He trained under Cedric Morris, and the hallucinatory realism of his early style hints at an admiration for Surrealism and Neue Sachlichkeit. His greatest influence, however, was Ingres. Freud emulated the meticulous draughtsmanship of the Frenchman, apparently attempting to depict every strand of hair on his sitters. His virtuoso skill was recognized when in 1951, his remarkable *Interior at Paddington* won a prize at the Festival of Britain.

Freud's style changed in the late 1950s, when he replaced his fine sable brushes with stiffer, hog-hair ones which led to a more painterly approach, in which the artist conveyed his flesh-tones through thicker slabs of colour. Freud's favourite subject matter has been the 'naked portrait': starkly realistic nudes, devoid of any picturesque or idealizing elements.

MOVEMENT
Realism, School of London
OTHER WORKS
Hotel Bedroom, Francis Bacon
INFLUENCES
Cedric Morris, Ingres, George Grosz

Lucian Freud *Born* 1922 Berlin, Germany
Painted in Britain

Courtesy of Private Collection/Christie's Images/© Lucian Freud

AFTER ART training in Munich and Berlin, Otto Freundlich settled in Paris in 1909, where he joined the avant-garde circle dominated by Picasso. In 1911 he exhibited at the Neue Sezession in Berlin, revealing the latest trends from France. He returned to Germany for military service in World War I, during which (1917) he joined the Aktion group of artists and between 1919–23 was associated with the Bauhaus. He returned to Paris in 1924 and latterly worked in Pontoise as a painter, graphic artist and sculptor. In 1929 he commenced the magazine *A bis Z*; a prolific writer, he was the intellectual voice of the avant-garde. In 1939 he was interned as an enemy alien, released on the intervention of Picasso, and moved to the Pyrenees, where he spent the next two years repainting from memory all those works which had been destroyed by the Nazis as degenerate art. Betrayed to the Gestapo in 1943, he was transported to Majdanek concentration camp where he died soon afterwards. Work on the restoration of the stained glass in Chartres Cathedral (1914) inspired his kaleidoscopic paintings which anticipated the Op Art of the 1960s.

MOVEMENTS
Abstract Art, Orphism

OTHER WORKS
Diptych, La Rosace, Composition avec Trois Personnages

INFLUENCES
Picasso, Kandinsky, Paul Klee, Robert Delaunay, Max Ernst

Otto Freundlich *Born* 1878 Pomerania (now Poland) *Painted in* Munich, Berlin, Paris, Pontoise and the Pyrenees *Died* 1943 Majdanek, Lublin, Poland

Courtesy of Private Collection/Christie's Images

Friedrich, Caspar David

The Wanderer above the Sea of Clouds, 1818

CASPAR DAVID FRIEDRICH studied drawing under J. G. Quistorp in Greifswald before going to the Copenhagen Academy between 1794–98. On his return to Germany he settled in Dresden, where he spent the rest of his life. His drawings in pen and ink were admired by Goethe and won him a Weimar Art Society prize in 1805. His first major commission came two years later in the form of an altarpiece for Count Thun's castle in Teschen, Silesia, entitled *Crucifixion in Mountain Scenery*. This set the tone of many later works, in which dramatic landscapes expressed moods, emotions and atmosphere. Appointed a professor of the Dresden Academy in 1824, he influenced many of the young German and Scandinavian artists of the mid nineteenth century and as a result he ranks high among the formative figures of the Romantic movement. For many years his works were neglected, but in the early 1900s they were rediscovered and revived.

MOVEMENT
Romanticism
OTHER WORKS
The Wreck of the Hope, The Stages of Life, Graveyard in Snow
INFLUENCES
Albrecht Altdorfer, Turner

Caspar David Friedrich *Born* 1774 Germany
Painted in Dresden, Germany
Died 1840 Dresden

Courtesy of Hamburg Kunsthalle, Hamburg, Germany/Bridgeman Art Library

Fuseli, Henry (Johann Heinrich Füssli)

The Birth of Sin

SWISS PAINTER and graphic artist; a key figure in the English Romantic movement. Born in Zurich, the son of a town clerk and amateur painter, Fuseli trained as a minister in the Swiss Reformed Church. He was ordained in 1761, but turned to art in 1768, after receiving encouragement from Sir Joshua Reynolds. Pursuing this ambition, he spent several years in Italy (1770–78), where he was impressed, above all, by Michelangelo's vision of the Sublime – a mood which he tried to capture in many of his own paintings.

In 1778, Fuseli moved to London, making this his principal artistic base. He cemented his reputation with *The Nightmare*, which was exhibited at the Royal Academy in 1782. Fuseli made several versions of this haunting image, which is undoubtedly his most famous work. Although the picture may have had a purely personal meaning for him – the expression of his unrequited passion for a Swiss girl – it has become one of the landmarks of Romanticism. In it, as in his other works, the artist focused on the darker side of the imagination, weaving together elements of horror, fantasy and eroticism.

MOVEMENT
Romanticism
OTHER WORKS
Titania's Awakening, The Ladies of Hastings
INFLUENCES
Michelangelo, William Blake, Sir Joshua Reynolds

Henry Fuseli *Born* 1741 Switzerland
Painted in England, Italy, Switzerland and Germany
Died 1825

Courtesy of Private Collection/Christie's Images

BORN IN Sudbury, Suffolk Gainsborough displayed precocious artistic skills. According to family legend, he helped catch a pear-thief in a neighbour's orchard by accurately sketching the culprit. Recognizing his obvious talent, his family sent him to London at the age of 13, where he was trained by the French Rococo artist Hubert Gravelot. In 1745, Gainsborough set up in business hoping to make a living selling landscapes, but the venture failed and he returned to Suffolk. Gainsborough preferred landscapes to 'face-painting', but found that portraiture was far more profitable. With

this in mind, he eventually moved from Suffolk to the fashionable resort of Bath, where he was employed by a rich and illustrious clientele. Here, Gainsborough honed his skills to perfection, often painting by candlelight, in order to give his brushwork its distinctive, flickering appearance. By 1768, he was so famous that he was invited to become one of the founder members of the Royal Academy. Gainsborough accepted, and spent the final years of his career in London, vying with Reynolds for supremacy in the field of portraiture.

MOVEMENT
Rococo
OTHER WORKS
The Morning Walk, The Painter's Daughters Chasing a Butterfly
INFLUENCES
Hubert Gravelot, Van Dyck, Francis Hayman

Thomas Gainsborough   *Born* 1727 England
Painted in England
Died 1788

Courtesy of Private Collection/Christie's Images

Gallen-Kallela, Akseli

IN THE period before Finland gained its independence at the end of World War I, Akseli Valdemar Gallen-Kallela played a major role in the revival of the national spirit, especially among the Finnish-speaking population. Hitherto the art establishment of the Grand Duchy was predominantly Swedish speaking and culturally oriented to Sweden. Gallen-Kallela studied in Paris from 1884 onwards and spent much of his life there prior to 1920, but throughout this period took a keen interest in the rebirth of Finnish culture. Although he is best known for his paintings of scenes from the great epic poem *Kalevala*, he produced numerous landscapes, the most evocative being of the lakes and forests of Finland in winter. He was also an accomplished portraitist and painted one of the best likenesses of Maxim Gorky. The disparate strands of his artistry came together in his great masterpiece, the triptych telling the story of Aino and Väinämöinen from Finnish mythology. He executed works in black and white, notably the sensitive and lively illustrations for the writings of Aleksis Kivi (1906–07).

MOVEMENT
Finnish School
OTHER WORKS
Head of a Young Girl, The Fratricide, Peace
INFLUENCES
August Ahlstedt, Karl Peter Mazer, Gustaf Albert Edelfelt

Akseli Gallen-Kallela *Born* 1865 Pori, Finland
Painted in France and Finland
Died 1931 Helsinki, Finland

Courtesy of Christie's Images/Bridgeman Art Library

Gauguin, Paul

ALTHOUGH HE was born in Paris, Gauguin spent his early childhood in Peru, returning to France in 1855. He worked for a time as a stockbroker, painting only as a hobby, until the stock market crash of 1882 prompted a dramatic change of career. His first pictures were in the Impressionist style, influenced in particular by his friend, Camille Pissarro. Increasingly, though, Gauguin became dissatisfied with the purely visual emphasis of the movement, and tried to introduce a greater degree of symbolism and spirituality into his work. Inspired by Japanese prints, he also developed a new style,

coupling bold splashes of bright, unmixed colour with simplified, linear designs. At the same time, haunted by memories of his Peruvian childhood, Gauguin developed a growing fascination for exotic and 'primitive' cultures. Initially, he was able to satisfy this need in Brittany where, inspired by the region's distinctive Celtic traditions, he produced *The Vision after the Sermon*, his first great masterpiece. Then in 1891, he moved to the French colony of Tahiti. Dogged by poverty and ill health, he spent most of his later life in this area, producing the paintings for which he is best known today.

MOVEMENT
Post-Impressionism, Impressionism, Symbolism
OTHER WORKS
Where Do We Come From? What Are We? Where Are We Going To?
INFLUENCES
Camille Pissarro, Emile Bernard, Vincent Van Gogh

Paul Gauguin *Born* 1848 Paris, France
Painted in France, Denmark, Martinique Tahiti
Died 1903

NAVE NAVE MOE

Courtesy of Hermitage, St Petersburg/Bridgeman/Christie's Images

Gentileschi, Artemisia

REGARDED BY many as the finest of all female artists, Artemisia was born in Rome, where she was trained by her father, Orazio. Both artists were heavily influenced by Caravaggio, sharing his fondness for unflinching realism and dramatic lighting effects. During her lifetime, Gentileschi was best known as a portraitist, but she has since become more famous for her powerful religious scenes. In these, she tended to focus on Biblical women, such as Susanna, Bathsheba and Esther but her favourite subject was Judith, the Jewish heroine who saved her people by killing an enemy general. Gentileschi produced at least six versions of this story and, although the theme was popular with other female artists of the time, hers are undoubtedly the goriest. This has often been ascribed to a trauma in her own life for, at the age of 19, she claimed that she was raped by an artist from her father's workshop. A five-month trial ensued, during which Gentileschi was tortured with thumbscrews, in order to 'verify' her evidence.

During her career, Artemisia worked in Florence, Naples, Venice. and also spent some time in London helping her father complete a commission for Charles I.

MOVEMENT
Baroque, Caravaggism
OTHER WORKS
Susanna and the Elders, Self-Portrait as the Allegory of Painting
INFLUENCES
Caravaggio, Orazio Gentileschi, the Carracci

Artemisia Gentileschi   *Born* 1593 Rome, Italy
Painted in Italy and England
Died c. 1652

Courtesy of Galleria degli Uffizi, Florence, Italy/Bridgeman Art Library

Géricault, Théodore

Homme Nu a Mi-Corps Man (Naked to the Waist)

JEAN LOUIS André Théodore Géricault studied under Carle Vernet and Pierre Narcisse Guérin, although he was frequently at odds with the latter because of his passion for Rubens and his unconventional approach in interpreting nature. He made his debut at the Salon of 1812 with his spirited portrait of a cavalry officer on horseback, and followed this with the *Wounded Cuirassier* (1814), subjects which were immensely popular at the height of the Napoleonic Empire. During the Hundred Days, he served as a volunteer in a Royalist regiment, witnessing soldiers and horses at close quarters. He travelled and studied in Italy in 1816–19, and on his return to Paris embarked on the large-scale works which established his reputation as one of the leading French Romantics. For an artist renowned for his equestrian subjects it is ironic that he died as the result of a fall from his horse.

MOVEMENT
Romanticism
OTHER WORKS
Officer of the Hussars, Coirse des Chevaux Libres
INFLUENCES
Carle Vernet, Pierre Narcisse Guérin

Théodore Géricault   *Born* 1791 Rouen, France
Painted in Paris
Died 1824 Rouen

Courtesy of Private Collection/Christie's Images

DOMENICO GHIRLANDAIO was the son of Tommaso Bigordi, under whom he trained as a goldsmith; he later studied painting and the art of mosaic under his uncle Alesso Bigordi. None of his early works has survived, but from 1475 onwards he was renowned as a painter of wood panels and frescoes mainly for church decoration. In 1481 Pope Sixtus VI summoned him to Rome, where he painted a number of frescoes as well as individual religious works in which the subject was placed in a secular setting, often with figures of contemporary personalities as spectators on the sidelines. Ghirlandaio ran a large workshop, employing many pupils (including the young Michelangelo). Although these frescoes incorporate numerous portraits, there are relatively few individual works by Ghirlandaio in this genre. The best of these, however, is the touching portrait of an old man with his grandson; the identity of the sitters is unknown.

MOVEMENT
Florentine School
OTHER WORKS
Adoration of the Magi, The Visitation, Virgin and Saints
INFLUENCES
Alesso Bigordi

Domenico Ghirlandaio *Born* 1449 Italy
Painted in Florence and Rome
Died 1494 Florence

Courtesy of Ashmolean Museum, Oxford, UK/Bridgeman Art Library

Giacometti, Alberto

ALBERTO GIACOMETTI studied in Geneva but worked mostly in Paris, where he settled in 1922, working for some time primarily as a sculptor with Antoine Bourdelle. He moved in the intellectual circle dominated by Jean-Paul Sartre and was an enthusiastic disciple of Existentialism. In his painting he was originally drawn to the Cubists but in 1930 he embraced Surrealism as preached by André Breton, although he was expelled from the movement five years later. This was a defining moment, which resulted in a radical departure from previous styles and the evolution of strange, wraith-like figures. Although he is best remembered as a sculptor for his semi-abstract bronzes such as the *Thin Man* series and even more skeletal, spidery figures of the immediate postwar period, the same qualities are evident in his paintings – mostly portraits of real people executed in an abstract fashion.

MOVEMENT
Surrealism

OTHER WORKS
Jean Genet, Portrait of Yanaihara

INFLUENCES
Bourdelle, Antoine, Andre Breton

Alberto Giacometti   *Born* 1901 Switzerland
Painted in Paris
Died 1966 Chur, Switzerland

Courtesy of Private Collection/Bridgeman Art Library/© ADAGP, Paris and DACS, London 2002

Gilbert and George

ITALIAN-BORN Gilbert Proesch first met George Pasmore when they were both students at St Martin's School of Art in London and have worked together since graduating in 1969. George had previously studied at Dartington Hall and the Oxford School of Art, while Gilbert had attended the Academy of Art in Munich. Since the late 1960s they have worked as performance artists, principally as living sculptures, their faces and hands covered with gold paint and holding the same pose for hours on end. Subsequently they developed two-dimensional art, often comprising a series of framed photographs which are integrated to form a single entity. Their very conservative images in these collaborative works often clash with the subject matter, in which bodily functions and overt references to homosexuality feature prominently. Controversy surrounds their work, which is often seen as promoting rather than condemning fascist or racist attitudes, although they claim to be attempting to define the 'new morality'.

MOVEMENT
Modern British School
OTHER WORKS
Fear, Flying Shit, England, The Nature of Our Looking
INFLUENCES
Op Art, Performance Art

Gilbert Proesch *Born* 1942 Dolomites, Italy
Worked in Italy, Germany and England
George Pasmore *Born* 1943 Devon, England
Painted in England

Courtesy of Private Collection/Christie's Images

BORN IN Castelfranco, Italy he is sometimes known as Giorgio da Castelfranco or even Giorgio Barbarelli, from the unsubstantiated legend that he was the natural son of the scion of the powerful family of that name. Giorgione (often spelled Zorzon in the Venetian dialect) is a somewhat shadowy figure, a man of apparently considerable musical and poetic talents whose career was cut short by the plague. His output consisted largely of frescoes which have not survived, but his reputation rests mainly on the small, intimate paintings of Christ, the saints and some contemporary figures. He was also responsible for great improvements in the depiction of figures in landscapes and an ability to convey senses and moods in these pictures. He learned his craft from Bellini and, in turn, passed on his expertise to Titian. Many paintings once attributed to Giorgione have since been disproved, but the few that remain confirm his position among the foremost artists of the early sixteenth century.

MOVEMENT
Venetian School

OTHER WORKS
The Sleeping Venus, The Tempest

INFLUENCES
Giovanni Bellini

Giorgione *Born c* 1478 Castelfranco, Italy
Painted in Venice
Died 1510 Venice

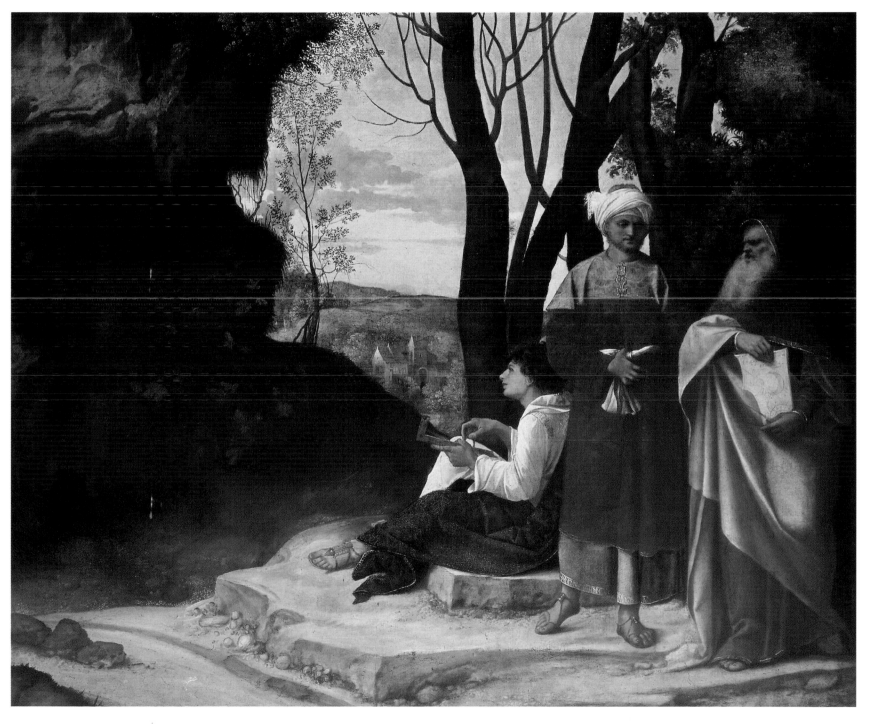

Courtesy of Kunsthistorisches Museum, Vienna, Austria/Bridgeman Art Library

Giotto (Giotto di Bondone)

ONE OF the founding fathers of the Renaissance, Giotto was revered by early commentators as the greatest artist since antiquity, and it is clear that he was still influencing painters more than a century after his death. His greatest achievement was to rid Italian art of the repetitive stylizations deriving from Byzantine painting. In the process, he became one of the first Western artists to stamp his own personality on his work. In particular, Giotto displayed an unparalleled degree of naturalism, both in his ability to depict solid, three dimensional forms and in his grasp of human psychology. He was also a gifted storyteller, conveying his religious narratives with absolute clarity and simplicity.

The details of Giotto's own life are, however a mystery. There is a tale that his master, Cimabue, first spotted his talent when he saw him as a shepherd-boy, sketching a lamb on a slab of rock. This is probably apocryphal, however, and the identification of Giotto's pictures presents even greater problems. The marvellous frescoes in the Arena Chapel, Padua, are usually cited as his masterpiece, but most other attributions are hotly disputed. Even his three signed altarpieces may only be workshop pieces.

MOVEMENT
Renaissance
OTHER WORKS
Arena Chapel Frescos, Madonna and Child, Ognissanti Madonna
INFLUENCES
Cimabue, Pietro Cavallini

Giotto   *Born c.* 1267
Painted in Italy
Died 1337

Courtesy of Scrovegni (Arena) Chapel, Padua, Italy/Bridgeman Giraudon

Girodet de Roussy-Trioson, Anne-Louis   Portrait of Mustapha, 1819

VERSATILE FRENCH painter and illustrator. Girodet was probably the illegitimate son of Dr Trioson, adopting his surname in 1806. After a false start in architecture, he trained as a painter under David, rapidly becoming one of his most talented followers. Girodet won the Prix de Rome in 1789, working in Italy until 1795. His smooth, sculptural finish linked him with Neoclassicism, but his choice of subject matter became increasingly Romantic. He often opted for poetic, nocturnal themes or for literary subjects, such as Chateaubriand's story of Atala. More Romantic still was his most famous picture *Ossian*, which was

commissioned for Bonaparte's country retreat at Malmaison. This exploited the contemporary craze for Celtic matters, and depicted a misty scene with a bard-like figure welcoming Napoleon's generals into paradise. Girodet also produced coolly erotic nudes, which betrayed his fondness for Mannerist artists such as Correggio. Girodet had a waspish personality, which occasionally landed him in trouble. There were frequent clashes with David and his scurrilous portrait of Mademoiselle Lange created a public scandal. In later life, he inherited a considerable fortune and his artistic output diminished.

MOVEMENT
Neoclassicism, Romanticism
OTHER WORKS
The Entombment of Atala, Mlle Lange as Danaë
INFLUENCES
David, Prud'hon, Correggio, Primaticcio

Anne-Louis Girodet de Roussy-Trioson   *Born* 1767
Painted in France and Italy *Died* 1824

Courtesy of Musee Girodet, Montargis, France/Bridgeman Art Library

Girtin, Thomas

Dunstanborough Castle, *c.* 1797

THOMAS GIRTIN served his apprenticeship in London as a mezzotint engraver under Edward Dayes, through whom he made the acquaintance of J. M. W. Turner who, being shown Girtin's architectural and topographical sketches, encouraged him to develop his talents as a landscape painter. His early death from tuberculosis brought a very promising career to an untimely end, but even by that date he had established a high reputation as an etcher. Hitherto watercolours had been used almost entirely for tinting engravings, but to Girtin goes the credit for establishing watercolour painting as a major art form in its own right. From 1794 onwards he exhibited his great watercolour landscapes at the annual Royal Academy exhibitions and this helped to develop the fashion for this medium from the beginning of the nineteenth century. Girtin collaborated with Turner in making a series of copies of architectural paintings for Dr Monro, notably works by Canaletto.

MOVEMENT
English School
OTHER WORKS
A Winding Estuary, Porte St Denis
INFLUENCES
Turner

Thomas Girtin   *Born* 1775 London, England
Painted in London
Died 1802 London

Courtesy of Private Collection/Christie's Images

A LEADING Post-Impressionist and forerunner of Expressionism. Vincent's first job was for a firm of art dealers, but he was sacked after a failed affair affected his ability to work. After a brief stint as a teacher, he became a lay preacher in a Belgian mining district. Here again he was fired when the Church became concerned at his over-zealous attempts to help the poor. Vincent had at least found his true vocation: illustrating the plight of the local peasantry.

Previously influenced by Millet, in 1886 Van Gogh went to Paris where his style changed dramatically. Under the combined impact of Impressionism and Japanese prints, his palette lightened and he began to employ bold simplifications of form. Like Gauguin, he also used colours symbolically, rather than naturalistically. With financial help from his brother, Theo, Vincent moved to the south of France. Gauguin joined him but the pair soon clashed, hastening Van Gogh's mental collapse. Despite his illness he continued working at a frenzied pace until his suicide in July 1890. Van Gogh sold only one painting in his lifetime, but his work has since become the most popular and sought-after of any modern artist.

MOVEMENT
Post-Impressionism

OTHER WORKS
Starry Night, Sunflowers, The Potato Eaters

INFLUENCES
Jean-François Millet, Louis Anquetin, Gauguin

Vincent van Gogh *Born* 1853
Painted in France, Holland and Belgium
Died 1890

Courtesy of Private Collection/Christie's Images

NATALIA GONTCHAROVA originally studied science but later changed direction and enrolled at the Moscow Academy of Art and trained as a sculptor. She turned to painting in 1904, attracted to the naive folk art of Russia and emulating the flat colours and primitive forms in which these paintings were expressed, combined with concepts borrowed from the Fauves and Cubists. All the elements in these pictures were reduced to simple circles and rectangles or flat shapes that complemented each other (as, for example, the woman's hat and the back of the carriage in her most famous painting). From 1911 she was a member of the German avant-garde movement known as Der Blaue Reiter. In 1915 she and her husband Mikhail Larionov moved to Geneva in order to design ballet costumes and sets for Diaghilev and never returned to Russia after the Revolution. Instead, she settled in Paris in 1921 where she continued to work mainly as a designer, and became a naturalized French citizen in 1938.

MOVEMENT
Der Blaue Reiter
OTHER WORKS
The Cyclist, The Ice Cutters
INFLUENCES
Mikhail Larionov, Picasso

Natalia Gontcharova   *Born* 1881 Russia
Painted in Moscow and Paris
Died 1962 Paris

Courtesy of Private Collection/Christie's Images © ADAGP, Paris and DACS, London 2002

ORIGINALLY NAMED Vosdanig Manoog Adoian, Gorky was born at Khorkom Vari in Turkish Armenia. He survived the genocide perpetrated on the Armenians by the Turks during World War I and escaped to the West, settling in the USA in 1920. The death of his mother during one of the Turkish atrocities had a profound influence on his art. It was at this time that he adopted his new name, taking the surname from the celebrated Russian writer Maxim Gorky. In America he trained at the Rhode Island School of Design and continued his studies in Boston. For several years his style was a heady but eclectic mixture of elements drawn from Miró, Cezanne, Picasso, Motta and André Breton, and it was from the latter that he was attracted to Surrealism, concentrating on biomorphism (the creation of organic abstracts), but later he developed his own distinctive style which promoted Abstract Expressionism.

MOVEMENT
Abstract Expressionism
OTHER WORKS
Agony, Waterfall
INFLUENCES
Joan Miró, Picasso, Cézanne

Arshile Gorky   *Born* 1904 Khorkom Vari, Turkey
Painted in USA
Died 1948 Sherman, Connecticut, USA

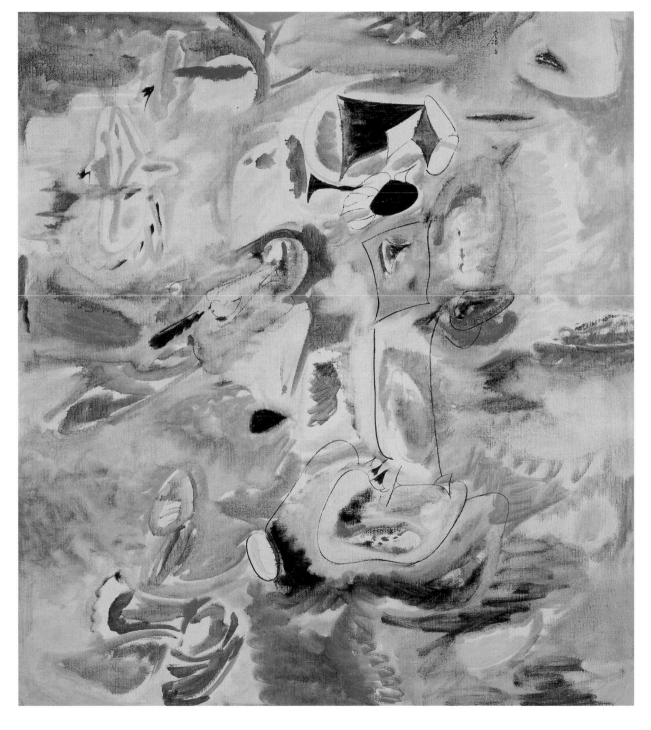

Courtesy of Private Collection/Christie's Images © ADAGP, Paris and DACS, London 2002

Goya, Francisco

FRANCISCO JOSÉ de Goya y Lucientes was raised in the small town of Fuendetodos near Saragossa, Spain. Frequently involved in parochial gang fights, he fled to Madrid in 1765 after a brawl in which three youths were killed. As a result of continued sparring he left Madrid precipitately, joining a troupe of itinerant bull-fighters and eventually reaching Rome, where he resumed his studies in art. In 1798 he returned to Spain as a designer for the royal tapestry factory and executed a number of frescoes drawn from contemporary life, as well as a series of satirical etchings. In 1799 he was appointed court painter to Charles IV, which resulted in some of his most notable portraits. After the French invasion (1808) he sided at first with the invaders, but secretly sketched their atrocities, which resulted in both full-scale canvasses and numerous etchings. In 1824 he moved to Bordeaux where, in old age, he produced some of his finest genre paintings.

MOVEMENT
Spanish School
OTHER WORKS
Execution of the Defenders of Madrid, The Naked Maja
INFLUENCES
Anton Raphael Mengs, Tiepolo

Francisco Goya   *Born* 1746 Fuendetodos, Spain
Painted in Madrid and Bordeaux
Died 1828 Bordeaux

Courtesy of Prado, Madrid, Bridgeman Art Library/Christie's Images

BORN BENOZZO di Lese di Sandro, he studied painting under Fra Angelico and assisted his master in the decoration of the Palazzo Medici-Riccardi in 1456–60. Gozzoli's major contribution was the *Journey of the Magi*, an ambitious work crammed with the portraits of the Florentine council and members of the Medici family. Later he moved with his master to Rome and later worked in Orvieto, also executing numerous frescoes and large murals for churches in Gimignano and Pisa. After leaving Angelico he went to Montefalco in Umbria, where he painted a number of smaller, individual works and altarpieces. As well as the obligatory religious subjects he painted a number of portraits, including Dante, Petrarch and Giotto. His paintings are characterized by their light, lively appearance, their vivacity enhanced by his use of bright, brilliant colours.

MOVEMENT
Florentine School
OTHER WORKS
St Thomas Receiving the Girdle of the Virgin
INFLUENCES
Fra Angelico

Benozzo Gozzoli   *Born* 1420 Florence, Italy
Painted in Florence, Rome, Orvieto and Montefalco
Gimignano and Pisa *Died* 1497 Pistoia

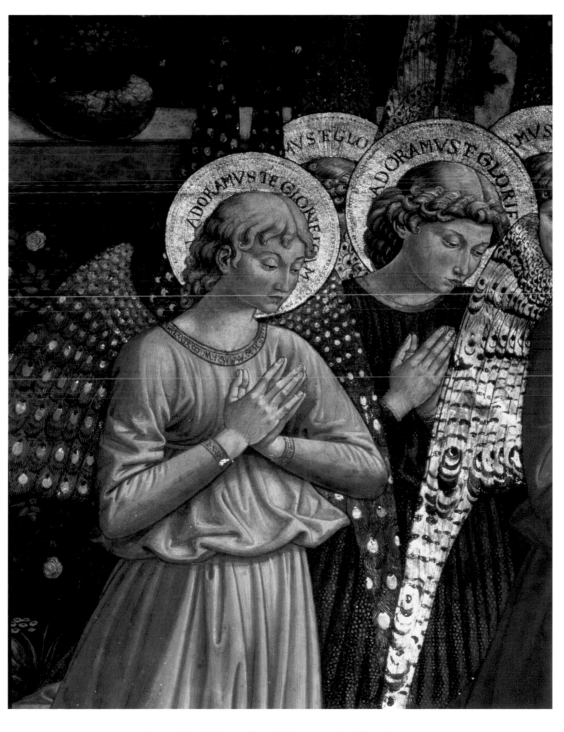

Courtesy of K & B News Foto, Florence/Bridgeman Art Library/Christie's Images

SPECIALIZING IN sentimental and melodramatic genre scenes. Greuze was taught by Grandon in Lyon, before completing his artistic training at the Académie in Paris. Apart from a brief spell in Italy (1755–57), Greuze's career revolved around his exhibits at the Salon. There, he achieved his first notable success in 1755 and soon carved out a niche for himself. Profiting from the contemporary cult of sensibility, he created a unique combination of Dutch-style domesticity and lachrymose sentiment or sermonizing. This approach caught the mood of the times and it won the approval of the influential critic Diderot, who described Greuze's pictures as 'morality in paint'. These moralizing overtones were somewhat ironic, given that the artist's own marriage was a disaster due to the extravagance and infidelity of his wife.

The vogue for Greuze's work was short-lived. Conscious of the growing popularity of sober Neoclassical themes, he tried to emulate this in *Septimus Severus*, but the move backfired. The picture was universally mocked and Greuze was only admitted to the Academy in the demeaning category of 'genre painter'. By the time of the Revolution, he was a forgotten man.

MOVEMENT
Rococo, Neoclassicism
OTHER WORKS
A Father's Curse, Girl with a Dead Bird
INFLUENCES
Chardin, François Boucher, Joseph-Marie Vien

Jean-Baptiste Greuze *Born* 1725 France
Painted in France and Italy
Died 1805

"Girl with a pet dog."

Courtesy of Private Collection/Christie's Images

BORN JOSÉ Victoriano Gonzalez, Gris began his art studies in Madrid before going to Paris in 1906 to work as a magazine illustrator. An early associate of Picasso and Matisse, he became one of the leading exponents of Synthetic Cubism from 1912 onwards, the majority of his paintings involving the deliberate distortion and rearrangement of the elements. He also made extensive use of collage, such as strips of newspaper cut up and rearranged. He moved to Boulogne after World War I and in the 1920s designed costumes and sets for several of Diaghilev's Ballets Russes as well as working as a book illustrator. In his later years he experimented with brighter, contrasting colours and also produced a number of multicoloured sculptures.

MOVEMENT
Synthetic Cubism

OTHER WORKS
Glasses, Newspaper and a Bottle of Wine, The Bay

INFLUENCES
Matisse, Picasso

Juan Gris *Born* 1887 Madrid, Spain
Painted in Paris and Boulogne
Died 1927 Paris

Courtesy of Private Collection/Christie's Images

Gros, Antoine-Jean   Napoleon Bonaparte Visiting the Plague Stricken of Jaffa, 1799

THE SON of a miniature painter, Antoine-Jean Gros studied under Jacques-Louis David. Following the death of his father in 1791 he went to Italy and it was there that he met Josephine Beauharnais, who introduced him to Napoleon, whom he accompanied on his Italian campaign. He was an eye-witness of the dramatic scene when Bonaparte planted the Tricolour on the bridge at Arcole in November 1796 and the dramatic painting that recorded this incident gave Gros a sense of purpose. Thereafter, as a war artist, he chronicled on canvas the exploits of the Napoleonic arms down to the campaign of 1811, and it is on these heroic paintings that his reputation is largely based, earning him the Napoleonic title of Baron in the process. The downfall of Napoleon robbed Gros of his true vocation. In the aftermath of Waterloo he returned to his classicist roots and concentrated on such works as *Hercules and Diomedes*, but by now he was fighting a losing battle against the rising tide of Romanticism.

MOVEMENT
French Classicism
OTHER WORKS
The Departure of Louis XVIII
INFLUENCES
David

Antoine-Jean Gros   *Born* 1771 Paris, France
Painted in France and Italy
Died 1835 Bas-Meudon, France

Courtesy of Louvre, Paris, France/Bridgeman Art Library

Grosz, George

GEORGE GROSZ studied in Dresden and Berlin before being drafted into the army at the outbreak of World War I. In 1917 he was discharged as permanently unfit for service, traumatized by the horrors of trench warfare. In the same year he became associated with the German Dadaists and was an eye-witness of the moral disintegration of Germany through the Spartakist uprising of 1918–19 and the violent street battles between Communists and Nazis in the 1920s. These events, combined with the corruption of the Weimar Republic, provided Grosz with endless material for his ruthlessly satirical and savage attacks on German militarism and the decadence of the middle classes. Garish colours and grossly distorted images, especially faces, were his main weapons. Grosz left Germany in 1932 and settled in the USA where he became naturalized in 1938. In his American period he concentrated on paintings of a more symbolic, less strident, nature. He returned to Germany in 1959, shortly before his death.

MOVEMENT
Dada

OTHER WORKS
Pillars of Society, Suicide

INFLUENCES
Giorgio de Chirico, Carlo Carrà

George Grosz *Born* 1893 Berlin, Germany
Painted in Berlin and USA
Died 1959 Berlin

Courtesy of Private Collection/Christie's Images © DACS 2002

Grünewald, Matthias

Mary Magdalene from Isenheim Altarpiece, 1510–15

BORN MATHIS Gothardt-Neithardt, probably in Würzburg, he flourished at Frankfurt, Mainz, Aschaffenburg and Upper Alsace between 1500 and 1528, where he worked as an architect and engineer. Very little is known of his origins and early life, and he only came to artistic prominence in 1508 when he was appointed court painter at Mainz, taking up a similar post at the court of the Elector of Brandenburg in 1515. It was during the latter period that he undertook the great altarpiece at Isenheim, now preserved in the Colmar Musem. In his heyday he was ranked equal with Dürer and Cranach and is regarded as the last great exponent of German Gothic art, at a time when the ideas of the Italian Renaissance were making inroads into northern Europe.

MOVEMENT
German Gothic
OTHER WORKS
The Crucifixion, The Mocking of Christ
INFLUENCES
Albrecht Dürer

Matthias Grünewald *Born c.* 1470 Bavaria, Germany *Painted in* Frankfurt, Aschaffenburg, Mainz, and Colmar *Died* 1528 Halle

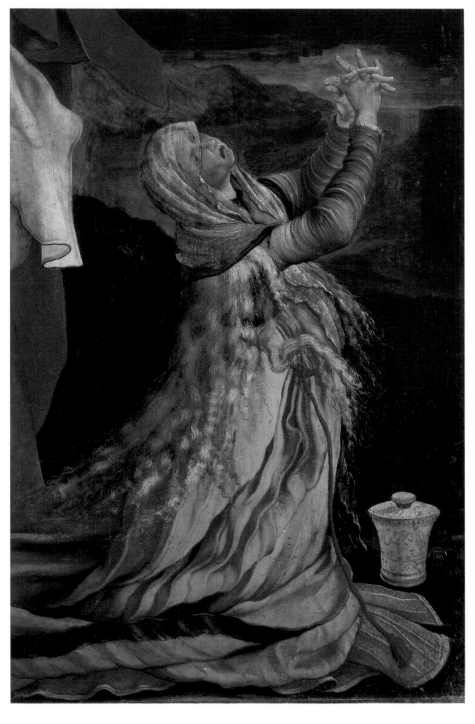

Courtesy of Musee d'Unterlinden, Colmar, France/Bridgeman Giraudon

FRANCESCO GUARDI was a near-contemporary of Canaletto and probably also studied under him; certainly the latter's influence was strongly evident in Guardi's numerous paintings of Venetian scenes, but exceeding his master in his deft handling of lighting effects and above all his application of dazzling colours. Apart from his landscapes, Guardi excelled in interiors and architectural subjects, although he was also a master of the large and majestic subject, notably his paintings of great contemporary spectacles such as the Doge embarking in his state barge or the early balloon ascents of fellow-Venetian Vincenzo Lunardi. Guardi departed from the mathematical precision of Canaletto and developed a more impressionistic approach, anticipating the paintings of Turner. Guardi also produced a number of religious works in collaboration with his brother Giovanni. His brother-in-law was Giovanni Battista Ticpolo.

MOVEMENT
Venetian School
OTHER WORKS
Masquerade in the Ridotto
INFLUENCES
Canaletto

Francesco Guardi   *Born* 1712, Venice, Italy
Painted in Venice
Died 1793, Venice

Courtesy of Private Collection/Christie's Images

BORN GIOVANNI Francesco Barbieri, he is invariably known by his nickname, which means 'squint-eyed', but in spite of this handicap he showed early promise for sketching and drawing. He was trained in the rigorous classical mode at the Carracci Academy but was later influenced by the realism of Caravaggio, whose lighting techniques he modified by the richness of his colours. Like most artists of his generation he specialized in religious works – his major project being the fresco of Aurora which decorated the ceiling at the Villa Ludovisi, commissioned by Pope Gregory XV. From 1642 onwards he was the leading painter in Bologna, where he died. His oil paintings matched the rich density of their colours with the knack of conveying a wide range of emotions which heighten the dramatic impact of his work. There is invariably a dominant central figure, set against a background in the best Baroque tradition.

MOVEMENT
School of Bologna
OTHER WORKS
Jacob Receiving Joseph's Coat
INFLUENCES
Caravaggio

Il Guercino   *Born* 1602 Cento, Italy
Painted in Rome and Bologna
Died 1666 Bologna

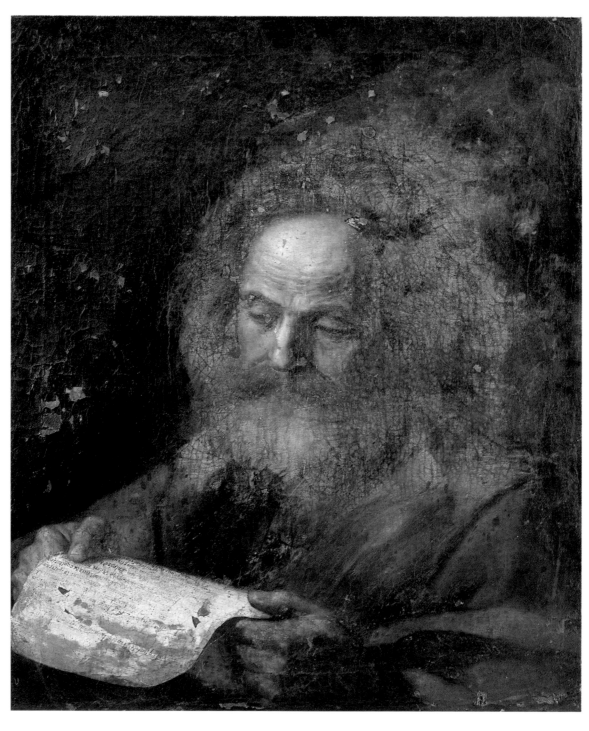

Courtesy of Private Collection/Christie's Images

BORN AT Antwerp about 1580, Frans Hals moved with his family to Haarlem at an early age and spent the whole of his life there. It is believed that he received his earliest instruction from Adam Van Noort in Antwerp but continued his studies under Van Mander. None of his earliest works appears to have survived, but from 1618 onwards, when he painted *Two Boys Playing and Singing* and *Arquebusiers of St George*, his works show great technical mastery allied to that spirit and passion which made him the equal of Rembrandt in portraiture.

His most famous work, *The Laughing Cavalier* is universally recognized, but it is only one of many expressive portraits, distinguished by a liveliness that was far ahead of its time and anticipating the work of the Impressionists. After 1640 his work mellowed and he adopted a darker and more contemplative style.

MOVEMENT
Dutch School
OTHER WORKS
Man with a Cane, Regents of the Company of St Elisabeth
INFLUENCES
Van Noort, Van Mander

Frans Hals *Born c.* 1580 Antwerp, Holland
Painted in Antwerp and Haarlem
Died 1666 Haarlem

Courtesy of Private Collection/Christie's Images

Haring, Keith

KEITH HARING received his formal training at the Ivy School of Art in Pittsburgh, followed in 1978 by a year at the New York School of Visual Arts. In this period he was influenced by Keith Sonnler and Joseph Kossuth, who encouraged him to experiment with form and colour, and to develop as a Conceptualist. His informal (though, in the long run the most influential) art education came through the medium of comic strips and television cartoons as well as the graffiti of the New York streets. He himself spent some time covering the commercial advertisements on the New York subway with flamboyant graffiti executed with coloured chalks and marker pens. Prolific and far-ranging, his work reflected the age in which he grew up. In the 1980s he graduated from the sidewalk to commercial art, producing motifs reproduced on T-shirts and badges, and then posters and murals, drawing on the fertile mix of cultures in his adopted city.

MOVEMENT
Conceptualism
OTHER WORKS
Ignorance-Fear, Silence-Death, Untitled
INFLUENCES
Keith Sonnler, Joseph Kossuth

Keith Haring *Born* 1958 Pennsylvania, USA
Painted in New York
Died 1990 New York

Courtesy of Private Collection/Christie's Images

Harris, Lawren

ONE OF the leaders of the modern Canadian movement, Lawren Harris worked as a commercial artist in Toronto. In 1908 he joined the newly formed Arts and Letters Club, which brought him into contact with other graphic designers and would-be artists, such as Arthur Lismer, Tom Thomson and J. E. H. MacDonald. But it was Harris who apparently took the lead in proposing that they should adopt a distinctive Canadian style – abandoning preconceived ideas, especially the classicism of English and European art – and paint nature as they found it. With the help of an art patron, Dr James McCallum, Harris founded the Studio Building for Canadian Art, to encourage graphic artists to concentrate on landscape painting. He also organized painting expeditions to Algonquin Park, Georgian Bay and the Laurentian Highlands. Though derided as the 'Hot Mush School', out of this eventually emerged the Group of Seven which revolutionized Canadian art. Later he joined the Theosophical Society, believing that art must express spiritual values as well as depicting the visual world.

MOVEMENT
Modern Canadian School

OTHER WORKS
Northern Lake, Kempenfelt Bay, Early Houses

INFLUENCES
J. E. H. MacDonald, Tom Thomson

Lawren Harris   *Born* 1885, Ontario, Canada
Painted in Canada
Died 1970 Toronto, Ontario

Courtesy of Art Gallery of Ontario, Toronto, Canada/Bridgeman Art Library

VERY LITTLE is known about the life of Abul Hasan, other than that he was one of the leading Muslim painters at the court of the Mughal emperors and was particularly esteemed by the Emperor Jahangir (1605–27), who conferred on him the special title of Nadir -uz-zaman. He appears to have been born about 1570 and came to prominence in the last years of the Emperor Akbar, but continued to paint in the reign of Shah Jahan (1627–58). He painted portraits of the emperors, courtiers and officials, as well as genre subjects and charming little studies of birds and animals. His technique matured from 1610 onwards and he was undoubtedly responsible for raising the standards of Indo-Persian painting to new levels. The old aggressive colouring was toned down and a general refinement of style and execution was cultivated. In the portraits of men and animals a little shading was introduced by a few delicate strokes, just enough to suggest solidity and roundness, in marked contrast to the flat, two-dimensional profile painting of the previous generation.

MOVEMENT
Indo-Persian School

OTHER WORKS
Elephant in a Palace Courtyard

INFLUENCES
Daswanth, Basawan

Abul Hasan   *Born c.* 1570 India
Painted in India
Died c. 1640 Delhi, India

Courtesy of British Library, UK/Bridgeman Art Library

FAIK HASSAN studied at the Institute of Fine Arts in Baghdad, Iraq, then won a scholarship to the École des Beaux-Arts in Paris, from which he graduated in 1938. On his return to Iraq he established and directed the department of painting and sculpture at the Institute of Fine Arts. During his time in France he came under the influence of the Cubists and Impressionists, which are reflected in many of his own paintings, although he also explored abstract art and painted landscapes and genre scenes in a relatively conventional style. He established the Pioneers Group in 1950 but withdrew from it in 1962 and five years later formed the Corners Group (Al Zawiya), whose aim was to serve the nation through their art, hence his many pictures with a strong social or political theme. After Iraq became a republic in 1958 he created the colossal mosaic mural entitled *Celebration of Victory* located in Tiran Square. In the last decade of his life he resumed painting in the Impressionist style.

MOVEMENT
Modern Iraqi School
OTHER WORKS
Celebration of Victory (Mosaic mural in Baghdad)
INFLUENCES
Picasso, Pierre Bonnard

Faik Hassan   *Born* 1914 Baghdad, Iraq
Painted in Baghdad and Paris
Died 1992 Baghdad

Courtesy of Sotheby's Picture Library

Hawkins, William

ONE OF the foremost practitioners of American Vernacular and Outsider Art to emerge in the late twentieth century, William Hawkins was barely able to read or write and had no art training at all. Despite this he produced an extraordinary range of paintings. He migrated to Columbus, Ohio in 1916, where he held a wide variety of jobs, from truck-driver to brothel-keeper. Although he began drawing in the 1930s, he did not begin painting in the style that made him famous until the late 1970s. His technique evolved naturally – dripping paint on to cardboard or plywood tilted to 'watch the painting make itself'. Vivid imagery combined motifs seen in newspapers with memories of his native Kentucky countryside. From his early years he had a deep knowledge of animals, an awareness that informs even his most fantastic dinosaur paintings. Latterly he combined paint with pieces of wood, gravel or found objects. His pictures often have elaborate borders including his full name with date and place of birth.

MOVEMENT
American Vernacular, Outsider School
OTHER WORKS
Abstract, The Last Supper, Prancing Horse, Country House
INFLUENCES
None

William Hawkins   *Born* 1895 Kentucky, USA
Painted in Columbus, Ohio
Died 1990 Columbus, Ohio

© Ricco/Maresca Gallery / Art Resource, NY

Heckel, Erich

ERICH HECKEL studied architecture in Dresden from 1904 to 1906 and it was during this period that he met Ernst Ludwig Kirchner and Karl Schmidt-Rottluf, with whom he formed the avant-garde group known as Die Brücke ('The Bridge'). They were strongly influenced by Edvard Munch, Cézanne and Van Gogh, and this was reflected in the vigorous quasi-primitive approach which they adopted in their paintings and prints – well suited to works which invariably had a strongly radical character. The group was dissolved in 1913 and the following year Heckel was drafted into the German Army, serving as a medical orderly throughout the war. Like many of his contemporaries, his wartime experiences influenced his paintings in the postwar period. Vilified by the Nazis when they came to power, he continued to live in Berlin but from 1949 to 1956 he was professor at the Karlsruhe Academy of Art. He was noted for his nudes, his style mellowing and becoming more decorative in his later years.

MOVEMENT
German Expressionism
OTHER WORKS
Bathers, Sleeping Negress, Landscape in Thunderstorm
INFLUENCES
Ernst Ludwig Kirchner, Edvard Munch

Erich Heckel   *Born* 1883 Döbeln, Germany
Painted in Dresden, Berlin and Karlsruhe
Died 1970 Hemmenhofen, Switzerland

Courtesy of Wilhelm Lehmbruck Museum, Duisburg, Germany/Bridgeman Art Library/© DACS 2002

BORN IN CINCINNATI, Ohio in 1865, Robert Henri enrolled at the Pennsylvania Academy of Fine Arts, Philadelphia, in 1886 and two years later went to Paris where he studied at the École des Beaux Arts. His formal training was rounded off by extensive travels in Italy and Spain. On his return to the USA in 1891 he became a teacher at the Women's School of Design, Philadelphia. He worked in Paris again from 1896 to 1901, but later settled in New York where he taught at the Art Students' League. He was a fervent believer in realism, which led critics to deride his 'Ashcan School', but he wielded enormous influence on the next generation of American artists. Despite his teaching commitments he was a prolific artist. In 1908 he founded his own art school in New York and formed the group known as 'The Eight'.

MOVEMENT
American Realism
OTHER WORKS
La Neige, The Equestrian, Young Woman in Black
INFLUENCES
Manet, Renoir

Robert Henri   *Born* 1865 Cincinnati, Ohio, USA
Painted in Paris, Philadelphia and New York, USA
Died 1929 New York

Courtesy of Private Collection/Christie's Images

Hiroshige, Ando

HIROSHIGE'S FAMILY name was Ando Tokitaro, but according to the custom of the time, his professional name was derived from the fact that he was a pupil of Toyohiro. He was a child prodigy, whose sketch of a procession, drawn at the age of 10, was regarded as one of the marvels of the Japanese capital in the early nineteenth century. On the death of his master in 1828, Hiroshige established his own studio, but discouraged by the lack of custom he moved to Kyoto where he produced a series of landscapes. Returning to Edo (now Tokyo) he became immensely popular and widely imitated. His landscapes in the style of Hokusai (whom he greatly admired) were executed as prints with clearly incised lines and solid blocks of colour which featured every aspect of the scenery along the Tokaido road linking Edo to Kyoto, as well as landmarks in and around the cities where he worked.

MOVEMENT
Ukiyo-e
OTHER WORKS
Moonlight at Nagakubo, Fifty-Three Stages of the Tokaido
INFLUENCES
Hokusai

Ando Hiroshige   *Born* 1797 Edo Japan
Painted in Edo and Kyoto, Japan
Died 1858

Courtesy of Private Collection/Christie's Images

IVON HITCHENS studied at the Royal Academy in London and had his first one-man exhibition in 1925. In the early part of his career he painted panoramic landscapes which reflected the influence of Cézanne but by 1936 he was veering towards a Cubist approach, inspired by Matisse, combining natural forms with a more abstract quality. In 1940 he settled at Selsey Bill in West Sussex and this area on England's south coast would provide him with the inspiration and subject matter for many of his later paintings. This gave him the opportunity to explore ways and means of interpreting the subject, conjuring up mood and atmosphere rather than a purely objective view. The 'tone poems' which he created have a timeless quality transcending time and place.

MOVEMENT
Modern English School
OTHER WORKS
Garden Cove, Flower Piece, Winter Lawn and Fir Trees
INFLUENCES
Cézanne, Matisse

Ivon Hitchens   *Born* 1893 London, England
Painted in London and Sussex
Died 1943 Selsey Bill, West Sussex

Courtesy of Christie's Images

Hobbema, Meindert A River Landscape with a Ruined Building and Figures, c. 1660s

ORIGINALLY NAMED Meindert Lubbertszoon, Hobbema studied under Jacob van Ruysdael in his native city. They were close friends and often painted the same subjects; as Hobbema lacked his master's genius in raising the dramatic temperature in his landscapes, Hobbema languished in his shadow. This must also have been the attitude of the picture-buying public at the time, for eventually Hobbema was obliged to forsake painting and work as an excise man, an arduous occupation that left him little time or inclination for art. While it is true that many of his paintings are not particularly distinguished Hobbema at his best could be sublime, and in recent times his painting has been the subject of considerable re-appraisal. It is generally recognized that his greatest achievement was *The Avenue, Middelharnis* – deceptively simple, yet a painting of immense subtlety and complex detail.

MOVEMENT
Dutch School

OTHER WORKS
Stormy Landscape, Road on a Dyke, Watermill with a Red Roof

INFLUENCES
Jacob and Salomon van Ruysdael

Meindert Hobbema *Born* 1638 Amsterdam, Holland *Painted in* Amsterdam
Died 1709 Amsterdam

Courtesy of Private Collection/Christie's Images

Hockney, David

BRITISH PAINTER, photographer and designer. Hockney was born in Bradford, Yorkshire, and trained at the Royal College of Art. There, his fellow students included Allen Jones, Derek Boshier and R. B. Kitaj, and together they all exhibited at the Young Contemporaries exhibition of 1961, a landmark show which marked the arrival of British Pop Art. Hockney himself denies belonging to this movement, even though his early work contained many references to popular culture. Instead, his style may be better defined as New Figuration – a blanket term, relating to the revival of figurative art in the 1960s.

Hockney has travelled widely in Europe, but his main passion has been for the States, especially Los Angeles where he settled in 1976. Throughout his career, autobiographical subjects have featured heavily in his paintings, ranging from friends, such as the Clarks, lovers sunbathing by swimming pools, to an entire book of pictures devoted to his dogs. Hockney has also been a prolific stage designer, creating sets and costumes for *The Rake's Progress*, *The Magic Flute* and *Parade*. In recent years, he has also experimented with photo-work, producing elaborate 'photocollages' from hundreds of photographic prints.

MOVEMENT
Pop Art, New Figuration
OTHER WORKS
A Bigger Splash, Mr. and Mrs. Clark and Percy
INFLUENCES
Picasso, Matisse, Jean Dubuffet

David Hockney   *Born* 1937 Yorkshire, England
Painted in Britain, USA and France

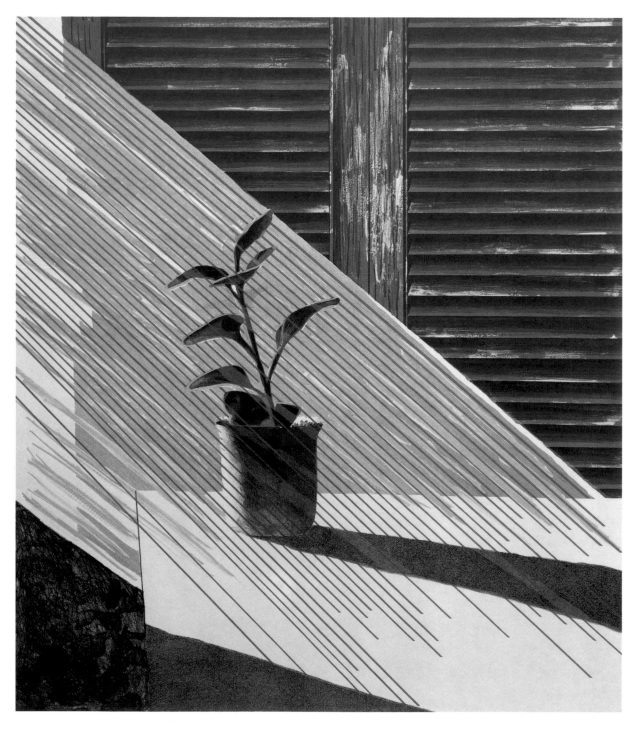

Courtesy of Christie's Images © David Hockney/Gemini G. E. L

Hodgkin, Sir Howard

HOWARD HODGKIN studied at the Camberwell School of Art in London and then Bath Academy of Art, where he later taught (1956–66). Although his painting does not fit neatly into any particular movement he was influenced by William Scott, his teacher at Bath, to regard painting as a physical object. An early but lifelong attraction to the Mughal art of India is also evident in the range of brilliant, contrasting colour. His paintings have a superficial impression of being abstract, but a closer examination reveals that they are truly representational, mostly of interiors or encounters, with figures caught in a split second, and these qualities are evoked strongly in his masterpiece *Dinner at Smith Square*, painted in oil on wood between 1975 and 1979, now in the Tate Gallery. He was awarded the Turner Prize for contemporary British art in 1985 and was knighted in 1992.

MOVEMENT
Modern English
OTHER WORKS
Lovers, Menswear, Interior at Oakwood Court
INFLUENCES
William Scott, Mughal art

Sir Howard Hodgkin *Born* 1932 London, England
Painted in London

Courtesy of Private Collection/Christie's Images

Hodgkins, Frances Mary

FRANCES MARY HODGKINS studied art in Dunedin, New Zealand and achieved a high reputation in her native country with charming genre studies of Maori life as well as landscapes and still-life studies. Her early success enabled her to travel all over the world, especially throughout Europe, spending considerable periods furthering her studies and perfecting her technique in Paris and London, where she eventually settled. At the beginning of the twentieth century she came under the influence of Henri Matisse in his Impressionistic period and this is reflected in her paintings which explored the harmonious use of flat colours. Although much older than most of her contemporaries in English art circles between the World Wars she was regarded as one of the leading figures in the Romanticism of that period.

MOVEMENT
Romanticism
OTHER WORKS
Maori Woman and Child, Hilltop, Barn in Picardy
INFLUENCES
Matisse

Frances Mary Hodgkins   *Born* 1869 New Zealand *Painted in* New Zealand, France and England *Died* 1947 London, England

Courtesy of Private Collection/Christie's Images

HANS HOFMANN studied art in Munich before settling in Paris at the beginning of the twentieth century. Here he came under the influence of the Impressionists, Fauves and Cubists in turn, imbibing their ideas and selecting the aspects of their art which suited him best. On the outbreak of World War I he returned to Munich, where he established his own art school in 1915. In 1930 he immigrated to the United States where, the following year, he opened the Hofmann School of Fine Art in New York City. He introduced to America the techniques of improvisation, which he had pioneered in Germany. He strove to translate the feelings of the artist into light, colour and form; texture was of major importance and he revelled in exploring this aspect of painting. These experiments conducted over many years finally evolved in the distinctive style which he practiced in America and was to have a profound influence on the development of Abstract Expressionism in his adopted country.

MOVEMENT
Abstract Expressionism
OTHER WORKS
Apparition, Nulli Secundus, The Prey, Exuberance
INFLUENCES
Matisse, Picasso

Hans Hoffman   *Born* 1880, Weissenburg, Germany
Painted in Munich, Paris and New York
Died 1966, New York

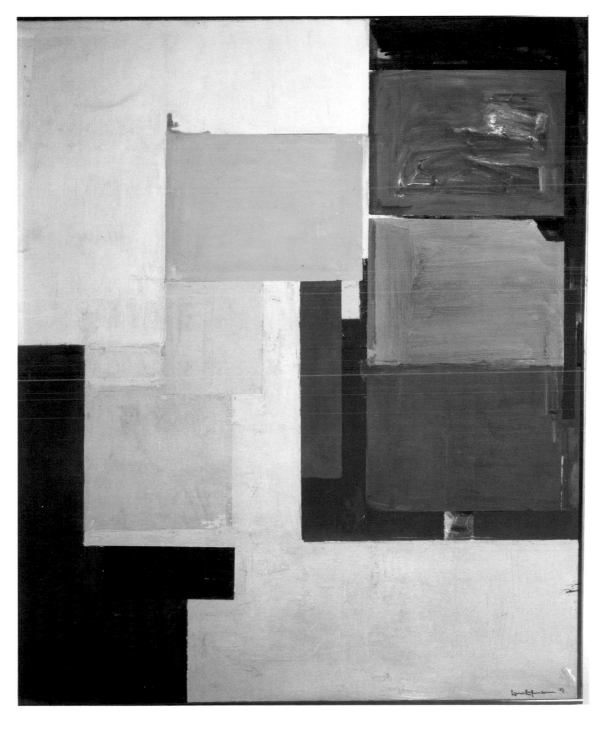

Courtesy of Metropolitan Museum of Art, New York, USA/Bridgeman Art Library/© ARS, NY and DACS, London 2002

WILLIAM HOGARTH became the greatest English satirical artist of his generation. He was apprenticed to a silver-plate engraver, Ellis Gamble, and established his own business in 1720. Seeking to diversify into the more lucrative business of copper-plate engraving, however he took lessons in draughtsmanship under Sir James Thornhill. His early work consisted mainly of ornamental bill-heads and business cards, but by 1724 he was designing plates for booksellers and from this he progressed to individual prints, before turning to portrait painting by 1730. Within a few years he had begun to concentrate on the great satirical works on which his reputation now rests. His canvasses are absolutely crammed with figures and minute detail, sub-plots and side issues to the main theme. Following a visit to Paris in 1743 he produced several prints of low life and moral subjects. He also executed a number of portraits and oils of genre subjects.

MOVEMENT
English School
OTHER WORKS
Marriage à la Mode, Industry and Idleness, Garrick as Richard III
INFLUENCES
Sir James Thornhill

William Hogarth *Born* 1697 London, England
Painted in London
Died 1764 London

Courtesy of Private Collection/Christie's Images

Hokusai, Katsushika

BORN AT Edo (modern Tokyo), the son of a mirror-maker, Hokusai learned the craft of wood-engraving before entering the studio of the painter Katsugawa Shunsho. Disagreement with his master over artistic techniques and principles resulted in his dismissal in 1785. Thereafter he worked on his own as a book illustrator and print-maker, using the Japanese techniques of block printing. His illustrations of everyday life executed for the encyclopaedic *Mangwa* established his reputation as the leading exponent of *ukiyo-e* ('pictures of the passing world') whose charm is exceeded only by their technical accomplishment. Of his prolific series of colour prints, the best known are *Thirty-six Views of Mount Fuji* (1823–29) and *Hundred Views of Mount Fuji* (1834–35), but he also produced several shorter sets and individual works. His prints had a tremendous impact on the Western world. Quite by chance, some of his prints were used as packing material for some china sent to Felix Bracquemond in 1856, triggering off the enthusiasm for Japanese art which strongly influenced the Impressionists.

MOVEMENT
Ukiyo-e
OTHER WORKS
The Dream of the Fisherman's Wife
INFLUENCES
Hishikawa Moronobu, Ando Hiroshige

Katsushika Hokusai
Born 1760 Edo (now Tokyo), Japan
Painted in Edo
Died 1849 Edo

Courtesy of Private Collection/Christie's Images

Holbein, Hans

BORN AT Augsburg, Germany, the son of Hans Holbein the Elder, he studied under his father and then went to Basle with his brother Ambrosius as apprentice to Hans Herbst. Subsequently he worked also in Zurich and Lucerne. He returned to Basle in 1519, married and settled there. To his Swiss period belong his mostly religious works. In 1524 he went to France and thence to England in 1526, where he finally took up residence six years later. There being no demand for religious paintings in England at that time, he concentrated on portraiture, producing outstanding portraits of Sir Thomas More and Henry VIII, whose service he entered officially in 1537. From then until his death he produced numerous sensitive and lively studies of the King and his wives, his courtiers and high officials of state. He also designed stained-glass windows and executed woodcuts.

MOVEMENT
German School
OTHER WORKS
Dead Christ, The Triumphs of Wealth and Poverty,
INFLUENCES
Hans Holbein the Elder, Hans Herbst

Hans Holbein   *Born* 1497 Augsuburg, Germany
Painted in Germany. Switzerland, France and England
Died 1543 London, England

Courtesy of Private Collection/Christie's Images

BORN AT Boston, Massachusetts, Winslow Homer served his apprenticeship there as a lithographer, but following the outbreak of the American Civil War he accompanied the Union forces and contributed sketches from the battlefront to *Harper's Weekly* as well as executing his earliest full-scale paintings, *Home Sweet Home* and *Prisoners from the Front*. He spent two years (1881–83) in England, mainly at Tynemouth, painting nautical subjects. Following his return to the USA he continued to paint the sea – apart from occasional genre subjects such as *The Fox Hunt*. During the last two decades of his life he lived at Prout's Neck on the coast of Maine, where he concentrated on watercolours of fishermen in the eternal struggle against the elements. Occasional forays to Florida, the Bahamas and Bermuda provided more exotic material but invariably with a maritime theme.

MOVEMENT
American School
OTHER WORKS
The Gulf Stream, Fishing Boats at Key West, Bearing Up
INFLUENCES
John Frederick Kensett, Fitz Hugh Lane

Winslow Homer *Born* 1836 Boston, USA
Painted in USA and England
Died 1910 Maine, USA

Courtesy of Private Collection/Christie's Images

Honthorst, Gerrit van

An Arcadian double portrait of two Ladies as Shepherdesses

GERARD OR GERRIT van Honthorst studied under Bloemart in Utrecht, then went to Italy where he studied the naturalism of Caravaggio. Returning to Holland in 1620 he entered the Guild of St Luke, of which he became Dean. Queen Elizabeth of Bohemia, then in exile in Holland, employed him to teach her children drawing and, through her, Honthorst was introduced to her brother Charles I. During two periods in England he painted the royal family and members of the royal court in the style of Van Dyck, as

well as a huge allegory of Diana, Apollo and Mercury with the Bohemian rulers and the Duke of Buckingham, now at Hampton Court. At Utrecht in 1631 he completed a large work of the Bohemian royal family. At the other end of the spectrum he also painted genre scenes of candlelit taverns and their customers in the style of Caravaggio which were renowned for their realism.

MOVEMENT
Dutch School
OTHER WORKS
Christ Before Pilate, Charles I and Queen Henrietta Maria
INFLUENCES
Caravaggio, Van Dyck

Gerrit van Honthorst *Born* 1590 Utrecht, Holland *Painted in* Holland, Italy and England *Died* 1656 Utrecht

Courtesy of Christie's Images / Bridgeman Art Library

PIETER DE HOOCH spent his early life in Rotterdam but when he married in 1654 he settled in Delft. Here he came under the influence of Carel Fabritius shortly before the latter's untimely death in the explosion of the Delft Arsenal. De Hooch was subsequently influenced by the late artist's gifted pupil Jan Vermeer. De Hooch himself became one of the leading masters of paintings showing domestic interiors or courtyard scenes, with the emphasis on order, domestic virtue, cleanliness to the point of ascetism and benign tranquillity, shown through the careful arrangement of furniture and figures. His pictures are characterized by a dark foreground, often a doorway or gateway, leading to a bright interior suffused with light and colour. He was an accomplished technician, noted for his complete mastery of perspective which enabled him to create an almost three-dimensional effect.

MOVEMENT
Dutch School
OTHER WORKS
Woman and a Maid with a Pail in a Courtyard
INFLUENCES
Carel Fabritius, Vermeer

Pieter de Hooch   *Born* 1629 Rotterdam, Holland *Painted in* Rotterdam and Delft, Holland *Died* 1684 Amsterdam

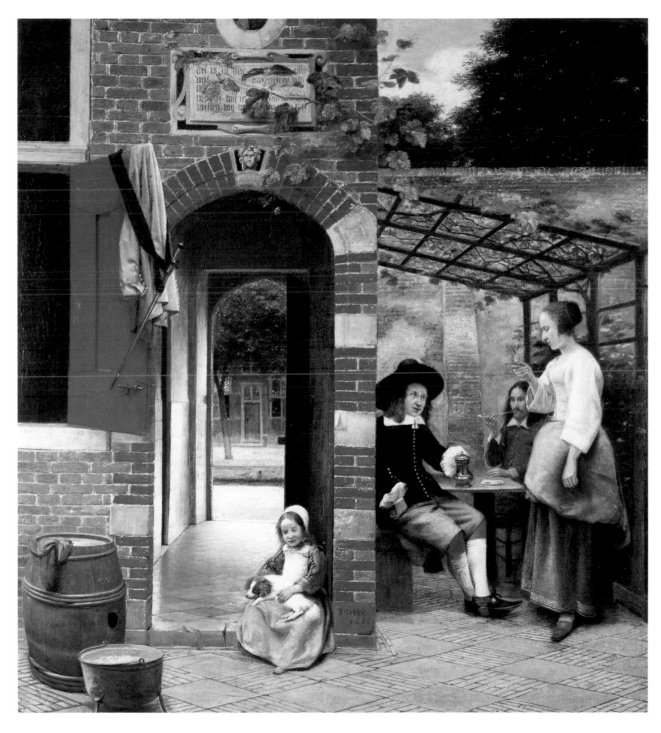

Courtesy of Noortman, Maastricht, Netherlands/Bridgeman Art Library

EDWARD HOPPER studied in New York City under Robert Henri between 1900 and 1906 and then travelled in Europe over the ensuing four years. The artistic atmosphere in Paris (1909–10) had a major impact on him and his paintings up to the mid-1920s reflect the influence of the French Impressionists. In this period he worked mainly as an illustrator, but from 1924 he concentrated on large-scale works which drew upon contemporary American life for their inspiration, from diners and gas stations to hotel lobbies and late-night bars. This emphasis on scenes which were instantly recognizable, coupled with the strong interplay of light and shadow, left an indelible impression – so much so that Hopper's art has come to represent urban America of the interwar years and had a major impact on the Pop Art of more recent years.

MOVEMENT
American School
OTHER WORKS
Room in New York, People in the Sun
INFLUENCES
Robert Henri

Edward Hopper *Born* 1882 New York, USA
Painted in New York
Died 1967 New York

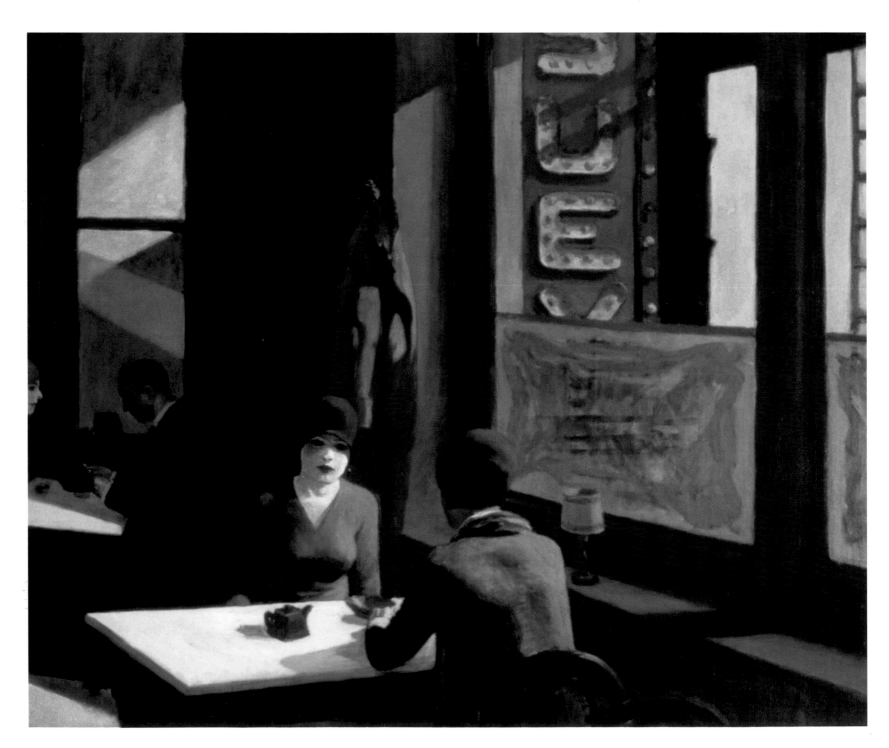

Courtesy of Whitney Museum of American Art, New York, USA/Bridgeman Art Library

ALTHOUGH BORN in London, Peter Howson trained at the Glasgow School of Art from 1975 to 1981 and has since lived in Scotland, apart from forays abroad as an official war artist. His style is essentially figurative, but he took the lead in creating the New Image, which has had a tremendous impact on British art since the late 1980s. Living and working in Glasgow – a city which was then in the process of re-inventing itself in the aftermath of post-industrial decay – he was strongly influenced by the prevailing socio-economic conditions and his paintings have echoes of the Social Realism of the 1930s. His figures, though recognizable, are often monstrous in appearance, reflecting the harshness of living and working conditions. This stark realism came to fruition in his paintings from the Balkan conflicts of the 1990s when, as a war artist, he did not pull his punches on the atrocities and appalling hardships he witnessed. An uncompromising, often fearful, reality pervades his work.

MOVEMENT
Modern British School
OTHER WORKS
A Night That Never Ends, Plum Grove, Patriots
INFLUENCES
Stanley Spencer

Peter Howson *Born* 1958, London, England
Painted in England, Scotland and the Balkans

Courtesy of The Fleming-Wyfold Art Foundation/Bridgeman Art Library/Courtesy of Angela Flowers Gallery

ENGLISH PAINTER; one of the founders of the Pre-Raphaelite movement. Born in London, the son of a warehouse manager, Hunt worked as a clerk before entering the Royal Academy School in 1844. There, he met Millais and, together with Rossetti, they formed the core of the Pre-Raphaelite Brotherhood. Hunt's meticulous attention to detail and his fondness for symbolism accorded well with the aims of the group, but his deeply felt religious convictions led him away from the British art scene. In January 1854, he embarked on a two-year expedition to Egypt and the Holy Land, believing that this was the only way to produce realistic images of biblical themes.

The critical response to this enterprise was mixed. *The Scapegoat* was greeted with puzzlement, but *The Finding of the Saviour in the Temple* was received far more enthusiastically, securing Hunt's reputation as a religious painter. Further trips to the East followed, although these were not always happy affairs. In 1866, his wife died in Florence, shortly after giving birth to their son. Hunt later married her sister. In 1905, he wrote his memoirs, which have become a primary source document for the Pre-Raphaelite movement.

MOVEMENT
Pre-Raphaelite Brotherhood
OTHER WORKS
The Hireling Shepherd, The Light of the World
INFLUENCES
Dante Gabriel Rossetti, Augustus Egg, John Everett Millais

William Holman Hunt   *Born* 1827
Painted in England, Egypt and the Holy Land
Died 1910

Courtesy of Private Collection/Christie's Images

Ingres, Jean-Auguste-Dominique

FRENCH PAINTER and draughtsman, a champion of academic art. Ingres' father was a minor painter and sculptor and, with parental encouragement, he displayed a talent for both drawing and music at a very early age. Opting for the former, he moved to Paris in 1797 and entered David's studio. There, inspired by his teacher and by Flaxman's engravings of antique vases, Ingres developed a meticulous Neo-classical style, notable for impeccable draughtsmanship and a smooth, enamel-like finish. This helped him to win the Prix de Rome in 1801, and brought him a succession of lucrative portrait commissions.

Ingres worked extensively in Italy after 1806, although he continued to exhibit at the Salon and rapidly became the epitome of the academic establishment. This was most obvious in the 1820s, when his pictures were contrasted with those of Delacroix, in the 'battle' between Classicism and Romanticism. While his style was a model of classical correctness, however, Ingres' subject matter was often distinctly Romantic. This is particularly evident in the exotic eroticism of Oriental scenes, such as *La Grande Odalisque* and *The Turkish Bath*.

MOVEMENT
Neoclassicism, Romanticism
OTHER WORKS
Madame Moitessier, The Apotheosis of Homer
INFLUENCES
David, Raphael, John Flaxman

Jean-Auguste-Dominique Ingres
Born 1780 *Painted in* France and Italy
Died 1867

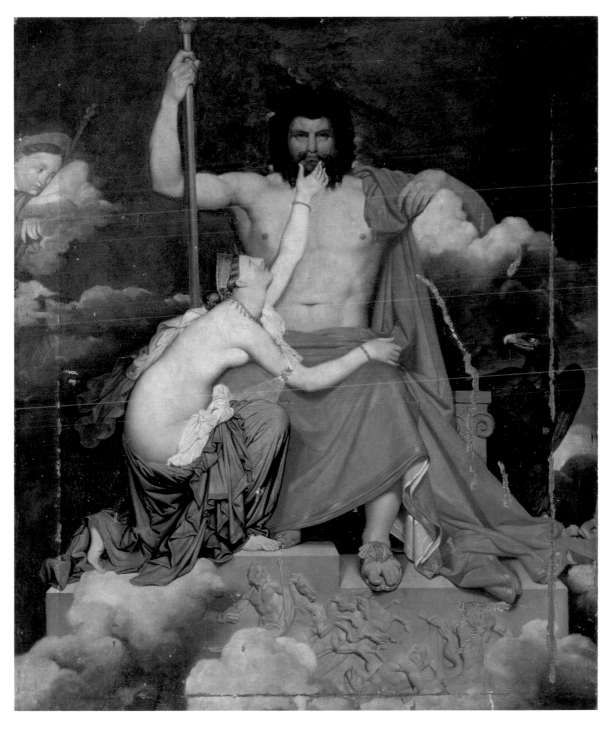

Courtesy of Private Collection/Christie's Images

Jackson, A.Y.

ONE OF the most influential Canadian artists of the twentieth century, Alexander Young Jackson originally worked as a commercial artist in Montreal (1895–1906), before moving to Chicago. While continuing in the same profession, he attended classes at the Art Institute of Chicago and then went to Paris in 1907, where he studied under Jean-Paul Laurens at the Académie Julian. He returned to Canada in 1909 and settled in Toronto in 1913, where he became one of the leaders of the Group of Seven, founded in 1920. In World War I he was wounded in action but later became a war artist. He resumed his work as a landscape painter in 1919, becoming the leading advocate for a distinctive Canadian style of painting, his words as eloquent as his paintings were striking. He travelled to every part of Canada, including the Arctic, to record the rich variety of landscape.

MOVEMENT
Modern Canadian School
OTHER WORKS
Terre Sauvage, Springtime in Picardy, First Snow
INFLUENCES
Jean-Paul Lauren, Lawren Harris, Tom Thomson

A.Y. Jackson *Born* 1882 Montreal, Canada
Painted in Canada and France
Died 1974 Kleinburg, Ontario, Canada

Courtesy of Art Gallery of Ontario, Toronto, Canada/Bridgeman Art Library

Jawlensky, Alexei

THE SCION of a Russian aristocratic family, Alexei Jawlensky served as an officer in the Imperial Guard before abandoning a military career in favour of art. He enrolled at the St Petersburg Academy and then moved to Germany in 1896, completing his education in Munich, where he met fellow Russian Wassily Kandinsky; under his guidance evolved his own highly distinctive brand of Fauvism. He spent some time painting in Brittany and Provence in about 1905. During a visit to Paris in 1913, however, he came under the influence of Matisse and Picasso and embraced Cubism, initially adapting it to his style of portraiture, which owed much to the religious icons of his native country. Later, however, his paintings became much less figurative and gradually switched to a more overtly abstract character, relying on simple geometric patterns in more muted colours than those that had been the hallmark of his Fauvist period. After World War I he settled in Wiesbaden, Germany, where he joined the group known as the Blaue Vier ('Blue Four') with Kandinsky, Klee and Feininger. Jawlensky used colour in a lyrical sense, believing that tones and shades corresponded to notes and chords.

MOVEMENT
Fauvism, Cubism
OTHER WORKS
The White Feather, Abstract Head
INFLUENCES
Kandinsky, Matisse, Paul Klee

Alexei Jawlensky *Born* 1864 Kuslovo, Russia
Painted in Russia, France and Germany
Died 1941 Wiesbaden, Germany

Courtesy of Private Collection/Christie's Images/© DACS 2002

John, Augustus

AUGUSTUS EDWIN John studied at the Slade School of Art and the University of London under Fred Brown and Henry Tonks, winning a scholarship with his *Moses and the Brazen Serpent* (1896). He went to Paris in 1900 and later travelled in the Netherlands, Belgium and Provence. His early work was influenced by Rembrandt, El Greco and the Post-Impressionists. A colourful, larger-than-life character, John hit the headlines when he roamed around England in a horse and cart, painting gypsy scenes. His later style was marked by the use of bold, bright colours, his first major oil being *The Smiling Woman* (1908) the first of many paintings in which his wife Dorelia was the model. During World War I he served as a war artist with the Canadians. From the 1920s onwards he painted numerous portraits. He became a member of the Royal Academy in 1928, resigned in protest in 1938, was re-elected in 1940 and in 1942 was awarded the Order of Merit. His genre scenes are full of wry humor.

MOVEMENT
English School
OTHER WORKS
Canadians Opposite Lens, The Smiling Woman
INFLUENCES
Rembrandt, El Greco

Augustus John   *Born* 1878 Wales
Painted in England
Died 1961 Hampshire, England

Courtesy of The Artists Estate/Bridgeman Art Library/Christie's Images

WELSH PAINTER, the greatest female artist of her age. John trained at the Slade School in London, together with her brother Augustus, who also went on to become a famous artist. She then moved to Paris to study under Whistler, from whom she derived her delicate sense of tonality. In 1903, John planned to walk to Rome with a friend, but they only got as far as France, where she decided to settle. For a time she worked as a model in Paris and, through this, met the sculptor Rodin, who became her lover. He urged her to paint more, but John's output was small and it was only through the generosity of her chief patron, an American lawyer named John Quinn, that she was able to give up modelling and devote herself to her art.

Quiet and retiring, John lived alone and rarely exhibited her work. In her solitude, she developed a unique style, painting intimate, small-scale subjects – usually female portraits or corners of her studio – in thin layers of exquisitely muted colours. At first glance, these often appear frail and insubstantial but, like the artist herself, they also exude an inner calm and strength.

MOVEMENT
Intimisme
OTHER WORKS
The Convalescent, Girl Reading at the Window, Nude Girl
INFLUENCES
Whistler, Henry Tonks

Gwen John *Born* 1876
Painted in England and France
Died 1939

Courtesy of Private Collection/Christie's Images © Estate of Gwen John 2002. All Rights Reserved, DACS 2002

JASPER JOHNS studied at the University of South Carolina, Columbia. In 1952 he settled in New York City and there he met Robert Rauschenberg, who shared his views on the brash banality of contemporary culture, which they exploited in the development of Pop Art. By taking the familiar, the mundane and everyday icons such as the Stars and Stripes and the numerals on football jerseys he created works of art that put them in an entirely new light. The influence of Dada is evident as he deliberately set himself against the tenets of conventional art. Thus originality is eschewed by taking previously existing and immediately recognizable objects and emphasizing their very ordinariness. Johns is a versatile artist, working in oils, encaustic, plaster and other materials in various media.

MOVEMENT
Pop Art
OTHER WORKS
Device, Zero Through Nine, Zone
INFLUENCES
Marcel Duchamp

Jasper Johns *Born* 1930 Augusta, Georgia, USA
Painted in New York

Courtesy of Private Collection/Christie's Images © Jasper Johns / VAGA, New York/DACS, London 2002

Johnson, William H

BORN IN South Carolina in 1901, William Henry Johnson migrated to New York in 1918 and settled in Harlem. For five years he studied art at the National Academy of Design and later moved to Denmark, after marrying the Danish weaver and potter Holche Krake in 1930. He later spent some time in Norway before returning to the USA shortly before World War II. In 1943 they lost everything as a result of a house fire, and soon afterwards his wife died. Johnson had a mental breakdown and by 1947 had to be committed to an

institution. In 1967 he gave his collected works, amounting to some 800 oils and watercolours and about 400 sketches and drawings, to the National Museum of American Art. He died three years later, and it is only since the 1970s that his achievement has been fully recognized and his importance in the development of contemporary American art fully appreciated. His paintings are characterized by their passion and exuberance, with echoes of Van Gogh and the Constructivists as well as the influence of African tribal sculpture and textile patterns.

MOVEMENT
African-American School
OTHER WORKS
Lamentation, Cagnes-sur-Mer, Minnie, Jacobia Hotel, Jitterbugs
INFLUENCES
Van Gogh, Kasimir Malevich

William H. Johnson *Born* 1901 South Carolina, USA *Painted in* Denmark, Norway and USA *Died* 1970 Long Island, New York

Courtesy of Smithsonian American Art Museum, Washington, DC/Art Resource, NY

NOTHING IS known of the birth or origins of Joshua Johnston and it is likely that he was born into slavery. He may have been a slave owned by the Peale family and perhaps received his artistic training from Charles Peale Polk, whose style he closely resembles. He first appears in the Baltimore directories in 1796, and by that time must have purchased his freedom. From then until 1824 he is listed as a limner or portrait painter, and many of his paintings are still in the possession of Baltimore's oldest families. He is regarded as the first African American to become a professional artist. The portraits have a curiously naive appearance, the figures very rigid, the faces expressionless with eyes staring straight off the canvas and tightly-pursed lips. What Johnston lacked in conveying the expression of his figures was compensated in the detail of clothing and furniture in the background, and the resulting portraits and groups have a definite charm.

MOVEMENT
American School of Portraiture
OTHER WORKS
Letitia Grace McCurdy, The Westwood Children
INFLUENCES
Charles Peale Polk, Charles Wilson Peale, Rembrandt

Joshua Johnston   *Born c.* 1770
Painted in Maryland, USA
Died 1832 Baltimore, Maryland

© The Newark Museum / Art Resource, NY

Jordaens, Jakob

BORN AT Antwerp in the Spanish Netherlands (now Belgium), Jakob Jordaens studied under Adam Van Noort, whose daughter he married in 1616. Unlike his fellow pupil Rubens, he did not go to Italy to further his studies but remained in Antwerp, where he continued to paint in the purely Flemish convention of exaggerated form and rather earthy humor, characterized by warm, glowing colour and the ruddy faces of the subjects. Although a Protestant by religion he gladly accepted commissions from the King of Spain

for religious paintings and altarpieces for Catholic churches. Later he produced large canvasses of historic scenes and in 1652 painted the heroic frescoes for the Huis ten Bosch near The Hague. After the death of Rubens in 1640 he was regarded as the greatest artist in Flanders. He also produced designs for tapestries and engravings.

MOVEMENT
Flemish School
OTHER WORKS
The Four Evangelists, The Victory of Time
INFLUENCES
Adam Van Noort, Rubens

Jakob Jordaens   *Born* 1593 Antwerp, Belgium
Painted in Antwerp
Died 1678 Antwerp

Courtesy of Private Collection/Christie's Images

Kahlo, Frida

Autoretrato en la Frontera entre Mexico y los Estados, 1932

BORN AT Coyoicoan near Mexico City, Frida Kahlo had the misfortune to be in a streetcar crash at the age of 15. During the long convalescence from her terrible injuries she took up painting and submitted samples of her work to Diego Rivera, whom she married in 1928. Artistic temperament resulted in a stormy relationship that ended in divorce in 1939, and many of Kahlo's self-portraits in this period are wracked with the pain she suffered all her adult life, as well as reflecting anger at her husband's numerous infidelities. Indeed, pain and the suffering of women in general were dominant features of her paintings, endlessly explored and revisited in canvases that verge on the surreal and often shock with their savage intensity. André Breton, the arch-apostle of Surrealism, neatly described her art as 'like a ribbon tied around a bomb'.

MOVEMENT
Surrealism
OTHER WORKS
Self-Portrait with Cropped Hair, Self-Portrait with Monkey
INFLUENCES
Diego Rivera

Frida Kahlo *Born* 1907 Coyoicoan, Mexico
Painted in Mexico City
Died 1954 Mexico City

Courtesy of Private Collection/Christie's Images/2002 Banco de Mexico Diego Rivera & Frida Kahlo Museums Trust. Av. Cinco de Mayo No.2, Col. Centro, Del. Cuauhtemoc 06059, Mexico, D.F.

Kalf, Willem

WILLEM KALF had a conventional art training in Rotterdam and then settled in Amsterdam, where he worked throughout his long but surprisingly undistinguished career. Very little is known of his life and work and although he had some recognition in his lifetime he appears to have not been particularly efficient at selling himself or his paintings. His work was all but forgotten until the twentieth century, when art historians restored his reputation. He is believed to have been influenced by his younger contemporary Jan Vermeer, whose own reputation had suffered similar vagaries in subsequent

centuries. Kalf specialized in still-life compositions in which he delighted in placing unusual and exotic objects in unlikely juxtaposition. Rich, dark backgrounds contrast with the subtly lit objects painted in brilliant colours and exhibiting a wonderful mastery of intricate detail. The filigree work on silver ornament or the rich jewels set against a Turkish carpet really come to life and jump off the canvas in their intense realism – the kind of subjects which would have appealed to the rich bourgeoisie of seventeenth century Holland.

MOVEMENT
Dutch School
OTHER WORKS
Still Life with Lobster, Drinking Horn and Glasses
INFLUENCES
Vermeer, Pieter Claesz

Willem Kalf *Born* 1622 Rotterdam, Holland
Painted in Rotterdam and Amsterdam, Holland
Died 1693 Amsterdam, Holland

Courtesy of Private Collection/Christie's Images

BORN IN Moscow, Kandinsky trained as a lawyer, but turned to art after visiting an exhibition of Monet's work. He moved to Munich, where he studied under Franz von Stuck. Here, he demonstrated his talent for organizing groups of artists, when he founded influential Der Blaue Reiter ('The Blue Rider'), an association of Expressionist artists, which included Franz Marc, August Macke and Paul Klee.

Kandinsky's personal style went through many phases, ranging from Jugenstil (the German equivalent of Art Nouveau) to Fauvism and Expressionism. He is most celebrated, however, for his advances towards abstraction. This came about after he returned to his studio one evening, and was enchanted by a picture he did not recognize. It turned out to be one of his own paintings lying on its side. Kandinsky immediately realized that subject matter lessened the impact of his pictures, and he strove to remove this from future compositions.

In later life, Kandinsky taught at the Bauhaus, until it was closed down by the Nazis in 1933. He spent his final years in France, becoming a French citizen in 1939.

MOVEMENT
Expressionism, Abstract Art
OTHER WORKS
Swinging, Composition IV (Battle), Cossacks
INFLUENCES
Claude Monet, Paul Klee, Franz Marc

Wassily Kandinsky   *Born* 1866, Moscow, Russia
Painted in Russia, Germany, France and Holland
Died 1944

Courtesy of Private Collection/Christie's Images/© ADAGP, Paris and DACS, London 2002

MARIA ANNA CATHARINA Angelica Kauffmann was a child prodigy, whose reputation as an artist and musician was well established by the age of eleven. Taught by her father, John Joseph Kauffmann, with whom she travelled to Italy, she developed her own highly distinctive version of Rococo portraiture. In 1766 she came to London where she was befriended by Sir Joshua Reynolds (they painted each other's portrait) and became a pillar of the artistic establishment and a founder member of the Royal Academy in 1769. In 1781 she married the Venetian artist Antonio Zucchi and returned with him to Italy soon afterwards, settling in Rome. As well as a large number of portraits, she executed a number of wall paintings for Robert Adam; she also decorated St Paul's and the Royal Academy's lecture room at Somerset House.

MOVEMENT
Rococo and Classicism
OTHER WORKS
David Garrick, Joshua Reynolds Aged 48
INFLUENCES
Sir Joshua Reynolds

Angelica Kauffmann   *Born* 1741 Switzerland
Painted in Switzerland, Rome and London
Died 1807 Rome, Italy

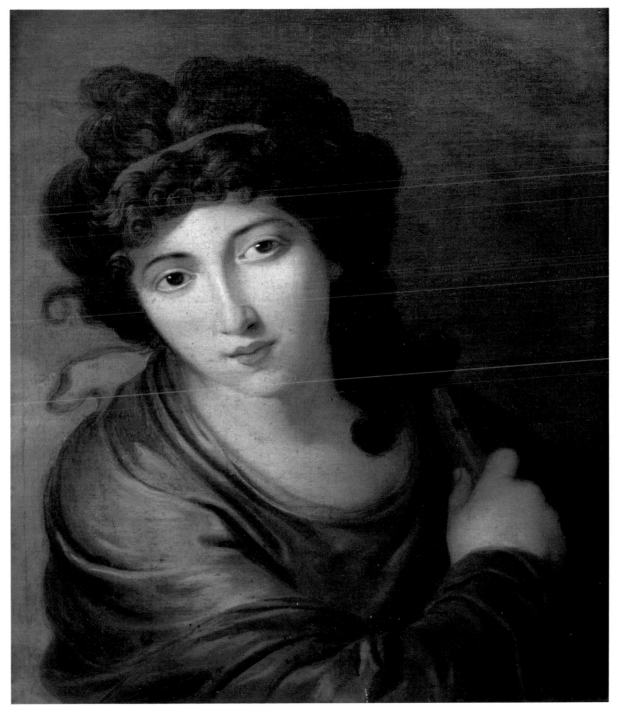

Courtesy of Private Collection/Christie's Images

Khadda, Muhammad

THOUGH BORN in Algeria, Muhammad Khadda lived in France, where he worked as a printer. His employment in the artisticmilieu of Paris inevitably brought him into contact with a number of painters from whom he picked up techniques and ideas on form, colour and composition, although he never had any formal art training. He made his debut in 1955 at the Jeune Peintre Exhibition and also at the Salon des Réalités Nouvelles (1955–58). Two years later he returned to Algeria, where he established himself as a full-time painter, graphic designer and engraver. As well as painting he has designed theater sets in recent years. In his work he explores traditional Berber-Arab art forms of North Africa and the Middle East, often incorporating calligraphy in the manner of the medieval Arab artists, although more figural and representational and with a highly developed sense of colour, reflecting the French influence.

MOVEMENT
Modern Algerian School
OTHER WORKS
Kabylie, Mediterranean Olive Tree
INFLUENCES
Traditional Arab-Berber art

Muhammad Khadda   *Born* 1930
Mostaganem, Algeria
Painted in France and Algeria   *Died* 1991

Courtesy of Sotheby's Picture Library

Kiefer, Anselm

ONE OF the leading artists to emerge in Germany in recent years, Anselm Kiefer originally studied law, but switched to art around 1965 and had his first one-man show five years later. Between 1970 and 1972 he studied under Joseph Beuys, but did not embrace either Minimalism or Conceptual Art as did so many of his contemporaries. In subsequent years he developed large-scale paintings, executed on paper or burlap, mounted on canvas, and using charcoal or black paint to create a starkly etched effect with muted tones of yellow and brown, which drew upon the myths and legends of Germany. Although controversial (and sometimes accused of fascist overtones) Kiefer's monumental paintings are inspired by the works of Caspar David Friedrich and the operas of Wagner. In addition to his paintings, Kiefer has produced numerous drawings and etchings and well as massive 'books' in wood or lead, engraved and worked over.

MOVEMENT
Neo-Expressionism

OTHER WORKS
Spiritual Heroes of Germany, Parsifal series, Lilith

INFLUENCES
Joseph Beuys, Caspar David Friedrich

Anselm Kiefer   *Born* 1945, Donaueschingen, Germany
Painted in Germany

Courtesy of Private Collection/Christie's Images

Kirchner, Ernst Ludwig

BORN IN Aschaffenburg, Germany in 1880, Kirchner studied architecture in Dresden before turning to painting as a result of encouragement from fellow students Erich Heckel and Karl Schmidt-Ruttluf. In 1905 these three artists formed the movement known as Die Brücke ('the Bridge'), which continued until 1913. The name signified the fact that they spanned the art of the past and present, and derived inspiration from a variety of disparate sources, from primitive tribal art to Van Gogh. Kirchner was the dominant personality in this group, which sought to give direct expression to human feelings. Kirchner evolved a distinctly angular style highlighted by bold, contrasting colours. Like so many other artists drafted into the infantry, Kirchner suffered a severe nervous breakdown and while convalescing in Switzerland he concentrated on Alpine landscapes as an antidote to the horrors of trench warfare. His postwar paintings grew more abstract in the time leading up to his suicide in 1938.

MOVEMENTS
Die Brücke, Expressionism
OTHER WORKS
Striding Into the Sea, Berlin Street Scene, The Red Tower in Halle
INFLUENCES
Van Gogh, Edvard Munch, Gauguin

Ernst Ludwig Kirchner   *Born* 1880 Germany
Painted in Germany and Switzerland
Died 1938 Davos, Switzerland

Courtesy of Private Collection/Christie's Images/© by Dr. Wolfgang & Ingeborg Henze-Ketterer, Wichtrach/Bern

BORN IN Cleveland, Ohio, in 1932, Ronald Brooks Kitaj travelled the world as a merchant seaman (1951–55) but after service in the US Army he went to Oxford to study art. In 1960 he enrolled at the Royal College of Art in London. Older and infinitely more worldly wise that his fellow students, he was an outstanding figure with a charismatic personality who played a leading role in introducing Pop Art to Britain in the 1960s. An abiding friendship with David Hockney was forged in this period. The strident colours and brashness of Pop Art belie the intellectual depth of Kitaj's work, which draws on many disparate sources, from his Hungarian Jewish ancestry to the ethnic art of the countries he visited as a seaman. The result is often a riotously eclectic mixture of patterns and images. Most of his work up to 1975 was executed in oils but in more recent years he has concentrated on pastels, a trend encouraged by his second wife, Sandra Fisher. This is cleverly demonstrated in his masterpiece *The Wedding* which celebrates their marriage.

MOVEMENT
Pop Art
OTHER WORKS
If Not, Not
INFLUENCES
Arthur Boyd, Edward Burra

R. B. Kitaj   *Born* 1932 Cleveland, Ohio
Painted in London, England

Courtesy of Private Collection/Christie's Images/The Artist courtesy of Marlborough Fine Art

Kiyonaga, Torii

THE SON of an Edo (Tokyo) bookseller, Kiyonaga was the star pupil of Kiyomitsu, last of great masters of the Torii line. In due course he succeeded as head of the Torii school, his adopted names reflecting the great influences on him. A very large part of his prolific output consisted of prints of the Kabuki theatre but he also painted genre subjects of everyday life in the capital. Kiyonaga introduced a note of greater realism and less idealism which revolutionized *ukiyo-e* ('pictures of the passing world') and paved the way for the mordant style of Sharaku and his followers. By the late 1770s Kiyonaga was spearheading the movement for a more naturalistic approach, with figures that were much more fully rounded and better proportioned than previously. It was Kiyonaga's style that influenced Utamaro, but when the latter overtook him in the 1790s Kiyonaga returned to Kabuki paintings and produced very few prints in his later years.

MOVEMENT
Ukiyo-e
OTHER WORKS
Kabuki Scene, Ladies and Young Man Walking
INFLUENCES
Kiyomitsu

Torii Kiyonaga   *Born* 1752 Edo
(now Tokyo) Japan *Painted in* Edo
Died 1815 Edo

Courtesy of British Library, UK/Bridgeman Art Library

PAUL KLEE studied in Munich and worked there as an etcher. In 1911 he joined with Feininger, Kandinsky and Jawlensky in the Blaue Reiter group founded by August Macke; up to that time he had worked mainly in watercolours, painting in an Expressionist manner with overtones of Blake and Beardsley, but subsequently he veered towards Cubism under the influence of Robert Delaunay and from 1919 onwards painted mostly in oils. In 1920 he became a teacher at the Bauhaus and in the ensuing period his paintings mingled the figural with the abstract as he explored subtle combinations of colours and shapes, often deriving elements from folk art and even children's drawings. He severed his connections with the Bauhaus and returned to Switzerland when the Nazis came to power in 1933 and condemned his works as degenerate art.

MOVEMENTS
Expressionism, Cubism

OTHER WORKS
The Castle in a Garden, At the Sign of the Hunter's Tree

INFLUENCES
August Macke, Robert Delaunay

Paul Klee *Born* 1879 Münchenbuschsee, Switzerland
Painted in Berne and Munich
Died 1940 Muralto-Locarno, Switzerland

Courtesy of Private Collection/Christie's Images © DACS 2002

KLIMT WAS born in Vienna and became one of the leading lights in the city's most dazzling, artistic period. The son of a goldsmith, he trained at the School of Applied Arts and started work as a decorative painter. He achieved early success with the schemes at the Burgtheater and the Kunsthistorisches Museum, but future commissions were threatened by his growing fascination with avant-garde art. Faced with official opposition, Klimt resigned from the Viennese Artists' Association in 1897 and founded the Vienna Sezession, becoming its first president. This coincided with protracted disputes about his

decorations for the university, a project that he abandoned in 1905.

Klimt's style was a compelling blend of Art Nouveau and Symbolist elements. From the former, he derived his taste for sinuous, decorative lines, while from the latter he borrowed his erotic subject matter and, in particular, his interest in the theme of the *femme fatale*. It was this blatant eroticism which troubled the authorities, though it did not seriously damage Klimt's career. He was always in great demand as a portraitist, and he continued to receive private commissions for decorative schemes.

MOVEMENT
Vienna Sezession
OTHER WORKS
The Kiss, Judith I, The Beethoven Frieze
INFLUENCES
Hans Makart, Edvard Munch, Franz von Stuck

Gustav Klimt   *Born* 1862, Vienna, Austria
Painted in Austria-Hungary, Belgium
Died 1918

Courtesy of Osterreichische Galerie, Vienna, Austria/Bridgeman Art Library

Kngwarreye, Emily Kame

EMILY KAME KNGWARREYE was an elder of the Alhalkere tribe and did not take up painting until her seventies. About 1977 she became a member of the Utopia Women's Batik group and showed artistic promise in her unusual treatment of traditional Aboriginal patterns. As a painter, she made her debut in the summer of 1988 with a series of pictures painted in acrylics on canvas and distinguished by their combination of traditional Amnatyerre ceremonial body designs and art forms. She used strong, linear designs, overlaid with fields of dots, in essence a miniaturization of the large ground paintings associated with tribal ceremonies. Although reduced to the confines of the canvas, however, her paintings possess great strength and vitality. Images are abstracted from several sources and coalesced in powerful motifs inspired by the mythological Aboriginal Dreamtime.

MOVEMENT
Utopia Australian School
OTHER WORKS
Emu Woman
INFLUENCES
Louie Pwerle

Emily Kame Kngwarreye *Born c.* 1910
Northern Territory, Australia *Painted in* Australia
Died 1996 Northern Territory, Australia

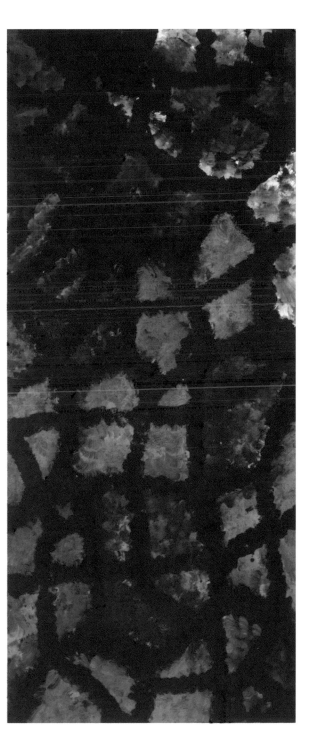

Courtesy of Private Collection/Dreamtime Gallery, London/Bridgeman Art Library/© DACS 2002

Kokoschka, Oskar

OSKAR KOKOSCHKA studied at the Vienna School of Arts and Crafts (1905–09) and joined the Wiener Werkstätte, where he produced lithographs distinguished by their strong graphic sense. His drawings contributed to the German avant-garde magazine *Der Sturm* reveal a highly original approach to Expressionism. After military service in World War I, in which he was seriously wounded, he taught at the Dresden Academy of Art from 1919 until 1924 but subsequently he travelled extensively in Europe and North America before settling in Prague. When the Nazis dismembered Czechoslovakia in 1938 he moved to England, becoming naturalized in 1947, but six years later he settled in Switzerland, where he died in 1980. A versatile artist, he painted landscapes and urban scenes but it is for his very expressive portraits, in which disparate colours bring out the psychological profile of the sitter, that he will be remembered.

MOVEMENT
Expressionism
OTHER WORKS
Portrait of a 'Degenerate Artist', *Children Playing*
INFLUENCES
Klimt, Max Beckmann

Oskar Kokoschka *Born* 1886 Pöchlarn, Austria
Painted in Vienna, Dresden, Prague and London
Died 1980 Montreux, Switzerland

Courtesy of Christie's Images/© DACS 2002

BORN KÄTHE SCHMIDT at Königsberg, East Prussia (now Kaliningrad, Russia), she studied there and later in Berlin, where she married Karl Kollwitz, a doctor who ran a children's clinic in a slum district. Through this connection the artist witnessed at close quarters the poverty and deprivation of the Berlin poor at the turn of the century, and this influenced her painting and sculpture, in which she concentrated on subjects with a strong social message. After her youngest son was killed in World War I she sculpted a large granite memorial, later erected at Dixmuiden in Flanders as a monument to all the young men who fell in battle. In 1928 she became the first woman elected to the Prussian Academy of Arts, but she was expelled by the Nazis in 1933. Her home, studio and most of her works were destroyed in an air raid in 1943. Although best known for her stone carvings and bronze sculptures, she also produced paintings, posters and lithographs with a powerful social message.

MOVEMENT
German Realism

OTHER WORKS
Weavers' Revolt, No More War

INFLUENCES
Otto Nagel

Käthe Kollwitz *Born* 1867 Königsberg, East Prussia
Painted in Berlin, Germany
Died 1945 Berlin

Courtesy of Private Collection/Christie's Images/© DACS 2002

BORN IN the Netherlands, Willem de Kooning was apprenticed to a firm of commercial artists at the tender age of 12 but shortly after receiving his diploma from the Rotterdam Academy of Fine Arts in 1925 he emigrated to the United States and settled in New York, where he worked as a house painter and commercial artist. From the early 1930s he shared a studio with Arshile Gorky and made painting a full-time career from about 1936. Through Gorky he was introduced to Surrealism, reflected in the predominantly black and white paintings of his early period. In the immediate postwar period, under the influence of Adolph Gottlieb, he turned to colour and painted female figures, tending towards Abstract Expressionism. He became one of the foremost exponents of this movement, especially as expressed in his action paintings. In the last years of his long life, however, he turned to modelling figures in clay.

MOVEMENT
Abstract Expressionism
OTHER WORKS
The Visit, Marilyn Monroe
INFLUENCES
Arshile Gorky, Adolph Gottlieb

Willem de Kooning *Born* 1904 Holland
Painted in New York, USA
Died 1997 New York

Courtesy of Private Collection/Christie's Images/© Willem de Kooning Revocable Trust / ARS, NY and DACS, London 2002

BORN AT Edo (now Tokyo), Ogata Korin came from an upper-middle-class Japanese merchant family, noted for their wealth and ostentation. He was once reprimanded by the court for flamboyant extravagance when at a party he wrote verses on gold leaf and floated them down a stream. He represented the rise of the merchant class in the Genroku era (1688–1703), which resulted in a distinctive culture and art forms. His paintings were carefully constructed and his brushwork shows great discipline, characterized by precise delineation and the even distribution of colour. His great masterpieces are the pair of six-fold screens featuring irises now preserved in the Nezu Art Museum, Tokyo. Like his kinsman and predecessor Koetsu, Korin worked in lacquer and ceramics as well as paint, producing boxes for writing implements or the tea ceremony, with delicate figure compositions worked in gold.

MOVEMENT
Rinpa School of Japanese Decorative Painting
OTHER WORKS
Irises, Birds, White and Red Prunus in the Spring
INFLUENCES
Honami Koetsu, Tawaraya Sotatsu

Ogata Korin *Born* 1658 Edo (now Tokyo)
Painted in Edo
Died 1716 Edo

© 1992 The Detroit Institute of Arts

Krieghoff, Cornelius

CORNELIUS DAVID Krieghoff was taught by his father, but in around 1830 he enrolled at the Academy of Fine Arts in Düsseldorf, Germany. Five years later he immigrated to the USA and joined the army, but in 1840 he settled in Montreal as a painter and musician. He later worked in Rochester, New York (1842–43) and studied in Paris (1844–45) before returning to Canada, where he worked at various times in Toronto, Montreal and Quebec City. From 1864 to 1867 he was in Paris and Munich, but continued to paint Canadian scenes there. Subsequently he worked in Quebec, concentrating on genre subjects. Though chiefly renowned for his landscapes (notably the panoramic murals in the Quebec Parliament building), he produced lively and colourful paintings of French-Canadian and Native American life in a style reminiscent of the seventeenth century Dutch masters, imparting a romantic flavor which has never been equalled. He also painted portraits of leading Canadian figures.

MOVEMENT
Nineteenth Century Canadian School
OTHER WORKS
Merrymaking, Gentlemen's Sleigh, Lorette Falls near Quebec
INFLUENCES
Jacob van Ruysdael, Gerrit van Honthorst

Cornelius Krieghoff   *Born* 1815 Holland
Painted in Canada and USA
Died 1872 Chicago, Illinois, USA

Courtesy of Christie's Images/Bridgeman Art Library

Lam, Wifredo

WIFREDO OSCAR de la Concepcion Lam y Castilla was the son of a Chinese immigrant and a woman of Afro-Cuban origin. In his art he strove to combine the disparate elements in the artistic traditions of these three different cultures. He enrolled at the Escuela de Bellas Artes in Havana and went to Madrid in 1923, where he studied under Fernandez Alvarez de Sotomayor and at the Academia Libre. Caught up in the Spanish Civil War, Lam fought with the Republicans in the defence of Madrid (1937). Escaping to Paris, he met Picasso and joined the Surrealists in 1940. On his return to Cuba in 1942 he began painting pictures that combined the dreamlike qualities of Surrealism with elements derived from Cubism and indigenous Afro-Cuban art. For a time he lived in Haiti before settling in Paris again in 1952, though continuing to travel back and forth between Europe and the Caribbean. His greatest masterpiece, *The Jungle* (1943) draws on Afro-Cuban myth and ritual, sugar cane stalks merging with human limbs in a hallucinatory effect.

MOVEMENT
Surrealism
OTHER WORKS
All Souls
INFLUENCES
Picasso, Michel Leiris, André Breton

Wifredo Lam   *Born* 1902 Sagua la Granda, Cuba
Painted in Cuba, France and Spain
Died 1992 Havana, Cuba

Courtesy of Private Collection/Christie's Images/© ADAGP, Paris and DACS, London 2002

EDWIN HENRY LANDSEER was taught by his father to sketch animals from life. From the age of 13 he exhibited at the Royal Academy and became one of the most fashionable painters of the mid-Victorian period, specializing in pictures of dogs with humanoid expressions and deer, usually set in misty, romantic Highland glens or moorland made popular by the novels of Scott and Queen Victoria's passion for Balmoral. Landseer's paintings attained even wider prominence as a result of the fine engravings of them produced by his brother Thomas. One of the Queen's favourite artists, he was knighted in 1850. He modelled the four lions, cast in bronze, which sit at the foot of Nelson's Column in Trafalgar Square, London, unveiled in 1867. Landseer's posthumous reputation was dented by accusations of sentimentalizing animals and, in more recent years, of political incorrectness in glorifying blood sports, but he wielded enormous influence on a later generation of British artists.

MOVEMENT
English School
OTHER WORKS
Monarch of the Glen, The Old Shepherd's Chief Mourner
INFLUENCES
George Stubbs

Sir Edwin Landseer *Born* 1802 London
Painted in London
Died 1873 London

Courtesy of Private Collection, Christie's Images

ORPHANED AT the age of three, John Lavery, born in Belfast, was raised by relatives in Scotland and began his artistic career retouching photographs. When the studio burned down he used the insurance money to acquire an artistic education in London and Paris. Returning to Glasgow in 1885 he founded the group known as the Glasgow School, which promoted the techniques of French Impressionism in Britain. He excelled in landscapes and genre subjects but it was his skill as a portraitist that earned him his biggest commission, to paint the visit of Queen Victoria in 1888, a task that involved over 250 sitters and took two years to complete. The most cosmopolitan British artist of his generation, he spent much of his time in Brittany. He was knighted in 1918 but later devoted much of his energies to promoting better relations between Ireland and Britain. His portrait of his wife Hazel adorned the Irish banknotes for many years.

MOVEMENT
Modern British School
OTHER WORKS
The Unfinished Harmony, George Bernard Shaw
INFLUENCES
Pre-Raphaelites, French Impressionists

Sir John Lavery   *Born* 1856 Belfast, Ireland
Painted in Britain, France, Ireland and USA
Died 1941 Kilkenny, Ireland

Courtesy of Private Collection/Christie's Images/By Courtesy of Felix Rosentiel's Widow & Son Ltd, London on behalf of the Estate of Sir John Lavery

JACOB LAWRENCE was brought up in Harlem, New York City, where he attended the Harlem Art Workshop and studied under Charles Alston. In 1937 he went to the American Artists' School and the following year became a painter in the WPA Federal Art Project. In the 1930s and 1940s Lawrence painted a series of portraits of historical scenes illustrating the lives of black personalities such as Frederick Douglass and Harriet Tubman, and traced the migration northward of African Americans after the Civil War. Wartime service in the Coast Guard provided material for paintings in the late 1940s, but in the ensuing decades he has dedicated his art to the civil rights movement and such causes as the desegregation of the South. A visit to Nigeria in 1964 enabled him to explore a purely African idiom. His late work was less explicit in its social commentary and more engaged with universal concerns and abstract ideals.

MOVEMENT
American Modernism
OTHER WORKS
The Migration of the Negro
INFLUENCES
Charles Alston, Augusta Savage, Orozco, Giotto, Cimabue

Jacob Lawrence   *Born* 1917 New Jersey, USA
Painted in New York and Seattle
Died 2000 Seattle

Courtesy of Private Collection New York/Christie's Images/Artwork © Gwendolyn Knight Lawrence, Courtesy of the Jacob and Gwendolyn Lawrence Foundation

Lawrence, Sir Thomas

Portrait of Mrs Robert Burne-Jones

THE SON of an innkeeper, Thomas Lawrence amazed and amused guests from the age of six by sketching their portraits. When his father became bankrupt four years later, it was the infant prodigy who became the family's breadwinner. At the age of 18, he went to London to study at the Royal Academy and exhibited almost immediately. On the death of Reynolds in 1792 he was appointed Painter in Ordinary to King George III and became the most fashionable portrait painter of the ensuing decades. He was knighted in 1815 and embarked on a European career, during which he painted all the royalty and most of the nobility of the Continent. As President of the Royal Academy (1820–30) he was the leader of the British art establishment. Ironically, he was no better a businessman than his father, and his prolific output barely kept pace with his immense debts.

MOVEMENT
British School

OTHER WORKS
The Duke of Wellington, Pinkie, Mrs Siddons, Princess Lieven

INFLUENCES
Sir Joshua Reynolds

Sir Thomas Lawrence *Born* 1769 Bristol, England *Painted in* England and Europe *Died* 1830 London, England

Courtesy of Private Collection/Christie's Images

Léger, Fernand

FERNAND LÉGER studied architecture in Caen and painting at the Académie Julien in Paris from 1903. Through Braque and Picasso he was introduced to Cubism in around 1910, but he soon developed his own distinctive brand of art described as the 'aesthetic of the machine', already evident in his work by 1913 but more fully developed after World War I. In this period he designed costumes and sets for the Swedish Ballet and collaborated with Man Ray on the first abstract film, *Le Ballet Mécanique* (1924). During World War II he lived in the USA where he taught at Yale and painted mainly acrobats and cyclists as well as working on the murals for the UN headquarters building in New York. After returning to France he concentrated on large paintings of men and machinery, earning the epithet of the 'Primitive of the Machine Age'.

MOVEMENT

Cubism

OTHER WORKS

The Construction Workers, The Builders, Still Life with a Beer Mug

INFLUENCES

Georges Braque, Picasso

Fernand Léger   *Born* 1881 Argentan, France

Painted in France and USA

Died 1955 Gif-sur-Yvette, France

Courtesy of Private Collection/Christie's Images © ADAGP, Paris and DACS, London 2002

BORN PIETER VAN DER FAES at Soest, Holland, he studied under Pieter de Gebber at Haarlem before settling in London in 1641, where he anglicized his name and adopted his father's nickname Lely as a surname. He rapidly became one of the most fashionable artists of the mid seventeenth century and managed to steer clear of politics, being patronized by both Charles I and subsequently Oliver Cromwell. In this early period he concentrated mainly on landscapes or historical and religious subjects, although a hint of things to come was given by his sensitive studies of the royal family during their imprisonment at Hampton Court. Following the Restoration of the monarchy in 1660 he was appointed court painter by Charles II in 1661 and changed his style of painting. Thereafter portraiture became the dominant theme, evinced in the magnificent series of *Windsor Beauties* now at Hampton Court, and the 13 portraits of British admirals at Greenwich. Lely was knighted in 1679.

MOVEMENT
English School

OTHER WORKS
Two Ladies of the Lake Family, Flagmen, Susannah and the Elders

INFLUENCES
Pieter de Gebber, Van Dyck

Sir Peter Lely *Born* 1618 Soest, Holland
Painted in London, England
Died 1680 London

Courtesy of Private Collection/Christie's Images

Lempicka, Tamara de

TAMARA DE Lempicka came from a Polish upper-class family, which gave her an excellent all-round international education. In 1918 she and her Russian husband fled the Russian Revolution to Paris. Here Lempicka came under the influence of the avant-garde artists, notably Fernand Léger. However, the painter whose work most impressed her and whose style is reflected in her own female nudes was Paul Cézanne, then near the end of his long career. Lempicka became one of the most fashionable portrait painters in Paris in the interwar period, her work emphasizing the glamour and ostentatious wealth of her patrons, idealizing their beauty and elegance. The other side of Lempicka, however, was her homosexuality – which was reflected in her extraordinary studies of female nudes, always fully representational (and often devastatingly so) yet with overtones of Cubism in the use of simplified anatomy and the geometric patterns of the background. The result was electrifying and highly distinctive.

MOVEMENT
Cubism
OTHER WORKS
The Two Friends
INFLUENCES
Cézanne, Fernand Léger

Tamara de Lempicka   *Born* 1898 Warsaw, Poland
Painted in Paris and Mexico
Died 1980 Cuernavaca, Mexico

Courtesy of Private Collection/Christie's Images/© ADAGP, Paris and DACS, London 2002

Leonardo da Vinci

FLORENTINE PAINTER, scientist and inventor; the supreme genius of the Renaissance. Leonardo was the illegitimate son of a notary and probably trained under Verrocchio. In 1482 he moved to Milan, where he worked for the Sforzas. His chief work from this period was a majestic version of *The Last Supper*. The composition dazzled contemporaries, but Leonardo's experimental fresco technique failed and the picture deteriorated rapidly. This was symptomatic of Leonardo's attitude to painting: the intellectual challenge of creation fascinated him, but the execution was a chore.

and many of his artistic projects were left unfinished. Leonardo returned to Florence in 1500, where he produced some of his most famous pictures, most notably the *Mona Lisa*. These were particularly remarkable for their *sfumato* – a blending of tones so exquisite that the forms seem to have no lines or borders. Leonardo spent a second period in Milan, before ending his days in France. Leonardo's genius lay in the breadth of his interests and his infinite curiosity. In addition to his art, his notebooks display a fascination for aeronautics, engineering, mathematics and the natural world.

MOVEMENT
Renaissance
OTHER WORKS
Mona Lisa, Virgin of the Rocks, The Last Supper
INFLUENCES
Verrocchio

Leonardo da Vinci   *Born* 1452 Italy
Painted in Italy and France
Died 1519

Courtesy of Louvre, Paris/Bridgeman Art Library/Christie's Images

Lewis, Norman

BORN IN New York Norman Lewis was one of the few natives of that city to gain early prominence as the artistic chronicler of African American life in Harlem. Under the WPA scheme of the 1930s, he was able to study at Columbia University and was later a pupil of Augusta Savage. His WPA assignment consisted of the decorations of the Harlem Art Centre, which put him in touch with other black American artists. In the late 1930s he began painting in a semi-abstract manner, reducing the human figure to geometric lines. Later he veered towards Abstract Expressionism. In the 1960s he belonged to the Spiral Group, which gave artistic interpretation to the civil rights movement. In 1971, while working at the Art Students' League, he formed the Cinque Gallery with Ernie Crichlow and Romare Bearden, with the aim of exhibiting the art of young people from ethnic minorities.

MOVEMENT
Abstract Expressionism
OTHER WORK
Yellow Hat, Ovum, Processional, Every Atom Glows
INFLUENCES
Augusta Savage

Norman Lewis   *Born* 1909 New York, USA
Painted in New York
Died 1979 New York

© Smithsonian American Art Museum, Washington, DC / Art Resource, NY

Lewis, Percy Wyndham

PERCY WYNDHAM LEWIS was born in Canada, but following the break-up of his parents' marriage when he was 10 years old he moved with his mother to England, where he enrolled at the Slade School of Art (1898–1901). For six years he travelled extensively in Europe, painting and continuing his studies before settling in London, where he joined the Camden Group of avant-garde artists in 1911 and the Omega Workshops in 1913. One of the most articulate and intellectual painters of his group, he edited their magazine *Blast*, in which he published his Vorticist Manifesto in 1914. This, the only distinctively British art movement to emerge in the early twentieth century, was short-lived. Lewis volunteered for active service on the outbreak of World War I and subsequently became an official war artist. Nevertheless, there are echoes of Vorticism in his powerful war paintings as well as in the great series of canvasses in the postwar period inspired by characters from classical mythology. In 1939 he returned to Canada and also worked for a time in the USA before going back to England in the last years of his life. Although blind in his old age he continued to teach and write.

MOVEMENT
Vorticism
OTHER WORKS
The Dancers, A Battery Shelled, A Reading of Ovid
INFLUENCES
Albert Gleizes, George Grosz

Percy Wyndham Lewis   *Born* 1882 Canada
Painted in England, Canada and USA
Died 1957 London, England

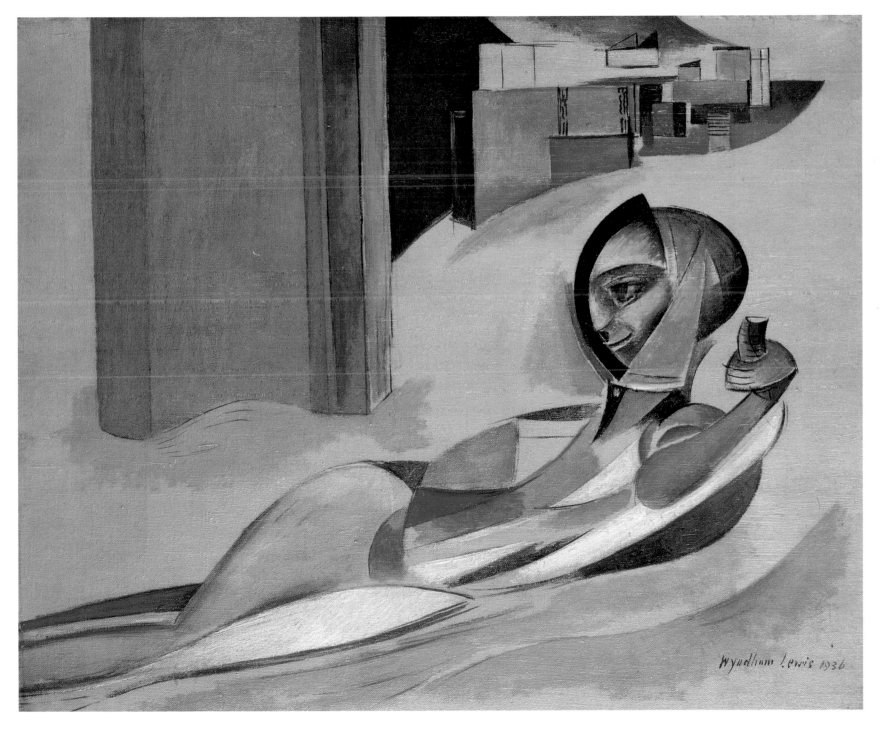

Courtesy of Private Collection/Christie's Images/© Estate of Mrs G. A. Wyndham Lewis

Leyster, Judith

JUDITH LEYSTER was a child prodigy, but nothing is known about her formal art training, although after her family moved to Utrecht in 1628 she came under the influence of Terbrugghen and Honthorst. On her return to Haarlem the following year she studied under Frans Hals. She became a member of the Guild of St Luke in 1633 and by 1635 had several pupils of her own. In 1636 she married fellow artist Jan Miense Molenaer and they moved to Amsterdam. She specialized in genre subjects noted for the

spontaneity of expression and her realism, heightened by her skilful control of light, tone and texture. These paintings ranged from little moments of domestic drama to exuberant scenes of revelry which have an underlying humour that sometimes bordered on the risqué. In addition she painted a few half-length portraits.

MOVEMENT
Dutch School
OTHER WORKS
Self Portrait, The Flute Player, The Gay Cavaliers
INFLUENCES
Hendrick Terbrugghen, Gerrit van Honthorst

Judith Leyster   *Born* 1609 Haarlem, Holland
Painted in Haarlem, Utrecht and Amsterdam
Died 1660 Amsterdam, Holland

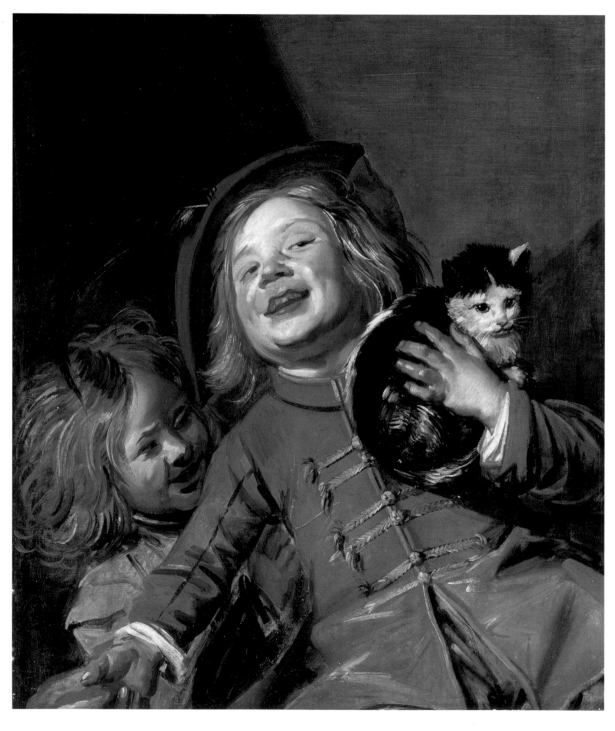

Courtesy Private Collection/Christie's Images

Lichtenstein, Roy

ROY LICHTENSTEIN enrolled at the Art Students' League (1939) and later studied at Ohio State College. After military service (1943–46) he returned to Ohio State as a teacher, and later taught at New York State and Rutgers Universities. He began exhibiting in 1949, his early works inspired by aspects of American history, strongly influenced by Cubism, though later he tended towards Abstract Expressionism. While teaching at Rutgers he met Allan Kaprow, who opened his eyes to the artistic possibilities inherent in consumerism and from about 1960 he developed what later came to be known as Pop Art, in which images are painted in the style of the comic strip. Even the dots of the screening process used in the production of comic books is meticulously reproduced in Lichtenstein's highly stylized paintings.

MOVEMENT
Pop Art
OTHER WORKS
In the Car, M-Maybe, Whaam!
INFLUENCES
Allan Kaprow

Roy Lichtenstein *Born* 1923 New York, USA
Painted in USA
Died 1997 New York

Courtesy of Private Collection/Christie's Images/© The Estate of Roy Lichtenstein/DACS 2002

Liebermann, Max

Bathers on the Beach at Scheveningen, *c.* 1897–98

AFTER HIS early training in Weimar, Germany, Max Liebermann continued his studies in Amsterdam and Paris, one of the first German artists of his generation to go abroad and come under the influence of foreign painters – in his case Courbet, Millet and the Barbizon School. Returning to Germany in 1878 Liebermann quickly established himself as the leading Impressionist, noted for his canvasses of mundane subjects in which elderly people and peasants predominate, although he also produced some noteworthy paintings of more sophisticated subjects, especially the outdoor cafés.

Liebermann played a major role in the establishment of the Berlin Secession in 1899. A major innovator in his heyday, he failed to move with the times and was later eclipsed by the younger avant-garde artists, led by Emil Nolde. Nevertheless, he remained a highly influential figure in German art, where the fashion for the heroic and romantic assured his works a substantial following.

MOVEMENT
German Impressionism
OTHER WORKS
The Parrot Keeper, Haarlem Pig Market
INFLUENCES
Courbet, Millet

Max Liebermann *Born* 1847 Berlin, Germany
Painted in France, Holland and Germany
Died 1935 Berlin

Courtesy of Private Collection/Christie's Images/© DACS 2002

Linnell, John

JOHN LINNELL studied in London under John Varley and was also influenced by the Irish portraitist William Mulready, a fellow pupil though seven years older. In the early part of his career he worked mainly as a painter of portraits but later he turned to landscapes, especially after 1852 when he moved from London to Redhill in Surrey, where he spent the last 30 years of his long and very productive life. A prolific artist, his work often suffered from repetitiveness, largely due to his method of painting from various sketches and studies rather than direct from nature. But at his best, his landscapes remarkably evoked the spirit and atmosphere of the English countryside, especially his series of paintings showing harvesters towards sunset, when the skies were brilliantly lit by his bold use of colour. Skies are what Linnell did best and they give his landscapes their distinctive and immediately recognizable character.

MOVEMENT
English School
OTHER WORKS
The Last Gleam Before the Storm, View of Hanson Toot
INFLUENCES
John Varley, William Mulready

John Linnell   *Born* 1792 London, England
Painted in London and Redhill
Died 1882 Redhill England

Courtesy of Private Collection/Christie's Images

Lowry, L. S. (Laurence Stephen)

DISTINCTIVE BRITISH painter, famous for his pictures of 'matchstick men'. Lowry was born in Old Trafford, Manchester, and lived in or near the city throughout his life. He failed to gain entry to the local art school and, instead, took on office work and painted in the evenings. Initially, he was employed by an insurance company and, after 1910, as a rent collector for a property firm. In later years, much of his time was also devoted to the care of his invalid mother. They were very close and Lowry was devastated when she died in 1939.

The childlike qualities of Lowry art have often been classified as naive, but technically this is untrue, since he had a succession of teachers at evening school. The most significant of these was Adolphe Valette, who also painted urban townscapes. From an early stage, Lowry began producing unglamorous views of the local, industrial scene, focusing in particular on details of everyday life. These ranged from the grotesque to the humorous. Lowry's style baffled the art establishment — he was conspicuously omitted from the Royal Academy's survey of twentieth century British art — but his paintings sold well and he has remained unfailingly popular with the public.

MOVEMENT
Naive Art
OTHER WORKS
Our Town, Man Lying on a Wall, Sudden Illness, The Pond
INFLUENCES
Adolphe Valette, Camden Town School

L. S. Lowry   *Born* 1887 Manchester, England
Painted in England
Died 1976 Glossop, England

Courtesy of Private Collection/Christie's Images/Reproduced by kind permission of Carol Lowry, copyright proprietor

BORN CLAUDE FRANÇOIS, Luc trained under Simon Vouet between 1627 and 1634, when he went to Rome to study the great Masters. He returned to Paris in 1639, working on the decoration of the Louvre. In 1641 he joined the Franciscan Order, taking the name of Frère Luc and thereafter most of his paintings were devoted to the life and works of St Francis of Assisi, which he executed for various monasteries. In 1670 he went to Quebec, mainly as the architect in charge of the rebuilding of the monastery there.

At the end of 1671 he returned to Paris and resumed his work as a painter of religious works. He is now chiefly of interest for the work he produced whilst in Quebec. These paintings influenced later generations of French-Canadian artists.

MOVEMENT
French-Canadian School
OTHER WORKS
Assumption, Guardian Angel
INFLUENCES
Raphael, Guido Reni, Girolamo Muziano

Frère Luc *Born* 1614 Amiens, France
Painted in France, Italy and Canada
Died 1685 Paris, France

Courtesy of National Gallery of Canada, Ottawa

MacDonald, J. E. H.　　　Clearing after Rain, Maganatawan River, Ontario, 1910

JAMES EDWARD HERVEY MACDONALD was born in England of Scottish-Canadian parents, and at the age of 14 he settled with them in Hamilton, Ontario. He studied art there and later in Toronto, and in 1894 joined the leading Toronto graphic art company Grip, where he remained until 1912. He was the doyen of the extremely talented group of artists working for this firm, including Tom Thomson, Arthur Lismer, Frederick Varley and Franklin Carmichael. MacDonald was a founder member of the

Arts and Letters Club (1908) which, under his leadership rapidly became the forum for Canadian avant-garde artists. Notoriety came his way in 1916 when he exhibited seven paintings at the Toronto annual show; his painting *The Tangled Garden* was ferociously attacked by the newspaper critics. After Thomson's untimely death in 1917, MacDonald continued to be the guiding light and the prime mover in establishing the Group of Seven in 1920. Significantly, the Group broke up after his death.

MOVEMENT
Modern Canadian School
OTHER WORKS
Mist Fantasy, Autumn, Algoma
INFLUENCES
Henry Thoreau, Walt Whitman

J. E. H. MacDonald　*Born* 1873 London, England
Painted in Canada
Died 1932 Toronto, Ontario, Canada

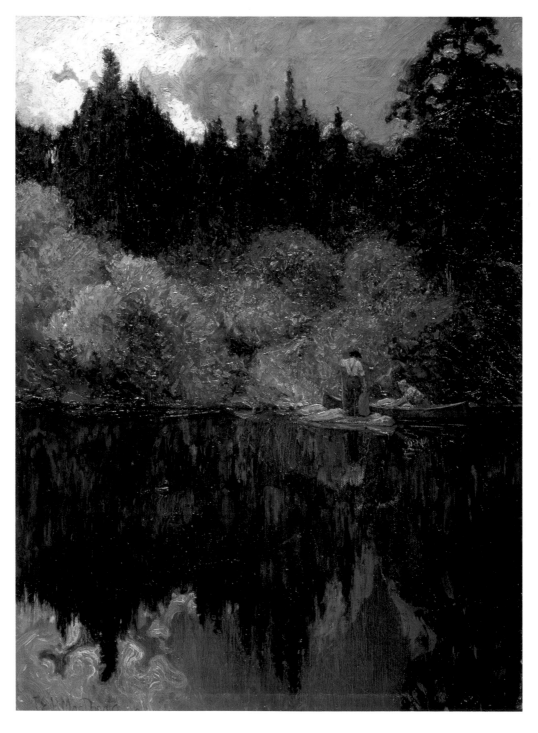

Courtesy of Christie's Images, London, UK/Bridgeman Art Library

Maeda, Seison

AFTER A conventional education Seison Maeda went to Tokyo in 1901, where he enrolled at the art school run by Hanko Kajita and formed a close friendship with Kokei Kobayashi, whose style influenced his own painting. From 1914 onwards Maeda was a prominent figure in the Inten (Japan Art Institute exhibitions). In 1922 he travelled to Italy where he was fascinated by the frescoes of the Early Renaissance which left an indelible mark on his later work, although Maeda continued to paint in the traditional

Japanese style. He was a prolific and versatile artist, excelling in landscapes and genre scenes, although his reputation rests mainly on his mastery of figures. He was very highly regarded by his contemporaries, being appointed to the Imperial Art Academy in 1935 and awarded the Order of Cultural Merit in 1955. He published his autobiography in 1969.

MOVEMENT
Modern Japanese School
OTHER WORKS
Yoritomo in the Cave, Awaiting the Outset
INFLUENCES
Hank Kajita, Kokei Kobayashi, Masaccio, Fra Angelico

Seison Maeda *Born* 1901 Gifu, Japan
Painted in Japan
Died 1977 Kanagawa, Japan

Courtesy of Private Collection/Bridgeman Art Library

THE GREAT Surrealist master René François Ghislain Magritte studied at the Académie Royale des Beaux-Arts in Brussels (1916–18) and became a commercial artist for fashion magazines and a designer of wallpaper. His paintings were initially influenced by Futurism and Cubism, but later he was attracted to the work of Giorgio de Chirico. In 1924 he became a founder member of the Belgian Surrealist group, which provided an escape from the dull routine of his everyday work. From 1927 to 1930 he lived in Paris to better continue his study of the Surrealists, then returned to Brussels where he built his reputation for paintings of dreamlike incongruity, in which themes and objects are jumbled in bizarre, nonsensical situations, often showing paintings within paintings. He is regarded in the United States as a forerunner of Pop Art.

MOVEMENT
Surrealism
OTHER WORKS
Rape, The Reckless Sleeper, The Treachery of Images
INFLUENCES
Giorgio de Chirico

René Magritte   *Born* 1898 Lessines, Belgium
Painted in Belgium
Died 1967 Brussels, Belgium

Courtesy of Christie's Images © ADAGP, Paris and DACS, London 2002

Malevich, Kasimir

The Carpenter III, 1910

KASIMIR SEVERINOVICH MALEVICH studied in Moscow from 1902 to 1905 and came under the influence of the French Impressionists. In 1912 Mikhail Larionov invited him to take part in the inaugural Knave of Diamonds exhibition. Later the same year he visited Paris and immediately converted to Cubism, attacking this new style with zeal and improving and refining it in a style which he called Suprematism. His exhibition of Suprematist art in 1915 gained a mixed reception and he subsequently modified his style, rejecting the stark minimalism of such works as *Black Square* and injecting a great deal of colour. But he reverted to his ideals in 1918 with a series of paintings entitled *White on White*, the ultimate example of minimalism. Thereafter he abandoned painting and concentrated on sculpture, becoming one of the leading Constructivists of the early Soviet era.

The sidebar info box.

MOVEMENTS
Cubism, Suprematism
OTHER WORKS
Dynamic Suprematism, Woman with Buckets
INFLUENCES
Mikhail Larionov, Picasso

Kasimir Malevich   *Born* 1878 Kiev, Ukraine
Painted in Moscow, Russia
Died 1935 Leningrad (now St Petersburg), Russia

Courtesy of State Russian Museum, St. Petersburg, Russia/Bridgeman Art Library

Manet, Edouard

INFLUENTIAL FRENCH painter, regarded by many as the inspirational force behind the Impressionist movement. Coming from a wealthy family, Manet trained under the history painter Couture, but was chiefly influenced by his study of the Old Masters, particularly Velázquez. His aim was to achieve conventional success through the Salon, but ironically two controversial pictures cast him in the role of artistic rebel. *Le Déjeuner sur l'Herbe* and *Olympia* were both updated versions of Renaissance masterpieces, but the combination of classical nudes and a modern context scandalized Parisian critics. This very modernity, however, appealed strongly to a group of younger artists, who were determined to paint scenes of modern life, rather than subjects from the past. This circle of friends who gathered round Manet at the Café Guerbois were to become the Impressionists.

Manet was equivocal about the new movement. He enjoyed the attention of his protégés, but still hoped for official success and, as a result, did not participate in the Impressionist exhibitions. Even so, he was eventually persuaded to try open-air painting, and his later pictures display a lighter palette and a freer touch.

MOVEMENTS
Realism, Impressionism

OTHER WORKS
A Bar at the Folies-Bergère

INFLUENCES
Velázquez, Gustave Courbet

Edouard Manet   *Born* 1832 France
Painted in France
Died 1883 France

Courtesy of Getty Museum/Christie's Images

ANDREA MANTEGNA was originally apprenticed to Francisco Squarcione, a tailor in Padua who later adopted him. Squarcione was a self-taught painter and it was from him that the young Mantegna learned the rudiments of art. About 1450 he completed an altarpiece for the church of Santa Lucia, which immediately established his reputation. Later he studied the works of Donatello in Florence and Castagno in Venice and mastered the newly developed techniques of perspective. He worked in Verona and elsewhere, executing religious paintings. In 1459 he was recruited by Ludvico Gonzaga, Duke of Mantua, to decorate his palaces and to the subsequent period belong his great masterpieces, the series of tempera paintings of the Triumph of Caesar, executed between 1482 and 1492, later purchased by Charles I and now preserved at Hampton Court.

MOVEMENT
Italian Renaissance
OTHER WORKS
The Dead Christ, The Agony in the Garden
INFLUENCES
Francisco Squarcione, Andrea del Castagno, Donatello

Andrea Mantegna   *Born c.* 1431 Vicenza, Italy
Painted in Italy
Died 1506 Mantua, Italy

Courtesy of Private Collection/Christie's Images

Maqhubela, Louis Khela

LOUIS KHELA Maqhubela studied at the Polly Street Art Centre in Durban under Cecil Skomes and Sydney Kumalo, imbibing the disparate strands of conventional genre painting and the more symbolic, abstract style which was becoming very fashionable in South Africa in the 1950s. These influences melded in Maqhubela's lively depiction of everyday life in the black townships, and the exhibition of his paintings in the Johannesburg galleries was a way of breaking through the barrier of apartheid in the 1960s. A prize as one of the most promising young artists of his time enabled him to travel to England to study under the South African abstract painter Douglas Portway. Maqhubela later studied at Goldsmiths College and the Slade School of Art (1985–87). Since then he has had a studio in London and now commutes between there and Johannesburg, a prominent figure in the modern movement since the downfall of the apartheid system.

MOVEMENT
Modern South African School
OTHER WORKS
Equilibrium
INFLUENCES
Douglas Portway, Cecil Skomes, Sydney Kumalo

Louis Khela Maqhubela *Born* 1939
Durban, Natal, South Africa
Painted in South Africa and England

Image with permission of "The Haenggi Foundation Inc., Johannesburg/Basel" (Gallery 21 London archives).

Marc, Franz

FRANZ MARC studied theology in Munich, intending to enter the Church, but switched to art, which he regarded as an intensely spiritual activity. He studied painting in Italy and France before returning to Munich where, with Kandinsky, he founded the Blaue Reiter group in 1911. An intensely religious man, he believed that animals were more in harmony with nature than human beings and therefore he concentrated on paintings in which animals, notably horses and foxes, featured prominently.

In his earlier works the animals form the dominant subject but later they merged into the landscape as though an integral part of it. He speculated on how animals perceived the world and this influenced his later Expressionist work, which was almost devoid of figural motifs and explored the emotional potential of colour. He returned to Germany on the outbreak of World War I; his death in action brought to an abrupt end one of the most promising artists of the early twentieth century.

MOVEMENTS
Impressionism, Expressionism
OTHER WORKS
Tiger, Deer in Wood, Foxes, Tower of the Blue Horses
INFLUENCES
August Macke, Kandinsky

Franz Marc   Born 1880 Munich, Germany
Painted in Munich and Paris
Died 1916 Verdun, France

Courtesy of Private Collection/Christie's Images

Marin, John

JOHN MARIN studied architecture at the Pennsylvania Academy in Philadelphia and the Art Students' League of New York and subsequently pursued this profession, while gradually becoming involved in painting under the influence of James McNeill Whistler. Between 1905 and 1910 he travelled extensively in Europe, continuing his art studies in Paris, Rome and London. In 1909 he exhibited his work for the first time at the 291 Gallery in New York – run by Alfred Stieglitz – and as a result he came into contact with

the Stieglitz Circle, an avant-garde group. Subsequently he went through phases of flirting with Fauvism and Cubism, both of which left their mark on his later paintings, although interpreted from a purely American standpoint. Although he occasionally worked in oils on canvas his preferred medium was watercolours. He was also a prolific etcher, his landscapes rendered in a highly individualistic style.

MOVEMENTS
Fauvism, Cubism
OTHER WORKS
Maine Islands, Four-Master off the Cape Maine Coast
INFLUENCES
James McNeill Whistler, Raoul Dufy, Emil Nolde

John Marin *Born* 1870 New York, USA
Painted in USA
Died 1953 Addison, Maine, USA

Courtesy of Private Collection/Christie's Images © A.R.S, NY and DACS, London 2002

Martin, John

Sunset over Rocky Bay, 1830

JOHN MARTIN trained as a heraldic painter in Newcastle, producing coats of arms for the nobility and gentry, and mainly worked in enamels to decorate their coach panels. Influenced by the flaming sunsets of his native Northumberland and inspired by the Book of Revelations and the apocalyptic poetry of John Milton, he began creating vast paintings which captured the end of the world and earned for him the nickname of Mad Martin. He made his debut at the Royal Academy annual exhibition in

1812 with *Sadak in Search of the Waters of Oblivion* in which the hero appeared as a tiny figure at the foot of the canvas, overwhelmed by mountains and beetling crags suffused with fiery light. His later paintings have all the qualities of some Hollywood epic and had immense appeal to the English Romantics. He also illustrated editions of Milton and produced a series of biblical illustrations.

MOVEMENT
English Romantic School
OTHER WORKS
The Great Day of His Wrath, Eve of the Deluge, Belshazzar's Feast
INFLUENCES
Hieronymus Bosch

John Martin   *Born* 1789 Northumberland, England
Painted in Northumberland and Isle of Man
Died 1854 Douglas, Isle of Man

Courtesy of Private Collection/Christie's Images

BORN TOMMASO de Giovanni di Simone Guidi at Castel San Giovanni di Altura in the duchy of Milan, he was nicknamed Masaccio ('massive') to distinguish him from another Tommaso who worked in the same studio. Who taught him is not recorded, but Masaccio was one of the most brilliant innovators of his generation, ranking with Brunelleschi and Donatello in revolutionizing painting in Italy. Biblical figures and scenes became infinitely more realistic in his hands. The human body is more fully rounded than before and

Masaccio's handling of perspective is a marked improvement over his predecessors. He wielded enormous influence over his contemporaries and successors, notably Michelangelo. His greatest work consisted of the series of frescoes for the Brancacci Chapel in the Church of Santa Maria del Carmine in Florence (1424–27).

MOVEMENTS
Italian Renaissance, Florentine School
OTHER WORKS
The Virgin and Child, The Trinity with the Virgin and St John
INFLUENCES
Donatello

Tommaso Masaccio   *Born* 1401 Italy
Painted in Milan and Florence
Died 1428 Rome

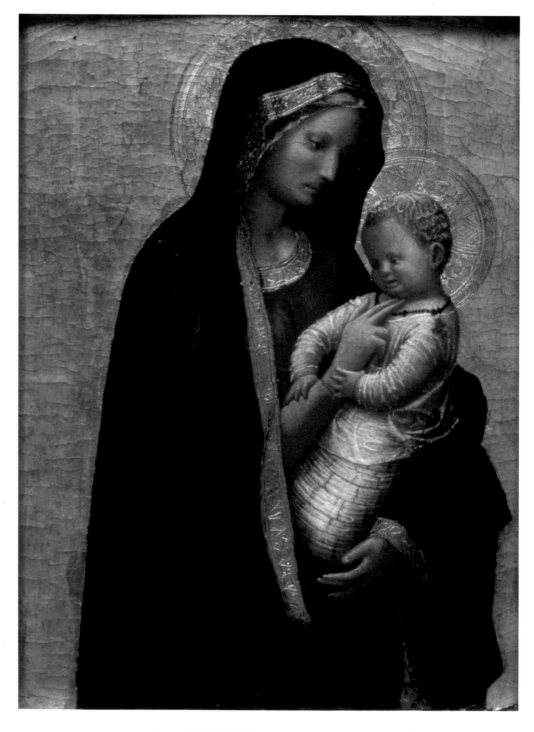

Courtesy of Galleria degli Uffizi, Florence, Italy/Bridgeman Art Library

JOSEPH MATAR was educated at the Marist Brothers' School in Jounieh and began working as an artist in Beirut. He received his art training under Omar Onsi, Rachid Webbe and George Corm between 1951 and 1957, while studying at the Italian Cultural Centre in Beirut (1955–57) and anatomy at the Beirut Faculty of Medicine (1958). Travelling scholarships enabled him to continue his studies at the San Fernando School of Fine Arts in Madrid (1961–63), Rome (1973) and the University of Paris (1963 and 1985). He began teaching art in 1954 at both high-school and university levels and has held a number of professorships since 1980. He has had more than 60 one-man shows around the world and his paintings are in major collections in many countries. Matar paints in oils and watercolours, both abstracts and landscapes. In addition to being the Lebanon's foremost contemporary painter he is a poet of considerable merit, recognized by an award for outstanding achievement from the International Library of Poetry, 2001.

MOVEMENT
Modern Lebanese School
OTHER WORKS
Corner of the Galaxy, Marriage Feast at Cana, Harvest, Temple
INFLUENCES
Omar Onsi, Rachid Wehbe, George Corm

Joseph Matar   *Born* 1935 Ghadir, Lebanon
Painted in Lebanon, Spain, France and Italy

All Joseph Matar works are © by the artist and LebanonArt - Germinal ltd

FRENCH PAINTER, printmaker and designer; the dominant figure in the Fauvist movement. Initially a lawyer's clerk, Matisse turned to art in 1890. His first teacher, Bouguereau, was a disappointment, but he learned a great deal from his second master, Gustave Moreau, a Symbolist painter with a taste for exotic colouring. Matisse's early works were mainly Impressionist or Neo-Impressionist in character but, after painting trips to the Mediterranean, he began to employ more vivid colours; using them to create an emotional impact, rather than simply to transcribe nature.

After years of failure, Matisse and his friends made their breakthrough at the Salon d'Automne of 1905. Critics were overwhelmed by the dazzling canvasses on display and dubbed the group *Les Fauves* ('the wild beasts').

Matisse continued to find his greatest inspiration from painting on the Riviera, but he also travelled widely, visiting Morocco, America and Spain. He decorated a chapel in Vence in southern France, in gratitude for a nun who had nursed him, and experimented with 'cut-outs' (pictures formed from coloured paper shapes, rather than paint).

MOVEMENT
Fauvism
OTHER WORKS
The Dance, Luxe, Calme et Volupte, The Blue Window
INFLUENCES
Paul Signac, Henri-Edmond Cross, Gustave Moreau, Cézanne

Henri Matisse   *Born* 1869 France
Painted in France and Morocco
Died 1954

Courtesy of Private Collection/Christie's Images/© Succession H Matisse/DACS 2002

Matta, Roberto

BORN ROBERTO Sebastian Matta Echaurren, he trained as an architect in his native city of Santiago and continued his studies under Le Corbusier in Paris. He took up painting in 1937 and was immediately attracted to Surrealism, of which he became one of the outstanding figures over the ensuing decade. He moved to the United States in 1939 and made his debut at the Julien Levy Gallery the following year. His work had an enormous impact on the younger generation of American artists, his approach to Surrealism being markedly different from that of Dalí and the other main European exponents. His technique of apparently random brushstrokes without rational control influenced such painters as Arshile Gorky and Jackson Pollock. From Abstract Expressionism he gradually moved towards what he termed as 'transparent Cubism' in the late 1940s, bringing back figural elements.

MOVEMENTS
Surrealism, Abstract Expressionism
OTHER WORKS
Invasion of the Night, Disasters of Mysticism, Abstraction, Untitled
INFLUENCES
Hans Bellmer

Roberto Matta   *Born* 1911 Santiago, Chile
Painted in Chile and US

Courtesy of Christie's Images/Private Collection © ADAGP, Paris and DACS, London 2002

Memling, Hans

Adoration of the Magi (Centrel Panel of Triptych), *c* 1470

ALTHOUGH BORN in Germany Memling spent most of his life in Bruges (now in Belgium), where he was probably a pupil of Rogier van der Weyden. This is borne out by the great triptych, whose central panel was painted by Rogier but the wings by 'Master Hans'. Bruges, which had been the commercial centre of the duchy of Burgundy, was then in decline and it has been said that Memling's genius alone brought lustre to the city. He was certainly residing in Bruges by 1463 and four years later enrolled in the painter's guild. In 1468 he painted the triptych showing the Virgin enthroned, flanked by the family of the donor, Sir John Donne, who was in Burgundy for the wedding of Charles the Bold that year. Although best known for his altarpieces and other religious paintings, Memling also produced a number of secular pieces, mostly portraits of his contemporaries. His paintings are characterized by an air of serenity and gentle piety enhanced by the use of vivid colours and sumptuous texture.

MOVEMENT
Flemish School
OTHER WORKS
The Mystic Marriage of St Catherine, The Virgin Ethroned
INFLUENCES
Rogier van der Weyden

Hans Memling   *Born c.* 1433, Germany
Painted in Bruges Belgium
Died 1494 Bruges

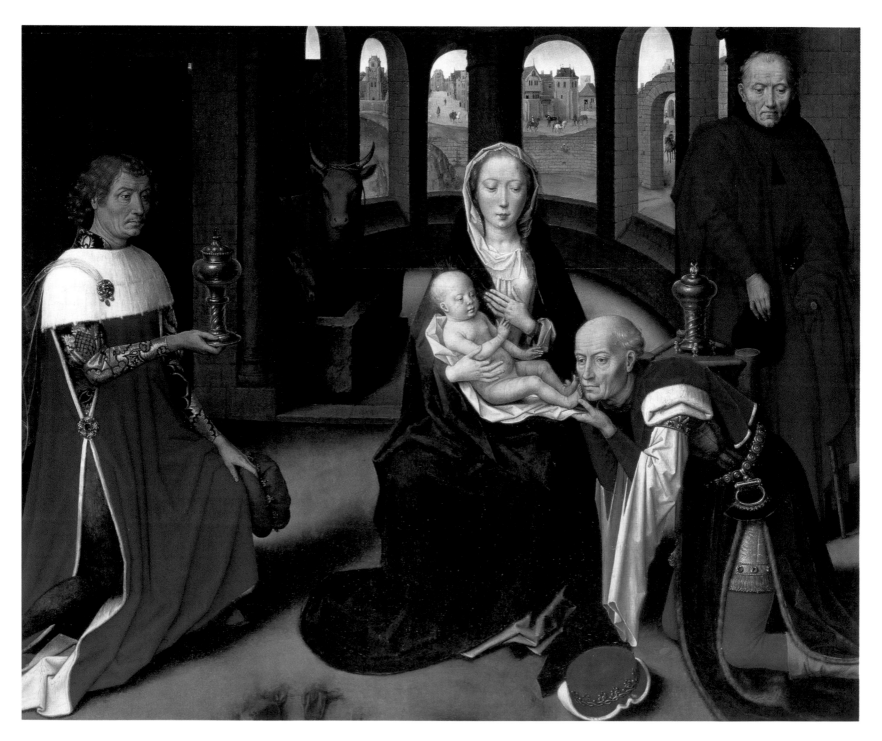

Courtesy of Prado, Madrid, Spain/Bridgeman Art Library

Menon, Anjolie Ela

ANJOLIE ELA MENON studied at the Sir J J School of Art in Mumbai (Bombay) before going on to Delhi University, where she majored in English Literature. As a result of highly successful exhibitions in Mumbai and Delhi in the late 1950s, she was awarded a French government scholarship and continued her studies at the École Nationale des Beaux-Arts in Paris. Before returning to India she travelled all over Europe and the Middle East, studying the classical art of Rome, Greece and Byzantium. One of the most cosmopolitan of modern Indian artists, she has since lived and worked in Britain, Germany, Russia and the USA, although she now resides in New Delhi, where she served on advisory committees of the National Gallery of Modern Art. She is regarded as India's foremost female painter of the present day; although renowned for her large murals she has also produced numerous easel paintings, landscapes, portraits and genre subjects – often reflecting traditional Indian motifs.

MOVEMENT
Modern Indian School
OTHER WORKS
Portrait, Malabar, The Fisherman's Tale
INFLUENCES
Amrita Sher-Gil, Rabindranath Tagore

Anjolie Ela Menon *Born* 1940, India
Painted in India, France, Britain, Russia and USA

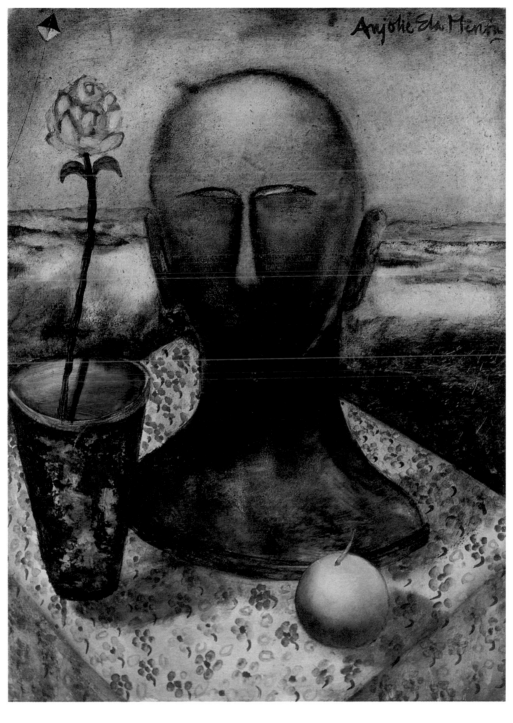

Courtesy of Private Collection/Christie's Images

Messina, Antonello da

PROBABLY BORN at Messina, Sicily, whence he derived his surname, Antonello travelled in north-western Europe and spent some time in the Netherlands where he studied the techniques of the pupils of Jan Van Eyck, taking them back to Messina about 1465. Subsequently he worked in Milan and then in 1472 settled at Venice, where he executed commissions for the Council of Ten. His paintings are remarkable for their blend of Italian simplicity and the Flemish delight in meticulous detail, although some of his earlier works do not always result in a perfect blend of techniques. The majority of his extant authentic works are religious subjects, mainly painted in oils on wood panels, but he also produced a number of half-length portraits of Venetian dignitaries in the last years of his life. By introducing Flemish characteristics Antonello transformed Italian painting, notably in the use of oil paints, which revolutionized technique.

MOVEMENT
Italian Renaissance
OTHER WORKS
Ecce Homo, Madonna
INFLUENCES
Jan Van Eyck, the Flemish School

Antonello da Messina *Born c.* 1430 Italy
Painted in Messina and Venice
Died 1479 Messina

Courtesy of National Gallery, London/Bridgeman Art Library

Michelangelo

ITALIAN PAINTER, sculptor and poet, one of the greatest artists of the Renaissance and a forerunner of Mannerism. Michelangelo was raised in Florence, where he trained briefly under Ghirlandaio. Soon his obvious talent brought him to the notice of important patrons. By 1490, he was producing sculpture for Lorenzo di Medici and, a few years later, he began his long association with the papacy.

Michelangelo's fame proved a double-edged sword. He was often inveigled into accepting huge commissions, which either lasted years or went unfinished. The most notorious of these projects was the Tomb of Julius II, which occupied the artist for over 40 years.

Michelangelo always considered himself primarily a sculptor, and he was extremely reluctant to take on the decoration of the Sistine Chapel. Fortunately, he was persuaded, and the resulting frescoes are among the greatest creations in Western art. The ceiling alone took four years (1508–12), while the *Last Judgment* (1536–41) was added later on the altar wall. In these, Michelangelo displayed the sculptural forms and the *terribilità* ('awesome power'), which made him the most revered artist of his time.

MOVEMENTS
Renaissance, Mannerism
OTHER WORKS
David, Pietà
INFLUENCES
Ghirlandaio, Giotto, Masaccio

Michelangelo   *Born* 1475 Italy
Painted in Italy
Died 1564 Italy

Courtesy of Vatican Museums and Galleries, Rome, Bridgeman Art Library/Christie's Images

Michelangelo

ENGLISH PAINTER and illustrator, a founding member of the Pre-Raphaelite Brotherhood. Born in Southampton, Millais was a child prodigy and, at the age of 11 became the youngest-ever pupil at the Royal Academy Schools. With Rossetti and Hunt, he formed the nucleus of the Pre-Raphaelite Brotherhood. His *Christ in the Carpenter's Shop* was pilloried by the critics, although his work was vigorously defended by John Ruskin. Millais' relations with this influential critic were initially very cordial, until he fell in love with Ruskin's wife, Effie.

Millais' rift with the art establishment did not last long. He continued painting dreamy Pre-Raphaelite themes until around 1860, but found that they did not sell well and took too long to complete. So gradually he adopted a more commercial style and subject matter, specializing in imposing portraits, sentimental narrative pictures, and mawkish studies of children. He also became a prolific book illustrator. This approach won Millais many honors – he was raised to the peerage and became President of the Royal Academy – but damaged his long-term artistic reputation.

MOVEMENT
Pre-Raphaelite Brotherhood
OTHER WORKS
Ophelia, Sir Isumbras at the Ford, Bubbles
INFLUENCES
William Holman Hunt, Dante Gabriel Rossetti

Sir John Everett Millais   *Born* 1829, England
Painted in England and Scotland
Died 1896 London, England

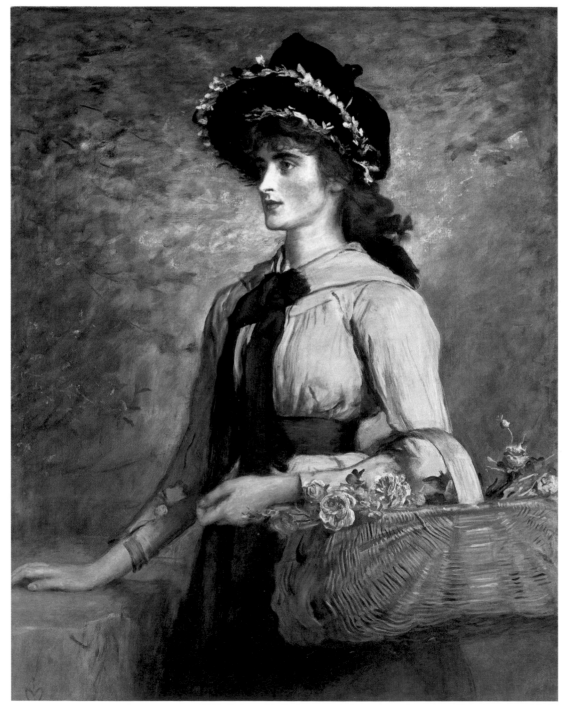

Courtesy of Private Collection/Christie's Images

MILLET WAS born near the city of Cherbourg, which granted him a scholarship to train in Paris, under Delaroche. His early paintings were mainly portraits or pastoral idylls, but by the 1840s he was producing more naturalistic scenes of the countryside. These drew on his own experience, since he came from peasant stock, but the pictures disturbed some critics, because of their unglamorous view of rustic life.

In the 1850s Millet's work attracted genuine hostility. In part, this was due to fears that his paintings were political. Memories of the 1848 Revolution were still very fresh, and the authorities were nervous about any images with socialist overtones. Millet declined to express his political views, but *The Gleaners*, for example, was a compelling portrait of rural poverty. Some critics also linked his work with the Realist movement, launched by Courbet, which was widely seen as an attack on the academic establishment.

After 1849, Millet was mainly based at Barbizon, where he befriended Rousseau and other members of the Barbizon School. Under their influence, he devoted the latter part of his career to landscape painting.

MOVEMENTS
Naturalism, Barbizon School
OTHER WORKS
The Winnower, Man with a Hoe
INFLUENCES
Rousseau, the Le Nain brothers, Gustave Courbert

Jean-François Millet   *Born* 1814 France
Painted in France
Died 1875 France

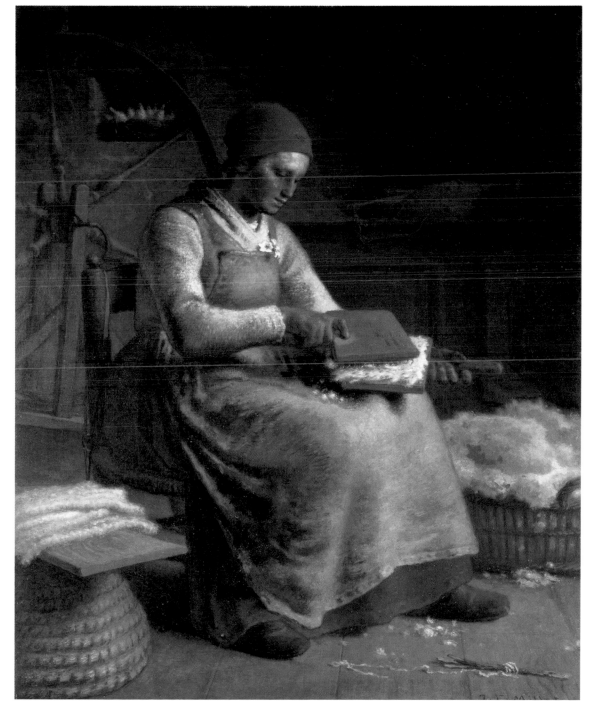

Courtesy of Private Collection/Christie's Images

Miró, Joan

SPANISH PAINTER, ceramist and graphic artist; a key member of the Surrealists. Miró trained under Francisco Galì. His early work showed traces of Fauvism and Cubism, but his first one-man show was a disaster. Undeterred, Miró decided to travel to Paris, the acknowledged home of the avant-garde. There, he contacted Picasso, who introduced him to the most radical artists and poets of the day. These included the blossoming Surrealist group, which Miró joined in 1924.

Miró was fascinated by the challenge of using art as a channel to the subconscious and, from the mid-1920s, he began to fill his canvasses with biomorphic, semi-abstract forms. Nevertheless, he felt suspicious of some of the more outlandish, Surrealist doctrines and remained at the fringes of the group. He moved to France during the Spanish Civil War, producing patriotic material for the struggle against Franco, but was obliged to return south in 1940 after the Nazi invasion. By this stage, Miró's work was much in demand, particularly in the US, where he received commissions for large-scale murals. Increasingly, these featured ceramic elements, which played a growing part in the artist's later style.

MOVEMENT
Surrealism
OTHER WORKS
Dog Barking at the Moon, Aidez l'Espagne
INFLUENCES
Picasso, Hans Arp, Paul Klee

Joan Miró   *Born* 1893 Barcelona, Spain
Painted in Spain, France, USA and Holland
Died 1983

Courtesy of Private Collection/Christie's Images © ADAGP, Paris and DACS, London 2002

Modersohn-Becker, Paula   Brustbild einer Jungen Frau mit offenem Haar

BORN PAULA BECKER, she was largely self-taught, although she was encouraged by her parents to develop her art by sending her to Paris on several occasions, during which she became familiar with the works of Cézanne, Gauguin and Van Gogh. What formal training she had she received at the classes held by the Association of Berlin Women Artists in 1893 95, but three years later she joined the artists' colony at Worpswede, where she spent most of the last nine years of her short life. Her early paintings concentrated largely on landscapes and peasant genre subjects. In 1901 she married Otto Modersohn, a widower 11 years her senior, and the more mature style of her later paintings may owe something to his advice and example. To her last years belong a number of portraits which reflect the influence of the Expressionists. Unable to cope with her domineering husband she fled to Paris in 1906 and died early the following year while giving birth to her daughter Mathilde.

MOVEMENT
German Expressionism
OTHER WORKS
Old Poorhouse Woman with a Glass Bottle
INFLUENCES
Cézanne, Gauguin, Van Gogh

Paula Modersohn-Becker   *Born* 1876
Germany *Painted in* Dresden, Berlin and Worpswede
Died 1907 Wopswede, Germany

Courtesy of Private Collection/Christie's Images

Modigliani, Amedeo

MODIGLIANI WAS born into a Jewish family in Livorno, Italy. Although educated in Florence and Venice he spent most of his career in France. His highly individual style combined the linear elegance of Botticelli, whose work he had studied in Italy, with the avant-garde ideas that were circulating in pre-war Paris. The key influence was the Romanian sculptor Brancusi, whom he met in 1909. Under his guidance, Modigliani produced an impressive series of African-influenced stone figures.

After the outbreak of war, the raw materials for sculpture became scarce, so Modigliani turned to painting. Most of his subjects were sensual nudes or portraits, featuring slender, elongated figures. These received little attention from the critics; he was better known for his self-destructive, bohemian lifestyle, a lifestyle which caused the breakdown of his health. Modigliani died of tuberculosis at the age of 35. Tragically, Jeanne Hébuterne, his mistress and favourite model, committed suicide on the following day, while pregnant with the artist's child. Modigliani's reputation was only secured posthumously, through a retrospective exhibition in Paris in 1922.

MOVEMENT
School of Paris
OTHER WORKS
Seated Nude, The Little Peasant, Portrait of Jeanne Hébuterne
INFLUENCES
Botticelli, Cézanne, Brancusi

Amedeo Modigliani   *Born* 1884, Italy
Painted in Italy and France
Died 1920 Paris, France

Courtesy of Private Collection/Christie's Images

LÁSZLÓ MOHOLY-NAGY studied law in Budapest, but never practiced. Instead he dabbled in photography and turned to painting after World War I, associating with Dadaists and Constructivists in Vienna and Berlin and constructing what he termed 'photograms': non-representational photographic images made directly from the subject without a camera. In 1925 he joined the Bauhaus under Gropius and established his reputation in the ensuing decade as the foremost exponent of the New Photographers' movement. In 1935 he moved to London, where he designed the futuristic sets for fellow-Hungarian Alexander Korda's film, *Things to Come*. In 1937 he went to the USA where he was appointed head of the Bauhaus School in Chicago, later renamed the Institute of Design. He became an American citizen at the end of World War II. Although primarily associated with photography, he also worked as a sculptor, designer and painter, often using collage and photo-montage.

MOVEMENT
Constructivism
OTHER WORKS
CHX, Composition A II, Jealousy
INFLUENCES
Naum Gabo, Kasimir Malevich

László Moholy-Nagy   *Born* 1895 Hungary
Painted in Vienna, Berlin, Weimar, London and Chicago
Died 1946 Chicago, USA

Courtesy of Christie's Images/© DACS 2002

Mondrian, Piet

Composition with Red, Blue and Yellow, 1930

BORN PIETER Cornelis Mondriaan, he simplified his name in 1909 when he moved to Paris, where he came under the influence of the Cubists, notably Henri Matisse. From still life, his work became progressively more abstract, his paintings distinguished by tightly regimented geometric shape and contrasting bright colours. In 1917 he became a founder member of De Stijl, the movement which derived its name from the journal which provided a forum for the Dutch avant-garde artists. Through this medium he propounded the theories which had a profound effect on a later generation as well as his contemporaries, and led to the development of the movement known as Neoplasticism. Mondrian was the arch-apostle of the abstract in its purest, simplest form. He moved to London in 1938, but after his studio was destroyed in the Blitz he settled in New York.

MOVEMENTS
De Stijl, Neoplasticism
OTHER WORKS
Composition with Red, Yellow and Blue, Broadway Boogie Woogie
INFLUENCES
Henri Matisse

Piet Mondrian   *Born* 1872 Amersfoot, Holland
Painted in Holland, London, England and New York
Died 1944 New York

Courtesy of Private Collection/Christie's Images/© Piet Mondrian 2002 Mondrian/Holtzman Trust c/o Beeldrecht, Hoofddorp & DACS, London

Monet, Claude

FRENCH PAINTER; a founding member of the Impressionist circle. Monet was born in Paris, but grew up on the Normandy coast, where he developed an early interest in landscape painting. His early mentors were Jongkind and Boudin, and the latter encouraged Claude to paint outdoors rather than in the studio. This was to be one of the key principles of Impressionism.

While a student in Paris, he met Pissarro, Renoir and Sisley, and together they formulated the basic ideas of the movement. One of Monet's paintings, *Impression:Sunrise* gave the group its name.

The Impressionists staged their own shows, holding eight exhibitions between 1874 and 1886. Initially, these attracted savage criticism, causing genuine financial hardship to Monet and his friends. His most distinctive innovation was the 'series' painting. Here, Monet depicted the same subject again and again, at different times of the day or in different seasons. In these pictures, his real aim was not to portray a physical object – whether a row of poplars or the façade of Rouen cathedral – but to capture the changing light and atmospheric conditions.

MOVEMENT
Impressionism
OTHER WORKS
Waterlilies, Wild Poppies, Rouen Cathedral
INFLUENCES
Eugène Boudin, Johan Barthold Jongkind, Renoir

Claude Monet   *Born* 1840 Paris, France
Painted in France, England and Italy
Died 1926

Courtesy of Private Collection/Christie's Images

ONE OF the leading female Impressionists. The daughter of a high-ranking civil servant, Morisot received art lessons from Corot. Then in 1859, she met Fantin-Latour, who would later introduce her to future members of the Impressionist circle. Before this, she had already made her mark at the Salon, winning favourable reviews for two landscapes shown at the 1864 exhibition. Conventional success beckoned, but a meeting with Manet in 1868 altered the course of Morisot's career. She was strongly influenced by his radical style, and appeared as a model in several of his paintings. For her part, she also had an impact on Manet's art, by persuading him to experiment with *plein-air* painting. The close links between the two artists were further reinforced when Morisot married Manet's brother in 1874.

Morisot proved to be one of the most committed members of the Impressionist group, exhibiting in all but one of their shows. She concentrated principally on quiet, domestic scenes, typified by *The Cradle*, which depicts her sister Edma with her newborn child. These canvasses displayed Morisot's gift for spontaneous brushwork and her feeling for the different nuances of light.

MOVEMENT
Impressionism
OTHER WORKS
Summer's Day, The Lake in the Bois de Boulogne
INFLUENCES
Manet, Renoir, Corot

Berthe Morisot   *Born* 1841
Painted in France and England
Died 1895

Courtesy of Private Collection/Christie's Images

Morrisseau, Norval

NATIVE NORTH AMERICAN painter and graphic artist. Born in Fort William, Canada, Morrisseau hails from the Ojibwa tribe and has made this the focus of his art. Awareness of Native American traditions blossomed during the 1960s, as a by-product of the civil rights movement, and Morrisseau belonged to the generation that spearheaded this revival. He held his first one-man exhibition at the Pollock Gallery, Toronto, in 1962, and the success of this show established him as the leader of a new school. This has been variously described as the Woodlands or Algonquian school of legend painting.

Morrisseau took his basic subject matter from Ojibwa folk traditions. Many of these had been preserved as pictographs on birchbark scrolls. Traditionally, non-Native Americans were not permitted to see these images, but Morrisseau broke this taboo. He also combined the legends with more universal, Native American symbolism and European forms. Much of his work has a strong, spiritual basis, dealing with such themes as soul travel and self-transformation. It reached its widest audience in Montreal, when Morrisseau and Carl Ray designed the Indian Pavilion for Expo 67.

MOVEMENT
Algonquian Legend Painters
OTHER WORKS
Thunderbird, Loon Totem and Evil Fish, The Creation of the Earth
INFLUENCES
Midewiwin birchbark scrolls, aboriginal rock art, Ojibwa folklore

Norval Morrisseau   *Born* 1931
Painted in Canada, USA

Courtesy of Collection of the Dennos Museum Center, Northwestern Michigan College, Traverse City, Michigan

Motherwell, Robert

ROBERT BURNS MOTHERWELL briefly attended the California School of Fine Arts in San Francisco before studying philosophy at Stanford, Harvard, Grenoble and Columbia universities. This unusual combination of academic training enabled him to write authoritatively on various aspects and theories of modern art, more especially the American brand of Abstract Expressionism which he helped to formulate in the 1940s. He only took up painting professionally in 1941, due to the influence of Roberto Matta.

Motherwell's large paintings were often characterized by unconscious doodles, a concept which arose from his interest in Freudian psychoanalysis and the interpretation of dreams. With Mark Rothko and others he founded the Subjects of the Artist movement to encourage the development of the next generation, and was also preoccupied with aspects of Symbolism.

MOVEMENT
Abstract Expressionism
OTHER WORKS
Elegies to the Spanish Republic, Bolton Landing Elegy
INFLUENCES
Roberto Matta

Robert Motherwell   *Born* 1915 USA
Painted in New York, USA
Died 1991 Cape Cod, Maine, USA

Courtesy of Private Collection/Christie's Images © Dedalus Foundation, Inc/VAGA, New York/DACS, London 2002

Motley Jr, Archibald

ARCHIBALD MOTLEY JR moved from New Orleans to Chicago in his youth and took various labouring occupations. Largely self-taught, he won a Guggenheim Fellowship in 1929 which enabled him to travel and study in Paris, where he also produced a number of paintings of the lively black music scene. A one-man show in New York in 1928 showed his deep interest in African-American culture, tinged with mysticism, voodoo and the spirit world, but after his Paris sojourn he concentrated on living subjects and genre scenes crammed with figures, full of action and movement, with a lively portrayal of the gambling and illegal drinking in the Prohibition era. Unlike many other African-American artists, Motley was not concerned so much with the racial consciousness of the Harlem Renaissance, but belonged more to the Ashcan School in his depiction of ordinary, often seedy, activities of people regardless of ethnic origin.

MOVEMENT
Modern American School
OTHER WORKS
Old Snuff Dipper, The Picnic in the Green, Chicken Shack
INFLUENCES
Ashcan School

Archibald Motley Jr   *Born* 1891 USA
Painted in Chicago, USA
Died 1980 Chicago

Courtesy of The Art Institute of Chicago, Mary Leigh Block Fund for Acquisitions, 1977.27

Moudarres, Fateh

ORIGINALLY A self-taught painter working in a realistic style, Fateh Moudarres subsequently came under the spell of the Surrealists and took part in public exhibitions, at which he explained his paintings in verse. Between 1954 and 1960 he studied at the Accademia di Belle Arti in Rome and on returning to Syria he developed a style which he describes as 'surrealistic and figurative with a strong element of abstraction'. Powerful influences in his work are the icons of the Orthodox Church and Syriac art, but from the early 1960s onwards his painting became increasingly abstract. Due to contemporary events, however, he returned to a more representational style from 1967 onwards, painting works with a strong political theme. A period in Paris (1969–72) studying at the École des Beaux Arts has resulted in a much more confident touch, with greater technical mastery of composition and colour. As Professor of Fine Arts in the University of Damascus, Moudarres has been a major influence over the rising generation of Syrian artists.

MOVEMENT
Modern Syrian School
OTHER WORKS
Christ the Child of Palestine
INFLUENCES
Salvador Dali

Fateh Moudarres   *Born* 1922 Aleppo, Syria
Painted in Damascus, Rome and Paris

Courtesy of Sotheby's Picture Library

Mukarobgwa, Thomas

ENTIRELY SELF-TAUGHT, Thomas Mukarobgwa worked as an attendant in the Rhodesian National Gallery; surrounded by so many paintings in different styles and from different periods he was encouraged to try his hand. His early drawings were childlike and ill-executed, but Frank McEwen, the Director of the Gallery, felt that they showed promise. Under McEwen's guidance, Mukarobgwa emerged in the early 1960s as one of the most important painters in Africa, his mature paintings a far cry from his 'adult child art' of the 1950s and since hailed as 'masterly and involved sophistication'. He paints in an almost abstract style in which the shapes of trees are simplified and the contours of landscapes rounded. Human figures are seldom encountered and when they appear they are clumsy little men in shadowy form, giving the impression of having strayed on to the canvas. His work has been likened to that of Nolde and the German Expressionists.

MOVEMENT
Modern African School
OTHER WORKS
Very Important Bush, Enemy People, Old Man Afraid to Cross
INFLUENCES
Frank McEwen

Thomas Mukarobgwa

Born 1924 Zimbabwe
Painted in Rhodesia (now Zimbabwe)
Died 1991

Courtesy of Private Collection/Bridgeman Art Library

Munch, Edvard

EDVARD MUNCH studied in Christiania (now Oslo) and travelled in Germany, Italy and France before settling in Oslo. During his time in Paris (1908) he came under the influence of Gauguin and had immense sympathy for Van Gogh due to the bouts of mental illness which both of them suffered. In fact, this would have a profound effect on the development of Munch as an artist and explains the extraordinary passion that pervades his work. Life, love and death are the themes that he endlessly explored in his paintings, rendered in an Expressionist symbolic style. His use of swirling lines and strident colours emphasize the angst that lies behind his paintings. He also produced etchings, lithographs and woodcut engravings which influenced the German artists of the movement known as Die Brücke.

MOVEMENT
Expressionism
OTHER WORKS
Puberty, The Dance of Life, The Madonna, Ashes
INFLUENCES
Gauguin, Van Gogh

Edvard Munch *Born* 1863 Loten, Norway
Painted in Oslo, Norway
Died 1944 Oslo

Courtesy of Nasuonal Galleriet, Oslo/Bridgeman/Christie's Images/© Munch Museum/Munch - Ellingsen Group, BONO, Oslo, DACS, London 2002

Murillo, Bartolomé Esteban

A GREAT master of sentimental religious paintings, Bartolomé Estebán Murillo received his brief artistic training from Juan de Castillo, but when his master moved to Cadiz Murillo scraped a living by painting cheap religious daubs, hawked at public fairs. It was an inauspicious start for the man who would co-found the Seville Academy in 1660 and become its first president. His career took off in 1648 when he went to Madrid and met his fellow townsman Velázquez, who not only helped him but also introduced his work to the royal court. Many of his earlier paintings were portraits of Franciscan saints, executed for the Franciscan monastery in Seville, but he went on to produce numerous works of a more general religious nature. In addition he produced many genre subjects, such as beggars, street urchins, fruit-sellers and other aspects of low life which reflect the hardships of his youth. He died from injuries sustained in a fall from scaffolding while painting an altarpiece at Cadiz in 1682.

MOVEMENT
Spanish School

OTHER WORKS
The Immaculate Conception of the Escorial

INFLUENCES
Juan de Castillo, Velázquez

Bartolomé Esteban Murillo *Born* 1618
Seville, Spain *Painted in* Seville
Died 1682 Seville

Courtesy of Private Collection/Christie's Images

Newman, Barnett

BARNETT NEWMAN trained at the Art Students' League in New York City while also studying at the City College in the early 1920s. Many years later, in the last decade of his life, he taught at the universities of Saskatchewan and Pennsylvania. In between he began his professional career as an Abstract Expressionist about 1930, but gradually developed his own highly distinctive style which eschewed the loose techniques of Expressionism for a more disciplined, rigorous approach. At the same time, the range of his palette gradually decreased as he moved towards a more monochrome treatment, relieved only by one or two vertical bands of contrasting colour which Newman styled as 'zips' from their resemblance to zip-fasteners on clothing. Ultimately, between 1952 and 1962, Newman painted in black and white, the minimalism of his pictures relieved only by the subtleties of shade and density, but in his last years he utilized colours of extraordinary depth and tone. From about 1965 he also produced a number of steel sculptures.

MOVEMENT
Abstract Expressionism
OTHER WORKS
Moment, Adam, Covenant, Onement III
INFLUENCES
Piet Mondrian, Mark Rothko

Barnett Newman *Born* 1905 New York, USA
Painted in New York
Died 1970 New York

Courtesy of Private Collection/Christie's Images/© ARS, NY and DACS, London 2002

A PIONEERING figure in the development of British Abstract Art. Both of Nicholson's parents were artists, but he was slow to discover his own vocation. He studied briefly at the Slade School, but spent most of his time there playing billiards with Paul Nash, and did not begin painting seriously until 1920. Initially, he painted naive landscapes and sturdy still lifes, which were reminiscent of his father's work. Increasingly, though, he turned to abstraction, joining a number of avant-garde groups. These included the Seven & Five Society, Unit One and the Abstraction-Création circle.

The primary influence on Nicholson's abstracts came from Cubism. Early examples featured motifs – guitars, jars, glasses – used by Picasso and Braque. After visiting Mondrian's studio in Paris, however, he began to banish figurative objects from his pictures, echoing the austere, geometric style favoured by the Dutchman.

Nicholson married three times, and both his wives – Winifred Nicholson and Barbara Hepworth – were distinguished artists in their own right. With the latter, he moved down to St Ives in Cornwall in 1939, where they became the focus of a famous artists' colony.

MOVEMENT
Abstract Art, Cubism, St Ives School
OTHER WORKS
1928 (Cornwall), 1933 (milk and plain chocolate)
INFLUENCES
Sir William Nicholson, Piet Mondrian, Georges Braque

Ben Nicholson *Born* 1894
Painted in England, France and Switzerland
Died 1982

Courtesy of Private Collection/Christie's Images © Angela Verren-Taunt 2002 All rights reserved, DACS

Nolan, Sir Sidney

SIDNEY ROBERT NOLAN had no formal art training. A self-taught amateur, he took up full-time professional painting in 1938, experimenting with abstract forms before turning in the early 1940s to the subject which would make him famous, the exploits of the bush-ranger Ned Kelly and his gang. This series of paintings, executed in a naive style, was followed by canvasses charting the exploits of the explorers Burke and Wills in the mid-nineteenth century. He travelled to Europe in 1950, studying the art of Italy and working in Greece and North Africa before settling in London where he continued to paint, developing a more mature style which combined figuration with the abstract. He designed sets for a number of Covent Garden operas and ballets from 1962 onwards. He also worked as a book illustrator and in 1972 published a volume of his own poetry illustrated with drawings and paintings. He was knighted in 1981.

MOVEMENT
Modern Australian School
OTHER WORKS
Burke and Wills Expedition 'Gray Sick', The Leda Suite
INFLUENCES
R. B. Kitaj, Arthur Boyd

Sir Sidney Nolan *Born* 1917 Australia
Painted in Australia, Greece, North Africa and England
Died 1992 London, England

Courtesy of Private Collection/Christie's Images

BORN EMIL HANSEN in Nolde, Germany, he later adopted the name of his birthplace. He trained as a wood-carver but later studied painting in Munich, where he was briefly a member of the Expressionist group known as Die Brücke ('The Bridge') in 1906–07 as well as Die Blaue Reiter ('the Blue Rider'). He was, however far too rugged an individualist ever to conform too closely to any particular movement, and developed his own distinctive Blut und Boden ('blood and soil') style of painting, originally confined largely to religious themes expressed with distorted images and violent brushstrokes, but later extended to landscapes, seascapes, still life and flowers. Most of his work was done in a remote area of the German North Sea coast where he lived increasingly as a recluse. His last work, a series entitled Unpainted Pictures, was completed in secrecy as he suffered the delusion of still being harassed by the Nazis. He was also a prolific producer of etchings, lithographs and woodcuts.

MOVEMENT
Expressionism
OTHER WORKS
The Life of Christ, Meeting on the Beach, Red Poppies
INFLUENCES
James Ensor, Vlaminck

Emil Nolde   *Born* 1867 Nolde, Germany
Painted Germany
Died 1956 Seebüll, Germany

Courtesy of Private Collection/Christie's Images/© The Nolde-Foundation 2002/© Nolde-Stiftung Seebüll

O'Brien, Lucius

AFTER A career as a civil engineer, Lucius Richard O'Brien took up painting full-time at the age of 40. An interest in the effects of sunlight on rock faces developed out of his work as a builder of roads and railways across the barren wilderness of Canada and this is reflected in his paintings, where colours were used to create the most startlingly luminous effects. In the 1880s he paid several visits to the Canadian Rockies and the great canvasses which resulted rank among the masterpieces of modern landscape painting.

Similarly, a trip to British Columbia in 1888 provided him with numerous subjects illustrative of the Pacific North West. Apart from his painting, he was a tireless promoter of a greater public awareness and appreciation of art. He was a founder member of the Royal Canadian Academy of Art, and its first President. As editor of *Picturesque Canada* (1882) he commissioned numerous artists to depict every part of Canada – one of the most ambitious projects of its kind ever undertaken.

MOVEMENT
Modern Canadian School
OTHER WORKS
Mountain Lake, British Columbian Forest
INFLUENCES
Albert Bierstadt, American Luminist School

Lucius O'Brien   *Born* 1832 Ontario, Canada
Painted in Canada
Died 1899 Toronto, Canada

© National Gallery of Canada, Ottawa/Royal Canadian Academy of Arts diploma work, deposited by the artist, Toronto, 1880

GEORGIA O'KEEFFE studied at the Art Institute of Chicago in 1905–06 and then the Art Students' League in New York City (1907–08), where she met her future husband Alfred Stieglitz, the founder of the avant-garde circle that bears his name. She was an early convert to Abstract Art and, with Stieglitz, did much to spread the gospel among American artists from 1915 onwards. In the 1920s, however, she developed a more figurative style, concentrating on architectural or floral motifs but injecting a note of Surrealism into her paintings. Her work was characterized by sharply defined images that explored geometric patterns and earned for her work the epithet of Precisionism. She travelled all over the world, drawing on her experiences in many of her later works. In her last years she resided in New Mexico, whose monumental scenery found expression in a number of her landscapes.

MOVEMENT
Modern American School

OTHER WORKS
Radiator Building, Cow's Skull with Calico Roses

INFLUENCES
Alfred Stieglitz

Georgia O'Keeffe *Born* 1887 Wisconsin, USA
Painted in USA
Died 1986 Santa Fé, New Mexico, USA

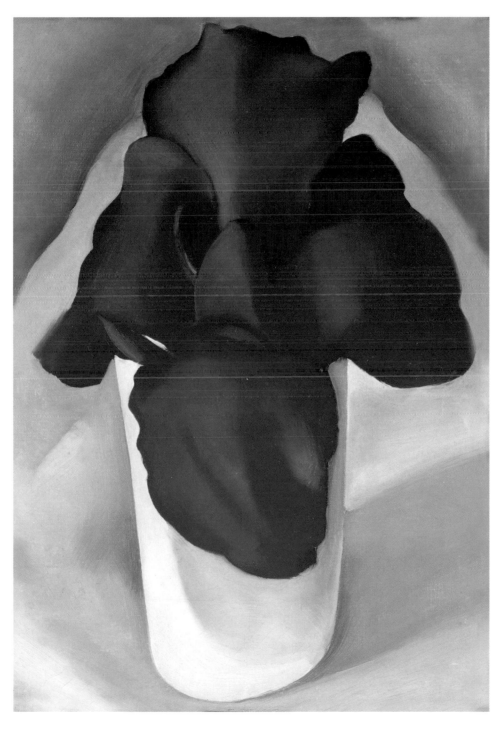

Courtesy of Private Collection/Christie's Images/© ARS, NY and DACS, London 2002

BORN IN Russia, Jules Olitski studied art in Paris before immigrating to the United States and continuing his studies in New York, where he subsequently taught and worked as a sculptor. By his background and training he thus combined elements of the avant-garde from both sides of the Atlantic. Originally he was strongly influenced by the colour-field painters and the vigorous abstracts of Hans Hoffman. In the 1960s, as many of his contemporaries were turning to Pop Art, he remained true to Abstract Expressionism while, along with Helen Frankenthaler, developing the style which came to be known as Post-Painterly Abstraction. This involved the staining of the canvas with paint in order to avoid brush-strokes. From this he moved on to spraying the canvas with acrylics to achieve a completely smooth surface with central abstract motifs of stridently contrasting colours, often with a narrow surround of bare canvas. Since the late 1970s, however, he has returned to the mainstream, producing thickly textured abstracts more reminiscent of the works of Hoffmann.

MOVEMENT
Post-Painterly Abstraction
OTHER WORKS
Yaksi Juice, Thigh Smoke, Green Jazz
INFLUENCES
Hans Hoffman, Helen Frankenthaler

Jules Olitski *Born* 1922, Gomel, Russia
Painted in Paris and New York

Courtesy of Private Collection/Christie's Images/© DACS, LondonVAGA, New York 2002

Onus, Lin

LIN ONUS was completely self-taught and began painting full-time in 1974. He had his first one-man exhibition the following year at the Aborigines Advancement League in Melbourne, and has since had regular shows in Melbourne, Canberra and Sydney. His work is represented in all the major Australian national and state art galleries and he has had many commissions from institutions and corporate collections. He is currently Chairman of the Aboriginal Arts Committee of the Australian Council, although he is at pains to stress that he should not be regarded purely as an Aboriginal artist and finds the labelling of his painting in this manner rather irksome. He is best known for his extraordinary blend of traditional Aboriginal imagery and photorealist landscapes, which he describes as 'a natural convergence of Aboriginal and non–Aboriginal techniques'. In more recent years he has also produced a series of fiberglass sculptures of dingoes.

MOVEMENT
Modern Australian School
OTHER WORKS
Arafura Swamp
INFLUENCES
Traditional Aboriginal art forms

Lin Onus *Born* 1948 Melbourne, Australia
Painted in Melbourne
Died 1996

Courtesy of National Gallery of Australia, Canberra, purchased from Gallery admission charges 1988/© DACS 2002

Oonark, Jessie

JESSIE OONARK spent her entire life in the Baker Lake community of Inuit in northern Canada, learning her skills in needlework from her mother. She excelled in the art of sewing duffel parkas intricately embroidered with figures, but it was not until 1963 that she was encouraged to apply these skills to wall-hangings. These are noted for the brilliant colours of the images and their striking resemblance to the frescoes of Pharaonic Egypt, although executed without any knowledge of Egyptian art. Jessie Oonark

also produced a vast number of drawings, many of which began as preliminary sketches for her embroideries but were later regarded as works of art in their own right. Her large wall-hangings were worked in mixed media, involving duffel, felt and embroidery floss with strips of caribou hide to create an almost three-dimensional effect. She combined traditional Inuit images dating back many centuries with the changes wrought by exposure to twentieth century civilization, but always in a truly unique and individual manner.

MOVEMENT
Modern Canadian School
OTHER WORKS
What the Shaman Can Do, Angagok Conjuring, Day Spirit
INFLUENCES
Inuit Tribal Art

Jessie Oonark *Born* 1906 Canada
Painted in Baker Lake, Canada
Died 1985 Churchill, Manitoba, Canada

Courtesy of Collection of the Dennos Museum Center, Northwestern Michigan College, Traverse City, Michigan/The Artist

MERET OPPENHEIM was raised by her grandparents in Switzerland during World War I. At the age of 18 she went to Paris, where she enrolled at the Académie de la Grande Chaumière. She met Giacometti and Arp, who introduced her to Surrealism and she even modelled for Man Ray. Oppenheim began contributing her own three-dimensional objects to the Surrealist exhibitions in 1933 and achieved critical acclaim three years later with *Object, Fur Breakfast*: a cup, saucer and teaspoon covered with gazelle fur. This typified much of her later work, in which ordinary, everyday objects were transformed into articles with fetishistic or sado-masochistic undertones. In her paintings and sculptures she explored female sexuality and woman's role as a male sex object. One of the few female Surrealists, she was certainly the most highly original of them. On one occasion she even staged a banquet in which a nude female formed the centrepiece of the table decoration.

MOVEMENT
Surrealism
OTHER WORKS
The Governess (My Nurse), Red Head, Blue Body,
INFLUENCES
Marcel Duchamp, Louise Bourgeois

Meret Oppenheim   *Born* 1913 Berlin, Germany
Painted in Switzerland
Died 1985 Basle, Switzerland

Courtesy of AKG, London © DACS 2002

Orozco, José Clemente

JOSÉ CLEMENTE OROZCO studied engineering and architecture in Mexico City and later art at the Academia San Carlos.
Although schooled in the Spanish classical tradition, Orozco was
strongly influenced by his studies of the art and architecture of the
Toltecs and Mayas and this was reflected in his paintings, which
also imbibed much from the European Expressionists. At the
same time, he was an ardent revolutionary and a lifelong political
activist, and as a result his canvasses often have an emphatic social
message. Many of his paintings deal with dramatic events in
Mexico's turbulent history – the revolution of 1911 and the
subsequent civil war providing a fertile source of material.
Orozco's passion for the sweeping social and economic changes
wrought in the 1920s and 1930s also comes across very vividly
in his work. He worked at various times between 1917 and 1934
in the United States and painted the murals and other decorations
for several public buildings.

MOVEMENTS
Expressionism, Social Realism
OTHER WORKS
Table of Universal Brotherhood, Modern Migration of the Spirit
INFLUENCES
Diego Rivera

José Clemente Orozco *Born* 1883 Mexico
Painted in Mexico and USA
Died 1949 Mexico City

Courtesy of Private Collection/Christie's Images © DACS 2002

Ozenfant, Amédée

Nature Morte aux Verres, Bouteilles et Pot Blanc

AMÉDÉE OZENFANT was not only a painter, but also a very articulate propagandist for modern art and a prolific writer on the subject. After a conventional art education he collaborated in Paris with Le Corbusier in the development of a post-Cubist style known as Purism, and together they published the Purist manifesto entitled *Après le Cubisme* ('After Cubism') in 1919. Later they published an avant-garde art periodical *Esprit nouveau* ('New Spirit') from 1921 to 1925 and co-authored *La Peinture moderne* in 1925. An English

translation under the title *Foundations of Modern Art* appeared in 1931 and was widely acclaimed as an imaginative account by a practicing artist. Ozenfant spread the gospel of Purism abroad, founding art schools in London (1935) and New York (1938) for this purpose. His paintings were mainly of still life, characterized by sinuous curvilinear elements reduced to their bare essentials, revealing his gradual departure from an early decorative style to the clear-cut forms of Purism.

MOVEMENT
Purism
OTHER WORKS
Smoking Room
INFLUENCES
Le Corbusier

Amédée Ozenfant   *Born* 1886 France
Painted in France
Died 1966 Cannes, France

Courtesy of Private Collection/Christie's Images/© ADAGP, Paris and DACS, London 2002

Palmer, Samuel

BORN IN London, the son of an eccentric bookseller, Palmer revealed his artistic talent at a very early stage. In 1819, aged just 14, he exhibited at the Royal Academy and the British Institution, selling a painting at the latter. Three years later he met the painter John Linnell, who gave him some instruction. More importantly, perhaps, Linnell also introduced Palmer to William Blake – a meeting which only served to intensify the youngster's mystical outlook.

In 1824, the same year as his encounter with Blake, Palmer started painting at Shoreham, in Kent. In this rural retreat, he began to produce the strange, pastoral idylls, which made his name. Using nothing more than ink and a sepia wash, he conjured up a worldly paradise, stocked with dozing shepherds, carefree animals and luxuriant foliage. In 1826, Palmer settled in Shoreham, where he was soon joined by a group of like-minded artists, who came to be known as the Ancients. Sadly, Palmer's period of poetic inspiration was short-lived. By the mid-1830s, his paintings had become disappointingly conventional, although his etchings retained some of his earlier, lyrical power.

MOVEMENTS
Romanticism, the Ancients

OTHER WORKS
The Sleeping Shepherd, Coming from Evening Church

INFLUENCES
William Blake, John Linnell, Edward Calvert

Samuel Palmer   *Born* 1805 London, England
Painted in England and Italy
Died 1881

Courtesy of Private Collection/Christie's Images

Parmigiano

GIROLAMO FRANCESCO Maria Mazzola was generally known as Parmigianino ('the little Parmesan') or Parmigiano from his birthplace of Parma. His father and two uncles were painters and from them he learned his craft. Later he followed the style of Correggio, who settled in Parma, and they worked together on a number of frescoes for churches in Parma. Around 1523 he went to Rome, where he worked on the ceiling of the Sala dei Pontifici and painted his earliest individual work, *Vision of St Jerome*. Following the sack of Rome in 1527 he fled to Bologna, where he painted the great Madonna altarpiece for the convent of St Margaret. He returned to Parma in 1531 and was commissioned to paint a series of church frescoes, but defaulting on the job resulted in his imprisonment. On his release he decamped to Cremona, where he died in 1540. His few surviving paintings are distinguished by their grace and serenity.

MOVEMENT
Lombard School
OTHER WORKS
Madonna with St Zacharias, Madonna with the Long Neck
INFLUENCES
Correggio, El Greco

Parmigiano   *Born* 1503 Parma, Italy
Painted in Parma, Rome and Bologona
Died 1540 Cremona, Italy

Courtesy of Kunsthistorisches Museum, Vienna, Austria/Ali Meyer/Bridgeman Art Library

Pechstein, Max

MAX HERMANN PECHSTEIN studied art in Dresden, where he joined Die Brücke ('The Bridge') in 1906. The only member of this avant-garde group to have received a formal art education, he had a formulative influence on his contemporaries. Later he co-founded the Neue Sezession in Berlin and was the first of that group to achieve widespread popularity, mainly because his paintings were more decorative than those of his fellow artists. He was profoundly influenced by Van Gogh, Matisse and the Fauves,

reflected in his vibrant colours and dramatic composition. Later he was also attracted to primitive art, evident in the greater angularity of his figures in the 1920s and 1930s. Bright, contrasting colours are emphasized by thick black lines creating an almost stained-glass effect. Pechstein taught at the Berlin Academy from 1923 until 1933, when he was dismissed by the Nazis, but he survived the Third Reich and was reinstated in 1945.

MOVEMENT
German Expressionism
OTHER WORKS
Meadow at Moritzburg, Tale of the Sea, Seated Female Nude
INFLUENCES
Van Gogh, Matisse

Max Pechstein   *Born* 1881 Zwickau, Germany
Painted in Dresden and Berlin
Died 1955 Berlin, Germany

Courtesy of Private Collection/Christie's Images/© DACS 2002

BORN PIETRO DI Cristoforo Vannucci, he is better known by his nickname, from Perugia, the chief city of the district where he grew up and spent much of his working life. Apprenticed to a Perugian painter at the tender age of nine, he showed precocious aptitude. Later he worked under Piero della Francesca at Arrezzo and then was a fellow-pupil of Leonardo under Verrocchio at Florence. In 1480-82 he worked on the frescoes in the Sistine Chapel, Rome, before returning to Perugia, but thereafter worked on various church commissions, occasionally in Rome but mainly in Florence where he had Raphael as one of his pupils for several years. Apart from frescoes and altarpieces he was a prolific painter of individual works, mainly religious subjects but also including a few contemporary portraits.

MOVEMENT
Umbrian School
OTHER WORKS
The Virgin and Child with Saints, Francesco dell' Opera
INFLUENCES
Piero della Francesco, Andrea del Verrocchio

Pietro Perugino *Born c.* 1450 Città delle Pieve, Umbria, Italy
Painted in Parma, Florence and Rome
Died 1523 Fontigano, Italy

Courtesy of Private Collection/Christie's Images

SPANISH PAINTER, sculptor, draughtsman and ceramicist; the most versatile and influential artist of the twentieth century. Having studied in Barcelona, Picasso finally settled in Paris in 1904. His Blue (1901–04) and Rose (1904–06) periods produced his popular scenes of vagrants and circus performers, which were loosely inspired by Puvis and the Symbolists. Then, in 1907, he produced *Les Demoiselles d'Avignon*, the most influential painting of the twentieth century. Named after the red-light district in Barcelona and drawing inspiration from African sculpture, it opened the way for the Cubist movement, which Picasso spearheaded with Braque.

In the 1920s he ushered in a Classical revival, while also being hailed as an inspiration by the Surrealists. Increasingly, though, his paintings displayed a pessimistic strain, brought on by the collapse of his marriage and the deteriorating political situation. This culminated in his most celebrated picture, *Guernica*, which commemorated an atrocity in the Spanish Civil War. Picasso's ongoing hostility to the Franco regime led him to make France, rather than Spain, the base for his later artistic activities.

MOVEMENT
Cubism, Surrealism, Classical Revival
OTHER WORKS
Three Musicians
INFLUENCES
Cézanne, Georges Braque, Toulouse-Lautrec

Pablo Picasso   *Born* 1881 Spain
Painted in Spain, France and Italy
Died 1973

Courtesy of Christie's Images © Succession Picasso/DACS 2002

Pick, Seraphine

THE PAKEHA artist Seraphine Pick attended the Bay of Islands College from 1978 to 1982 before going to Christchurch to study at the Canterbury School of Fine Arts (1984–87), then trained as a teacher. She began painting professionally in 1988 and won the Olivia Spencer Bower Foundation Art Award (1994) and was Rita Angus Artist in Residence at Wellington the following year. She then went on to work and teach in Auckland in 1997–98 and won the Frances Hodgkins Fellowship in Dunedin in 1999 – the country's most prestigious art award.

Her earliest 'mature' works depict simple, domestic objects recalled in a dreamlike, almost naïve manner suggestive of childhood memories, creating an atmosphere that is somewhat nostalgic and somewhat surreal. Since then the surrealism has been fleshed out into dynamic, chaotic and strongly figurative paintings, more reminiscent of Hieronymous Bosch which explore themes of sexual playfulness and social confusion, with an emphasis on the acceptance of humankind's animal nature, alongside the 'higher' themes of traditional Western fine art.

MOVEMENT
Contemporary New Zealand School
OTHER WORKS
Sound, Space Junk, Riki & Ruru, Summer's Wind
INFLUENCES
Goya, Hieronymous Bosch, Sidney Nolan, Remedios Varo

Seraphine Pick *Born* 1964 New Zealand.
Painted in Christchurch, Wellington, Auckland and Dunedin, New Zealand

Courtesy of Collection of the Museum of New Zealand Te Papa Tongarewa/© The Artist

Pierneef, Jacob Hendrik

CAUGHT UP in the struggle of the Anglo–Boer War, Jacob Hendrik Pierneef fled from the Transvaal and went into exile in Holland in 1900–02, and it was there that he began attending evening classes in drawing at Hilversum, followed by a year at the Rotterdam Academy. Returning to Pretoria, he began working as a painter and print-maker in his spare time, but became a full-time artist in 1924. A second visit to Holland (1925–26) acquainted him with the art theories of Willem van Konijnenburg, which led him to apply geometric principles to his own highly formalized landscapes, as exemplified in the series of 32 large murals commissioned for Johannesburg Railway Station. In these he created a stylization bordering on the abstract, to which the vast panoramic landscapes of the Transvaal were ideally suited. These qualities are also evident in his easel paintings of the Veld.

MOVEMENT
Modern South African School
OTHER WORKS
Composition in Blue, The Bushveld, Cape Homestead
INFLUENCES
Willem van Konijnenburg

Jacob Hendrik Pierneef *Born* 1886, Pretoria, South Africa *Painted in* Holland and South Africa *Died* 1957 Pretoria

Courtesy of Bonhams, UK/Bridgeman Art Library

Piero della Francesca

PIERO DELLA FRANCESCA began his career as a pupil of Veneziano in Florence, although he spent most of his working life in his home town of Borgo San Sepolcro, where he attained some eminence in civic affairs. Although strongly influenced by Donatello, Masaccio and Uccello, he was fascinated with mathematics and problems of perspective. Indeed, from 1470 onwards, he abandoned painting and concentrated on these subjects, writing treatises dealing with geometry and perspective. He was a rather slow, perhaps dilatory, artist who took a long time to complete commissions – one of his greatest masterpieces being the unfinished *Nativity* now in the National Gallery, London. His work was neglected and underrated for many years, but he was rediscovered in the nineteenth century and his stature as one of the major artists of the Renaissance has been re-established.

MOVEMENT
Florentine School

OTHER WORKS
Resurrection, The Legend of the True Cross, Constantine's Dream

INFLUENCES
Veneziano, Donatello, Masaccio, Uccello

Piero della Francesca *Born* c. 1420 Italy
Painted in Florence and Borgo San Sepolcro
Died 1492 Borgo San Sepolcro

Courtesy of National Gallery, UK/Bridgeman Art Library

Piero di Cosimo

BORN PIERO DI LORENZO, he was a pupil of Cosimo Rosselli, whose name he adopted. In 1482 he accompanied his master to Rome, where they worked on the frescoes of the Sistine Chapel, and it was during this period that he became imbued with the images of classical mythology which, along with the obligatory religious themes, dominated much of his later work. He also painted a number of portraits and landscapes which are notable for their cheerful accessories. His later style was influenced to some extent by Signorelli and Leonardo da Vinci, although he developed his own highly distinctive approach which his contemporaries regarded as rather eccentric; his interpretation of certain subject matters being, at times rather strange. His reclusive character and diet of hard-boiled eggs tended to reinforce this opinion. Nevertheless, his paintings are distinguished by their mastery of light and composition.

MOVEMENT
Florentine School
OTHER WORKS
A Satyr Mourning Over a Nymph, Immaculate Conception
INFLUENCES
Cosimo Rosselli, Luca Signorelli, Leonardo da Vinci

Piero di Cosimo   *Born c.* 1462 Florence, Italy
Painted in Florence and Rome
Died c. 1521 Florence

Courtesy of Dulwich Picture Gallery, London, UK/Bridgeman Art Library

Piper, John

ENGLISH PAINTER, graphic artist, writer and designer. The son of a solicitor, Piper only turned to art after his father's death in 1926. After training at the Royal College of Art, his early work was predominantly abstract. He joined the London Group (1933) and the Seven & Five Society (1934), while also working on the avant-garde journal *Axis* with his future wife, Myfanwy Evans. But, in common with other Neo Romantic painters, Piper found abstraction an artistic cul-de-sac. Instead, inspired by the late works of Turner, he began to celebrate the glories of the English countryside and its architecture.

In part, the visionary landscapes produced by Piper and his Neo-Romantic colleagues were prompted by the threat of wartime destruction. Accordingly, Piper became a war artist and contributed to the 'Recording Britain' scheme by painting war-damaged buildings. He also produced marvellous, brooding studies of Renishaw and Windsor Castle. In later years, Piper's interests diversified. He designed stained glass windows for Coventry Cathedral, devised stage sets for Benjamin Britten and created a notable tapestry for Chichester Cathedral.

MOVEMENT
Neo-Romanticism
OTHER WORKS
Forms on Dark Blue, Seaton Delaval, The Gothic Archway
INFLUENCES
Turner, Georges Braque, Picasso, John Sell Cotman

John Piper   *Born* 1903 Surrey, England
Painted in England, Wales, Italy and France
Died 1992

Courtesy of Private Collection/Christie's Images/The Piper Estate

HORACE PIPPIN began drawing at the age of seven, but in his youth he held a variety of menial jobs before joining the army in 1917. He returned to West Chester in 1920, his right arm badly damaged by a sniper's bullet and as part of his therapy he began executing pictures in pokerwork on wood panels. In 1929 he took up painting and without any formal training developed into one of America's leading primitive painters, his work being compared to that of Henri 'Douanier' Rousseau. He started by painting the grim scenes from his experiences on the Western Front, vividly conveying the psychological trauma of trench warfare. Later he turned to historic events, biblical subjects and genre paintings derived from childhood incidents. A recurring feature of his work is his own highly personal interpretation of events and personalities. His last paintings were the *Holy Mountain* series, four versions of the same subject, painted in 1944.

MOVEMENT
African American School
OTHER WORKS
The End of War: Starting Home, Night Call, Buffalo Hunt
INFLUENCES
Renoir

Horace Pippin *Born* 1888 Pennsylvania USA
Painted in West Chester, Pennsylvania
Died 1946 West Chester, Pennsylvania

Courtesy of Private Collection/Christie's Images

FRENCH PAINTER, one of the founding fathers of Impressionism. Born at St Thomas in the West Indies, Pissarro was schooled in Paris and enjoyed a brief interlude in Venezuela, before eventually settling in France in 1855. There, he was initially influenced by Corot, whose landscapes he admired at the Universal Exhibition. He also studied at the Académie Suisse, where he met Monet, who introduced him to the future Impressionist circle at the Café Guerbois. Pissarro remained in close contact with Monet in 1870–71, when both men took refuge in London during the Franco-Prussian War.

Pissarro was slightly older than the other Impressionists and this, together with his ability as a teacher, enabled him to assume a guru-like authority within the group. In the mid-1880s, Pissarro flirted briefly with Seurat's Neo-Impressionist techniques, before reverting to his traditional style. In later years, he had increasing trouble with his eyesight and could no longer paint out of doors. Instead, he took to painting lively street scenes from rented hotel rooms. His son Lucien also became a successful artist.

MOVEMENT
Impressionism
OTHER WORKS
View of Pontoise, A Road in Louveciennes, Red Roofs
INFLUENCES
Corot, Monet, Seurat

Camille Pissarro *Born* 1830
Painted in France, England and Venezuela
Died 1903

Courtesy of Private Collection/Christie's Images

Pollock, Jackson

POLLOCK GREW up in the American West, becoming familiar with Native American art at an early age. He was briefly influenced by Benton and the Regionalists, but learned more from Siqueiros and the Mexican muralists. He was impressed by their expressive, almost violent use of paint. Pollock also began to explore the possibilities of Jungian psychology. This started as an aspect of his private life – psychotherapy was one of the many treatments he tried for his long-term alcoholism – but it also fuelled his art. For, like the Surrealists, he adopted the idea of automatic painting, as a mirror of the subconscious.

After years of isolation and critical neglect, Pollock's experiments bore fruit in the late 1940s. By 1947, he had perfected the 'drip' technique which made him famous. He placed his canvas on the floor and covered it in trails of paint, poured directly from the can. This process was carried out in an artistic frenzy, comparable with the Indian ritual dances which he had witnessed as a boy. Pollock's output slowed in the 1950s, and he was killed in a car crash in 1956.

MOVEMENT
Abstract Expressionism
OTHER WORKS
Convergence, Autumn Rhythm, Lavender Mist
INFLUENCES
André Masson, Thomas Hart Benton, David Siqueiros

Jackson Pollock   *Born* 1912 USA
Painted in USA
Died 1956

Courtesy of Private Collection/Christie's Images/© ARS, NY and DACS, London 2002

BORN LIUBOV Sergeyevna Eding on the outskirts of Moscow, Popova studied in Paris shortly before the outbreak of World War I. On her return to Russia in 1914 she met Vladimir Tatlin, who would later become the founder of Soviet Constructivism, and whose principles are very evident in her paintings immediately after the Revolution. In the last years of her life she designed costumes and sets for the theater as well as patterns for the First State Textile Factory in Moscow, which put on a major retrospective exhibition of her works shortly after her sudden death from scarlet fever in 1924. Her paintings broke new ground in their exploration of spatial possibilities and in their colour values, characterized by overlapping circles, curved, diagonal lines and geometric shapes in which the colours merge or contrast sharply. She fervently believed that art should not be merely decorative but should serve some useful purpose, and but for her untimely death she would undoubtedly have become one of the major forces in Soviet art.

MOVEMENT
Constructivism
OTHER WORKS
Space-Force Construction, Cubist Nude
INFLUENCES
Vladimir Tatlin, Alexander Archipenko

Liubov Popova   *Born* 1889 Moscow, Russia
Painted in Moscow
Died 1924 Moscow

Courtesy of Private Collection/Christie's Images

Poussin, Nicolas

ONE OF the leading exponents of Baroque painting, Nicolas Poussin settled in Paris in 1612. Ignoring the Mannerist painting then fashionable, he took as his model Raphael and studied the great Classical works of the Italian Renaissance. He left Paris in 1623 and began travelling in Italy, studying the works of the Italian masters at first hand. He settled in Rome the following year. Apart from a brief sojourn in Paris (1640–42) he spent the rest of his life in Rome, executing commissions for Cardinal Barberini. Eschewing the increasingly popular Baroque style, he clung to the Classical style and became its greatest French exponent. He drew upon the rich store of Greek and Roman mythology for his subjects, while utilizing the techniques of colour developed by Titian. His greatest canvasses deal with vast subjects, crowd scenes crammed with action and detail. Later on he tended to concentrate more on landscapes, although still steeped in the Classical tradition.

MOVEMENT
Classicism
OTHER WORKS
The Rape of the Sabines, The Worship of the Golden Calf
INFLUENCES
Raphael, Bernini

Nicolas Poussin *Born* 1594 Les Andelys, France
Painted in Paris and Rome
Died 1665 Rome

Courtesy of Dulwich Picture Gallery, London, UK/Bridgeman Art Library

Pozzo, Andrea

The Entry of St Ignatius into Paradise, *c.* 1707

ONE OF the most brilliant painters and architects of his generation, Andrea Pozzo was the pupil of an unknown master whom he accompanied to Milan, where he became a Jesuit lay brother. In this connection he was responsible for the decorations of religious festivals and from this graduated to theatrical sets.

In 1676 he painted the frescoes for the church of San Francisco Saverio in Modovi, a masterpiece of *trompe l'oeil*. This was a foretaste of his greatest illusionistic masterpiece, the ceiling of the church of Sant'Ignazio which, by an ingenious use of perspective, appears to expand the interior by hundreds of feet. In this immense achievement he united his talents as painter, architect and sculptor to great effect. In 1695 he designed the elaborate tomb of Ignatius Loyola, founder of the Society of Jesus. He worked on the decoration of many other churches in Italy and from 1703 onwards was similarly employed in Vienna.

MOVEMENT
Italian Baroque
OTHER WORKS
St Francis Xavier Preaching, Investiture of St Francesco Borgia
INFLUENCES
Andrea Sacchi, Pietro da Cortona, Bernini

Andrea Pozzo   *Born* 1642 Trento, Italy
Painted in Mondovi, Rome and Vienna
Died 1709 Vienna

Courtesy of Church of St. Ignatius, Rome, Italy/Bridgeman Art Library

Qiu Ying

Zhao Mengfu Writing the Heart Sutra in Exchange for Tea

REGARDED AS one of the Four Great Masters of the Ming Dynasty (along with Shen Zhou, Wen Zhengming and Tang Yin), Qiu Ying was by far the most versatile of the four. In contrast to his great contemporaries, he was born of humble peasant parents, but his aptitude enabled him to study painting in the Wu School at Suzhou. Unlike the scholar-painters, he relied solely on commissions from wealthy patrons and for that reason he was always more alive to the slightest change in fashion or taste. He painted flowers, gardens, figures, religious subjects and landscapes that revelled in colour and form, very much in line with the sensuousness then prevailing in Ming society. A prolific artist, he frequently copied works of earlier masters or incorporated elements of their work into his own. His technique likewise varied considerably and his palette ranged from the deep, bright colours which give his sensuous and erotic paintings a jewel-like quality, to the paler, more muted shades found in many of his scroll paintings of landscapes, imparting a poetic or contemplative character.

MOVEMENT
Chinese Landscape School
OTHER WORKS
Golden Valley Garden, Landscape after Li Tang
INFLUENCES
Shen Zhou, Zhou Chen

Qiu Ying   *Born c.* 1494, Taicang, Jiangsu, China
Painted in Suzhou, China
Died c. 1552, Suzhou

Courtesy of Private Collection/Bridgeman Art Library

Raeburn, Sir Henry   The Reverend Robert Walker skating on Duddington Loch, 1784

HENRY RAEBURN was originally apprenticed to a goldsmith but began painting portrait miniatures and soon expanded to full-scale oil paintings, though entirely self-taught. After marrying one of his sitters, a wealthy widow, he was enabled to travel to Italy to study for two years, mainly under Pompeo Batoni. He returned to Edinburgh in 1787 and established himself as the most fashionable portraitist of his generation. Unlike Ramsay, he spent most of his life in Edinburgh and seldom visited London. He became a full member of the Royal Academy in 1815. In 1823 he was appointed His Majesty's Limner for Scotland and was knighted the same year. Although his contemporaries judged him less successful in his female subjects, his portraits of both men and women are full of vigour and liveliness and had a profound influence on the development of Scottish art in the nineteenth century.

MOVEMENT
British School of Portraiture
OTHER WORKS
Self-Portrait, Sir Walter Scott, Mrs Robert Bell
INFLUENCES
Allan Ramsay, Pompeo Batoni, Sir Joshua Reynolds

Sir Henry Raeburn   *Born* 1756 Scotland
Painted in Edinburgh and Rome
Died 1823 Edinburgh

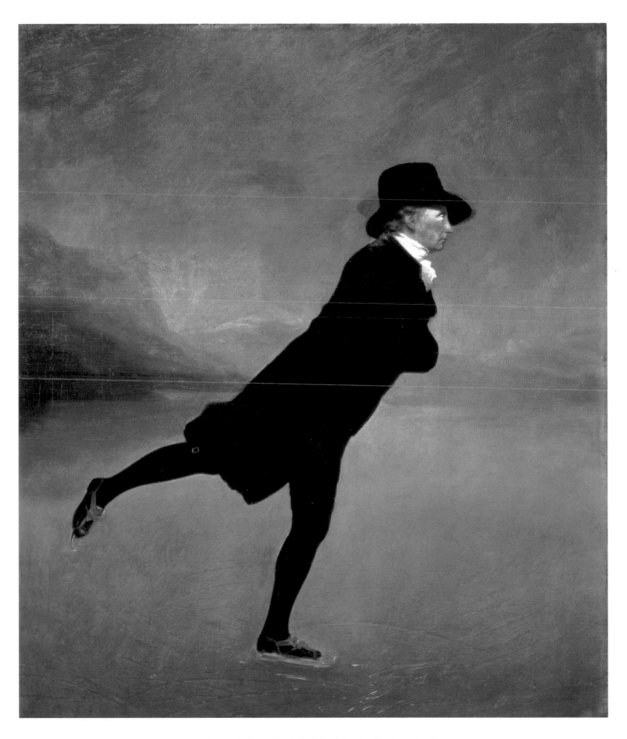

Courtesy of National Gallery of Scotland, Edinburgh, Scotland/Bridgeman Art Library

THE SON of the celebrated Scottish poet of the same name, Allan Ramsay was raised in Edinburgh and was one of the best-educated and most intellectual artists in Europe in his day. He trained in Edinburgh and Rome and was influenced by Pompeo Batoni, the most fashionable of the Italian portraitists. Ramsay settled in London in 1762 and was appointed Principal Painter to King George III in 1767. The following year he became one of the co-founders of the Royal Academy. Ramsay was one of the outstanding portrait painters of his generation, the rival of Reynolds and Gainsborough.

In his lifetime he enjoyed an international reputation for the sensitive and expressive qualities of his portraits, especially of women. However, Ramsay was not content with mere likeness but conveyed the feelings and emotions of his subjects in a manner which had seldom been achieved before. He was a prolific artist whose canvasses are a veritable portrait gallery of British society, but include a number of European celebrities. Living in the shadow of his father, Ramsay had literary ambitions and published a number of polemical and philosophical essays.

MOVEMENT
British School of Portraiture
OTHER WORKS
Queen Charlotte and her Children, David Hume
INFLUENCES
François Boucher, Pompeo Batoni

Allan Ramsay   *Born* 1713 Edinburgh
Painted in Edinburgh, London, Rome and Paris
Died 1784 Dover, England

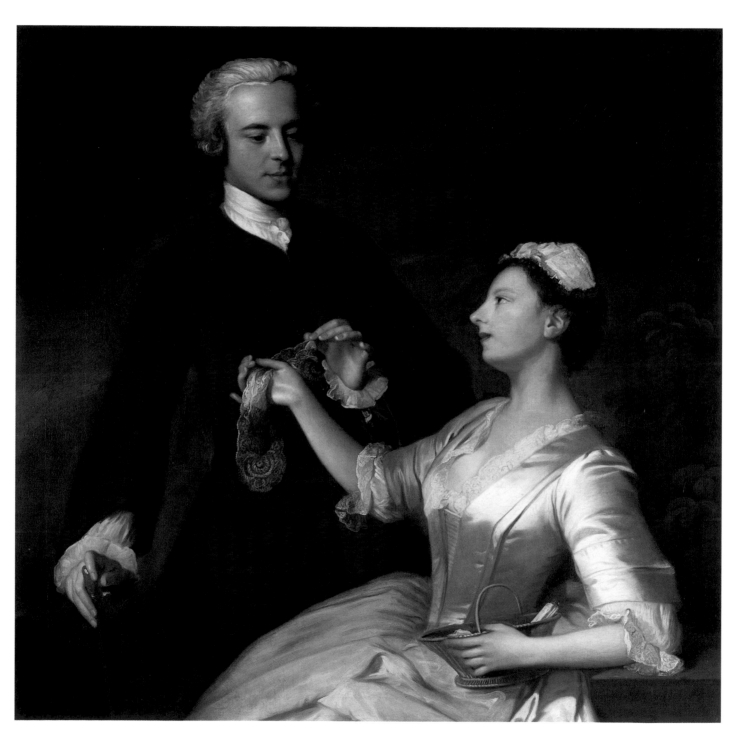

Courtesy of Private Collection/Christie's Images

Raphael (Raffaello Sanzio)

THE ARCHETYPAL artist of the High Renaissance, Raphael received his education in Perugino. In 1504, he moved to Florence, where he received many commissions for portraits and pictures of the Virgin and Child. Soon, his reputation reached the ears of Pope Julius II, who summoned him to Rome in 1508. Deeply influenced by Michelangelo he added a new sense of grandeur to his compositions and greater solidity to his figures. Michelangelo grew jealous of his young rival, accusing him of stealing his ideas, but Raphael's charming manner won him powerful friends and numerous commissions.

The most prestigious of these jobs was the decoration of the Stanze, the papal apartments in the Vatican. This was a huge task, which occupied the artist for the remainder of his life. *The School of Athens* is the most famous of these frescoes. Other commissions included a majestic series of cartoons for a set of tapestries, which were destined for the Sistine Chapel, and a cycle of frescoes for the banker, Agostino Chigi. In the midst of this frantic activity, however, Raphael caught a fever and died, at the tragically young age of 37.

MOVEMENT
Renaissance
OTHER WORKS
Galatea, The Sistine Madonna
INFLUENCES
Pietro Perugino, Leonardo da Vinci, Michelangelo

Raphael *Born* 1483 Urbino, Italy
Painted in Italy
Died 1520

Courtesy of Vatican Museums and Galleries, Vatican City, Italy/Bridgeman Art Library

Rapira-Davies, Shona   Song for 900 Children: Tautoko for the Black Womin, 1986

BORN IN the Northland province of New Zealand, Shona Rapira-Davies is one of the most promising of the younger female Maori artists, working as a painter and sculptor. Like several of her contemporaries she evinces a concern for contemporary social issues, particularly those that affect women and families and the problems of a Maori community struggling to retain its traditional culture and values in a rapidly changing world. Her paintings reflect her passionate interest in the traditions of rural communities and the deracinated Maori caught up in an increasingly urban environment. Her work is not afraid to tackle such matters as racism and sexism, while reflecting the revival of Maori pride in its distinctive culture.

MOVEMENT
Modern New Zealand School
OTHER WORKS
Nga Morehu, Taku Whanau Motvairhe Aotea
INFLUENCES
Kura Te Waru Rewiri, Emare Karaka

Shona Rapira-Davies   *Born* 1951
Painted in New Zealand

Courtesy of Collection of the Museum of New Zealand Te Papa Tongarewa © The Artist

Rauschenberg, Robert

ROBERT RAUSCHENBERG studied at the Kansas City Art Institute and at Black Mountain College, North Carolina, where he was strongly influenced by Joseph Albers. In 1948 he crossed the Atlantic and enrolled at the Académie Julien in Paris (1948). His friendship with the avant-garde composer John Cage led to their collaboration in *Happenings,* in which Cage supplied the music and Rauschenberg the visual entertainment, later extended from collages to painting entirely in one colour (black, white or red). From such minimalism in the early 1950s he moved on to highly controversial pictures, which were not only unusual in colour and surface treatment, but also incorporated scraps of ephemera and even three-dimensional objects such as stuffed birds, rusty metal, rubber tyres, pieces of discarded clothing and any old junk, often dripping with paint. The results are unsettling and unnerving, but always thought-provoking.

MOVEMENTS
American Abstract, Pop Art
OTHER WORKS
The Red Painting, Canyon, Bed, Reservoir
INFLUENCES
Joseph Albers, Marcel Duchamp

Robert Rauschenberg *Born* 1925 USA
Painted in France and USA

Courtesy of Christie's Images/© Robert Rauschenberg/DACS, London/VAGA, New York 2002

Redon, Odilon

ODILON REDON'S ambitions to become an architect were thwarted by ill health; instead he became apprenticed to Rodolphe ·Bresdin, a master lithographer and engraver. The first 20 years of Redon's career were almost entirely devoted to working in monochrome, producing a vast number of charcoal drawings and lithographs, and it was not until the late 1870s that he turned to colour, mainly using pastels. He was very friendly with a botanist named Clavand, whose microscopic researches on plant structures fired his imagination and encouraged him to explore their artistic potential. These Redon later utilized in his Symbolist paintings. From about 1900 these developed a dreamlike quality, which is regarded as a precursor of the Surrealists. In his later years Redon also produced portraits that were a riot of colour. A recluse who shunned the limelight, Redon nevertheless became a role model for the next generation of French artists.

MOVEMENTS
Symbolism, Surrealism
OTHER WORKS
Portrait of Gauguin, The Marsh Flower, The Red Sphinx
INFLUENCES
Rodolphe Bresdin, Gauguin, Gustave Moreau

Odilon Redon   *Born* 1840 Bordeaux, France
Painted in Paris
Died 1916 Paris

Courtesy of Private Collection/Christie's Images

Rego was born in Lisbon, but her father worked for Marconi in Essex, and she was educated at an English school. In 1952, she entered the Slade School of Art, where she trained under Coldstream. There she met Victor Willing, a fellow painter, who became her husband in 1959. They lived in Portugal until 1963, after which they resided principally in England.

Rego's early work was strongly influenced by Dubuffet. She also produced semi-abstract collages, sometimes with political overtones. Increasingly, though, she turned to figurative painting, drawing much of her inspiration from children's illustration, nursery rhymes and her own memories of childhood. In mature works, such as *The Maids*, these playful elements are transposed into unsettling contexts, hinting at games of a very sinister kind. Rego's paintings have brought her success, both in Portugal and the UK. She has twice represented her native land at the Bienal in São Paolo, and on one occasion for Britain. In 1990, she became the first Associate Artist of the National Gallery in London.

MOVEMENT
Symbolist Figuration

OTHER WORKS
Crivelli's Garden, The Policeman's Daughter

INFLUENCES
Jean Dubuffet, Picasso, Walt Disney, James Gillray

Paula Rego *Born* 1935 Lisbon, Portugal
Painted in Britain and Portugal

Courtesy of Private Collection/Bridgeman Art Library/© The Artist

Reinhardt, Ad

Untitled Gouache on Paper 1949

BORN ADOLPH Frederick Reinhardt, he studied at the National Academy of Design in New York City (1936) before joining the American Abstract Artists, an avant-garde group which advocated hard-edged abstraction. He soon broke away from this New York group, whose brand of Abstract Expressionism he found alien to him. Instead he was attracted to the art of India, seeking to develop a style that would be 'breathless, timeless, styleless, lifeless, deathless, endless'. To his way of thinking, Oriental art rejected anything that

was 'irrational, momentary, spontaneous, primitive, expressionist…' Consequently he developed a geometric form of abstraction, but contact with Rothko and Newman in the 1940s led him to concentrate on canvasses covered with paint on which he worked up rectangles of different sizes. Out of this arose his Minimalist art, which would be highly influential in the 1960s.

MOVEMENT
Minimalism
OTHER WORKS
Painting, Abstract Painting, Black Painting No 34
INFLUENCES
Mark Rothko, Barnett Newman, Constantin Brancusi

Ad Reinhardt *Born* 1913, New York, USA
Painted in New York
Died 1967 New York

Courtesy of Private Collection/Christie's Images © ARS, NY and DACS, London 2002

Rembrandt, Harmensz van Rijn

ONE OF Holland's greatest and most versatile artists, Rembrandt trained under several painters, the most influential of these being Pieter Lastman. For a time he shared a studio with Jan Lievens, but by the early 1630s he had moved to Amsterdam, where he established a formidable reputation as a portraitist. Rembrandt's approach to group portraiture, in particular, was extremely ambitious. He showed the anatomist, Dr Tulp actually performing a dissection, while his most famous canvas, *The Night Watch*, is a stunningly complex composition, portraying a local militia group.

As the 1640s progressed, Rembrandt's art entered a more reflective phase. He painted fewer fashionable portraits, preferring instead to depict the inner life. This can be seen in his magnificent religious paintings, in his intimate, unidealized portrayals of his two wives, Saskia and Hendrickje, and in a penetrating series of self-portraits – perhaps the finest ever produced by any artist. Rembrandt's later work was less commercially successful, and although this led to insolvency the popular image of him as a reclusive pauper is entirely fictitious.

MOVEMENT
Baroque
OTHER WORKS
The Night Watch, The Anatomy Lesson of Dr. Tulp, The Jewish Bride
INFLUENCES
Pieter Lastman, Jan Lievens, Rubens

Rembrandt   *Born* 1606 Leiden, Holland
Painted in Holland
Died 1669

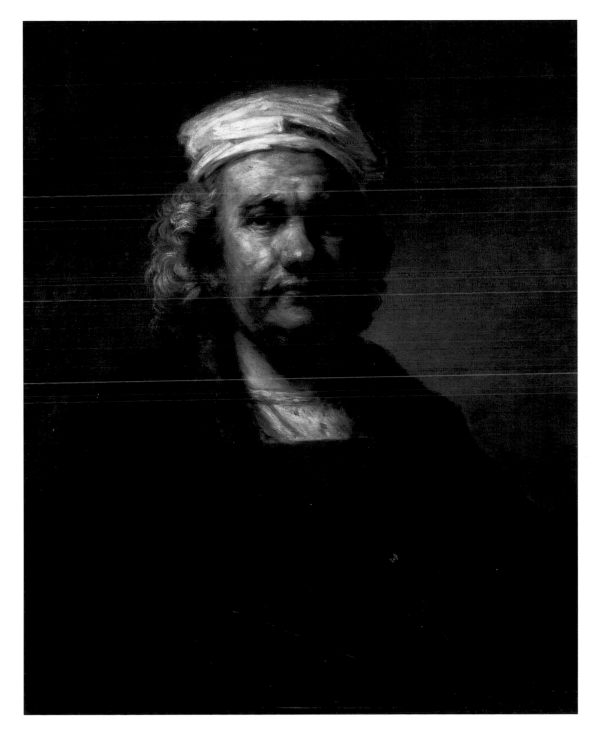

Courtesy of Prado, Madrid/Bridgeman Art Library/Christie's Images

GUIDO RENI studied at the Carracci Academy in his native city of Bologna and acquired a mastery of drawing from life. In 1600 he went to Rome, where he studied the works of Raphael, but he was also strongly influenced by the paintings of other masters working on classical and mythological themes. Reni later painted frescoes, of which his *Aurora and the Hours* (1613–14) for the Borghese family is regarded as his masterpiece. After Carracci's death Reni became the most fashionable painter in Bologna and operated a large studio with numerous assistants. The pious sentimentality of his great religious canvasses had an enormous impact on later generations, although he went on to eclipse in the nineteenth century and has been restored to favour in more recent times, his technical mastery of lighting and composition being appreciated once more.

MOVEMENT
Bolognese School
OTHER WORKS
Massacre of the Innocents, Saint Jerome and the Angel, The Nativity
INFLUENCES
Raphael, Annibale Carracci

Guido Reni *Born* 1575 Bologna, Italy
Painted in Bologna
Died 1642 Bologna

Courtesy of Private Collection/Christie's Images

Renoir, Pierre-Auguste

FRENCH IMPRESSIONIST. Born in Limoges, Renoir trained as a porcelain-painter before entering the studio of Gleyre in 1862. He learnt little from this master, but did meet future members of the Impressionist circle who were fellow-pupils. Together they attended the meetings at the Café Guerbois, where Manet held court. Initially, Renoir was particularly close to Monet, and the pair often painted side by side on the River Seine. Although both were desperately poor, these early, apparently carefree pictures are often cited as the purest distillation of Impressionist principles.

Renoir participated at four of the Impressionist shows, but gradually distanced himself from the movement. This was partly because of his growing success as a portraitist, and partly because he had never lost his affection for Old Masters such as Rubens and Boucher. In the early 1880s, he reached a watershed in his career. He married Aline Charigot, one of his models, and travelled widely in Europe and North Africa, reaffirming his taste for the art of the past. In his subsequent work, he moved away from traditional Impressionist themes, concentrating instead on sumptuous nudes.

MOVEMENT
Impressionism
OTHER WORKS
The Luncheon of the Boating Party, The Bathers, The Umbrellas,
INFLUENCES
Monet, François Boucher, Rubens

Pierre-Auguste Renoir *Born* 1841 France
Painted in France
Died 1919

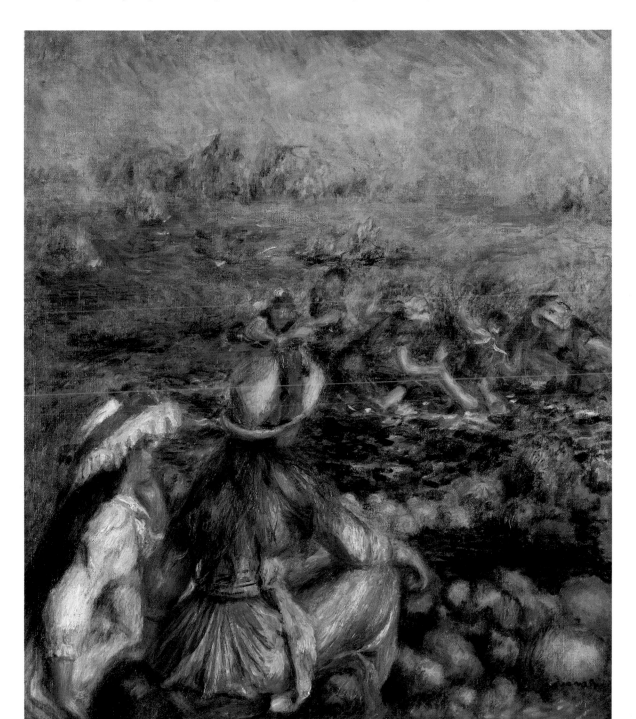

Courtesy of Private Collection/Christie's Images

BORN AT Chuguyev near Kharkov of poor peasant parents, Ilya Yefimovich Repin learned his trade under Bunakov, a painter of icons. In 1863 he won a scholarship to the Academy of Fine Arts in St Petersburg, where he remained for six years, winning the gold medal and a travelling scholarship which enabled him to continue his studies in France and Italy. On his return, he concentrated on paintings in the heroic mold and was appointed Professor of Historical Painting at St Petersburg in 1894. Moving with the times, he later painted large canvasses with a strong social message and, with his peasant background, he thus fitted the ideals expressed by the Revolution. Even his historical paintings struck a chord with the strongly nationalist feelings of Russians in the early 1920s. His social realism was much admired by both Lenin and Stalin and influenced the artists working in the Soviet Union throughout the 1930s and 1940s.

MOVEMENT
Russian School

OTHER WORKS
Procession in the Government of Kiev

INFLUENCES
Alexei Venetsianov, Grigori Soroka

Ilya Repin *Born* 1844 Chuguyev, Kharkov, Russia
Painted in St Petersburg, Russia
Died 1930 St Petersburg

Courtesy of Private Collection/Christie's Images

Rewiri, Kura Te Waru   I nga haerenga me nga hokinga mai (Coming and going), 2001

KURA TE WARU REWIRI studied at the Canterbury School of Fine Arts in Christchurch, from which she graduated in 1973. She had a conventional art training in Western Expressionism, but was strongly influenced by Rudolf Gopas, who told her that she should never forget that she was a Maori. This has shaped the pattern of her art in the subsequent period, both in subject matter and in the style of her painting. She uses strongly contrasting colours in vivid compositions which, while figural, have underlying symbolism and

hidden meanings. A typical example of this is her great painting of the Treaty of Waitangi, negotiated between the British and the Maori chiefs in 1840. By placing the cross in the centre of the picture she suggests the sacrifice of her people and the role of the Christian missionaries in undermining Maori culture. In more recent years she has turned more and more to traditional art forms, notably godstick figures.

MOVEMENT
Modern Maori School, New Zealand
OTHER WORKS
Nga Tohu O Te Tiriti, Whenua Wahine Whenua
INFLUENCES
Rudolf Gopas

Kura Te Waru Rewiri   *Born* 1950
Painted in New Zealand

Courtesy of Private Collection/Artist & Ferner Galleries - New Zealand

BORN IN Plympton, Devon, Joshua Reynolds was apprenticed in London to Thomas Hudson, a second-rate portrait painter, from whom he learned the rudiments of his craft. In 1743 Reynolds settled in Plymouth, but in 1744 he returned to London where his portrait of Captain John Hamilton, brought him recognition. Reynolds spent two years in Rome perfecting his technique, then visited other Italian art centres, before returning to England in 1752. By 1760 he was the most fashionable portrait painter in London, becoming the first President of the Royal Academy in 1768 and knighted a year later. A prolific artist, he produced over 2,000 portraits, many of which were subsequently published as engravings that further enhanced his reputation.

MOVEMENT
English School
OTHER WORKS
Nelly O'Brien, Samuel Johnson
INFLUENCES
Thomas Hudson, Sir Peter Lely

Sir Joshua Reynolds   *Born* 1723 England
Painted in London, England
Died 1792 London

Courtesy of Private Collection/Christie's Images

Ribera, Jusepe

JUSEPE RIBERA, nicknamed Lo Spagnoletto ('the little Spaniard'), studied under Francisco Ribalta in Valencia and then went to Rome to study the frescoes of Raphael, and to Parma to learn from Correggio's works. He settled at Naples, where his paintings caught the eye of the Spanish viceroy. As a result his career was assured and he became a prolific painter of intensely realistic religious and genre subjects. He delighted in the gory details of the martyrdom of the saints, thus provoking Lord Byron in *Don Juan* to quip that 'Spagnoletto tainted his brush with all the blood of all the sainted'. He was also fascinated with the bizarre or grotesque in contemporary life; but by the 1630s his work assumed a more reflective, tranquil approach. Nevertheless it was the fervent spirituality of his earlier paintings that appealed to his predominantly Spanish clientele.

MOVEMENT
Spanish and Neapolitan Schools
OTHER WORKS
Saint Paul the Hermit, Portrait of a Bearded Woman
INFLUENCES
Raphael, Correggio

Jusepe Ribera   *Born* 1591 Jeatiba, Spain
Painted in Naples, Italy
Died 1652 Naples

Courtesy of Private Collection/Christie's Images

GERHARD RICHTER studied in his native city of Dresden and Düsseldorf before engaging in a career as a designer of sets for the stage and then working as a commercial artist in advertising. His early paintings were mostly figurative, but from 1962 onwards he produced paintings that were derived from blurred photographic images. Many of his paintings have been produced in series, exploring particular themes that continually flit back and forward between the camera and the canvas, and hover between figuration and the abstract. In particular, he painted a series of oils derived from aerial photographs of cities. His most recent work has consisted of enormous canvasses, more purely abstract in character, with emphasis on the artist rather than the subject. Noted for his range and versatility, coupled with absolute mastery of his technique, he has an infinite capacity to rediscover or reinvent the medium. A great innovator, he has had a tremendous influence on postwar German art.

MOVEMENT
Modern German
OTHER WORKS
Abstraktes Bild, Stag, Betty, Colour Streaks, Townscape series
INFLUENCES
Otto Dix

Gerhard Richter   *Born* 1932 Dresden, Germany
Painted in Germany

Courtesy of Private Collection/Christie's Images/© Gerhard Richter

Riley, Bridget

BRIDGET RILEY studied at Goldsmith's College of Art (1949–52) and the Royal College of Art (1952–55) in London. She had her first one-woman exhibition at Gallery One, London, in 1962 and has had many other shows all over the world in subsequent years. Influenced by the Futurists Giacomo Balla and Umberto Boccioni, she began to develop an optical style in the 1960s – now known as Op Art – in which hallucinatory images were created in black and white, in geometric or curvilinear patterns endlessly repeated to produce the illusion of rippling or undulating movement. By 1966 she had moved into colour, which enabled her to widen the scope of these images considerably; her colours vary in depth and tone and add subtlety to the overall pattern. Widely acclaimed in England, she made an impact on the international scene in 1968 when she became the first British artist to win the top award for painting at the Venice Biennale.

MOVEMENT
Op Art
OTHER WORKS
Cataract I, In Attendance, Fission, Fall
INFLUENCES
Giacomo Balla, Umberto Boccioni, Joseph Albers

Bridget Riley   *Born* 1931 London, England
Painted in London

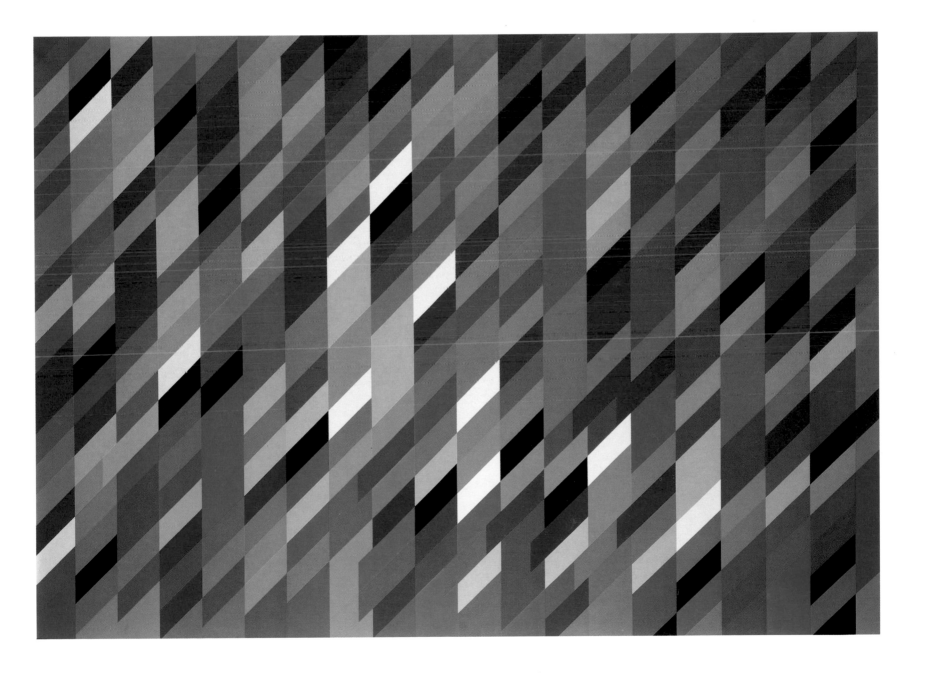

Courtesy of Private Collection/Christie's Images 2002 © Bridget Riley, all rights reserved Courtesy Karsten Schubert, London

Riopelle, Jean-Paul

Composition (non-representational), 1958

ALTHOUGH HE painted landscapes from early childhood, Riopelle studied at the Montreal Polytechnic (1939–41), but later concentrated for some time on architecture. In 1943 he resumed his art studies at the Montreal École des Beaux Arts and the École du Meuble, where he studied furniture design. Under the influence of Paul-Emile Borduas he developed an interest in Abstraction, Surrealism and mechanical techniques used by the group of French-Canadian artists known as Les Automatistes. In 1947 he settled in Paris, where he came into close contact with Duchamp and the other Surrealists. For a time he painted in the tachiste manner, but after 1950 he evolved a technique in which blobs of paint were squeezed direct from the tube on to the canvas, then about 1953 he turned to the palette knife to create almost sculptural effects. In turn this was followed by a fragmented, mosaic effect, which eventually gave way to a more representational style. From 1958 onwards he also modelled figures, cast in bronze. Since 1970 he has experimented with collages, employing a wide range of materials and techniques.

MOVEMENT
Modern Canadian School

OTHER WORKS
Green Parrot, Composition, Blue Night, Pavane

INFLUENCES
Paul-Emile Borduas, Marcel Duchamp

Jean-Paul Riopelle *Born* 1923 Montreal, Quebec, Canada
Painted in Canada and France

Courtesy of Private Collection/Christie's Images/© ADAGP, Paris and DACS, London 2002

THE OUTSTANDING muralist of Latin America, Diego Rivera studied art in Mexico City and Madrid; he went to Paris in 1911, where he met Picasso and began painting Cubist works, which were strongly influenced by Gris and Braque. By contrast, a sojourn in Italy studying the frescoes of the Renaissance Masters made such an impact on him that, on his return to Mexico in 1921, he concentrated on large murals decorating the walls of public buildings. These depicted every aspect of life in Mexico and drew on the turbulent history of its people. Rivera's best work was carried out during a period when Mexico was dominated by left-wing, anti-clerical governments, which regarded Rivera as the leading revolutionary artist. He also worked in the USA where he painted murals extolling the industrial proletariat and preaching social messages. He evolved his own brand of folk art with overtones of such disparate elements as Aztec symbolism and Byzantine icons.

MOVEMENT
Mexican Modernism

OTHER WORKS
Court of the Inquisition, Workers of the Revolution

INFLUENCES
Juan Gris, Georges Braque

Diego Rivera *Born* 1886 Guanajuato, Mexico
Painted in Mexico and USA
Died 1957 Mexico City

Courtesy of Private Collection/Christie's Images/2002 Banco de Mexico Diego Rivera & Frida Kahlo Museums Trust. Av. Cinco de Mayo No. 2, Col. Centro, Del. Cuauhtemoc 06059, Mexico, D.F.

Robert, Hubert

HUBERT ROBERT was trained in the Classical tradition but grew up in a world in which the Rococo style was at the height of fashion. Coming under the influence of Watteau, Boucher and Fragonard in turn, his style gradually developed away from the Rococo to a greater realism. Although his skill in composition and mastery of colour were acknowledged, Robert's chief contribution to French art in the latter part of the 18th century was his incisiveness and the liveliness with which he presented his subjects.

He made an immense impression on his contemporaries, not the least of whom was Voltaire, who commissioned Robert to decorate his theatre at Ferney as well as design sets. Robert painted portraits and genre subjects, but it was his skill as a landscape artist and creator of historical tableaux that had the greatest impact and many of his larger canvasses are preserved in the Louvre.

MOVEMENT
French School
OTHER WORKS
Landscape with Ruins, The Mouth of a Cave
INFLUENCES
Jean-Antoine Watteau, François Boucher, Fragonard

Hubert Robert *Born* 1733 Paris, France
Painted in France
Died 1808 Paris

Courtesy of Christie's Images

Romney, George

Portrait of Emma, Lady Hamilton, 1786

ENGLISH PAINTER, specializing in portraits. Romney was born in Lancashire, the son of a cabinet maker, and trained under an itinerant portraitist named Christopher Steele. For a time, he picked up commissions by travelling from town to town, before making his base in Kendal. Moving to London in 1762, he established a reputation as a fashionable portrait painter, although his style did not really mature until after his tour of Italy (1773–75). There, his study of Classical and Renaissance art paid huge dividends, and most of his best paintings were produced in the decade after his return to England.

Romney, like Gainsborough, was deeply dissatisfied with portraiture. His ambition of becoming a history painter was never fulfilled, perhaps partly because of his nervous, introspective character, and partly because of his reluctance to exhibit. His later career was marred by his obsession with Emma Hart (later Lady Hamilton, Nelson's mistress). Romney met her in 1781 and, in the years which followed, produced dozens of pictures of her, usually masquerading as a character from mythology. As his reputation began to wane, the artist returned to Kendal, where he suffered a serious mental decline.

MOVEMENTS
Neoclassicism, Romanticism

OTHER WORKS
The Parson's Daughter, The Beaumont Family, Lady Rodbard

INFLUENCES
Sir Joshua Reynolds, Henry Fuseli, Joseph Highmore

George Romney *Born* 1734 England
Painted in England and Italy
Died 1802

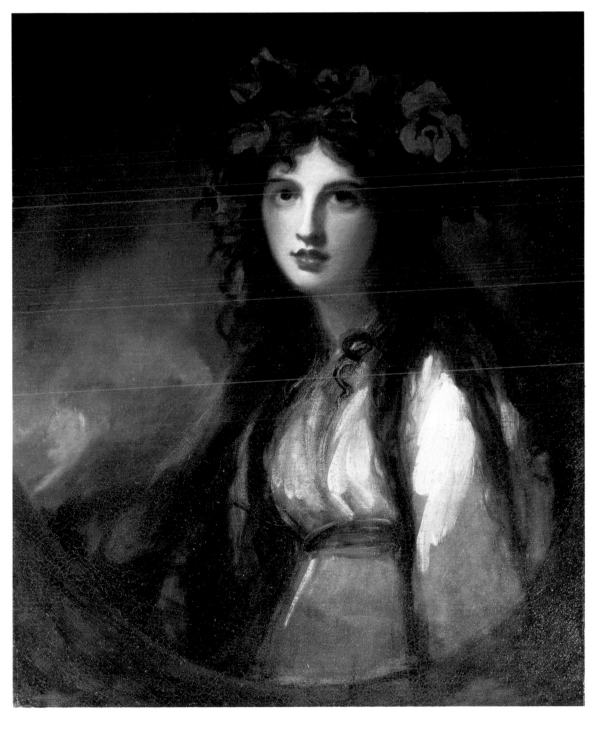

Courtesy of Philip Mould, Historical Portraits Ltd, London, UK/Bridgeman Art Library

Rossetti, Dante Gabriel

ROSSETTI CAME from a hugely talented family. His father was a noted scholar while his sister Christina became a celebrated poet. For years Dante wavered between a career in art or literature, before devoting himself to painting. While still only 20, he helped to found the Pre-Raphaelite Brotherhood, the radical group that shook the Victorian art world with their controversial exhibits at the Royal Academy in 1848. The Pre-Raphaelites were appalled by the dominant influence of sterile, academic art, which they linked with the teachings of Raphael – then regarded as the greatest Western painter. In its place, they called for a return to the purity and simplicity of medieval and early Renaissance art.

Although championed by the critic Ruskin the Pre-Raphaelites' efforts were greeted with derision and this discouraged Rossetti from exhibiting again. During the 1850s, he concentrated largely on watercolours, but in the following decade he began producing sensuous oils of women. These were given exotic and mysterious titles, such as *Monna Vanna* and were effectively the precursors of the *femmes fatales*, which were so admired by the Symbolists.

MOVEMENT
Pre-Raphaelite Brotherhood
OTHER WORKS
Beata Beatrix, Proserpine
INFLUENCES
Ford Madox Brown, William Bell Scott

Dante Gabriel Rossetti *Born* 1828
Painted in England
Died 1882

Courtesy of Christie's Images

BORN MARCUS Rothkovitch in Dvinsk, Russia, Rothko emigrated to the US in 1913. He studied briefly at Yale and at the Art Student's League in New York, although he considered his formal training to have had little influence on his development as a painter. Rothko's personal style took many years to take form and his income for much of his life came from teaching. His early works included portraits and strange, urban landscapes, which he exhibited with American Expressionist group The Ten. Following this, Rothko went through a Surrealist phase, working in a similar vein to Arshile Gorky.

By the mid-1940s, Rothko was linked with the Abstract Expressionist circle and, in 1947, he began to create the enormous Colour Field paintings, with which he has become most closely associated. These huge canvasses, with their asymmetric, blurred patches of colour, have a soothing effect on the viewer when seen under the muted lighting that Rothko insisted upon. However, Rothko's private life was anything but tranquil; prone to depression and heavy drinking, his irritable manner alienated friends and colleagues alike and, eventually, he committed suicide.

MOVEMENT
Abstract Expressionism, Colour Field Painting
OTHER WORKS
Central Green, Blue, Orange, Red, Number 118
INFLUENCES
Barnett Newman, Arshile Gorky, Clyfford Still

Mark Rothko   *Born* 1903 Russia
Painted in USA
Died 1970 USA

Courtesy of Private Collection/Christie's Images/© Kate Rothko Prizel and Christopher Rothko/DACS 2002.

GEORGES HENRI ROUALT was originally apprenticed to a stained-glass designer and the vivid colours of this material left their mark on his later work as a painter, in which forms and shapes were sharply outlined in black, rather like leaded windows. In 1892 he took up painting, studying under Gustave Moreau at the École des Beaux-Arts, where he met Matisse. About 1904 he joined the Fauves, but their violent colours were at odds with Roualt's preference for strong, dark shades. He had his first one-man show six years later. Apart from painting, he designed ballet sets and costumes and textiles, notably tapestry. Brought up in a staunchly Catholic environment, Roualt had a crisis of faith in about 1902, which led him to paint somber pictures with harsh motifs that symbolized man's fall from grace. He returned to a much purer form of religious art during World War I and this dominated his output during the global conflict of the 1940s. A prolific artist, he also illustrated books and designed ceramics.

MOVEMENT
French Expressionism
OTHER WORKS
Bust of a Woman Wearing a Necklace, The Three Judges
INFLUENCES
Gustave Moreau, Matisse

Georges Roualt *Born* 1871 Paris, France
Painted in Paris
Died 1958 Paris

Courtesy of Private Collection/Christie's Images/© ADAGP, Paris and DACS, London 2002

Rousseau, Henri Vue de L'isle Saint-Louis, Prise du Port Saint-Nicolas Le Soir

FRENCH PAINTER, perhaps the most famous of all Naive artists. Rousseau came from a poor background and he went through a succession of menial jobs, before turning to art late in life. Among other things he was a clerk, a soldier and a toll-collector. While working as the latter, he began painting as a hobby and, in 1893, he took early retirement, in order to pursue his artistic ambitions.

Rousseau was entirely self-taught, although he did take advice from academic artists such as Clément and Gérôme. He copied many of the individual elements in his pictures from book illustrations, using a mechanical device called a pantograph. But it was his dreamlike combination of images and his intuitive sense of colour which gave his art its unique appeal.

Rousseau began exhibiting his paintings from the mid-1880s, using avant-garde bodies such as the Salon des Indépendants, for the simple reason that they had no selection committee. He never achieved great success, but his guileless personality won him many friends in the art world, among them Picasso, Apollinaire and Delaunay. Posthumously, his work was an important influence on the Surrealists.

MOVEMENT
Naive Art
OTHER WORKS
Surprised! (Tropical Storm with a Tiger), The Sleeping Gypsy
INFLUENCES
Jean-Léon Gérôme, Félix Clément

Henri Rousseau *Born* 1844 France
Painted in France
Died 1910 Paris, France

Courtesy of Private Collection/Christie's Images

Rousseau, Théodore

A Wooded Landscape at Sunset with a Faggot Gatherer

FRENCH LANDSCAPE painter, hailed as the leader of the Barbizon School. The son of a clothier, Rousseau developed a deep love of the countryside at an early age. After working briefly in a sawmill, he decided to take up landscape painting and trained with Joseph Rémond. The latter produced classical landscapes, however, and Rousseau's naturalistic tendencies were better served by the study of foreign artists, such as Ruisdael and Constable. He adopted the practice of making sketches outdoor - a foretaste of Impressionism - although he still preferred to finish his paintings in the studio.

Rousseau's favourite location was the Barbizon region, at the edge of the Forest of Fontainebleau. By the late 1840s, this area had become the focus for a group of like-minded artists known as the Barbizon School. Headed by Rousseau, this circle included Corot, Daubigny, Diaz and Millet. In the 1850s, Rousseau's work achieved widespread recognition, fetching high prices, but he preferred to remain in Barbizon, campaigning to preserve the character of the forest. He died in his cottage, in the arms of fellow landscapist Jean-François Millet.

MOVEMENT
Barbizon School
OTHER WORKS
Edge of a Forest – Sunset, Farm in the Landes
INFLUENCES
Jacob van Ruisdael, Constable

Théodore Rousseau *Born* 1812 Paris, France
Painted in France
Died 1867 Paris

Courtesy of Christie's Images

BORN AT Siegen, Westphalia, now part of Germany, Peter Paul Rubens was brought up in Antwerp in the Spanish Netherlands. Originally intended for the law, he studied painting under Tobias Verhaecht, Adam Van Noort and Otto Vaenius and was admitted into the Antwerp painters' guild in 1598. From 1600 to 1608 he was court painter to Vincenzo Gonzaga, Duke of Mantua, and travelled all over Italy and Spain, furthering his studies and also executing paintings for various churches. Shortly after his return to Antwerp he was appointed court painter to Archduke Albrecht of the Netherlands. In the last years of his life he combined painting with diplomatic missions which took him to France, Spain and England and resulted in many fine portraits, as well as his larger religious pieces. He was knighted by both Charles I and Philip IV of Spain. In 1630 he retired from the court to Steen and devoted the last years of his life to landscape painting.

MOVEMENT
Flemish School
OTHER WORKS
Samson and Delilah, The Descent from the Cross, Peace and War
INFLUENCES
Tobias Verhaecht, Adam Van Noort

Peter Paul Rubens   *Born* 1577 Siegen, Germany
Painted in Antwerp, Rome, Madrid, Paris and London
Died 1640 Antwerp, Belgium

Courtesy of Private Collection/Christie's Images

Rublev, Andrei

RUBLEV (OR RUBLYOV) was born in Russia around the middle of the fourteenth century, during the upsurge of church-building in Russia and the desire for extravagant murals, mosaics and, above all, icons, whose human scale appealed to the Russian psyche far more than large frescoes. In Russia the icon was liberated from the strictures imposed upon it by the Greek Orthodox hierarchy and became much more humanist. To Rublev, a humble monk in the Andryonikov monastery near Moscow, fell the honor of transforming the icon and raising it to the status of fine art, combining intense realism with serenity and a sense of absolute devotion. Nothing is known about his origins, but his aptitude for drawing and painting came to the attention of the Greek master icon painter Theophanes, under whom Rublev worked from 1405 till 1422. He then settled in the Troitsky Sergieva monastery, where he produced his greatest works, establishing a reputation as the greatest icon painter of his era.

MOVEMENT
Russian Icon Painting
OTHER WORKS
The Saviour, The Trinity
INFLUENCES
Theophanes

Andrei Rublev   *Born c.* 1360 Russia
Painted in Moscow, Russia
Died c. 1430 Moscow

Courtesy of Tretyakov Gallery, Moscow, Russia/Bridgeman Art Library

Ruysch, Rachel

A Carnation Morning Glory with Other Flowers, *c.* 1695

RACHEL RUYSCH had a conventional art education in the Classicist tradition, but was strongly influenced by Willem Kalf and Jan Vermeer – not only in the techniques of light and shade, but also in subject matter. Nevertheless she added her own distinctive contribution to the art of the still life, specializing in bouquets or vases of flowers made more interesting by the subtle inclusion of bees, butterflies or other insects. The vivid colours of the blossom contrasted with the muted tones of the backgrounds, which often featured classical buildings. She excelled in the painting of crystal vases, which positively sparkle and exquisitely set off the flowers, whose meticulous detail gives them an intensely realistic appearance and explains the popularity of Ruysch's work right up to the present time. Floral paintings were very fashionable in Holland in the late seventeenth and early eighteenth centuries, symbolizing the brevity of all life that is doomed to death and decay. Ruysch's bouquets have a sumptuous quality that has become timeless. She spent her entire life in Amsterdam.

MOVEMENT
Dutch School
OTHER WORKS
Still Life of Flowers
INFLUENCES
Willem Kalf, Vermeer

Rachel Ruysch   *Born* 1664 Amsterdam, Holland
Painted in Amsterdam
Died 1750 Amsterdam

Courtesy of Private Collection/Christie's Images

BORN AT Naarden in Gooiland, Salomon Jacobsz van Ruysdael was originally Salomon de Gooyer, but he and his brother Isaack (1599–77) adopted the name 'Ruysdael' from a castle near their father's home. Salomon joined the painters' guild at Haarlem in 1623, becoming Dean in 1648. From 1651 he also had a business supplying blue dyes to the Haarlem bleachworks. His earliest dated works belong to 1626 and within two years of this his reputation as a landscape painter was assured. Although he remained in Haarlem all his life, he made occasional forays to other parts of the Netherlands in search of landscape subjects, noted for their fine tonal qualities, and laying the foundations for the great paintings of his much more famous nephew Jacob van Ruysdael. As well as his tranquil landscapes and river scenes, he produced a number of still-life paintings towards the end of his career.

MOVEMENT
Dutch School
OTHER WORKS
Pellekussenpoort, Utrecht, Still Life
INFLUENCES
Esaias van de Velde, Jan van Goyen

Salomon van Ruysdael   *Born c.* 1600 Holland *Painted in* Haarlem, Holland *Died* 1670 Haarlem

Courtesy of Private Collection/Christie's Images

ALBERT PINKHAM RYDER came from a long line of seafarers and whalers, but his formal education was terminated as a result of an illness which gravely affected his eyesight, and it has been suggested that his dark, moonlit pictures and vague forms may have resulted from his impaired vision. To while away the time his father bought him paints and a few lessons from a local amateur got him started. Not until he moved to New York in 1867 was he able to improve his skills under William Edgar Marshall and four years later he succeeded at the second attempt in enrolling at the National Academy of Design. Although he visited Europe several times, neither the Old Masters nor contemporary artists had any influence on his work, which consisted mostly of small landscapes. In the 1880s he turned to more metaphysical paintings inspired by poetry and the Bible, becoming a recluse in his last years

MOVEMENT
American Expressionism
OTHER WORKS
The Watering Place
INFLUENCES
William Edgar Marshall

Albert Pinkham Ryder   *Born* 1847 USA
Painted in New Bedford and New York, USA
Died 1917 New Bedford

Courtesy of Private Collection/Christie's Images

JAWAD SALIM hailed from a family of painters, which included his father Muhammad, brother Nizar and sister Naziha. The family came from the vilayet of Mosul, which became part of Iraq on the break-up of the Ottoman Empire. He trained under his father and then continued his studies in Paris and Rome (1938–40). During World War II he was employed in the Archaeological Museum in Baghdad, where he gained an abiding interest in sculpture. From 1946 to 1949 he studied painting and sculpture at the Slade School of Art in London and on his return to Iraq was appointed head of the sculpture department at the Institute of Fine Arts. When Iraq became a republic in 1958 he was commissioned to create the Monument to Liberty – one of the largest sculptures in the Middle East. This has tended to overshadow his achievement as a painter, but he strove to create a distinctive Iraqi idiom that combined modern styles with ancient Mesopotamian symbols and mythology. He also worked as a graphic artist and book illustrator.

MOVEMENT
Modern Iraqi School
OTHER WORKS
Fishermen Hauling Boat, Festive Crowd, Bazaar
INFLUENCES
Haji Muhammad Salim al-Mosuli

Jawad Salim *Born* 1920 Ankara, Turkey
Painted in Baghdad, Iraq
Died 1961 Baghdad

Courtesy of Sotheby's Picture Library

Samba, Chéri

IN COLONIAL times it was axiomatic that aspiring African artists had to receive a good grounding in European styles and techniques, but gradually it dawned that such an influence was often negative or counterproductive. Fortunately for Chéri Samba, he was entirely self-taught and if he had been influenced in any way by European art it was through the medium of the cartoons and graphic art in contemporary newspapers. In 1975 he graduated from drawing cartoons to painting them on canvas, but without compromising his direct, crystal-clear approach. Every painting tells a story, the images generally enhanced by words, an unconscious borrowing from the art of China and Japan. Detail is painstaking, brushwork is crisp and outlines are hard-edged, enhancing the impact of his work. One of the most prominent of the naive painters to emerge in post-colonial Africa, his paintings with their undertones of social realism are now in many international collections.

MOVEMENT
Modern African School
OTHER WORKS
Mr Poor's Family
INFLUENCES
Henri Rousseau, Gino Severini

Chéri Samba *Born* 1956 Kinto M'Vulia, Zaire (now Congo)
Painted in Congo

Courtesy of Galerie Peter Herrmann, Berlin/© Chéri Samba

BORN OF American parents in Florence, Italy, John Singer Sargent was brought up in Nice, Rome and Dresden – giving him a rather sporadic education but a very cosmopolitan outlook. He studied painting and drawing in each of these cities, but his only formal schooling came at the Accademia in Florence, where he won a prize in 1873, and in the studio of Carolus-Duran in Paris (1874). In 1876 he paid the first of many trips to the USA, re-affirming his American citizenship in that Centennial year. He painted landscapes, but it was his early portraits that earned him acclaim. However, the scurrilous treatment of him by the French press over a décolleté portrait of Madame Gautreau induced him to leave France in 1885 and settle in London, where he spent most of his life. As well as portraits he produced large decorative works for public buildings from 1910 onwards. Some of his most evocative paintings were produced as a war artist in 1914–18.

MOVEMENT
Anglo-American School
OTHER WORKS
The Lady of the Rose, Carmencita, Gassed
INFLUENCES
Carolus-Duran, Frans Hals, Velázquez

John Singer Sargent   *Born* 1856 Florence, Italy
Painted in France, England and USA
Died 1925 London, England

Courtesy of Private Collection/Christie's Images

EGON SCHIELE studied at the Vienna Academy of Fine Arts in 1906 and the following year he met Gustave Klimt, whose Vienna Sezession movement he joined in 1908. A disciple of Sigmund Freud, Schiele sought to explore the deeper recesses of the human psyche, especially the sexual aspects. He developed a particularly stark style of Expressionism – distinguished by figures, often naked and usually emaciated – with harsh outlines, filling the canvas with contorted limbs and anguished features.

Long before the Nazis were denouncing his paintings as degenerate art, the Austrian authorities were confiscating and destroying his works. In 1912 he was actually arrested, convicted of offences against public morals and briefly imprisoned. After his marriage in 1915 his art mellowed, taking on a brighter and more sensuous form, and it is interesting to conjecture how this trend might have developed had he not died in the influenza pandemic of 1918.

MOVEMENT
Austrian Expressionism
OTHER WORKS
The Embrace, Recumbent Female Nude with Legs Apart
INFLUENCES
Klimt

Egon Schiele   *Born* 1890 Tulln, Austria
Painted in Vienna, Austria
Died 1918 Vienna

Courtesy of Private Collection/Christie's Images

Schnabel, Julian

ALTHOUGH A native of New York City, Schnabel studied art at the University of Texas from 1969 to 1972. After moving back to New York, he began exhibiting in 1976, creating enormous canvasses in which layers of paint are applied in different ways in order to create interesting and unusual textures. A later development on these lines includes the use of shards of pottery to break up the surfaces and heighten dramatic effect. Unfortunately this combination of paint and crockery is friable and inherently unstable, creating numerous problems for curators and conservators of art galleries housing these monumental works. More recently he has also created paintings on velvet. Apart from re-inventing Action Painting, Schnabel has experimented with imagery on the grand scale, creating extraordinary works which incorporate numerous images and portraits mingled with allusions to history and emotions. Since the early 1980s he has enjoyed phenomenal commercial success.

MOVEMENT
Action Painting
OTHER WORKS
Blue Nude with Sword, Humanity Asleep, St Francis in Ecstasy
INFLUENCES
Robert Motherwell, Robert Rauschenberg

Julian Schnabel   *Born* 1951 New York, USA
Painted in New York

Courtesy of Private Collection/Christie's Images

KURT SCHWITTERS studied at the Dresden Academy and worked as a painter, designer, architect, typographer, writer and publisher, disparate occupations and disciplines which he combined with remarkable flair. He was intrigued by Cubism very early on and produced a number of abstract paintings in this style, but was then attracted to Dadaism and strongly influenced by Hausmann, Arp and other leading exponents. During this phase he produced montages of totally unrelated objects and incongruous fragments of junk and ephemera, such as discarded leaflets, bus tickets and used stamps torn off envelopes. After 1920 he took this notion a step further, incorporating street rubbish in enormous three-dimensional collages which he termed Merzbau ('cast-off construction'). This led to the Dadaist magazine *Merz*, which he ran from 1923 until 1932. When the Nazis came to power he fled to Norway and from there moved in 1940 to England, where he died in 1948.

MOVEMENT
Dada
OTHER WORKS
Chocolate, Spring Picture, Circle
INFLUENCES
Jean Arp, Marcel Duchamp, Raoul Hausmann

Kurt Schwitters *Born* 1887 Hanover, Germany
Painted in Germany, Norway and England
Died 1948 Ambleside, Cumbria, England

Courtesy of Private Collection/Christie's Images/© DACS 2002

Scully, Sean

ALTHOUGH BORN in Dublin, Ireland, Sean Scully was raised in London, where he studied at the Croydon College of Art (1965–68) and Newcastle University (1968–72). He continued his art education at Harvard University before settling permanently in the United States in 1975. Such a rich and varied training is reflected in his paintings, which provide an interesting blend of elements derived from Minimalism and Conceptual Art on the one hand and the Abstract Expressionism of his adopted country. This is manifest in his most characteristic works, in which the dominant features are vertical or horizontal bands of contrasting colours, generally muted shades of brown, beige and deep reds alternating with black. At first glance they may appear Minimal, but closer examination reveals the rich textures and layers of colour. Scully styles these works triptychs, and this is true in so far as they comprise three pieces of canvas whose juxtaposition is deliberately uneven. The use of a term more commonly associated with medieval religious works is a reflection of Scully's regard for the spiritual qualities of abstract painting.

MOVEMENT
Abstract Expressionism
OTHER WORKS
Paul, The Fall, White Window, Why and What
INFLUENCES
Noel Foster, Mark Rothko, Barnett Newman

Sean Scully *Born* 1945 Dublin, Ireland
Painted in London and New York

Courtesy of Christie's Images

Sekoto, Gerard

GERARD SEKOTO trained as a school teacher, and it was in the course of his training that he was introduced to painting and drawing. Although this instruction was quite rudimentary it was sufficient to launch him on an artistic career. Within a few years he gave up teaching and moved to Johannesburg to concentrate on painting full-time. His early landscapes and genre scenes drew on the everyday life of the black townships. One of these, exhibited in the South African Academy show of 1940, was purchased by the Johannesburg Art Gallery – the one and only painting by a black African artist in any South African museum for more than two decades. Sekoto went to Paris in 1947 to further his education, but settled in France where he spent the rest of life. Nevertheless, his subjects remained firmly South African, although his interpretation of them showed the influence of the various art movements with which he now came into contact, from Impressionism to Cubism and Orphism.

MOVEMENT
Black South African School
OTHER WORKS
Yellow Houses: a Street in Sophiatown, Eastwood Memories
INFLUENCES
Cézanne, Picasso, Robert Delaunay

Gerard Sekoto   *Born* 1913 South Africa
Painted in Johannesburg, Eastwood, Transvaal and Paris
Died 1993 Paris

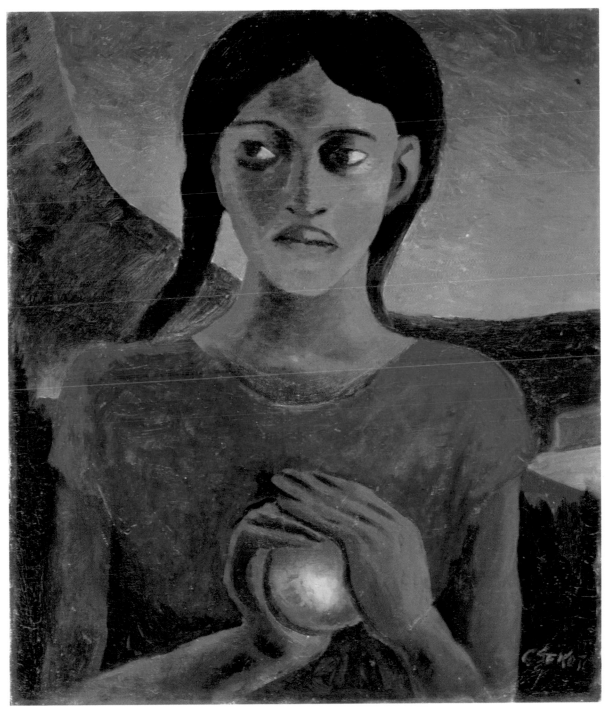

Courtesy of Johannesburg Art Gallery, South Africa/Bridgeman Art Library/© The Gerard Sekoto Foundation

GEORGES PIERRE SEURAT studied at the École des Beaux-Arts and was influenced by the precise draughtsmanship of Ingres, as well as with Chevreul's theories on colour. He combined the Classicist tradition with the newer ideas of the Impressionists. In particular, he painted in a very distinctive style using a multitude of different-coloured dots to build up the impression of the subject, much as the half-tone process or multicolour photogravure use a screen of dots of varying intensity and depth to achieve the overall image. This extremely precise method he termed Divisionism, and it was instrumental in the subsequent development of Pointillism. There is not much evidence of this technique, however, in his first major work depicting bathers at Asnières (1884), but it became almost a trademark in his later paintings. Always meticulous in the execution of his work, Seurat was also painstaking in the preparation, often spending months on preliminary sketches for each canvas.

MOVEMENT
French Impressionism
OTHER WORKS
The Can-Can, Sunday Afternoon on the Island of the Grande Jatte
INFLUENCES
Ingres, Eugène Chevreul

Georges Seurat   *Born* 1859 Paris, France
Painted in France
Died 1891 Paris

Courtesy of Private Collection/Christie's Images

Sharaku, Toshusai   Portrait of Sakata Hangoro III as Fujikawa Mizuema, 1794

NOTHING APPEARS to be known regarding the origins or early career of Toshusai Sharaku, other than that he came from a noble family and had been an actor in the Kabuki theater before taking up art. In the brief period of only 10 months in 1794–95 he produced some 159 caricatures and portraits of Kabuki actors, drawn with extraordinary power and originality, coupled with savage satirical qualities which had not been witnessed in Japanese art since the Kamakura period (1185–1333). Sharaku mastered the new technique of tinted mica backgrounds extremely effectively, so that the silhouettes of the posturing actors almost jump out at the spectator. Sharaku's harsh, uncompromising pictures shocked the public, more accustomed to the simpering beauties of Masanobu or Utamaro, and not surprisingly they were unpopular. The exaggerated features of the subjects may have given offence to the actors themselves and perhaps concerted action on their part helped bring Sharaku's enterprise to an abrupt end.

MOVEMENT
Ukiyo-e
OTHER WORKS
Otani Oniji III as Edohei, Iwai Hanshiro IV as Shigenoi
INFLUENCES
Kitagawa Utamaro, Suzuki Harunobu

Toshusai Sharaku   *Born c.* 1750 Edo (now Tokyo), Japan *Painted in* Edo *Died* 1801 Edo

Courtesy of Private Collection/Christie's Images

Shouping, Yun

A NOTABLE poet and calligrapher, Yun Shouping was second only to Wu Li among the Chinese painters who were neither orthodox nor individualist, and therefore he does not fit into any exact category. He has often been dismissed merely as a flower painter, but this does not do justice to his art as a landscape painter. Of course, more than any other artist of his period, he loved to decorate his pictures with masses of flowers, but this does not detract from the fact that his landscapes themselves are among the most serenely beautiful and perfect productions among the later Chinese artists. In his studies of flowers and plants as such, however, he was unsurpassed for the delicacy and clarity of his draughtsmanship and the care he took with his compositions. He preferred a very wet brush so that the ink flowed freely, producing a very sharp, clean-cut line. His landscape paintings are very similar to those of the four Wangs and Wu Li, but it is in his use of floral ornament that he stands out from his contemporaries.

MOVEMENT
Early Ming Period, China
OTHER WORKS
Bamboo and Old Tree, Peonies, Plum Blossoms
INFLUENCES
Wang Yuanqi, Wang Hui, Wu Li

Yun Shouping   *Born* 1633 Wujin, Jiangsu, China
Painted in Changzhou, China
Died 1690 Changzhou

Courtesy of Osaka Museum of Fine Arts, Japan/Bridgeman Art Library

Sickert, Walter

BORN IN Munich, Bavaria, Walter Richard Sickert was the son of the painter Oswald Adalbert Sickert and grandson of the painter and lithographer Johannes Sickert. With such an artistic pedigree it was almost inevitable that he should follow the family tradition. In 1868 his parents moved to London, where he later studied at the Slade School of Art and took lessons from Whistler, whose limited tonal range is reflected in much of Sickert's work. On the advice of Degas – whom he met while studying in Paris – he made detailed preliminary drawings for his paintings rather than paint from life. As a youth, Sickert had been an actor and he had a lifelong interest in the theater, reflected in many of his paintings. He was a competent all-rounder, painting portraits, rather seedy genre subjects and murky landscapes, and as a teacher he wielded enormous influence on the British artists of the early twentieth century.

MOVEMENT
British Impressionism

OTHER WORKS
Mornington Crescent Nude, La Hollandaise Nude

INFLUENCES
James McNeill Whistler, Degas

Sickert, Walter *Born* 1860 Munich, Germany
Painted in London, Dieppe, and Venice
Died 1942 Bathampton, Avon, England

Courtesy of Private Collection/Christie's Images/© Estate of Walter R. Sickert 2002. All Rights Reserved, DACS

MEXICAN PAINTER and political activist, best known for his murals. Siqueiros was born in Chihuahua, the son of a lawyer. In his youth, he became involved in the Mexican Revolution and, as a reward, was given a scholarship to study in Europe (1919–22). There he met Rivera, a fellow muralist and future rival. The revival of mural-painting was deliberate government policy, aimed at bringing art to the people. Siqueiros received a commission to decorate the Preparatoria, but work was halted by student riots and, in fact, he did not complete a mural in his homeland until 1939.

Although a late developer, Siqueiros proved hugely influential as a teacher. In 1936, he ran an experimental workshop in New York, which did much to shape the Abstract Expressionism of Jackson Pollock. The latter was particularly impressed by Siqueiros's theories about the potential of 'pictorial accidents' and his use of industrial materials. These included spray-guns, blow-torches and the pyroxylin paints used in car manufacture. In the artist's own work, these were seen to best effect in the massive *March of Humanity in Latin America* and his extraordinar, multimedia creation the *Polyforum Siqueiros*.

MOVEMENT
Mexican Muralists
OTHER WORKS
Portrait of the Bourgeoisie, The Victory of Science over Cancer
INFLUENCES
Diego Rivera, Amado de la Cueva

David Alfaro Siqueiros *Born* 1896 Mexico
Painted in Mexico, USA, Uruguay and Chile
Died 1974 Mexico City

Courtesy of Private Collection/Christie's Images © DACS 2002

Sisley, Alfred

BORN IN Paris of English parents, Alfred Sisley had a conventional art education in Paris and at first was strongly influenced by Corot. In 1862 he entered the studio of Charles Gleyre, where he was a fellow pupil with Monet and Renoir, whom he joined on sketching and painting expeditions to Fontainebleau. The range of colours employed by Sisley lightened significantly under the influence of his companions. From 1874 onwards he exhibited regularly with the Impressionists and is regarded as the painter who remained most steadfast to the aims and ideals of that movement. The vast majority of his works are landscapes, drawing on the valleys of the Loire, Seine and Thames for most of his subjects. Sisley revelled in the subtleties of cloud formations and the effects of light, especially in the darting reflection of water. Hopeless at the business aspects of his art and largely dependent on his father for money, Sisley spent his last years in great poverty. Like Van Gogh, interest in his paintings only developed after his death.

MOVEMENT
Impressionism
OTHER WORKS
Wooden Bridge at Argenteuil, Snow at Veneux-Nadon
INFLUENCES
Corot, Paul Renoir, Monet, Charles Gleyre

Alfred Sisley   *Born* 1839, Paris, France
Painted in France and England
Died 1899 Moret-sur-Loing, France

Courtesy of Private Collection/Christie's Images

Smith, Jaune Quick-to-see

Modern Times on the Rez, *c*.1992-93

JAUNE SMITH derives her unusual name from her Shoshoni grandmother, being herself also of Cree and Métis descent. She followed the Famous American art course in high school then took degrees in fine art at Olympic College, Bremerton, Framingham State College and the University of New Mexico. Since the 1960s she has lived at Corrales, New Mexico, where she paints in a wide range of media, though preferring oils and acrylics. Her paintings, which she describes as 'nomad art' vary enormously in subject from figures and genre studies to landscapes and semi-abstract works. One of the most articulate of Native American artists, she emerged in the 1980s as one of the foremost Native American artists. Her paintings reflect a long-term commitment to feminist issues and the problems of the indigenous peoples of North America.

MOVEMENT
Native American School
OTHER WORKS
Ghost Dance Dress
INFLUENCES
Miró, Kandinsky, Paul Klee

Jaune Quick-to-see Smith   *Born* 1940
St Ignatius Flathead Reservation, Montana, USA
Painted in New Mexico, USA

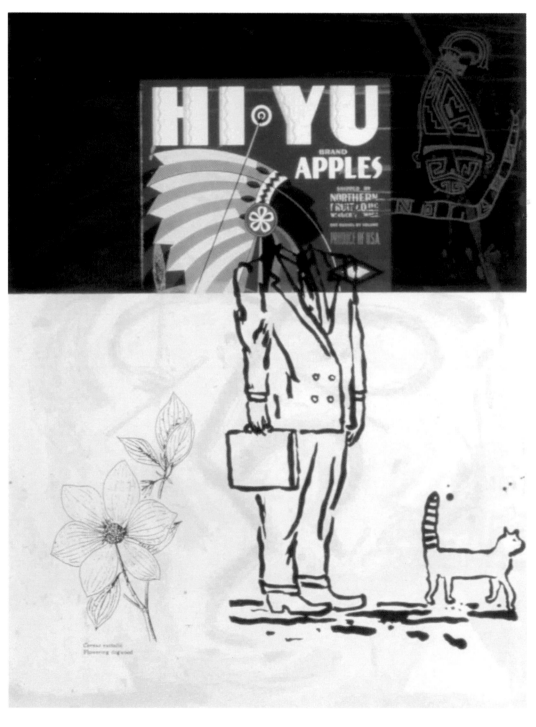

Courtesy of Contemporary American Indian Art Collection, Art Museum of Missoula. Donated by the Artist/© The Artist

TAWARAYA SOTATSU operated a print shop in Kyoto that specialized in painted fans, but in 1621 he was commissioned to paint a set of sliding screens depicting pine trees and this appears to have been a major turning point in his career. Later he was closely associated with Ogata Korin in the Rinpa School, but as a result his own contribution to the development of Japanese art in the early seventeenth century was largely overlooked until relatively recently. A pair of two-fold screens depicting the gods of thunder and wind, however, reveals quite a radical departure from the style of the Momoyama painters, much bolder and ascetic, with greater emphasis on asymmetry and overall simplicity, coupled with greater use of colour. Rejecting the styles imported from China, he went back to earlier Japanese traditions both in subject matter and treatment. He also collaborated with Honami Koetsu in founding Takagamine, an artists' colony which reinvigorated Japanese art.

MOVEMENT
Rinpa School, Japan
OTHER WORKS
Deer Scroll, Zen Priest Choka, The Tale of Genji
INFLUENCES
Ogata Korin, Honami Koetsu

Tawaraya Sotatsu *Born* 1576 Kyoto, Japan
Painted in Kyoto
Died 1643 Kyoto

Courtesy of British Library. London, UK/Bridgeman Art Library

Soutine, Chaim

BORN AT Smilovich, Russian Poland (now Belarus), Chaim Soutine studied in Vilnius and travelled to Paris in 1911, where he was befriended by fellow Russian Jew Marc Chagall. Modigliani introduced him to the Expressionist school in Paris and he, in turn, exerted an exotic influence on its development, adding a dash of Fauvism and the German approach to Expressionism. Soutine delighted in painting the carcasses of animals, much to the disgust and annoyance of neighbours, who habitually complained of the stench of rotting flesh that emanated from his studio. Apart from studies of dead birds and decomposing sides of beef, Soutine painted portraits whose emaciated features and deathly expression bear a gruesome resemblance to the living dead of Belsen and Auschwitz. Soutine, who continued to live in Paris after the fall of France, managed to evade deportation to the camps and died in Paris in 1943.

MOVEMENT

French Expressionism

OTHER WORKS

The Boy in Black, Pageboy at Maxim's, Portrait of Modigliani

INFLUENCES

Emil Nolde, Matisse, Chagall

Chaim Soutine   *Born* 1893 Smilovich, Russia

Painted in Paris

Died 1943 Paris

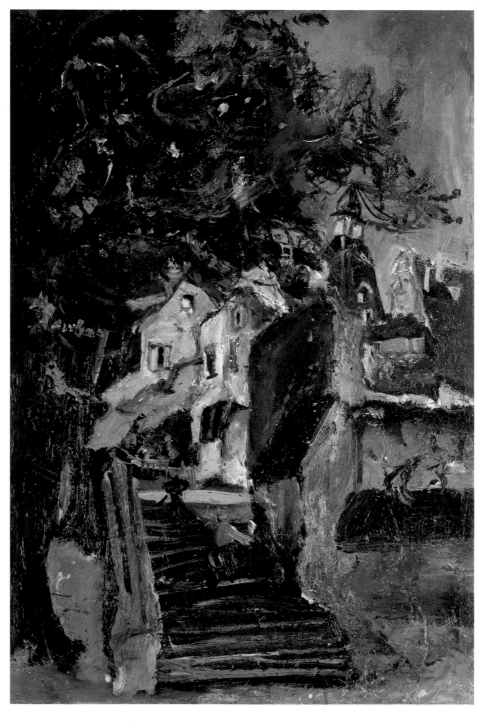

Courtesy of Private Collection/Christie's Images/© ADAGP, Paris and DACS, London 2002

Spencer, Sir Stanley

STANLEY SPENCER spent most of his life in the Berkshire village of Cookham, which provided him with most of his inspiration. He studied at the Slade School of Art in London from 1909 to 1912 but appears not to have been affected by any of the avant-garde developments in that period. Apart from military service in World War I, and a period during World War II spent on Clydeside recording the toil of shipyards, he remained very close to his roots – a familiar sight in Cookham, painting or sketching. Often dismissed as an eccentric, he worked outside the artistic mainstream, but inevitably some trends in art found a reflection in his paintings, notably his use of distorted anatomy and space. A profoundly religious man, his paintings often have biblical connotations, although events such as the Resurrection are placed in the context of Cookham or Clydeside. He covered his enormous canvasses with drawings of the subjects, which were then painted over. He was knighted shortly before he died.

MOVEMENT
Modern English School
OTHER WORKS
The Resurrection, The Crucifixion, Self-Portrait with Patricia
INFLUENCES
Pre-Raphaelites

Sir Stanley Spencer *Born* 1891 England
Painted in Cookham and Port Glasgow, Scotland
Died 1959 Cookham

Courtesy of Private Collection/Christie's Images/© Estate Stanley Spencer 2002. All Rights Reserved, DACS

Stella, Frank

FRANK PHILIP STELLA studied at Phillips Academy in Andover, Maine (1950–54) and Princeton University (1954–58). After university he went to New York City, where he worked as a house painter, an experience which influenced his art. He began painting in the Minimalist style in 1959, using a broad brush in order to eliminate the brushstrokes typical of art, and created works which were often virtually solid blocks of black, relieved only by a few contrasting stripes. Later he evolved polychrome patterns of straight lines or concentric rings and curves using the same technique of eliminating brushstrokes, which would have detracted from the overall effect. These paintings have a decidedly Art Deco character, reflecting Stella's admiration of the Bauhaus designs of the 1920s. His method is to cut templates and assemble them in reliefs painted in day-glo and metallic paints. His more recent work, in fact, verges on the sculptural, with its multicoloured, three-dimensional effects.

MOVEMENTS
Minimalism, Abstract Expressionism
OTHER WORKS
Agbatana II, Tuxedo Park Junction, Harewa, Jarama II
INFLUENCES
Josef Albers, Gwen John

Frank Stella   *Born* 1936 Malden, Massachusetts, USA
Painted in New York

Courtesy of Musee d'Art et d'Industrie, St. Etienne, France/Bridgeman Giraudon/© ARS, NY and DACS, London 2002

RAISED IN the American Midwest, Clyfford Still studied art at Spokane University, Washington, graduating in 1933 when the United States was still recovering from the Depression. Eschewing the social realism of his contemporaries, he strove to evolve his own distinctive style, embracing elements of Biomorphism in which organic forms predominated. In 1941 he settled in San Francisco and subsequently taught at the California School of Fine Arts (1946–50). During this period he emerged as one of the leading exponents of Abstract Expressionism. Heavily influenced by Barnett Newman and Mark Rothko, he favoured large canvasses in which a single colour predominated; the variations in colour, form and content being largely confined to the periphery. Interest and variety in the principal colour was imparted by its rich texture and brushwork. Many of his works were either completely untitled or only given the most cryptic of titles. Thus it was mainly left to the viewer to divine the significance of the detail at the edges of his canvas, although Still himself was a past-master in the art of making pretentious statements that allegedly explained the metaphor of his work.

MOVEMENT
Abstract Expressionism
OTHER WORKS
Untitled, No 1, Untitled 1953
INFLUENCES
Barnett Newman, Mark Rothko

Clyfford Still   *Born* 1904
Painted in Spokane, Washington, San Francisco, California, USA
Died 1980, New Windsor, Maryland, USA

Courtesy of Peggy Guggenheim Foundation, Venice, Italy/Bridgeman Art Library

Streeton, Sir Arthur

ARTHUR ERNEST STREETON studied at the National Gallery School in Melbourne and worked as a lithographer. In 1885 Tom Roberts returned from Europe and together with Frederick McCubbin and Streeton, founded the Heidelberg School of artists, who painted from nature. Later Streeton founded a permanent artists' colony at Eaglemont, where he perfected his techniques of landscape painting, noted for its realism and sense of atmosphere. He travelled extensively in Egypt and Europe and worked in London (1898–1906), where he studied the works of Turner and Constable and exhibited at the Royal Academy. He was back in Australia in 1906–07, then worked in England and became a war artist on the Western Front. From 1919 onwards he lived mainly in Australia, travelling all over the country and painting prolifically. He was knighted in 1937. As well as landscapes he painted powerful scenes of men at work, making a major contribution to the art of social realism.

MOVEMENT
Modern Australian School
OTHER WORKS
Still Glides the Stream, Fire's On
INFLUENCES
Turner, Constable, Philip Wilson Steer

Sir Arthur Streeton   *Born* 1867 Australia
Painted in Australia and Europe
Died 1943 Olinda, Victoria, Australia

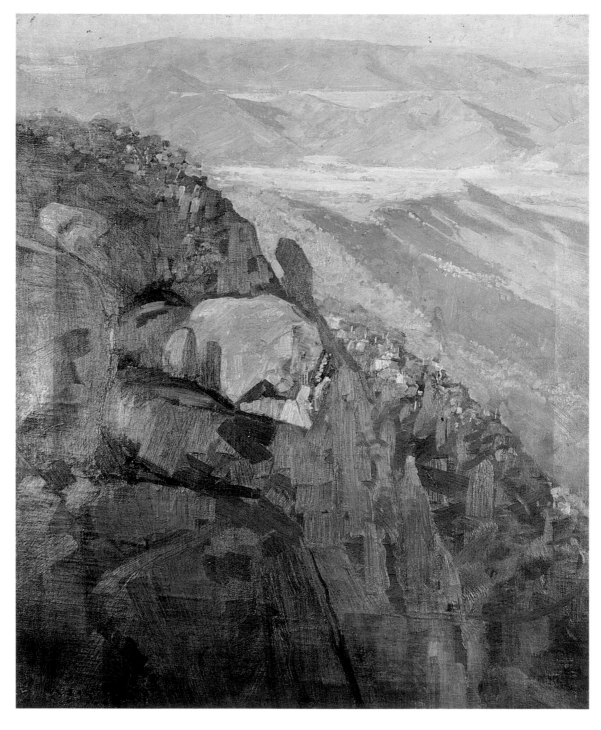

Courtesy of The Art Archive

Sugai, Kumi

KUMI SUGAI received his early art education in his home town of Kobe, Japan, but after military service in World War II he resumed his studies and travelled to Europe, where he eventually settled in Paris and worked from 1952 onwards as a painter, print-maker and sculptor. After a period producing conventional oils on canvas he concentrated on prints, combining the traditional techniques of the *ukiyo-e* school of Japan with Western ideas and modern materials. Over a period of three decades he produced over 400 different prints. From about 1962 there was a noticeable change in his style, as he adopted the hard-edge geometric imagery of Max Pechstein, a marked contrast to the softer style of his earlier prints, reflecting the influence of the great Japanese masters of the eighteenth and nineteenth centuries.

MOVEMENT
Modern Japanese School
OTHER WORKS
The Flying Deer, Devil's Chain, Alea, Printemps
INFLUENCES
Ukiyo-e, Max Pechstein

Kumi Sugai   *Born* 1919 Kobe, Japan
Painted in Kobe, Tokyo, and Paris
Died 1996 Paris

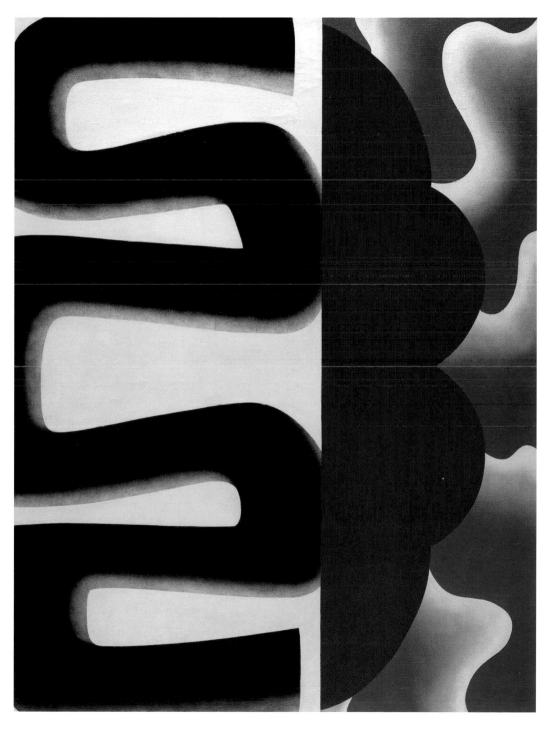

Courtesy of Private Collection/Christie's Images

Sutherland, Graham

GRAHAM VIVIAN SUTHERLAND originally intended to become a railway engineer, but switched courses and studied art at Goldsmiths College in London. Influenced by the visionary artist Samuel Palmer, he worked mainly as an etcher, but the market for prints collapsed in the aftermath of the stock-market crash of 1929, and as a result Sutherland took up painting instead. A visit to south-west Wales in 1934 introduced him to the astonishing diversity of the Pembrokeshire scenery which would provide endless subject matter for his later paintings.

Sutherland's great landscapes combined elements of the romantic with the abstract. From 1941 until 1945 he was employed as an official war artist, and in the postwar period he produced a number of memorable (if occasionally controversial) portraits, including that of Sir Winston Churchill (1955). True to his original training, Sutherland also produced posters, ceramic designs and textiles, the best known being the extraordinary tapestry *Christ in Majesty*, which he executed for the new Coventry Cathedral in 1962.

MOVEMENT
Modern English Landscape School
OTHER WORKS
Red Landscape, Entrance to a Lane, Devastation: House in Wales
INFLUENCES
Samuel Palmer, Picasso, Odilon Redon

Graham Sutherland   *Born* 1903 England
Painted in England and Wales
Died 1980 London

Courtesy of Private Collection/Christie's Images

Tagore, Rabindranath

BORN AT Calcutta of a princely family, Rabindranath Tagore was educated privately in India, then sent to England to study law, but before 1900 he began writing poetry and essays for Bengali periodicals. In 1901 he established the Santineketan at Bolpur, an unconventional educational institute. A prolific writer of poetry, novels and plays, he was awarded the Nobel Prize for literature in 1913 and was knighted in 1915. Tagore took up painting in 1929, but in the decade preceding his death he produced a number of major works which influenced a later generation of Indian artists. Like his writings, his paintings are suffused by a visionary quality. Although his work is executed in a Western style, it contains elements derived from Bengali art, a delicate blend of East and West. He worked mainly in ink on paper, building up an image from lines, doodles, smudges and blots with minimal use of secondary colours. His work suggests the influence of Symbolism.

MOVEMENT
Symbolism
OTHER WORKS
Untitled Portraits
INFLUENCES
Bengali art

Rabindranath Tagore *Born* 1861 Calcutta, India
Painted in Bengal, India
Died 1941 Calcutta

Courtesy of National Museum of India, New Delhi, India/Bridgeman Giraudon/Lauros

Tanguy, Yves

GOING TO sea as a teenager, and later serving in the French Army, Yves Tanguy did not take up painting until his return to Paris in 1922. Without any formal training, he was influenced by the work of Giorgio de Chirico and joined the Surrealists in 1925, subsequently concentrating on that style known as Biomorphism because its images were derived from living organisms. Inevitably, Tanguy's paintings in the ensuing period drew heavily on memories of naval and military service. In 1939 he immigrated to the United States, where he married fellow-artist Kay Sage and settled in Woodbury, Connecticut. In his last years his work took on a darker character, suggestive of dream sequences which reflected his fascination with the Freudian theories of psychoanalysis. His paintings were non-figurative, inhabited by small objects, often boney-like but defying description and suggestive of some other world.

MOVEMENTS
Biomorphism, Surrealism
OTHER WORKS
Dehors, The Invisible, The Rapidity of Sleep
INFLUENCES
Giorgio de Chirico, Salvador Dalí

Yves Tanguy   *Born* 1900, Paris, France
Painted in Paris, France and Woodbury, Connecticut, USA
Died 1955, Woodbury

Courtesy of Private Collection/Christie's Images/© ARS, NY and DACS, London, 2002

HENRY OSSAWA TANNER was educated in Philadelphia, where his father was bishop of the African Methodist Church. Against strong parental opposition he decided to pursue a career in art, enrolling at the Pennsylvania Academy of Fine Arts and studying under Thomas Eakins, who also taught him photography. In 1888 Tanner moved to Atlanta, Georgia and opened a photographic studio, but the business failed and he scraped a living as a part-time art teacher, supplementing his meagre salary by painting portraits.

In 1891 he moved to Paris where he continued his studies at the Académie Julien, and later travelled round the Middle East, gaining material for his religious paintings. He continued to live mainly in Paris, working for the Red Cross in World War I and becoming a Chevalier of the Legion d'Honneur.

MOVEMENT
Modern American School
OTHER WORKS
Daniel in the Lions' Den, The Disciples of Emmaus
INFLUENCES
Thomas Eakins, Benjamin Constant, Jean-Paul Laurens

Henry Ossawa Tanner   *Born* 1859 USA
Painted in USA, France and Middle East
Died 1937 Paris, France

Courtesy of Private Collection/Christie's Images

Tanning, Dorothea

DOROTHEA TANNING worked as a librarian in her home town of Galesburg, Illinois. In 1930 she went to work in Chicago and attended a two-week course of evening classes in art at the Academy of Fine Art, before going to New York in 1936, where she found employment as a commercial artist. Her earliest paintings drew on childhood nostalgia interpreted in a surreal manner, and this brought her to the attention of the American Surrealists. In 1946 she married Max Ernst, the German Dadaist then living in exile in the USA, and together they settled in France, where she worked as a painter, graphic artist and designer of theatrical sets and costumes. Tanning's later work has a more fully rounded character but still essentially explores the female psyche and sexuality through the medium of dreams. Her paintings often combine a superficial childhood innocence with rather disturbing sexual undertones and morbid symbolism.

MOVEMENT
Surrealism
OTHER WORKS
Born A Little Night Music, A Very Happy Picture, A Family Portrait
INFLUENCES
Max Ernst

Dorothea Tanning   *Born* 1910 Galesburg, Illinois, USA
Painted in Chicago, New York and Paris

Courtesy of Private Collection/Christie's Images/© ADAGP, Paris and DACS, London 2002

ANTONI TÀPIES studied law in Barcelona in 1943–46 but then gave up his studies to concentrate on painting, in which he was almost entirely self-taught. He became a founder member of the Catalan group of avant-garde writers and artists known as Dau al Set ('Seven on the Die'). His paintings reflect a diversity of influences, from the abstract radicalism of Catalonia in the Civil War period to the philosophy of the Surrealists and the lyrical qualities of Robert Motherwell and Joan Miro. He had his first one-man show in America in 1953 and thereafter made an impact on the international scene, winning many prizes. Since 1955 he has concentrated on 'matter' painting, influenced by such French artists as Fautrier. At first this consisted of mixing paints and varnish with unusual substances such as marble dust, pieces of cloth, straw and strips of metal. Taking this to its logical conclusion he eventually replaced canvas with solid objects, as in his 'Desk with Straw'.

MOVEMENT
Modern Spanish School

OTHER WORKS
Violet Grey with Wrinkles, Perforated Body, Peintre Grise et Verte

INFLUENCES
Alberto Burri, Robert Motherwell, Miró, Jean Fautrier

Antoni Tàpies *Born* 1923 Barcelona, Spain
Painted in Barcelona

Courtesy of Private Collection/Christie's Images/© Foundation Antoni Tapies, Barcelona/ADAGP, Paris and DACS, London 2002

HENDRICK TERBRUGGHEN studied in Utrecht and in around 1612 went to Italy, where he was influenced by the paintings of Caravaggio and Lorenzo Lotto. Returning to the Netherlands in 1615 he settled in Utrecht, where he built up a reputation for his religious and genre paintings. He and Gerrit van Honthorst were mainly responsible for importing to the Netherlands the techniques of chiaroscuro and the dramatic use of light and shade which they had seen in Rome. Terbrugghen made a thorough study of anatomy, which he put to good advantage in his paintings and this, with his attention to detail in such matters as clothing and drapery, brought a new realism to Dutch painting. Dutch paintings in the early seventeenth century tended to have some underlying allegorical concept and it may be that *The Flute Player*, Terbrugghen's most famous work, executed towards the end of his career, was meant to symbolize Music.

MOVEMENT
Utrecht School
OTHER WORKS
Jacob and Laban
INFLUENCES
Lorenzo Lotto, Caravaggio

Hendrick Terbrugghen *Born c.* 1588 Holland
Painted in Utrecht, Holland
Died 1629 Utrecht

Courtesy of Private Collection/Christie's Images

WAYNE THIEBAUD originally worked as a sign-painter and later a freelance cartoonist in New York before turning to fine art in 1949. His expertise in his earlier vocations stood him in good stead, for his paintings are both witty and executed with a clarity and deftness that make them instantly recognizable. His reputation has been built largely on the series of paintings of American junk food, pies, cakes, sweets, ice-cream and other delicacies, which often strike a nostalgic note but are invariably presented in a humorously deadpan manner. He injects realism by laying on the paint in thick slabs so that the icing or frosting on cakes looks good enough to eat. More recently he has painted figures of women, harshly lit in artificial light or the bright sunlight of California where he now lives, but here again he incorporates a wide range of minor objects, all painted against severely plain backgrounds.

MOVEMENT
Pop Art
OTHER WORKS
Refrigerator Pies, Woman and Cosmetics, Various Cakes
INFLUENCES
Pierre Bonnard, Man Ray, Edward Ruscha

Wayne Thiebaud   *Born* 1920 Mesa, Arizona, USA
Painted in New York, Sacramento and San Francisco

Courtesy of Private Collection/Christie's Images/© DACS, London VAGA, New York 2002

Thomas, Alma

ALMA THOMAS moved with her family to Washington, DC in 1906 following race riots in the South. She came from a black professional, middle-class family and trained as a kindergarten teacher. After a spell in Wilmington, Delaware she returned to Washington in 1921 and became the first art graduate of Howard University. She taught art at Shaw Junior High School until her retirement in 1959. A spell in New York City, taking a teacher's postgraduate course at Columbia, brought her into contact with avant-garde art, but it was not until 1949 that she took a painting course at American University, and only when she retired in her sixties did she take up painting seriously. In the last decade of her life she painted prolifically in watercolours and acrylic, emerging as one of the greatest colourists of her generation. Always independent, she did not conform to any particular style but used colour in her own distinctive manner.

MOVEMENT
Abstract Art
OTHER WORKS
Pinks of Cherry Blossom, Light Blue Nursery
INFLUENCES
Kandinsky

Alma Thomas   *Born* 1891 Columbia, Georgia
Painted in Washington, DC
Died 1978 Washington, DC

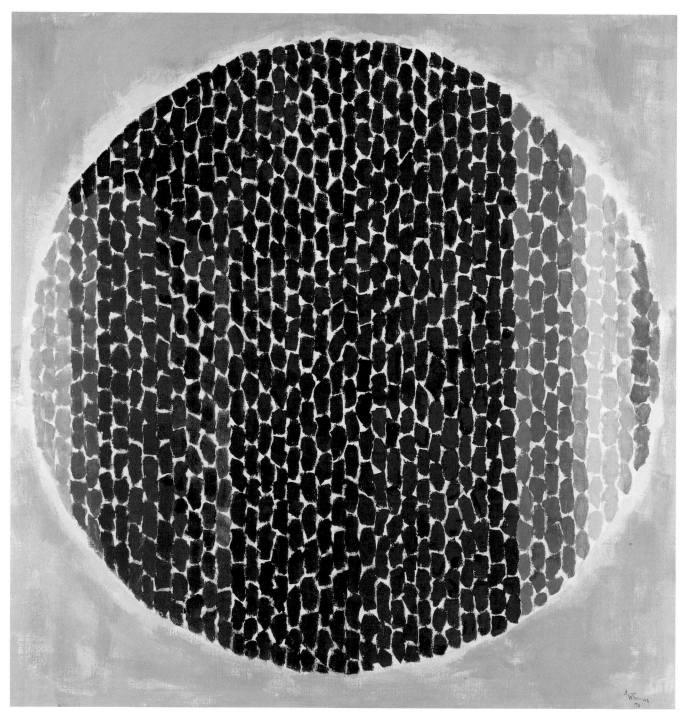

© Smithsonian American Art Museum, Washington, DC / Art Resource, NY

THOMAS JOHN THOMSON originally worked as an engraver and draughtsman at Grip Limited in Toronto, illustrating books and periodicals, and it was not until 1906 that he took up painting seriously. While working at Grip he was encouraged by co-workers J. E. H. MacDonald and Arthur Lismer to develop his painting. Other artists who were subsequently employed as graphic designers at Grip included Frederick Varley, Frank Johnston and Franklin Carmichael, who all made their name as painters; never before or since has any commercial firm employed such a talented group.

While many of his younger colleagues became official war artists, Thomson remained behind, but it was his tragic death in mysterious circumstances – drowned near Wapomeo island in Canoe Lake in 1917 – which had a major impact on the post-war development of Canadian art. His death shocked his friends but increased their determination to paint Canada their way. A. Y. Jackson summed this up when he wrote, 'he was the guide, the interpreter, and we the guests partaking of his hospitality so generously given'.

MOVEMENT
Modern Canadian School
OTHER WORKS
Pine Island, Snow in the Woods, Sunrise
INFLUENCES
A. Y. Jackson, J. E. H. MacDonald, Arthur Lismer

Tom Thomson *Born* 1877 Ontario, Canada
Painted in Canada
Died 1917 Wapomeo Island and Canoe Lake, Ontario

© National Gallery of Canada, Ottawa Purchased 1918

Tintoretto

BORN JACOPO ROBUSTI, he derived his nickname, meaning 'little dyer', from his father's trade. He was very briefly a pupil of Titian (who is said to have been jealous of the boy's talents) and though largely self-taught, was influenced by his master as well as Michelangelo and Sansovino. Apart from two trips to Mantua he spent his entire working life in Venice, painting religious subjects and contemporary portraits. His most ambitious project was the series of 50 paintings for the Church and School of San Rocco, but his fame rests on the spectacular *Paradise* (1588), a huge work crammed with figures. He was a master of dark tones illumined by adroit gleams of light. Three of his children became artists, including his daughter Marietta, known as La Tintoretta. His output was phenomenal and he painted with great rapidity and sureness of brushstrokes, earning him a second nickname of 'Il Furioso'.

MOVEMENT
Venetian School

OTHER WORKS
The Annunciation, The Last Supper, The Nine Muses

INFLUENCES
Michelangelo, Titian, Sansovino

Tintoretto *Born* 1518 Venice, Italy
Painted in Venice and Mantua
Died 1594 Venice

Courtesy of Private Collection/Christie's Images

Titian (Tiziano Vecellio)   Venus & Adonis, 1555–60

THE GREATEST and most versatile artist of the Venetian Renaissance, Titian excelled equally at portraiture, religious pictures and mythological scenes. Born in the Dolomite region, he arrived in Venice as a boy and was apprenticed to a mosaicist. Turning to painting, he entered the studio of Giovanni Bellini, before joining forces with Giorgione. After Giorgione's premature death (1510), Titian's star rose quickly. He gained a major commission for frescoes in Padua (1511) and, in 1516, was appointed as the official painter of the Venetian Republic.

This honor enhanced Titian's international reputation and, soon, offers of work began to flow in from the princely rulers of Ferrara, Urbino and Mantua. The painter did not always accept these commissions, as he was notoriously reluctant to travel, but some patrons could not be refused. The most distinguished of these was the Emperor Charles V. After their initial meeting in 1529, Titian was appointed Court Painter in 1533 and given the rank of Count Palatine. In 1548, he worked at the Imperial Court at Augsburg, and his services were also prized by Charles's successor, Philip II.

MOVEMENT
Renaissance
OTHER WORKS
Bacchus and Ariadne, Man with a Glove, Sacred and Profane Love
INFLUENCES
Bellini, Giorgione

Titian *Born c.* 1485
Painted in Italy and Germany
Died 1576

Courtesy of Private Collection/Christie's Images

Tjapaltjarri, Clifford Possum

CLIFFORD POSSUM TJAPALTJARRI had no formal art training in the conventional Western sense, but he inherited an Aboriginal artistic and spiritual tradition stretching back thousands of years. He belongs to the group of Aboriginal artists known as the Western Desert Painters, who have adapted their tribal art forms to the Western world only in so far as they use westernized materials and techniques, instead of wood, bark, sand or indigenous dyes. Tjapaltjarri works in acrylic paints on canvas, but otherwise much of his work clings steadfastly to the imagery and expression practiced by his ancestors. A large part of his oeuvre centres on the Dreamtime, the sacred world of the tribe's ancestral spirits, whom the Aborigines regard as the creators of all living things. Superficially, his paintings may seem abstract, but they are actually a carefully constructed and systematized map or chart of a particular tribal or community site.

MOVEMENT
Australian Aboriginal
OTHER WORKS
Kangaroo Dreaming
INFLUENCES
Tribal art

Clifford Possum Tjapaltjarri *Born* 1932
Nabberby Creek, Central Australia
Painted in Central Australia

Courtesy of Corbally Stourton Contemporary Art, London, UK/Bridgeman Art Library © Aborginal Artists Agency, Sydney

HENRI MARIE RAYMOND de Toulouse-Lautrec-Monfa was the scion of one of France's oldest noble families who had been rulers of Navarre in the Middle Ages. Henri was a chronically sick child whose legs, broken at the age of 14, stopped growing and left him physically deformed. In 1882 he went to Paris to study art and settled in Montmartre, where he sketched and painted the cabaret performers, can-can dancers, clowns, barmaids and prostitutes, although occasionally he painted more conventional subjects as well. He played a prominent part in raising the lithographic poster to a recognized art form. He worked rapidly and feverishly from life, seldom using posed models. He belonged to the artistic milieu in which Impressionists and Post-Impressionists mingled and both schools left their mark on his work. Alcoholism led to a complete breakdown and confinement in a sanatorium (1899) but he recovered sufficiently for a last frenzied bout of hard work.

MOVEMENT
Post-Impressionism

OTHER WORKS
At the Moulin Rouge, The Bar, At the Races, Jane Avril

INFLUENCES
Degas

Henri de Toulouse-Lautrec   *Born* 1864
France *Painted in* Paris
Died 1901 Paris

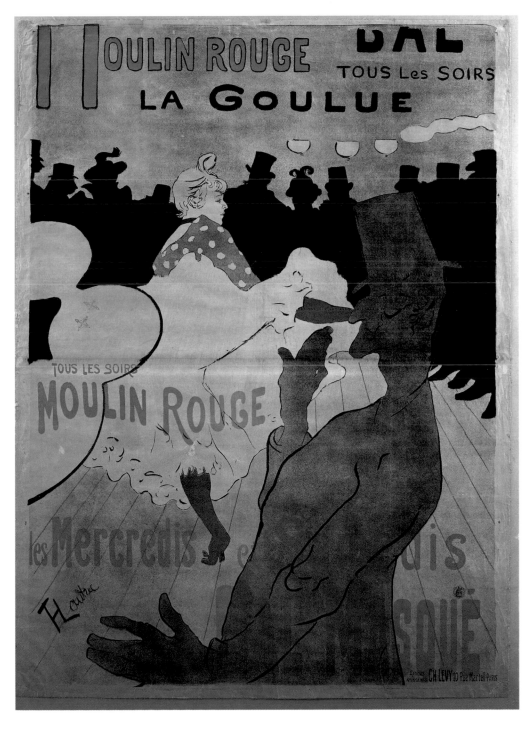

Courtesy of Christie's Images

Tour, Georges De La

BORN AT Vic-sur-Seille, France, in 1593, Georges de la Tour established himself at Luneville about 1620, where he received many important commissions from the Duke of Lorraine. He also presented one of his paintings to King Louis XIII, who was so enchanted by it that he decided to remove paintings by all other artists from his private apartments. De la Tour concentrated on religious subjects, many of which were rather sombre with large areas of dark shadows and muted colours subtly illumined by a

candle to create dark, dramatic and essentially realistic scenes. In this regard he was heavily influenced by Caravaggio and was, indeed, the leading French exponent of his particular brand of naturalism, although eschewing Caravaggio's penchant for the macabre. De la Tour's paintings exude serenity in keeping with their subject matter. Like his paintings, however, he languished in obscurity for many years and was not rediscovered until 1915.

MOVEMENT
French School
OTHER WORKS
St Peter Denying Christ
INFLUENCES
Caravaggio

Georges de la Tour   *Born* 1593 France
Painted in Luneville and Paris
Died 1652 Paris

Courtesy of Musee des Beaux-Arts, Rennes, France/Bridgeman Art Library

Traylor, Bill

ONE OF the earliest artists belonging to the American Vernacular and Outsider tradition, without any training or outside influences whatsoever, Bill Traylor was born a slave and for many years after Emancipation continued to work as a field hand on a plantation in rural Alabama. Later he moved to Montgomery as an unskilled factory worker and latterly was a homeless down-and-out, an outsider both artistically and in reality, sleeping rough and existing on welfare hand-outs. He took up drawing and painting in 1939 and in three years he produced over 1,800 pictures, executed on cardboard. His technique developed rapidly from simple geometric shapes to complex abstract constructions inhabited by tiny moving figures. He drew on his memories and imagination as well as keenly observing the people and scenes around him. Although his work had come to the notice of the Museum of Modern Art in 1941, it is only within more recent years that it has been recognized as one of the major triumphs of self-taught art.

MOVEMENT
American Vernacular and Outsider School
OTHER WORKS
Fish, Cat, Man, Plant Pot, Dog and Figures
INFLUENCES
None

Bill Traylor   *Born c.* 1854 Benton, Alabama, USA
Painted in Montgomery, Alabama
Died 1946 Montgomery, Alabama

© Smithsonian American Art Museum, Washington, DC / Art Resource, NY

JOSEPH MALLORD WILLIAM TURNER entered the Royal Academy School in 1789 and began exhibiting the following year. He travelled all over England, filling sketch-books with drawings of scenery and landmarks which would later provide the raw material for his oils and watercolours. He collaborated with Girtin on a three-year watercolour project but later turned to oils. After his first trip to Italy (1819) his paintings showed a marked Classical influence and following his second (1829) his art entered its greatest phase with paintings such as *Rain, Steam and Speed* (1844), which were the precursors of Impressionism. A solitary, rather reclusive man who never married, Turner bequeathed over 300 oils and some 20,000 watercolours and drawings to the nation. A prolific artist, he ranks with Constable as one of the greatest British landscape painters of all time and his career marks a turning-point in the development of modern British art.

MOVEMENT
English School
OTHER WORKS
The Fighting Téméraire, Norham Castle, Sunrise with Sea Monsters
INFLUENCES
Claude Lorraine

J. M. W. Turner *Born* 1775 London, England
Painted in England
Died 1851 London

Courtesy of Private Collection/Christie's Images

Uccello, Paolo

The Flood and the Subsidence of the Waters, 1447–8

PAOLO DI DONO acquired his nickname from his love of painting birds. At the age of 10 he was apprenticed to Lorenzo Ghiberti, who was then working on the doors of the Florentine Baptistry, but it is not known from whom Paolo received his instruction in painting. He went to Venice in 1425 and worked on mosaics. In 1433 he painted the figure of Sir John Hawkswood, a fourteenth century knight errant, for Florence cathedral, the first equestrian painting of the Renaissance. Most of his work consisted of frescoes, few of which have survived intact, but he also painted tempera on pane, sufficient of which have come down to posterity to reveal Uccello as a master of perspective and foreshortening. He also made a major contribution to the art of showing natural objects in three-dimensional space.

MOVEMENT
Florentine School
OTHER WORKS
The Battle of San Romano, St George and the Dragon
INFLUENCES
Donatello

Paolo Uccello *Born* 1397 Pratovecchio, Italy
Painted in Florence and Venice
Died 1475 Florence

Courtesy of Santa Maria Novella, Florence, Italy/Bridgeman Art Library

Utamaro, Kitagawa

KITAGAWA NEBSUYOSHI received a conventional art training but raised it to an entirely new level, earning for him the epithet of *Ukiyo-ye Chuko-no-so* ('great master of the popular school'). A versatile artist who painted flowers, birds, fish and insects in meticulous detail as well as great sweeping landscapes, he specialized in portraits and genre scenes involving the ladies of the court. No one ever surpassed him in the precise delineation of faces, figures and flowing robes that capture the gracefulness and elegance of the courtesans and professional beauties of the Shogunate at the height of its prestige. Though he painted in oils, his fame rests mainly on the colour prints, which had immense appeal not only for the Japanese but also for the Dutch community at Nagasaki, whence his work was brought to Europe and had a tremendous influence on many artists of the nineteenth century.

MOVEMENT
Ukiyo-e
OTHER WORKS
Lovers, Girl Playing Glass Flute, Women Working in the Kitchen
INFLUENCES
Hishikawa Moronobu, Ando Hiroshige

Kitagawa Utamaro *Born* 1753 Kawayoye near Edo (now Tokyo), Japan *Painted in* Edo
Died 1806 Edo

Courtesy of Private Collection/Christie's Images

Utrillo, Maurice

THE ILLEGIMITATE son of the painter Suzanne Valadon, Maurice Utrillo led an extremely Bohemian life. Despite alcoholism and drug addiction, however, he was a prolific painter, turning out vast numbers of Parisian street scenes, especially in and around Montmartre, where he lived. Except what he learned from his mother, he had no formal art training and, in fact, only took up painting as a form of therapy during one of his periodic spells in a detoxification clinic. He started off by making copies of Parisian picture postcards

and this is reflected in the meticulous, almost photographic, quality of all his work. He began exhibiting in 1909 and thereafter was closely associated with the Impressionists, especially Camille Pissarro, although Utrillo left his own indelible mark – 'a wild thirst for reality' was how he succinctly described it himself. In his 'white period' (1909–16) his palette consisted of very light colours, but thereafter they became much deeper and richer in tone. A reformed alcoholic, Utrillo became extremely devout in old age.

MOVEMENT
Impressionism
OTHER WORKS
La Place du Tertre, Street in a Paris Suburb with Trees
INFLUENCES
Suzanne Valadon, Camille Pissarro

Maurice Utrillo   *Born* 1883 Paris, France
Painted in Paris
Died 1955 Dax, France

Courtesy of Private Collection/Christie's Images © ADAGP, Paris and DACS, London 2002

Van der Goes, Hugo

HUGO VAN DER GOES was the Dean of the painters' guild in that city from 1467 to 1475, before retiring to the monastery of Rouge Cloître near Brussels, where he continued to execute religious paintings. The outstanding Flemish artist of his generation, his reputation rests mainly on a single work: the magnificent altarpiece which was commissioned by Tommaso Portinari for the chapel in the hospital of Santa Maria at Florence. It is a vast triptych, crammed with figures, the great centrepiece representing the Adoration of the Shepherds, while the wings portray Portinari and his sons praying under the protection of Saints Anthony and Matthew and Protinari's wife and daughters on the other, protected by Saints Margaret and Mary Magdalen. A number of easel paintings have been attributed to this artist, while he also designed stained-glass windows and frescoes.

MOVEMENT
Flemish School

OTHER WORKS
Fall and Deposition, Adoration of the Magi, Death of the Virgin

INFLUENCES
Rogier van der Weyden

Hugo van der Goes *Born c.* 1440 Ghent, Belgium
Painted in Ghent
Died 1482 Ghent

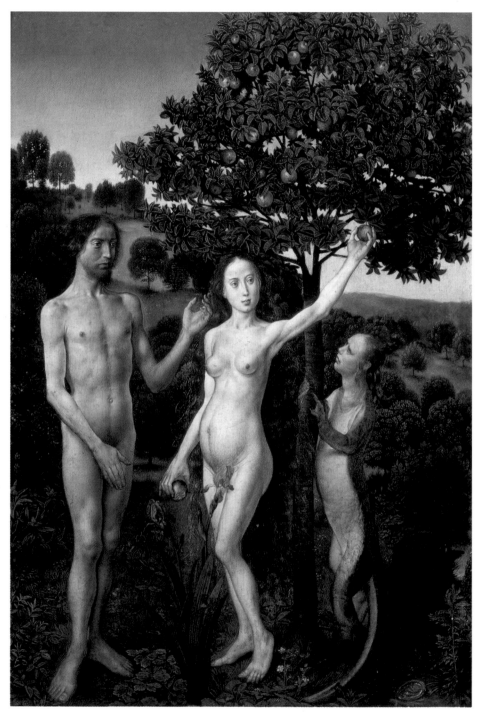

Courtesy of Kunsthistorisches Museum, Vienna, Austria/Bridgeman Art Library

ROGIER VAN DER WEYDEN studied under Robert Campin in his native city of Tournai before going to Brussels, where he made his mark both as an artist and as a prominent citizen. From 1436 he was the official painter to the city as well as the Burgundian Court. Although he visited Rome in 1450 it had no impact on his style. A very accomplished technician, he excelled not only in form and composition but also in his use of colour. But his main contribution to the progress of art was in his highly expressive portraiture, one of the first painters to convey the character and psychological profile of the model or the subject. He combined deep religious feeling with a desire to make the maximum impact on the spectator and in this he succeeded admirably. He wielded enormous influence over his contemporaries and the ensuing generation of Flemish artists.

MOVEMENT
Flemish School
OTHER WORKS
Deposition, The Last Judgment
INFLUENCES
Robert Campin

Rogier van der Weyden   *Born* 1399 Belgium
Painted in Tournai and Brussels
Died 1464 Brussels

Courtesy of Prado, Madrid, Spain/Bridgeman Art Library

Van Dyck, Sir Anthony (circle of) Self Portrait with a Sunflower, after 1632

ANTHONY VAN DYCK worked under Rubens and later travelled all over Italy, where he painted portraits and religious subjects. He first visited England in 1620 and was invited back in 1632 by King Charles I, who knighted him and appointed him Painter-in-Ordinary. Apart from a two-year period (1634–35) when he was back in Antwerp, Van Dyck spent the rest of his life in England and on his return to London he embarked on the most prolific phase of his career. He not only painted numerous portraits of King Charles, Queen Henrietta Maria and their children, but also many pictures of courtiers and other notable figures, creating a veritable portrait gallery of the great and good of the period. His immense popularity was due not only to his technical mastery, but also his ability to give his sitters an expressiveness, grace and elegance, which few other artists have ever equalled.

MOVEMENT
Flemish School
OTHER WORKS
Charles I in Hunting Dress, The Three Royal Children
INFLUENCES
Peter Paul Rubens

Sir Anthony Van Dyck *Born* 1599 Belgium
Painted in Antwerp and London
Died 1641 London

Courtesy of Private Collection/Philip Mould, Historical Portraits Ltd, London, UK/Bridgeman Art Library

Van Eyck, Jan

Portrait of Giovanni Arnolfini and Wife (Arnolfini Marr), 1434

JAN VAN EYCK settled in Bruges in 1431, where he became the leading painter of his generation and founder of the Bruges School. He and his elder brother Hubert are credited with the invention of oil painting. Van Eyck's paintings have a startlingly fresh quality about them, not only in the dazzling use of light and colour but also in their expression and realism, which was something of a quantum leap in portraiture. Van Eyck was very much a pillar of the establishment, being successively court painter to John of Bavaria,

Count of Holland, and Philip the Good of Burgundy. He was equally versatile in painting interiors and outdoor scenes, and exhibited a greater attention to detail than in the works of his predecessors. It is not surprising that he should not only sign and date his paintings but add his motto *Als ich kan* ('as I can').

MOVEMENT
Bruges School of Flemish Painting
OTHER WORKS
A Man in a Turban
INFLUENCES
Hubert van Eyck

Jan van Eyck *Born* c. 1389 Maastricht, Holland
Painted in Maastricht and Bruges
Died 1441 Bruges

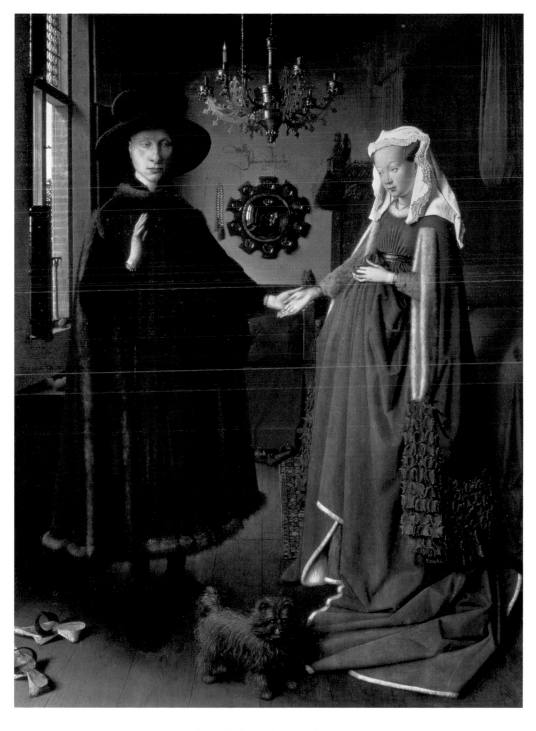

Courtesy of National Gallery, London, UK/Bridgeman Art Library

Van Goyen, Jan

JAN VAN GOYEN visited France in his youth and may have been influenced by the painters in that country, but he also travelled all over Holland and imbibed the ideas of his older contemporaries. With Salomon van Ruysdael he helped to establish the Dutch School of landscape painters, and he had numerous pupils and imitators. In his travels he made countless sketches and drawings that formed the basis of his later oil paintings. He was a prolific artist but a poor businessman and died in debt. His landscapes divide into two periods, those dating from 1630 onwards being in more muted colours, predominantly shades of brown, but much more atmospheric. Towards the end of his life he began using a much greater range of colours again, coupled with that poetic sensibility which was the hallmark of the next generation of Dutch artists.

MOVEMENT
Dutch School
OTHER WORKS
A Castle by a River with Shipping at a Quay
INFLUENCES
Esaias van de Velde, Jan Porcellis

Jan van Goyen   *Born* 1596 Leyden, Holland
Painted in Leyden and The Hague
Died 1656 The Hague

Courtesy of Private Collection/Christie's Images

DIEGO RODRIGUEZ de Silva y Velázquez was the son of a prominent lawyer and studied languages and philosophy with the intention of following his father, but his aptitude for drawing induced him to become the pupil of Herera and then Pacheco, whose daughter he married in 1618. His earliest works were domestic genre subjects but after he moved to Madrid in 1623, and especially as a result of a visit to Italy (1629–31), he adopted a much more colourful approach. As the leading court painter of his day he produced numerous portraits of the Spanish royal family and nobility as well as scenes derived from classical mythology. Considering that he is now regarded as one of the greatest painters of all time, it is surprising that his work was little known outside Spain until the early nineteenth century, but his mastery of light and atmosphere had enormous impact on the Impressionists.

MOVEMENT
Spanish School
OTHER WORKS
The Tapestry Weavers, Venus and Cupid
INFLUENCES
Francisco Pacheco

Diego Velázquez *Born* 1599 Seville, Spain
Painted in Seville and Madrid
Died 1660 Madrid

Courtesy of Christie's Images

Vermeer, Jan

JAN VERMEER studied painting under Carel Fabritius. In 1653 he entered the Guild of St Luke taking the role of head there in 1662 and 1670. Diffident and a poor businessman, he died young, leaving a widow and eight children destitute. He was almost entirely forgotten until 1860, when he was rediscovered and works which had previously been attributed to other artists were properly identified as coming from his brush. He specialized in small paintings of domestic scenes, distinguished by their perspective and clever use of light to create subtle tones, as well as the fact that, unusual for the time, the figures in them are self-absorbed. Only about 40 paintings have definitely been credited to him, but they are sufficient to establish him as one of the more original and innovative painters of his time – second only to Rembrandt.

MOVEMENT
Dutch School
OTHER WORKS
Lady Seated at a Virginal, The Painter in his Studio, View of Delft
INFLUENCES
Carel Fabritius

Jan Vermeer   *Born* 1632 Delft, Holland
Painted in Delft
Died 1675 Delft

Courtesy of Mauritshuis, The Hague, Netherlands/Bridgeman Art Library

Verner, Frederick

FREDERICK ARTHUR VERNER was self-taught, but in 1856 he went to England and enrolled at Heatherley's Academy in London. During the French invasion scare of 1858 he enlisted in the Yorkshire Militia and this gave him a taste for soldiering, for he joined the British Legion which fought alongside Garibaldi for the unification of Italy in 1860. He returned to Canada in 1862, where he found employment as a colourist in a photographic studio in Toronto, but spent all his spare time travelling in the wilds, sketching the Indian tribal communities and subsequently transferring these

vivid images to canvas. He excelled in genre paintings of the Native Canadians, infusing an element of Romanticism, making his work immensely popular, especially in England. He was a founder member of the Ontario Society of Artists (1872) and a regular exhibitor in its early years. In 1880 he settled in England, but continued to paint Indian scenes, which were much in demand, and periodically visited Manitoba and British Columbia as well as Ontario in search of fresh material. At best, his paintings are intensely atmospheric.

MOVEMENT
Modern Canadian School
OTHER WORKS
Ojibway Camp, Northern Shore of Lake Huron
INFLUENCES
Paul Kane

Frederick Verner   *Born* 1836 Ontario, Canada
Painted in Canada and England
Died 1928 London

© National Gallery of Canada, Ottawa Purchased 1958

Veronese, Paolo

Christ and the Widow of Nain/Woman taken in Adultery

PAOLO CALIARI or Cagliari is invariably known by his birthplace. He was the son of a stone-cutter and originally trained as a stone-carver, but he showed more of an aptitude for painting and therefore switched to the profession of his uncle, Antonio Badile. According to Vasari he studied under Giovanni Caroto – though this left no mark on his style. He worked in Verona and Mantua before settling in Venice in 1555, where he ranked with Titian and Tintoretto in his range and technical virtuosity, reinforced by a visit to Rome (1560). He was a skilful master of genre subjects, which he used to imbue his religious works with humanity, but as a result of his painting *The Feast in the House of Levi* (1573), he fell foul of the Inquisition on a charge of trivializing religious subjects. His undoubted masterpiece is the colossal *Marriage at Cana*, which has over 120 portraits, including royalty and celebrities of the period.

MOVEMENT
Venetian School
OTHER WORKS
The Adoration of the Magi, The Holy Family and St John
INFLUENCES
Domenico Brussasorci, Paolo Farinato

Paolo Veronese   *Born* 1528 Verona, Italy
Painted in Verona, Mantua and Venice
Died 1588 Venice

Courtesy of Christie's Images

Vigée-Lebrun, Louise Elisabeth   Marie Antoinette and her Four Children, 1787

MARIE LOUISE Elisabeth Vigée-Lebrun was the daughter of an artist from whom she received her early training, but later benefited from the help of several fellow-painters. By the age of 20 she had already made her mark with portraits of Count Orloff and the Duchess of Orleans. In 1783 she was admitted to the Academy on the strength of her allegorical masterpiece *Peace Bringing Back Abundance*. Following the outbreak of the Revolution she fled to Italy and worked in Rome and Naples, later visiting Vienna, Berlin and St Petersburg. She returned briefly to Paris in 1802 but went to London the same year, where she painted the Prince of Wales and Lord Byron. She was a prolific portraitist, and a score of her paintings portray Marie-Antoinette alone.

MOVEMENT
French School
OTHER WORKS
Portrait of the Artist and her Daughter
INFLUENCES
Joseph Vernet, Jean Baptiste Grueze, Jean Baptiste Lebrun

Elisabeth Vigée-Lebrun   *Born* 1755 France
Painted in France, England and Europe
Died 1842 Paris

Courtesy of Chateau de Versailles, France/Bridgeman Art Library

ALTHOUGH LARGELY self-taught, this exuberant, highly extrovert artist wielded a considerable influence over the development of avant-garde styles at the beginning of the twentieth century. Influenced by the expressive quality in the paintings of Van Gogh and Gauguin, he was later closely associated with André Derain and Henri Matisse, with whom he established Fauvism, painting flat patterns in the most extravagantly brilliant colours. Subsequently he came under the influence of Paul Cézanne and between 1908 and World War I produced landscapes that were more in the mainstream Realist manner and much more restrained in their use of colour. War service left its mark on him and in his later years he withdrew to a remote part of the country, where he developed a form of brooding Expressionism characterized by more sombre colours.

MOVEMENT
Fauvism, Realism

OTHER WORKS
Landscape with Red Trees, The River, Summer Landscape

INFLUENCES
André Derain, Matisse, Cézanne

Vlaminck, Maurice de   *Born* 1876 Paris, France
Painted in France
Died 1958 Rueil-la-Gadelière, France

Courtesy of Private Collection/Christie's Images/© ADAGP, Paris and DACS, London 2002

Von Menzel, Adolph

THE SON of a schoolmaster and lithographer, Adolph von Menzel was taught by his father and made his debut at an exhibition in Breslau in 1828 with a drawing of a tigress. The family moved to Berlin in 1830, where Adolph was employed in his father's business as a draughtsman and book illustrator. At the Berlin Academy show (1833) he exhibited illustrations for the works of Goethe. Later he produced a series showing the uniforms of the Prussian Army and woodcut engravings of historical subjects. Inspired by the Revolution of 1848 he painted his first great historic work, *The Lying in State of the March Fallen* – the first German political painting. Later he produced numerous portraits and historical scenes, and was employed as a war artist during the Seven Weeks' War (1866) and the Franco-German War (1870–71), for which he was awarded the Ordre Pour le Mérite, Prussia's highest decoration. A pillar of the establishment, he influenced the heroic style of German painting in the late nineteenth century.

MOVEMENT
German Romanticism
OTHER WORKS
Chess Players, Coronation of Wilhelm I in Königsberg
INFLUENCES
Claude Monet

Adolph von Menzel *Born* 1815 Breslau, Germany (now Wroclaw, Poland) *Painted in* Berlin *Died* 1905 Berlin

Courtesy of Private Collection/Christie's Images

JEAN EDOUARD VUILLARD studied at the Académie Julien in Paris and shared a studio with Pierre Bonnard. Both artists were inspired by Sérusier's theories derived from the works of Gauguin and became founder members of the Nabis in 1889. Vuillard was also influenced by the fashion for Japanese prints and this was reflected in his paintings of flowers and domestic interiors, executed with a keen sense of tone, colour and light. He was also a prolific designer of textiles, wallpaper and decorative features for public buildings. His paintings of cozy domestic subjects show a tremendous feeling for texture and patterning, a skill he picked up from his mother, who was a dressmaker. The bolts of brightly coloured cloth that surrounded him as a child found an echo in his own textile designs. His later paintings were more naturalistic, aided by photography, which he employed to capture the fleeting moment.

MOVEMENT
Les Nabis
OTHER WORKS
Femme Lisant, Le Soir, Two Schoolboys, Mother and Child
INFLUENCES
Paul Sérusier, Gauguin

Edouard Vuillard   *Born* 1868 Cuiseaux, France
Painted in France
Died 1940 La Baule, France

Courtesy of Christie's Images © ADAGP, Paris and DACS, London 2002

KAY WALKINGSTICK studied at Beaver College, Glenside, Pennsylvania and the Brooklyn art school. She had her first one-woman exhibition at the New Jersey State Museum in Trenton in 1975 and has since exhibited all over the United States as well as overseas, and her paintings are in many of the world's major art collections. She was director of an art gallery in New Jersey before taking up a series of teaching posts in Colourado, Ohio and New York and was latterly professor at Stony Brook. Her paintings are executed in oils or acrylic and she also models in wax. Her pictures cover a wide range of subjects and reflect her background as a Winnebago Cherokee Indian. She also designed the Memorial to the Cherokee Nation in Oklahoma.

MOVEMENT
Modern American School
OTHER WORKS
Magical Night, Happy Trails
INFLUENCES
Figurative Art

Kay WalkingStick   *Born* 1935 New York, USA
Painted in New Jersey, New York, Colourado and Ohio

© National Gallery Canada, Ottawa Purchased 1993/Kay WalkingStick

Warhol, Andy

AMERICAN ARTIST specializing in printmaking and films. Warhol was born in Pittsburgh, the son of Czech immigrants. In 1949 he moved to New York, where he became a successful commercial artist. This gave him a solid grounding in silkscreen printing techniques and taught him the value of self-promotion – both of which were to feature heavily in his art. Warhol's breakthrough came when he began to make paintings of familiar, everyday objects, such as soup cans, dollar bills and brillo pads. Early examples were hand-painted, but Warhol soon decided to use mechanical processes as far as possible. His aim, in this respect, was to free the image from any connotations of craftsmanship, aesthetics or individuality. He further emphasized this by describing his studio as 'The Factory'.

Warhol rapidly extended his references to popular culture by portraying celebrities (Marilyn Monroe, Marlon Brando), as well as more sinister items, such as news clippings with car crashes or the electric chair. He also associated himself with other branches of the mass media, notably through his links with the rock band The Velvet Underground, and through his controversial films.

MOVEMENT
Pop Art
OTHER WORKS
Campbell's Soup Can, Marilyn Monroe, Brillo
INFLUENCES
Roy Lichtenstein, Jasper Johns

Andy Warhol *Born* 1928
Painted in USA
Died 1987

Courtesy of Christie's Images/© The Andy Warhol Foundation for the Visual Arts, Inc./ARS, NY and DACS, London 2002

Waring, Laura Wheeler

A NATIVE of Connecticut, Laura Wheeler Waring attended the art school in Hartford before going to the Pennsylvania Academy of Fine Arts in Philadelphia from which she won a travelling scholarship in 1914. Her studies were interrupted by World War I, but in 1924–25 she attended classes at the Académie de la Grande Chaumière in Paris. Later she taught art in the Cheney State Teachers College, Pennsylvania. Her portraiture contained elements of Expressionism but she was also influenced by the Romantics, resulting in an unusual blend of the two styles, which had a much livelier appearance than normally associated with wholly representational portraits of the interwar period. At the same time, although her portraits are sensitive, they manage to avoid the cloying sentimentality often associated with the Romantics. She also worked as an illustrator.

MOVEMENT
African American School

OTHER WORKS
Portrait of a Child, Frankie

INFLUENCES
Henry Ossawa Tanner

Laura Wheeler Waring   Born 1887 USA
Painted in Pennsylvania and Paris
Died 1948 Philadelphia, Pennsylvania, USA

© Smithsonian American Art Museum, Washington, DC/Art Resource NY

Waterhouse, John William

ENGLISH PAINTER, whose dreamy mythological paintings represent one of the last flowerings of Romanticism in Britain. Born in Rome, the son of a minor artist, Waterhouse moved to England with his family in 1854. He trained at the Royal Academy Schools and began exhibiting there in 1874. Initially, he painted in a traditional, academic vein, specializing in decorative, classical themes, which recall the work of Alma-Tadema and Leighton. By the late 1880s, however, elements of Symbolism and *plein-air* painting began to enter his work.

The pivotal work in Waterhouse's career was *The Lady of Shalott*. Painted in 1888, this was a typically Pre-Raphaelite subject – the kind of theme which he favoured increasingly, in his later years. The style, however, was more modern. The landscape background, in particular, displays a freshness and a robust handling, which underlines Waterhouse's links with the Newlyn School and his debt to continental, *plein-air* painting. During the same period, he also began to paint sirens, mermaids and other *femmes fatales*, drawing his inspiration from the French Symbolists.

MOVEMENTS
Late Romantic, Symbolism
OTHER WORKS
Hylas and the Nymphs, St Eulalia, Echo and Narcissus
INFLUENCES
Frederic Leighton, Alma-Tadema, Sir Edward Burne-Jones

John William Waterhouse   *Born* 1849
Painted in England and Italy
Died 1917

Courtesy of Private Collection/Christie's Images

Watteau, Jean-Antoine

JEAN-ANTOINE WATTEAU studied under Gérin but learned more from the paintings of Ostade and Teniers. On his master's death, Watteau went to Paris, where he worked for the scene-painter Métayer and then in a factory where he turned out cheap religious pictures by the dozen. He was rescued from this drudgery by Claude Gillot and later worked under Claude Audran. The turning point came when he won second prize in a Prix de Rome competition (1709). He became an associate of the Academy in 1712 and a full member in 1717. He led the revolt against the pompous classicism of the Louis XIV period, and broke new ground with his realism and lively imagination. His early works were mainly military subjects, but later he concentrated on rustic idylls which were very fashionable in the early eighteenth century.

MOVEMENT
French School
OTHER WORKS
The Music Party, Embarkation for the Isle of Cythera
INFLUENCES
Claude Audran, David Teniers

Jean-Antoine Watteau   *Born* 1684 France
Painted in Valenciennes and Paris
Died 1721 Nogent-sur-Marne, France

Courtesy of Dulwich Picture Gallery, London; UK/Bridgeman Art Library

Wen Zhengming (and Qui Ying) The Student Chang bidding farewell to his lover Ying Ying at the Rest Pavilion

ALTHOUGH HE pursued his career as a mandarin (senior civil servant), Wen Zhengming retired early to devote the rest of his life to art, which had hitherto merely been a leisure pursuit. He was fortunate to study under Shen Zhou, the great master of the Wu School, and eventually emerged as one of the greatest scholar-painters of the Ming Dynasty. His early work was eclectic, drawing on many different periods, sources and styles for inspiration and, in effect, creating an extraordinary – if subconscious – commentary on the art of his predecessors. His artistic career, however, reflects the transition from the relatively small range of muted colours to a much more colourful style of realism in landscape painting, ultimately employing colour to convey a sense of perspective, a radical departure from traditional techniques in composition. This was a major breakthrough, opening up new aspects of pictorial representation which would be more fully developed by later generations of Chinese painters.

MOVEMENT
Chinese Landscape School
OTHER WORKS
Lofty Leisure Below a Sheer Cliff
INFLUENCES
Shen Zhou, Ni Zan

**Wen Zhengming 1470–1559
(Qui Ying 1494–1552)**
Painted in China

Courtesy of Private Collection/Bridgeman Art Library

West, Benjamin

A Group Portrait of a Lady and her two Children

BORN AT Springfield, Pennsylvania in 1738, Benjamin West came from an old Quaker family originating in Buckinghamshire. He showed a talent for drawing when very young, and at the age of 18 settled in Philadelphia as a portrait painter. Later he worked in New York and in 1760 travelled to Italy, where he lived for almost three years. In 1763 he settled in London as a painter specializing in historical subjects which brought him the patronage of King George III, who appointed him his historical painter in 1772. In 1768 he was one of the four artists who submitted a plan to the King for the establishment of the Royal Academy, which came to fruition the following year. In 1792 he succeeded Reynolds as President and was for many years a prominent figure in the English art establishment, producing numerous religious, allegorical and historical works. His adoption of modern dress in his great masterpiece *The Death of General Wolfe* was an innovation in English historical painting.

MOVEMENT
English School
OTHER WORKS
Self Portrait, Treaty of William Penn with the Indians
INFLUENCES
John Smibert, John Wollaston

Benjamin West   *Born* 1738 Pennsylvania, USA
Painted in Philadelphia, New York and London
Died 1820 London

Courtesy of Christie's Images, London, UK/Bridgeman Art Library

Whistler, James

JAMES ABBOTT MCNEILL WHISTLER was originally intended for a career in the army and studied at West Point from 1851 to 1854, then worked for a year as a Navy map-maker before going to Paris to take up art instead. He met Courbet and Fantin-Latour, and joined their group of Realist painters. He copied paintings in the Louvre and fell in love with Japanese art, which was then a novelty. In 1859 he settled in London, where he began painting in a style which combined these influences rather than following the English narrative convention. He strove to present a harmonious composition of tone and colour, doing in paint what a composer might do in music. This analogy was evident in the titles of these paintings, which Whistler called *Nocturnes*. Not surprisingly, his work got a very mixed reception, John Ruskin being his most vociferous critic and accusing him of 'flinging a pot of paint in the public's face'. Nevertheless his views gradually gained ground and influenced the next generation of British artists.

MOVEMENT
Realism
OTHER WORKS
Nocturne in Blue and Gold, Old Battersea Bridge
INFLUENCES
Gustave Courbet, Henri Fantin-Latour

James Whistler   *Born* 1834 Massachusetts, USA
Painted in Paris and London
Died 1903 London

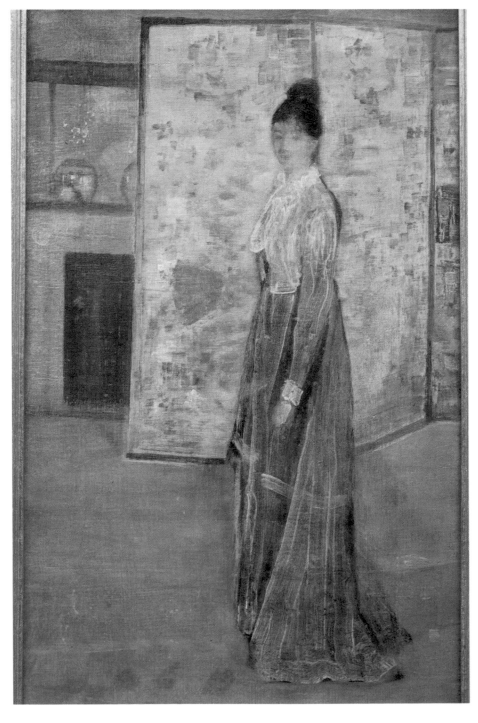

Courtesy of Christie's Images

CHARLES WHITE was largely self-taught but from an early age he was imbued with the desire to depict the African American heroes whose exploits formed a large part of the folklore of the 1920s when he was growing up. His reputation was assured by one of his most ambitious early works, the mural entitled *Five Great American Negroes*, which was commissioned for the Chicago Public Library. In this great work can be seen the tension and emotion, the realistic depiction of persecution, injustice and struggle, that characterized much of his later work. The passion is more restrained in the tempera mural completed in 1943 for Hampton University illustrating the contribution of the Negro to American democracy – a mural whose vast expanse is crammed with portraits large and small. Features and forms are sharply outlined with a geometric, angular style that adds to their rugged character, and this intensely graphic quality came to fruition in White's later works, from murals to individual portraits.

MOVEMENT
African American School

OTHER WORKS
Frederick Douglass, Booker T. Washington, In Memoriam

INFLUENCES
Charles Alston, Hale Woodruff

Charles White   *Born* 1918 Chicago, Illinois, USA
Painted in Chicago and Los Angeles
Died 1979

Courtesy of National Academy of Design, New York, USA/Bridgeman Art Library

Wilkie, Sir David

The Death of the Red Deer, 1821

THE SON of the parish minister of Cults in Fife, David Wilkie enrolled at the Trustees' Academy, Edinburgh in 1799 and was strongly influenced by Alexander Carse and David Allan, who were the first Scottish artists to paint scenes of peasant life. Wilkie frequented markets and country fairs, sketching the raw material for his great genre paintings. In 1805 he went to London and studied in the Royal Academy schools, making his debut in 1806 with *Village Politicians*. In 1830 he succeeded Sir Thomas Lawrence as Painter-in-Ordinary

to King William IV and was knighted six years later. Wilkie did not flatter his sitters, but injected a note of realism into his portraiture, which had a marked effect on the next generation of British artists. His reputation rests mainly on his genre paintings, noted for their detail, somber colours and wry humor tinged with pathos.

MOVEMENT
British School
OTHER WORKS
Blind Fiddler, Rent Day, Card-players, The Penny Wedding
INFLUENCES
David Teniers, Adriaen van Ostade, David Allan

Sir David Wilkie *Born* 1785 Cults, Fife, Scotland
Painted in Scotland and England
Died 1841 off Gibraltar

Courtesy of Private Collection/Christie's Images

BORN AT Anamosa, Iowa, Grant Wood spent his entire life in this small town in the American Midwest, and his paintings are a chronicle of the people and the scenery of the district. In the 1920s, however, he travelled to France and the Netherlands where he studied the works of the Old Masters, especially the Gothic, Romanesque, Renaissance and Flemish School, all of which had a strong influence on his own paintings. His best-known painting, *American Gothic*, is aptly named, for in it Wood depicts a cottage in his home town whose Gothic window appealed to him. In the foreground stands a typical Midwestern farmer and his wife, actually Wood's sister and his dentist, who served as his models. He was severely criticized at the time for lampooning the values of Middle America but he defended himself, insisting that the painting was intended as a sincere tribute to the simple dignity of rural communities. Wood was the foremost of the Regionalists, a group of American artists who rejected the abstract in favour of the realism of ordinary people and their locale.

MOVEMENT
Regionalism
OTHER WORKS
Haying
INFLUENCES
Van Eyck, Rogier van der Weyden

Grant Wood *Born* 1892 Anamosa, Iowa, USA
Painted in Iowa
Died 1942 Anamosa

Courtesy of Private Collection/Christie's Images © Estate of Grant Wood/VAGA, New York/DACS, London 2002

Woodruff, Hale

ALTHOUGH BORN in Illinois, Hale Woodruff was raised in Tennessee and witnessed the persecution of African Americans at close quarters. He studied at the John Herron Art Institute in Indianapolis and won a Harmon scholarship that enabled him to continue his studies at the Académie de la Grande Chaumière in Paris (1927–31). His later Expressionist paintings reflect the influence of this period. On his return to America he taught at Atlanta and New York Universities. He was one of the foremost creators of large murals on an epic scale, illustrating episodes in the history of African Americans, notably the Amistad Mutiny panels for the Savery Library of Talladega College, Alabama. The Amistad mutiny was a defining moment in the history of Black Americans and it was the turning point in Woodruff's career. Subsequent murals were commissioned for Atlanta University but in the latter part of his working life Woodruff turned from representational painting to Abstract Expressionism.

MOVEMENT
African American School
OTHER WORKS
The Mutiny Aboard the Amistad, Leda, Landscape with Green Sun
INFLUENCES
Diego Rivera, José Clemente Orozco

Hale Woodruff *Born* 1900 Cairo, Illinois, USA
Painted in Alabama, Georgia and Tennessee
Died 1980 USA

© Smithsonian American Art Museum, Washington, DC / Art Resource, NY

KNOWN AS Wright of Derby because he spent his entire life in that town, Joseph Wright was the first English painter of any significance to work in the provinces, although even he had to go to London for his formal art education. He established his own studio, where he flourished as a portraitist, and it was probably as a result of his contact with the rising industrialists of the 1760s and 1770s, such as Richard Arkwright and Josiah Wedgwood (whose portraits he painted), that his career eventually changed direction quite dramatically. Wright, in fact, was *the* artist of the Industrial Revolution, the right man in the right place at the right time, and it is for his spectacular canvasses depicting the wonders of modern science and technology in their infancy that he is chiefly remembered. His attention to the details of machinery was matched by his uncanny mastery of artificial lighting, which he used to good effect.

MOVEMENT
British School
OTHER WORKS
The Air Pump, A Philosopher Giving a Lecture on the Orrery
INFLUENCES
Gerrit van Honthorst

Joseph Wright   *Born* 1734 Derby, England
Painted in Derby
Died 1797 Derby

Courtesy of National Gallery, London, UK/Bridgeman Art Library

Wyeth, Andrew

ANDREW NEWEL WYETH studied under his father, the book illustrator Newel Convers Wyeth, and closely followed his style until 1945, when his father was killed in a level-crossing accident. The sense of bereavement led Wyeth to change his artistic direction and concentrate on landscapes, executed mainly in drybrush watercolours or tempera rather than oils. Both methods are slow and laborious and Wyeth even went to the length of mixing his own pigments, often combining them with earth to achieve the special subdued tones which are characteristic of his pictures. Like Grant Wood, he was concerned to depict the ordinary people and scenes of rural America, particularly in Pennsylvania and Maine. His landscapes often pose a solitary figure in a corner against a vast expanse, conveying an uneasy sense of desolation and pathos. His paintings have a compelling realism, almost photographic in their painstaking detail, which accounts for their tremendous popular appeal.

MOVEMENT
Regionalism
OTHER WORKS
Up in the Studio, Field Hand, That Gentleman
INFLUENCES
Winslow Homer, Thomas Eakins, Grant Wood

Andrew Wyeth *Born* 1917 Chadds Ford, Pennsylvania, USA
Painted in Pennsylvania and Maine

Purchased for the Brandywine River Museum by John T. Dorrance, Jr.; Mr. and Mrs. Felix du Pont; Mr. and Mrs. James P. Mills; Mr and Mrs. Bayard Sharp; two anonymous donors; and the Pew Memorial Trust © 2002 Brandywine Conservancy

Xian, Gong

BORN IN China about 1619, Gong Xian is ranked among the greatest of the Individualists working in the Qing period. Although his was the most limited style, it was also the most forceful and dramatic in compact. His paintings have been described as gloomy, funereal and full of foreboding, peopled by ghosts and wraiths; or alternatively as the expression of a monumental genius of somber and passionate temperament. His preferred medium was the hanging scroll, painted in the richest, deepest, most sumptuous shades of black to be found in any Chinese painting, shading subtly in tones of grey, and contrasting with the sunless whites of clouds and mists. He painted empty landscapes; no figures either human or animal disturb the scene. In his experiments with light and shade he went far beyond any of his contemporaries, far less his predecessors and it has been suggested that this reveals the influence of Western artists whose work was beginning to enter China in his lifetime.

MOVEMENTS
Individualist School, Qing Dynasty

OTHER WORKS
A Thousand Peaks and Myriad Ravines

INFLUENCES
Yuan Ji, Zhu Da, Kun-Can

Gong Xian *Born c.* 1619 China
Painted in China
Died 1689 China

Courtesy of Private Collection/Christie's Images

HUA YAN painted horses and figures, usually set in misty or windy weather. This created an atmospheric sense which was very rare in Chinese painting prior to that time, but had immense impact on the artists of the eighteenth and nineteenth centuries. His paintings evoked a realism and immediacy that was radically opposed to the timeless quality for which the painters of the classical tradition invariably strove. Hua Yan was one of the new generation of artists who were not employed in court circles and were thus free from the constraints of their predecessors, and therefore known as the Eccentrics. His works appealed to the rising middle classes of China and, unlike the dilettante artists in court circles, he had a keen sense of the value of his paintings. They found a ready market and he apparently made a fortune from the small pictures which he turned out in vast quantities.

MOVEMENT
Chinese Eccentric School
OTHER WORKS
The Red Bird
INFLUENCES
Wang Fu, Badashanren, Shi Tao

Hua Yan   *Born* 1682 near Yangzhou, China
Painted in Yangzhou
Died 1756 Yangzhou

Courtesy of Private Collection/Christie's Images

JOHN BUTLER YEATS was the son of an Irish painter and younger brother of the celebrated Irish poet and playwright William Butler Yeats. Though born in London, he was raised in Co. Sligo and spent most of his life in Ireland. His earliest artistic efforts were strip cartoons and illustrations for children's comics, but he did not turn to painting until 1915. In the aftermath of the Easter Rising the following year, his art took on a much more serious tone; his style became increasingly violent and revelling in strident colours as he strove to give an Expressionist interpretation to the Irish Troubles, often using religious metaphors. Unlike his brother, he did not involve himself in Irish politics, but his passionate loyalty to his country leaps off the canvas. Later he adapted his Expressionism to mellower subjects that chronicled life in rural Ireland, and he also went back to the roots of Irish culture, exploring scenes from Celtic myths and legends.

MOVEMENT
Modern Irish School
OTHER WORKS
Waiting for the Long Car, The Rogues' March
INFLUENCES
Oskar Kokoschka

Jack B. Yeats   *Born* 1871 London, England
Painted in Ireland
Died 1957 Dublin, Ireland

Courtesy of Private Collection/Christie's Images

Yin, Tang   The Immortal Ge Changgeng Sitting on his Three-legged Toad, 1506–10

AN EXACT contemporary of Wen Zhengming, Tang Yin came from a prosperous middle-class family and had a brilliant academic education. Under the patronage of Wen Lin (Wen Zhengming's father) he seemed destined for the highest ranks in the civil service but he was caught trying to bribe the examiner, imprisoned and later returned to Suzhou in disgrace. His hopes of becoming a mandarin now dashed, Tang Yin took up painting and excelled to such an extent that he came to be regarded as one of the Four

Great Masters of the Wu School. Studying under Zhou Chen, he achieved mastery of a very wide range of styles and subjects. Apart from handscrolls and wall hangings, Tang Yin was adept at the difficult art of painting on bamboo. He painted landscapes, scenes from Chinese mythology and portraits of beautiful women with equal skill. Most of his work was executed on paper using pen and ink with restrained use of colour, but combined with poetry and calligraphy in the finest tradition of the scholar-painters.

MOVEMENT
Wu School of China
OTHER WORKS
Moon Goddess Chang-e
INFLUENCES
Zhou Chen, Wen Zhengming

Tang Yin   *Born* 1470 Suzhou, China
Painted in Suzhou
Died 1524 Suzhou

Courtesy of Private Collection/Bridgeman Art Library

ANDERS LEONHARD ZORN began as a watercolourist in the manner of Egron Lundgren, under whom he studied. He achieved instant fame with the portrait of a girl entitled *Mourning*, which was exhibited in 1880, after which he received numerous commissions for portraits. His fortune assured, he travelled widely, studying the art of England, Spain, Eastern Europe and North Africa – experiences which resulted in some of his finest landscapes and genre paintings. He resided in Paris from 1887 to 1893 and switched direction by taking up oil painting and rejecting his early realism in favour of Impressionism. From 1893 onwards he made frequent trips to the United States and specialized in portraits of American tycoons and leading political figures. In his later years he spent more time in the Swedish countryside concentrating on landscapes and genre scenes. He was also one of the most accomplished etchers of the turn of the century, as well as a fine sculptor.

MOVEMENT
Modern Swedish School
OTHER WORKS
Our Daily Bread, Mona, Self-Portrait, Dagmar, By Lake Siljan
INFLUENCES
Max Liebermann

Anders Zorn   *Born* 1860, Mora, Sweden
Painted in Sweden, England, Spain, Algiers and USA
Died 1920 Mora

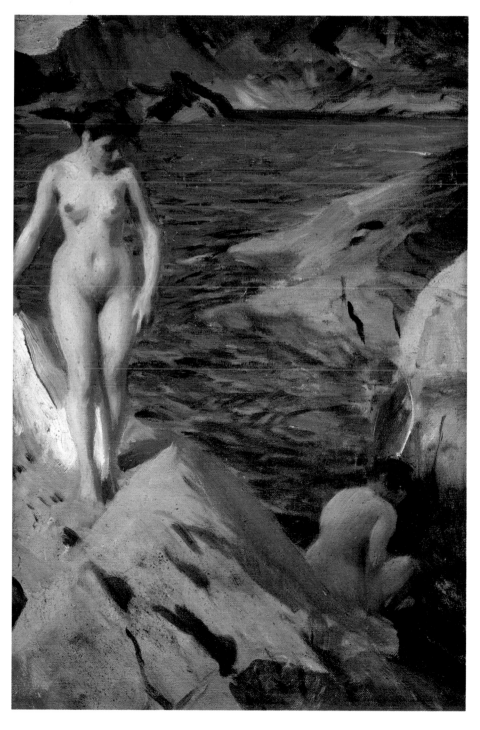

Courtesy of Private Collection/Christie's Images

Resources

INSTITUTIONS AND MUSEUMS

Africa
Johannesburg Art Gallery
King George Street
Joubert Park
Tel: 725 3130 8081

National Gallery of
Zimbabwe
Park Lane,
Harare
Tel: 00 263 14 70 4666

Australia
Art Gallery of New South
Wales
Art Gallery Road
The Domain
Sydney NSW 2000
Tel: 00 61 2 9225 1700

National Gallery of Australia
Parkes Place
Canberra
ACT 2601
Tel: 00 61 2 6240 6502

National Gallery of Victoria
180 St Kilda Road
Melbourne
3004 Victoria
Tel: 0061 3 627 411

Austria
Österrechische Galerie
Prinz Eugen-strasse 27
1037 Vienna
Tel: 00 43 1 7955 7134

Kunsthistorisches Museum
Burgring 5
1010 Wien
Tel: 00 43 1 222 52177

Belgium
Koninklink Museum voor
Schone Kunsten
(Musée Royal des Beaux-
Arts)
Plaatnijdersstrasse 2
2000 Antwerp
Tel: 0032 3 238 7809

Musée Royaux des Beaux-
Arts
(Musée d'Art Ancien)
Rue de la Régence 3
1000 Bruxelles
Tel: 0032 2 508 3211

Brazil
Museo de Arte
Contemporaneo
Rua da Reitoria, 160
Cidade Universitária
05508-900 São Paulo
Tel: 00 55 11 3091 3039

Museu de Arte de Sao Paulo
'Assis Chateaubriand'
Avenida Paulista 1578
01310 Sao Paulo
Tel: 0055 11 251 5644

Canada
National Gallery of Canada
380 Sussex Drive
Box 427, Station A
Ottawa, Ontario
Canada
K1N 9N4
Tel: 00 1 613 990-1985

Art Gallery of Ontario
317 Dundas Street W
Toronto
Ontario
M5T IG4
Tel: 001 416 977 0414

China/North Asia
Beijing Art Museum
Wanshou Temple,
North of West 3rd-ring Road,
Beijing,
P.R. China
Tel: 00 86 10 68479391

Hong Kong Museum of Art
10 Salisbury Road,
Tsimshatsui,
Kowloon
Tel: 00 85 2 2721 0116

Taiwan Museum of Art
2, Sec. 1, Wu Chuan W. Rd.,
Taichung 403
Taiwan, R.O.C.
Tel: 00 88 6 4 23723552

Czech Republic
Národni Galerie v Praze
(National Gallery in Prague)
Hrad anské nám sti 15
Praha
Tel: 0042 2 2451 0594

Denmark
Louisiana Museum of
Modern Art
Gl Standvej 13
3056 Humlebaek
Tel: 00 45 49 190 719

NY Carlsberg Glyptothek
Dantes Plads 7
1556 København
Tel: 0045 33 418141

Finland
Finnish National Gallery
Kaivokatu 2
00100 Helsinki
Tel: 00 358 91 73361

France
Musée National Auguste
Rodin
77 Rue de Varenne
75007 Paris
Tel: 00 33 1 4705 0134

Musée National du Château
de Versailles
78000 Versailles
Tel: 00 33 1 3084 7400

Centre National d'Art et de
Culture Georges Pompidou
19 Rue de Renard
75191 Paris
Tel: 0033 1 447 81233

Musée d'art Moderne de la
Ville de Paris
11 ave du President Wilson
751116 Paris
Tel: 0033 1 472 36 127

Musée du Louvre
34-36 Quai du Louvre
75058 Paris
Tel: 00 33 1 402 05 009

Musée d'Orsay
62 rue de Lille
75007 Paris
Tel: 0033 1 404 94814

Germany
Germanische
Nationalmuseum
Kartänsergasse I
90402 Nürn
Tel: 00 49 911 13310

Hamburg Kunsthalle
Glockengiesserwall
2000 Hamburg 1
Tel: 00 49 40 2486 2612

Alte Pinakothek
Barer Strasse 27
80333 München
Tel: 00 49 89 238 05216

Germanisches
Nationalmuseum
Kartänsergasse I
90402 Nürn

Kunstammlung Nordrhein-
Westfalen
Grabbeplatz 5
40213 Düsseldorf
Tel: 0049 211 83810

Ludwig Forum für
Internationale Kunst
J'licher Stasse 97-109
52050 Aachen
Tel: 0049 24 18070

Neue Nationalgalerie
Potsdamerstrasse 50
10785 Berlin
Tel: 0049 30 266 2651

Holland
Rijksmuseum
Stadhouderskade 42
Postbus 74888
1070 DN
Amsterdam
Tel: 00 31 20 673 2121

Rijksmuseum Vincent
Van Gogh
Paulus Potterstraat 7
Postbus 75366
1070 AJ
Amsterdam
Tel: 00 31 20 570 5200

Stedelijk Museum of
Modern Art
Paulus Potterstraat 13
Postbus 75082
1070 AB
Amsterdam
Tel: 00 31 20 573 2911

Hungary
Magyar Nemzeti Galéria
Szent György tér 2
Budávári Pálota Pf31 (1250)
Tel: 00 36 1 757 533

Indian Sub-Continent
National Gallery of Modern
Art
Jaipur House, near India Gate,
New Delhi
Tel: 00 91 11 3383032

National Museum of India
National Museum,
Janpath,
New Delhi 110 011
Tel: 00 91 011 3018415

Ireland
National Gallery of Ireland
Merrion Square West
Dublin 2
Tel: 00 353 1 661 5133

Italy
Galleria Borghese
Piazza Scipione Borghese 5
00197 Rome
Tel: 00 39 6 858 577

Galleria Degli Uffizi
Piazza degli Uffizi
50122 Florence
Tel: 00 39 55 238 8651

Museo Nazionale del Bargello
Palazzo del Bargello
Via del Proconsolo 4
50122 Florence
Tel: 00 39 55 238 85

Pinacoteca di Brera
Via Brera 28
20121 Milan
Tel: 00 39 2 800 985

Vatican Museums and
Galleries
00120 Vatican City
Tel: 00 1 39 6 481 4430

Japan
National Museum of Art,
Osaka
10-4 Expo Park
Senri
Suita
565-0826
Tel: 81 6 6876 2481

National Museum of Modern
Art, Kyoto
Enshoji-cho
Okazaki
Sakyoto-ku
Kyoto
606-8344
Tel: 075 761 4111
075 761 9900

Mexico
Museo Nacional de Arte
Calle Tacuba 8
Mexico City
Tel: 5 512 3224

Palacio de Bellas Artes
Avenida Juarez
Mexico City
Tel: 5 512 2593
5 521 9251

Middle East
Egyptian Museum
Maydan at-Tahrir,
Cairo
Tel. 00 20 2 5742681

Egyptian Museum of
Modern Art
Gazirah Exibition Grounds
Cairo
Tel. 00 20 2 3416667

Israel Museum
Ruppin Blvd.
Jerusalem 91710
Tel: 00 97 2 2670 8811

New Zealand
Auckland Art Gallery
Corner of Wellesley and
Kitchener Streets
Auckland
Phone: 64 9 307 7700

Te Papa Tongarewa
Cable Street
Wellington
Tel: 00 64-4-381-7000

Norway
Nasjonalgalleriet
Universitetsgaten 13
0033 Oslo 1
Tel: 00 47 2 200 404

Poland
Muzeum Narodowe w
Warzawie
Al. Jerozolimski 3
00-495 Warsaw
Tel: 00 48 22 621 1031

Portugal
Musea Nacional de Arte
Antiga
Rua Das Janelas Verdes
1293 Lisbon
Tel: 00 351 1 397 6001

Romania
Muzeul de Arta
Calea Unirii 15
1100 Craiova
Tel: 00 40 41 12342

Muzeul National de Art al
Romaniei
Calea Victoriei nr. 49-53
70101 Bucharest
Tel: 00 40 1 615 5193

Russia
Gosud Arstvennaja
Tretjakovskaja Galerija
Lavrushinskij Per 10
117049 Moscow
Tel: 00 7 095 230 7788

Hermitage Gosudarstvennij
Ermitaj
Dworcowaja Nabereshnaja
34-36
St Petersburgh 191065
Tel: 00 7 812 212 9545

Pushkin Museum
12 Volkhonka str
121019 Moscow
Tel: 00 7 095 203-79-98

Spain
Fundació Joan Miró
Barcelona
Tel: 00 34 93 329 1908

Museo Nacional del Prado
Paseo del Prado
28014 Madrid
Tel: 00 34 91 486 0950

Museu Nacional d'Art
de Catalunya
Palacio Nacional
Parc de Montjuic
08038 Barcelona
Tel: 00 34 3 325 5635

South East Asia
Agung Rai Museum of Art
Ubud,
Bali, 80571,
Tel: 62-361-974-228

Contempory Art Museum of
the Phillippines
Roxas Boulevard
1000 Manila
Philippines
Tel: 00 63 2 8321125

Malaysian National Art
Gallery
Pengarah
Balai Seni Lukis Negara
Jalan Temerloh
Off Jalan Tun Razak
50400 Kuala Lumpur.
Tel: 00 60 3-425 4989

Thavibu Gallery
Silom Galleria Building,
3rd Floor
Suite 308, 919/1 Silom Rd.
Bangkok 10500,
Thailand
Tel: 00 66 2 266 5454

Sweden
Göteborgs Konstmuseum
Göt aplatsen
41256 Göteborg
Tel: 00 46 31 612 980

Modern Museet
Birger Jarlsgatan 57
10327 Stockholm
Tel: 00 46 8 666 4250

Nationalmuseum
Södra Blasieholmshamnen
10324 Stockholm
Tel: 00 46 8 666 4250

Switzerland
Musée d'Art et d'Histoire
2 rue Charles Galland
1211 Geneva 3
Tel: 00 41 22 311 4340

Taiwan
Taiwan Museum of Art
2, Sec. 1,
Wu Chuan W R d ,
Taichung
403 Taiwan, R.O.C.
Tel:00 886-4-23723552

United Kingdom
Ashmolean Museum
Beaumont Street
Oxford
Oxfordshire
OX1 2PH
Tel: 00 44 1865 278 000

Courtauld Institute of Art
Courtauld Gallery
Somerset House
Strand
London
WC2R 0RN
Tel: 00 44 20 7873 2526

Dulwich Picture Gallery
College Road
London
SE21 7AD
Tel: 00 44 20 8693 5254

National Gallery
Trafalgar Square
London
WC2N 5DN
Tel: 00 44 20 7839 3321

National Gallery of Scotland
The Mound
Edinburgh
Scotland EH2 2EL
Tel: 00 44 131 624 6200

National Museum and
Gallery Cardiff
Cathays Park
Cardiff CF1 3NP
Tel: 00 44 1222 397 951

National Portrait Gallery
St Martin's Place
London
WC2H 0HE
Tel: 00 44 20 7306 0055

Royal Academy of Arts
Burlington House
Piccadilly
London
W1V 0DS
Tel: 00 44 20 7300 8000

School of Art Gallery
and Museum
University of Wales
Buarth Mawr
Aberystwyth
Ceredigion SY23 1NE
Tel: 00 44 1970 622 460

Scottish National Gallery
of Modern Art
Belford Road
Edinburgh
Scotland EH4 3DR
Tel: 00 44 131 624 6200

Scottish National Portrait
Gallery
1 Queen Street
Edinburgh
Scotland EH2 1JD
Tel: 00 44 131 642 6200

Tate Modern
Bankside
London SE1 9TG
Tel: 00 44 20 7887 8000

Victoria and Albert Museum
Cromwell Road
South Kensington
London SW7 2RL
Tel. 00 44 20 7938 8500

United States
Albright Knox Art Gallery
1285 Elmwood Avenue
Buffalo
NY 14222
Tel: 00 1 716 882 8700

Art Institute of Chicago
111 Michigan Avenue
Chicago
IL 60603
Tel. 00 1 312 443 3600

Cleveland Museum of Art
University Circle
11150 E Boulevard
Cleveland
OH 44106-1797
Tel: 00 1 216 421 7340

Detroit Institute of Arts
5200 Woodward Avenue
Detroit, Michigan
MI 48202
Tel: 00 1 313 833 7900

J Paul Getty Museum
17985 Pacific Coast Highway
Malibu
CA 90265
Tel: 00 1 310 458 2003

Metropolitan Museum of Art
1000 Fifth Avenue
NY 10028
New York
Tel: 00 1 212 879 5500

Museum of Fine Arts
465 Huntingdon Avenue
Boston
MA 02115
Tel: 00 1 617 267 9300

Museum of Modern Art
11 West 53rd Street
NY 10019
New York
Tel: 00 1 212 708 9480

National Gallery of Art
4th Street and Constitution
Avenue
Washington DC 20565
Tel: 00 1 202 737 4215

National Museum of
American Art
Eighth and G Streets NW
Washington
DC 20560
Tel: 00 1 202 357 2700

Philadelphia Museum of Art
26th Street at Benjamin
Franklin Parkway
Philadelphia
PA 19130
Tel: 00 1 215 763 8100

Smithsonian Institute
1000 Jefferson Drive
Washington
DC 200009-1090
Tel: 00 1 202 357 2700

Whitney Museum
American Art
945 Madison Avenue
New York, NY 10021
Tel: 00 1 212 570 3600

BIBLIOGRAPHY

Adams, S., *The Barbizon School and the Origins of Impressionism,* Phaidon Press, 1994
Akurgal, E., *The Art of the Hittites,* Thames and Hudson, 1962
Aldred, C., *The Development of Ancient Egyptian Art from 3200 to 1315 BC,* 3 vols, Tiranti, 1973
Ames-Lewis, F. and Rogers, M. eds., *Concepts of Beauty in Renaissance Art,* Ashgate Publishing Limited, 1998
Amiet, P., *Art of the Ancient Near East,* New York, 1980
Archer, M., *Art since 1960,* Thames and Hudson, 1997
Arribas, A., *The Iberians,* Thames & Hudson, 1964
Atil, Ed., *Turkish Art,* Smithsonian Institute Press, Washington DC/New York, 1980
Barnhart, R.M. et al., *Three Thousand Years of Chinese Painting,* Yale University Press, 1997

Berenson, B., *The Italian Painters of the Renaissance 1894—1907,* Cornell University Press, 1980
Berger, J., *Ways of Seeing,* Penguin Books, 1990
Berlo, J.C. and Wilson L.A., *Arts of Africa, Oceania and the Americas,* Englewood Cliffs, NJ, 1993
Berrin, K. and Pasztory, E. eds., *Teotihuacán: Art from the City of the Gods,* San Francisco/London, 1993
Blurton, T.R., *Hindu Art,* British Museum Press, 1992
Boardman, J., *The Oxford History of Classical Art,* Oxford University Press, 1993
Boardman, J., *Greek Art,* Thames and Hudson, 1996
Boardman, J., *Pre-classical: From Crete to Archaic Greece,* Penguin Books, 1967
Boime, A., *Art in the Age of Revolution 1750—1800,* University of Chicago Press, 1987
Bomford, D. et al., *Impressionism,* National Gallery Company Ltd, 1990
Brilliant, R., *Roman Art from the Republic to Constantine,* Praeger Pub Text, 19/4
Brown, J., *The Golden Age of Painting in Spain,* Yale University Press, 1991
Buckton, D. ed., *Byzantium,* London, 1994
Camille, M., *Gothic Art,* US Imports & PHIPEs, 1996
Campbell, L., *Renaissance Portraits,* Yale University Press, 1990
Canby, S.R., *Persian Painting,* British Museum Press, 1993
Carpenter, R., *Greek Art,* Philadelphia, 1962
Caruana, W., *Aboriginal Art,* Thames and Hudson, 1993
Charbonneaux, J., *Hellenistic Art,* George Braziller, 1973
Chastel, A., *French Art: The Renaissance 1430—1620,* Paris, 1995
Clarke, G., *The Photograph,* Oxford University Press, 1997
Clunas, C., *Art in China,* Oxford Paperbacks, 1997
Collon, D., *Ancient Near Eastern Art,* British Museum Press, 1995
Craven, R.C., *Indian Art* (1976) Thames and Hudson, 1997
Crichton, R.A., *The Floating World: Japanese Popular Prints 1700—1900,* London, 1973

Cumming, R., *Annotated Great Artist,* Dorling Kindersley, 1998
D'Alleva, A., *Art of the Pacific,* Weidenfeld Nicolson, London/New York, 1998
Davies, D. ed., *Harrap's Illustrated Dictionary of Art and Artists,* Harrap Books Ltd, 1990
Deepwell, K. ed., *Women Artists and Modernism,* Manchester/New York, 1998
Duro, P. and Greenhalgh, M., *Essential Art History,* Bloomsbury, 1992
Eisenman, S.E., *Nineteenth Century Art: A Critical History,* Thames and Hudson, 1994
Evans, H.C. and Wixom, W.D. eds., *The Glory of Byzantium,* Harry N. Abrams, Inc., 1997
Eyo, E. and Willett, F., *Treasures of Ancient Nigeria,* Collins, 1982
Fer, B., *On Abstract Art,* Yale University Press, 2000
Fong, Wen C., *Beyond Representation,* Yale University Press, 1992
Frankfort, H., *The Art and Architecture of the Ancient Orient,* Yale University Press, 1996
Fry, E.F., *Cubism,* Thames and Hudson, 1966
Gale, M., *Dada and Surrealism,* Phaidon Press, 1997
Gaze, D. ed., *Dictionary of Women Artists,* Fitzroy Dearborn, 1997
Geidion, S., *The Eternal Present: The Beginning of Art,* Oxford University Press, 1962
Gilbert, C., *History of Renaissance Art throughout Europe,* Abrams, 1973
Gillon, W., *A Short History of African Art,* Penguin Books, 1991
Godfrey, T., *Conceptual Art,* Phaidon Press, 1998
Gombrich, E.H., *Art and Illusion,* Phaidon Press, 2002
Goodman, C., *Digital Visions, Computers and Art,* Harry N. Abrams, 1987
Gordon, E.D., *Expressionism, Art and Idea* (1987) New Haven/London, 1991
Grabar, A., *Early Christian Art,* London, 1968
Hanfmann, G., *Roman Art,* W. W. Norton, 1975
Haskell, F., *History and its Images,* Yale University Press, 1993
Hauser, A., *The Social History of Art,* Routledge, 1985
Held, J. and Posner, D., *17th and 18th Century Art,* Harry N. Abrams, Inc, 1972

Art

Henderson, G., *Early Medieval,* University of Toronto Press Inc, 1993

Hessel, I., *Inuit Art: An Introduction,* British Museum Press, 1998

Honour, H., *Neoclassicism,* Penguin, 1968

Honour, H., *Romanticism,* Viking, 1979

Howard, J., *Art Nouveau: International and National Styles in Europe,* Manchester University Press, 1996

Irwin, R., *Islamic Art,* Laurence King Publishing, 1997

James, T.G.H., *An Introduction to Ancient Egypt,* British Museum Publications, 1979

Jantzen, H., *High Gothic,* Princeton University Press, 1984

Kaplan, P. and Manso, S. eds., *Major European Art Movements 1900—1945,* E P Dutton, 1977

Kemp, M., *The Science of Art,* Yale University Press, 1990

Klindt-Jensen, O., *Viking Art,* University of Minnesota Press, 1980

Kramrisch, S., *The Art of India through the Ages,* Motilal Banarsidass, 2002

Kubler, G., *The Art and Architecture of Ancient America,* Yale University Press, 1992

Laing, L. and Laing, J., *Art of the Celts,* Thames and Hudson, 1992

Lee, S.E. and Richard, N., *A History of Far Eastern Art,* Thames and Hudson, 1997

Leroi-Gourhan, A., *The Art of Prehistoric Man in Western Europe,* Thames and Hudson, 1967

Leroi-Gourhan, A., *The Dawn of European Art,* Cambridge University Press, 1982

Levey, M., *High Renaissance,* Penguin, 1975

Levey, M., *The Early Renaissance,* Harmondsworth, 1967

Livingstone, M. ed., *Pop Art: A Continuing History,* Harry N Abrams, 1990

Lodder, C., *Russian Constructivism,* Yale University Press, 1998

Loevren, S., *The Genesis of Modernism,* Hacker Art Books Inc, 1983

Lowden, J., *Early Christian and Byzantine Art,* Phaidon Press, 1997

Lynton, N., *The Story of Modern Art,* Phaidon Press, 1992

Martin, J.R., *Baroque,* Westview Press, 1977

Mason, P., *History of Japanese Art,* Harry N. Abrams, Inc., 1993

Miller, M.E., *The Art of Mesoamerica,* Thames and Hudson, 2001

Morphy, H., *Aboriginal Art,* Phaidon Press, 1998

Nochlin, L., *Realism,* Penguin Books, 1991

Noma, S., *The Arts of Japan,* Kodansha America, 1978

Osborne, R., *Archiac and Classical Greek Art,* Oxford University Press, 1998

Pächt, O. et al., *Book Illumination in the Middle Ages,* Harvey Miller Publishers, 1994

Panofsky, E., *Meaning in the Visual Arts,* Peter Smith Pub, 1988

Panofsky, E., *Renaissance and Renascences in Western Art,* Paladin, 1970

Partridge, L., *The Art of Renaissance Rome,* US Imports & PHIPEs, 1996

Phillips, P., *The Prehistory of Europe,* Viking, 1980

Phillips, T. ed., *Africa: The Art of a Continent,* Prestel Publishing Ltd, 1999

Piotrovsky, B. et al., *Scythian Art,* Phaidon Press, 1993

Pollitt, J.J., *Art and Experience in Classical Greece,* Cambridge University Press, 1972

Powell, R.J., *Black Art and Culture in the Twentieth Century,* Thames and Hudson, 1997

Rampage, N.H. & A., *The Cambridge Illustrated History of Roman Art,* Cambridge, 1991

Rawson, J., *The British Museum Book of Chinese Art,* British Museum Press, 1992

Rewald, J., *The History of Impressionism,* Secker & Warburg, 1980

Richter, G., *A Handbook of Greek Art,* Phaidon Press 1987

Rosen, C. and Zerner, H., *Romanticism and Realism,* Faber and Faber, 1984

Rosen, R. et al., *Making Their Mark: Women Artists Move into the Mainstream,* Abbeville Press, 1991

Rosenblum, R. and Janson, H.W., *19ᵗʰ Century Art,* Thames and Hudson, 1984

Rosenblum, R., *Transformations in Late Eighteenth Century Art,* Princeton University Press, 1992

Roskill, M., *What is Art History?* University of Massachusetts Press, 1989

Rowland, B., *The Evolution of the Buddha Image,* Arno P, New York, 1976

Sandler, I., *Art of the Postmodern Era,* Icon Editions, 1996

Schäfer, H., *Principles of Egyptian Art,* Aris & Phillips, 1986

Schapiro, M., *Modern Art, 19th and 20th Centuries,* George Braziller, 1978

Singer, J.C. and Denwood, P. eds., *Tibetan Art: Towards a Definition of Style,* Laurence King Publishing, 1997

Spivey, N., *Etruscan Art,* Thames and Hudson, 1997

Stanley-Baker, J., *Japanese Art,* Thames and Hudson, 2000

Starzecka, D.C. ed., *Maori: Art and Culture,* British Museum Press, 1998

Stone-Miller, R., *Art of the Andes,* Thames and Hudson, 1995

Strong, D.E., *Roman Art,* Yale University Press, 1992

Ucko, P. and Rosenfeld, A., *Palaeolithic Cave Art,* Weidenfeld & Nicolson, 1967

Vermeule, C.V., *Roman Art: Early Republic to Late Empire,* Boston, 1979

Watson, W., *The Arts of China to AD 900,* Yale University Press, 2000

Welch, S.C., *Art of Moghul India,* Arno P, NY, 1976

Whelte, K., *The Materials and Techniques of Painting,* Van Nost, Reinhold, New York, 1975

Willett, F. *African Art: An Introduction,* Harcourt School Pub, 1971

Wölfflin, G. *Principles of Art History,* G Bell, 1950

Wollheim, H. *Painting as an Art,* Thames and Hudson, 1990

Yonemura, A. et al., *Twelve Centuries of Japanese Art from the Imperial Collections,* Smithsonian Institution Press, 1998

Zarnecki, G. *Romanesque,* Herbert Press, 1989

WEBSITES

About.com
http://arttech.about.com
http://arthistory.about.com

Academic Info: Art and Art History
www.academicinfo.net/art.html

Ancient Greece
www.medie
www.art-bridge.com/directory/abdir.htm

Art Channel
www.art4net.com

Art Daily.com
www.artdaily.com

Art Galleries and Museums Worldwide
http://link.bubL.ac.uk/artgalleriesworldwide

Art History Network
www.arthistory.net

Art History: Resources on the Web
http://witcombe.sbc.edu/ARTH Links.html

Art Museum Network
www.amn.org

Art Quest
www.artquest.com/index2.asp

Art Related Bookmarks
www-ah.st-and.ac.uk

Art Resources
www.geocities.com/rr17bb

Art Seek
www.artseek.com

Art Source
www.ilpi.com/artsource/welcome.html

Artchive
www.artchive.com

Artcyclopedia
www.artcyclopedia.com

Artlex Art Dictionary
www.artlex.com

Artsiteguide.com
www.artsiteguide.com

Artworlddealers.com
www.artworlddealers.com

Bartleby.com
www.bartleby.com

BBC
www.bbc.co.uk/arts/digital/index.shtml

Chinese Art Net
www.chineseartnet.com/artinst.htm

Cornucopia
www.cornucopia.org.uk

Encyclopedia Britannica
www.britannica.com

Fine Art History Quick Reference
www.finearthistory.com

Galleryguide.org
www.galleryguide.org

Hunt for: Art History
www.huntfor.com/arthistory

Internet Art Resources
www.artresources.com

Internet Public Library Reference Centre

www.ipl.org/ref

Mother of all Art and Art History link pages
www.art-design.umich.edu/mother

Nixnet Medieval
www.medievalarthistory.com

Refdesk.com
www.refdesk.com/culture.html

The Gallery Channel
www.thegallerychannel.com

The World Wide Art Gallery
www.theartgallery.com.au

The World Wide Web Virtual Library: History of Art
www.chart.ac.uk/vlib

Virtual Guggenheim
www.guggenheim.org/exhibitions/virtual

Virtual Library Museum pages
http://vlmp.museophile.com

Worldwide Art Resources
http://wwar.com/index.html

www Art Guide
www.artcents.com/artguide

Xrefer
www.xrefer.com

Yahoo, Art History
http://dir.yahoo.com/Arts/Art History

AUTHOR BIOGRAPHIES

Dr Robert Belton
Author of *The Beribboned Bomb: The Image of Women in Male Surrealist Art,* *Sights of Resistance* and *The Theatre of the Self: The Life and Art of William Ronald,* Dr Robert Belton is the Associate Dean of Arts at Okanagan University College in Kelowna, British Columbia. He has received the Alma Mater Society Frank Knox Award for Teaching Excellence and the Arts and Science Undergraduate Award for Teaching Excellence.

Christopher Rothko
Christopher Rothko is Mark Rothko's second child. He holds a B.A. in Literature from Yale University and a Ph.D. in Psychology from The University of Michigan. He has worked to organize and present most of his father's recent exhibitions around the globe. He has written extensively as a classical music critic and, when work and children allow, likes to write fiction.

Tom Middlemost
Tom Middlemost is an art curator who specialises in Australian Art. In June 2001 he began a three month internship with the former director Lars Nittve, one of the world's leading art curators, in the Tate Modern, London, to develop the Charles Sturt University's art collection. Tom is passionate about making art accessible to people in country regions of Australia.

Dr James Mackay
Dr James Mackay is a journalist and broadcaster, biographer and historian. A former salesroom correspondent for the *Financial Times,* he has also written numerous books on art, sculpture, antiques and collectables, including *Dictionary of Sculptures in Bronze* and *Animaliers.* A graduate of Glasgow University, he is regarded as the world's leading authority on Robert Burns.

Iain Zaczek
Born in Dundee and educated at Wadham College, Oxford and the Courtauld Institute of Art in England, Ian Zaczek, has written numerous art books, some of which include *Lovers in Art, Impressionists* and *Celtic Art and Design.* His most recent book, published in 2002, is entitled *Women in Art.*

Dr Julia Kelly
Dr Julia Kelly is currently a lecturer at Manchester University. Educated at Oxford and the Courtauld Institute of Art in England, she specialises in twentieth-century art, with a particular interest in Surrealism and the inter-war period. Her PhD thesis was in the art writings of Michel Leiris, and she has published works on Picasso and Francis Bacon.

William Matar
The son of the famous Lebanese artist, Joseph Matar, William is the site owner and director of LebanonArt.net. He and his other experienced editorial staff have provided invaluable help in choosing the Middle Eastern Art represented in this book.

GENERAL INDEX

Main entries are in **bold** type.
Illustrations are in *italic* type.

Art